Programming Microsoft® LINQ

Paolo Pialorsi and Marco Russo

PUBLISHED BY
Microsoft Press
A Division of Microsoft Corporation
One Microsoft Way
Redmond, Washington 98052-6399

Library of Congress Control Number: 2008923655

Printed and bound in the United States of America.

1 2 3 4 5 6 7 8 9 QWT 3 2 1 0 9 8

Distributed in Canada by H.B. Fenn and Company Ltd.

A CIP catalogue record for this book is available from the British Library.

Microsoft Press books are available through booksellers and distributors worldwide. For further information about international editions, contact your local Microsoft Corporation office or contact Microsoft Press International directly at fax (425) 936-7329. Visit our Web site at www.microsoft.com/mspress. Send comments to mspinput@microsoft.com.

Acquisitions Editor: Ben Ryan
Developmental Editor: Devon Musgrave
Project Editor: Valerie Woolley
Editorial Production: ICC Macmillan, Inc.
Technical Reviewer: Christophe Nasarre; Technical Review services provided by Content Master,
                 a member of CM Group, Ltd.
Cover: Tom Draper Design

Body Part No. X14-71509

Dedication

To Elena, Riccardo, and Alessandra

– Marco

To Andrea, who makes me and Paola deeply enjoy our lives!

– Paolo

Contents at a Glance

Table of Contents

What do you think of this book? We want to hear from you!

Microsoft is interested in hearing your feedback so we can continually improve our books and learning resources for you. To participate in a brief online survey, please visit:

www.microsoft.com/learning/booksurvey/

What do you think of this book? We want to hear from you!

Microsoft is interested in hearing your feedback so we can continually improve our books and learning resources for you. To participate in a brief online survey, please visit:

www.microsoft.com/learning/booksurvey/

Foreword

LINQ changes how you write code. At least it did that for me.

It is not the well-publicized object relational aspect of LINQ that does it. Don't get me wrong, I love the object relational piece. I have been involved in shipping object relational frameworks at Microsoft for the better part of the past eight years. I adore the technology, and I'm thrilled that we have shipped it. It is a *very useful* framework. But it doesn't change the way you think about your code. It allows you to use an object-oriented paradigm when interacting with your relational data, but you were using an object-oriented paradigm in your programming language all along.

It is not even LINQ to XML that brings about the paradigm shift. Granted, that is a fantastic library. I can finally write XML code and understand it the next day. In Visual Basic, I can just look at it; in C# I have to look a little harder. But it is still just a library, even though it's sprinkled with Anders Hejlsberg's design magic. It helps you write better XML code, but it doesn't change how you think about your code.

What changed how I write code is the functional aspect of LINQ. And that is not easy. I've been writing code for a very long time, and you sort of calcify in your ways (in my case pure object-oriented ways). You get good at it. Or you think you do ...

But the elegance of the LINQ operators and how they compose won me over. Very rarely in my own code have I been able to achieve it. As the design evolved, it became evident to me that we were creating something more than just a bunch of good libraries and a nice syntax to represent queries. We were crafting a blueprint of what new libraries might look like. We were giving people the tools to create these new libraries. We were working in the frontier of the integration between functional and object-oriented programming. Now the way I write my code is different.

Sure, similar things have been done in research-oriented languages before. But this is the first time, to my knowledge, that these paradigms have been mixed in a mainstream programming language to create a framework that tackles very fundamental scenarios such as databases, XML, and parallel computing.

Therefore, use this very fine book to learn how to use LINQ. Let my fellow countrymen Marco and Paolo guide you to discover all the details of LINQ to Objects, LINQ to SQL, LINQ to XML, and everything else that LINQ comprises. But don't lose track of the overall design; take time to understand the basic concepts (that is, lambda expressions, expression trees, extension methods, and such). Delve into Chapter 12 on extending LINQ. You can be just a passive user of LINQ, or you can deeply understand how it works. I suggest the latter as a more rewarding path.

Luca Bolognese
LINQ Principal Program Manager
Microsoft Corporation

Preface

We saw Language Integrated Query (LINQ) for the first time in September 2005, when the LINQ Project was announced during the Professional Developers Conference (PDC 2005). We immediately realized the importance and the implications of LINQ for the long term. At the same time, we felt it would be a huge error to look to LINQ only for its capability to wrap access to relational data. This would be an error because the important concept introduced by LINQ is the growth in code abstraction that comes from using a consistent pattern that makes code more readable, without having to pay in terms of loss of control. We liked LINQ, we could foresee widespread use for it, but we were worried about the possible misperception of its key points. For these reasons, we started to think about writing a book about LINQ.

We had the great opportunity to write such a book when our proposal was accepted by Microsoft Press. We wrote an initial short version of this book, *Introducing Microsoft LINQ*, which was based on beta 1 code. We incorrectly assumed that writing the first book put us halfway to completing this comprehensive book, but we were only about one-third (or, more likely, one-quarter) of the way there. We got a lot of feedback from readers of *Introducing Microsoft LINQ*, and the most important feedback was the negative feedback. Today, we are writing the preface to *Programming Microsoft LINQ*, which we really think is the book we would like to buy if we had not already written it!

After spending almost three years working on it, this book is a great goal for us to have reached, but it is just the beginning for you. LINQ introduces a more declarative style of programming that is not a temporary trend. Anders Hejlsberg, the chief designer of C#, said that LINQ tries to solve the impedance mismatch between code and data. We think that LINQ is probably already one step ahead of other methods of resolving that dilemma because it can also be used to write parallel algorithms, such as when using the Parallel LINQ (PLINQ) implementation.

LINQ can be pervasive in software architectures because it can be used in any tier of an application; however, just like any other tool, it can be used effectively or not. We tried to address how to use LINQ in the most beneficial ways throughout the book. However, after all this work, we still feel LINQ is a "new" technology. We think that at the beginning, you, like us, will find it natural to use LINQ where a query to a relational database is required. The turning point is writing an algorithm operating on in-memory data using a LINQ to Objects query. This should be easy. In fact, after only three chapters of this book, you will already have the knowledge to do that. But in reality, this is the hardest part, because you need to change the way you think about your code. You need to start thinking in LINQ. We have not found a magic formula to teach this. Probably, like any big change, you will need time and practice to metabolize it.

Enjoy the reading!

Acknowledgments

A book is the result of the work of many people. Unfortunately, only the authors have their names on the cover. This section is only partial compensation for other individuals who helped out.

First, we want to thank Luca Bolognese for his efforts in giving us resources and contacts that helped us to write this book. Moreover, Luca has honored us by writing the foreword for this book. To find the right words to express our gratitude, we take the license to use our mother language. Grazie, Luca!

We also want to thank all the people from Microsoft who answered our questions along the way—in particular, Mads Torgersen, Amanda Silver, Erick Thompson, Joe Duffy, Ed Essey, Yuan Yu, Dinesh Kulkarni, and Luke Hoban. Moreover, Charlie Calvert deserves special mention for his great and precious help.

If you understand what we wrote, we do not deserve all the credit. We had the good fortune to have some great people at Microsoft Press edit our drafts: John Pierce and Roger LeBlanc. John has followed this project since we first had the idea for it; he helped us to stay on track, answered all our questions, remained tolerant of our delays, and improved a lot of our drafts. Roger has been so accurate and patient in his editing work that we really do not have words to explain the exceptional value of the job he did.

We want to thank the main technical reviewer, Christophe Nasarre, who has found errors that otherwise we would have missed. We also want to thank the many people who had the patience to read our drafts and suggest improvements and corrections. Big thanks to Alberto Ferrari, Bill Ryan, Cristian Civera, Diego Colombo, Luca Regnicoli, Roberto Brunetti, and Sergio Murru for their reviews.

Finally, we would like to thank Francesco Balena and Giovanni Librando, who supported us three years ago when we decided to try writing a book in English.

Introduction

This book covers Language Integrated Query (LINQ) deeply and widely. The main goal is to give you a complete understanding of what LINQ is, as well as what to do and what not to do with LINQ. The target audience for this book is .NET developers with a good knowledge of Microsoft .NET 2.0 who are wondering whether to upgrade their expertise to Microsoft .NET 3.5.

To start working with LINQ, you need to install Microsoft .NET Framework 3.5 and Microsoft Visual Studio 2008 on your development machine.

This book has been written against the released to market (RTM) edition of LINQ and Microsoft .NET 3.5. However, some topics, such as LINQ to Entities, the ADO.NET Entity Framework, and Parallel LINQ, are still in beta versions. Some features of these technologies might be changed, removed, or added between now and their final release. We are providing a Web site (*http://www.programminglinq.com/*) where we will maintain a change list, a revision history, corrections, and a blog about what is going on with the LINQ Project and this book. We also have a Web page (*http://www.programminglinq.com/booklinks.aspx*) with all the URLs contained in this book, sorted by page, so that you do not need to copy these URLs by hand.

About This Book

This book is divided into five parts that group a total of 18 chapters, followed by 3 appendixes.

If you are new to C# 3.0, Visual Basic 2008, or both, we suggest you start by reading Appendix B or Appendix C, respectively. These appendixes cover new features introduced in these languages to provide full support for LINQ. If you are already familiar with these new versions of the languages, you can use these appendixes as a reference if you have some doubts about the language syntax when using LINQ. We use C# as the principal language in our examples, but almost all the LINQ features we show are available in Visual Basic 2008 too. Where appropriate, we use Visual Basic 2008 because it has some features that are not available in C# 3.0.

The first part of the book, "LINQ Foundations," introduces LINQ, explains its syntax, and gives all the information you need to start using LINQ with in-memory objects. It is important to learn LINQ to Objects before any other LINQ implementation because many of its features are used in the other LINQ implementations described in this book. We strongly suggest reading the three chapters of this part first.

The second part of this book, "LINQ to Relational Data," is dedicated to all the LINQ implementations that provide access to relational stores of data. The LINQ to SQL implementation is divided into three chapters. In Chapter 4, "LINQ to SQL: Querying Data," you will learn the basics for mapping relational data to LINQ entities and how to build LINQ queries that will be transformed into SQL queries. In Chapter 5, "LINQ to SQL: Managing Data," you will learn how to handle changes to data extracted from a database using the entities of LINQ to SQL. Chapter 6, "Tools for LINQ to SQL," is a guide to the tools available for helping you define data models for LINQ to SQL. We suggest that you read all the LINQ to SQL chapters if you are interested in using it in your applications.

Chapter 7, "LINQ to DataSet," covers the implementation of LINQ that targets ADO.NET DataSets. If you have an application that makes use of DataSets, this chapter will teach you how to integrate LINQ, or at least how to progressively migrate from DataSets to a domain model handled with LINQ to SQL or LINQ to Entities.

Chapter 8, "LINQ to Entities," offers a description of the LINQ implementation that wraps access to the ADO.NET Entity Framework. We suggest that you read this chapter after the LINQ to SQL chapters because concepts that are similar for the two implementations are often referred to in the later chapter. In this chapter, we assume you already know about the ADO.NET Entity Framework. If you do not have sufficient experience, we have provided an appendix that you can read first.

The third part, "LINQ and XML," includes two chapters about LINQ to XML: Chapter 9, "LINQ to XML: Managing Infoset," and Chapter 10, "LINQ TO XML: Querying Nodes." We suggest reading these chapters before you start any development that reads or manipulates data in XML.

The fourth part, "Advanced LINQ," includes the most complex topics of the book. In Chapter 11, "Inside Expression Trees," you can learn how to handle, produce, and simply read an expression tree. Chapter 12, "Extending LINQ," provides information about how to extend LINQ by using your own data structures, by wrapping an existing service, and finally by creating a custom LINQ provider. Chapter 13, "Parallel LINQ," describes a LINQ interface to the Parallel Framework for .NET. Finally, Chapter 14, "Other LINQ Implementations," offers an overview of the most significant LINQ components available from third-party vendors. You can read any chapter of this part independently from the others. The only chapter that references another chapter in the section is Chapter 12, which makes some references to Chapter 11.

The fifth part, "Applied LINQ," is dedicated to the use of LINQ in several different scenarios of a distributed application. Chapter 15, "LINQ in a Multitier Solution," is interesting for everyone because it is a very architectural-focused chapter that will help you make the right design decisions for your applications. Chapters 16, 17, and 18 present relevant information about the use of LINQ with existing libraries such as ASP.NET, Windows Presentation Foundation, Silverlight, and Windows Communication Foundation. We suggest that you read Chapter 15 before going into details of specific libraries. You can skip one or more chapters among Chapters 16, 17, and 18 if you do not use the corresponding technology.

Find Additional Content Online   As new or updated material becomes available that complements your book, it will be posted online on the Microsoft Press Online Developer Tools Web site. The type of material you might find includes updates to book content, articles, links to companion content, errata, sample chapters, and more. This Web site will be available soon at www.microsoft.com/learning/books/online/developer, and will be updated periodically.

System Requirements

The following system requirements are needed to work with LINQ and to manage the sample code we provide:

- Supported operating systems: Microsoft Windows Server 2003, Windows Server 2008, Windows Vista, Windows XP with Service Pack 2
- Microsoft Visual Studio 2008

The Companion Web Site

This book features a companion Web site that makes available to you all the code used in the book. This code is organized by topic, and you can download it from the companion site at this address: *http://www.microsoft.com/mspress/companion/9780735624009*.

Support for This Book

Every effort has been made to ensure the accuracy of this book. Microsoft Press provides corrections for books through the World Wide Web at the following address: *http://www.microsoft.com/mspress/support/*.

If you have comments, questions, or ideas about this book, please send them to Microsoft Press using either of the following methods:

Postal Mail:

Microsoft Press
Attn: Editor, Programming Microsoft LINQ
One Microsoft Way
Redmond, WA 98052-6399

E-mail:
mspinput@microsoft.com

Please note that product support isn't offered through the mail addresses. For support information, visit Microsoft's Web site at *http://support.microsoft.com/*.

Part I
LINQ FOUNDATIONS

Chapter 1
LINQ Introduction

By surfing the Web, you can find several descriptions of Language Integrated Query (LINQ), including these:

- LINQ is a uniform programming model for any kind of data. LINQ enables you to query and manipulate data by using a consistent model that is independent of data sources.
- LINQ is another tool for embedding SQL queries into code.
- LINQ is another data abstraction layer.

All of these descriptions are correct to a degree, but they each focus on only a single aspect of LINQ. LINQ can do a lot more than embed SQL queries, it is much easier to use than a "uniform programming model," and it is far from being just another set of rules for modeling data.

What Is LINQ?

LINQ is a programming model that introduces queries as a first-class concept into any Microsoft .NET language. Complete support for LINQ, however, requires some extensions in the language you are using. These extensions boost developer productivity, thereby providing a shorter, more meaningful, and expressive syntax with which to manipulate data.

> **More Info**   Details about language extensions are contained in Appendix B, "C# 3.0: New Language Features," and Appendix C, "Visual Basic 2008: New Language Features."

LINQ provides a methodology that simplifies and unifies the implementation of any kind of data access. LINQ does not force you to use a specific architecture; it facilitates the implementation of several existing architectures for accessing data, for example:

- RAD/prototype
- Client/server
- N-tier
- Smart client

LINQ made its first appearance in September 2005 as a technical preview. Since then it has evolved from an extension of Microsoft Visual Studio 2005 to an integrated part of the .NET Framework 3.5 and Visual Studio 2008, both released to manufacturing in November 2007. The first released version of LINQ directly supports several data sources. It does not include LINQ to Entities, which will be released with the ADO.NET Entity Framework during 2008.

In this book, we describe current and upcoming LINQ implementations from Microsoft that are used to access several data sources:

- LINQ to Objects
- LINQ to ADO.NET
  - ❑ LINQ to SQL
  - ❑ LINQ to DataSet
  - ❑ LINQ to Entities (see note below)
- LINQ to XML

> **Important**   We describe LINQ to Entities in this book based on beta code. We have tried to update the content as much as we could with the final specification and will provide news, book corrections, and updated code samples at *http://www.programminglinq.com*.

Extending LINQ

LINQ can be extended to support other data sources. Possible extensions might be something like LINQ to SharePoint, LINQ to Exchange, and LINQ to LDAP, just to name a few examples. Actually, some possible implementations are already available using LINQ to Objects. We describe a possible LINQ to Reflection query in the "LINQ to Objects" section of this chapter. More advanced extensions of LINQ are discussed in Chapter 12, "Extending LINQ." Some of the existing LINQ Implementations are shown in Chapter 14, "Other LINQ Implementations."

LINQ is likely to have an impact on the way applications are coded. It would be incorrect to think that LINQ will change application architectures because its goal is to provide a set of tools that improve code implementation by adapting to several different architectures. However, we expect that LINQ will affect some critical parts of the layers of an *n*-tier solution. For example, we envision the use of LINQ in a SQLCLR stored procedure, with a direct transfer of the query expression to the SQL engine instead of using an SQL statement.

Many possible evolutions could originate from LINQ, but we should not forget that SQL is a widely adopted standard that cannot be easily replaced by another, just for performance reasons. Nevertheless, LINQ is an interesting step in the evolution of current mainstream programming languages. The declarative nature of its syntax might be interesting for uses other than data access, such as the parallel programming that is offered by Parallel LINQ (PLINQ). Many other services can be offered by an execution framework to a program written using a higher level of abstraction such as the one offered by LINQ. A good understanding of this new technology is important to have today, but it could become fundamental tomorrow.

> **More Info**   Parallel LINQ (PLINQ) is covered in Chapter 13, "Parallel LINQ."

Why Do We Need LINQ?

Today, data managed by a program can be originated from various data sources: an array, an object graph, an XML document, a database, a text file, a registry key, an e-mail message, Simple Object Access Protocol (SOAP) message content, a Microsoft Office Excel file.... The list is long.

Each data source has its own specific data access model. When you have to query a database, you typically use SQL. You navigate XML data by using the Document Object Model (DOM) or XPath/XQuery. You iterate an array and build algorithms to navigate an object graph. You use specific application programming interfaces (APIs) to access other data sources, such as an Excel file, an e-mail message, or the Windows registry. In the end, you use different programming models to access different data sources.

The unification of data access techniques into a single comprehensive model has been attempted in many ways. For example, Open Database Connectivity (ODBC) providers allow you to query an Excel file as you would a Windows Management Instrumentation (WMI) repository. With ODBC, you use an SQL-like language to access data represented through a relational model.

Sometimes, however, data is represented more effectively in a hierarchical or network model instead of a relational one. Moreover, if a data model is not tied to a specific language, you probably need to manage different type systems. All these differences create an "impedance mismatch" between data and code.

LINQ addresses these issues by offering a uniform way to access and manage data without forcing the adoption of a "one size fits all" model. LINQ makes use of common capabilities in the *operations* in different data models instead of flattening the different *structures* between them. In other words, by using LINQ you keep existing heterogeneous data structures, such as classes or tables, but you get a uniform syntax to query all these data types regardless of their physical representation. Think about the differences between a graph of in-memory objects and relational tables with proper relationships. With LINQ you can use the same query syntax over both models.

Here is a simple LINQ query for a typical software solution that returns the names of customers in Italy. (Do not worry about the syntax and keywords such as *var* for now.)

```
var query =
    from   c in Customers
    where  c.Country == "Italy"
    select c.CompanyName;
```

The result of this query is a list of strings. You can enumerate these values with a *foreach* loop in C#:

```
foreach ( string name in query ) {
    Console.WriteLine( name );
}
```

Both the *query* definition and the *foreach* loop are regular C# 3.0 statements, but what is *Customers*? At this point, you might be wondering what it is we are querying. Is this query a new form of Embedded SQL? Not at all. You can apply the same query (and the *foreach* loop) to an SQL database, to a *DataSet* object, to an array of objects in memory, to a remote service, or to many other kinds of data.

Customers could be a collection of objects, for example.

```
Customer[] Customers;
```

Customers could be a *DataTable* in a *DataSet*:

```
DataSet ds = GetDataSet();
DataTable Customers = ds.Tables["Customers"];
```

Customers could be an entity class that describes a physical table in a relational database:

```
DataContext db = new DataContext( ConnectionString );
Table<Customer> Customers = db.GetTable<Customer>();
```

Or *Customers* could be an entity class that describes a conceptual model and is mapped to a relational database:

```
NorthwindModel dataModel = new NorthwindModel();
ObjectQuery<Customer> Customers = dataModel.Customers;
```

How LINQ Works

As you will learn in Chapter 2, "LINQ Syntax Fundamentals," the SQL-like syntax used in LINQ is called a *query expression*. A SQL-like query mixed with the syntax of a program written in a language that is not SQL is typically called Embedded SQL, but languages that implement it do so by using a simplified syntax. In Embedded SQL, these statements are not integrated into the language's native syntax and type system because they have a different syntax and several restrictions related to their interaction. Moreover, LINQ is not limited to querying databases, as Embedded SQL is. LINQ provides much more than Embedded SQL does--a query syntax that is integrated into a language. But how does LINQ work?

When you write the following code using LINQ

```
Customer[] Customers = GetCustomers();
var query =
    from   c in Customers
    where  c.Country == "Italy"
    select c;
```

the compiler generates this code:

```
Customer[] Customers = GetCustomers();
IEnumerable<Customer> query =
      Customers
        .Where( c => c.Country == "Italy" );
```

When the query becomes more complex, as you can see here (from now on, we will skip the *Customers* declaration for the sake of brevity):

```
var query =
      from    c in Customers
      where   c.Country == "Italy"
      orderby c.Name
      select  new { c.Name, c.City };
```

the generated code is more complex too:

```
var query =
        Customers
          .Where( c => c.Country == "Italy" );
          .OrderBy( c => c.Name )
          .Select( c => new { c.Name, c.City } );
```

As you can see, the code apparently calls instance members on the object returned from the previous call: *Where* is called on *Customers*, *OrderBy* is called on the object returned by *Where*, and finally *Select* is called on the object returned by *OrderBy*. You will see that this behavior is regulated by what are known as *extension methods* in the host language (C# in this case). The implementation of the *Where*, *OrderBy*, and *Select* methods–called by the sample query–depends on the type of *Customers* and on namespaces specified in relevant *using* statements. Extension methods are a fundamental syntax feature that is used by LINQ to operate with different data sources by using the same syntax.

More Info   An extension method appears to extend a class (the class *Customers* in our examples), but in reality a method of an external type receives the instance of the class that seems to be extended as the first argument. The *var* keyword used to declare *query* infers the variable type declaration from the initial assignment, which in this case will return an *IEnumerable<T>* type. Further descriptions of these and other language extensions are contained in Appendix B and Appendix C.

Another important concept is the timing of operations over data. In general, a LINQ query is not executed until the result of the query is required for some reason. That query describes a set of operations that will be performed only when the result is actually accessed by the program. In the following example, this access is performed only when the *foreach* loop is executed:

```
var query = from c in Customers ...
foreach ( string name in query ) ...
```

There are also methods that iterate a LINQ query result, producing a persistent copy of data in memory. For example, the *ToList* method produces a typed *List<T>* collection:

```
var query = from c in Customers ...
List<Customer> customers = query.ToList();
```

When the LINQ query operates on data that is in a relational database (such as a Microsoft SQL Server database), it generates an equivalent SQL statement instead of operating with in-memory copies of data tables. The query execution on the database is delayed until the first access to the query results. Therefore, if in the last two examples *Customers* was a *Table<Customer>* type (a physical table in a relational database) or an *ObjectQuery<Customer>* type (a conceptual entity mapped to a relational database), the equivalent SQL query would not be sent to the database until the *foreach* loop was executed or the *ToList* method was called. The LINQ query can be manipulated and composed in different ways until those events occur.

> **More Info**   A LINQ query can be represented as an expression tree. In Chapter 11, "Inside Expression Trees," we describe how to visit and dynamically build an expression tree, thus a LINQ query too.

Relational Model vs. Hierarchical/Network Model

At first sight, LINQ might appear to be just another SQL dialect. This similarity has its roots in the way a LINQ query can describe a relationship between entities, as shown in the following code:

```
var query =
    from   c in Customers
    join   o in Orders
           on c.CustomerID equals o.CustomerID
    select new { c.CustomerID, c.CompanyName, o.OrderID };
```

This syntax is similar to the regular way of querying data in a relational model using a SQL *join* clause. However, LINQ is not limited to a single data representation model like the relational one, where relationships between entities are expressed inside a query but not in the data model. (Foreign keys keep referential integrity but do not participate in a query.) In a hierarchical or network model, parent/child relationships are part of the data structure. For example, suppose that each customer has its own set of orders, and each order has its own list of products. In LINQ, we can get the list of products ordered by each customer in this way:

```
var query =
    from   c in Customers
    from   o in c.Orders
    select new { c.Name, o.Quantity, o.Product.ProductName };
```

This query contains no joins. The relationship between *Customers* and *Orders* is expressed by the second *from* clause, which uses *c.Orders* to say "get all *Orders* of the *c Customer*." The relationship between *Orders* and *Products* is expressed by the *Product* member of the *Order* instance. The result projects the product name for each order row using *o.Product.Product-Name.*

Hierarchical and network relationships are expressed in type definitions through references to other objects. (Throughout, we will use the phrase "graph of objects" to generically refer to hierarchical or network models.) To support the previous query, we would have classes similar to those in Listing 1-1.

Listing 1-1   Type declarations with simple relationships

```
public class Customer {
    public string Name;
    public string City;
    public Order[] Orders;
}
public struct Order {
    public int Quantity;
    public Product Product;
}
public class Product {
    public int IdProduct;
    public decimal Price;
    public string ProductName;
}
```

However, chances are that we want to use the same *Product* instance for many different *Orders* of the same product. We probably also want to filter *Orders* or *Products* without accessing them through *Customer*. A common scenario is the one shown in Listing 1-2.

Listing 1-2   Type declarations with two-way relationships

```
public class Customer {
    public string Name;
    public string City;
    public Order[] Orders;
}
public struct Order {
    public int Quantity;
    public Product Product;
    public Customer Customer;
}
public class Product {
    public int IdProduct;
    public decimal Price;
    public string ProductName;
    public Order[] Orders;
}
```

By having an array of all products declared as follows:

```
Product[] products;
```

We can query the graph of objects, asking for the list of orders for the single product with an ID equal to 3:

```
var query =
    from    p in products
    where   p.IdProduct == 3
    from    o in p.Orders
    select o;
```

With the same query language, we are querying different data models. When you do not have a relationship defined between the entities used in a LINQ query, you can always rely on subqueries and joins that are available in LINQ syntax just as in an SQL language. However, when your data model already defines entity relationships, you can use them, avoiding replication of (and possible mistakes in) the same information.

If you have entity relationships in your data model, you can still use explicit relationships in a LINQ query—for example, when you want to force some condition, or when you simply want to relate entities that do not have native relationships. For instance, imagine that you want to find customers and suppliers who live in the same city. Your data model might not provide an explicit relationship between these attributes, but with LINQ you can write the following:

```
var query =
    from    c in Customers
    join    s in Suppliers
            on c.City equals s.City
    select new { c.City, c.Name, SupplierName = s.Name };
```

Data like the following will be returned:

```
City=Torino     Name=Marco      SupplierName=Trucker
City=Dallas     Name=James      SupplierName=FastDelivery
City=Dallas     Name=James      SupplierName=Horizon
City=Seattle    Name=Frank      SupplierName=WayFaster
```

If you have experience using SQL queries, you probably assume that a query result is always a "rectangular" table, one that repeats the data of some columns many times in a join like the previous one. However, often a query contains several entities with one or more one-to-many relationships. With LINQ, you can write queries like the following one that return a graph of objects:

```
var query =
    from    c in Customers
    join    s in Suppliers
            on c.City equals s.City
            into customerSuppliers
    select new { c.City, c.Name, customerSuppliers };
```

This query returns a row for each customer, each containing a list of suppliers available in the same city as the customer. This result can be queried again, just as any other object graph with LINQ. Here is how the *hierarchized* results might appear:

```
City=Torino      Name=Marco       customerSuppliers=...
   customerSuppliers: Name=Trucker         City=Torino
City=Dallas      Name=James       customerSuppliers=...
   customerSuppliers: Name=FastDelivery    City=Dallas
   customerSuppliers: Name=Horizon         City=Dallas
City=Seattle     Name=Frank       customerSuppliers=...
   customerSuppliers: Name=WayFaster       City=Seattle
```

If you want to get a list of customers and provide each customer with the list of products he ordered at least one time and the list of suppliers in the same city, you can write a query like this:

```
var query =
    from   c in Customers
    select new {
        c.City,
        c.Name,
        Products = (from   o in c.Orders
                    select new { o.Product.IdProduct,
                                 o.Product.Price }).Distinct(),
        CustomerSuppliers = from   s in Suppliers
                            where  s.City == c.City
                            select s };
```

You can take a look at the results for a couple of customers to understand how data is returned from the previous single LINQ query:

```
City=Torino      Name=Marco       Products=...    CustomerSuppliers=...
   Products: IdProduct=1    Price=10
   Products: IdProduct=3    Price=30
   CustomerSuppliers: Name=Trucker         City=Torino
City=Dallas      Name=James       Products=...    CustomerSuppliers=...
   Products: IdProduct=3    Price=30
   CustomerSuppliers: Name=FastDelivery    City=Dallas
   CustomerSuppliers: Name=Horizon         City=Dallas
```

This type of result would be hard to obtain with one or more SQL queries because it would require an analysis of query results to build the desired objects graph. LINQ offers an easy way to move data from one model to another and different ways to get the same results.

LINQ requires you to describe your data in terms of entities that are also types in the language. When you build a LINQ query, it is always a set of operations on instances of some classes. These objects might be the real container of data, or they might be a simple description (in terms of metadata) of the external entity you are going to manipulate. A query can be sent to a database through an SQL command only if it is applied to a set of types that map tables and relationships contained in the database. After you have defined entity classes, you can use *both* approaches we described (joins and entity relationships navigation). The conversion of all these operations into SQL commands is the responsibility of the LINQ engine.

> **Note**   You can create entity classes by using code-generation tools such as SQLMetal or the LINQ to SQL Designer in Microsoft Visual Studio. These tools are described in Chapter 6, "Tools for LINQ to SQL."

In Listing 1-3, you can see an example of a *Product* class that maps a relational table named Products, with five columns that correspond to public data members.

Listing 1-3   Class declaration mapped on a database table

```
[Table("Products")]
public class Product {
    [Column(IsPrimaryKey=true)] public int IdProduct;
    [Column(Name="UnitPrice")] public decimal Price;
    [Column()] public string ProductName;
    [Column()] public bool Taxable;
    [Column()] public decimal Tax;
}
```

When you work on entities that describe external data (such as database tables), you can create instances of these kinds of classes and manipulate in-memory objects just as if data from all tables were loaded in memory. These changes are submitted to the database through SQL commands when you call the *SubmitChanges* method, as you can see in Listing 1-4.

Listing 1-4   Database update calling the *SubmitChanges* method

```
var taxableProducts =
    from   p in db.Products
    where  p.Taxable == true
    select p;
foreach( Product product in taxableProducts ) {
    RecalculateTaxes( product );
}
db.SubmitChanges();
```

The *Product* class in the preceding example represents a row in the Products table of an external database. When *SubmitChanges* is called, all changed objects generate an SQL command to synchronize the corresponding data tables in the database—in this case, updating the corresponding rows in the table Products.

> **More Info**   Class entities that match tables and relationships in the database are further described in Chapter 4, "LINQ to SQL: Querying Data," in Chapter 5, "LINQ to SQL: Managing Data," and in Chapter 8, "LINQ to Entities."

XML Manipulation

LINQ has a different set of classes and extensions to support the manipulation of XML data. Imagine that your customers are able to send orders using XML files like the ORDERS.XML file shown in Listing 1-5.

Listing 1-5   A fragment of an XML file of orders

```
<?xml version="1.0" encoding="utf-8" ?>
<orders xmlns="http://schemas.devleap.com/Orders">
    <order idCustomer="ALFKI" idProduct="1" quantity="10" price="20.59"/>
    <order idCustomer="ANATR" idProduct="5" quantity="20" price="12.99"/>
    <order idCustomer="KOENE" idProduct="7" quantity="15" price="35.50"/>
</orders>
```

Using standard Microsoft .NET 2.0 *System.Xml* classes, you can load the file using a DOM approach or you can parse its contents using an implementation of *XmlReader*, as shown in Listing 1-6.

Listing 1-6   Reading the XML file of orders using an *XmlReader*

```
String nsUri = "http://schemas.devleap.com/Orders";
XmlReader xmlOrders = XmlReader.Create( "Orders.xml" );

List<Order> orders = new List<Order>();
Order order = null;
while (xmlOrders.Read()) {
    switch (xmlOrders.NodeType) {
        case XmlNodeType.Element:
            if ((xmlOrders.Name == "order") &&
            (xmlOrders.NamespaceURI == nsUri)) {
                order = new Order();
                order.CustomerID = xmlOrders.GetAttribute( "idCustomer" );
                order.Product = new Product();
                order.Product.IdProduct =
                    Int32.Parse( xmlOrders.GetAttribute( "idProduct" ) );
                order.Product.Price =
                    Decimal.Parse( xmlOrders.GetAttribute( "price" ) );
                order.Quantity =
                    Int32.Parse( xmlOrders.GetAttribute( "quantity" ) );
                orders.Add( order );
            }
            break;
    }
}
```

You can also use an XQuery like the following one to select nodes:

```
for $order in document("Orders.xml")/orders/order
return $order
```

However, XQuery also requires learning another language and syntax. Moreover, the result of the previous XQuery sample should be converted into a set of *Order* instances to be used within our code.

Regardless of the solution you choose, you must always consider nodes, node types, XML namespaces, and whatever else is related to the XML world. Many developers do not like working with XML because it requires knowledge of another domain of data structures and uses syntax of its own. For many of them, it is not very intuitive. As we have already said, LINQ provides a query engine suitable for any kind of source, even an XML document. By using LINQ queries, you can achieve the same result with less effort and with unified programming language syntax. Listing 1-7 shows a LINQ to XML query made over the orders file.

Listing 1-7   Reading the XML file using LINQ to XML

```
XDocument xmlOrders = XDocument.Load( "Orders.xml" );

XNamespace ns = "http://schemas.devleap.com/Orders";
var orders = from o in xmlOrders.Root.Elements( ns + "order" )
             select new Order {
                         CustomerID = (String)o.Attribute( "idCustomer" ),
                         Product = new Product {
                             IdProduct = (Int32)o.Attribute("idProduct"),
                             Price = (Decimal)o.Attribute("price") },
                         Quantity = (Int32)o.Attribute("quantity")
                     };
```

Using the new Microsoft Visual Basic 2008 syntax, you can reference XML nodes in your code by using an XPath-like syntax, as shown in Listing 1-8.

Listing 1-8   Reading the XML file using LINQ to XML and Visual Basic 2008 syntax

```
Imports <xmlns:o="http://schemas.devleap.com/Orders">
' ...

Dim xmlOrders As XDocument = XDocument.Load("Orders.xml")
Dim orders = _
    From o In xmlOrders.<o:orders>.<o:order> _
    Select New Order With {
        .CustomerID = o.@idCustomer, _
        .Product = New Product With {
            .IdProduct = o.@idProduct,
            .Price = o.@price}, _
        .Quantity = o.@quantity}
```

The result of these LINQ to XML queries could be used to transparently load a list of *Order* entities into a customer *Orders* property, using LINQ to SQL to submit the changes into the physical database layer:

```
customer.Orders.AddRange(
    From o In xmlOrders.<o:orders>.<o:order> _
    Where o.@idCustomer = customer.CustomerID _
```

```
Select New Order With {
    .CustomerID = o.@idCustomer, _
    .Product = New Product With {
        .IdProduct = o.@idProduct,
        .Price = o.@price}, _
    .Quantity = o.@quantity})
```

And if you need to generate an ORDERS.XML file starting from your customer's orders, you can at least leverage Visual Basic 2008 XML literals to define the output's XML structure. This is an exclusive feature of Visual Basic and does not have an equivalent syntax in C#. An example is shown in Listing 1-9.

Listing 1-9 Creating the XML for orders using Visual Basic 2008 XML literals

```
Dim xmlOrders = <o:orders>
    <%= From o In orders _
        Select <o:order idCustomer=<%= o.CustomerID %>
                        idProduct=<%= o.Product.IdProduct %>
                        quantity=<%= o.Quantity %>
                        price=<%= o.Product.Price %>/> %>
    </o:orders>
```

You can appreciate the power of this solution, which keeps the XML syntax without losing the stability of typed code and transforms a set of entities selected via LINQ to SQL into an XML *InfoSet*.

> **More Info** You will find more information about LINQ to XML syntax and its potential in Chapter 9, "LINQ to XML: Managing Infoset" and in Chapter 10, "LINQ to XML: Querying Nodes."

Language Integration

Language integration is a fundamental aspect of LINQ. The most visible part is the query expression feature, which is present in C# 3.0 and Visual Basic 2008. It allows you to write code such as you've seen earlier. For example, you can write the following code

```
var query =
    from    c in Customers
    where   c.Country == "Italy"
    orderby c.Name
    select  new { c.Name, c.City };
```

instead of writing this code:

```
var query =
    Customers
    .Where( c => c.Country == "Italy" );
    .OrderBy( c => c.Name )
    .Select( c => new { c.Name, c.City } );
```

Many people call this simplification *syntax sugaring* because it is just a simpler way to write code that defines a query over data. However, there is more to it than that. Many language constructs and syntaxes are necessary to support what seems to be just a few lines of code that query data. Under the cover of this simple query expression are local type inference, extension methods, lambda expressions, object initialization expressions, and anonymous types. All of these features are useful by themselves, but if you look at the overall picture you can see important steps in two directions: one moving to a more declarative style of coding, and one lowering the impedance mismatch between data and code.

Declarative Programming

What are the differences between an SQL query and an equivalent C# 2.0 or Visual Basic 2005 program that filters data contained in native storage (such as a table for SQL or an array for C# or Visual Basic)?

In SQL, you can write the following:

```
SELECT * FROM Customers WHERE Country = 'Italy'
```

In C#, you would probably write this:

```
public List<Customer> ItalianCustomers( Customer customers[] )
{
    List<Customer> result = new List<Customer>();
    foreach( Customer c in customers ) {
        if (c.Country == "Italy") result.Add( c );
    }
    return result;
}
```

 Note   This specific example could have been written in C# 2.0 using a *Find* predicate, but we are using it just as an example of the different programming patterns.

C# code takes longer to write and read. But the most important consideration is expressivity. In SQL, you describe *what* you want. In C#, you describe *how* to obtain the expected result. In SQL, the selection of the best algorithm to implement for how to get the result (which is more explicitly dealt with in C#) is the responsibility of the query engine. The SQL query engine has more freedom to apply optimizations than a C# compiler, which has many more constraints on how an operation is performed.

LINQ enables a more declarative style of coding for C# and Visual Basic. A LINQ query describes operations on data through a declarative construct instead of an iterative one. LINQ allows the intentions of programmers to be made more explicit, and this knowledge of programmer intent is fundamental to obtaining a higher level of services from the underlying framework. For example, think about parallelization. An SQL query can be split into several concurrent operations simply because it does not place any constraint on the kind of table scan algorithm applied. A C# *foreach* loop is harder to split into several loops over different parts of an array that could be executed in parallel by different processors.

> **More Info**   You will find more information about using LINQ to achieve parallelism in code execution in Chapter 13.

Declarative programming can take advantage of services offered by compilers and frameworks, and in general it is easier to read and maintain. This single feature of LINQ might be the most important because it boosts programmers' productivity. For example, suppose that you want to get a list of all static methods available in the current application domain that return an *IEnumerable<T>* interface. You can use LINQ to write a query over Reflection:

```
var query =
    from    assembly in AppDomain.CurrentDomain.GetAssemblies()
    from    type in assembly.GetTypes()
    from    method in type.GetMethods()
    where   method.IsStatic
            && method.ReturnType.GetInterface( "IEnumerable`1" ) != null
    orderby method.DeclaringType.Name, method.Name
    group   method by new { Class = method.DeclaringType.Name,
                            Method = method.Name };
```

The equivalent C# code that handles data takes more time to write, is harder to read, and is probably more error prone. You can see a version that is not particularly optimized in Listing 1-10.

Listing 1-10   C# code equivalent to a LINQ query over Reflection

```
List<String> results = new List<string>();
foreach( var assembly in AppDomain.CurrentDomain.GetAssemblies()) {
    foreach( var type in assembly.GetTypes() ) {
        foreach( var method in type.GetMethods()) {
            if (method.IsStatic &&
                method.ReturnType.GetInterface("IEnumerable`1") != null) {
                string fullName = String.Format( "{0}.{1}",
                                    method.DeclaringType.Name,
                                    method.Name );
                if (results.IndexOf( fullName ) < 0) {
                    results.Add( fullName );
                }
            }
        }
    }
}
results.Sort();
```

Type Checking

Another important aspect of language integration is type checking. Whenever data is manipulated by LINQ, no unsafe cast is necessary. The short syntax of a query expression makes no compromises with type checking: data is always strongly typed, including both the queried collections and the single entities that are read and returned.

The type checking of the languages that support LINQ (currently C# 3.0 and Visual Basic 2008) is preserved even when LINQ-specific features are used. This enables the use of Visual Studio features such as Microsoft IntelliSense and Refactoring, even with LINQ queries. These Visual Studio features are other important factors in programmers' productivity.

Transparency Across Different Type Systems

When you think about the type system of the Microsoft .NET Framework and the type system of Microsoft SQL Server, you realize they are different. Using LINQ, you give precedence to the .NET type system because it is the one supported by any language that hosts a LINQ query. However, most of your data will be saved in a relational database, and it is necessary to convert many types of data between these two worlds. LINQ handles this conversion for you automatically, making the differences in type systems almost completely transparent to the programmer.

> **More Info**   Some limitations exist in the capability to perform conversions between different type systems and LINQ. You will find some information about this topic throughout the book, and you can find a more detailed type system compatibilities table in the product documentation.

LINQ Implementations

LINQ is a technology that covers many data sources. Some of these sources are included in LINQ implementations that Microsoft provides as part of the .NET 3.5 Framework, as shown in Figure 1-1, which also includes LINQ to Entities (which will be released during 2008).

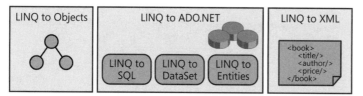

Figure 1-1   LINQ implementations provided by Microsoft within .NET 3.5

Each of these implementations is defined through a set of extension methods that implement the operators needed by LINQ to work with a particular data source. Access to these features is controlled by the imported namespaces.

LINQ to Objects

LINQ to Objects is designed to manipulate collections of objects, which can be related to each other to form a graph. From a certain point of view, LINQ to Objects is the default implementation used by a LINQ query. LINQ to Objects is enabled by including the *System.Linq* namespace.

More Info   The base concepts of LINQ are explained using LINQ to Objects as a reference implementation in Chapter 2.

It would be a mistake to think that LINQ to Objects queries are limited to collections of user-generated data. You can see why this is not true by analyzing Listing 1-11, which shows you a LINQ query over information extracted from the file system. The list of all files in a given directory is read in memory before being filtered by the LINQ query.

Listing 1-11   LINQ query that gets temporary files greater than 10,000 bytes, ordered by size

```
string tempPath = Path.GetTempPath();
DirectoryInfo dirInfo = new DirectoryInfo( tempPath );
var query =
    from    f in dirInfo.GetFiles()
    where   f.Length > 10000
    orderby f.Length descending
    select  f;
```

LINQ to ADO.NET

LINQ to ADO.NET includes different LINQ implementations that share the need to manipulate relational data. It also includes other technologies that are specific to each particular persistence layer:

- **LINQ to SQL**   Handles the mapping between custom types in .NET and the physical table schema.

- **LINQ to Entities**   Is in many ways similar to LINQ to SQL. However, instead of using the physical database as a persistence layer, it uses a conceptual Entity Data Model (EDM). The result is an abstraction layer that is independent from the physical data layer.

- **LINQ to DataSet**   Makes it possible to query a *DataSet* using LINQ.

LINQ to SQL and LINQ to Entities have similarities because they both access information stored in a relational database and operate on object entities that represent external data in memory. The main difference is that they operate at a different level of abstraction. While LINQ to SQL is tied to the physical database structure, LINQ to Entities operates over a conceptual model (business entities) that might be far from the physical structure (database tables).

The reason for these different options for accessing relational data through LINQ is that different models for database access are in use today. Some organizations implement all access through stored procedures, including any kind of database query, without using dynamic queries. Many others use stored procedures to insert, update, or delete data and dynamically build SELECT statements to query data. Some see the database as a simple object persistence layer, while others put some business logic into the database using triggers, stored procedures, or both. LINQ tries to offer help and improvement in database access without forcing everyone to adopt a single comprehensive model.

> **More Info**   The use of any LINQ to ADO.NET implementation depends on the inclusion of particular namespaces in the scope. LINQ to ADO.NET implementations and similar details are investigated in Chapter 4, Chapter 5, Chapter 7, "LINQ to DataSet," and Chapter 8.

LINQ to XML

LINQ to XML offers a slightly different syntax that operates on XML data, allowing query and data manipulation. A particular type of support for LINQ to XML is offered by Visual Basic 2008, which includes XML literals in the language. This enhanced support simplifies the code needed to manipulate XML data. In fact, you can write a query such as the following in Visual Basic 2008:

```
Dim book = _
    <Book Title="Programming  LINQ">
        <%= From person In team _
            Where person.Role = "Author" _
            Select <Author><%= person.Name %></Author> %>
    </Book>
```

This query corresponds to the following C# 3.0 syntax:

```
dim book =
    new XElement( "Book",
        new XAttribute( "Title", "Programming LINQ" ),
        from   person in team
        where  person.Role == "Author"
        select new XElement( "Author", person.Name ) );
```

More Info   You can find more information about LINQ to XML in Chapter 9 and Chapter 10. Other details about Visual Basic 2008 syntax are covered in Appendix C.

Summary

In this chapter, we introduced LINQ and discussed how it works. We also examined how different data sources can be queried and manipulated by using a uniform syntax that is integrated into current mainstream programming languages such as C# and Visual Basic. We took a look at the benefits offered by language integration, including declarative programming, type checking, and transparency across different type systems. We briefly presented the LINQ implementations available in .NET 3.5–LINQ to Objects, LINQ to ADO.NET, and LINQ to XML–and we will cover them in more detail in the remaining parts of the book.

Chapter 2
LINQ Syntax Fundamentals

Language Integrated Query (LINQ) allows developers to query and manage sequences of items (objects, entities, database records, XML nodes, and so on) within their software solutions by using a common syntax and a unique programming language regardless of the nature of the items handled. The key feature of LINQ is its integration with widely used programming languages, an integration made possible by the use of a syntax common to all kinds of content.

As we described in Chapter 1, "LINQ Introduction," LINQ provides a basic infrastructure for many different implementations of querying engines, including LINQ to Objects, LINQ to SQL, LINQ to DataSet, LINQ to Entities, LINQ to XML, and so on. All these query extensions are based on specialized extension methods and share a common set of keywords for query expression syntax that we will cover in this chapter.

Before we look at each keyword in detail, we'll walk through various aspects of a simple LINQ query and introduce you to fundamental elements of LINQ syntax.

LINQ Queries

LINQ is based on a set of query operators, defined as extension methods, that work with any object that implements the *IEnumerable<T>* or *IQueryable<T>* interface.

> **More Info**   For more details about extension methods, see Appendix B, "C# 3.0: New Language Features," and Appendix C, "Visual Basic 2008: New Language Features."

This approach makes LINQ a general-purpose querying framework because many collections or types implement *IEnumerable<T>* or *IQueryable<T>* and any developer can define her or his own implementation. This query infrastructure is also highly extensible, as you will see in Chapter 12 "Extending LINQ." Given the architecture of extension methods, developers can specialize a method's behavior based on the type of data they are querying. For instance, both LINQ to SQL and LINQ to XML have specialized LINQ operators to handle relational data and XML nodes, respectively.

Query Syntax

To introduce query syntax, we will start with a simple example. Imagine that you need to query an array of objects of a *Developer* type using LINQ to Objects and extract the names of the developers who use C# as their main programming language. The code you might use is shown in Listing 2-1.

Listing 2-1   A simple query expression in C# 3.0

```
using System;
using System.Linq;
using System.Collections.Generic;

public class Developer {
    public string Name;
    public string Language;
    public int Age;
}

class App {
    static void Main() {
        Developer[] developers = new Developer[] {
            new Developer {Name = "Paolo", Language = "C#"},
            new Developer {Name = "Marco", Language = "C#"},
            new Developer {Name = "Frank", Language = "VB.NET"}};

        var developersUsingCSharp =
            from    d in developers
            where   d.Language == "C#"
            select  d.Name;

        foreach (var item in developersUsingCSharp) {
            Console.WriteLine(item);
        }
    }
}
```

The result of running this code is the names *Paolo* and *Marco*.

In Visual Basic 2008 the same query, against the same *Developer* type, can be expressed with syntax such as that shown in Listing 2-2.

Listing 2-2   A simple query expression in Visual Basic 2008

```
Imports System
Imports System.Linq
Imports System.Collections.Generic

Public Class Developer
    Public Name As String
    Public Language As String
    Public Age As Integer
End Class
Module App
    Sub Main()

        Dim developers As New Developer() { _
            New Developer With {.Name = "Paolo", .Language = "C#"}, _
            New Developer With {.Name = "Marco", .Language = "C#"}, _
            New Developer With {.Name = "Frank", .Language = "VB.NET"}}
```

```
        Dim developersUsingCSharp = _
            From    d In developers _
            Where   d.Language = "C#" _
            Select d.Name

        For Each item in developersUsingCSharp
            Console.WriteLine(item)
        Next
    End Sub
End Module
```

The syntax of the queries (shown in bold in Listing 2-1 and Listing 2-2) is called a *query expression*. In some LINQ implementations, an in-memory representation of these queries is known as an *expression tree*. A query expression operates on one or more information sources by applying one or more query operators from either the group of standard query operators or domain-specific operators. In general, the evaluation of a query expression results in a sequence of values. A query expression is evaluated only when its contents are enumerated. For further details on query expressions and expression trees, refer to Chapter 11, "Inside Expression Trees."

Note   For the sake of simplicity, we will cover only the C# 3.0 syntax in the following examples; however, you can see that the Visual Basic 2008 version of this sample is very similar to the C# 3.0 one.

These queries read something like an SQL statement, although their style is a bit different. The sample expression we have defined consists of a selection command:

```
select d.Name
```

applied to a set of items:

```
from d in developers
```

where the *from* clause targets any instance of a class that implements the *IEnumerable<T>* interface. The selection applies a specific filtering condition:

```
where d.Language == "C#"
```

These clauses are translated by the language compilers into invocations of extension methods that are sequentially applied to the target of the query. The core library of LINQ, defined in assembly System.Core.dll, defines a set of extension methods grouped by target and purpose. For instance, the assembly includes a class named *Enumerable*, defined in the namespace *System.Linq*, that defines extension methods that can be applied to instances of types implementing the *IEnumerable<T>* interface.

The filtering condition (*where*) defined in our sample query translates into an invocation of the *Where* extension method of the *Enumerable* class. This method provides a couple of overloads, both of which accept a delegate to a *predicate* function that describes the filtering condition to check while partitioning the resulting data. In this case, the filtering *predicate* is a generic delegate that accepts an element of type *T*, which is the same type of the instances stored in the enumeration we are filtering. The delegate returns a *Boolean* result stating the membership of the item in the filtered result set.

```
public static IEnumerable<T> Where<T>(
    this IEnumerable<T> source,
    Func<T, bool> predicate);
```

As you can see from the method signature, you can invoke this method against any type that implements *IEnumerable<T>*; therefore, we can call it on our *developers* array as follows.

```
var filteredDevelopers = developers.Where(delegate (Developer d) {
    return (d.Language == "C#");
});
```

Here the *predicate* argument, passed to the *Where* method, represents an anonymous delegate to a function that is called for each item of type *Developer* taken from the source set of data (*developers*). The result of invoking the *Where* method will be a subset of items: all those that verify the *predicate* condition.

In C# 3.0 and Visual Basic 2008, an anonymous delegate can be defined in an easier way, using a lambda expression. Using a lambda expression, our sample filtering code can be rewritten in a more compact way:

```
var filteredDevelopers = developers.Where(d => d.Language == "C#");
```

Important   For further details on the syntax of extension methods, lambda expressions, anonymous delegates, and so on. Please refer to Appendix B and Appendix C.

The *select* statement is also an extension method (named *Select*) provided by the *Enumerable* class. Here is the signature of the *Select* method:

```
public static IEnumerable<TResult> Select<TSource, TResult>(
    this IEnumerable<TSource> source,
    Func<TSource, TResult> selector);
```

The *selector* argument is a projection that returns an enumeration of objects of type *TResult*, which is obtained from a set of source objects of type *TSource*. As we did previously, we can apply this method to the whole collection of *developers* by using a lambda expression. Or we can invoke it on the collection filtered by the programming language (named *filteredDevelopers*) because it is still a type implementing *IEnumerable<T>*:

```
var csharpDevelopersNames = filteredDevelopers.Select(d => d.Name);
```

Based on the sequence of statements we have just described, we can rewrite the sample query without using the query expression syntax:

```
IEnumerable<string> developersUsingCSharp =
    developers
    .Where(d => d.Language == "C#")
    .Select(d => d.Name);
```

The *Where* method and the *Select* method both receive lambda expressions as arguments. These lambda expressions translate to predicates and projections that are based on a set of generic delegate types defined within the *System* namespace, in the System.Core.dll assembly.

Here is the entire family of generic delegate types available. Many extension methods of the *Enumerable* class accept these delegates as arguments, and we will use them throughout the examples in this chapter.

```
public delegate TResult Func< TResult >();
public delegate TResult Func< T, TResult >( T arg );
public delegate TResult Func< T1, T2, TResult > (T1 arg1, T2 arg2 );
public delegate TResult Func< T1, T2, T3, TResult >
    ( T1 arg1, T2 arg2, T3 arg3 );
public delegate TResult Func< T1, T2, T3, T4, TResult >
    (T1 arg1, T2 arg2, T3 arg3, T4 arg4 );
```

A final version of our initial query might be something like Listing 2-3.

Listing 2-3   The first query expression translated into basic elements

```
Func<Developer, bool> filteringPredicate = d => d.Language == "C#";
Func<Developer, string> selectionPredicate = d => d.Name;
IEnumerable<string> developersUsingCSharp =
    developers
    .Where(filteringPredicate)
    .Select(selectionPredicate);
```

The C# 3.0 compiler, like the Visual Basic 2008 compiler, translates the LINQ query expressions (Listing 2-1 and Listing 2-2) into something like the statement shown in Listing 2-3. After you become familiar with the query expression syntax (Listing 2-1 and Listing 2-2), it is simpler and easier to write and manage this syntax, even if it is optional and you can always use the equivalent, more verbose version (Listing 2-3). Nevertheless, sometimes it is necessary to use the direct call to an extension method because query expression syntax does not cover all possible extension methods.

Important   In Chapter 3, "LINQ to Objects," we will cover in more detail all the extension methods available in the *Enumerable* class defined in the namespace *System.Linq*.

Full Query Syntax

In the previous section, we described a simple query over a list of objects. Query expression syntax, however, is more complete and articulate than shown in that example, providing many different language keywords that satisfy most common querying scenarios. Every query starts with a *from* clause and ends with either a *select* clause or a *group* clause. The reason to start with a *from* clause instead of a *select* statement, as in SQL syntax, is related (among other technical reasons) to the need to provide Microsoft IntelliSense capabilities within the remaining part of the query, which makes writing conditions, selections, and any other query expression clauses easier. A *select* clause projects the result of an expression into an enumerable object. A *group* clause projects the result of an expression into a set of groups, based on a grouping condition, where each group is an enumerable object. The following code shows a prototype of the full syntax of a query expression:

```
query-expression ::= from-clause query-body

query-body ::=
join-clause*
(from-clause join-clause* | let-clause | where-clause)*
orderby-clause?
(select-clause | groupby-clause)
    query-continuation?

from-clause ::= from itemName in srcExpr

select-clause ::= select selExpr

groupby-clause ::= group selExpr by keyExpr
```

The first *from* clause can be followed by zero or more *from*, *let*, or *where* clauses. A *let* clause applies a name to the result of an expression; it is useful whenever you need to reference the same expression many times within a query.

```
let-clause ::= let itemName = selExpr
```

A *where* clause, as we have already mentioned, defines a filter that is applied to include specific items in the results.

```
where-clause ::= where predExpr
```

Each *from* clause generates a local "range variable" that corresponds to each item in the source sequence on which query operators (such as the extension methods of *System.Linq.Enumerable*) are applied.

A *from* clause can be followed by any number of *join* clauses. The final *select* or *group* clause can be preceded by an *orderby* clause that applies an ordering to the results:

```
join-clause ::=
join itemName in srcExpr on keyExpr equals keyExpr
(into itemName)?
```

```
orderby-clause ::= orderby (keyExpr (ascending | descending)?)*

query-continuation ::= into itemName query-body
```

You'll see examples of query expressions throughout this book. You can refer to this section when you want to check specific elements of their syntax.

Query Keywords

In the following sections, we will describe in more detail the various query keywords available in query expression syntax.

From Clause

The first keyword is the *from* clause. It defines the data source of a query or subquery and a range variable that defines each single element to query from the data source. The data source can be any instance of a type implementing the interfaces *IEnumerable*, *IEnumerable<T>*, or *IQueryable<T>*, which implements *IEnumerable<T>*. In the following excerpt, you can see a sample C# 3.0 statement that uses this clause:

```
from rangeVariable in dataSource
```

The language compiler infers the type of the range variable from the type of the data source. For instance, if the data source is of type *IEnumerable<Developer>*, the range variable will be of type *Developer*. In cases in which you do not use a strongly typed data source—for instance an *ArrayList* of objects of type *Developer* that implements *IEnumerable*—you should explicitly provide the type of the range variable. In Listing 2-4, you can see an example of such a query with an explicit declaration of the *Developer* type for the range variable named *d*.

Listing 2-4   A query expression against a nongeneric data source, with type declaration for the range variable

```
ArrayList developers = new ArrayList();
developers.Add(new Developer { Name = "Paolo", Language = "C#" });
developers.Add(new Developer { Name = "Marco", Language = "C#" });
developers.Add(new Developer { Name = "Frank", Language = "VB.NET" });


var developersUsingCSharp =
    from    Developer d in developers
    where   d.Language == "C#"
    select  d.Name;

foreach (string item in developersUsingCSharp) {
    Console.WriteLine(item);
}
```

In the previous example, the casting is mandatory; otherwise, the query will not compile because the compiler cannot automatically infer the type of the range variable, thereby losing the ability to resolve the *Language* and *Name* member access in the same query.

Queries can have multiple *from* clauses in order to define joins between multiple data sources. In C# 3.0, each data source requires a *from* clause declaration, as you can see in Listing 2-5, where we join customers with their orders. Please note that the relationship between *Customer* and *Order* is physically defined by the presence of an *Orders* array of type *Order* in each instance of *Customer*.

> **Important**   When you use multiple *from* clauses, the "join condition" is determined by the structure of the data and is different from the concept of a join in a relational database. (For this, you need to use the *join* clause in a query expression, which we will cover later in this chapter.)

Listing 2-5   A C# 3.0 query expression with a join between a couple of data sources

```
public class Customer {
    public String Name { get; set; }
    public String City { get; set; }
    public Order[] Orders { get; set; }
}

public class Order {
    public Int32 IdOrder { get; set; }
    public Decimal EuroAmount { get; set; }
    public String Description { get; set; }
}

// ... code omitted ...

static void queryWithJoin() {
    Customer[] customers = new Customer[] {
        new Customer { Name = "Paolo", City = "Brescia",
            Orders = new Order[] {
                new Order { IdOrder = 1, EuroAmount = 100, Description = "Order 1" },
                new Order { IdOrder = 2, EuroAmount = 150, Description = "Order 2" },
                new Order { IdOrder = 3, EuroAmount = 230, Description = "Order 3" },
            }},
        new Customer { Name = "Marco", City = "Torino",
            Orders = new Order[] {
                new Order { IdOrder = 4, EuroAmount = 320, Description = "Order 4" },
                new Order { IdOrder = 5, EuroAmount = 170, Description = "Order 5" },
            }}};

    var ordersQuery =
        from   c in customers
        from   o in c.Orders
        select new { c.Name, o.IdOrder, o.EuroAmount };
```

```
        foreach (var item in ordersQuery) {
            Console.WriteLine(item);
        }
    }
}
```

In Visual Basic 2008, a single *From* clause can define multiple data sources, separated by commas, as you can see in Listing 2-6.

Listing 2-6   A Visual Basic 2008 query expression with a join between a couple of data sources

```
Dim customers As Customer() = { _
    New Customer With {.Name = "Paolo", .City = "Brescia", _
        .Orders = New Order() { _
            New Order With {.IdOrder = 1, .EuroAmount = 100, .Description = "Order 1"}, _
            New Order With {.IdOrder = 2, .EuroAmount = 150, .Description = "Order 2"}, _
            New Order With {.IdOrder = 3, .EuroAmount = 230, .Description = "Order 3"} _
        }}, _
    New Customer With {.Name = "Marco", .City = "Torino", _
        .Orders = New Order() { _
            New Order With {.IdOrder = 4, .EuroAmount = 320, .Description = "Order 4"}, _
            New Order With {.IdOrder = 5, .EuroAmount = 170, .Description = "Order 5"} _
}}}

Dim ordersQuery = _
    From    c In customers, _
            o In c.Orders _
    Select c.Name, o.IdOrder, o.EuroAmount

For Each item In ordersQuery
    Console.WriteLine(item)
Next
```

We will cover joins in more detail later in the chapter.

Where Clause

As we have already mentioned, the *where* clause specifies a filtering condition to apply to the data source. The predicate applies a Boolean condition to each item in the data source, extracting only those that evaluate to *true*. Within a single query, you can have multiple *where* clauses or a *where* clause with multiple predicates that are combined by using logical operators (*&&*, *||*, and *!* in C# 3.0, or *And*, *Or*, *AndAlso*, *OrElse*, *Is*, and *IsNot* in Visual Basic 2008). In Visual Basic 2008, the predicate can be any expression equivalent to a *Boolean* value, so you can also use a numeric expression that will be considered true if it is not equal to zero.

Consider the query in Listing 2-7, in which we use the *where* clause to extract all the orders with a *EuroAmount* greater than 200 Euros.

Listing 2-7   A C# 3.0 query expression with a *where* clause

```
var ordersQuery =
    from   c in customers
    from   o in c.Orders
    where  o.EuroAmount > 200
    select new { c.Name, o.IdOrder, o.EuroAmount };
```

In Listing 2-8, you can see the corresponding query syntax using Visual Basic 2008.

Listing 2-8   A Visual Basic 2008 query expression with a *where* clause

```
Dim ordersQuery = _
    From   c In customers, _
           o In c.Orders _
    Where  o.EuroAmount > 200 _
    Select c.Name, o.IdOrder, o.EuroAmount
```

Select Clause

The *select* clause specifies the shape of the query output. It is based on a projection that determines what to select from the result of the evaluation of all the clauses and expressions that precede it. In Visual Basic 2008, the *Select* clause is not mandatory. If it is not specified, the query returns a type that is based on the range variable identified for the current scope. In Listing 2-7 and Listing 2-8, we used the *select* clause to project anonymous types made up of properties or members of the range variables in scope. As you can see by comparing the C# 3.0 syntax (Listing 2-7) and the Visual Basic 2008 syntax (Listing 2-8), the latter looks more like an SQL statement in its select pattern, while the former appears more like the programming language syntax. In fact, in C# 3.0 you need to explicitly declare your intent to create a new anonymous type instance, while in Visual Basic 2008 the language syntax is lighter and hides the inner workings.

Group and *Into* Clauses

The *group* clause can be used to project a result grouped by a key. It can be used as an alternative to the *from* clause and allows you to use single value keys as well as multiple value keys. In Listing 2-9, you can see an example of a query that groups developers by programming language.

Listing 2-9   A C# 3.0 query expression to group developers by programming language

```
Developer[] developers = new Developer[] {
    new Developer { Name = "Paolo", Language = "C#" },
    new Developer { Name = "Marco", Language = "C#" },
    new Developer { Name = "Frank", Language = "VB.NET" },
};
```

```
var developersGroupedByLanguage =
    from  d in developers
    group d by d.Language;

foreach (var group in developersGroupedByLanguage) {
    Console.WriteLine("Language: {0}", group.Key);
    foreach (var item in group) {
        Console.WriteLine("\t{0}", item.Name);
    }
}
```

The output of the code excerpt in Listing 2-9 is the following one:

```
Language: C#
        Paolo
        Marco
Language: VB.NET
        Frank
```

As you can see in the code sample, the result of the query is an enumeration of groups identified by a key and made up of inner items. In fact, we enumerate each group in the result of the query, writing its *Key* property to the console and browsing the items in each group to extract their values. As we mentioned previously, you can group items by using a multiple value key that makes use of anonymous types. An example is shown in Listing 2-10, where we group developers by language and an age cluster.

Listing 2-10   A C# 3.0 query expression to group developers by programming language and age cluster

```
Developer[] developers = new Developer[] {
    new Developer { Name = "Paolo", Language = "C#", Age = 32 },
    new Developer { Name = "Marco", Language = "C#", Age = 37},
    new Developer { Name = "Frank", Language = "VB.NET", Age = 48 },
};

var developersGroupedByLanguage =
    from  d in developers
    group d by new { d.Language, AgeCluster = (d.Age / 10) * 10 };

foreach (var group in developersGroupedByLanguage) {
    Console.WriteLine("Language: {0}", group.Key);
    foreach (var item in group) {
        Console.WriteLine("\t{0}", item.Name);
    }
}
```

This time the output of the code excerpt in Listing 2-10 is the following:

```
Language: { Language = C#, AgeCluster = 30 }
        Paolo
        Marco
Language: { Language = VB.NET, AgeCluster = 40 }
        Frank
```

In this example, the *Key* for each group is an anonymous type defined by two properties: *Language* and *AgeCluster*.

Visual Basic 2008 also supports grouping of results by using the *Group By* clause. In Listing 2-11, you can see an example of a query that is equivalent to the one shown in Listing 2-9.

Listing 2-11   A Visual Basic 2008 query expression to group developers by programming language

```
Dim developers As Developer() = { _
    New Developer With {.Name = "Paolo", .Language = "C#", .Age = 32}, _
    New Developer With {.Name = "Marco", .Language = "C#", .Age = 37}, _
    New Developer With {.Name = "Frank", .Language = "VB.NET", .Age = 48}}

Dim developersGroupedByLanguage = _
    From   d In developers _
    Group  d By d.Language Into Group _
    Select Language, Group

For Each group In developersGroupedByLanguage
    Console.WriteLine("Language: {0}", group.Language)
    For Each item In group.Group
        Console.WriteLine("    {0}", item.Name)
    Next
Next
```

The Visual Basic 2008 syntax is a little bit more complex than the corresponding C# 3.0 syntax. In Visual Basic 2008, you need to project the grouping by using the *Into* clause to create a new *Group* object of items and then explicitly declare the selection pattern. However, the result of the grouping is easier to enumerate because the *Key* value keeps its name (*Language*).

C# 3.0 also provides an *into* clause that is useful in conjunction with the *group* keyword, even if it is not mandatory to use it. You can use the *into* keyword to store the results of a *select*, *group*, or *join* statement in a temporary variable. You might use this construction when you need to execute additional queries over the results. Because of this behavior, this keyword is also called a *continuation* clause. In Listing 2-12, you can see an example of a C# 3.0 query expression that uses the *into* clause.

Listing 2-12   A C# 3.0 query expression using the *into* clause

```
var developersGroupedByLanguage =
    from   d in developers
    group  d by d.Language into developersGrouped
    select new {
        Language = developersGrouped.Key,
        DevelopersCount = developersGrouped.Count()
    };

foreach (var group in developersGroupedByLanguage) {
    Console.WriteLine ("Language {0} contains {1} developers",
        group.Language, group.DevelopersCount);
}
```

Orderby Clause

The *orderby* clause, as you can assume from its name, allows you to sort the result of a query in either ascending or descending order. The ordering can be carried out by using one or more keys that combine different sorting directions. Listing 2-13 shows an example of a query to extract orders placed by customers, ordered by *EuroAmount*.

Listing 2-13   A C# 3.0 query expression with an *orderby* clause

```
var ordersSortedByEuroAmount =
    from    c in customers
    from    o in c.Orders
    orderby o.EuroAmount
    select  new { c.Name, o.IdOrder, o.EuroAmount };
```

Listing 2-14 shows an example of a query that selects orders sorted by customer *Name* and *EuroAmount* in descending order.

Listing 2-14   A C# 3.0 query expression with an *orderby* clause with multiple ordering conditions

```
var ordersSortedByCustomerAndEuroAmount =
    from    c in customers
    from    o in c.Orders
    orderby c.Name, o.EuroAmount descending
    select  new { c.Name, o.IdOrder, o.EuroAmount };
```

In Listing 2-15, you can see the corresponding query written in Visual Basic 2008.

Listing 2-15   A Visual Basic 2008 query expression with an *orderby* clause with multiple ordering conditions

```
Dim ordersSortedByCustomerAndEuroAmount = _
    From    c In customers, _
            o In c.Orders _
    Order   By c.Name, o.EuroAmount Descending _
    Select c.Name, o.IdOrder, o.EuroAmount
```

Here both languages have very similar syntax.

Join Clause

The *join* keyword allows you to associate different data sources on the basis of a member that can be compared for equivalency. It works similarly to a SQL equijoin statement. You cannot compare items to join by using comparisons such as "greater than," "less than," or "not equal to." You can define equality comparisons only by using a special *equals* keyword that has a different behavior from the == operator because the position of the operands matters. With *equals*, the left key consumes the outer source sequence and the right key consumes the inner source. The outer source is in scope only on the left side of *equals*, and the inner source sequence is in scope only on the right side. Here is this concept presented in pseudo-code.

```
join-clause ::= join innerItem in innerSequence on outerKey equals innerKey
```

By using the *join* clause, you can define inner joins, group joins, and left outer joins. An inner join is a join that returns a flat result mapping the outer data source elements with the corresponding inner data source. It skips outer data source elements that lack their corresponding inner data source elements. Listing 2-16 presents a simple query with an inner join between product categories and related products.

Listing 2-16   A C# 3.0 query expression with an inner join

```csharp
public class Category {
    public Int32 IdCategory { get; set; }
    public String Name { get; set; }
}

public class Product {
    public String IdProduct { get; set; }
    public Int32 IdCategory { get; set; }
    public String Description { get; set; }
}

// ... code omitted ...

Category[] categories = new Category[] {
    new Category { IdCategory = 1, Name = "Pasta"},
    new Category { IdCategory = 2, Name = "Beverages"},
    new Category { IdCategory = 3, Name = "Other food"},
};

Product[] products = new Product[] {
    new Product { IdProduct = "PASTA01", IdCategory = 1, Description = "Tortellini" },
    new Product { IdProduct = "PASTA02", IdCategory = 1, Description = "Spaghetti" },
    new Product { IdProduct = "PASTA03", IdCategory = 1, Description = "Fusilli" },
    new Product { IdProduct = "BEV01", IdCategory = 2, Description = "Water" },
    new Product { IdProduct = "BEV02", IdCategory = 2, Description = "Orange Juice" },
};

var categoriesAndProducts =
    from   c in categories
    join   p in products on c.IdCategory equals p.IdCategory
    select new {
        c.IdCategory,
        CategoryName = c.Name,
        Product = p.Description
    };

foreach (var item in categoriesAndProducts) {
    Console.WriteLine(item);
}
```

The output of this code excerpt is something like the following. Notice that the "Other food" category is missing because no products are included in it.

```
{ IdCategory = 1, CategoryName = Pasta, Product = Tortellini }
{ IdCategory = 1, CategoryName = Pasta, Product = Spaghetti }
{ IdCategory = 1, CategoryName = Pasta, Product = Fusilli }
{ IdCategory = 2, CategoryName = Beverages, Product = Water }
{ IdCategory = 2, CategoryName = Beverages, Product = Orange Juice }
```

A group join defines a join that produces a hierarchical result set, grouping the inner sequence elements with their corresponding outer sequence elements. In cases in which an outer sequence element is missing its corresponding inner sequence elements, the outer element will be joined with an empty array. A group join does not have a relational counterpart in SQL syntax because of its hierarchical result. In Listing 2-17, you can see an example of such a query. (You will see an expanded form of this type of query in Chapter 3.)

Listing 2-17   A C# 3.0 query expression with a group join

```
var categoriesAndProducts =
    from c in categories
    join p in products on c.IdCategory equals p.IdCategory
        into productsByCategory
    select new {
        c.IdCategory,
        CategoryName = c.Name,
        Products = productsByCategory
    };

foreach (var category in categoriesAndProducts) {
    Console.WriteLine("{0} - {1}", category.IdCategory, category.CategoryName);
    foreach (var product in category.Products) {
        Console.WriteLine("\t{0}", product.Description);
    }
}
```

Notice that this time the "Other food" category is present in the output, even if it is empty:

```
1 - Pasta
        Tortellini
        Spaghetti
        Fusilli
2 - Beverages
        Water
        Orange Juice
3 - Other food
```

Visual Basic 2008 provides a specific keyword called *Group Join* to define group joins in query expressions.

A left outer join returns a flat result set that includes any outer source element even if it is missing its corresponding inner source element. To produce this result, you need to use the *DefaultIfEmpty* extension method, which returns a default value in the case of an empty data source value. We will cover this and many other extension methods in more detail in Chapter 3. In Listing 2-18, you can see an example of this syntax.

Listing 2-18   A C# 3.0 query expression with a left outer join

```
var categoriesAndProducts =
    from c in categories
    join p in products on c.IdCategory equals p.IdCategory
        into productsByCategory
    from pc in productsByCategory.DefaultIfEmpty(
      new Product {
        IdProduct = String.Empty,
        Description = String.Empty,
        IdCategory = 0})
    select new {
        c.IdCategory,
        CategoryName = c.Name,
        Product = pc.Description
    };

foreach (var item in categoriesAndProducts) {
    Console.WriteLine(item);
}
```

This example produces the following output to the console:

```
{ IdCategory = 1, CategoryName = Pasta, Product = Tortellini }
{ IdCategory = 1, CategoryName = Pasta, Product = Spaghetti }
{ IdCategory = 1, CategoryName = Pasta, Product = Fusilli }
{ IdCategory = 2, CategoryName = Beverages, Product = Water }
{ IdCategory = 2, CategoryName = Beverages, Product = Orange Juice }
{ IdCategory = 3, CategoryName = Other food, Product =  }
```

Notice that the "Other food" category is present with an empty product, which is provided by the *DefaultIfEmpty* extension method.

One last point to emphasize about the join clause is that you can compare elements by using composite keys. You simply make use of anonymous types as we showed with the *group* keyword. For example, if you had a composite key in *Category* made up of *IdCategory* and *Year*, you could write the following statement with an anonymous type used in the *equals* condition:

```
from c in categories
join p in products
    on new { c.IdCategory, c.Year } equals new { p.IdCategory, p.Year }
    into productsByCategory
```

As you have already seen in this chapter, you can also get the results of joins by using nested *from* clauses, which is a useful approach whenever you need to define non-equijoin queries.

Visual Basic 2008 has syntax quite similar to C# 3.0, but it also offers some shortcuts to define joins more quickly. We can define implicit join statements by using multiple *In* clauses in the *From* statement and defining the equality conditions with a *Where* clause. In Listing 2-19, you can see an example of this syntax.

Listing 2-19   A Visual Basic 2008 implicit join statement

```
. Dim categoriesAndProducts = _
     From    c In categories, p In products _
     Where  c.IdCategory = p.IdCategory _
     Select c.IdCategory, CategoryName = c.Name, Product = p.Description

  For Each item In categoriesAndProducts
      Console.WriteLine(item)
  Next
```

In Listing 2-20, you can see the same query defined by using the standard explicit *join* syntax.

Listing 2-20   A Visual Basic 2008 explicit join statement

```
  Dim categoriesAndProducts = _
      From    c In categories Join p In products _
              On p.IdCategory Equals c.IdCategory _
      Select c.IdCategory, CategoryName = c.Name, Product = p.Description
```

Notice that in Visual Basic 2008 the order of elements in the equality comparison does not matter because the compiler will arrange them on its own, making the query syntax more relaxed, as happens in classic relational SQL.

Let Clause

The *let* clause allows you to store the result of a subexpression in a variable that can be used somewhere else in the query. This clause is useful when you need to reuse the same expression many times in the same query and you do not want to define it every single time you use it. Using the *let* clause, you can define a new range variable for that expression and reference it within the query. Once assigned, a range variable defined by a *let* clause cannot be changed. However, if the range variable holds a queryable type, it can be queried. In Listing 2-21, you can see an example of this clause applied to select the same product categories with the count of their products, sorted by the counter itself.

Listing 2-21   A C# 3.0 sample of usage of the *let* clause

```
  var categoriesByProductsNumberQuery =
      from    c in categories
      join    p in products on c.IdCategory equals p.IdCategory
          into productsByCategory
      let     ProductsCount = productsByCategory.Count()
      orderby ProductsCount
      select  new { c.IdCategory, ProductsCount};

  foreach (var item in categoriesByProductsNumberQuery) {
      Console.WriteLine(item);
  }
```

Here is the output of the previous code excerpt:

```
{ IdCategory = 3, ProductsCount = 0 }
{ IdCategory = 2, ProductsCount = 2 }
{ IdCategory = 1, ProductsCount = 3 }
```

Visual Basic 2008 uses syntax very similar to C# 3.0 and allows you to also define multiple aliases, separated by commas, within the same *let* clause.

Additional Visual Basic 2008 Keywords

Visual Basic 2008 includes additional query expression keywords that are available in C# 3.0 only by using extension methods. These keywords are described in the following list:

- *Aggregate*, which is useful for applying an aggregate function to a data source. It can be used to begin a new query instead of a *From* clause.

- *Distinct*, which can be used to eliminate duplicate values in query results.

- *Skip*, which can be used to skip the first *N* elements of a query result.

- *Skip While*, which can be used to skip the first elements of a query result that verify a predicate that is provided.

- *Take*, which can be used to take the first *N* elements of a query result.

- *Take While*, which can be used to take the first elements of a query result that verify a predicate that is provided.

Skip and *Take*, or *Skip While* and *Take While*, can be used together to paginate query results. We will come back to this matter with some examples in Chapter 3.

> ## More About Query Syntax
>
> By now, you have seen all the query keywords available through the programming languages. However, remember that each query expression is converted by the language compiler into an invocation of the corresponding extension methods. Whenever you need to query a data source by using LINQ and there is no keyword available for a particular operation in a query expression, you can use native or custom extension methods directly in conjunction with query expression syntax. If you use extension methods only (as shown in Listing 2-3), the syntax is called *method syntax*. When you use query syntax in conjunction with extension methods (as shown in Listing 2-17), the result is defined as *mixed query syntax*.

Deferred Query Evaluation and Extension Method Resolution

In this section, we want to examine two behaviors of a query expression: deferred query evaluation and extension method resolution. Both of these concepts are important for all LINQ implementations.

Deferred Query Evaluation

A query expression is not evaluated when it is defined but when it is used. Consider the example in Listing 2-22.

Listing 2-22   A sample LINQ query over a set of developers

```
List<Developer> developers = new List<Developer>(new Developer[] {
    new Developer { Name = "Paolo", Language = "C#", Age = 32 },
    new Developer { Name = "Marco", Language = "C#", Age = 37},
    new Developer { Name = "Frank", Language = "VB.NET", Age = 48  },
});

var query =
    from    d in developers
    where   d.Language == "C#"
    select new { d.Name, d.Age };

Console.WriteLine("There are {0} C# developers.", query.Count());
```

This code declares a very simple query that contains just two items, as you can see by reading the code that declares the list of developers or simply by checking the console output of the code that invokes the *Count* extension method.

```
There are 2 C# developers.
```

Now imagine that you want to change the content of the source sequence by adding a new *Developer* instance—after the *query* variable has been defined (as shown in Listing 2-23).

Listing 2-23   Sample code to modify the set of developers that we are querying

```
developers.Add(new Developer {
    Name = "Roberto", Language = "C#", Age = 35 });

Console.WriteLine("There are {0} C# developers.", query.Count());
```

If we enumerate the *query* variable again or just check its item count, as we do in Listing 2-23 after a new developer is added, the result is three. The developer we added is now included in the result even though it was added after the definition of *query*.

The reason for this behavior is that from a logical point of view, a query expression describes a kind of "query plan." It is not actually executed until it is used, and it will be executed again and again every time you run it. Some LINQ implementations—such as LINQ to Objects—implement this behavior through delegates. Others—such as LINQ to SQL—might use expression trees that leverage the *IQueryable<T>* interface. We call this behavior *deferred query evaluation*, and it is a fundamental concept in LINQ, regardless of the LINQ implementation you are using.

Deferred query evaluation is useful because you can define queries once and apply them several times: if the source sequence has been changed, the result will always be updated to the most recent content. However, consider a situation in which you want a snapshot of the result at a particular "safe point" to use many times, avoiding re-execution for performance reasons or to be independent of changes to the source sequence. You need to make a copy of the result, which you can do by using a set of operators, called conversion operators (such as *ToArray*, *ToList*, *ToDictionary*, *ToLookup*), that are specifically for this purpose. We will cover conversion operators in detail in Chapter 3.

Extension Method Resolution

Extension method resolution is one of the most important concepts to understand if you want to master LINQ. Consider the code in Listing 2-24, in which we define a custom list of type *Developer* (named *Developers*) and a class, *DevelopersExtension*, that provides an extension method named *Where* that applies specifically to instances of the *Developers* type.

Listing 2-24   Sample code to modify the set of developers that we are querying

```
public sealed class Developers : List<Developer> {
    public Developers(IEnumerable<Developer> items) : base(items) { }
}

public static class DevelopersExtension {
    public static IEnumerable<Developer> Where(
        this Developers source, Func<Developer, bool> predicate) {

        Console.WriteLine("Invoked Where extension method for Developers");
        return (source.AsEnumerable().Where(predicate));
    }

    public static IEnumerable<Developer> Where(
        this Developers source,
        Func<Developer, int, bool> predicate) {

        Console.WriteLine("Invoked Where extension method for Developers");
        return (source.AsEnumerable().Where(predicate));
    }
}
```

The only special work we do in the custom *Where* extension methods is to write to the console to indicate that they have executed. After that we pass the request to the *Where* extension methods defined for any standard instance of type *IEnumerable<T>*, converting the source with a method called *AsEnumerable*, which we will cover in Chapter 3.

If we use our usual *developers* array, the behavior of the query in Listing 2-25 is quite interesting.

Listing 2-25   A query expression over a custom list of type *Developers*

```
Developers developers = new Developers(new Developer[] {
    new Developer { Name = "Paolo", Language = "C#", Age = 32 },
    new Developer { Name = "Marco", Language = "C#", Age = 37},
    new Developer { Name = "Frank", Language = "VB.NET", Age = 48  },
});

var query =
    from   d in developers
    where  d.Language == "C#"
    select d;

Console.WriteLine("There are {0} C# developers.", query.Count());
```

The query expression will be converted by the compiler into the following code, as we saw early in this chapter:

```
Var expert =
    developers
    .Where (d => d.Language == "C#")
    .Select(d => d);
```

As a result of the presence of the *DevelopersExtension* class, the extension method *Where* is the one defined by *DevelopersExtension*, instead of the general-purpose one defined in *System.Linq.Enumerable*. (To be considered as an extension method container class, the *DevelopersExtension* class must be declared as *static* and defined in the current namespace or in any namespace included in active *using* directives.) The resulting code produced by the compiler resolving extension methods is the following.

```
var expr =
    Enumerable.Select(
        DevelopersExtension.Where(
            developers,
            d => d.Language == "C#"),
        d => d );
```

In the end, we are always calling static methods of a static class, but the syntax required is lighter and more intuitive with extension methods than by using the verbose static method explicit calls.

Now we are experiencing the real power of LINQ. Using extension methods, we are able to define custom behaviors for specific types. In the following chapters, we will discuss LINQ to SQL, LINQ to XML, and other implementations of LINQ. These implementations are just specific implementations of query operators, thanks to the extension method resolution realized by the compilers.

At this point, everything looks fine. But now imagine that you need to query the custom list of type *Developers* with the standard *Where* extension method rather than with the specialized one. You should convert the custom list to a more generalized one to divert the extension method resolution made by the compiler. This is another scenario that can benefit from conversion operators, which we will cover in Chapter 3.

Some Final Thoughts About LINQ Queries

In this section, we will cover a few more details about degenerate query expressions and exception handling.

Degenerate Query Expressions

Sometimes you need to iterate over the elements of a data source without any filtering, ordering, grouping, or custom projection. Consider for instance the query presented in Listing 2-26.

Listing 2-26   A degenerate query expression over a list of type *Developers*

```
Developer[] developers = new Developer[] {
    …
};

var query =
    from    d in developers
    select d;

foreach (var developer in query) {
    Console.WriteLine(developer.Name);
}
```

In this code excerpt, we simply iterate over the data source, so someone might wonder why we do not use the data source directly, as we do in Listing 2-27.

Listing 2-27   Iteration over a list of type *Developers*

```
Developer[] developers = new Developer[] {
    …
};

foreach (var developer in developers) {
    Console.WriteLine(developer.Name);
}
```

Apparently, the results of both Listing 2-26 and Listing 2-27 are the same. However, in Listing 2-26, the use of the query expression ensures that if a specific *Select* extension method for the data source exists, the custom method will be called and the result will be consistent as a result of the translation of the query expression into its corresponding method syntax.

A query that simply returns a result equal to the original data source (thus appearing trivial or useless) is called a *degenerate query expression*. On the other hand, iterating directly over the data source (as in Listing 2-27) skips the invocation of any custom *Select* extension method and does not guarantee the correct behavior unless you explicitly want to iterate over the data source without using LINQ.

Exception Handling

Query expressions can refer to external methods within their definition. Sometime those methods can fail. Consider the query defined in Listing 2-28, where we invoke the *DoSomething* method over each data source item.

Listing 2-28   A C# 3.0 query expression based on an external method throwing a fictitious exception

```
static Boolean DoSomething(Developer dev) {
    if (dev.Age > 40)
        throw new ArgumentOutOfRangeException("dev");

    return (dev.Language == "C#");
}

static void Main() {
    Developer[] developers = new Developer[] {
        ...
        new Developer { Name = "Frank", Language = "VB.NET", Age = 48  },
    };

    var query =
        from    d in developers
        let     SomethingResult = DoSomething(d)
        select new { d.Name, SomethingResult };

    foreach (var item in query) {
        Console.WriteLine(item);
    }
}
```

The *DoSomething* method throws a fictitious exception for any developer older than 40. We call this method from inside the query. During query execution, when the developer Frank, who is 48 years old, is iterated, the custom method will throw an exception.

First of all, you should think carefully about calling custom methods in query definitions because it is a dangerous habit, as you can see when executing this sample code. However, in cases in which you decide to call external methods, the best way to work with them is to wrap the enumeration of the query result with a *try ... catch* block. In fact, as you have just seen in the section "Deferred Query Evaluation," a query expression is executed each time it is enumerated and not when it is defined. Thus, the correct way of writing the code in Listing 2-28 is presented in Listing 2-29.

Listing 2-29   A C# 3.0 query expression used with exception handling

```
Developer[] developers = new Developer[] {
    ...
    new Developer { Name = "Frank", Language = "VB.NET", Age = 48  },
};

var query =
    from   d in developers
    let    SomethingResult = DoSomething(d)
    select new { d.Name, SomethingResult };

try {
    foreach (var item in query) {
        Console.WriteLine(item);
    }
}
catch (ArgumentOutOfRangeException e) {
    Console.WriteLine(e.Message);
}
```

In general, it is useless to wrap a query expression definition with a *try ... catch* block. Moreover, for the same reason you should avoid using the results of methods or constructors directly as data sources for a query expression and should instead assign their results to instance variables, wrapping the variable assignment with a *try ... catch* block as we do in Listing 2-30.

Listing 2-30   A C# 3.0 query expression with exception handling in local variables declaration

```
static void queryWithExceptionHandledInDataSourceDefinition() {
    Developer[] developers = null;

    try {
        developers = createDevelopersDataSource();
    }
    catch (InvalidOperationException e) {
        // Imagine that the createDevelopersDataSource
        // throws an InvalidOperationException in case of failure

        // Handle it somehow ...
        Console.WriteLine(e.Message);
    }

    if (developers != null)
    {
        var query =
            from   d in developers
```

```
            let    SomethingResult = DoSomething(d)
            select new { d.Name, SomethingResult };

        try {
            foreach (var item in query) {
                Console.WriteLine(item);
            }
        }
        catch (ArgumentOutOfRangeException e) {
            Console.WriteLine(e.Message);
        }
    }
}

private static Developer[] createDevelopersDataSource() {
    // Fictitious InvalidOperationException thrown
    throw new InvalidOperationException();
}
```

Summary

In this chapter, we discussed the principles of query expressions and their different flavors of syntax (query syntax, method syntax, and mixed syntax), as well as all the main query keywords available in C# 3.0 and Visual Basic 2008. We discussed two important LINQ features: deferred query evaluation and extension method resolution. You have seen as well examples of degenerate query expression and how to handle exceptions while enumerating query expressions. In the next chapter, we'll turn to LINQ to Objects in detail.

Chapter 3
LINQ to Objects

Modern programming languages and software development architectures are based more and more on object-oriented design and development. As a result, quite often we need to query and manage objects and collections rather than records and data tables. We also need tools and languages independent from specific data sources or persistence layers. LINQ to Objects is the main implementation of LINQ that can be used to query in-memory collections of objects, entities, and items.

In this chapter, we will describe the main classes and operators on which LINQ is based as a means of understanding its architecture and to learn its syntax. The examples in this chapter use LINQ to Objects so that we can focus on queries and operators.

Sample Data for Examples

We need to define some data that we will use in the examples in this chapter. We will use a set of *customers*, each of which has ordered *products*. The following code defines these types with C# 3.0 code.

```csharp
public enum Countries {
    USA,
    Italy,
}

public class Customer {
    public string Name;
    public string City;
    public Countries Country;
    public Order[] Orders;

    public override string ToString() {
        return String.Format("Name: {0} - City: {1} - Country: {2}",
        this.Name, this.City, this.Country );
    }
}

public class Order {
    public int IdOrder;
    public int Quantity;
    public bool Shipped;
    public string Month;
    public int IdProduct;

    public override string ToString() {
        return String.Format(    "IdOrder: {0} - IdProduct: {1} - " +
          "Quantity: {2} - Shipped: {3} - " +
```

```
            "Month: {4}", this.IdOrder, this.IdProduct,
            this.Quantity, this.Shipped, this.Month);
    }
}

public class Product {
    public int IdProduct;
    public decimal Price;

    public override string ToString() {
        return String.Format("IdProduct: {0} - Price: {1}", this.IdProduct, this.Price );
    }
}
```

The following code excerpt initializes some instances of these types.

```
// ---------------------------------------------------------
// Initialize a collection of customers with their orders:
// ---------------------------------------------------------
customers = new Customer[] {
  new Customer {Name = "Paolo", City = "Brescia",
            Country = Countries.Italy, Orders = new Order[] {
                new Order { IdOrder = 1, Quantity = 3, IdProduct = 1 ,
                            Shipped = false, Month = "January"},
                new Order { IdOrder = 2, Quantity = 5, IdProduct = 2 ,
                            Shipped = true, Month = "May"}}},
  new Customer {Name = "Marco", City = "Torino",
            Country = Countries.Italy, Orders = new Order[] {
                new Order { IdOrder = 3, Quantity = 10, IdProduct = 1 ,
                            Shipped = false, Month = "July"},
                new Order { IdOrder = 4, Quantity = 20, IdProduct = 3 ,
                            Shipped = true, Month = "December"}}},
  new Customer {Name = "James", City = "Dallas",
            Country = Countries.USA, Orders = new Order[] {
                new Order { IdOrder = 5, Quantity = 20, IdProduct = 3 ,
                            Shipped = true, Month = "December"}}},
  new Customer {Name = "Frank", City = "Seattle",
            Country = Countries.USA, Orders = new Order[] {
                new Order { IdOrder = 6, Quantity = 20, IdProduct = 5 ,
                            Shipped = false, Month = "July"}}}};

products = new Product[] {
    new Product {IdProduct = 1, Price = 10 },
    new Product {IdProduct = 2, Price = 20 },
    new Product {IdProduct = 3, Price = 30 },
    new Product {IdProduct = 4, Price = 40 },
    new Product {IdProduct = 5, Price = 50 },
    new Product {IdProduct = 6, Price = 60 }};
```

Here is the corresponding Visual Basic 2008 support code.

```vb
Public Enum Countries
    USA
    Italy
End Enum

Public Class Customer
    Public Name As String
    Public City As String
    Public Country As Countries
    Public Orders As Order()
    Public Overrides Function ToString() As String
        Return String.Format("Name: {0} - City: {1} - Country: {2}",
            Me.Name, Me.City, Me.Country)
    End Function
End Class

Public Class Order
    Public IdOrder As Integer
    Public Quantity As Integer
    Public Shipped As Boolean
    Public Month As String
    Public IdProduct As Integer

    Public Overrides Function ToString() As String
        Return String.Format ( _
        "IdOrder: {0} - IdProduct: {1} - " & _
        "Quantity: {2} - Shipped: {3} - " & _
        "Month: {4}",  Me.IdOrder, Me.IdProduct, _
        Me.Quantity, Me.Shipped, Me.Month)
    End Function
End Class

Public Class Product
    Public IdProduct As Integer
    Public Price As Decimal

    Public Overrides Function ToString() As String
        Return String.Format("IdProduct: {0} - Price: {1}", Me.IdProduct,
            Me.Price)
    End Function
End Class
```

And here is the corresponding Visual Basic 2008 initialization code.

```vb
' --------------------------------------------------------
' Initialize a collection of customers with their orders:
' --------------------------------------------------------

customers = New Customer() { _
    New Customer With {.Name = "Paolo", .City = "Brescia", _
```

```
            .Country = Countries.Italy, .Orders = New Order() { _
                New Order With {.IdOrder = 1, .Quantity = 3, .IdProduct = 1, _
                    .Shipped = False, .Month = "January"}, _
                New Order With {.IdOrder = 2, .Quantity = 5, .IdProduct = 2, _
                    .Shipped = True, .Month = "May"}}}, _
        New Customer With {.Name = "Marco", .City = "Torino", _
            .Country = Countries.Italy, .Orders = New Order() { _
                New Order With {.IdOrder = 3, .Quantity = 10, .IdProduct = 1, _
                    .Shipped = False, .Month = "July"}, _
                New Order With {.IdOrder = 4, .Quantity = 20, .IdProduct = 3, _
                    .Shipped = True, .Month = "December"}}}, _
        New Customer With {.Name = "James", .City = "Dallas", _
            .Country = Countries.USA, .Orders = New Order() { _
                New Order With {.IdOrder = 5, .Quantity = 20, .IdProduct = 3, _
                    .Shipped = True, .Month = "December"}}}, _
        New Customer With {.Name = "Frank", .City = "Seattle", _
            .Country = Countries.USA, .Orders = New Order() { _
                New Order With {.IdOrder = 6, .Quantity = 20, .IdProduct = 5, _
                    .Shipped = False, .Month = "July"}}}}

products = New Product() { _
    New Product With {.IdProduct = 1, .Price = 10}, _
    New Product With {.IdProduct = 2, .Price = 20}, _
    New Product With {.IdProduct = 3, .Price = 30}, _
    New Product With {.IdProduct = 4, .Price = 40}, _
    New Product With {.IdProduct = 5, .Price = 50}, _
    New Product With {.IdProduct = 6, .Price = 60}}
```

Query Operators

In this section we will describe the main methods and generic delegates provided by the *System.Linq* namespace, which is hosted by System.Core.dll, to query items with LINQ.

The *Where* Operator

Imagine that you need to list the names and cities of customers from Italy. To filter a set of items, you can use the *Where* operator, which is also called a restriction operator because it restricts a set of items. Listing 3-1 shows a simple example.

Listing 3-1   A query with a restriction

```
var expr =
    from   c in customers
    where  c.Country == Countries.Italy
    select new { c.Name, c.City };
```

Here are the signatures of the *Where* operator:

```
public static IEnumerable<TSource> Where<TSource>(
    this IEnumerable<TSource> source,
    Func<TSource, Boolean> predicate);
```

```
public static IEnumerable<TSource> Where<TSource>(
    this IEnumerable<TSource> source,
    Func<TSource, Int32, Boolean> predicate);
```

As you can see, two signatures are available. In Listing 3-1, we used the first one, which enumerates items of the *source* sequence and yields those that verify the predicate (*c.Country == Countries.Italy*). The second signature accepts an additional parameter of type *Int32* for the predicate. This argument is used as a zero-based index of the elements within the *source* sequence. Keep in mind that if you pass null arguments to the predicates, an *ArgumentNull-Exception* error will be thrown. You can use the index parameter to start filtering by a particular index, as shown in Listing 3-2.

Listing 3-2   A query with a restriction and an index-based filter

```
var expr =
    customers
    .Where((c, index) => (c.Country == Countries.Italy && index >= 1))
    .Select(c => c.Name);
```

> **Important**   In Listing 3-2, we use the method syntax because the version of *Where* that we want to call is not supported by an equivalent query expression clause. We will use both syntaxes from here onward.

The result of Listing 3-2 will be the list of Italian customers, skipping the first one. As you can see from the following console output, the *index*-based partitioning occurs over the data source already filtered by *Country*.

Marco

The capability to filter items of the *source* sequence by using their positional index is useful when you want to extract a specific page of data from a large sequence of items. Listing 3-3 shows an example.

Listing 3-3   A query with a paging restriction

```
int start = 5;
int end = 10;

var expr =
    customers
    .Where((c, index) => ((index >= start) && (index < end)))
    .Select(c => c.Name);
```

Keep in mind that it is generally not a good practice to store large sequences of data loaded from a database persistence layer in memory, thus in general you should not have to paginate data in memory. Usually, it is better to page data at the persistence layer level.

Projection Operators

The following sections describe how to use projection operators. These operators are used to select (or "project") contents from the source enumeration into the result.

Select

In Listing 3-1, you saw an example of defining the result of the query by using the *Select* operator. The signatures for the *Select* operator are shown here:

```
public static IEnumerable<TResult> Select<TSource, TResult>(
    this ILnumerable<ISource> source,
    Func<TSource, IResult> selector);
public static IEnumerable<TResult> Select<TSource, TResult>(
    this IEnumerable<TSource> source,
    Func<TSource, Int32, TResult> selector);
```

The *Select* operator is one of the projection operators because it projects the query results, making them available through an object that implements *IEnumerable<TResult>*. This object will enumerate items identified by the *selector* predicate. Like the *Where* operator, *Select* enumerates the *source* sequence and yields the result of the *selector* predicate. Consider the following predicate:

```
var expr = customers.Select(c => c.Name);
```

This predicate's result will be a sequence of customer names (*IEnumerable<String>*). Now consider this example:

```
var expr = customers.Select(c => new { c.Name, c.City });
```

This predicate projects a sequence of instances of an anonymous type, defined as a tuple of *Name* and *City*, for each customer object. With the second overload of *Select*, we can also provide an argument of type *Int32* for the predicate. This zero-based index is used to define the positional index of each item inserted in the resulting sequence. In Listing 3-4 you can see an example of using this overload.

Listing 3-4   A projection with an *index* argument in the *selector* predicate

```
var expr =
    customers
        .Select((c, index) => new { index, c.Name, c.Country } );

foreach (var item in expr) {
    Console.WriteLine(item);
}
```

The following is the result of this query:

```
{ index = 0, Name = Paolo, Country = Italy }
{ index = 1, Name = Marco, Country = Italy }
{ index = 2, Name = James, Country = USA }
[ index = 3, Name = Frank, Country  USA ]
```

As with the *Where* operator, the *Select* operator's simple overload is available as a query expression keyword, while the more complex overload needs to be invoked explicitly as an extension method.

As you have already seen in Chapter 2 "LINQ Syntax Fundamentals," the query expression syntax of the *Select* operator changes slightly between C# 3.0 and Visual Basic 2008 in respect to anonymous type projection. In Visual Basic 2008 the anonymous type creation is implicitly determined by the query syntax, while in C# 3.0 you need to explicitly declare that you want a *new* anonymous type.

SelectMany

Imagine that you want to select all the orders of customers from Italy. You could write the query shown in Listing 3-5 using the verbose method.

Listing 3-5   The list of orders made by Italian customers

```
var orders =
    customers
    .Where(c => c.Country == Countries.Italy)
    .Select(c => c.Orders);

foreach(var item in orders) { Console.WriteLine(item); }
```

Because of the behavior of the *Select* operator, the resulting type of this query will be *IEnumerable <Order[]>*, where each item in the resulting sequence represents the array of orders of a single customer. In fact, the *Orders* property of a *Customer* instance is of type *Order[]*. The output of the code in Listing 3-5 would be the following:

```
DevLeap.Linq.LinqToObjects.Operators.Order[]
DevLeap.Linq.LinqToObjects.Operators.Order[]
```

To have a "flat" *IEnumerable<Order>* result type, we need to use the *SelectMany* operator:

```
public static IEnumerable<TResult> SelectMany<TSource, TResult>(
    this IEnumerable<TSource> source,
    Func<TSource, IEnumerable<TResult>> selector);
public static IEnumerable<TResult> SelectMany<TSource, TResult>(
    this IEnumerable<TSource> source,
    Func<TSource, Int32, IEnumerable<TResult>> selector);
public static IEnumerable<TResult> SelectMany<TSource, TCollection, TResult>(
    this IEnumerable<TSource> source,
    Func<TSource, IEnumerable<TCollection>> collectionSelector,
    Func<TSource, TCollection, TResult> resultSelector);
public static IEnumerable<TResult> SelectMany<TSource, TCollection, TResult>(
    this IEnumerable<TSource> source,
    Func<TSource, Int32, IEnumerable<TCollection>> collectionSelector,
    Func<TSource, TCollection, TResult> resultSelector);
```

This operator enumerates the *source* sequence and merges the resulting items, providing them as a single enumerable sequence. The second overload available is analogous to the equivalent overload for *Select*, which allows a zero-based integer index for indexing purposes. Listing 3-6 shows an example.

Listing 3-6   The flattened list of orders made by Italian customers

```
var orders =
    customers
    .Where(c => c.Country == Countries.Italy)
    .SelectMany(c => c.Orders);
```

Using the query expression syntax, the query in Listing 3-6 can be written with the code shown in Listing 3-7.

Listing 3-7   The flattened list of orders made by Italian customers, written with a query expression

```
var orders =
    from   c in customers
    where  c.Country == Countries.Italy
        from   o in c.Orders
        select o;
```

Both Listing 3-6 and Listing 3-7 have the following output, where we leverage the *ToString* override of the *Order* type.

```
IdOrder: 1 - IdProduct: 1 - Quantity: 3 - Shipped: False - Month: January
IdOrder: 2 - IdProduct: 2 - Quantity: 5 - Shipped: True - Month: May
IdOrder: 3 - IdProduct: 1 - Quantity: 10 - Shipped: False - Month: July
IdOrder: 4 - IdProduct: 3 - Quantity: 20 - Shipped: True - Month: December
```

The *select* keyword in query expressions, for all but the initial *from* clause, is translated to invocations of *SelectMany*. In other words, every time you see a query expression with more than one *from* clause, you can apply this rule: the *select* over the first *from* clause is converted to an invocation of *Select*, and the other *select* commands are translated into a *SelectMany* call.

The third and fourth overloads of *SelectMany* are useful whenever you need to select a custom result from the source set of sequences instead of simply merging their items, as with the two previous overloads. These overloads invoke the *collectionSelector* projection over the *source* sequence and return the result of the *resultSelector* projection. The result is applied to each item in the collections selected by *collectionSelector* and eventually projects a zero-based integer index in the case of the last *SelectMany* overload shown. In Listing 3-8, you can see an example of the third method overload used to extract a new anonymous type made from the *Quantity* and *IdProduct* of each order by Italian customers.

Listing 3-8   The list of *Quantity* and *IdProduct* of orders made by Italian customers

```
var items = customers
  .Where(c => c.Country == Countries.Italy)
  .SelectMany(c => c.Orders,
    (c, o) => new { o.Quantity, o.IdProduct });
```

The query in Listing 3-8 can be written with the query expression shown in Listing 3-9.

Listing 3-9   The list of *Quantity* and *IdProduct* of orders made by Italian customers, written with a query expression

```
var items =
    from   c in customers
    where  c.Country == Countries.Italy
        from   o in c.Orders
        select new {o.Quantity, o.IdProduct};
```

Ordering Operators

Another useful set of operators is the ordering operators group. Ordering operators are used to determine the ordering and direction of elements in output sequences.

OrderBy and *OrderByDescending*

Sometimes it is helpful to apply an order to the results of a database query. LINQ can order the results of queries, in ascending or descending order, by using ordering operators, just as we do in SQL syntax. For instance, if you need to select the *Name* and *City* of all Italian customers in descending order by *Name*, you can write the corresponding query expression shown in Listing 3-10.

Listing 3-10   A query expression with a descending *orderby* clause

```
var expr =
    from   c in customers
    where  c.Country == Countries.Italy
    orderby c.Name descending
    select  new { c.Name, c.City };
```

The query expression syntax will translate the *orderby* keyword into one of the following ordering extension methods:

```
public static IOrderedEnumerable<TSource> OrderBy<TSource, TKey>(
    this IEnumerable<TSource> source,
    Func<TSource, TKey> keySelector);
public static IOrderedEnumerable<TSource> OrderBy<TSource, TKey>(
    this IEnumerable<TSource> source,
```

```
    Func<TSource, TKey> keySelector,
    IComparer<TKey> comparer);
public static IOrderedEnumerable<TSource> OrderByDescending<TSource, TKey>(
    this IEnumerable<TSource> source,
    Func<TSource, TKey> keySelector);
public static IOrderedEnumerable<TSource> OrderByDescending<TSource, TKey>(
    this IEnumerable<TSource> source,
    Func<TSource, TKey> keySelector,
    IComparer<TKey> comparer);
```

As you can see, the two main extension methods, *OrderBy* and *OrderByDescending*, both have two overloads. The methods' names suggest their objective: *OrderBy* is for ascending order, and *OrderByDescending* is for descending order. The *keySelector* argument represents a function that extracts a key, of type *TKey*, from each item of type *TSource*, taken from the *source* sequence. The extracted key represents the typed content to be compared by the comparer while ordering, and the *TSource* type describes the type of each item of the *source* sequence. Both methods have an overload that allows you to provide a custom comparer. If no comparer is provided or the *comparer* argument is null, the *Default* property of the *Comparer<T>* generic type is used (*Comparer<TKey>.Default*).

> **Important**   The default *Comparer* returned by *Comparer<T>.Default* uses the generic interface *IComparable<T>* to compare two objects. If type *T* does not implement the *System.IComparable<T>* generic interface, the *Default* property of *Comparer<T>* returns a *Comparer* that uses the *System.IComparable* interface. If the type of *T* does not implement either of these interfaces, the *Compare* method of the *Default* comparer will throw an exception.

It is important to emphasize that these ordering methods return not just *IEnumerable<TSource>* but *IOrderedEnumerable<TSource>*, which is an interface that extends *IEnumerable<T>*.

The query expression in Listing 3-10 will be translated to the following extension method calls:

```
var expr =
    customers
    .Where(c => c.Country == Countries.Italy)
    .OrderByDescending(c => c.Name)
    .Select(c => new { c.Name, c.City } );
```

As you can see from the previous code excerpt, the *OrderByDescending* method, as well as all the ordering methods, accepts a key selector lambda expression that selects the key value from the range variable (*c*) of the current context. The selector can extract any sorting field available in the range variable, even if it is not projected in the output by the *Select* method. For instance, you can sort customers by *Country* and select their *Name* and *City* properties.

ThenBy and *ThenByDescending*

Whenever you need to order data by many different keys, you can take advantage of the *ThenBy* and *ThenByDescending* operators. Here are their signatures:

```
public static IOrderedEnumerable<TSource> ThenBy<TSource, TKey>(
    this IOrderedEnumerable<TSource> source,
    Func<TSource, TKey> keySelector);
public static IOrderedEnumerable<TSource> ThenBy<TSource, TKey>(
    this IOrderedEnumerable<TSource> source,
    Func<TSource, TKey> keySelector,
    IComparer<TKey> comparer);
public static IOrderedEnumerable<TSource> ThenByDescending<TSource, TKey>(
    this IOrderedEnumerable<ISource> source,
    Func<TSource, TKey> keySelector);
public static IOrderedEnumerable<TSource> ThenByDescending<TSource, TKey>(
    this IOrderedEnumerable<TSource> source,
    Func<TSource, TKey> keySelector,
    IComparer<TKey> comparer);
```

These operators have signatures similar to *OrderBy* and *OrderByDescending*. The difference is that *ThenBy* and *ThenByDescending* can be applied only to *IOrderedEnumerable<T>* and not to any *IEnumerable<T>*. Therefore, you can use the *ThenBy* or *ThenByDescending* operators just after the first use of *OrderBy* or *OrderByDescending*. Here is an example:

```
var expr = customers
    .Where(c => c.Country == Countries.Italy)
    .OrderByDescending(c => c.Name)
    .ThenBy(c => c.City)
    .Select(c => new { c.Name, c.City } );
```

In Listing 3-11, you can see the corresponding query expression.

Listing 3-11   A query expression with *orderby* and *thenby*

```
var expr =
    from    c in customers
    where   c.Country == Countries.Italy
    orderby c.Name descending, c.City
    select  new { c.Name, c.City };
```

> **Important**   In the case of multiple occurrences of the same key within a sequence to be ordered, the result is not guaranteed to be "stable." In such conditions, the original ordering might not be preserved by the comparer.

A custom comparer might be useful when the items in your *source* sequence need to be ordered using custom logic. For instance, imagine that you want to select all the orders of your customers ordered by month, shown in Listing 3-12:

Listing 3-12   A query expression ordered using the comparer provided by *Comparer<T>.Default*

```
var expr =
    from c in customers
        from   o in c.Orders
        orderby o.Month
        select o;
```

If you apply the default comparer to the *Month* property of the orders, you will get a result alphabetically ordered because of the behavior of *Comparer<T>.Default* that we have described previously. The result is wrong because the *Month* property is just a string and not a number or a date:

```
IdOrder: 4 - IdProduct: 3 - Quantity: 20 - Shipped: True - Month: December
IdOrder: 5 - IdProduct: 3 - Quantity: 20 - Shipped: True - Month: December
IdOrder: 1 - IdProduct: 1 - Quantity: 3 - Shipped: False - Month: January
IdOrder: 3 - IdProduct: 1 - Quantity: 10 - Shipped: False - Month: July
IdOrder: 6 - IdProduct: 5 - Quantity: 20 - Shipped: False - Month: July
IdOrder: 2 - IdProduct: 2 - Quantity: 5 - Shipped: True - Month: May
```

You should use a custom *MonthComparer* that correctly compares months:

```
using System.Globalization;

class MonthComparer: IComparer<string> {
    public int Compare(string x, string y) {
        DateTime xDate = DateTime.ParseExact(x, "MMMM", new CultureInfo("en-US"));
        DateTime yDate = DateTime.ParseExact(y, "MMMM", new CultureInfo("en-US"));
        return(Comparer<DateTime>.Default.Compare(xDate, yDate)); } }
```

The newly defined custom *MonthComparer* could be passed as a parameter while invoking the *OrderBy* extension method, as in Listing 3-13.

Listing 3-13   A custom comparer used with an *OrderBy* operator

```
var orders =
    customers
    .SelectMany(c => c.Orders)
    .OrderBy(o => o.Month, new MonthComparer());
```

Now the result of Listing 3-13 will be the following one, correctly ordered by month.

```
IdOrder: 1 - IdProduct: 1 - Quantity: 3 - Shipped: False - Month: January
IdOrder: 2 - IdProduct: 2 - Quantity: 5 - Shipped: True - Month: May
IdOrder: 3 - IdProduct: 1 - Quantity: 10 - Shipped: False - Month: July
IdOrder: 6 - IdProduct: 5 - Quantity: 20 - Shipped: False - Month: July
IdOrder: 4 - IdProduct: 3 - Quantity: 20 - Shipped: True - Month: December
IdOrder: 5 - IdProduct: 3 - Quantity: 20 - Shipped: True - Month: December
```

Reverse Operator

Sometimes you need to reverse the result of a query, listing the last item in the result first. LINQ provides a last-ordering operator, called *Reverse*, which allows you to perform this operation:

```
public static IEnumerable<TSource> Reverse<TSource>(
    this IEnumerable<TSource> source);
```

The implementation of *Reverse* is quite simple. It just yields each item in the *source* sequence in reverse order. Listing 3-14 shows an example of its use.

Listing 3-14   The *Reverse* operator applied

```
var expr =
    customers
    .Where(c => c.Country == Countries.Italy)
    .OrderByDescending(c => c.Name)
    .ThenBy(c => c.City)
    .Select(c => new { c.Name, c.City } )
    .Reverse();
```

The *Reverse* operator, like many other operators, does not have a corresponding keyword in query expressions. However, you can merge query expression syntax with operators (as we described in Chapter 2) as shown in Listing 3-15.

Listing 3-15   The *Reverse* operator applied to a query expression with *orderby* and *thenby*

```
var expr =
    (from    c in customers
    where    c.Country == Countries.Italy
    orderby c.Name descending, c.City
    select  new { c.Name, c.City }
    ).Reverse();
```

As you can see, we apply the *Reverse* operator to the expression resulting from Listing 3-11. Under the covers, the inner query expression is first translated to the resulting list of extension methods, and then the *Reverse* method is applied at the end of the extension methods chain. It is just like Listing 3-14, but hopefully easier to write.

Grouping Operators

Now you have seen how to select, filter, and order sequences of items. Sometimes when querying contents, you also need to group results based on specific criteria. To realize content groupings, you use a grouping operator.

The *GroupBy* operator, also called a grouping operator, is the only operator of this family and provides a rich set of eight overloads. Here are the first four:

```
public static IEnumerable<IGrouping<TKey, TSource>> GroupBy<TSource, TKey>(
    this IEnumerable<TSource> source, Func<TSource, TKey> keySelector);
public static IEnumerable<IGrouping<TKey, TSource>> GroupBy<TSource, TKey>(
    this IEnumerable<TSource> source, Func<TSource, TKey> keySelector,
    IEqualityComparer<TKey> comparer);
public static IEnumerable<IGrouping<TKey, TElement>> GroupBy<TSource, TKey, TElement>(
    this IEnumerable<TSource> source, Func<TSource, TKey> keySelector,
    Func<TSource, TElement> elementSelector);
public static IEnumerable<IGrouping<TKey, TElement>> GroupBy<TSource, TKey, TElement>(
    this IEnumerable<TSource> source, Func<TSource, TKey> keySelector,
    Func<TSource, TElement> elementSelector,
    IEqualityComparer<TKey> comparer);
```

These *GroupBy* method's overloads select pairs of keys and items for each item in *source*. They use the *keySelector* predicate to extract the *Key* value from each item to group results based on the different *Key* values. The *elementSelector* argument, if present, defines a function that maps the source element within the *source* sequence to the destination element of the resulting sequence. If you do not specify the *elementSelector*, elements are mapped directly from the source to the destination. (You will see an example of this later in the chapter, in Listing 3-18.) Then they yield a sequence of *IGrouping<TKey, TElement>* objects, where each group consists of a sequence of items with a common *Key* value.

The *IGrouping<TKey, TElement>* generic interface is a specialized implementation of *IEnumerable<TElement>*. This implementation can return a specific *Key* of type *TKey* for each item within the enumeration:

```
public interface IGrouping<TKey, TElement> : IEnumerable<TElement> {
    TKey Key { get; }
}
```

From a practical point of view, a type that implements this generic interface is simply a typed enumeration with an identifying type *Key* for each item.

There are also four more signatures useful to shape a custom result projection.

```
public static IEnumerable<TResult> GroupBy<TSource, TKey, TResult>(
    this IEnumerable<TSource> source, Func<TSource, TKey> keySelector,
    Func<TKey, IEnumerable<TSource>, TResult> resultSelector);
public static IEnumerable<TResult> GroupBy<TSource, TKey, TElement, TResult>(
    this IEnumerable<TSource> source, Func<TSource, TKey> keySelector,
    Func<TSource, TElement> elementSelector,
    Func<TKey, IEnumerable<TSource>, TResult> resultSelector);
```

```
public static IEnumerable<TResult> GroupBy<TSource, TKey, TResult>(
    this IEnumerable<TSource> source, Func<TSource, TKey> keySelector,
    Func<TKey, IEnumerable<TSource>, TResult> resultSelector,
    IEqualityComparer<TKey> comparer);
public static IEnumerable<TResult> GroupBy<TSource, TKey, TElement, TResult>(
    this IEnumerable<TSource> source, Func<TSource, TKey> keySelector,
    Func<TSource, TElement> elementSelector,
    Func<TKey, IEnumerable<TSource>, TResult> resultSelector,
    IEqualityComparer<TKey> comparer);
```

The *resultSelector* argument present in these last signatures allows you to define a projection for the *GroupBy* operation, which enables you to return an *IEnumerable<TResult>*. This last set of overloads is useful for selecting a flattened enumeration of items, based on aggregations over the grouping sets. You will see an example of this syntax later in this section.

One last optional argument you can pass to some of these methods is a custom *comparer*, which is useful when you need to compare key values and define group membership. If no custom *comparer* is provided, the *EqualityComparer<TKey>.Default* is used. The order of keys and items within each group corresponds to their occurrence within the *source*. Listing 3-16 shows an example of using the *GroupBy* operator.

Listing 3-16   The *GroupBy* operator used to group customers by *Country*

```
var expr = customers.GroupBy(c => c.Country);

foreach(IGrouping<Countries, Customer> customerGroup in expr) {
    Console.WriteLine("Country: {0}", customerGroup.Key);
    foreach(var item in customerGroup) {
        Console.WriteLine("\t{0}", item);
    }
}
```

Here is the console output of Listing 3-16.

```
Country: Italy
        Name: Paolo - City: Brescia - Country: Italy
        Name: Marco - City: Torino - Country: Italy
Country: USA
        Name: James - City: Dallas - Country: USA
        Name: Frank - City: Seattle - Country: USA
```

As Listing 3-16 shows, you need to enumerate all group keys before iterating over the items contained within each group. Every group is an instance of a type that implements *IGrouping<Countries, Customer>*, because we are using the default *elementSelector* that directly projects the source *Customer* instances into the result. In query expressions, the *GroupBy* operator can be defined using the *group ... by ...* syntax, which is shown in Listing 3-17.

Listing 3-17   A query expression with a *group by* syntax

```
var expr =
    from  c in customers
    group c by c.Country;

foreach(IGrouping<Countries, Customer> customerGroup in expr) {
    Console.WriteLine("Country: {0}", customerGroup.Key);
    foreach(var item in customerGroup) {
        Console.WriteLine("\t{0}", item);
    }
}
```

The code defined in Listing 3-16 is semantically equivalent to the code shown in Listing 3-17.

Listing 3-18 is another example of grouping, this time with a custom *elementSelector*.

Listing 3-18   The *GroupBy* operator used to group customer names by *Country*

```
var expr =
    customers
    .GroupBy(c => c.Country, c => c.Name);
foreach(IGrouping<Countries, String> customerGroup in expr) {
    Console.WriteLine("Country: {0}", customerGroup.Key);
    foreach(var item in customerGroup) {
        Console.WriteLine("\t{0}", item);
    }
}
```

Here is the result of this code:

```
Country: Italy
  Paolo
  Marco
Country: USA
  James
  Frank
```

In this last example, the result is a class that implements *IGrouping<Countries, String>*, because the *elementSelector* predicate projects only the customers' names (of type *String*) into the output sequence.

In Listing 3-19 you can see an example of using the *GroupBy* operator with a *resultSelector* predicate argument.

Listing 3-19   The *GroupBy* operator used to group customer names by *Country*

```
var expr = customers
   .GroupBy(c => c.Country,
      (k, c) => new { Key = k, Count = c.Count()});
foreach (var group in expr) {
    Console.WriteLine("Key: {0} - Count: {1}", group.Key, group.Count);
}
```

In this last example we projected the *Key* value of each group and the *Count* of elements for each group. In cases when you need them, there are also *GroupBy* overloads that allow you to define both a *resultSelector* and a custom *elementSelector*. They are useful whenever you need to project groups, calculating aggregations on each group of items, but also having the single items through a custom *elementSelector* predicate. Listing 3-20 shows an example.

Listing 3-20   The *GroupBy* operator used to group customer names by *Country*, with a custom *resultSelector* and *elementSelector*

```
var expr = customers
    .GroupBy(
        c => c.Country, // keySelector
        c => new { OrdersCount = c.Orders.Count() }, // elementSelector
        (key, elements) => new { // resultSelector
            Key = key,
            Count = elements.Count(),
            OrdersCount = elements.Sum(item => item.OrdersCount) });

foreach (var group in expr) {
    Console.WriteLine("Key: {0} - Count: {1} - Orders Count: {2}",
        group.Key, group.Count , group.OrdersCount);
}
```

The code in Listing 3-20 shows an example of a query that returns a flat enumeration of items made of customers grouped by *Country*, the count of customers for each group, and the total count of orders executed by customers of each group. Notice that the result of the query is an *IEnumerable<TResult>* and not an *IGrouping<TKey, TElement>*. Here is the output of the code in Listing 3-20.

```
Key: Italy - Count: 2 - Orders Count: 4
Key: USA - Count: 2 - Orders Count: 2
```

Join Operators

Join operators are used to define relationships within sequences in query expressions. From a SQL and relational point of view, almost every query requires joining one or more tables. In LINQ, a set of join operators is defined to implement this behavior.

Join

The first operator of this group is, of course, the *Join* method, which is defined by the following signatures:

```
public static IEnumerable<TResult> Join<TOuter, TInner, TKey, TResult>(
    this IEnumerable<TOuter> outer,
    IEnumerable<TInner> inner,
    Func<TOuter, TKey> outerKeySelector,
    Func<TInner, TKey> innerKeySelector,
    Func<TOuter, TInner, TResult> resultSelector);
public static IEnumerable<TResult> Join<TOuter, TInner, TKey, TResult>(
    this IEnumerable<TOuter> outer,
    IEnumerable<TInner> inner,
    Func<TOuter, TKey> outerKeySelector,
    Func<TInner, TKey> innerKeySelector,
    Func<TOuter, TInner, TResult> resultSelector,
    IEqualityComparer<TKey> comparer);
```

Join requires a set of four generic types. The *TOuter* type represents the type of the *outer* source sequence, and the *TInner* type describes the type of the *inner* source sequence. The predicates *outerKeySelector* and *innerKeySelector* define how to extract the identifying keys from the *outer* and *inner* source sequence items, respectively. These keys are both of type *TKey*, and their equivalence defines the join condition. The *resultSelector* predicate defines what to project into the result sequence, which will be an implementation of *IEnumerable<TResult>*. *TResult* is the last generic type needed by the operator, and it defines the type of each single item in the join result sequence. The second overload of the method has an additional custom equality comparer, used to compare the keys. If the *comparer* argument is null or if the first overload of the method is invoked, a default key comparer (*EqualityComparer<TKey>.Default*) will be used.

Here is an example that will make the use of *Join* clearer. Think about our customers, with their orders and products. In Listing 3-21, a query joins orders with their corresponding products.

Listing 3-21   The *Join* operator used to map orders with products

```
var expr =
    customers
    .SelectMany(c => c.Orders)
    .Join( products,
           o => o.IdProduct,
           p => p.IdProduct,
           (o, p) => new {o.Month, o.Shipped, p.IdProduct, p.Price });
```

The following is the result of the query:

```
{Month = January, Shipped = False, IdProduct = 1, Price = 10}
{Month = May, Shipped = True, IdProduct = 2, Price = 20}
{Month = July, Shipped = False, IdProduct = 1, Price = 10}
{Month = December, Shipped = True, IdProduct = 3, Price = 30}
{Month = December, Shipped = True, IdProduct = 3, Price = 30}
{Month = July, Shipped = False, IdProduct = 5, Price = 50}
```

In this example, *orders* represents the outer sequence and *products* is the inner sequence. The *o* and *p* used in lambda expressions are of type *Order* and *Product*, respectively. Internally, the operator collects the elements of the *inner* sequence into a hash table, using their keys extracted with *innerKeySelector*. It then enumerates the *outer* sequence and maps its elements, based on the *Key* value extracted with *outerKeySelector*, to the hash table of items. Because of its implementation, the *Join* operator result sequence keeps the order of the *outer* sequence first, and then uses the order of the *inner* sequence for each *outer* sequence element.

From an SQL point of view, the example in Listing 3-21 can be thought of as an inner equi-join somewhat like the following SQL query:

```
SELECT     o.Month, o.Shipped, p.IdProduct, p.Price
FROM       Orders AS o
INNER JOIN Products AS p
     ON    o.IdProduct = p.IdProduct
```

If you want to translate the SQL syntax into the *Join* operator syntax, you can think about the columns selection in SQL as the *resultSelector* predicate, while the equality condition on *IdProduct* columns (of orders and products) corresponds to the pair of *innerKeySelector* and *outerKeySelector* predicates.

The *Join* operator has a corresponding query expression syntax, which is shown in Listing 3-22.

Listing 3-22   The *Join* operator query expression syntax

```
var expr =
    from c in customers
        from  o in c.Orders
        join  p in products
             on o.IdProduct equals p.IdProduct
        select new {o.Month, o.Shipped, p.IdProduct, p.Price };
```

Important   As we described in Chapter 2, the order of items to relate (*o.IdProduct equals p.IdProduct*) in query expression syntax must have the outer sequence first and the inner sequence after; otherwise, the query expression will not compile. This requirement is different from standard SQL queries, in which item ordering does not matter.

In Listing 3-23 you can see the Visual Basic 2008 syntax corresponding to Listing 3-22. Take a look at the SQL-like selection syntax.

Listing 3-23   The *Join* operator query expression syntax expressed in Visual Basic 2008

```
Dim expr = _
    From c In customers _
    From o In c.Orders _
    Join p In products _
        On o.IdProduct Equals p.IdProduct _
    Select o.Month, o.Shipped, p.IdProduct, p.Price
```

GroupJoin

In cases in which you need to define something similar to a LEFT OUTER JOIN or a RIGHT OUTER JOIN, you need to use the *GroupJoin* operator. Its signatures are quite similar to the *Join* operator:

```
public static IEnumerable<TResult>
    GroupJoin<TOuter, TInner, TKey, TResult>(
        this IEnumerable<TOuter> outer,
        IEnumerable<TInner> inner,
        Func<TOuter, TKey> outerKeySelector,
        Func<TInner, TKey> innerKeySelector,
        Func<TOuter, IEnumerable<TInner>, TResult> resultSelector);
public static IEnumerable<IResult>
    GroupJoin<TOuter, TInner, TKey, TResult>(
        this IEnumerable<TOuter> outer,
        IEnumerable<TInner> inner,
        Func<TOuter, TKey> outerKeySelector,
        Func<TInner, TKey> innerKeySelector,
        Func<TOuter, IEnumerable<TInner>, TResult> resultSelector,
        IEqualityComparer<TKey> comparer);
```

The only difference is the definition of the *resultSelector* projector. It requires an instance of *IEnumerable<TInner>*, instead of a single object of type *TInner*, because it projects a hierarchical result of type *IEnumerable<TResult>*. Each item of type *TResult* consists of an item extracted from the *outer* sequence and a group of items, of type *TInner*, joined from the *inner* sequence.

As a result of this behavior, the output is not a flattened outer equi-join, which would be produced by using the *Join* operator, but a hierarchical sequence of items. Nevertheless, you can define queries using *GroupJoin* with results equivalent to the *Join* operator whenever the mapping is a one-to-one relationship. In cases in which a corresponding element group in the *inner* sequence is absent, the *GroupJoin* operator extracts the *outer* sequence element paired with an empty sequence (*Count = 0*). In Listing 3-24, you can see an example of this operator.

Listing 3-24   The *GroupJoin* operator used to map products with orders, if present

```
var expr =
    products
    .GroupJoin(
        customers.SelectMany(c => c.Orders),
        p => p.IdProduct,
        o => o.IdProduct,
        (p, orders) => new { p.IdProduct, Orders = orders });

foreach(var item in expr) {
    Console.WriteLine("Product: {0}", item.IdProduct);
    foreach (var order in item.Orders) {
        Console.WriteLine("\t{0}", order); }}
```

The following is the result of Listing 3-24:

```
Product: 1
    IdOrder: 1 - IdProduct: 1 - Quantity: 3 - Shipped: False - Month: January
    IdOrder: 3 - IdProduct: 1 - Quantity: 10 - Shipped: False - Month: July
Product: 2
    IdOrder: 2 - IdProduct: 2 - Quantity: 5 - Shipped: True - Month: May
Product: 3
    IdOrder: 4 - IdProduct: 3 - Quantity: 20 - Shipped: True - Month: December
    IdOrder: 5 - IdProduct: 3 - Quantity: 20 - Shipped: True - Month: December
Product: 4
Product: 5
    IdOrder: 6 - IdProduct: 5 - Quantity: 20 - Shipped: False - Month: July
Product: 6
```

You can see that products 4 and 6 have no mapping orders, but the query returns them nonetheless. You can think about this operator like a SELECT ... FOR XML AUTO query in Transact-SQL in Microsoft SQL Server 2000 and 2005. In fact, it returns results hierarchically grouped like a set of XML nodes nested within their parent nodes, similar to the default result of a FOR XML AUTO query.

In a query expression, the *GroupJoin* operator is defined as a *join ... into ...* clause. The query expression shown in Listing 3-24 is equivalent to Listing 3-25.

Listing 3-25   A query expression with a *join ... into* clause

```
var customersOrders =
    from c in customers
        from o in c.Orders
        select o;

var expr =
    from   p in products
    join   o in customersOrders
              on p.IdProduct equals o.IdProduct
              into orders
    select new { p.IdProduct, Orders = orders };
```

In this example, we first define an expression called *customersOrders* to extract the flat list of orders. (This expression still uses the *SelectMany* operator because of the double *from* clause.) We could also define a single query expression, nesting the *customersOrders* expression within the main query. This approach is shown in Listing 3-26.

Listing 3-26   The query expression of Listing 3-25 in its compact version

```
var expr =
    from  p in products
    join  o in (
        from c in customers
            from  o in c.Orders
            select o
        ) on p.IdProduct equals o.IdProduct
        into orders
    select new { p.IdProduct, Orders = orders };
```

Set Operators

Our journey through LINQ operators continues with a group of methods that are used to handle sets of data, applying common set operations (*union*, *intersect*, and *except*) and selecting unique occurrences of items (*distinct*).

Distinct

Imagine that you want to extract all products that are mapped to orders, avoiding duplicates. This requirement could be solved in standard SQL by using a DISTINCT clause within a JOIN query. LINQ provides a *Distinct* operator too. Its signatures are quite simple. It requires just a *source* sequence, from which all the distinct occurrences of items will be yielded, and provides an overload with a custom *IEqualityComparer<TSource>*, which we will cover later.

```
public static IEnumerable<TSource> Distinct<TSource>(
    this IEnumerable<TSource> source);
public static IEnumerable<TSource> Distinct<TSource>(
    this IEnumerable<TSource> source,
    IEqualityComparer<TSource> comparer);
```

An example of the operator is shown in Listing 3-27.

Listing 3-27   The *Distinct* operator applied to the list of products used in orders

```
var expr =
    customers
    .SelectMany(c => c.Orders)
    .Join(products,
        o => o.IdProduct,
        p => p.IdProduct,
        (o, p) => p)
    .Distinct();
```

Distinct does not have an equivalent query expression clause; hence, as we did in Listing 3-15, we can apply this operator to the result of a query expression, as shown in Listing 3-28.

Listing 3-28   The *Distinct* operator applied to a query expression

```
var expr =
    (from c in customers
         from   o in c.Orders
         join   p in products
                on o.IdProduct equals p.IdProduct
         select p
    ).Distinct();
```

By default, *Distinct* compares and identifies elements using their *GetHashCode* and *Equals* methods because internally it uses a default comparer of type *EqualityComparer<T>.Default*. We can, if necessary, override our type behavior to change the *Distinct* result, or we can just use the second overload of the *Distinct* method.

```
public static IEnumerable<TSource> Distinct<TSource>(
    this IEnumerable<TSource> source,
    IEqualityComparer<TSource> comparer);
```

This last overload accepts a *comparer* argument, available to provide a custom comparer for instances of type *TSource*.

> **Note**   You will see an example of how to compare reference types in the *Union* operator in Listing 3-29.

Union, *Intersect*, and *Except*

Within the group of set operators, three more operators are useful for classic set operations. They are *Union*, *Intersect*, and *Except*, and they share a similar definition:

```
public static IEnumerable<TSource> Union<TSource>(
    this IEnumerable<TSource> first,
    IEnumerable<TSource> second);
public static IEnumerable<TSource> Union<TSource>(
    this IEnumerable<TSource> first,
    IEnumerable<TSource> second,
    IEqualityComparer<TSource> comparer);
public static IEnumerable<TSource> Intersect<TSource>(
    this IEnumerable<TSource> first,
    IEnumerable<TSource> second);
public static IEnumerable<TSource> Intersect<TSource>(
    this IEnumerable<TSource> first,
    IEnumerable<TSource> second,
    IEqualityComparer<TSource> comparer);
```

```
public static IEnumerable<TSource> Except<TSource>(
    this IEnumerable<TSource> first,
    IEnumerable<TSource> second);
public static IEnumerable<TSource> Except<TSource>(
    this IEnumerable<TSource> first,
    IEnumerable<TSource> second,
    IEqualityComparer<TSource> comparer);
```

The *Union* operator enumerates the *first* sequence and the *second* sequence in that order and yields each element that has not already been yielded. For instance, in Listing 3-29, you can see how to merge two sets of *Integer* numbers.

Listing 3-29   The *Union* operator applied to sets of *Integer* numbers

```
Int32[] setOne = {1, 5,  6, 9};
Int32[] setTwo = {4, 5, 7, 11};

var union = setOne.Union(setTwo);
foreach (var i in union) {
    Console.Write(i + ", ");
}
```

Here is the console output of Listing 3-29:

```
1, 5, 6, 9, 4, 7, 11,
```

As with the *Distinct* operator, in *Union*, *Intersect*, and *Except*, the elements are compared by using the *GetHashCode* and *Equals* methods in the first overload, or by using a custom *comparer* in the second overload. Consider the code excerpt of Listing 3-30.

Listing 3-30   The *Union* operator applied to a couple of sets of products

```
Product[] productSetOne = {
    new Product {IdProduct = 46, Price = 1000 },
    new Product {IdProduct = 27, Price = 2000 },
    new Product {IdProduct = 14, Price = 500}};
Product[] productSetTwo = {
    new Product {IdProduct = 11, Price = 350 },
    new Product {IdProduct = 46, Price = 1000 }};

var productsUnion = productSetOne.Union(productSetTwo);

foreach (var item in productsUnion) {
    Console.WriteLine(item);
}
```

Here is the console output of this code:

```
IdProduct: 46 - Price: 1000
IdProduct: 27 - Price: 2000
IdProduct: 14 - Price: 500
IdProduct: 11 - Price: 350
IdProduct: 46 - Price: 1000
```

The result might seem unexpected because we have two rows, the first and the last, that appear to be the same. However, if you look at the initialization code used in Listing 3-30, each product is a different instance of the *Product* reference type. Even if the second product of *productSetTwo* is semantically equal to the first product of *productSetOne*, they are different objects that have two different hash codes.

We have not defined a value type semantic for our *Product* reference type. To get the expected result, we can implement a value type semantic by overriding the *GetHashCode* and *Equals* implementations of the type to be compared. In this situation, it might be useful to do that, as you can see in this new *Product* implementation:

```
public class Product {
    public int IdProduct;
    public decimal Price;

    public override string ToString(){
        return String.Format("IdProduct: {0} - Price: {1}",
            this.IdProduct, this.Price);
    }

    public override bool Equals(object obj) {
        if (!(obj is Product))
            return false;
        else {
            Product p = (Product)obj;
            return (p.IdProduct == this.IdProduct &&
                p.Price == this.Price);
        }
    }

    public override int GetHashCode(){
        return String.Format("{0}|{1}", this.IdProduct, this.Price)
            .GetHashCode();
    }
}
```

Another way to get the correct result is to use the second overload of the *Union* method, providing a custom comparer for the *Product* type. A final way to get the expected distinct behavior is to define the *Product* type as a value type, using *struct* instead of *class* in its declaration. By the way, it is not always possible to define a *struct* because sometimes you need to implement an object-oriented infrastructure using type inheritance.

```
// Using struct instead of class, we get a value type
public struct Product {
    public int IdProduct;
    public decimal Price;
}
```

Remember that an anonymous type is defined as a reference type with a value type semantic. In other words, all anonymous types are defined as a class with an override of *GetHashCode* and *Equals* written by the compiler, with an implementation that leverages *GetHashCode* and *Equals* for each property of the anonymous type instance.

In Listing 3-31, you can find an example of using *Intersect* and *Except*.

Listing 3-31   The *Intersect* and *Except* operators applied to the same products set used in Listing 3-30

```
var expr = productSetOne.Intersect(productSetTwo);
var expr = productSetOne.Except(productSetTwo);
```

The *Intersect* operator yields only the elements that occur in both sequences, and the *Except* operator yields all the elements in the *first* sequence that are not present in the *second* sequence. Once again, there are no compact clauses to define set operators in query expressions, but we can apply them to query expression results, as in Listing 3-32.

Listing 3-32   Set operators applied to query expressions

```
var expr = (
    from c in customers
        from o in c.Orders
            join p in products on o.IdProduct equals p.IdProduct
    where c.Country == Countries.Italy
    select p)
    .Intersect(
    from c in customers
        from o in c.Orders
            join p in products on o.IdProduct equals p.IdProduct
    where c.Country == Countries.USA
    select p);
```

Value Type vs. Reference Type Semantic   Remember that all the considerations for *Union* and *Distinct* operators are also valid for *Intersect* and *Except*. In general, they are valid for each operation that involves a comparison of two items made by LINQ to Objects. The result of the *Intersect* operation illustrated in Listing 3-31 is an empty set whenever the *Product* type is a reference type with no override of the *GetHashCode* and *Equals* methods. If you define *Product* as a value type (using *struct* instead of *class*), you get a product (IdProduct: 46 - Price: 1000) as an *Intersection* result. Once again, we want to emphasize that when using LINQ, it is better to use types with a value type semantic, even if they are reference types, so that you get consistent behavior across all regular and anonymous types.

Aggregate Operators

At times, you need to make some aggregations over sequences to make calculations on source items. To accomplish this, LINQ provides the family of aggregate operators that implement the most common aggregate functions: *Count*, *LongCount*, *Sum*, *Min*, *Max*, *Average*, and *Aggregate*. Many of these operators are simple to use because their behavior is easy to understand. However, remember that LINQ to Objects works over in-memory instances of *IEnumerable<T>* types, thus the code working on this enumeration might have some performance issues in cases in which you need to browse the query result multiple times.

Count and LongCount

Imagine that you want to list all customers, each one followed by the number of orders the customer has placed. In Listing 3-33, you can see an equivalent syntax, based on the *Count* operator.

Listing 3-33   The *Count* operator applied to customer orders

```
var expr =
    from  c in customers
    select new {c.Name, c.Country, OrdersCount = c.Orders.Count() };
```

The *Count* operator provides a couple of signatures, as does the *LongCount* operator:

```
public static int Count<TSource>(
    this IEnumerable<TSource> source);
public static int Count<TSource>(
    this IEnumerable<TSource> source,
    Func<TSource, Boolean> predicate);
public static long LongCount<TSource>(
    this IEnumerable<TSource> source);
public static long LongCount<TSource>(
    this IEnumerable<TSource> source,
    Func<TSource, Boolean> predicate);
```

The signature shown in Listing 3-33 is the common and simpler one that simply counts items in the *source* sequence. The second method overload accepts a *predicate*, which is used to filter the items to count. *LongCount* variations simply return a *long* instead of an *integer*.

Sum

The *Sum* operator requires more attention because it has multiple definitions:

```
public static Numeric Sum(
    this IEnumerable<Numeric> source);
public static Numeric Sum<TSource>(
    this IEnumerable<TSource> source,
    Func<TSource, Numeric> selector);
```

We used *Numeric* in the syntax to generalize the return type of the *Sum* operator. In practice, it has many definitions, one for each of the main *Numeric* types: *Int32*, *Nullable<Int32>*, *Int64*, *Nullable<Int64>*, *Single*, *Nullable<Single>*, *Double*, *Nullable<Double>*, *Decimal*, and *Nullable<Decimal>*.

Important   Remember that in C# 2.0 and later, the question mark that appears after a value type name (*T?*) defines a nullable type (*Nullable<T>*) of this type. For instance, you can write *int?* instead of *Nullable<System.Int32>*.

The first implementation sums the *source* sequence items, assuming that the items are all of the same numeric type, and returns the result. In the case of an empty *source* sequence, zero is returned. This implementation can be used when the items can be summed directly. For example, we can sum an array of integers as in this code:

```
int[] values = { 1, 3, 9, 29 };
int   total  = values.Sum();
```

When the sequence is not made up of simple *Numeric* types, we need to extract values to be summed from each item in the *source* sequence. To do that, we can use the second overload, which accepts a *selector* argument. You can see an example of this syntax in Listing 3-34.

Listing 3-34   The *Sum* operator applied to customer orders

```
var customersOrders =
    from c in customers
        from  o in c.Orders
        join  p in products
              on o.IdProduct equals p.IdProduct
        select new { c.Name, OrderAmount = o.Quantity * p.Price };

foreach (var o in customersOrders) {
    Console.WriteLine(o);
}

Console.WriteLine();

var expr =
    from  c in customers
    join  o in customersOrders
          on c.Name equals o.Name
          into customersWithOrders
    select new { c.Name,
             TotalAmount = customersWithOrders.Sum(o => o.OrderAmount) };

foreach (var item in expr) {
    Console.WriteLine(item);
}
```

In Listing 3-34, we join customers into the *customersOrders* sequence to get the list of the customer names associated with the total amount of orders placed, with the result shown in the following output:

```
{ Name = Paolo, OrderAmount = 30 }
{ Name = Paolo, OrderAmount = 100 }
{ Name = Marco, OrderAmount = 100 }
{ Name = Marco, OrderAmount = 600 }
{ Name = James, OrderAmount = 600 }
{ Name = Frank, OrderAmount = 1000 }
```

Next, another join is used for each customer to get the total value of his orders, calculated with the *Sum* operator, with the following result:

```
{ Name = Paolo, TotalAmount = 130 }
{ Name = Marco, TotalAmount = 700 }
{ Name = James, TotalAmount = 600 }
{ Name = Frank, TotalAmount = 1000 }
```

As usual, we can collapse the previous code by using nested queries, which is the approach shown in Listing 3-35.

Listing 3-35   The *Sum* operator applied to customer orders, with a nested query

```
var expr =
    from    c in customers
    join    o in (
            from c in customers
                from    o in c.Orders
                join    p in products
                        on o.IdProduct equals p.IdProduct
                select new { c.Name, OrderAmount = o.Quantity * p.Price }
            ) on c.Name equals o.Name
            into customersWithOrders
    select new { c.Name,
            TotalAmount = customersWithOrders.Sum(o => o.OrderAmount) };
```

SQL vs. LINQ Query Expression Syntax

At this point, we want to make a comparison with SQL syntax because there are similarities but also important differences. The following is an SQL statement similar to the query expression in Listing 3-35, assuming that customer names are unique:

```
SELECT    c.Name, SUM(o.OrderAmount) AS OrderAmount
FROM      customers AS c
INNER JOIN (
    SELECT    c.Name, o.Quantity * p.Price AS OrderAmount
    FROM      customers AS c
    INNER JOIN orders AS o ON c.Name = o.Name
    INNER JOIN products AS p ON o.IdProduct = p.IdProduct
    ) AS o
ON        c.Name = o.Name
GROUP BY c.Name
```

You can see that this SQL syntax is redundant. In fact, we can obtain the same result with this simpler SQL query:

```
SELECT    c.Name, SUM(o.OrderAmount) AS OrderAmount
FROM      customers AS c
INNER JOIN (
    SELECT    o.Name, o.Quantity * p.Price AS OrderAmount
```

```
        FROM          orders AS o
        INNER JOIN products AS p ON o.IdProduct = p.IdProduct
        ) AS o
ON        c.Name = o.Name
GROUP BY c.Name
```

But it can be simpler and shorter still, as in the following SQL query:

```
SELECT    c.Name, SUM(o.Quantity * p.Price) AS OrderAmount
FROM      customers AS c
INNER JOIN orders AS o ON c.Name = o.Name
INNER JOIN products AS p ON o.IdProduct = p.IdProduct
GROUP RY   c.Name
```

If we started from this last SQL query and tried to write a corresponding query expression syntax using LINQ, we would probably encounter some difficulties. The reason is that SQL queries data through relationships, but all data is flat (in tables) until it is queried. On the other hand, LINQ handles data that can have native hierarchical relationships, just as our Customer/Orders/Products data. This difference implies that sometimes one approach has advantages over the other, depending on the kind of query and the kind of data you are working on.

For these reasons, the best expression of a query can appear differently in SQL and in LINQ query expression syntax, even if the query is obtaining the same results from the same data.

Min and Max

Within the set of aggregate operators, *Min* and *Max* calculate the minimum and maximum values of the source sequence, respectively. Both of these extension methods provide a rich set of overloads:

```
public static Numeric Min/Max(
    this IEnumerable<Numeric> source);
public static TSource Min<TSource>/Max<TSource>(
    this IEnumerable<TSource> source);
public static Numeric Min<TSource>/Max<TSource>(
    this IEnumerable<TSource> source,
    Func<TSource, Numeric> selector);
public static TResult Min<TSource, TResult>/Max<TSource, TResult>(
    this IEnumerable<TSource> source,
    Func<TSource, TResult> selector);
```

The first signature, as in the *Sum* operator, provides many definitions for the main numeric types (*Int32*, *Nullable<Int32>*, *Int64*, *Nullable<Int64>*, *Single*, *Nullable<Single>*, *Double*, *Nullable<Double>*, *Decimal*, and *Nullable<Decimal>*), and it computes the minimum or maximum value on an arithmetic basis, using the elements of the *source* sequence. This signature is useful when the source elements are numbers by themselves, as in Listing 3-36.

Listing 3-36   The *Min* operator applied to order quantities

```
var expr =
    (from c in customers
         from  o in c.Orders
         select o.Quantity
    ).Min();
```

The second signature computes the minimum or maximum value of the source elements regardless of their type. The comparison is made using the *IComparable<TSource>* interface implementation, if supported by the source elements, or the non-generic *IComparable* inter-face implementation. If the source type *TSource* does not implement either of these interfaces, an *ArgumentException* error will be thrown, with an *Exception.Message* equal to "At least one object must implement *IComparable*." To examine this situation, take a look at Listing 3-37, in which the resulting anonymous type does not implement either of the interfaces required by the *Min* operator.

Listing 3-37   The *Min* operator applied to wrong types (thereby throwing an *ArgumentException*)

```
var expr =
    (from c in customers
         from o in c.Orders
         select new { o.IdProduct, o.Quantity }
    ).Min();
```

In the case of an empty source or null values in the source sequence, the result will be null whenever the *Numeric* type is a nullable type; otherwise, an *InvalidOperationException* will be thrown. The *selector* predicate, available in the last two signatures, defines the function with which to extract values from the *source* sequence elements. For instance, you can use these overloads to avoid errors related to missing interface implementations (*ICompara-ble<T>/IComparable*), as in Listing 3-38.

Listing 3-38   The *Max* operator applied to custom types, with a value selector

```
var expr =
    (from c in customers
         from o in c.Orders
         select new { o.IdProduct, o.Quantity }
    ).Min(o => o.Quantity);
```

Average

The *Average* operator calculates the arithmetic average of a set of values, extracted from a source sequence. Like the previous operators, this function works with the source elements themselves or with values extracted using a custom *selector*:

```
public static Result Average(
    this IEnumerable<Numeric> source);
public static Result Average<TSource>(
    this IEnumerable<TSource> source,
    Func<TSource, Numeric> selector);
```

The *Numeric* type can be *Int32*, *Nullable<Int32>*, *Int64*, *Nullable<Int64>*, *Single*, *Nullable<Single>*, *Double*, *Nullable<Double>*, *Decimal*, and *Nullable<Decimal>*. The *Result* type always reflects the "nullability" of the numeric type. When the *Numeric* type is *Int32* or *Int64*, the *Result* type is *Double*. When the *Numeric* type is *Nullable<Int32>* or *Nullable<Int64>*, the *Result* type is *Nullable<Double>*. Otherwise, the *Numeric* and *Result* types are the same.

When the sum of the values used to compute the arithmetic average is too large for the result type, an *OverflowException* error is thrown. Because of its definition, the *Average* operator's first signature can be invoked only on a *Numeric* sequence. If you want to invoke it on a source sequence of non-numeric type instances, you need to provide a custom *selector*. In Listing 3-39, you can see an example of both of the overloads.

Listing 3-39   Both *Average* operator signatures applied to product prices

```
var expr =
    (from p in products
    select p.Price
    ).Average();
var expr =
    (from p in products
    select new { p.IdProduct, p.Price }
    ).Average(p => p.Price);
```

The second signature is useful when you are defining a query in which the average is just one of the results to extract. An example is shown in Listing 3-40, where we extract all customers and their average order amounts.

Listing 3-40   Customers and their average order amounts

```
var expr =
    from   c in customers
    join   o in (
        from c in customers
            from   o in c.Orders
            join   p in products
                   on o.IdProduct equals p.IdProduct
            select new { c.Name, OrderAmount = o.Quantity * p.Price }
        ) on c.Name equals o.Name
        into customersWithOrders
    select new { c.Name,
                AverageAmount = customersWithOrders.Average(o =>
    o.OrderAmount) };
```

The results will be similar to the following:

```
{ Name = Paolo, AverageAmount = 65 }
{ Name = Marco, AverageAmount = 350 }
{ Name = James, AverageAmount = 600 }
{ Name = Frank, AverageAmount = 1000 }
```

Aggregate

The last operator in this set is *Aggregate*. Take a look at its definition:

```
public static T Aggregate<TSource>(
    this IEnumerable<TSource> source,
    Func<TSource, TSource, TSource> func);
public static TAccumulate Aggregate<TSource, TAccumulate>(
    this IEnumerable<TSource> source,
    TAccumulate seed,
    Func<TAccumulate, TSource, TAccumulate> func);
public static TResult Aggregate<TSource, TAccumulate, TResult>(
    this IEnumerable< TSource > source,
    TAccumulate seed,
    Func<TAccumulate, TSource, TAccumulate> func,
    Func<TAccumulate, TResult> resultSelector);
```

This operator repeatedly invokes the *func* function, storing the result in an accumulator. Every step calls the function with the current accumulator value as the first argument, starting from *seed*, and the current element within the *source* sequence as the second argument. At the end of the iteration, the operator returns the final accumulator value.

The only difference between the first two signatures is that the second requires an explicit value for the *seed* of type *TAccumulator*. The first signature uses the first element in the *source* sequence as the *seed* and infers the *seed* type from the *source* sequence itself. The third signature looks like the second, but it requires a *resultSelector* predicate to call when extracting the final result.

In Listing 3-41, we use the *Aggregate* operator to extract the most expensive order for each customer.

Listing 3-41   Customers and their most expensive orders

```
var expr =
    from   c in customers
    join   o in (
        from c in customers
            from   o in c.Orders
            join   p in products
                   on o.IdProduct equals p.IdProduct
            select new { c.Name, o.IdProduct,
                             OrderAmount = o.Quantity * p.Price }
    ) on c.Name equals o.Name
    into orders
```

```
select new { c.Name,
             MaxOrderAmount =
                 orders
                 .Aggregate((a, o) => a.OrderAmount > o.OrderAmount ?
                                      a : o)
                 .OrderAmount };
```

As you can see, the function called by the *Aggregate* operator compares the *OrderAmount* property of each order executed by the current customer and keeps track of the more expensive one in the accumulator variable (*a*). At the end of each customer aggregation, the accumulator will contain the most expensive order, and its *OrderAmount* property will be projected into the final result, coupled with the customer *Name* property. The following is the output from this query:

```
{ Name = Paolo, MaxOrderAmount = 100 }
{ Name = Marco, MaxOrderAmount = 600 }
{ Name = James, MaxOrderAmount = 600 }
{ Name = Frank, MaxOrderAmount = 1000 }
```

In Listing 3-42, you can see another sample of aggregation. This example calculates the total amount ordered for each product.

Listing 3-42   Products and their ordered amounts

```
var expr =
    from   p in products
    join   o in (
           from c in customers
                from   o in c.Orders
                join   p in products
                       on o.IdProduct equals p.IdProduct
                select new { p.IdProduct, OrderAmount = o.Quantity * p.Price }
           ) on p.IdProduct equals o.IdProduct
           into orders
    select new { p.IdProduct,
                 TotalOrderedAmount =
                     orders
                     .Aggregate(0m, (a, o) => a += o.OrderAmount)};
```

Here is the output of this query:

```
{ IdProduct = 1, TotalOrderedAmount = 130 }
{ IdProduct = 2, TotalOrderedAmount = 100 }
{ IdProduct = 3, TotalOrderedAmount = 1200 }
{ IdProduct = 4, TotalOrderedAmount = 0 }
{ IdProduct = 5, TotalOrderedAmount = 1000 }
{ IdProduct = 6, TotalOrderedAmount = 0 }
```

In this second sample, the aggregate function uses an accumulator of *Decimal* type. It is initialized to zero (*seed = 0m*) and accumulates the *OrderAmount* values for every step. The result of this function will also be a *Decimal* type.

Both of the previous examples could also be defined by invoking the *Max* or *Sum* operators, respectively. They are shown in this section to help you learn about the *Aggregate* operator's behavior. In general, keep in mind that the *Aggregate* operator is useful whenever there are no specific aggregation operators available; otherwise, you should use an operator such as *Min*, *Max*, *Sum*, and so on. For instance, consider the example in Listing 3-43.

Listing 3-43   Customers and their most expensive orders paired with the month of execution

```
var expr =
    from    c in customers
    join    o in (
            from c in customers
                from    o in c.Orders
                join    p in products
                    on o.IdProduct equals p.IdProduct
                select new { c.Name, o.IdProduct, o.Month,
                            OrderAmount = o.Quantity * p.Price }
            ) on c.Name equals o.Name into orders
    select new { c.Name,
                MaxOrder =
                    orders
                    .Aggregate( new { Amount = 0m, Month = String.Empty },
                                (a, s) => a.Amount > s.OrderAmount
                                    ? a
                                    : new { Amount = s.OrderAmount,
                                            Month = s.Month })};
```

The result of Listing 3-43 is shown here:

```
{ Name = Paolo, MaxOrder = { Amount = 100, Month = May } }
{ Name = Marco, MaxOrder = { Amount = 600, Month = December } }
{ Name = James, MaxOrder = { Amount = 600, Month = December } }
{ Name = Frank, MaxOrder = { Amount = 1000, Month = July } }
```

In this example, the *Aggregate* operator returns a new anonymous type called *MaxOrder*: it is a tuple composed of the amount and month of the most expensive order made by each customer. The *Aggregate* operator used here cannot be replaced by any of the other predefined aggregate operators because of its specific behavior and result type.

Note   For further information about anonymous types, refer to Appendix B, "C# 3.0: New Language Features," or Appendix C, "Microsoft Visual Basic 2008: New Language Features."

The only way to produce a similar result using standard aggregate operators is to call two different aggregators. That would require two *source* sequence scannings: one to get the maximum amount and one to get its month. Be sure to pay attention to the *seed* definition, which declares the resulting anonymous type that will be used by the aggregation function as well.

Aggregate Operators in Visual Basic 2008

Visual Basic 2008 introduces a set of new keywords and clauses in LINQ query expression syntax in order to better and easily support aggregation over data items. In particular, there is the *Aggregate* clause that allows you to include aggregate functions in query expressions. Here is the syntax of this clause:

```
Aggregate element [As type] In collection _
    [, element2 [As type2] In collection2, [...]]
    [ clause ]
    Into expressionList
```

Here *element* is the item taken from an iteration over the source *collection* to use to execute the aggregation. The *clause* part of the syntax (which is optional) represents any query expression used to refine the items to aggregate. For instance, it could be a *Where* clause. The *expressionList* part of the syntax is mandatory and defines one or more comma-delimited expressions that identify an aggregate function to be applied to the *collection*. The standard aggregate functions that you can use are the *All*, *Any*, *Average*, *Count*, *LongCount*, *Max*, *Min*, and *Sum* functions.

In Listing 3-44 you can see an example of the *Aggregate* clause to get the average price of products ordered by customers.

Listing 3-44   Average price of products ordered by customers

```
Dim productsOrdered = _
    From c In customers _
    From o In c.Orders _
        Join p In products _
        On o.IdProduct Equals p.IdProduct _
    Select p
Dim expr = Aggregate p In productsOrdered _
    Into Average(p.Price)
```

As you saw earlier in this chapter in examples written in C# 3.0, you can merge the previous code in order to write a single query expression. In Listing 3-45 you can see the unique query solution.

Listing 3-45   Average price of products ordered by customers, determined with a unique query expression

```
Dim expr = Aggregate p In ( _
    From c In customers _
    From o In c.Orders _
        Join p In products _
        On o.IdProduct Equals p.IdProduct _
    Select p) _
    Into Average(p.Price)
```

The most interesting feature of the *Aggregate* clause is its capability to apply any kind of aggregate function, even custom ones that you define. Whenever you define a custom extension method, which extends *IEnumerable<T>*, this can be used in the *expressionList* within the *Aggregate* clause. In Listing 3-46 you can see an example of a custom aggregate function that calculates the standard deviation of a set of values describing the price of products.

Listing 3-46   Custom aggregate function to calculate the standard deviation of a set of *Double* values

```
<Extension()> _
Function StandardDeviation( _
    ByVal source As IEnumerable(Of Double)) As Double

    If source Is Nothing Then
        Throw New ArgumentNullException("source")
    End If

    If source.Count = 0 Then
        Throw New InvalidOperationException("Cannot compute Standard
        Deviation for an empty set.")
    End If

    Dim avg = Aggregate v In source Into Average(v)
    Dim accumulator As Double = 0

    For Each x In source
        accumulator += (x - avg) ^ 2
    Next

    Return Math.Sqrt(accumulator / (source.Count))

End Function

<Extension()> _
Function StandardDeviation(Of TSource)( _
        ByVal source As IEnumerable(Of TSource), _
        ByVal selector As Func(Of TSource, Double)) As Double

    Return (From element In source Select _
        selector(element)).StandardDeviation()

End Function

Sub Main()

    Dim expr = Aggregate p In products _
            Into StandardDeviation(p.Price)

End Sub
```

Generation Operators

When working with data by applying aggregates, arithmetic operations, and mathematical functions, sometimes you need to also iterate over numbers or item collections. For example, think about a query that needs to extract orders placed for a particular set of years, between 2000 and 2007, or a query that needs to repeat the same operation over the same data. The generation operators are useful for operations such as these.

Range

The first operator in this set is *Range*. It is a simple extension method that yields a set of *Integer* numbers, selected within a specified range of values, as shown in its signature:

```
public static IEnumerable<Int32> Range(
    Int32 start,
    Int32 count);
```

The code in Listing 3-47 illustrates a means to filter orders for the months between January and June.

> **Important**   Please note that in the following example, a *where* condition would be more appropriate because we are iterating *orders* many times. The example in Listing 3-47 is provided only for demonstration and is not the best solution for the specific query.

Listing 3-47   A set of months generated by the *Range* operator, used to filter orders

```
var expr = Enumerable.Range(1, 6)
    .SelectMany(x => (
        from o in (
            from c in customers
            from o in c.Orders
            select o)
        where o.Month ==
            new CultureInfo("en-US").DateTimeFormat.GetMonthName(x)
        select new { o.Month, o.IdProduct }));
```

The *Range* operator can also be used to implement classic mathematical operations. Listing 3-48 shows an example of using *Range* and *Aggregate* to calculate the factorial of a number.

Listing 3-48   A factorial of a number using the *Range* operator

```
static int Factorial(int number) {
    return (Enumerable.Range(0, number + 1)
        .Aggregate(0, (s, t) => t == 0 ? 1 : s *= t)); }
```

Repeat

Another generation operator is *Repeat*, which returns a set of *count* occurrences of *element*. When the *element* is an instance of a reference type, each repetition returns a reference to the same instance, not a copy of it.

```
public static IEnumerable<TResult> Repeat<TResult>(
    TResult element,
    int count);
```

The *Repeat* operator is useful for initializing enumerations (using the same element for all instances) or for repeating the same query many times. In Listing 3-49, we repeat the customer name selection two times.

Listing 3-49   The *Repeat* operator, used to repeat the same query many times

```
var expr =
    Enumerable.Repeat( ( from c in customers
                         select c.Name), 2)
    .SelectMany(x => x);
```

Please note that in this example, *Repeat* returns a sequence of sequences, formed by two lists of customer names. For this reason, we used *SelectMany* to get a flat list of names.

Empty

The last of the generation operators is *Empty*, which is used to create an empty enumeration of a particular type *TResult*. This operation can be useful to initialize empty sequences.

```
public static IEnumerable<TResult> Empty<TResult>();
```

Listing 3-50 provides an example that uses *Empty* to fill an empty enumeration of *Customer*.

Listing 3-50   The *Empty* operator used to initialize an empty set of customers

```
IEnumerable<Customer> customers = Enumerable.Empty<Customer>();
```

Quantifiers Operators

Imagine that you need to check for the existence of elements within a sequence by using conditions or selection rules. First you select items with *Restriction* operators, and then you use aggregate operators such as *Count* to determine whether any item that verifies the condition exists. There is, however, a set of operators, called quantifiers, specifically designed to check for existence conditions over sequences.

Any

The first operator we will describe in this group is the *Any* method. It provides a couple of overloads:

```
public static Boolean Any<TSource>(
    this IEnumerable<TSource> source,
    Func<TSource, Boolean> predicate);
public static Boolean Any<TSource>(
    this IEnumerable<TSource> source);
```

As you can see from the method's signatures, the method has an overload accepting a predicate. This overload returns *true* whenever an item exists in the *source* sequence that verifies the predicate provided. There is also a second overload that requires only the *source* sequence, without a predicate. This method returns *true* when at least one element in the *source* sequence exists or *false* if the *source* sequence is empty. To optimize its execution, *Any* returns as soon as a result is available. In Listing 3-51, you can see an example that determines whether there is any order of product one (*IdProduct* == 1) within all the customers' orders.

Listing 3-51   The *Any* operator applied to all customer orders to check orders of *IdProduct* == 1

```
bool result =
    (from c in customers
         from  o in c.Orders
         select o)
    .Any(o => o.IdProduct == 1);

result = Enumerable.Empty<Order>().Any();
```

In this example, the operator evaluates items only until the first order matching the condition (*IdProduct* == 1) is found. The second example in Listing 3-51 illustrates a trivial use of the *Any* operator with a *false* result, using the *Empty* operator described earlier.

> **Important**   The *Any* operator applied to an empty sequence will always return *false*. The internal operator implementation in LINQ to Objects enumerates all the *source* sequence items. It returns *true* as soon as an element that verifies the *predicate* is found. If the sequence is empty, the *predicate* is never called and the *false* value is returned.

All

When you want to determine whether all the items of a sequence verify a filtering condition, you can use the *All* operator. It returns a *true* result only if the condition is verified by all the elements in the *source* sequence:

```
public static Boolean All<TSource>(
    this IEnumerable<TSource> source,
    Func<TSource, Boolean> predicate);
```

For instance, in Listing 3-52 we determine whether every order has a positive quantity.

Listing 3-52   The *All* operator applied to all customer orders to check the quantity

```
bool result =
    (from c in customers
        from o in c.Orders
        select o)
    .All(o => o.Quantity > 0);

result = Enumerable.Empty<Order>().All(o => o.Quantity > 0);
```

> **Important**   The *All* operator applied to an empty sequence will always return *true*. The internal operator implementation in LINQ to Objects enumerates all the *source* sequence items. It returns *false* as soon as an element that does not verify the *predicate* is found. If the sequence is empty, the *predicate* is never called and the *true* value is returned.

Contains

The last quantifier operator is the *Contains* extension method, which determines whether a *source* sequence contains a specific item value:

```
public static Boolean Contains<TSource>(
    this IEnumerable<TSource> source,
    TSource value);
public static Boolean Contains<TSource>(
    this IEnumerable<TSource> source,
    TSource value,
    IEqualityComparer<TSource> comparer)
```

In the LINQ to Objects implementation, the method tries to use the *Contains* method of *ICollection<T>* if the *source* sequence implements this interface. In cases when *ICollection<T>* is not implemented, *Contains* enumerates all the items in *source*, comparing each one with the given *value* of type *TSource*. It uses a custom *comparer,* if provided with the second method overload, or *EqualityComparer<T>.Default* otherwise.

In Listing 3-53, you can see an example of the *Contains* method as it is used to check for the existence of a specific order within the collection of orders of a customer.

Listing 3-53   The *Contains* operator applied to the first customer's orders

```
// the first customer has an order with the following values
var orderOfProductOne = new Order {IdOrder = 1, Quantity = 3, IdProduct =
    1 , Shipped = false, Month = "January"};
bool result = customers[0].Orders.Contains(orderOfProductOne);
```

Unlike what you would expect, at the end of Listing 3-53 the result will be *false* even though an order exists for the first customer that contains the same values for each field. The *Contains* method returns *true* only if you use the same object as the one to compare. Otherwise, you need a custom *comparer* or a value type semantic for *Order* type (a reference type that over-loads the *GetHashCode* and *Equals* methods or a value type, as we have already described) to look for an equivalent order in the sequence.

Partitioning Operators

Selection and filtering operations sometimes need to be applied only to a subset of the elements of the source sequence. For instance, you might need to extract only the first *n* ele-ments that verify a condition. You can use the *Where* and *Select* operators with the zero-based index argument of their predicate, but this approach is not always useful and intuitive. It is better to have specific operators for these kinds of operations because they are performed quite frequently.

A set of partitioning operators is provided to satisfy these needs. *Take* and *TakeWhile* select the first *n* items or the first items that verify a predicate, respectively. *Skip* and *SkipWhile* complement the *Take* and *TakeWhile* operators, skipping the first *n* items or the first items that validate a predicate.

Take

We will start with the *Take* and *TakeWhile* family:

```
public static IEnumerable<TSource> Take<TSource>(
    this IEnumerable<TSource> source,
    Int32 count);
```

The *Take* operator requires a *count* argument that represents the number of items to take from the *source* sequence. Negative values of *count* determine an empty result; values over the sequence size return the full *source* sequence. This method is useful for all queries in which you need the top *n* items. For instance, you could use this method to select the top *n* customers based on their order amount, as shown in Listing 3-54.

Listing 3-54   The *Take* operator, applied to extract the two top customers ordered by order amount

```
var topTwoCustomers =
    (from   c in customers
     join   o in (
         from c in customers
             from   o in c.Orders
             join   p in products
                    on o.IdProduct equals p.IdProduct
             select new { c.Name, OrderAmount = o.Quantity * p.Price }
         ) on c.Name equals o.Name
         into customersWithOrders
```

```
    let     TotalAmount = customersWithOrders.Sum(o => o.OrderAmount)
    orderby TotalAmount descending
    select  new { c.Name, TotalAmount }
).Take(2);
```

As you can see, the *Take* operator clause is quite simple, while the whole query is more articulated. The query contains several of the basic elements and operators we have previously discussed. The *let* clause, in addition to *Take*, is the only clause that we have not already seen in action applied to a LINQ to Objects query. As you have seen in Chapter 2, the *let* keyword is useful for defining an alias for a value or for a variable representing a formula. In this sample, we need to use the sum of all order amounts on a customer basis as a value to project into the resulting anonymous type. At the same time, the same value is used as a sorting condition. Therefore, we defined an alias named *TotalAmount* to avoid duplicate formulas.

TakeWhile

The *TakeWhile* operator works like the *Take* operator, but it checks a formula to extract items instead of using a counter. Here are the method's signatures:

```
public static IEnumerable<TSource> TakeWhile<TSource>(
    this IEnumerable<TSource> source,
    Func<TSource, Boolean> predicate);
public static IEnumerable<TSource> TakeWhile<TSource>(
    this IEnumerable<TSource> source,
    Func<TSource, Int32, Boolean> predicate);
```

There are two overloads of the method. The first requires a *predicate* that will be evaluated on each *source* sequence item. The method enumerates the *source* sequence and yields items if the *predicate* is *true*; it stops the enumeration when the *predicate* result becomes *false*, or when the end of the *source* is reached. The second overload also requires a zero-based index for the *predicate* to indicate where the query should start evaluating the *source* sequence.

Imagine that you want to identify your top customers, generating a list that makes up a minimum aggregate amount of orders. The problem looks similar to the one we solved with the *Take* operator in Listing 3-54, but we do not know how many customers we need to examine. *TakeWhile* can solve the problem by using a predicate that calculates the aggregate amount and uses that number to stop the enumeration when the target is reached. The resulting query is shown in Listing 3-55.

Listing 3-55   The *TakeWhile* operator, applied to extract the top customers that form 80 percent of all orders

```
// globalAmount is the total amount for all the orders
var limitAmount = globalAmount * 0.8m;
var aggregated = 0m;
var topCustomers =
    (from    c in customers
     join    o in (
```

```
            from c in customers
                from   o in c.Orders
                join   p in products
                        on o.IdProduct equals p.IdProduct
                select new { c.Name, OrderAmount = o.Quantity * p.Price }
            ) on c.Name equals o.Name
            into customersWithOrders
    let     TotalAmount = customersWithOrders.Sum(o => o.OrderAmount)
    orderby TotalAmount descending
    select  new { c.Name, TotalAmount }
)
.TakeWhile( X => {
                bool result = aggregated < limitAmount;
                aggregated += X.TotalAmount;
                return result;
            } );
```

Skip and SkipWhile

The *Skip* and *SkipWhile* signatures are very similar to those for *Take* and *TakeWhile*:

```
public static IEnumerable<TSource> Skip<TSource>(
    this IEnumerable<TSource> source,
    Int32 count);
public static IEnumerable<TSource> SkipWhile<TSource>(
    this IEnumerable<TSource> source,
    Func<TSource, Boolean> predicate);
public static IEnumerable<TSource> SkipWhile<TSource>(
    this IEnumerable<TSource> source,
    Func<TSource, Int32, Boolean> predicate);
```

As we mentioned previously, these operators complement the *Take* and *TakeWhile* couple. In fact, the following code returns the full sequence of customers:

```
var result = customers.Take(3).Union(customers.Skip(3));
var result = customers.TakeWhile(p).Union(customers.SkipWhile(p));
```

The only point of interest is that *SkipWhile* skips the *source* sequence items while the *predicate* evaluates to *true* and starts yielding items as soon as the *predicate* result is *false*, suspending the *predicate* evaluation on all the remaining items.

Element Operators

Element operators are defined to work with single items of a sequence. They are designed to extract a specific element by position or by using a predicate, rather than by using a default value in case of missing elements.

First

We will start with the *First* method, which extracts the first element in the sequence by using a predicate or a positional rule:

```
public static TSource First<TSource>(
    this IEnumerable<TSource> source);
public static TSource First<TSource>(
    this IEnumerable<TSource> source,
    Func<TSource, Boolean> predicate);
```

The first overload returns the first element in the *source* sequence, and the second overload uses a *predicate* to identify the first element to return. If there are no elements that verify the *predicate* or there are no elements at all in the *source* sequence, the operator will throw an *InvalidOperationException* error. Listing 3-56 shows an example of the *First* operator.

Listing 3-56   The *First* operator, used to select the first U.S. customer

```
var item = customers.First(c => c.Country == Countries.USA);
```

Of course, this example could be defined by using a *Where* and *Take* operator. However, the *First* method better demonstrates the intention of the query, and it also guarantees a single (partial) scan of the *source* sequence.

FirstOrDefault

If you need to find the first element only if it exists, without any exception in case of failure, you can use the *FirstOrDefault* method. This method works like *First*, but if there are no elements that verify the predicate or if the *source* sequence is empty, it returns a default value:

```
public static TSource FirstOrDefault<TSource>(
    this IEnumerable<TSource> source);
public static TSource FirstOrDefault<TSource>(
    this IEnumerable<TSource> source,
    Func<TSource, Boolean> predicate);
```

The default returned is *default(TSource)* in the case of an empty *source*, where that *default(TSource)* returns *null* for reference types and nullable types. If no *predicate* argument is provided, the method returns the first element of the *source* if it exists. Examples are shown in Listing 3-57.

Listing 3-57   Examples of the *FirstOrDefault* operator syntax

```
var item = customers.FirstOrDefault(c => c.City == "Las Vegas");
Console.WriteLine(item == null ? "null" : item.ToString()); // returns null

IEnumerable<Customer> emptyCustomers = Enumerable.Empty<Customer>();
item = emptyCustomers.FirstOrDefault(c => c.City == "Las Vegas");
Console.WriteLine(item == null ? "null" : item.ToString()); // returns null
```

Last and LastOrDefault

The *Last* and *LastOrDefault* operators are complements of *First* and *FirstOrDefault*. The former have signatures and behaviors that mirror the latter:

```
public static TSource Last<TSource>(
    this IEnumerable<TSource> source);
public static TSource Last<TSource>(
    this IEnumerable<TSource> source,
    Func<TSource, Boolean> predicate);
public static TSource LastOrDefault<TSource>(
    this IEnumerable<TSource> source);
public static TSource LastOrDefault<TSource>(
    this IEnumerable<TSource> source,
    Func<TSource, Boolean> predicate);
```

These methods work like *First* and *FirstOrDefault*. The only difference is that they select the last element in *source* instead of the first.

Single

Whenever you need to select a specific and unique item from a *source* sequence, you can use the operators *Single* or *SingleOrDefault*:

```
public static TSource Single<TSource>(
    this IEnumerable<TSource> source);
public static TSource Single<TSource>(
    this IEnumerable<TSource> source,
    Func<TSource, Boolean> predicate);
```

If no *predicate* is provided, *Single* extracts from the *source* sequence the first single element. Otherwise, it extracts the single element that verifies the *predicate*. If there is no predicate and the source sequence contains more than one item, an *InvalidOperationException* error will be thrown. If there is a *predicate* and there are no matching elements or there is more than one match in the *source*, the method will throw an *InvalidOperationException* error, too. You can see some examples in Listing 3-58.

Listing 3-58   Examples of the *Single* operator syntax

```
// returns Product 1
var item = products.Single(p => p.IdProduct == 1);
Console.WriteLine(item == null ? "null" : item.ToString());

// InvalidOperationException
item = products.Single();
Console.WriteLine(item == null ? "null" : item.ToString());

// InvalidOperationException
IEnumerable<Product> emptyProducts = Enumerable.Empty<Product>();
item = emptyProducts.Single(p => p.IdProduct == 1);
Console.WriteLine(item == null ? "null" : item.ToString());
```

SingleOrDefault

The *SingleOrDefault* operator provides a default result value in the case of an empty sequence or no matching elements in *source*. Its signatures are like those for *Single*:

```
public static TSource SingleOrDefault<TSource>(
    this IEnumerable<TSource> source);
public static TSource SingleOrDefault<TSource>(
    this IEnumerable<TSource> source,
    Func<TSource, Boolean> predicate);
```

The default value returned by this method is *default(TSource)*, as in the *FirstOrDefault* and *LastOrDefault* extension methods.

> **Important**   The default value is returned only if no elements match the *predicate*. An *InvalidOperationException* error is thrown when the *source* sequence contains more than one matching item.

ElementAt and ElementAtOrDefault

Whenever you need to extract a specific item from a sequence based on its position, you can use the *ElementAt* or *ElementAtOrDefault* method:

```
public static TSource ElementAt<TSource>(
    this IEnumerable<TSource> source,
    Int32 index);
public static TSource ElementAtOrDefault<TSource>(
    this IEnumerable<TSource> source,
    Int32 index);
```

The *ElementAt* method requires an *index* argument that represents the position of the element to extract. The *index* is zero based; therefore, you need to provide a value of 2 to extract the third element. When the value of *index* is negative or greater than the size of the *source* sequence, an *ArgumentOutOfRangeException* error is thrown. The *ElementAtOrDefault* method differs from *ElementAt* because it returns a default value—*default(TSource)* for reference types and nullable types—in the case of a negative *index* or an *index* greater than the size of the *source* sequence. Listing 3-59 shows some examples of how to use these operators.

Listing 3-59   Examples of the *ElementAt* and *ElementAtOrDefault* operator syntax

```
// returns Product 2
var item = products.ElementAt(2);
Console.WriteLine(item == null ? "null" : item.ToString());

// returns null
item = Enumerable.Empty<Product>().ElementAtOrDefault(6);
Console.WriteLine(item == null ? "null" : item.ToString());

// returns null
item = products.ElementAtOrDefault(6);
Console.WriteLine(item == null ? "null" : item.ToString());
```

DefaultIfEmpty

DefaultIfEmpty returns a default element for an empty sequence:

```
public static IEnumerable<TSource> DefaultIfEmpty<TSource>(
    this IEnumerable<TSource> source);
public static IEnumerable<TSource> DefaultIfEmpty<TSource>(
    this IEnumerable<TSource> source,
    TSource defaultValue);
```

By default, it returns the list of items of a *source* sequence. In the case of an empty source, it returns a default value that is *default(TSource)* in the first overload or *defaultValue* if you use the second overload of the method.

Defining a specific default value can be helpful in many circumstances. For instance, imagine that you have a public static property named *Empty* that is used to return an empty instance of a *Customer*, as in the following code excerpt:

```
private static volatile Customer empty;
private static Object emptySyncLock = new Object();

public static Customer Empty {
    get {
        // Multithreaded singleton pattern
        if (empty == null) {
            lock (emptySyncLock) {
                if (empty == null) {
                    empty = new Customer();
                    empty.Name = String.Empty;
                    empty.Country = Countries.Italy;
                    empty.City = String.Empty;
                    empty.Orders = (new List<Order>(Enumerable.Empty<Order>())).ToArray();
                }
            }
        }
        return (empty);
    }
}
```

Sometime this is useful, especially when unit testing code. Another situation is when a query uses *GroupJoin* to realize a left outer join. The possible resulting nulls can be replaced by a default value chosen by the query author.

In Listing 3-60, you can see how to use *DefaultIfEmpty*, including a custom default value such as *Customer.Empty*.

Listing 3-60   Example of the *DefaultIfEmpty* operator syntax, both with *default(T)* and a custom default value

```
var expr = customers.DefaultIfEmpty();

var customers = Enumerable.Empty<Customer>(); // Empty array
IEnumerable<Customer> customersEmpty =
    customers.DefaultIfEmpty(Customer.Empty);
```

Other Operators

To complete our coverage of LINQ to Objects query operators, we will describe a few final extension methods in this section.

Concat

The first one is the concatenation operator, named *Concat*. As its name suggests, it simply appends one sequence to another, as we can see from its signature:

```
public static IEnumerable<TSource> Concat<TSource>(
    this IEnumerable<TSource> first,
    IEnumerable<TSource> second);
```

The only requirement for *Concat* arguments is that they enumerate the same type *TSource*. We can use this method to append any *IEnumerable<T>* sequence to another of the same type. Listing 3-61 shows an example of customer concatenation.

Listing 3-61   The *Concat* operator, used to concatenate Italian customers with customers from the United States

```
var italianCustomers =
    from   c in customers
    where  c.Country == Countries.Italy
    select c;

var americanCustomers =
    from   c in customers
    where  c.Country == Countries.USA
    select c;

var expr = italianCustomers.Concat(americanCustomers);
```

SequenceEqual

Another useful operator is the equality operator, which corresponds to the *SequenceEqual* extension method:

```
public static Boolean SequenceEqual<TSource>(
    this IEnumerable<TSource> first,
    IEnumerable<TSource> second);
public static Boolean SequenceEqual<TSource>(
    this IEnumerable<TSource> first,
    IEnumerable<TSource> second,
    IEqualityComparer<TSource> comparer);
```

This method compares each item in the first sequence with each corresponding item in the second sequence. If the two sequences have exactly the same number of items with equal items in every position, the two sequences are considered equal. Remember the possible issues of reference type semantics in this kind of comparison. You can consider overriding *GetHashCode* and *Equals* on the *TSource* type to drive the result of this operator, or you can use the second method overload, providing a custom implementation of *IEqualityComparer<T>*.

Conversion Operators

The methods included in the conversion operator set are *AsEnumerable*, *ToArray*, *ToList*, *ToDictionary*, *ToLookup*, *OfType*, and *Cast*. Conversion operators are mainly defined to solve the problems and the needs related to LINQ deferred query evaluation. (See Chapter 2 for more details on this topic.) Sometimes you might need a stable and immutable result from a query expression, or you might want to use a generic extension method operator instead of a more specialized one. In the following sections, we will describe the conversion operators in more detail.

AsEnumerable

The signature for *AsEnumerable* is shown here:

```
public static IEnumerable<TSource> AsEnumerable<TSource>(
    this IEnumerable<TSource> source);
```

The *AsEnumerable* operator simply returns the *source* sequence as an object of type *IEnumerable* *<TSource>*. This kind of "conversion on the fly" makes it possible to call the general-purpose extension methods over *source*, even if its type has specific implementations of them.

Consider a custom *Where* extension method for a type *Customers*, like the one defined in Listing 3-62.

Listing 3-62   A custom *Where* extension method defined for the type *Customers*.

```
public class Customers : List<Customer> {
    public Customers(IEnumerable<Customer> items): base(items) {
    }
}

public static class CustomersExtension {
    public static Customers Where(this Customers source,
        Func<Customer, Boolean> predicate) {
        Customers result = new Customers();

        Console.WriteLine("Custom Where extension method");
        foreach (var item in source) {
            if (predicate(item))
                result.Add(item);
        }
        return result;
    }
}
```

Notice the presence of the *Console.WriteLine* method call inside the sample code.

Important   In real solutions you would probably use a custom iterator instead of an explicit list to represent the result of this extension method, but for the sake of simplicity we decided not to do that in this quick example.

In Listing 3-63 you can see an example of a query expression executed over an instance of the type *Customers*.

Listing 3-63   A query expression over a list of *Customers*

```
Customers customersList = new Customers(customers);

var expr =
    from   c in customersList
    where  c.Country == Countries.Italy
    select c;

foreach (var item in expr) {
    Console.WriteLine(item);
}
```

The output of this sample code will be the following one.

```
Custom Where extension method
Name: Paolo - City: Brescia - Country: Italy - Orders Count: 2
Name: Marco - City: Torino - Country: Italy - Orders Count: 2
```

As you can see the output starts with the *Console.WriteLine* invoked in our custom *Where* extension method. In fact, as we have already described in Chapter 2, LINQ queries are translated into the corresponding extension methods, and for the *Customers* type, the *Where* extension method is the one that we defined ourselves.

Now imagine that you want to define a query over an instance of the *Customers* type without using the custom extension method; instead, you wan to use the default *Where* operator defined for the *IEnumerable<T>* type. The *AsEnumerable* extension method accomplishes this requirement for you, as you can see in Listing 3-64.

Listing 3-64   A query expression over a list of *Customers* converted with the *AsEnumerable* operator

```
Customers customersList = new Customers(customers);

var expr =
    from  c in customersList.AsEnumerable()
    where  c.City == "Brescia"
    select c;

foreach (var item in expr) {
    Console.WriteLine(item);
}
```

The code in Listing 3-64 will use the standard *Where* operator defined for *IEnumerable<T>* within *System.Linq.Enumerable*.

ToArray and *ToList*

Two other useful conversion operators are *ToArray* and *ToList*. They convert a source sequence of type *IEnumerable<TSource>* into an array of *TSource* (*TSource[]*) or into a generic list of *TSource* (*List<TSource>*), respectively:

```
public static TSource[] ToArray<TSource>(
    this IEnumerable<TSource> source);
public static List<TSource> ToList<TSource>(
    this IEnumerable<TSource> source);
```

The results of these operators are snapshots of the sequence. When they are applied inside a query expression, the result will be stable and unchanged, even if the *source* sequence does change. Listing 3-65 shows an example of using *ToList*.

Listing 3-65   A query expression over an immutable list of *Customers* obtained by the *ToList* operator

```
List<Customer> customersList = new List<Customer>(customers);

var expr = (
    from  c in customersList
    where  c.Country == Countries.Italy
    select c).ToList();
```

```
foreach (var item in expr) {
    Console.WriteLine(item);
}
```

These methods are also useful whenever you need to enumerate the result of a query many times, executing the query only once for performance reasons. Consider the sample in Listing 3-66. It would probably be inefficient to refresh the list of products to join with orders every time. Therefore, you can create a "copy" of the products query.

Listing 3-66   A query expression that uses *ToList* to copy the result of a query over products

```
var productsQuery =
    (from p in products
     where p.Price >= 30
     select p)
    .ToList();

var ordersWithProducts =
    from c in customers
        from   o in c.Orders
        join   p in productsQuery
               on o.IdProduct equals p.IdProduct
        select new { p.IdProduct, o.Quantity, p.Price,
                     TotalAmount = o.Quantity * p.Price};

foreach (var order in ordersWithProducts) {
    Console.WriteLine(order);
}
```

Every time you enumerate the *ordersWithProducts* expression—for instance, in a *foreach* block—the *productsQuery* expression will not be evaluated again.

ToDictionary

Another operator in this set is the *ToDictionary* extension method. It creates an instance of *Dictionary<TKey, TSource>*. The *keySelector* predicate identifies the key of each item. The *elementSelector*, if provided, is used to extract each single item. These predicates are defined through the available signatures:

```
public static Dictionary<TKey, TSource> ToDictionary<TSource, TKey>(
    this IEnumerable<TSource> source,
    Func<TSource, TKey> keySelector);
public static Dictionary<TKey, TSource> ToDictionary<TSource, TKey>(
    this IEnumerable<TSource> source,
    Func<TSource, TKey> keySelector,
    IEqualityComparer<TKey> comparer);
public static Dictionary<TKey, TElement> ToDictionary<TSource, TKey, TElement>(
        this IEnumerable<TSource> source,
        Func<TSource, TKey> keySelector,
        Func<TSource, TElement> elementSelector);
```

```
public static Dictionary<TKey, TElement> ToDictionary<TSource, TKey, TElement>(
        this IEnumerable<TSource> source,
        Func<TSource, TKey> keySelector,
        Func<TSource, TElement> elementSelector,
        IEqualityComparer<TKey> comparer);
```

When the method constructs the resulting dictionary, it assumes the uniqueness of each key extracted by invoking the *keySelector*. In cases of duplicate keys, an *ArgumentException* error will be thrown. The key values are compared using the *comparer* argument if provided or *EqualityComparer<TKey>.Default* if not. In Listing 3-67, we use this operator to create a dictionary of customers.

Listing 3-67   An example of the *ToDictionary* operator, applied to customers

```
var customersDictionary =
    customers
    .ToDictionary(c => c.Name,
                  c => new {c.Name, c.City});
```

The first argument of the operator is the *keySelector* predicate, which extracts the customer *Name* as the key. The second argument is *elementSelector*, which creates an anonymous type that consists of customer *Name* and *City* properties. Here is the result of the query in Listing 3-67:

```
[Paolo, { Name = Paolo, City = Brescia }]
[Marco, { Name = Marco, City = Torino }]
[James, { Name = James, City = Dallas }]
[Frank, { Name = Frank, City = Seattle }]
```

> **Important**   Like the *ToList* and *ToArray* operators, *ToDictionary* references the *source* sequence items in case they are reference types. The *ToDictionary* method in Listing 3-67 effectively evaluates the query expression and creates the output dictionary. Therefore, *customersDictionary* does not have a deferred query evaluation behavior; it is the result produced by a statement execution.

ToLookup

Another conversion operator is *ToLookup*, which can be used to create enumerations of type *Lookup<K, T>*, whose definition follows:

```
public class Lookup<K, T> : IEnumerable<IGrouping<K, T>> {
    public int Count { get; }
    public IEnumerable<T> this[K key] { get; }
    public bool Contains(K key);
    public IEnumerator<IGrouping<K, T>> GetEnumerator();
}
```

Each object of this type represents a one-to-many dictionary, which defines a tuple of keys and sequences of items, somewhat like the result of a *GroupJoin* method. Here are the available signatures:

```
public static Lookup<TKey, TSource> ToLookup<TSource, TKey>(
    this IEnumerable<TSource> source,
    Func<TSource, TKey> keySelector);
public static Lookup<TKey, TSource> ToLookup<TSource, TKey>(
    this IEnumerable<TSource> source,
    Func<TSource, TKey> keySelector,
    IEqualityComparer<TKey> comparer);
public static Lookup<TKey, TElement> ToLookup<TSource, TKey, TElement>(
    this IEnumerable<TSource> source,
    Func<TSource, TKey> keySelector,
    Func<TSource, TElement> elementSelector);
public static Lookup<TKey, TElement> ToLookup<TSource, TKey, TElement>(
    this IEnumerable<TSource> source,
    Func<TSource, TKey> keySelector,
    Func<TSource, TElement> elementSelector,
    IEqualityComparer<TKey> comparer);
```

As in *ToDictionary*, there is a *keySelector* predicate, an *elementSelector* predicate, and a *comparer*. The sample in Listing 3-68 demonstrates how to use this method to extract all orders for each product.

Listing 3-68   An example of the *ToLookup* operator, used to group orders by product

```
var ordersByProduct =
    (from c in customers
        from  o in c.Orders
        select o)
    .ToLookup(o => o.IdProduct);

Console.WriteLine( "\n\nNumber of orders for Product 1: {0}\n",
                   ordersByProduct[1].Count());

foreach (var product in ordersByProduct) {
    Console.WriteLine("Product: {0}", product.Key);
    foreach(var order in product) {
        Console.WriteLine("  {0}", order);
    }
}
```

As you can see, *Lookup<K, T>* is accessible through an item key (*ordersByProduct[1]*) or through enumeration (the *foreach* loop). The following is the output of this example:

```
Number of orders for Product 1: 2

Product: 1
  IdOrder: 1 - IdProduct: 1 - Quantity: 3 - Shipped: False - Month: January
  IdOrder: 3 - IdProduct: 1 - Quantity: 10 - Shipped: False - Month: July
```

```
Product: 2
  IdOrder: 2 - IdProduct: 2 - Quantity: 5 - Shipped: True - Month: May
Product: 3
  IdOrder: 4 - IdProduct: 3 - Quantity: 20 - Shipped: True - Month: December
  IdOrder: 5 - IdProduct: 3 - Quantity: 20 - Shipped: True - Month: December
Product: 5
  IdOrder: 6 - IdProduct: 5 - Quantity: 20 - Shipped: False - Month: July
```

OfType and *Cast*

The last two operators of this set are *OfType* and *Cast*. The first filters the source sequence, yielding only items of type *TResult*. It is useful in the case of sequences with items of different types. For instance, working with an object-oriented approach, you might have an object with a common base class and particular specialization in derived classes:

```
public static IEnumerable<TResult> OfType<TResult>(
    this IEnumerable source);
```

If you provide a type *TResult* that is not supported by any of the source items, the operator will return an empty sequence.

The *Cast* operator enumerates the source sequence and tries to yield each item, cast to type *TResult*. In the case of failure, an *InvalidCastException* error will be thrown. (See Listing 2-4 for a sample of this operator.)

```
public static IEnumerable<TResult> Cast<TResult>(
    this IEnumerable source);
```

Because of their signatures, which accept any *IEnumerable* sequence, these two methods can be used to convert old nongeneric types to newer *IEnumerable<T>* types. This conversion makes it possible to query these types with LINQ even if the types are unaware of LINQ.

Important   Each item returned by *OfType* and *Cast* is a reference to the original object and not a copy. *OfType* does not create a snapshot of a source; instead, it evaluates the source every time you enumerate the operator's result. This behavior is different from other conversion operators.

Summary

In this chapter, we discussed the principles of LINQ query expressions and the syntax rules behind them. We covered query operators and conversion operators. We used LINQ to Objects as a reference implementation, but all of the concepts are also valid for other LINQ implementations that we will cover in the following chapters.

Part II
LINQ to Relational Data

Chapter 4
LINQ to SQL: Querying Data

The first and most obvious application of LINQ is for querying an external relational database. LINQ to SQL is a component of the LINQ project that provides the capability to query a relational Microsoft SQL Server database, offering you an object model based on available entities. In other words, you can define a set of objects that represents a thin abstraction layer over the relational data, and you can query this object model by using LINQ queries that are converted into corresponding SQL queries by the LINQ to SQL engine. LINQ to SQL supports Microsoft SQL Server starting from SQL Server 2000 and Microsoft SQL Server Compact starting from version 3.5.

In LINQ to SQL, you can write a simple query like the following:

```
var query =
    from    c in Customers
    where   c.Country == "USA"
            && c.State == "WA"
    select  new {c.CustomerID, c.CompanyName, c.City };
```

This query is converted into an SQL query that is sent to the relational database:

```
SELECT CustomerID, CompanyName, City
FROM    Customers
WHERE   Country = 'USA'
  AND   Region = 'WA'
```

> **Important** The SQL queries generated by LINQ that we show in this chapter are only illustrative. Microsoft reserves the right to independently define the SQL that is generated by LINQ, and at times we use simplified queries in the text. Thus, you should not rely on the SQL that is shown.

At this point, you might be asking a few questions. First, how can the LINQ query be written using object names that are validated by the compiler? Second, when is the SQL query generated from the LINQ query? Third, when is the SQL query executed? To understand the answers to these questions, you need to understand the entity model in LINQ to SQL and then deferred query evaluation.

Entities in LINQ to SQL

Any external data must be described with appropriate metadata bound to class definitions. Each table must have a corresponding class decorated with particular attributes. That class corresponds to a row of data and describes all columns in terms of data members of the defined type. The type can be a complete or partial description of an existing physical table, view, or stored procedure result. Only the described fields can be used inside a LINQ query for both projection and filtering. Listing 4-1 shows a small and simple entity definition.

> **Important**   You need to include the *System.Data.Linq* assembly in your projects to use
> LINQ to SQL classes and attributes. The attributes used in Listing 4-1 are defined in
> the *System.Data.Linq.Mapping* namespace.

Listing 4-1   Entity definition for LINQ to SQL

```
using System.Data.Linq.Mapping;

[Table(Name="Customers")]
public class Customer {
    [Column] public string CustomerID;
    [Column] public string CompanyName;
    [Column] public string City;
    [Column(Name="Region")] public string State;
    [Column] public string Country;
}
```

The *Customer* type defines the content of a row, and each field or property decorated with *Column* corresponds to a column of the relational table. The *Name* parameter can specify a column name that is different from the data member name. (In this example, *State* corresponds to the Region table column.) The *Table* attribute specifies that the class is an entity representing data of a database table; its *Name* property can specify a table name that is different from the entity name. It is common to use the singular form for the name of the class (a single row) and the plural form for the name of the table (a set of rows).

You need a Customers table to build a LINQ to SQL query over Customers data. The *Table<T>* generic class is the right way to create such a type:

```
Table<Customer> Customers = ...;
// ...
var query =
    from    c in Customers
    // ...
```

> **Note**   To build a LINQ query on *Customers*, you need a class implementing *IEnumera-ble<T>*, using *Customer* as *T*. However, LINQ to SQL needs to implement extension methods in a different way than the LINQ to Objects implementation that we used in the Chapter 3, "LINQ to Objects." For this reason, you need to use an object implementing *IQueryable<T>* to build LINQ to SQL queries. The *Table<T>* class implements *IQueryable<T>*. To include the LINQ to SQL extension, the statement *using System.Data.Linq;* must be part of the source code.

The *Customers* table object has to be instantiated. To do that, you need an instance of the *DataContext* class, which defines the bridge between the LINQ world and the external relational database. The nearest concept to *DataContext* that comes to mind is a database connection—in fact, a mandatory parameter needed to create a *DataContext* instance is the connection string or the *Connection* object. Its *GetTable<T>* method returns a corresponding *Table<T>* for the specified type:

```
DataContext db = new DataContext("Database=Northwind");
Table<Customer> Customers = db.GetTable<Customer>();
```

Note   The *DataContext* class internally uses the *SqlConnection* class from ADO.NET. You can pass an existing *SqlConnection* to the *DataContext* constructor, and you can also read the connection used by a *DataContext* instance through its *Connection* property. All services related to the database connection, such as connection pooling (which is turned on by default), are accessible at the *SqlConnection* level and are not directly implemented in the *DataContext* class.

Listing 4-2 shows the resulting code when you put all the pieces together.

Listing 4-2   Simple LINQ to SQL query

```
DataContext db = new DataContext( ConnectionString );
Table<Customer> Customers = db.GetTable<Customer>();

var query =
    from    c in Customers
    where   c.Country == "USA"
            && c.State == "WA"
    select  new {c.CustomerID, c.CompanyName, c.City };

foreach( var row in query ) {
    Console.WriteLine( row );
}
```

The *query* variable is initialized with a query expression that forms an expression tree. An expression tree maintains a representation of the expression in memory instead of pointing to a method through a delegate. When the *foreach* loop enumerates data selected by the query, the expression tree is used to generate the corresponding SQL query, using all metadata and information you have in the entity classes and in the referenced *DataContext* instance.

Note   The *deferred execution* method used by LINQ to SQL converts the expression tree into an SQL query that is valid in the underlying relational database. The LINQ query is functionally equivalent to a string containing an SQL command, with at least two important differences. First, it is tied to the object model and not to the database structure. Second, its representation is semantically meaningful without requiring an SQL parser and without being tied to a specific SQL dialect. The expression tree can also be dynamically built in memory before its use, as we will show in Chapter 11, "Inside Expression Trees."

The data returned from the SQL query accessing *row* and placed into the *foreach* loop is then used to fill the projected anonymous type following the *select* keyword. In this sample, the *Customer* class is never instantiated, and it is used only by LINQ to analyze its metadata.

You can explore the generated SQL command by using the *GetCommand* method of the *DataContext* class. Accessing the *CommandText* property of the returned *DbCommand*, you can see the generated query in SQL language:

```
Console.WriteLine( db.GetCommand( query ).CommandText );
```

A simpler way to do this is to call *ToString* on a LINQ to SQL query: the overridden *ToString* method produces the same result as the *GetCommand(query).CommandText* statement.

```
Console.WriteLine( query );
```

The simple LINQ to SQL query in Listing 4-2 generates the following SQL query:

```
SELECT [t0].[CustomerID], [t0].[CompanyName], [t0].[City]
FROM    [Customers] AS [t0]
WHERE   ([t0].[Country] = @p0) AND ([t0].[Region] = @p1)
```

An alternative way to get a trace of all SQL statements sent to the database is to assign a value to the *Log* property of *DataContext*:

```
db.Log = Console.Out;
```

In the next section, you will see in more detail how to generate entity classes for LINQ to SQL.

External Mapping

The mapping between LINQ to SQL entities and database structures has to be described through metadata information. In Listing 4-1, you saw attributes on an entity definition fulfilling this rule. However, you can also use an external XML mapping file to decorate entity classes instead of using attributes. An XML mapping file looks like the following code sample:

```
<Database Name="Northwind">
   <Table Name="Products">
      <Type Name="Product">
         <Column Name="ProductID" Member="ProductID"
                 Storage="_ProductID" DbType="Int NOT NULL IDENTITY"
                 IsPrimaryKey="True" IsDbGenerated="True" />
```

The *Type* tag defines the relationship with an entity class, and the *Member* attribute of *Column* defines the corresponding member name of the class entity in case it is different from the column name of the table. By default, *Member* is not required and it is assumed to be the same as the *Name* attribute of *Column*. This XML file usually has a *dbml* filename extension and is produced by some of the tools described in Chapter 6, "Tools for LINQ to SQL."

The XML file can be loaded using an *XmlMappingSource* instance generated by calling its *FromXml* static method and passing it to the *DataContext* derived class constructor. The following example shows how to use such syntax:

```
string path = "Northwind.dbml";
XmlMappingSource prodMapping =
        XmlMappingSource.FromXml(File.ReadAllText(path));
Northwind db = new Northwind(
        "Database=Test_Northwind;Trusted_Connection=yes",
        prodMapping
    );
```

One possible use of this technique is in a scenario in which different databases must be mapped to a specific data model. Differences in databases might be table and field names (for example, localized versions of the database). In general, consider this option when you need to realize a light decoupling of mapping between entity classes and the physical data structure of the database.

> **More Info**   It is beyond the scope of this book to describe the details of the XML grammar for a .dbml file. This syntax is described in the LinqToSqlMapping.xsd and DbmlSchema.xsd files that are contained in the Microsoft Visual Studio 9.0\Xml\Schemas directory of your program files directory if you installed Visual Studio 2008. If you do not have either of these files, you can copy the code from the product documentation page at *http://msdn2.microsoft.com/en-us/library/bb386907.aspx* and *http://msdn2.microsoft.com/en-us/library/bb399400.aspx*.

Data Modeling

The set of entity classes that LINQ to SQL requires is a thin abstraction layer over the relational model. Each entity class defines an accessible table of data, which can be queried and modified. Entity instances that are modified can apply their changes on data contained in the relational database. You will see the options for data updates in Chapter 5, "LINQ to SQL: Managing Data." In this section, you will learn how to build a data model for LINQ to SQL.

DataContext

The *DataContext* class handles the communication between LINQ and external relational data sources. Each instance has a single *Connection* property that refers to a relational database. Its type is *IDbConnection*; therefore, it should not be specific to a particular database product. However, the LINQ to SQL implementation supports only Microsoft SQL Server databases. Choosing between specific versions of SQL Server depends only on the connection string passed to the *DataContext* constructor.

Important   The architecture of LINQ to SQL supports many data providers so that it can map to different underlying relational databases. A provider is a class that implements the *System.Data.Linq.Provider.IProvider* interface. However, that interface is declared as internal and is not documented. Microsoft supports only a Microsoft SQL Server provider. The .NET Framework 3.5 supports SQL Server 2000 and SQL Server 2005 for both 32-bit and 64-bit executables. At the time of this writing, SQL Server Compact 3.5 is also supported, but only for 32-bit executables, because SQL Server Compact 3.5 is still not available for 64-bit platforms. (It will probably be supported in a future release.) Future versions of SQL Server are also likely to be supported.

DataContext uses metadata information to map the physical structure of relational data on which the SQL code generation is based. *DataContext* can also be used to call a stored procedure and persist data changes in entity class instances in the relational database.

Classes that specialize access for a particular database can be derived from *DataContext*. Such classes offer an easier way to access relational data, including members that represent available tables. You can define fields referencing existing tables in the database simply by declaring them, without a specific initialization, as in the following code:

```
public class SampleDb : DataContext {
    public SampleDb(IDbConnection connection)
            : base( connection ) {}
    public SampleDb(string fileOrServerOrConnection)
            : base( fileOrServerOrConnection ) {}
    public SampleDb(IDbConnection connection, MappingSource mapping)
            : base( connection, mapping ) {}

    public Table<Customer> Customers;
}
```

Note   Table members are initialized automatically by the *DataContext* base constructor, which examines the type at execution time through Reflection, finds those members, and initializes them based on the mapping metadata.

Entity Classes

An entity class has two roles. The first role is to provide metadata to the LINQ query engine; for this purpose, an entity class is not instantiated. The second role is to provide storage for data read from the relational data source, as well as to track possible updates and support their submission back to the relational data source.

An entity class is any reference type definition decorated with the *Table* attribute. A struct (value type) cannot be used for this. The *Table* attribute can have a *Name* parameter that defines the name of the corresponding table in the database. If *Name* is omitted, the name of the class is used as the default:

```
[Table(Name="Products")] public class Product { ... }
```

> **Note**   Although the term commonly used is *table*, nothing prevents you from using an updatable view in place of a table name in the *Name* parameter. Using a nonupdatable view will work too, at least until you try to update data without using that entity class.

Inside an entity class, there can be any number and type of members. Only data members or properties decorated with the *Column* attribute are significant in defining the mapping between the entity class and the corresponding table in the database:

```
[Column] public int ProductID;
```

An entity class should have a unique key. This key is necessary to support unique identity (more on this later), to identify corresponding rows in database tables, and to generate SQL statements that update data. If you do not have a primary key, instances of the entity class can be created but are not modifiable. The Boolean *IsPrimaryKey* property of the *Column* attribute, set to *true*, states that the column belongs to the primary key of the table. If the primary key used is a composite key, all the columns that form the primary key will have *IsPrimary-Key=true* in their parameters:

```
[Column(IsPrimaryKey=true)] public int ProductID;
```

By default, a column is mapped using the same name of the member to which the *Column* attribute is applied. You can use a different name, specifying a value for the *Name* parameter. For example, the following *Price* member corresponds to the *UnitPrice* field in the database table:

```
[Column(Name="UnitPrice")] public decimal Price;
```

If you want to filter data access through member property accessors, you have to specify the underlying storage member with the *Storage* parameter. If you specify a *Storage* parameter, LINQ to SQL bypasses the public property accessor and interacts directly with the underlying value. Understanding this is particularly important if you want to track only the modifications made by your code and not the read/write operations made by the LINQ framework. In the following code, the *ProductName* property is accessed for each read/write operation made by your code; a direct read/write operation on the *_ProductName* data member is made when a LINQ operation is executed:

```
[Column(Storage="_ProductName")]
public string ProductName {
    get { return this._ProductName; }
    set { this.OnPropertyChanging("ProductName");
          this._ProductName = value;
          this.OnPropertyChanged("ProductName");
    }
}
```

The correspondence between relational type and .NET type is made assuming a default relational type corresponding to the .NET type that is used. Whenever you need to define a different type, you can use the *DBType* parameter, specifying a valid type by using a valid SQL syntax for the relational data source. This property is used only if you want to create a database schema starting from entity class definitions (a process we will describe in Chapter 5):

```
[Column(DBType="NVARCHAR(20)")] public string QuantityPerUnit;
```

If a column value is autogenerated by the database (which is a service offered by the IDENTITY keyword in SQL Server), you might want to synchronize the entity class member with the generated value whenever you insert an entity instance into the database. To get this behavior, you need to set the *IsDBGenerated* parameter to *true*, and you also need to adapt the *DBType* accordingly—for example, by adding the *IDENTITY* modifier for SQL Server tables:

```
[Column(DBType="INT NOT NULL IDENTITY",
       IsPrimaryKey=true, IsDBGenerated=true)]
public int ProductID;
```

It is worth mentioning that a specific *CanBeNull* parameter exists. It is used to specify that the value can contain the null value, but it is important to note that the *NOT NULL* clause in *DBType* is still necessary if you want to create such a condition in a database created by LINQ to SQL:

```
[Column(DBType="INT NOT NULL IDENTITY", CanBeNull=false,
       IsPrimaryKey=true, IsDBGenerated=true)]
public int ProductID;
```

Other parameters that are relevant in updating data are *AutoSync*, *Expression*, *IsVersion*, and *UpdateCheck*. You will see a more detailed explanation of *IsDBGenerated*, *IsVersion*, and *UpdateCheck* in Chapter 5.

Entity Inheritance

Sometimes a single table contains many types of entities. For example, imagine a list of contacts—some of them can be customers, others can be suppliers, and others can be company employees. From a data point of view, each entity can have some specific fields. (For example, a customer can have a discount field, which is not relevant for employees and suppliers.) From a business logic point of view, each entity can implement different business rules. The best way to model this kind of data in an object-oriented environment is by leveraging inheritance to create a hierarchy of specialized classes. LINQ to SQL allows a set of classes derived from the same base class to map to the same relational table.

The *InheritanceMapping* attribute decorates the base class of a hierarchy, indicating the corresponding derived classes that are based on the value of a special *discriminator column*. The *Code* parameter defines a possible value, and the *Type* parameter defines the corresponding derived type. The discriminator column is defined by the *IsDiscriminator* argument being set to *true* in the *Column* attribute specification.

Listing 4-3 provides an example of a hierarchy based on the Contacts table of the Northwind sample database.

Listing 4-3   Hierarchy of classes based on contacts

```
[Table(Name="Contacts")]
[InheritanceMapping(Code = "Customer", Type = typeof(CustomerContact))]
[InheritanceMapping(Code = "Supplier", Type = typeof(SupplierContact))]
[InheritanceMapping(Code = "Shipper", Type = typeof(ShipperContact))]
[InheritanceMapping(Code = "Employee", Type = typeof(Contact), IsDefault = true)]
public class Contact {
    [Column(IsPrimaryKey=true)] public int ContactID;
    [Column(Name="ContactName")] public string Name;
    [Column] public string Phone;
    [Column(IsDiscriminator = true)] public string ContactType;
}

public class CompanyContact : Contact {
    [Column(Name="CompanyName")] public string Company;
}

public class CustomerContact : CompanyContact {
}

public class SupplierContact : CompanyContact {
}

public class ShipperContact : CompanyContact {
    public string Shipper {
        get { return Company; }
        set { Company = value; }
    }
}
```

Contact is the base class of the hierarchy. If the contact is a *Customer, Supplier,* or *Shipper,* the corresponding classes derive from an intermediate *CompanyContact,* which defines the *Company* field corresponding to the CompanyName column in the source table. The *CompanyContact* intermediate class is necessary because you cannot reference the same column (CompanyName) in more than one field, even if this happens in different classes in the same hierarchy. The *ShipperContact* class defines a *Shipper* property that exposes the same value of *Company* but with a different semantic meaning.

Important   This approach requires that you flatten the union of all possible data columns for the whole hierarchy into a single table. If you have a normalized database, you might have data for different entities separated in different tables. You can define a view to use LINQ to SQL to support entity hierarchy, but to update data you must make the view updatable.

The level of abstraction offered by having different entity classes in the same hierarchy is well described by the sample queries shown in Listing 4-4. The *queryTyped* query uses the *OfType* operator, while *queryFiltered* relies on a standard *where* condition to filter out contacts that are not customers.

Listing 4-4   Queries using a hierarchy of entity classes

```
var queryTyped =
    from    c in contacts.OfType<CustomerContact>()
    select  c;

var queryFiltered =
    from    c in contacts
    where   c is CustomerContact
    select  c;

foreach( var row in queryTyped ) {
    Console.WriteLine( row.Company );
}

// We need an explicit cast to access the CustumerContact members
foreach( CustomerContact row in queryFiltered ) {
    Console.WriteLine( row.Company );
}
```

The SQL queries produced by these LINQ queries are functionally identical to the following one. (The actual query is different because of generalization coding.)

```
SELECT [t0].[ContactType], [t0].[CompanyName] AS [Company],
       [t0].[ContactID], [t0].[ContactName] AS [Name],
       [t0].[Phone]
FROM   [Contacts] AS [t0]
WHERE  [t0].[ContactType] = 'Customer'
```

The difference between *queryTyped* and *queryFiltered* queries lies in the returned type. A *queryTyped* query returns a sequence of *CustomerContact* instances, while *queryFiltered* returns a sequence of the base class *Contact*. With *queryFiltered*, you need to explicitly cast the result into a *CustomerContact* type if you want to access the *Company* property.

Unique Object Identity

An instance of an entity class stores an in-memory representation of table row data. If you try to instantiate two different entities containing the same row from the same *DataContext*, you obtain a reference to the same in-memory object. In other words, object identity (same references) maintains data identity (same table row) using the entity unique key. The LINQ to SQL engine ensures that the same object reference is used when an entity instantiated from a query result coming from the same *DataContext* is already in memory. This check does not happen if you create an instance of an entity by yourself or in a different *DataContext* (regardless of the real data source). In Listing 4-5, you can see that *c1* and *c2* reference the same *Contact* instance, even if they originate from two different queries, while *c3* is a different object, even if its content is equivalent to the others.

> **Note**   If you want to force reloading data from the database using the same *DataContext*, you must use the *Refresh* method of the *DataContext* class. You will find more about this in Chapter 5.

Listing 4-5   Object identity

```
var queryTyped =
    from    c in contacts.OfType<CustomerContact>()
    orderby c.ContactID
    select  c;

var queryFiltered =
    from    c in contacts
    where   c is CustomerContact
    orderby c.ContactID
    select  c;

Contact c1 = null;
Contact c2 = null;
foreach( var row in queryTyped.Take(1) ) {
    c1 = row;
}
foreach( var row in queryFiltered.Take(1) ) {
    c2 = row;
}
Contact c3 = new Contact();
c3.ContactID = c1.ContactID;
c3.ContactType = c1.ContactType;
c3.Name = c1.Name;
c3.Phone = c1.Phone;
Debug.Assert( c1 == c2 ); // same instance
Debug.Assert( c1 != c3 ); // different objects
```

Entity Constraints

Entity classes support the maintenance of valid relationships between entities, just like the support offered by foreign keys in a standard relational environment. However, the entity classes cannot represent all possible check constraints of a relational table. No attributes are available to specify the same alternate keys (unique constraint), triggers, and check expressions that can be defined in a relational database. This fact is relevant when you start to manipulate data using entity classes because you cannot guarantee that an updated value will be accepted by the underlying database. (For example, it could have a duplicate unique key.) However, because you can load into entity instances only parts (rows) of the whole table, these kinds of checks are not possible without accessing the relational database anyway.

Associations Between Entities

Relationships between entities in a relational database are modeled on the concept of foreign keys referring to primary keys of a table. Class entities can use the same concept through the *Association* attribute, which can describe both sides of a *one-to-many* relationship described by a foreign key.

EntityRef

Let's start with the concept of *lookup*, which is the typical operation used to get the customer related to one order. Lookup can be seen as the direct translation into the entity model of the foreign key relationship existing between the CustomerID column of the Orders table and the primary key of the Customers table. In our entity model, the *Order* entity class will have a *Customer* property (of type *Customer*) that shows the customer data. This property is decorated with the *Association* attribute and stores its information in an *EntityRef<Customer>* member (named *_Customer*), which enables the deferred loading of references that you will see shortly. Listing 4-6 shows the definition of this association.

Listing 4-6 *Association EntityRef*

```
[Table(Name="Orders")]
public class Order {
    [Column(IsPrimaryKey=true)] public int OrderID;
    [Column] private string CustomerID;
    [Column] public DateTime? OrderDate;

    [Association(Storage="_Customer", ThisKey="CustomerID", IsForeignKey=true)]
    public Customer Customer {
        get { return this._Customer.Entity; }
        set { this._Customer.Entity = value; }
    }

    private EntityRef<Customer> _Customer;
}
```

As you can see, the CustomerID column must be defined in *Order* because otherwise it would not be possible to obtain the related *Customer*. The *IsForeignKey* argument specifies that we are in the child side of a parent-child relationship, and the *ThisKey* argument of the *Association* attribute indicates the "foreign key" column (which would be a comma-separated list if more columns were involved for a composite key) that is used to define the relationship between entities. If you want to hide this detail in the entity properties, you can declare that column as private, just as in the *Order* class shown earlier.

Note   There are two other arguments for the *Association* attribute. One is *IsUnique*, which must be true whenever the foreign key also has a uniqueness constraint. In that case, the relationship with the parent table is one-to-one instead of many-to-one. The other argument is *Name*, and it is used just to define the name of the constraint if a database is generated from the metadata using the *DataContext.CreateDatabase* method, which will be described in Chapter 5.

Using the *Order* class in a LINQ query, you can specify a *Customer* property in a filter without the need to write a join between *Customer* and *Order* entities. In the following query, the *Country* member of the related *Customer* is used to filter orders that come from customers of a particular *Country*:

```
Table<Order> Orders = db.GetTable<Order>();
var query =
    from   o in Orders
    where  o.Customer.Country == "USA"
    select o.OrderID;
```

The previous query is translated into an SQL JOIN like the following one:

```
SELECT    [t0].[OrderID]
FROM      [Orders] AS [t0]
LEFT JOIN [Customers] AS [t1]
      ON [t1].[CustomerID] = [t0].[CustomerID]
WHERE     [t1].[Country] = "USA"
```

Until now, we have used entity relationships only for their metadata in building LINQ queries. When an instance of an entity class is created, a reference to another entity (such as the previous *Customer* property) works with a technique called *deferred loading*. The related *Customer* entity is not instantiated and loaded into memory from the database until it is accessed either in read or write mode.

Note   *EntityRef<T>* is a wrapper class that is instantiated with the container object (a *DataContext* derived class) to give a valid reference for any access to the referenced entity. Each read/write operation is filtered by a property *getter* and *setter*, which execute a query to load data from the database the first time this entity is accessed if it is not already in memory.

In other words, to generate an SQL query to populate the *Customer*-related entity when the *Country* property is accessed, you use the following code:

```
var query =
    from   o in Orders
    where  o.OrderID == 10528
    select o;

foreach( var row in query ) {
    Console.WriteLine( row.Customer.Country );
}
```

The process of accessing the *Customer* property involves checking to determine whether the related *Customer* entity is already in memory for the current *DataContext*. If it is, that entity is accessed; otherwise, the following SQL query is executed and the corresponding *Customer* entity is loaded in memory and then accessed:

```
SELECT [t0].[Country], [t0].[CustomerID], [t0].[CompanyName]
FROM   [Customers] AS [t0]
WHERE  [t0].[CustomerID] = "GREAL"
```

The GREAL string is the *CustomerID* value for order 10528. As you can see, the SELECT statement queries all columns declared in the *Customer* entity, even if they are not used in the expression that accessed the *Customer* entity. (In this case, the executed code never referenced the *CompanyName* member.)

EntitySet

The other side of an association is a table that is referenced from another table through its primary key. Although this is an implicit consequence of the foreign key constraint in a relational model, you need to explicitly define this association in the entity model. If the Customers table is referenced from the Orders table, you can define an *Orders* property in the *Customer* class that represents the set of *Order* entities related to a given *Customer*. The relationship is implemented by an instance of *EntitySet<Order>*, which is a wrapper class over the sequence of related orders. You might want to directly expose this *EntitySet<T>* type, as in the code shown in Listing 4-7. In that code, the *OtherKey* argument of the *Association* attribute specifies the name of the member on the related type (*Order*) that defines the association between *Customer* and the set of *Order* entities.

Listing 4-7   *Association EntitySet* (visible)

```
[Table(Name="Customers")]
public class Customer {
    [Column(IsPrimaryKey=true)] public string CustomerID;
    [Column] public string CompanyName;
    [Column] public string Country;

    [Association(OtherKey="CustomerID")]
    public EntitySet<Order> Orders;
}
```

You might also decide to expose *Orders* as a property, as in the declaration shown in Listing 4-8. In this case, the *Storage* argument of the *Association* attribute specifies the *EntitySet<T>* for physical storage. You might also choose to make only an *ICollection<Order>* visible outside the *Customer* class, instead of an *EntitySet<Order>*, but this is not a common practice.

Listing 4-8   *Association EntitySet* (hidden)

```
public class Customer {
    [Column(IsPrimaryKey=true)] public string CustomerID;
    [Column] public string CompanyName;
    [Column] public string Country;

    private EntitySet<Order> _Orders;

    [Association(OtherKey="CustomerID", Storage="_Orders")]
    public EntitySet<Order> Orders {
        get { return this._Orders; }
        set { this._Orders.Assign(value); }
    }
    public Customer() {
```

```
        this._Orders = new EntitySet<Order>();
    }
}
```

With both models of association declaration, you can use the *Customer* class in a LINQ query, accessing the related *Order* entities without the need to write a join. You simply specify the *Orders* property. The next query returns the names of customers who placed more than 20 orders:

```
Table<Customer> Customers = db.GetTable<Customer>();
var query =
    from   c in Customers
    where  c.Orders.Count > 20
    select c.CompanyName;
```

The previous LINQ query is translated into an SQL query like the following one:

```
SELECT [t0].[CompanyName]
FROM    [Customers] AS [t0]
WHERE ( SELECT COUNT(*)
        FROM [Orders] AS [t1]
        WHERE [t1].[CustomerID] = [t0].[CustomerID]
      ) > 20
```

In this case, no instances of the *Order* entity are created. The *Orders* property serves only as a metadata source to generate the desired SQL query. If you return a *Customer* entity from a LINQ query, you can access the *Orders* of a customer on demand:

```
var query =
    from   c in Customers
    where  c.Orders.Count > 20
    select c;

foreach( var row in query ) {
    Console.WriteLine( row.CompanyName );
    foreach( var order in row.Orders ) {
        Console.WriteLine( order.OrderID );
    }
}
```

In the preceding code, you are using deferred loading. Each time you access the *Orders* property of a customer for the first time (as indicated by the highlighted code), a query like the following one (which uses @p0 as the parameter to filter *CustomerID*) is sent to the database:

```
SELECT [t0].[OrderID], [t0].[CustomerID]
FROM    [Orders] AS [t0]
WHERE   [t0].[CustomerID] = @p0
```

If you want to load all orders for all customers into memory using only one query to the database, you need to request *immediate loading* instead of deferred loading. To do that, you have two options. The first approach, which is demonstrated in Listing 4-9, is to force the inclusion of an *EntitySet* using a *DataLoadOptions* instance and the call to its *LoadWith<T>* method.

Listing 4-9   Use of *DataLoadOptions* and *LoadWith<T>*

```
DataContext db = new DataContext( ConnectionString );
Table<Customer> Customers = db.GetTable<Customer>();

DataLoadOptions loadOptions = new DataLoadOptions();
loadOptions.LoadWith<Customer>( c => c.Orders );
db.LoadOptions = loadOptions;
var query =
    from   c in Customers
    where  c.Orders.Count > 20
    select c;
```

The second option is to return a new entity that explicitly includes the *Orders* property for the *Customer*:

```
var query =
    from   c in Customers
    where  c.Orders.Count > 20
    select new { c.CompanyName, c.Orders };
```

These LINQ queries send an SQL query to the database to get all customers who placed more than 20 orders, including the entire order list for each customer. That SQL query might be similar to the one shown in the following code:

```
SELECT [t0].[CompanyName], [t1].[OrderID], [t1].[CustomerID], (
    SELECT COUNT(*)
    FROM [Orders] AS [t3]
    WHERE [t3].[CustomerID] = [t0].[CustomerID]
    ) AS [value]
FROM [Customers] AS [t0]
LEFT OUTER JOIN [Orders] AS [t1] ON [t1].[CustomerID] = [t0].[CustomerID]
WHERE (
    SELECT COUNT(*)
    FROM [Orders] AS [t2]
    WHERE [t2].[CustomerID] = [t0].[CustomerID]
    ) > 20
ORDER BY [t0].[CustomerID], [t1].[OrderID]
```

Note   You can see that there is a single SQL statement here and the LINQ to SQL engine parses the result, extracting different entities (Customers and Orders). Keeping the result ordered by *CustomerID*, the engine can build in-memory entities and relationships in a faster way.

You can filter the subquery produced by relationship navigation. Suppose you want to see only customers who placed at least five orders in 1997, and you want to load and see only these orders. You can use the *AssociateWith<T>* method of the *DataLoadOptions* class to do that, as demonstrated in Listing 4-10.

Listing 4-10 Use of *DataLoadOptions* and *AssociateWith<T>*

```
DataLoadOptions loadOptions = new DataLoadOptions();
loadOptions.AssociateWith<Customer>(
    c => from   o in c.Orders
         where o.OrderDate.Value.Year == 1997
         select o);
db.LoadOptions = loadOptions;
var query =
    from   c in Customers
    where  c.Orders.Count > 5
    select c;
```

You will appreciate that the C# filter condition (*o.OrderDate.Value.Year == 1997*) is translated into the following SQL expression:

```
(DATEPART(Year, [t2].[OrderDate]) = 1997)
```

AssociateWith<T> can also control the initial ordering of the collection. To do that, you can simply add an order condition into the query passed as an argument to *AssociateWith<T>*. For example, if you want to get the orders for each customer starting from the newest one, add the *orderby* line highlighted in the following code:

```
loadOptions.AssociateWith<Customer>(
    c => from   o in c.Orders
         where o.OrderDate.Value.Year == 1997
         orderby o.OrderDate descending
         select o);
```

Using *AssociateWith<T>* alone does not apply the immediate loading behavior. If you want both immediate loading and filtering through a relationship, you have to call both the *Load-With<T>* and *AssociateWith<T>* methods. The order of these calls is not relevant. For example, you can write the following code:

```
DataLoadOptions loadOptions = new DataLoadOptions();
loadOptions.AssociateWith<Customer>(
    c => from   o in c.Orders
         where o.OrderDate.Value.Year == 1997
         select o);
loadOptions.LoadWith<Customer>( c => c.Orders );
db.LoadOptions = loadOptions;
```

Loading all data into memory using a single query might be a better approach if you are sure you will access all data that is loaded, because you will spend less time in round-trip latency. However, this technique will consume more memory and bandwidth when the typical access to a graph of entities is random. Think about these details when you decide how to query your data model.

Graph Consistency

Relationships are bidirectional between entities—when an update is made on one side, the other side should be kept synchronized. LINQ to SQL does not automatically manage this kind of synchronization, which has to be done by the class entity implementation. LINQ to

SQL offers an implementation pattern that is also used by code-generation tools such as SQLMetal, a tool that is part of the Microsoft .NET 3.5 Software Development Kit (SDK), or the LINQ to SQL class generator that is included in Visual Studio 2008. Both these tools will be described in Chapter 6. This pattern is based on the *EntitySet<T>* class on one side and on the complex *setter* accessor on the other side. Take a look at the tools-generated code if you are interested in implementation details of this pattern.

Change Notification

You will see in Chapter 5 that LINQ to SQL is able to track changes in entities, submitting equivalent changes to the database. This process is implemented by default through an algorithm that compares an object's content with its original values, requiring a copy of each tracked object. The memory consumption can be high, but it can be optimized if entities participate in the change tracking service by announcing when an object has been changed.

The implementation of change notification requires an entity to expose all its data through properties implementing the *System.ComponentModel.INotifyPropertyChanging* interface. Each property *setter* needs to call the *PropertyChanging* method of *DataContext*. Further details are available in the product documentation. Tools-generated code for entities (such as that emitted by SQLMetal and Visual Studio 2008) already implement this pattern.

Relational Model vs. Hierarchical Model

The entity model used by LINQ to SQL defines a set of objects that maps the database tables into objects that can be used and manipulated by LINQ queries. The resulting model represents a paradigm shift that has been revealed in describing associations between entities. We moved from a relational model (tables in a database) to a hierarchical or graph model (objects in memory).

A hierarchical/graph model is the natural way to manipulate objects in a program written in C# or Microsoft Visual Basic. When you try to consider how to translate an existing SQL query into a LINQ query, this is the major conceptual obstacle you encounter. In LINQ, you can write a query using joins between separate entities, just as you do in SQL. However, you can also write a query leveraging the existing relationships between entities, as we did with *EntitySet* and *EntityRef* associations.

 Important   Remember that SQL does not make use of relationships between entities when querying data. Those relationships exist only to define the data integrity conditions. LINQ does not have the concept of *referential integrity*, but it makes use of relationships to define possible navigation paths into the data.

Data Querying

A LINQ to SQL query is sent to the database only when the program needs to read data. For example, the following *foreach* loop iterates rows returned from a table:

```
var query =
    from    c in Customers
    where   c.Country == "USA"
    select  c.CompanyName;
 foreach( var company in query ) {
    Console.WriteLine( company );
}
```

The code generated by the *foreach* statement is equivalent to the following code. The exact moment the query is executed corresponds to the call to *GetEnumerator*:

```
// GetEnumerator sends the query to the database
IEnumerator<string> enumerator = query.GetEnumerator();
while (enumerator.MoveNext()) {
    Console.WriteLine( enumerator.Current );
}
```

Writing more *foreach* loops in the same query generates an equal number of calls to *Get-Enumerator*, and thus an equal number of repeated executions of the same query. If you want to iterate the same data many times, you might prefer to cache data in memory. Using *ToList* or *ToArray*, you can convert the results of a query into a *List* or an *Array*, respectively. When you call these methods, the SQL query is sent to the database:

```
// ToList() sends the query to the database var companyNames = query.ToList();
```

You might want to send the query to the database several times when you manipulate the LINQ query between data iterations. For example, you might have an interactive user interface that allows the user to add a new filter condition for each iteration of data. In Listing 4-11, the *DisplayTop* method shows only the first few rows of the result; query manipulation between calls to *DisplayTop* simulates a user interaction that ends in a new filter condition each time.

> **More Info**   Listing 4-11 shows a very simple technique for query manipulation, which adds more restrictive filter conditions to an existing query represented by an *IQueryable<T>* object. Chapter 11 describes the techniques to dynamically build a query tree in a more flexible way.

Listing 4-11   Query manipulation

```
static void QueryManipulation() {
    DataContext db = new DataContext( ConnectionString );
    Table<Customer> Customers = db.GetTable<Customer>();
    db.Log = Console.Out;
```

```
        // All Customers
        var query =
            from    c in Customers
            select  new {c.CompanyName, c.State, c.Country };

        DisplayTop( query, 10 );

        // User interaction add a filter
        // to the previous query
        // Customers from USA
        query =
            from    c in query
            where   c.Country == "USA"
            select c;

        DisplayTop( query, 10 );

        // User interaction add another
        // filter to the previous query
        // Customers from WA, USA
        query =
            from    c in query
            where   c.State == "WA"
            select c;

        DisplayTop( query, 10 );
    }

    static void DisplayTop<T>( IQueryable<T> query, int rows ) {
        foreach( var row in query.Take(rows)) {
            Console.WriteLine( row );
        }
    }
}
```

Important   In the previous example, we used *IQueryable<T>* as the *DisplayTop* parameter. If you pass *IEnumerable<T>* instead, the results would appear identical, but the query sent to the database would not contain the *TOP (rows)* clause to filter data directly on the database. When using *IEnumerable<T>*, you use a different set of extension methods to resolve the *Take* operator without generating a new expression tree. Refer to Chapter 2, "LINQ Syntax Fundamentals," for an introduction to the differences between *IEnumerable<T>* and *IQueryable<T>*.

A common query used for accessing a database is the reading of a single row from a table, defining a condition that is guaranteed to be unique, such as a record key. Here is a typical query:

```
var query =
    from    c in db.Customers
    where   c.CustomerID == "ANATR"
    select  c;
```

```
var enumerator = query.GetEnumerator();
if (enumerator.MoveNext()) {
    var customer = enumerator.Current;
    Console.WriteLine( "{0} {1}", customer.CustomerID, customer.CompanyName );
}
```

In this case, it might be shorter and more explicit to state your intention by using the *Single* operator. The previous query can be written in this more compact way:

```
var customer = db.Customers.Single( c => c.CustomerID == "ANATR" );
Console.WriteLine( "{0} {1}", customer.CustomerID, customer.CompanyName );
```

However, it is important to note that calling *Single* has a different semantic than the previous equivalent *query*. Calling *Single* generates a query to the database only if the desired entity (in this case, the *Customer* with *ANATR* as *CustomerID*) is not already in memory. If you want to read the data from the database, you need to call the *DataContext.Refresh* method:

```
db.Refresh(RefreshMode.OverwriteCurrentValues, customer);
```

You will find more information about an entity life cycle in Chapter 5.

Projections

The transformation from an expression tree to an SQL query requires the complete understanding of the query operations sent to the LINQ to SQL engine. This transformation affects the use of object initializers. You can use projections through the *select* keyword, as in the following example:

```
var query =
    from    c in Customers
    where   c.Country == "USA"
    select  new {c.CustomerID, Name = c.CompanyName.ToUpper()} into r
    orderby r.Name
    select  r;
```

The whole LINQ query is translated into this SQL statement:

```
SELECT [t1].[CustomerID], [t1].[value] AS [Name]
FROM ( SELECT [t0].[CustomerID],
              UPPER([t0].[CompanyName]) AS [value],
              [t0].[Country]
       FROM [Customers] AS [t0]
     ) AS [t1]
WHERE    [t1].[Country] = "USA"
ORDER BY [t1].[value]
```

As you can see, the *ToUpper* method has been translated into an UPPER T-SQL function call. To do that, the LINQ to SQL engine needs a deep knowledge of the meaning of any operation in the expression tree. Consider this query:

```
var queryBad =
    from    c in Customers
```

```
    where   c.Country == "USA"
    select  new CustomerData( c.CustomerID, c.CompanyName.ToUpper()) into r
    orderby r.Name
    select  r;
```

In this case, we call a constructor of the *CustomerData* type that can do anything a piece of Intermediate Language (IL) code can do. In other words, there is no semantic value in calling a constructor other than the initial assignment of the instance created. The consequence is that LINQ to SQL cannot correctly translate this syntax into equivalent SQL code, and it throws an exception if you try to execute the query. However, you can safely use a parameterized constructor in the final projection of a query, as in the following sample:

```
var queryParamConstructor =
    from    c in Customers
    where   c.Country == "USA"
    orderby c.CompanyName
    select  new CustomerData( c.CustomerID, c.CompanyName.ToUpper() );
```

If you only need to initialize an object, use the object initializers instead of a parameterized constructor call, as in following query:

```
var queryGood =
    from    c in Customers
    where   c.Country == "USA"
    select  new CustomerData { CustomerID = c.CustomerID,
                               Name = c.CompanyName.ToUpper() } into r
    orderby r.Name
    select  r;
```

Important   Always use object initializers to encode projections in LINQ to SQL. Use parameterized constructors only in the final projection of a query.

Stored Procedures and User-Defined Functions

Accessing data through stored procedures and user-defined functions (UDFs) requires the definition of corresponding methods decorated with attributes. This enables you to write LINQ queries in a strongly typed form. From the point of view of LINQ, there is no difference if a stored procedure or UDF is written in T-SQL or SQLCLR, but there are some details you have to know to handle differences between stored procedures and UDFs.

Note   Considering that many of you will automatically generate specialized *DataContext* derived classes, we will focus our attention on the most important concepts to know to effectively use these objects. If you want to manually create these wrappers, please refer to the product documentation for a detailed list of the attributes and their arguments.

Stored Procedures

Consider the *Customers by City* stored procedure:

```
CREATE PROCEDURE [dbo].[Customers By City]( @param1 NVARCHAR(20) )
AS BEGIN
    SET NOCOUNT ON;
    SELECT CustomerID, ContactName, CompanyName, City
    FROM   Customers AS c
    WHERE  c.City = @param1
END
```

You can define a method decorated with a *Function* attribute that calls the stored procedure through the *ExecuteMethodCall* method of the *DataContext* class. In Listing 4-12, we define *CustomersByCity* as a member of a class derived from *DataContext*.

Listing 4-12   Stored procedure declaration

```
class SampleDb : DataContext {
    // ...
    [Function(Name = "Customers by City", IsComposable = false)]
    public ISingleResult<CustomerInfo> CustomersByCity(string param1) {
        IExecuteResult executeResult =
            this.ExecuteMethodCall(
                    this,
                    (MethodInfo) (MethodInfo.GetCurrentMethod()),
                    param1);
        ISingleResult<CustomerInfo> result =
            (ISingleResult<CustomerInfo>) executeResult.ReturnValue;
        return result;
    }
}
```

The *ExecuteMethodCall* is declared in this way:

```
IExecuteResult ExecuteMethodCall( object instance,
                                  MethodInfo methodInfo,
                                  params object[] parameters)
```

The method's first parameter is the instance (which is not required if you call a static method). The second parameter is a metadata description of the method to call, which could be obtained through Reflection as we do in Listing 4-12. The third parameter is an array containing parameters to pass to the method that is called.

CustomersByCity returns an instance of *ISingleResult<CustomerInfo>*, which implements *IEnumerable<CustomerInfo>* and can be enumerated in a *foreach* statement like this one:

```
SampleDb db = new SampleDb( ConnectionString );
foreach( var row in db.CustomersByCity( "London" )) {
    Console.WriteLine( "{0} {1}", row.CustomerID, row.CompanyName );
}
```

As you can see in Listing 4-12, we had to access the *IExecuteResult* interface returned by *ExecuteMethodCall* to get the desired result. This requires a further explanation here. We use the same *Function* attribute to decorate a method wrapping either a stored procedure or a UDF. The discrimination between these constructs is made by the *IsComposable* argument of the *Function* attribute: if it is *false*, the following method wraps a stored procedure; if it is *true*, a user-defined function will be called.

> **Note**   The name *IsComposable* relates to the composability of user-defined functions in a query expression. You will see an example of this when describing the mapping of UDFs in the next section of this chapter.

The *IExecuteResult* interface has a simple definition:

```
public interface IExecuteResult : IDisposable {
    object GetParameterValue(int parameterIndex);
    object ReturnValue { get; }
}
```

The *GetParameterValue* method allows access to the output parameters of a stored procedure. You need to cast this result to the correct type, also passing the ordinal position of the output parameter in *parameterIndex*.

The *ReturnValue* read-only property is used to access the return value of a stored procedure or UDF. The scalar value returned is accessible with a cast to the correct type: a stored procedure always returns an integer, while the type of a UDF function can be different. However, when the results are tabular, *ISingleResult<T>* is used to access a single resultset, while *IMultiple-Results* is used to access multiple resultsets.

You always need to know the metadata of all possible returned resultsets, applying the right type to the generic interfaces used to return data. *ISingleResult<T>* is a simple wrapper of *IEnumerable<T>* that also implements *IFunctionResult*, which has a *ReturnValue* read-only property acting as the *IExecuteResult.ReturnValue* property we have already seen:

```
public interface IFunctionResult {
    object ReturnValue { get; }
}
public interface ISingleResult<T> :
    IEnumerable<T>, IEnumerable, IFunctionResult, IDisposable { }
```

You saw an example of *ISingleResult<T>* in Listing 4-12. We wrote the *CustomersByCity* wrapper in a verbose way to better illustrate the internal steps necessary to access the returning data.

Whenever you have multiple resultsets from a stored procedure, you will call the *IMultiple-Result.GetResult<T>* method for each resultset sequentially and specify the correct *T* type for the expected result. *IMultipleResults* also implements *IFunctionResult*, thus it also offers a *ReturnValue* read-only property.

```
public interface IMultipleResults : IFunctionResult, IDisposable {
    IEnumerable<TElement> GetResult<TElement>();
}
```

Consider the following stored procedure that returns two resultsets with different structures:

```
CREATE PROCEDURE TwoCustomerGroups
AS BEGIN
    SELECT  CustomerID, ContactName, CompanyName, City
    FROM    Customers AS c
    WHERE   c.City = 'London'

    SELECT  CustomerID, CompanyName, City
    FROM    Customers AS c
    WHERE   c.City = 'Torino'
END
```

The results returned from this stored procedure can be stored in the following *CustomerInfo* and *CustomerShortInfo* types, which do not require any attribute in their declaration:

```
public class CustomerInfo {
    public string CustomerID;
    public string CompanyName;
    public string City;
    public string ContactName;
}

public class CustomerShortInfo {
    public string CustomerID;
    public string CompanyName;
    public string City;
}
```

The declaration of the LINQ counterpart of the *TwoCustomerGroups* stored procedure should be like the one shown in Listing 4-13.

Listing 4-13 Stored procedure with multiple results

```
class SampleDb : DataContext {
    // ...
    [Function(Name = "TwoCustomerGroups", IsComposable = false)]
    [ResultType(typeof(CustomerInfo))]
    [ResultType(typeof(CustomerShortInfo))]
    public IMultipleResults TwoCustomerGroups() {
        IExecuteResult executeResult =
                this.ExecuteMethodCall(
                    this,
                    (MethodInfo) (MethodInfo.GetCurrentMethod()));
        IMultipleResults result =
            (IMultipleResults) executeResult.ReturnValue;
        return result;
    }
}
```

Each resultset has a different type. When calling each *GetResult<T>*, you need to specify the correct type, which needs at least a public member with the same name for each returned column. If you specify a type with more public members than available columns, the "missing" members will have a default value. Moreover, each returned type has to be declared by using a *ResultType* attribute that decorates the *TwoCustomerGroups* method, as you can see in Listing 4-13. In the next sample, the first resultset must match the *CustomerInfo* type, while the second resultset must correspond to the *CustomerShortInfo* type:

```
IMultipleResults results = db.TwoCustomerGroups();
foreach( var row in results.GetResult<CustomerInfo>()) {
    // Access to CustomerInfo instance
}
foreach( var row in results.GetResult<CustomerShortInfo>()) {
    // Access to CustomerShortInfo instance
}
```

Remember that the order of *ResultType* attributes is not relevant, but you have to pay attention to the order of the *GetResult<T>* calls. The first resultset will be mapped from the first *GetResult<T>* call, and so on, regardless of the parameter type used. For example, if you invert the previous two calls, asking for *CustomerShortInfo* before *CustomerInfo*, you get no error, but you get an empty string for the *ContactName* of the second resultset mapped to *CustomerInfo*.

> **Important**   The order of *GetResult<T>* calls is relevant and must correspond to the order of returned resultsets. Conversely, the order of *ResultType* attributes applied to the method representing a stored procedure is not relevant.

Another use of *IMultipleResults* is the case in which a stored procedure can return different types based on parameters. For example, consider the following stored procedure:

```
CREATE PROCEDURE ChooseResultType( @resultType INT )
AS BEGIN
    IF @resultType = 1
        SELECT * FROM [Customers]
    ELSE IF @resultType = 2
        SELECT * FROM [Products]
END
```

Such a stored procedure will always return a single result, but its type might be different on each call. We do not like this use of stored procedures and prefer to avoid this situation. However, if you have to handle this case, decorating the method with both possible *ResultType* attributes allows you to handle both situations:

```
[Function(Name = "ChooseResultType", IsComposable = false)]
[ResultType(typeof(Customer))]
[ResultType(typeof(Product))]
public IMultipleResults ChooseResultType( int resultType ) {
    IExecuteResult executeResult =
            this.ExecuteMethodCall(
```

```
                this,
                (MethodInfo) (MethodInfo.GetCurrentMethod()),
                resultType );
    IMultipleResults result =
        (IMultipleResults) executeResult.ReturnValue;
    return result;
}
```

In the single *GetResult<T>* call you have to specify the type that correctly corresponds to what the stored procedure will return:

```
IMultipleResults results = db.ChooseResultType( 1 );
foreach( var row in results.GetResult<Customer>()) {
    // Access to Customer instance
}
```

If you have a similar scenario, it would be better to encapsulate the stored procedure call (*ChooseResultType* in this case) in several methods, one for each possible returned type, so that you limit the risk of mismatching the relationship between parameter and result type:

```
public IEnumerable<Customer> ChooseCustomer() {
    IMultipleResults results = db.ChooseResultType( 1 );
    return results.GetResult<Customer>();
}

public IEnumerable<Product> ChooseProduct() {
    IMultipleResults results = db.ChooseResultType( 2 );
    return results.GetResult<Product>();
}
```

Before turning to user-defined functions, we want to take a look at what happens when you call a stored procedure in a LINQ query. Consider the following code:

```
var query =
    from   c in db.CustomersByCity("London")
    where  c.CompanyName.Length > 15
    select new { c.CustomerID, c.CompanyName };
```

Apparently, this query can be completely converted into a SQL query. However, all the data returned from *CustomersByCity* is passed from the SQL server to the client, as you can see from the generated SQL statement:

```
EXEC @RETURN_VALUE = [Customers by City] @param1 = 'London'
```

Both the filter (*where*) and projection (*select*) operations are made by LINQ to Objects, filtering data that has been transmitted to the client and enumerating only rows that have a *CompanyName* value longer than 15 characters. Thus, stored procedures are not composable into a single SQL query. To make this kind of composition, you need to use user-defined functions.

User-Defined Functions

To be used in LINQ, a user-defined function needs the same kind of declaration as a stored procedure. When a UDF is used inside a LINQ query, the LINQ to SQL engine must consider it in the construction of the SQL statement, adding a UDF call to the generated SQL code if the UDF is called inside the LINQ query. The capability of a UDF to be used in a LINQ query is what we mean by composability–the capability to compose different queries and/or operators into a single query. Because the same *Function* attribute is used for both stored procedures and UDFs, the *IsComposable* argument is set to *true* to map a UDF, and is set to *false* to map a stored procedure. Remember that there is no difference if a UDF is written in T-SQL or SQLCLR.

Listing 4-14 provides an example of a LINQ declaration of the scalar-valued UDF *MinUnit-PriceByCategory* that is defined in the sample Northwind database.

Listing 4-14   Scalar-valued user-defined function

```
class SampleDb : DataContext {
    // ...
    [Function(Name = "dbo.MinUnitPriceByCategory", IsComposable = true)]
    public decimal? MinUnitPriceByCategory( int? categoryID) {
        IExecuteResult executeResult =
            this.ExecuteMethodCall(
                this,
                ((MethodInfo) (MethodInfo.GetCurrentMethod())),
                categoryID);
        decimal? result = (decimal?) executeResult.ReturnValue;
        return result;
    }
}
```

The call to a UDF as an isolated expression generates a single SQL query invocation. You can also use a UDF in a LINQ query such as the following one:

```
var query =
    from   c in Categories
    select new { c.CategoryID,
                 c.CategoryName,
                 MinPrice = db.MinUnitPriceByCategory( c.CategoryID )};
```

The generated SQL statement *composes* the LINQ query with the UDF that is called, resulting in a SQL query like this:

```
SELECT [t0].[CategoryID],
       [t0].[CategoryName],
       dbo.MinUnitPriceByCategory([t0].[CategoryID]) AS [value]
FROM   [Categories] AS [t0]
```

There are some differences in table-valued UDF wrappers. Consider the following UDF:

```
CREATE FUNCTION [dbo].[CustomersByCountry] ( @country NVARCHAR(15) )
RETURNS TABLE
AS RETURN
    SELECT  CustomerID,
            ContactName,
            CompanyName,
            City
    FROM    Customers c
    WHERE   c.Country = @country
```

To use this UDF in LINQ, you need to declare a *CustomersByCountry* method as shown in Listing 4-15. A table-valued UDF always sets *IsComposable* to *true* in *Function* arguments, but it calls the *DataContext.CreateMethodCallQuery* instead of *DataContext.ExecuteMethodCall*.

Listing 4-15   Table-valued user-defined function

```
class SampleDb : DataContext {
    // ...
    [Function(Name = "dbo.CustomersByCountry", IsComposable = true)]
    public IQueryable<Customer> CustomersByCountry(string country) {
        return this.CreateMethodCallQuery<Customer>(
            this,
            ((MethodInfo) (MethodInfo.GetCurrentMethod())),
            country);
    }
]
```

A table-valued UDF can be used like any other table in a LINQ query. For example, you can join customers returned by the previous UDF with the orders they placed, as in the following query:

```
Table<Order> Orders = db.GetTable<Order>();
var queryCustomers =
    from   c in db.CustomersByCountry( "USA" )
    join   o in Orders
           on c.CustomerID equals o.CustomerID
           into orders
    select new { c.CustomerID, c.CompanyName, orders };
```

The generated SQL query will be similar to this one:

```
SELECT [t0].[CustomerID], [t0].[CompanyName],
       [t1].[OrderID], [t1].[CustomerID] AS [CustomerID2],
       (SELECT COUNT(*)
        FROM [Orders] AS [t2]
        WHERE [t0].[CustomerID] = [t2].[CustomerID]
        ) AS [value]
FROM dbo.CustomersByCountry('USA') AS [t0]
LEFT OUTER JOIN [Orders] AS [t1] ON [t0].[CustomerID] = [t1].[CustomerID]
ORDER BY [t1].[OrderID]
```

Compiled Queries

If you need to repeat the same query many times, eventually with different argument values, you might be worried about the multiple query construction. Several databases, such as SQL Server, try to parameterize received SQL queries automatically to optimize the compilation of the query execution plan. However, the program that sends a parameterized query to SQL Server will get better performance because SQL Server does not spend time to analyze it if the query is similar to another one already processed. LINQ already does a fine job of query optimization, but each time that the same query tree is evaluated, the LINQ to SQL engine parses the query tree to build the equivalent SQL code. You can optimize this behavior by using the *CompiledQuery* class.

> **More Info**   The built-in SQL Server provider sends parameterized queries to the database. Every time you see a constant value in the SQL code presented in this chapter, keep in mind that the real SQL query sent to the database has a parameter for each constant in the query. That constant can be the result of an expression that is independent of the query execution. This kind of expression is resolved by the host language (C# in this case). When you use the *CompiledQuery* class, the parsing of the query tree and the creation of the equivalent SQL code is the operation that is not repeated every time LINQ has to process the same query. You might be asking what is the break-even point that justifies the use of the *CompiledQuery* class. Rico Mariani did a performance test that is described in this blog post: *http://blogs.msdn.com/ricom/archive/2008/01/14/performance-quiz-13-linq-to-sql-compiled-query-cost-solution.aspx*. The response from his benchmark is that with at least two calls for the query, the use of the *CompiledQuery* class produces a performance advantage.

To compile a query, you can use one of the *CompiledQuery.Compile* static methods. This approach passes the LINQ query as a parameter in the form of an expression tree, and then obtains a delegate with arguments corresponding to both the *DataContext* on which you want to operate and the parameters of the query. Listing 4-16 illustrates the compiled query declaration and use.

Listing 4-16   Compiled query in a local scope

```
static void CompiledQueriesLocal() {
    DataContext db = new DataContext( ConnectionString );
    Table<Customer> Customers = db.GetTable<Customer>();

    var query =
        CompiledQuery.Compile(
            ( DataContext context, string filterCountry ) =>
                from   c in Customers
                where  c.Country == filterCountry
                select new { c.CustomerID, c.CompanyName, c.City } );

    foreach (var row in query( db, "USA" )) {
        Console.WriteLine( row );
    }
}
```

```
        foreach (var row in query( db, "Italy" )) {
            Console.WriteLine( row );
        }
    }
```

As you can see in Listing 4-16, the *Compile* method requires a lambda expression whose first argument is a *DataContext* instance. That argument defines the connection over which the query will be executed. In this case, we do not use that argument inside our lambda expression. Assigning the *CompiledQuery.Compile* result to a local variable is easy (because you declare that variable with *var*), but you will not encounter this situation very frequently. Chances are that you will need to store the delegate returned from *CompiledQuery.Compile* in an instance or a static member to easily reuse it several times. To do that, you need to know the correct declaration syntax.

A compiled query is stored in a *Func* delegate, where the first argument must be an instance of *DataContext* (or a class derived from *DataContext*) and the last argument must be the type returned from the query. You can define up to three arguments in the middle that will be arguments of the compiled query and will need to be specified for each compiled query invocation. Listing 4-17 shows the syntax you can use in this scenario to create the compiled query and then use it.

Listing 4-17   Compiled query assigned to a static member

```
    public static Func< nwind.Northwind, string, IQueryable<nwind.Customer>>
        CustomerByCountry =
            CompiledQuery.Compile(
                ( nwind.Northwind db, string filterCountry ) =>
                    from   c in db.Customers
                    where  c.Country == filterCountry
                    select c );

    static void CompiledQueriesStatic() {
        nwind.Northwind db = new nwind.Northwind( ConnectionString );

        foreach (var row in CustomerByCountry( db, "USA" )) {
            Console.WriteLine( row.CustomerID );
        }

        foreach (var row in CustomerByCountry( db, "Italy" )) {
            Console.WriteLine( row.CustomerID );
        }
    }
```

Because the *Func* delegate that holds the compiled query needs the result type in its declaration, you cannot use an anonymous type as the result type of a compiled query. This is possible only when the compiled query is stored in a local variable, as you saw in Listing 4-16.

Different Approaches to Querying Data

When using LINQ to SQL entities, you have two approaches for querying the same data. The classic way to navigate a relational schema is to write associative queries, just as you can do in SQL. The alternative way offered by LINQ to SQL is through graph traversal. Given the same query result, we might obtain different SQL queries and a different level of performance using different LINQ approaches.

Consider this SQL query that calculates the total quantity of orders for a product (in this case, Chocolade, which is a localized name in the Northwind database):

```
SELECT    SUM( od.Quantity ) AS TotalQuantity
FROM      [Products] p
LEFT JOIN [Order Details] od
    ON    od.[ProductID] = p.[ProductID]
WHERE     p.ProductName = 'Chocolade'
```

The natural conversion into a LINQ query is shown in Listing 4-18. The *Single* operator gets the first row and puts it into *quantityJoin*, which is used to display the result.

Listing 4-18   Query with *Join*

```
var queryJoin =
    from  p in db.Products
    join  o in db.Order_Details
          on p.ProductID equals o.ProductID
          into OrdersProduct
    where p.ProductName == "Chocolade"
    select OrdersProduct.Sum( o => o.Quantity );
var quantityJoin = queryJoin.Single();
Console.WriteLine( quantityJoin );
```

As you can see, the associative query in LINQ can explicitly require the join between *Products* and *Order_Details* through *ProductID* equivalency. By leveraging entities, you can implicitly use the relationship between *Products* and *Order_Details* defined in the *Product* class, as shown in Listing 4-19.

Listing 4-19   Query using *Association*

```
var queryAssociation =
    from  p in db.Products
    where p.ProductName == "Chocolade"
    select p.Order_Details.Sum( o => o.Quantity );
var quantityAssociation = queryAssociation.Single();
Console.WriteLine( quantityAssociation );
```

The single SQL queries produced by both of these LINQ queries are identical. The LINQ query with *join* is more explicit about the access to data, while the query that uses the association between *Product* and *Order_Details* is more implicit in this regard. Using implicit associations results in shorter queries that are less error-prone (because you cannot be wrong about the join condition). At first, you might find that a shorter query is less easy to read. However, this perception might arise because you are accustomed to seeing lengthier queries, and your comfort level with shorter ones might change over time.

> **Note**   The SQL query produced by the LINQ queries in Listings 4-18 and 4-19 is different between SQL Server 2000 and SQL Server 2005 or later versions. With SQL Server 2005, the OUTER APPLY join is used. This is the result of an internal implementation of the provider, but the final result is the same.

Examining this further, you can observe that reading a single product does not require a query expression. You can apply the *Single* operator directly on the *Products* table, as shown in Listing 4-20. Apparently, we get the same results. However, the internal process is much different because this kind of access generates instances of the *Product* and *Order_Details* entities in memory, even if you do not use them in your program.

Listing 4-20   Access through *Entity*

```
var chocolade = db.Products.Single( p => p.ProductName == "Chocolade" );
var quantityValue = chocolade.Order_Details.Sum( o => o.Quantity );
Console.WriteLine( quantityValue );
```

This is a two-step operation that sends two SQL queries to the database. The first one retrieves the *Product* entity. The second one accesses the Order Details table to get *all* the Order Details rows for the required product and sums up the *Quantity* value in memory for the required product. The following are the SQL statements generated:

```
SELECT [t0].[ProductID], [t0].[ProductName], [t0].[SupplierID],
       [t0].[CategoryID], [t0].[QuantityPerUnit], [t0].[UnitPrice],
       [t0].[UnitsInStock], [t0].[UnitsOnOrder], [t0].[ReorderLevel],
       [t0].[Discontinued]
FROM   [dbo].[Products] AS [t0]
WHERE  [t0].[ProductName] = "Chocolade"

SELECT [t0].[OrderID], [t0].[ProductID], [t0].[UnitPrice], [t0].[Quantity],
       [t0].[Discount]
FROM   [dbo].[Order Details] AS [t0]
WHERE  [t0].[ProductID] = "Chocolade"
```

Code that uses this kind of access is shorter to write compared to a query, but its performance is worse if your need is only to get the total *Quantity* value, without the need to get *Product* and *Order_Detail* entities in memory to make further operations.

The queries in Listings 4-18 and 4-19 did not create *Product* or *Order_Details* instances because only the total for the product was required as output. From this point of view, if we already had the required *Product* and *Order_Details* instances for Chocolade in memory, the performance of those queries would be worse because they unnecessarily access the database to get data that is already in memory. On the other hand, a second access to get the sum *Quantity* could be faster if you use the entity approach. Consider this code:

```
var chocolade = db.Products.Single( p => p.ProductName == "Chocolade" );
var quantityValue = chocolade.Order_Details.Sum( o => o.Quantity );
Console.WriteLine( quantityValue );
var repeatCalc = chocolade.Order_Details.Sum( o => o.Quantity );
Console.WriteLine( repeatCalc );
```

The *quantityValue* evaluation requires a database query to create *Order_Details* entities, while the *repeatCalc* evaluation is made on the in-memory entities without the need to read other data from SQL Server.

> **Note**   If you want to understand what the behavior of the code is, you can analyze the SQL queries that are produced. In the previous examples, we wrote a *Sum* in a LINQ query. When the generated SQL query does contain a SUM aggregation operation, we are not reading entities in memory. When the generated SQL query does not contain the same aggregation operation we requested, that aggregation will be made in memory on corresponding entities.

A final thought on the number of generated queries. You might think that we generated two queries when accessing data through the *Product* entity because we had two distinct statements—one to assign the *chocolade* variable, and the other to assign a value to *quantityEntity*. This assumption is not completely true. Even if you write a single statement, the use of a *Product* entity (the results from the *Single* operator call) generates a separate query. Listing 4-21 produces the same results (in terms of memory objects and SQL queries) as Listing 4-20.

Listing 4-21   Access through *Entity* with a single statement

```
var quantityChocolade = db.Products.Single( p => p.ProductName == "Chang" )
                        .Order_Details.Sum( o => o.Quantity );
Console.WriteLine( quantityChocolade );
```

Finding a better way to access data really depends on the whole set of operations performed by a program. If you extensively use entities in your code to store data in memory, access to data through graph traversal based on entity access might offer better performance. On the other hand, if you always transform query results in anonymous types and never manipulate entities in memory, you might prefer an approach based on LINQ queries. As always, the right answer is, "It depends."

Direct Queries

Sometimes you might need access to database SQL features that are not available with LINQ. For example, imagine that you want to use Common Table Expressions (CTEs) or the PIVOT command with SQL Server. LINQ does not have an explicit constructor to do that, even if its SQL Server provider could use these features to optimize some queries. Listing 4-22 shows

how you can use the *ExecuteQuery<T>* method of the *DataContext* class to send a query
directly to the database. The *T* in *ExecuteQuery<T>* is an entity class that represents a
returned row.

Listing 4-22   Direct query

```
var query = db.ExecuteQuery<EmployeeInfo>( @"
    WITH EmployeeHierarchy (EmployeeID, LastName, FirstName,
                            ReportsTo, HierarchyLevel) AS
    ( SELECT EmployeeID,LastName, FirstName,
             ReportsTo, 1 as HierarchyLevel
      FROM    Employees
      WHERE   ReportsTo IS NULL

      UNION ALL

      SELECT    e.EmployeeID, e.LastName, e.FirstName,
                e.ReportsTo, eh.HierarchyLevel + 1 AS HierarchyLevel
      FROM      Employees e
      INNER JOIN  EmployeeHierarchy eh
             ON  e.ReportsTo = eh.EmployeeID
    )
    SELECT  *
    FROM    EmployeeHierarchy
    ORDER BY HierarchyLevel, LastName, FirstName" );
```

As you can see, we need a type to get direct query results. We used *EmployeeInfo*, which is
declared as follows:

```
public class EmployeeInfo {
    public int EmployeeID;
    public string LastName;
    public string FirstName;
    public int? ReportsTo; // int? Corresponds to Nullable<int>
    public int HierarchyLevel;
}
```

The names and types of *EmployeeInfo* members must match the names and types of the
columns returned by the executed query. Please note that if a column can return a NULL
value, you need to use a nullable type, as we did for the *ReportsTo* member that is declared as
int? (which corresponds to *Nullable<int>*).

Warning   Columns in the resulting rows that do not match entity attributes are ignored.
Entity members that do not have corresponding columns are initialized with the default
value. If the *EmployeeInfo* class contains a mismatched column name, that member will not be
assigned without an error. Be careful and check name correspondence in the result when
some column or member values are not filled in.

The *ExecuteQuery* method can also receive parameters using the same curly notation used by *Console.WriteLine* and *String.Format*, but with a different behavior. Parameters are not replaced in the string sent to the database; they are substituted with parameter names that are automatically generated (@p0, @p1, @p2, ...) and are sent to SQL Server as arguments of the parametric query.

The code in Listing 4-23 shows the call to *ExecuteQuery<T>* using a SQL statement with two parameters. The parameters are used to filter the customers who made their first order within a specified range of dates.

Listing 4-23   Direct query with parameters

```
var query = db.ExecuteQuery<CompanyOrders>(@"
        SELECT    c.CompanyName,
                  MIN( o.OrderDate ) AS FirstOrderDate,
                  MAX( o.OrderDate ) AS LastOrderDate
        FROM      Customers c
        LEFT JOIN Orders o
              ON o.CustomerID = c.CustomerID
        GROUP BY  c.CustomerID, c.CompanyName
        HAVING    COUNT(o.OrderDate) > 0
            AND   MIN( o.OrderDate ) BETWEEN {0} AND {1}
        ORDER BY  FirstOrderDate ASC",
      new DateTime( 1997, 1, 1 ),
      new DateTime( 1997, 12, 31 ) );
```

The parameters are identified by the *{0}* and *{1}* format items. The generated SQL query simply substitutes them with @p0 and @p1. The results are returned in instances of the *CompanyOrders* class, declared as follows:

```
public class CompanyOrders {
    public string CompanyName;
    public DateTime FirstOrderDate;
    public DateTime LastOrderDate;
}
```

Deferred Loading of Entities

We have seen that using graph traversal to query data is a very comfortable way to proceed. However, sometimes you might want to stop the LINQ to SQL provider from automatically deciding what entities have to be read from the database and when, thereby taking control over that part of the process. You can do this by using the *DeferredLoadingEnabled* and *LoadOptions* properties of the *DataContext* class.

The code in Listing 4-24 makes the same *QueryOrder* call under three different conditions, driven by the code in the *DemoDeferredLoading* method.

Listing 4-24   Deferred loading of entities

```
public static void DemoDeferredLoading() {
    Console.Write("DeferredLoadingEnabled=true  ");
    DemoDeferredLoading(true);
    Console.Write("DeferredLoadingEnabled=false ");
    DemoDeferredLoading(false);
    Console.Write("Using LoadOptions           ");
    DemoLoadWith();
}

static void DemoDeferredLoading(bool deferredLoadingEnabled) {
    nwDataContext db = new nwDataContext(Connections.ConnectionString);
    db.DeferredLoadingEnabled = deferredLoadingEnabled;

    QueryOrder(db);
}

static void DemoLoadWith() {
    nwDataContext db = new nwDataContext(Connections.ConnectionString);
    db.DeferredLoadingEnabled = false;

    DataLoadOptions loadOptions = new DataLoadOptions();
    loadOptions.LoadWith<Order>(o => o.Order_Details);
    db.LoadOptions = loadOptions;

    QueryOrder(db);
}

static void QueryOrder(nwDataContext db) {
    var order = db.Orders.Single((o) => o.OrderID == 10251);
    var orderValue = order.Order_Details.Sum(od => od.Quantity * od.UnitPrice);
    Console.WriteLine(orderValue);
}
```

The call to *DemoDeferredLoading(true)* sets the *DeferredLoadingEnabled* property to *true*, which is the default condition for a *DataContext* instance. The call to *DemoDeferredLoading(false)* disables the *DeferredLoadingEnabled* property. Any access to the related entities does not automatically load data from the database, and the sum of *Order_Details* entities shows a total of 0. Finally, the call to *DemoLoadWith* also disables *DeferredLoadingEnabled*, but it sets the *LoadOptions* property of the *DataContext*, requesting the loading of *Order_Details* entities related to an *Order* instance. The execution of the *DemoDeferredLoading* method in Listing 4-24 produces the following output:

```
DeferredLoadingEnabled=true  670,8000
DeferredLoadingEnabled=false 0
Using LoadOptions            670,8000
```

Remember that the use of *LoadOptions* is possible regardless of the state of *DeferredLoading-Enabled*, and it is useful for improving performance when early loading of related entities (rather than deferred loading) is an advantage for your application. The use of *DeferredLoadingEnabled* should be carefully considered because it does not produce any error, but it limits the navigability of your data model through graph traversal. However, you must remember that *DeferredLoadingEnabled* is automatically considered to be *false* whenever the *ObjectTracking-Enabled* property (discussed in the next section) is disabled too.

Deferred Loading of Properties

LINQ to SQL provides a deferred loading mechanism that acts at the property level, loading data only when that property is accessed for the first time. You can use this mechanism when you need to load a large number of entities in memory, which usually requires space to accommodate all the properties of the class that correspond to table columns of the database. If a certain field is very large and is not always accessed for every entity, you can delay the loading of that property.

To request the deferred loading of a property, you simply use the *Link<T>* type to declare the storage variable for the table column, as you can see in Listing 4-25.

Listing 4-25   Deferred loading of properties

```
[Table(Name = "Customers")]
public class DelayCustomer {
    private Link<string> _Address;

    [Column(IsPrimaryKey = true)] public string CustomerID;
    [Column] public string CompanyName;
    [Column] public string Country;

    [Column(Storage = "_Address")]
    public string Address {
        get { return _Address.Value; }
        set { _Address.Value = value; }
    }
}

public static class DeferredLoading {
    public static void DelayLoadProperty() {
        DataContext db = new DataContext(Connections.ConnectionString);
        Table<DelayCustomer> Customers = db.GetTable<DelayCustomer>();
        db.Log = Console.Out;

        var query =
            from   c in Customers
            where  c.Country == "Italy"
            select c;

        foreach (var row in query) {
            Console.WriteLine(
                "{0} - {1}",
                row.CompanyName,
                row.Address);
        }
    }
}
```

The query that is sent to the database to get the list of Italian customers is the following one:

```
SELECT [t0].[CustomerID], [t0].[CompanyName], [t0].[Country]
FROM   [Customers] AS [t0]
WHERE  [t0].[Country] = "Italy"
```

This query does not retrieve the *Address* field. When the result of the query is iterated in the *foreach* loop, the *Address* property of the current *Customer* is accessed for each customer for the first time, and this produces a query to the database like the following one to get the *Address* value:

```
SELECT [t0].[Address]
FROM   [Customers] AS [t0]
WHERE  [t0].[CustomerID] - @p0
```

The *Link<T>* type should be used only when the content of a field is very large (which should not be the case for the *Address* field that we used in our example) and when that field is accessed very few times. A field of the SQL type *VARCHAR(MAX)* is generally a good candidate, as long as its value is displayed only in a detailed form visible on demand and not on the main grid that shows query results. Using the LINQ to SQL class generator included in Visual Studio 2008, you can use *Link<T>* and set to *true* the *Delay Loaded* property of the desired member property.

> **Important**   You need to use the *Link<T>* type on the storage variable for a property of type *T* mapped to the column, as we did in Listing 4-25. You cannot use the *Link<T>* type directly on a public data member mapped to a table column (like all the other fields); if you do, you will get an exception during execution. In the RTM version, that run-time error is of type *VerificationException*. A more analytical exception might be used in future versions.

Read-Only *DataContext* Access

If you need to access data exclusively in a read-only way, you might want to improve performance by disabling a *DataContext* service that supports data modification:

```
DataContext db = new DataContext( ConnectionString );
db.ObjectTrackingEnabled = false;
var query = ...
```

The *ObjectTrackingEnabled* property controls the change tracking service that we will describe in the next chapter. By default, *ObjectTrackingEnabled* is set to *true*.

> **Important**   Disabling object tracking also disables the deferred loading feature of the same *DataContext* instance. If you want to optimize performance by disabling the object tracking feature, you must be aware of the side effects of disabling deferred loading too. Refer to the earlier "Deferred Loading of Entities" section for further details.

Limitations of LINQ to SQL

LINQ to SQL has some limitations when converting a LINQ query into a corresponding SQL statement. For this reason, some valid LINQ to Objects statements are not supported in LINQ to SQL. In this section, we cover the most important operators that cannot be used in a LINQ to SQL query.

> **More Info**   A complete list of unsupported methods and types is available in the product documentation, "Data Types and Functions (LINQ to SQL)," which is available at *http://msdn2.microsoft.com/en-us/library/bb386970.aspx*.

Aggregate Operators

The general-purpose *Aggregate* operator is not supported. However, specialized aggregate operators such as *Count*, *LongCount*, *Sum*, *Min*, *Max*, and *Average* are fully supported.

Any aggregate operator other than *Count* and *LongCount* requires particular care to avoid an exception if the result is *null*. If the entity class has a member of a non-nullable type and you make an aggregation on it, a null result (for example when no rows are aggregated) throws an exception. You need to cast the aggregated value to a nullable type before considering it in the aggregation function in order to avoid that exception. You can see an example of the necessary cast in Listing 4-26.

Listing 4-26   Null handling with aggregate operators

```
decimal? totalFreight =
    (from    o in Orders
     where   o.CustomerID == "NOTEXIST"
     select o).Min( o => (decimal?) o.Freight );
```

This cast is necessary only if you declared the *Freight* property with *decimal*:

```
[Table(Name = "Orders")]
public class Order {
    [Column] public decimal Freight;
}
```

Another solution is declaring *Freight* as a nullable type using *decimal?*, but it is not a good idea to have different nullable settings between entities and corresponding tables in the database.

> **More Info**   You can find a more complete discussion about this issue in this post written by Ian Griffiths: *http://www.interact-sw.co.uk/iangblog/2007/09/10/linq-aggregates*.

Partitioning Operators

The *TakeWhile* and *SkipWhile* operators are not supported. *Take* and *Skip* operators are supported, but be careful with *Skip* because the generated SQL query could be complex and not very efficient when there are a large number of rows to skip, particularly if the target database is SQL Server 2000.

Element Operators

The following operators are not supported: *ElementAt*, *ElementAtOrDefault*, *Last*, and *Last-OrDefault*.

String Methods

Many of the .NET *String* type methods are supported in LINQ to SQL because there is a corresponding method in T-SQL. However, there is no support for methods that are culture-aware (those that receive arguments of type *CultureInfo*, *StringComparison*, and *IFormat-Provider*) and for methods that receive or return a *char* array.

DateTime Methods

There are differences between the *DateTime* type in .NET and the *DATETIME* and *SMALL-DATETIME* types in SQL Server. The range of values and the precision is greater in .NET than in SQL Server, allowing for a correct representation of SQL Server types in .NET, but not the opposite. Moreover, *DATETIME* in SQL Server does not have the notion of a time zone, thus it cannot be supported by LINQ to SQL. Finally, some .NET *DateTime* methods are not supported, mainly because of the lack of a corresponding function in T-SQL.

Unsupported SQL Functionalities

LINQ to SQL does not have syntax to make use of the SQL *LIKE* operator and *STDDEV* aggregation.

Thinking in LINQ to SQL

When you start working with LINQ to SQL, you might have to rethink the ways in which you are used to writing queries, especially if you try to find the equivalent LINQ syntax for a well-known SQL statement. Moreover, a verbose LINQ query might be reduced when the corresponding SQL query is produced. You need to be aware of this change, and you have to fully understand it to be productive in LINQ to SQL. In the final part of this chapter, we introduce you to thinking in LINQ to SQL.

The IN/EXISTS Clause

One of the best examples of the syntactic differences between T-SQL and LINQ is the NOT IN clause that you can use in SQL. This clause is not found in LINQ, which makes you wonder whether there is any way to express the same concept in LINQ. In fact, there is not always a direct translation for each single SQL keyword, but you can get the same result with semantically equivalent statements, sometimes with equal or better performance.

Consider this code, which returns all the customers who do not have an order in the Orders table. Here is one SQL query that returns that value:

```
SELECT *
FROM    [dbo].[Customers] AS [t0]
WHERE   [t0].[CustomerID] NOT IN (
    SELECT [t1].[CustomerID]
    FROM    [dbo].[Orders] AS [t1]
)
```

This is not the fastest way to get the desired result. (Using NOT EXISTS is our favorite way—more on this shortly.) Anyhow, LINQ does not have an operator directly equivalent to IN or NOT IN, but it offers a *Contains* operator that allows you to write the code in Listing 4-27. Pay attention to the not operator (*!*) applied to the *where* predicate, which negates the *Contains* condition that follows.

Listing 4-27   Use of *Contains* to get an EXISTS/IN equivalent statement

```
public static void DemoContains() {
    nwDataContext db = new nwDataContext(Connections.ConnectionString);
    db.Log = Console.Out;

    var query =
        from c in db.Customers
        where !(from o in db.Orders
                select o.CustomerID)
            .Contains(c.CustomerID)
        select new { c.CustomerID, c.CompanyName };

    foreach (var c in query) {
        Console.WriteLine(c);
    }
}
```

The following code is the SQL query generated by LINQ to SQL:

```
SELECT [t0].[CustomerID], [t0].[CompanyName]
FROM    [dbo].[Customers] AS [t0]
WHERE   NOT (EXISTS(
    SELECT NULL AS [EMPTY]
    FROM    [dbo].[Orders] AS [t1]
    WHERE   [t1].[CustomerID] = [t0].[CustomerID]
    ))
```

Using this approach to generate SQL code is not only semantically equivalent, but it also executes faster. If you look at the I/O operation made by SQL Server 2005, the first query (using NOT IN) executes 364 logical reads on the Orders table, while the second query (using NOT EXISTS) requests only 5 logical reads on the same Orders table. This is a big difference, and in this case LINQ to SQL is the best choice for you.

The same *Contains* operator might generate an IN operator in SQL, for example, if it is applied to a list of constants, as in Listing 4-28.

Listing 4-28   Use of *Contains* with a list of constants

```
public static void DemoContainsConstants() {
    nwDataContext db = new nwDataContext(Connections.ConnectionString);

    var query =
        from   c in db.Customers
        where  (new string[] { "London", "Seattle" }).Contains(c.City)
        select new { c.CustomerID, c.CompanyName, c.City };

    Console.WriteLine(query);

    foreach (var c in query) {
        Console.WriteLine(c);
    }
}
```

The SQL code generated by LINQ to SQL is simpler to read than the original query:

```
SELECT [t0].[CustomerID], [t0].[CompanyName], [t0].[City]
FROM   [dbo].[Customers] AS [t0]
WHERE  [t0].[City] IN ("London", "Seattle")
```

What is counterintuitive in the LINQ query is that you have to specify the *Contains* operator on the list of constants, passing the value to look for as an argument, exactly the opposite of what you need to do in SQL:

```
where (new string[] { "London", "Seattle" }).Contains(c.City)
```

After years of experience in SQL, we are more comfortable with a hypothetical *IsIn* syntax such as this:

```
where c.City.IsIn( new string[] { "London", "Seattle" } )
```

However, it is probably only a question of time before we get used to the new syntax. In fact, the semantics of *Contains* corresponds exactly to the argument's position. To make the code clearer, we could simply separate the declaration of the list of constants outside the query declaration, in a *cities* array, making the code more readable:

```
var cities = new string[] { "London", "Seattle" };
var query =
    from   c in db.Customers
    where  cities.Contains(c.City)
    select new { c.CustomerID, c.CompanyName, c.City };
```

> **Note** Creating the *cities* array outside the query instead of putting it into the *where* predicate simply improves code readability, at least in LINQ to SQL. From a performance point of view, only one *string* array is created in both cases. The reason is that in LINQ to SQL, the query only defines an expression tree and the array is created only once to produce the SQL statement. In LINQ to SQL, unless you execute the same query many times, performance is equivalent under either approach (object creation inside or outside a predicate). This is different in LINQ to Objects. In that case the predicate condition in the *where* clause would be executed for each row of the data source.

SQL Query Reduction

Every LINQ to SQL query is initially represented in memory as an expression tree. The engine of LINQ to SQL converts this tree into an equivalent SQL query, visiting the tree and generating the corresponding code. However, theoretically this translation can be made in many ways, all producing the same results, even if not all the translations are equally readable or perform as well. The actual implementation of LINQ to SQL generates good SQL code, favoring performance over query readability, although this last characteristic is often more than acceptable too.

> **More Info** You can find more information about query reduction in a LINQ provider in this post from Matt Warren: *http://blogs.msdn.com/mattwar/archive/2008/01/16/ linq-building-an-iqueryable-provider-part-ix.aspx*. Implementation of a query provider is covered in Chapter 12, "Extending LINQ."

We described this quality of LINQ to SQL because it is important to know that unnecessary parts of the query are removed before the query is sent to SQL Server. This knowledge allows you to compose LINQ queries in many ways—for example, by appending new predicates and projections to an originally large selection of rows and columns, without worrying too much about unnecessary elements left in the query.

The LINQ query in Listing 4-29 is built by making a first query on Customers that filters only the customers with a *CompanyName* longer than 10 characters. These companies are then filtered by *Country*, operating on the anonymous type generated by the inner query.

Listing 4-29 Example of query reduction

```
var query =
    from s in (
        from   c in db.Customers
        where  c.CompanyName.Length > 10
        select new { c.CustomerID, c.CompanyName, c.ContactName, c.City,
```

```
                    c.Country, c.ContactTitle, c.Address }
    )
    where s.Country == "UK"
    select new { s.CustomerID, s.CompanyName, s.City };
```

The SQL query generated is the following one:

```
SELECT [t0].[CustomerID], [t0].[CompanyName], [t0].[City]
FROM   [dbo].[Customers] AS [t0]
WHERE  ([t0].[Country] = @p0) AND (LEN([t0].[CompanyName]) > @p1)
```

There are two important reductions that were made. First, there is a single table on which *FROM* operates, instead of a *SELECT ... FROM (SELECT ... FROM ...)* composition that would normally be made when translating the original query tree. Second, unnecessary fields have been removed; only *CustomerID*, *CompanyName*, and *City* are part of the SELECT projection because they are the only fields necessary to the consumer of the LINQ query. The first reduction improves query readability; the second one improves performance because it reduces the amount of data that is transferred from the database server to the client.

Mixing .NET Code with SQL Queries

LINQ to SQL queries are represented as an expression tree that is translated into an equivalent SQL statement. We previously noted that there are some known limitations of LINQ to SQL with regard to using the full range of .NET features, which cannot be entirely translated into corresponding T-SQL operations. This does not necessarily mean that you cannot write a query containing an unsupported method, but you should be aware that such a method cannot be translated into T-SQL and will be executed locally on the client. The side effect of this can be that sections of the query tree depending on a .NET method that does not have a SQL translation will be completely maintained as a LINQ to Objects operation, requiring all the data to be transferred to the client to apply required operators.

We can see this effect with some examples. Consider the LINQ query in Listing 4-30.

Listing 4-30   LINQ query with a native string manipulation in the projection

```
var query1 =
    from   p in db.Products
    where  p.UnitPrice > 50
    select new {
        ProductName = "** " + p.ProductName + " **",
        p.UnitPrice };
```

The generated SQL embodies the string manipulation of the *ProductName*:

```
SELECT ("** " + [t0].[ProductName]) + " **" AS [ProductName],
       [t0].[UnitPrice]
FROM [dbo].[Products] AS [t0]
WHERE [t0].[UnitPrice] > 50
```

We try to move the string manipulation operation into a .NET extension method, like that shown in Listing 4-31.

Listing 4-31   String manipulation extension method

```
static public class Extensions {
    public static string Highlight(this string s) {
        return "** " + s + " **";
    }
}
```

In Listing 4-32, we modify the LINQ query using the *Highlight* method defined in Listing 4-31.

Listing 4-32   LINQ query calling a .NET method in the projection

```
var query2 =
    from   p in db.Products
    where  p.UnitPrice > 50
    select new {
        ProductName = p.ProductName.Highlight(),
        p.UnitPrice };
```

The result produced by *query2* in Listing 4-32 is the same as the one produced by *query1* in Listing 4-30. However, the SQL query sent to the database is different because it lacks the string manipulation operation:

```
SELECT [t0].[ProductName] AS [s],
       [t0].[UnitPrice]
FROM   [dbo].[Products] AS [t0]
WHERE  [t0].[UnitPrice] > 50
```

The *ProductName* field is returned as *s* and will be used as an argument to the *Highlight* call. For each row, a call to the .NET *Highlight* method will be made. This is not an issue if we directly consume the *query2* results. However, if we turn the same operation into a subquery, all dependent queries cannot be translated into a native SQL statement. For example, consider *query3* in Listing 4-33.

Listing 4-33   LINQ query combining native and custom string manipulation

```
var query3 =
    from a in (
        from   p in db.Products
        where  p.UnitPrice > 50
        select new {
            ProductName = p.ProductName.Highlight(),
            p.UnitsInStock,
            p.UnitPrice
        }
    )
    select new {
        ProductName = a.ProductName.ToLower(),
        a.UnitPrice };
```

The SQL query produced by *query3* in Listing 4-33 is the same as the one produced by *query2* in Listing 4-32, despite the addition of another string manipulation (*ToLower*) to *ProductName*:

```
SELECT [t0].[ProductName] AS [s],
       [t0].[UnitPrice]
FROM   [dbo].[Products] AS [t0]
WHERE  [t0].[UnitPrice] > 50
```

If we remove the call to *Highlight* and restore the original string manipulation directly inside the LINQ query, we will get a complete native SQL query again, as shown in Listing 4-34.

Listing 4-34 LINQ query using native string manipulation

```
var query4 =
    from a in (
              from   p in db.Products
              where  p.UnitPrice > 50
              select new {
                    ProductName = "** " + p.ProductName + " **",
                    p.UnitPrice
              }
    )
    select new {
        ProductName = a.ProductName.ToLower(),
        a.UnitPrice
    };
```

The *query4* in Listing 4-34 produces the following SQL query, which does not require further manipulations by .NET code:

```
SELECT LOWER([t1].[value]) AS [ProductName], [t1].[UnitPrice]
FROM (
    SELECT ("** " + [t0].[ProductName]) + " **" AS [value],
           [t0].[UnitPrice]
    FROM [dbo].[Products] AS [t0]
    ) AS [t1]
WHERE [t1].[UnitPrice] > 50
```

Until now, we have seen that there is a possible performance implication only when using a .NET method that does not have a corresponding SQL counterpart. However, there are situations that cannot be handled by the LINQ to SQL engine and for which an exception is thrown at execution time—for example, if we try to use the result of the *Highlight* call in a *where* predicate as shown in Listing 4-35.

Listing 4-35 LINQ query calling a .NET method in a *where* predicate

```
var query5 =
    from   p in db.Products
    where  p.ProductName.Highlight().Length > 20
    select new {
        ProductName = p.ProductName.Highlight(),
        p.UnitPrice
    };
```

At execution time, trying to access to the *query5* result (or asking for the generated SQL query) will raise the following exception:

```
System.NotSupportedException
Method 'System.String Highlight(System.String)'
has no supported translation to SQL.
```

As you have seen, it is important to understand what operators are supported by LINQ to SQL, because the code could work or break at execution time, depending on the use of such operators. It is hard to define a rule of thumb other than to avoid the use of unsupported operators. If you think that a LINQ query is composable and can be used as a source to build another query, the only safe guideline is to use operators supported by LINQ to SQL.

Summary

In this chapter, we discussed the LINQ to SQL features used to query data. LINQ to SQL enables you to query a relational structure stored in a Microsoft SQL Server database so that you can convert LINQ queries into native SQL queries and access UDFs and stored procedures if required. LINQ to SQL handles entity classes that map an underlying physical database structure through attributes or external XML files. Stored procedures and UDFs can be mapped to methods of a class representing a SQL Server database. LINQ to SQL supports most of the basic LINQ features that we saw in Chapter 3.

Chapter 5
LINQ to SQL: Managing Data

In the previous chapter, you saw mainly how to read data with LINQ to SQL. The next step is understanding how to modify the data in a database using LINQ to SQL.

Luckily, by using entities, updating a column for a certain row in a table is as simple as changing a property of an entity instance. For example, the following code reads a product, increases its price by 5 percent by modifying the *UnitPrice* property, and then applies the in-memory changes to the database by calling *SubmitChanges*:

```
Product product = db.Products.Single(p => p.ProductID == 42);
product.UnitPrice *= 1.05M;
db.SubmitChanges();
```

In this chapter, you will learn how to handle entity updates applied to the database, concurrency, transactions, exceptions, and entity serialization.

CRUD and CUD Operations

The term CRUD means Create, Read, Update, and Delete. These are the fundamental operations provided by a storage system, and they correspond to the SQL statements *INSERT*, *SELECT*, *UPDATE*, and *DELETE*, respectively. Using LINQ to SQL, read operations are typically performed in an indirect way, by executing LINQ queries or by accessing LINQ entities through their relationships without a direct call of the *SELECT* SQL statement. For this reason, in LINQ to SQL documentation you will find another acronym, CUD (Create, Update, and Delete) to describe all the operations that manipulate data through entities. In this chapter, we will focus on CUD operations performed by operating on LINQ to SQL entities.

By default, all entity instances in LINQ to SQL are tracked by the *identity management service* of LINQ to SQL to maintain a unique instance of a row of data. This service is guaranteed only for objects created or handled by a single *DataContext* instance. (This behavior has implications that you will see shortly.) Keeping a single instance of a row of data allows a *DataContext* instance to manipulate in-memory objects without concern for potential data inconsistencies or duplication in memory. We will analyze how to deal with concurrent operations later.

 Important Remember that a class entity must have at least a column with the *IsPrimaryKey=true* setting in the *Column* attribute; otherwise, it cannot be tracked by the identity management service, and data manipulation is not allowed.

Entity Updates

Changing data members and properties of an entity instance is an operation tracked by the *change tracking service* of LINQ to SQL. This service retains the original value of a modified entity. With this information, the service generates a corresponding list of SQL statements that make the same changes on the database. You can see the list of delete, update, and insert operations that will be applied to the relational database by calling the *GetChangeSet* method on the *DataContext*:

```
var customer = db.Customers.Single( c => c.CustomerID == "FRANS" );
customer.ContactName = "Marco Russo";
Helper.DumpChanges(db.GetChangeSet());
db.SubmitChanges();
```

The *Helper.DumpChanges* method shown in Listing 5-1 simply inspects the *ChangeSet* instance to display the planned operations. If you run the preceding code, you get the following output:

```
** UPDATES **
CustomerID=FRANS, CompanyName=Franchi S.p.A.
{Inserts: 0, Deletes: 0, Updates: 1}
```

At the end, the call to the *SubmitChanges* method sends a single UPDATE statement to the relational database:

```
UPDATE [Customers]
SET    [ContactName] = "Marco Russo"
FROM   [Customers]
WHERE  ...
```

We will discuss the *WHERE* condition later. Remember that no SQL statement is sent to the database until the call to the *SubmitChanges* method is made.

Listing 5-1   Helper methods *DumpChanges* and *Dump*

```
public static void DumpChanges(ChangeSet changeSet) {
    if (changeSet.Deletes.Count > 0) {
        Console.WriteLine("** DELETES **");
        foreach (var del in changeSet.Deletes) {
            Console.WriteLine(Dump(del));
        }
    }
    if (changeSet.Updates.Count > 0) {
        Console.WriteLine("** UPDATES **");
        foreach (var upd in changeSet.Updates) {
            Console.WriteLine(Dump(upd));
        }
    }
    if (changeSet.Inserts.Count > 0) {
        Console.WriteLine("** INSERTS **");
        foreach (var ins in changeSet.Inserts) {
            Console.WriteLine(Dump(ins));
        }
```

```
        }
        Console.WriteLine(changeSet);
    }

    public static string Dump(this object data) {
        if (data is Customer) {
            Customer customer = (Customer) data;
            return String.Format(
                "CustomerID={0}, CompanyName={1}",
                customer.CustomerID, customer.CompanyName);
        }
        else {
            throw new NotSupportedException(
                String.Format(
                    "Dump is not supported on {0}",
                    data.GetType().FullName) );
        }
    }
}
```

If you want to add a record to a table or remove a record from a table, creating or deleting an object in memory is not enough. The *DataContext* instance must also be notified. You can do this directly by calling *InsertOnSubmit* or *DeleteOnSubmit* on the corresponding *Table* collection. (These methods operate on the in-memory copy of the data; a subsequent *Submit-Changes* call will forward the SQL commands to the database.) The following code illustrates this process:

```
var newCustomer = new Customer {
                      CustomerID = "DLEAP",
                      CompanyName = "DevLeap",
                      Country = "Italy" };
db.Customers.InsertOnSubmit(newCustomer);

var oldDetail = db.Order_Details.Single(
        od => od.OrderID == 10422
              && od.ProductID == 26);
db.Order_Details.DeleteOnSubmit(oldDetail);
```

Looking at the generated SQL statements, you can see that single SQL INSERT and DELETE statements are generated:

```
INSERT INTO [Customers](CustomerID, CompanyName, ...)
VALUES("DLEAP", "DevLeap", ...)

DELETE FROM [dbo].[Order Details]
WHERE [OrderID] = 10422 AND [ProductID] = 26 AND ...
```

Whenever the deleted entity is referenced by other entities, these references have to be checked too. You have to remove related entities or change their relationship. We will talk about this process later in the section "Cascading Deletes and Updates."

> **Note**   Calling *InsertOnSubmit* or *DeleteOnSubmit* several times for the same object (entities have a unique identity) will not generate the same SQL statement multiple times. If the same entity is inserted or deleted many times, the change-tracking service ignores redundant calls.

Another way to notify the *DataContext* of a new entity is to attach the new entity to an existing object already tracked by *DataContext*:

```
var newCustomer = new Customer {
                    CustomerID = "DLEAP",
                    CompanyName = "DevLeap",
                    Country = "Italy" };
var order = db.Orders.Single( o => o.OrderID == 10248 );
order.Customer = newCustomer;
```

The examples just shown introduce the need to understand how relationships between entities work when updates are applied to the database. Relationships are bidirectional between entities, and when an update is made on one side, the other side should be kept synchronized. Synchronization has to be done by the class entity implementation. Entity classes generated by code-generation tools (such as SQLMetal and Microsoft Visual Studio 2008, which will be covered in Chapter 6, "Tools for LINQ to SQL") usually offer this level of service.

The previous operation inserted a customer tied to order 10248. If you explore the *newCustomer* entity after the *order.Customer* assignment, you will see that its *Orders* properties contain order 10248. Executing the following code displays one row containing the order 10248:

```
foreach( var o in newCustomer.Orders ) {
    Console.WriteLine( "{0}-{1}", o.CustomerID, o.OrderID );
}
```

You can work in the opposite way, assigning an order to the *Orders* property of a customer. Consequently, the *Customer* property of the assigned order will be updated:

```
var oldCustomer = db.Customers.Single( c => c.CustomerID == "VINET" );
var newCustomer = new Customer {
                    CustomerID = "DLEAP",
                    CompanyName = "DevLeap",
                    Country = "Italy" };
db.Customers.Add( newCustomer );
var order = oldCustomer.Orders.Single( o => o.OrderID == 10248 );
oldCustomer.Orders.Remove( order );
newCustomer.Orders.Add( order );
```

Regardless of the way you modified the object model, the result is that you create a new *Customer* entity instance and modify an *Order* entity instance. Therefore, the generated SQL statements sent to the database on a *SubmitChanges* call are an INSERT followed by an UPDATE:

```
INSERT INTO [Customers](CustomerID, CompanyName, ...)
VALUES("DEVLEAP", "DevLeap", ...)

UPDATE [dbo].[Orders]
SET [CustomerID] = "DLEAP"
WHERE [OrderID] = 10248 AND ...
```

Even if a *Customer* is no longer referenced by other entities in memory, it is not automatically deleted by the change tracking service. You need to call *DeleteOnSubmit* on a *Table<T>* collection to delete a row in a database table.

Finally, there are dedicated methods to insert or delete a sequence of entities of the same type, called *InsertAllOnSubmit<T>* and *DeleteAllOnSubmit<T>*, respectively.

Important   As you saw in Chapter 4, "LINQ to SQL: Querying Data," you can disable the change-tracking service for a *DataContext* by specifying *false* on its *ObjectTrackingEnabled* property. Whenever you need to get data exclusively in a read-only mode—for example, to display a report or a Web page in a noninteractive state—this setting will improve overall performance.

Cascading Deletes and Updates

You have seen that there are two ways to add a record to a table (one direct and one indirect). However, if you need to remove a row, you always have to do this in a direct way, calling the *DeleteOnSubmit* method on the corresponding *Table* collection. When you remove an object, you need to be sure that there are no more entities referencing it; otherwise, an exception will be thrown when *SubmitChanges* is called, because the SQL *DELETE* statement will violate some referential integrity constraint (such as *FOREIGN KEY* being declared in the database). You can unbind related entities by setting their foreign key to NULL, but this might throw an exception if constraints do not allow NULL values. Another option is to remove the child objects from an object you want to remove by calling the *DeleteOnSubmit* method on them. You can do that by leveraging the *DeleteAllOnSubmit* method:

```
var order = db.Orders.Single( o => o.OrderID == 10248 );
db.Orders.DeleteOnSubmit( order );
db.Order_Details.DeleteAllOnSubmit( order.Order_Details );
```

At the moment of calling *SubmitChanges* this update generates SQL statements that respect the referential integrity constraints shown in the following statements:

```
DELETE FROM [Order Details] WHERE ([OrderID] = 10248) AND ([ProductID] = 11) AND ...
DELETE FROM [Order Details] WHERE ([OrderID] = 10248) AND ([ProductID] = 42) AND ...
DELETE FROM [Order Details] WHERE ([OrderID] = 10248) AND ([ProductID] = 72) AND ...
DELETE FROM [Orders] WHERE [OrderID] = 10248 AND ...
```

The order of *DeleteOnSubmit* and *DeleteAllOnSubmit* calls is not relevant. As you can see, the deletion of rows in the Order Details table precedes the deletion in the Orders table, despite the fact that the order of deletion of LINQ entities was the opposite. LINQ to SQL automatically handles the correct order of SQL statements so that referential integrity constraints are respected during deletion.

> **Note**   After a call to *SubmitChanges*, deleted entities are not removed from the *Table* collection and are still in memory, with a particular state that we will describe in the upcoming "Entity States" section.

Another cascading operation that is possible on a relational database is the cascading update. For example, changing the primary key of a *Customer* changes all the foreign keys in related entities referring to that *Customer*. However, LINQ to SQL does not allow changing the primary key of an entity. You need to create a new *Customer*, change the references from the old *Customer* to the new one, and finally remove the old *Customer*. This operation is shown in Listing 5-2.

Listing 5-2   Replace a *Customer* on existing orders

```
var oldCustomer = db.Customers.Single(c => c.CustomerID == "FRANS");
Customer newCustomer = new Customer();
newCustomer.CustomerID = "CHNGE";
newCustomer.Address = oldCustomer.Address;
newCustomer.City = oldCustomer.City;
newCustomer.CompanyName = oldCustomer.CompanyName;
newCustomer.ContactName = oldCustomer.ContactName;
newCustomer.ContactTitle = oldCustomer.ContactTitle;
newCustomer.Country = oldCustomer.Country;
newCustomer.Fax = oldCustomer.Fax;
newCustomer.Orders = oldCustomer.Orders;
newCustomer.Phone = oldCustomer.Phone;
newCustomer.PostalCode = oldCustomer.PostalCode;
newCustomer.Region = oldCustomer.Region;
```

The code in Listing 5-2 shows the substitution of the customer FRANS with a new customer that is identical to FRANS, except for the primary key that is set equal to CHNGE. All entity properties are copied from the old to the new entity, but the most interesting part is the assignment to the *Orders* property:

```
newCustomer.Orders = oldCustomer.Orders;
```

Assigning an *EntitySet<T>* property propagates the assignment to the *EntityRef* property of *T* entities, which corresponds to the foreign key of the related table. In other words, all entities in *Orders* are changed, setting their *Customer* property to *newCustomer*. This synchronization is implemented by the *Customer* entity class generated by SQLMetal or Visual Studio 2008, which contains the code necessary to make the synchronization work.

> **Warning**   LINQ to SQL does not support cascading operations. If a foreign key in the relational database is declared with the ON DELETE CASCADE or ON UPDATE CASCADE option, the updates automatically made on the database are not propagated into the object model of LINQ to SQL if the affected entities have already been loaded in memory. However, that kind of update should be the result of a direct SQL statement and not of SQL code generated by LINQ to SQL, because in the latter case it means that the LINQ to SQL entities are not declared with the same associations corresponding to existing foreign keys in the relational database.

Entity States

An entity instance has a state in a *DataContext* that defines its synchronization state in relation to the relational database. Each operation on an entity modifies its state to reflect the necessary operation to synchronize the relational database with an in-memory entity instance. The possible states of an instance are represented in Figure 5-1.

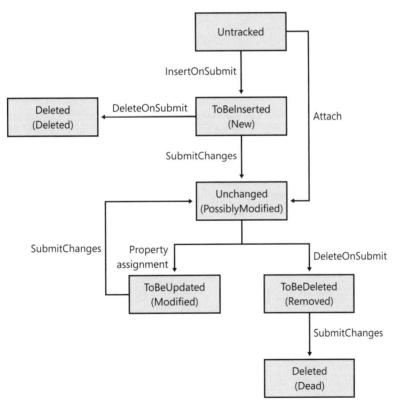

Figure 5-1   Possible states of an entity

In Figure 5-1, we used for each state the name used by LINQ to SQL documentation and within parentheses we used the name of the *StandardChangeTracker.StandardTrackedObject.State* enumeration, which is an internal implementation mapped to LINQ to SQL. The following is a list of definitions of these states:

- **Untracked**   This is not a true state. It identifies an object that is not tracked by LINQ to SQL. A newly created object is always in this state until it is not attached to a *DataContext*. Because this state is the relationship of an entity in a given *DataContext*, an entity created as a result of a query of a *DataContext* instance is *Untracked* by other *DataContext* instances. Finally, after deserialization, an entity instance is always *Untracked*.

- **Unchanged**   The initial state of an object retrieved by using the current *DataContext*.

- **PossiblyModified**   An object attached to a *DataContext*. In Figure 5-1, the two states *Unchanged* and *PossiblyModified* are represented by the same box (state).

- **ToBeInserted**   An object not retrieved by using the current *DataContext*. This is a newly created object that has been added with an *InsertOnSubmit* to a *Table<T>* collection, or that has been added to an *EntitySet<T>* of an existing entity instance.

- **ToBeUpdated**   An object that has been modified since it was retrieved. This state is set by a change to any property of an entity retrieved by using the current *DataContext*.

- **ToBeDeleted**   An object marked for deletion by calling *DeleteOnSubmit*.

- **Deleted**   An object that has been deleted in the database. The entity instance for this object still exists in memory with this particular state. If you want to use the same primary key of a *Deleted* entity, you need to define a new entity in a different *DataContext*.

Later in this chapter, we will discuss how to manipulate and customize entity classes. At this stage, you should understand that the LINQ to SQL engine needs to keep track of entity states to correctly update the relational database. You cannot directly access and manipulate the state of an entity.

Entity Synchronization

After you write an entity to the database by calling *SubmitChanges*, it is possible that changes are made directly on the database to some column of the table. Identities, triggers, and time stamps are all cases in which the actual value written on the database cannot be known in advance by the entity itself and needs to be read from the database after the *SubmitChanges* call. If you use an entity after the call to *SubmitChanges*, you probably need to update these values by reading the entity from the database. LINQ to SQL helps automate this process by providing the *AutoSync* parameter to the *Column* attribute that decorates entity properties. For each column, this parameter can have one of the following values provided by the *System.Data.Linq.Mapping.AutoSync* enumeration:

- **Default**   There is an automatic handling of the entity update, based on known metadata of the column itself. For example, an *IsDbGenerated* column will be read after an *Insert* operation, and an *IsVersion* column will be updated after any *Update* or *Insert* operation.

- **Always**   The column is always updated from the database after any *SubmitChanges* call.

- **Never**   The column is never updated from the database.

- **OnInsert**   The column is updated from the database after the *SubmitChanges* call that inserts the entity.

- **OnUpdate**   The column is updated from the database after the *SubmitChanges* call that updates the entity.

The *AutoSync.Default* value should be a good choice most of the time because it defines a behavior that is consistent with the metadata defined for your entities. However, if you have triggers operating on a table that modify columns as part of their work, you might need to set the *AutoSync* property to a specific value. Remember that this synchronization system cannot automatically create and read new entities; it can only modify existing ones. If you have a trigger that adds new rows into a table as a result of a database operation, you need to read those entities by executing a specific query to the database.

Database Updates

With LINQ to SQL, many SQL queries are sent to the database in a transparent and implicit way. On the other hand, all SQL commands that modify the state of the database are sent only when you decide to send them by calling *SubmitChanges* on the *DataContext* object (which is eventually derived), as shown in Listing 5-3. The *Northwind* class here is derived from *DataContext*.

Listing 5-3   Submit changes to the database

```
Northwind db = new Northwind( Program.ConnectionString );
var customer = db.Customers.Single( c => c.CustomerID == "FRANS" );
customer.ContactName = "Marco Russo";
db.SubmitChanges();
```

The instance of *DataContext* (or the derived class) is similar to a database connection. It embeds all tracking information in addition to connection data. Despite its features, a *Data-Context* instance is a lightweight object that can be used in both a client-server and an n-tier application. In the first case, the *DataContext* object might be created on the client side and kept alive for the entire lifetime of the application. In an n-tier application, the data layer (where LINQ to SQL could be used) is typically a stateless intermediate layer. The *DataContext* class has been conceived with all these scenarios in mind. Its activation cost at runtime has a small performance impact, and this allows for the creation of new *DataContext* instances on demand, without the need for having a complex cache system.

More Info   You will find more information about the n-tier architecture in Chapter 15, "LINQ in a Multitier Solution."

The role of *SubmitChanges* is simply to send to the database a set of INSERT, UPDATE, and DELETE SQL statements, handling update conflicts at the database level. (Conflict handling will be discussed later in this chapter in the "Exceptions" section.) These statements are generated starting from the list of entities that need to be deleted, updated, and inserted. That list is accessible through a *ChangeSet* instance returned by the *DataContext.GetChangeSet* method, as you saw earlier in this chapter. This list of updated entities loses the number and order of changes applied to the entities. What is preserved is the final result of all these modifications. We call this set of updated entities a *unit of work*.

> **More Info**   See *http://www.martinfowler.com/eaaCatalog/unitOfWork.html* for a definition of the unit of work pattern by Martin Fowler.

The default implementation of *SubmitChanges* transforms the list of updated entities in a set of SQL statements and sends these commands in a particular order, following the requirements enforced by existing relationships between entities. For example, you can add and update *Order Order_Detail* instances in any order in your object model. However, an Order_Details row will be inserted in the relational database only after the parent Orders row has been inserted. In this way, the foreign key relationship for OrderID will be observed. As we said, the default *SubmitChanges* implementation provides the right SQL statement order by analyzing these dependencies. However, *SubmitChanges* is a virtual method that can be overridden if you need to control this logic deeply or to change its behavior.

Overriding *SubmitChanges*

The *DataContext.SubmitChanges* instance method is virtual and can be overridden if you want to modify its behavior or simply intercept calls to it. For example, you can intercept updated entities to create a log of them, as shown in Listing 5-4. (The *Helper.DumpChanges* method called in Listing 5-4 was shown earlier in Listing 5-1.)

Listing 5-4   Specialized *SubmitChanges* to log modified entities

```
public class CustomNorthwind : Northwind {
    public CustomNorthwind(string connectionString) :
        base(connectionString) { }

    public override void SubmitChanges(ConflictMode failureMode) {
        Helper.DumpChanges(this.GetChangeSet());
        base.SubmitChanges(failureMode);
    }
}
```

You might want to change the entities contained in the *ChangeSet* result returned by *GetChangeSet*. For example, the following code could be an interesting pattern to use to populate audit fields in some entity:

```
public partial class MyDataContext : DataContext {
    public override void SubmitChanges(ConflictMode failureMode) {
```

```
        ChangeSet cs = this.GetChangeSet();
        foreach(object entity in cs.Inserts) {
            if (entity is Employee) {
                Employee e = (Employee)entity;
                e.CreatedByUser = GetCurrentUser();
                e.CreationTime = DateTime.Now;
            }
        }
        base.SubmitChanges(failureMode);
    }
}
```

The previous code is applicable when the same action is used on entities of different types. Whenever you need to intercept a particular operation (insert, update, or delete) of a particular entity type (*Employee*, in this case), you can implement either the *UpdateTYPE*, *InsertTYPE*, or *DeleteTYPE* method, which we describe later in the "Stored Procedures" section of this chapter.

A more complex operation that can be performed in *SubmitChanges* is the resolution of circular references. The standard implementation of *SubmitChanges* throws an exception if a circular reference is detected when the relationships between affected entities are evaluated. For example, consider the following code that creates two instances of *Employee*:

```
Northwind db = new CustomNorthwind(Connections.ConnectionString);
Employee empMarco = new Employee();
db.Employees.InsertOnSubmit(empMarco);
empMarco.FirstName = "Marco";
empMarco.LastName = "Russo";
Employee empPaolo = new Employee();
empPaolo.FirstName = "Paolo";
empPaolo.LastName = "Pialorsi";
empPaolo.Employees.Add(empMarco);
empMarco.Employees.Add(empPaolo);
```

We are describing a situation where *empMarco* reports to *empPaolo* and vice versa. This scenario could be nonsensical in the real world most of the time, but there are situations where circular references between entities could be meaningful. Thus, we will use the well-known Employees table to construct an example. If you try to call *SubmitChanges* for this code, the following exception will be thrown:

```
System.InvalidOperationException: A cycle was detected in the set of changes
```

If you want to build such a relationship, you need to break the cycle using two *SubmitChanges*, as in the following code:

```
Northwind db = new CustomNorthwind(Connections.ConnectionString);
Employee empMarco = new Employee();
db.Employees.InsertOnSubmit(empMarco);
empMarco.FirstName = "Marco";
empMarco.LastName = "Russo";
Employee empPaolo = new Employee();
```

```
empPaolo.FirstName = "Paolo";
empPaolo.LastName = "Pialorsi";
empPaolo.Employees.Add(empMarco);
db.SubmitChanges();
empMarco.Employees.Add(empPaolo);
db.SubmitChanges();
```

You can build a custom *SubmitChanges* implementation that automatically handles your possible source of cycles. Please note that solving cycles in a proper way requires you to make some assumptions about the kind of intermediate operations that are allowed. For this reason, there is not a general-purpose solution to this kind of problem. Listing 5-5 shows a possible implementation of *SubmitChanges*.

Listing 5-5 Specialized *SubmitChanges* to solve circular references of *Employee* entities

```
public class CircularReferenceNorthwind : Northwind {
    public CircularReferenceNorthwind(string connectionString) :
        base(connectionString) { }

    public override void SubmitChanges(ConflictMode failureMode) {
        Dictionary<Employee, Employee> employeeReferences;
        employeeReferences = new Dictionary<Employee, Employee>();

        // Remove and save references to other employees
        ChangeSet cs = this.GetChangeSet();
        foreach (object entity in cs.Inserts) {
            if (entity is Employee) {
                Employee e = (Employee) entity;
                employeeReferences.Add(e, e.Employee1);
                e.Employee1 = null;
            }
        }
        // Save Employees without references to other employees
        base.SubmitChanges(failureMode);

        // Restore references to other employees
        foreach (var item in employeeReferences) {
            item.Key.Employee1 = item.Value;
        }

        // Update Employees with references to other employees
        base.SubmitChanges(failureMode);
    }
}
```

This implementation makes an initial *SubmitChanges* call using *Employee* entities without references to other employees (which are saved in temporary objects), and then it makes a second *SubmitChanges* call after the original employee references have been restored. The second *SubmitChanges* call sends two UPDATE SQL statements that modify the two employees inserted with the first *SubmitChanges* call.

Customizing Insert, Update, and Delete

You can override the default insert, update, and delete SQL statements generated by LINQ to SQL when submitting changes. To do that, you can define one or more methods with specific signatures and pattern names. Here is the syntax to use. Note that you need to replace the name of the modified type to *TYPE*:

```
public void UpdateTYPE(TYPE original, TYPE current) { ... }
public void InsertTYPE(TYPE inserted) { ... }
public void DeleteTYPE(TYPE deleted) { ... }
```

> **Important**   The name of the method is important. The LINQ to SQL engine looks for a method with a matching signature and that has a name that starts with the word corresponding to the operation you override (*Update, Insert,* or *Delete*) followed by the name of the modified type.

Stored Procedures

Usually, these particular overrides are used to call stored procedures instead of sending SQL statements to execute data manipulation on the database. These methods have to be defined on the *DataContext*-derived class. Because a derived class is already generated by a tool (such as SQLMetal or the Object Relational Designer in Microsoft Visual Studio 2008), which also creates partial methods with the correct signatures, you can add your methods by using the *partial* class syntax, as shown in Listing 5-6. In this case, we assume that only changes in *UnitsInStock* properties are necessary to be tracked and we call a particular stored procedure that updates only that value. In this sample, we also get the original version of the *Product* entity using the *GetOriginalEntityState* method, which we will discuss in more detail in the upcoming "Concurrent Operations" section in this chapter.

Listing 5-6   Stored procedure to override an update

```
public partial class Northwind {
    partial void UpdateProduct(Product current) {
        Product original = ((Product) (Products.GetOriginalEntityState(current)));

        // Execute the stored procedure for UnitsInStock update
        if (original.UnitsInStock != current.UnitsInStock) {
            int rowCount = this.ExecuteCommand(
                        "exec UpdateProductStock " +
                        "@id={0}, @originalUnits={1}, @decrement={2}",
                        original.ProductID,
                        original.UnitsInStock,
                        (original.UnitsInStock - current.UnitsInStock));
            if (rowCount < 1) {
                throw new ChangeConflictException();
            }
        }
    }
}
```

> **Important**   Conflict detection is your responsibility if you decide to override insert, update, and delete methods.

Interception of Insert, Update, and Delete

The implementation of an UpdateTYPE, InsertTYPE, or DeleteTYPE method replaces the regular dynamic SQL statement generation. However, you can still leverage that behavior by calling *ExecuteDynamicUpdate*, *ExecuteDynamicInsert*, or *ExecuteDynamicDelete*, respectively. This allows you to intercept the original process of an entity by placing your own code just before and after the dynamic SQL statement execution. For example, you can populate audit fields in an entity just as you did before overriding the *SubmitChanges* method: in this case, you have already filtered for only the desired entities. You can see the customization of *InsertEmployee* in the following excerpt:

```
public partial class Northwind : DataContext {
    partial void InsertEmployee(Employee employee) {
        employee.CreatedByUser = GetCurrentUser();
        employee.CreationTime = DateTime.Now;
        base.ExecuteDynamicUpdate(employee);
    }
}
```

Database Interaction

The interaction with the database involves the handling of concurrent operations, transactions, and exceptions. In this part of the chapter, we will examine what you need to know to properly write code using LINQ to SQL to interact with a database.

Concurrent Operations

Operating with in-memory entities in LINQ is a form of disconnected operations on data. In these cases, you always have to deal with concurrent operations made by other users or connections between the reading of data and its successive updates. Usually, you operate with optimistic concurrency. In the case of a conflict, a *ChangeConflictException* error is thrown by default. This exception contains a *ChangeConflicts* collection of *ObjectChangeConflict* instances that explains the reasons for the error. (There can be several conflicts on different tables in a single *SubmitChanges* call.) Each *ObjectChangeConflict* instance describes the conflict on an entity (a row of a table) and contains a list of affected members in *MemberConflicts*. Listing 5-7 provides a demonstration, displaying information about a conflict by using the *Display-ChangeConflict* method.

Listing 5-7   Retry loop for a concurrency conflict

```
public static void ConcurrentUpdates() {
    // ...
    Northwind db2 = new Northwind(Connections.ConnectionString);
    var customer2 = db2.Customers.Single(c => c.CustomerID == "FRANS");
    customer2.ContactName = "Paolo Pialorsi";

    for (int retry = 1; retry < 4; retry++) {
        Console.WriteLine("Retry loop {0}", retry);

        try {
            db2.SubmitChanges(); // Throws exception
            break;               // Exit from while if submit succeed
        }
        catch (ChangeConflictException ex) {
            Console.WriteLine(ex.Message);
            DisplayChangeConflict(db2);
            db2.Refresh(RefreshMode.KeepChanges,customer2);
        }
    }
    // ...
}

private static void DisplayChangeConflict(Northwind db) {
    foreach (ObjectChangeConflict occ in db.ChangeConflicts) {
        MetaTable metatable = db.Mapping.GetTable(occ.Object.GetType());
        Customer entityInConflict = occ.Object as Customer;

        Console.WriteLine(
            "Table={0}, IsResolved={1}",
            metatable.TableName, occ.IsResolved);
        foreach (MemberChangeConflict mcc in occ.MemberConflicts) {
            object currVal = mcc.CurrentValue;
            object origVal = mcc.OriginalValue;
            object databaseVal = mcc.DatabaseValue;
            MemberInfo mi = mcc.Member;
            Console.WriteLine("Member: {0}", mi.Name);
            Console.WriteLine("current value: {0}", currVal);
            Console.WriteLine("original value: {0}", origVal);
            Console.WriteLine("database value: {0}", databaseVal);
        }
    }
}
```

For each conflicting member there are three values available, which are members of a *Member-ChangeConflict* instance:

- ■ **CurrentValue**   The value of the member in the entity instance that you wanted to write in the current *DataContext*.

- **OriginalValue**   The original value of the member when the entity was read from the database before its modification in the current *DataContext*.

- **DatabaseValue**   The value of the member that is currently stored in the database. The database has changed from *OriginalValue* to *DatabaseValue* since you have read the entity, and you have to make a decision about what value you want to write.

After a conflict, you might decide to re-read all the data or rely on the *Refresh* method, as demonstrated in the previous code sample. The *Refresh* method updates data in memory according to the argument passed, which can have three possible values:

- **RefreshMode.KeepChanges**   Only the *CurrentValue* values that are different from *OriginalValue* are preserved. All other *CurrentValue* values are equal to *OriginalValue*, and they are both updated to *DatabaseValue*.

- **RefreshMode.KeepCurrentValue**   Keeps the *CurrentValue*, assigning the *DatabaseValue* to the *OriginalValue*. In other words, after *Refresh*, the original entity state is set to the current database values. Current entity values are unchanged after this *Refresh*; thus, the following call to *SubmitChanges* attempts to save the *CurrentValue* on the relational database.

- **RefreshMode.OverwriteCurrentValues**   Discards any change made on the entity, replacing *OriginalValue* and *CurrentValue* with the *DatabaseValue*.

The difference between *KeepChanges* and *KeepCurrentValue* is the following: they are identical for the changed values, but they differ in how they handle unchanged values. *KeepCurrentValue* overwrites any database change to the entity made since the original read, while *KeepChanges* merges the updates made to the entity with the updates made to the relational database.

For example, assume you are executing the code in Listing 5-7 in the following scenario. You read the *Customer* entity, which has a *ContactName* equal to Paolo Accorti and *City* equal to Torino. This is the *OriginalValue* of your entity, which you have modified by setting *ContactName* to Paolo Pialorsi. At this point, you have an entity in memory that has the *CurrentValue* of *ContactName* set to Paolo Pialorsi, while the *City* property is still set to Torino. In the meantime, someone else modifies the database, setting *ContactName* to Marco Russo and *City* to Milano.

If you look at Table 5-1, you will find this situation described in the first row with a gray background. This is the state that you have when you get a *ChangeConflictException* when trying to call the *SubmitChanges* method. At this point, any *Refresh* call will change the *OriginalValue* of your entity, setting it to the current *DatabaseValue*, because this is the only way to make a successful *SubmitChanges* later. The different values of the *RefreshMode* enumeration passed to *Refresh* determine the final state of the *CurrentValue* of your entity, which will correspond to what will be saved to the database in an ensuing call to *SubmitChanges*. As you can see in Table 5-1, all possible combinations can be handled by choosing the value for this parameter.

Table 5-1   Effects of *RefreshMode* argument to *Refresh*

	CurrentValue	*OriginalValue*	*DatabaseValue*
ChangeConflictException	Paolo Pialorsi Torino	Paolo Accorti Torino	**Marco Russo** **Milano**
KeepChanges	Paolo Pialorsi **Milano**	Marco Russo Milano	Marco Russo Milano
KeepCurrentValues	Paolo Pialorsi Torino	Marco Russo Milano	Marco Russo Milano
OverwriteCurrentValues	**Marco Russo** **Milano**	Marco Russo Milano	Marco Russo Milano

SubmitChanges can have a parameter specifying whether you want to stop at the first conflict or try all updates regardless of the conflict. The default is to stop at the first conflict:

```
db.SubmitChanges(ConflictMode.FailOnFirstConflict);
db.SubmitChanges(ConflictMode.ContinueOnConflict);
```

Column Attributes for Concurrency Control

You can control how a concurrency conflict is determined by using an entity class definition. Each *Column* attribute can have an *UpdateCheck* argument that can have one of the following three values:

- **Always**   Always use this column (which is the default) for conflict detection.

- **Never**   Never use this column for conflict detection.

- **WhenChanged**   Use this column only when the member has been changed by the application.

> **Note**   If a column is not considered for conflict detection, shorter and faster SQL queries are generated when updating entities. However, remember that, by default, columns that are not checked for conflict detection are not updated in the entities whenever they are changed in the database after the initial read. Check the *AutoSync* column setting to get this kind of update; otherwise, you have to be sure that you do not make use of such columns after the *Submit-Changes* call, because those columns might not reflect the actual state of the database.

Other options for column definitions are represented by two Boolean flags: *IsDBGenerated* indicates that the value is autogenerated by the database, and *IsVersion* identifies a database timestamp or a version number. If a column has *IsVersion* set to *true*, the concurrency conflict is identified and only the entity's unique key and its timestamp/version column are compared. A typical use of *IsVersion* is for a *LastUpdate* column of type *TIMESTAMP* that is defined in the SQL Server database. (In this case, *IsDbGenerated* is set to *true* too, because a *TIMESTAMP* value is generated from SQL Server.)

```
[Column(Storage="_lastUpdate", AutoSync=AutoSync.Always,
        CanBeNull=false, IsDbGenerated=true, IsVersion=true)]
```

```
public System.Data.Linq.Binary LastUpdate {
    get { return this._lastUpdate; }
}

private Binary _lastUpdate = default(Binary);
```

> **Note**   Updates and deletes can have a long WHERE condition if an *IsVersion* column is not specified. Using *IsVersion* simplifies the query sent to the database to check concurrency conflicts. Only the column having *IsVersion* set to *true* is part of the WHERE condition that tries to match the record previously read. If that record has been changed in the meantime, a *ChangeConflictException* will be thrown.
>
> *IsDBGenerated* and *IsVersion* require a SELECT statement to be submitted after the UPDATE or INSERT operation. The advantages and disadvantages between having an *IsVersion* column or not having one depend on the number and complexity of table columns.

Transactions

A *SubmitChanges* call automatically starts a database-explicit transaction unless a transaction is already active in the connection being used. *SubmitChanges* eventually calls *IDbConnection.BeginTransaction* and then applies all changes made in memory to the database, inside the same transaction. Using the *TransactionScope* class contained in the *System.Transactions* library since .NET 2.0, you can add any standard command to the database or change any other transactional resource in the same transaction, which eventually will be transparently promoted to a distributed transaction. Listing 5-8 is an example of a transaction controlled in this way.

Listing 5-8   Transaction controlled by *TransactionScope*

```
Northwind db = new Northwind(Connections.ConnectionString);
Order_Detail orderDetail = db.Order_Details.Single(
                             o => o.OrderID == 10248
                                  && o.ProductID == 42);

if (orderDetail.Quantity >= 10) {
    orderDetail.Discount = 0.05F;
}

using (TransactionScope ts = new TransactionScope()) {
    db.SubmitChanges();
    ts.Complete();
}
```

In the case of an exception, the database transaction is canceled. If you do not call the *Complete* method on the *TransactionScope* instance, there is an automatic rollback of the transaction when the *TransactionScope* instance is disposed of. (This happens when *ts* goes out of scope—the *using* statement makes an automatic call to *Dispose*.)

If you have an existing ADO.NET application that does not use *System.Transactions*, you can control database transactions by accessing the *Transaction* property of *DataContext*. In Listing 5-9, you can see how to implement direct control of the transaction. In this case, the *Transaction.Commit* call is equivalent to the *TransactionScope.Complete* call made in Listing 5-8. However, usually you will use this technique when the connection (and the transaction) encloses direct ADO.NET calls.

Listing 5-9   Transaction controlled through the *DataContext.Transaction* property

```
Northwind db = new Northwind(Connections.ConnectionString);
db.Connection.Open();
Order_Detail orderDetail = db.Order_Details.Single(
                              o => o.OrderID == 10248
                                   && o.ProductID == 42);

if (orderDetail.Quantity >= 10) {
    orderDetail.Discount = 0.05F;
}
 using (db.Transaction = db.Connection.BeginTransaction())
 {
    db.SubmitChanges();       db.Transaction.Commit();
 }
```

Exceptions

LINQ to SQL does not have a dedicated set of exception types. You might have to handle exceptions of different types, thrown in different parts of your program. The following are the most critical points.

DataContext Construction

When you call the constructor of a *DataContext*-derived class, some errors in the attribute definitions of entities tied to the *DataContext* could throw a runtime exception. Usually these kinds of errors cannot be recovered because you do not have a valid model to work with—for example, as with an incorrect storage definition like the following one:

```
private EntitySet<Order> _Orders;

[Association(OtherKey="CustomerID", Storage="_Wrong")]
public EntitySet<Order> Orders {
    get { return this._Orders; }
    set { this._Orders.Assign(value); }
}
```

This definition maps *_Wrong* instead of *_Orders* and produces the following exception:

```
System.InvalidOperationException: Bad Storage property: '_Order_Details1'
on member 'DevLeap.Linq.LinqToSql.Product.Order_Details'.
```

These kinds of errors will not occur if you generate the LINQ to SQL entities using a tool such as SQLMetal or Visual Studio 2008. However, if you manually build your own queries, remember that the C# compiler cannot identify such errors at compile time.

Database Reads

Every time you access the database, you might have an exception: SQL Server might not be active, data tables might have a different structure than you expected, and so on. Given the nature of LINQ to SQL, you might access the database in a very indirect way. For example, accessing a property might require the reading of an entity from the database because it is not already in a cache. The following code might throw an exception when accessing the *Customer* property of an *Order* for the first time because it might require access to the database:

```
public static void WriteOrderDestination(Order order) {
    Console.WriteLine(order.Customer.City);
}
```

The beauty of database access abstraction comes at a price: you cannot identify a specific point at which to access the database, as you can do in a data layer. If you distribute LINQ to SQL entities across the logical tiers of your application, you will have access to the database at several points. In a small application with a local database, this might not be an issue, but you might want to avoid such loss of control in a more complex application.

More Info   You can be sure you have all required entities in memory by leveraging *DataContext.LoadOptions* and disabling deferred loading by using its *DeferredLoadingEnabled* setting. These options and settings are discussed in Chapter 4.

Database Writes

LINQ to SQL entities are written to the database only at very specific and controlled points. Only when you call *DataContext.SubmitChanges* are new and updated entities written to the database, and entities that have been removed from the *DataContext* tables deleted. To highlight this behavior, *Table<T>* methods are named *InsertOnSubmit* and *DeleteOnSubmit*. However, remember that many more entities can be affected in a *SubmitChanges* call than the ones that have been directly added or removed by calling these methods.

When you call *SubmitChanges*, you might expect any ADO.NET database access-related exception. Moreover, a specific *ChangeConflictException* is thrown by the LINQ to SQL engine whenever the entity you tried to write to the database has been changed since its original read. We described *ChangeConflictException* handling earlier in this chapter, in the "Concurrent Operations" section.

Entity Manipulation

Creating and manipulating entities might throw exceptions when there is an attempt to perform an operation not allowed by the change-tracking service. Two exceptions that might be thrown when accessing entity properties are the following:

- *DuplicateKeyException*   Thrown when an attempt is made to add an object to the identity cache by using a key that is already being used—for example, when you try to add two different entities to a table having the same primary key.

- *ForeignKeyReferenceAlreadyHasValueException*   Thrown when an attempt is made to change a foreign key but the entity is already loaded. This exception is thrown by the entity code generated by tools such as SQLMetal and Visual Studio 2008.

Database and Entities

Any update operation on the database made through LINQ to SQL requires the definition of proper entities describing the underlying database structure. In this final part of the chapter, we will cover important details about entity definitions and manipulation that are useful in implementing a real-world application using LINQ to SQL.

Entity Attributes to Maintain Valid Relationships

Entity classes can have relationships with other entities, just as tables can in a relational database. While a relational database declares the parent-child relationship only by declaring a foreign key on the child side, LINQ to SQL entities can show the relationship on both sides. The *Association* attribute is used to decorate properties that define relationships with other entities. Its use was explained in Chapter 4. The implementation of properties decorated with *Association* requires some code to establish the synchronization between in-memory entities while they are manipulated. Thanks to this bidirectional synchronization, the programmer needs to update only one side of the relationship. The other side will be synchronized by the entity code. Usually, that entity's code is generated by a tool such as SQLMetal or Visual Studio 2008.

For example, if you have two entities, *Product* and *Category*, there is probably a one-to-many relationship between *Category* and *Product*. Each *Product* can belong to one *Category*, and each *Category* has a set of related *Products*. The code generated by tools for the *Category* property in the *Product* class will be like that shown in the following block of code. It updates the *Products* set in the *Category*-related entities, removing the product from the old *Category* and adding the product to the assigned *Category*. In other words, assigning the *Category* property to a *Product* instance also updates the *Products* property of the referenced *Category* instance.

```
public partial class Product {
    [Association(Name = "Category_Product", Storage = "_Category",
                 ThisKey = "CategoryID", IsForeignKey = true)]
    public Category Category {
        get { return this._Category.Entity; }
        set {
            Category previousValue = this._Category.Entity;
            if (((previousValue != value)
                || (this._Category.HasLoadedOrAssignedValue == false))) {
                this.SendPropertyChanging();
                if ((previousValue != null)) {
                    this._Category.Entity = null;
                    previousValue.Products.Remove(this);
                }
                this._Category.Entity = value;
                if ((value != null)) {
                    value.Products.Add(this);
                    this._CategoryID = value.CategoryID;
                }
                else {
                    this._CategoryID = default(Nullable<int>);
                }
                this.SendPropertyChanged("Category");
            }
        }
    }
}
```

The remaining part of the synchronization process yields the assignment of the *Category*
property of a *Product* instance whenever that *Product* instance is added to a *Products* property
of a *Category* instance. This assignment is made through the *EntitySet<T>* type, which has to
be correctly initialized with the actions to be called to maintain that synchronization. The
following example shows the tool-generated code for the *Products* property of the *Category*
class:

```
public partial class Category {
    private EntitySet<Product> _Products;

    public Category() {
        this._Products = new EntitySet<Product>(
                        new Action<Product>(this.attach_Products),
                        new Action<Product>(this.detach_Products));
        OnCreated();
    }

    [Association(Name="Category_Product", Storage="_Products",
                OtherKey="CategoryID")]
    public EntitySet<Product> Products {
        get { return this._Products; }
        set { this._Products.Assign(value); }
    }
}
```

```
    private void attach_Products(Product entity) {
        this.SendPropertyChanging();
        entity.Category = this;
    }

    private void detach_Products(Product entity) {
        this.SendPropertyChanging();
        entity.Category = null;
    }
}
```

If a programmer manually assigns both sides of a relationship, the second assignment will simply be redundant.

Deriving Entity Classes

In Chapter 4, you saw how to define an entity class derived from another one, as in the following code:

```
[Table(Name="Contacts")]
[InheritanceMapping(Code = "Customer", Type = typeof(CustomerContact))]
[InheritanceMapping(Code = "Supplier", Type = typeof(SupplierContact))]
[InheritanceMapping(Code = "Employee", Type = typeof(Employee), IsDefault = true)]
public class Contact {
    [Column(IsPrimaryKey=true)] public int ContactID;
    [Column(IsDiscriminator = true)] public string ContactType;
    // ...
}

public class CompanyContact : Contact {
    [Column(Name="CompanyName")] public string Company;
}
public class CustomerContact : CompanyContact {
}

public class SupplierContact : CompanyContact {
}

public class Employee : Contact {
    [Column] public string PhotoPath;
    [Column(UpdateChack=UpdateCheck.Never)] public Binary Photo;
}
```

These classes can be graphically represented with the hierarchy shown in Figure 5-2.

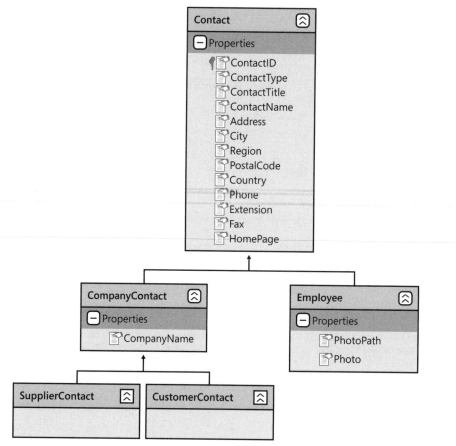

Figure 5-2   Example of an entity hierarchy

With this hierarchy, you have three different types used by your program: *SupplierContact*, *CustomerContact*, and *Employee*. There are also two classes, *Contact* and *CompanyContact*, which would be "abstract" from a C# point of view, even if a tool-generated class is always a type that can be instantiated. In reality, these types are stored in the same table (Contact), with some column that is used only by some types and not by others. There are several advantages to making this choice:

- **Strong type check**   You create and manipulate entities of the right type corresponding to the discriminator field value.

- **Centralization of discrimination logic**   There is only one point (in the model) where the discriminating field is defined. You do not have dispatching logic potentially duplicated in your code.

- **Code clearness**   You can write methods (and extension methods) operating on fields that are specific to certain types of records, without writing conditional code to check the value of the discriminator field.

Every time you have very similar entities stored in the same table, which differs in terms of the use of some fields that are specific to a certain group of records, consider using entity inheritance in LINQ to SQL as a way to design your domain model.

> **Warning**   There are some issues related to applying entity inheritance to derived entities in a parent-child relationship. The Object Relational Designer included in Visual Studio 2008 allows you to create relationships only by using properties defined in the entities you are associating. The designer does not support inherited properties. However, you can still modify the DBML file by hand and it will generate the right entity class code. After such an *Association* is created, it can be maintained through the Object Relational Designer, except for changing the participating properties.

Another important consideration about entity inheritance is that it has the capability to derive a class entity from an existing class. Tools such as SQLMetal and Object Relational Designer build entity classes that do not derive from any other class. (Technically, they still derive from *System.Object*.) However, you can derive your entity classes from the base class that you want. You can establish this definition by leveraging the *partial class* definition used by these tools. For example, if you place the following declaration in your code

```
public partial class Contact : EntityBase { }
```

the *Contact* class will derive from your own *EntityBase* class, and therefore all *Contact*-derived classes will also inherit the *EntityBase* behaviors. The same partial declaration can also be used to add class attributes to an entity class. Unfortunately, there is no syntax sugar with which to add attributes at the member level, such as a property already decorated with *Column* in the tool-generated code. In fact, it is not possible to declare a partial property.

Attaching Entities

If you want to manipulate an entity in a disconnected way, you need to serialize entities and attach them to a *DataContext* instance, possibly an instance different from the one that originally created the entities.

Entity Serialization

Entities used by LINQ to SQL can be serialized using particular attributes that are defined in the *System.Runtime.Serialization* namespace: *DataContract* and *DataMember*. These attributes are applied to the class and property definitions, respectively. By default, SQLMetal and Visual Studio 2008 do not generate serializable entity classes; thus, classes and properties are not decorated with *DataContract* and *DataMember*. However, this behavior is controlled by the "/serialization:unidirectional" parameter at the command line of the SQLMetal invocation, or with the Serialization Mode designer property of the *DataContext* class edited with the Object Relational Designer in Visual Studio 2008. That property is set to *None* by default, but by using *Unidirectional* you get the same behavior as you do with the "/serialization:unidirectional" parameter in SQLMetal.

The *Unidirectional* serialization setting means that an entity is serialized with only a one-way association property so as to avoid a cycle. Only the property on the parent side of a parent-child relationship is marked for serialization (the property of type *EntitySet<T>*), while the other side in a bidirectional association is not serialized (usually a property stored on a member of type *EntityRef<T>*). You can see an example of serialization in Listing 5-10.

Listing 5-10   Entity serialization

```
Northwind db = new Northwind(Connections.ConnectionString);
var customer = db.Customers.Single(c => c.CustomerID == "WHITC");
DataContractSerializer dcs = new DataContractSerializer(typeof(Customer));
StringBuilder sb = new StringBuilder();
using (XmlWriter writer = XmlWriter.Create(sb)) {
    dcs.WriteObject(writer, customer);
}
string xml = sb.ToString();
Console.WriteLine(xml);
```

The serialized entity results in the XML you see in Listing 5-11.

Listing 5-11   Serialized *Customer* entity

```
<?xml version="1.0" encoding="utf-16"?>
<Customer xmlns:i="http://www.w3.org/2001/XMLSchema-instance"
 xmlns="http://schemas.datacontract.org/2004/07/DevLeap.Linq.LinqToSql">
    <CustomerID>WHITC</CustomerID>
    <CompanyName>White Clover Markets</CompanyName>
    <ContactName>Karl Jablonski</ContactName>
    <ContactTitle>Owner</ContactTitle>
    <Address>305 - 14th Ave. S. Suite 3B</Address>
    <City>Seattle</City>
    <Region>WA</Region>
    <PostalCode>98128</PostalCode>
    <Country>USA</Country>
    <Phone>(206) 555-4112</Phone>
    <Fax>(206) 555-4115</Fax>
</Customer>
```

At this point, the serialized entity can be easily transmitted to an external tier of a distributed architecture. When it comes back, you will need to deserialize and attach it to a new *DataContext* instance, because the same *DataContext* cannot have two entities with the same key. You will see how to handle this in the following section.

More Info   A further discussion of LINQ to SQL entity serialization is included in Chapter 18, "LINQ and the Windows Communication Foundation." Because most of the time serialization is used to transfer entities between layers of a distributed application, we included a more practical discussion of this topic in the chapter dedicated to Windows Communication Foundation.

Attach Operation

A typical scenario that involves entity serialization is one in which a service provides instances of an entity class on demand. Data consumers might update that entity and send it back to the service, asking for an update of the corresponding data source. If your service uses SQL Server as data source and LINQ to SQL as the data access layer, you need to create LINQ to SQL entity instances that will make the desired database updates.

In the scenario we have been working with, the service sends a consumer a *Customer* entity serialized by the code you saw in Listing 5-10. You do not care how the consumer internally manipulates the *Customer* entity it receives because it can also be code written with a different platform than the .NET Framework. What is important is that you receive an XML document representing the possibly modified *Customer* entity you originally sent. Listing 5-12 shows an XML document that you could receive: the *ContactName* tag content is highlighted because it is the changed part of the original entity you saw in Listing 5-11. The *ContactName* has been changed from Karl Jablonski to John Smith.

Listing 5-12   *Customer* entity modified

```xml
<?xml version="1.0" encoding="utf-16"?>
<Customer xmlns:i="http://www.w3.org/2001/XMLSchema-instance"
 xmlns="http://schemas.datacontract.org/2004/07/DevLeap.Linq.LinqToSql">
    <CustomerID>WHITC</CustomerID>
    <CompanyName>White Clover Markets</CompanyName>
    <ContactName>John Smith</ContactName>
    <ContactTitle>Owner</ContactTitle>
    <Address>305 - 14th Ave. S. Suite 3B</Address>
    <City>Seattle</City>
    <Region>WA</Region>
    <PostalCode>98128</PostalCode>
    <Country>USA</Country>
    <Phone>(206) 555-4112</Phone>
    <Fax>(206) 555-4115</Fax>
</Customer>
```

In Listing 5-13, you can see how to deserialize into a new *Customer* instance the XML document shown in Listing 5-12. Using the *Attach* method, you add that instance to the *Customers* table in the *Northwind* data context. Note that this is a different instance of the *Northwind* class than the one you used to get the original *Customer* entity in Listing 5-11.

Listing 5-13   Attach an entity to a *DataContext*, providing its original state for optimistic concurrency

```csharp
Northwind nw = new Northwind(Connections.ConnectionString);
nw.Log = Console.Out;

Customer deserializedCustomer;
using (XmlTextReader reader = new XmlTextReader(new StringReader(xml))) {
    deserializedCustomer = (Customer) dcs.ReadObject(reader, true);
    }
```

```
nw.Customers.Attach(deserializedCustomer, customer);
Console.WriteLine(
    "ContactName Original={0}, Updated={1}\n",
    customer.ContactName,
    deserializedCustomer.ContactName);

nw.SubmitChanges();
```

You know that the instance you received might be changed, but you do not know what the changed fields are. In fact, the XML document you receive does not contain the original state of the *ContactName* tag content. As we said earlier in this chapter, you have several ways to handle concurrency. If you want to use optimistic concurrency, you need to provide to the *DataContext* two versions of the same entity: the original version and the updated one. The example in Listing 5-13 uses the original customer instance cached by the original query made in Listing 5-10 and its execution provides the following result:

```
ContactName Original=Karl Jablonski, Updated=John Smith
```

```
UPDATE [dbo].[Customers]
SET     [ContactName] = 'John Smith'
WHERE  ([CustomerID] = 'WHITC')
AND ([ContactName] = 'Karl Jablonski')
AND ...
```

Important   The *DataContext* class is designed to be created and destroyed frequently. It is good practice to create a new *DataContext* instance for each service request.

Making a cache of all the entities provided by a service would make the service itself stateful, and we know that in the Service Oriented Architecture (SOA) world a service should be stateless. However, note that the code in Listing 5-13 uses the *customer* instance obtained from another *DataContext* as the original entity version calling the *Attach* method. The same approach is not possible for the updated entity. You can pass only a new (or deserialized) entity to the *Attach* method, because using an entity obtained from a different *DataContext* results in a *NotSupportedException*.

If you do not want to use the *Attach* method with two *Customer* instances as arguments (for current and original entity values), you can pass a single entity instance to *Attach*, asking the change tracking service to ignore original values and to consider the object as modified. In this case, your entity must have either a field tagged with *IsVersion=true* on *Column* attributes, or all the fields tagged with *UpdateCheck=Never* on *Column* attributes. In the latter case, a column with *IsPrimary=true* must also exist. In any of these cases, you would have called the *Attach* method with the following syntax (the second argument is the *asModified* setting):

```
nw.Customers.Attach(deserializedCustomer, true);
```

Finally, you can also attach an entity, assuming it is unmodified, and then modify that instance and leave the change-tracking service the work of finding updated fields. Of course, even in this case we are assuming you have the original entity available, and this might not be the common case with SOA. In these cases, you need to call *Attach* with either syntax shown here:

```
nw.Customers.Attach(customer, false);
nw.Customers.Attach(customer);
```

Whenever you have a sequence of entities of the same type to attach to a *DataContext*, you might consider using the *DataContext.AttachAll* method. Both the *Attach* and *AttachAll* methods work only if *ObjectTrackingEnabled* is *true*.

 More Info   Other information about the use of LINQ in a multitier architecture is contained in Chapter 15.

Binding Metadata

The mapping between LINQ to SQL entities and database structures has to be described through metadata information. Until now, you have seen attributes within entity definitions fulfilling this rule. There is an alternative way to do this (using an external XML mapping file), and there are tools and methods that automate the generation of entity classes starting from a database and vice versa.

External XML Mapping File

If you do not want to use attribute-based mapping information, you can put all binding metadata in an external XML file. For example, consider a *Customer* entity class like the one in Listing 5-14, used in the *Northwind* class derived by *DataContext*.

Listing 5-14   Entity class with binding information saved in an external XML file

```
public class Customer {
    public string CustomerID;
    public string CompanyName;
    public string City;
    public string State;
    public string Country;
}

public class Northwind : DataContext {
    public Northwind(string connection) :
        this(connection, GetMapping()) { }

    public Northwind(string connection, MappingSource mapping) :
        base(connection, mapping) { }

    static MappingSource GetMapping() {
```

```
        using (StreamReader reader = new StreamReader("Northwind.xml")) {
            return XmlMappingSource.FromReader(new XmlTextReader(reader));
        }
    }

    public System.Data.Linq.Table<Customer> Customers {
        get { return this.GetTable<Customer>(); }
    }

}
```

The *Northwind* class can be used without specifying a mapping file, implicitly using the *GetMapping* static method, as shown in Listing 5-15.

Listing 5-15   Entity class with binding information saved in an external XML file

```
public static void SimpleQuery() {
    Northwind db = new Northwind(Connections.ConnectionString);
    var query = from   c in db.Customers
                where  c.City == "Seattle"
                select c;

    foreach( var customer in query ) {
        Console.WriteLine(
            "Customer={0}, State={1}",
            customer.CompanyName,
            customer.State);
    }
}
```

Using a second argument in the *Northwind* constructor call you can specify different mapping information. The *Northwind.GetMapping* static method returns an *XmlMappingSource* instance, which reads the binding information contained in the Northwind.xml file shown in Listing 5-16.

Listing 5-16   Entity class with binding information saved in an external XML file

```
<?xml version="1.0" encoding="utf-8" ?>
<Database Name="Northwind"
  xmlns="http://schemas.microsoft.com/linqtosql/mapping/2007">
    <Table Name="dbo.Customers" Member="Customers">
        <Type Name="Customer">
            <Column Name="CustomerID" Member="CustomerID"
                    IsPrimaryKey="true" />
            <Column Name="CompanyName" Member="CompanyName"/>
            <Column Name="City" Member="City"/>
            <Column Name="Region" Member="State"/>
            <Column Name="Country" Member="Country"/>
        </Type>
    </Table>
</Database>
```

Decoupling the binding information in an external file allows you to map an entity to different database schemas, handling differences such as different naming conventions, translated table and column names, or versioning between database schemas. For example, an older version of the database might not have some newer column. In that case, different mapping files can be used to best match different versions of the database.

Creating a Database from Entities

An application that automatically installs itself on a computer might have a reason to create a database that can persist its objects graph. This is a typical situation—you need to handle simple configurations that are represented by a graph of objects.

If you have a class derived from *DataContext* that contains entity definitions decorated with *Table* and *Column* attributes, you can create the corresponding database by calling the *CreateDatabase* method. This method sends the necessary CREATE DATABASE statement, as well as the subsequent CREATE TABLE and ALTER TABLE statements:

```
const string ConnectionString =
    "Database=Test_Northwind;Trusted_Connection=yes";
public static void Create() {
    Northwind db = new Northwind( ConnectionString );
    db.CreateDatabase(); }
```

You can also drop a database and check for its existence. The name of the database is inferred from the connection string. You can duplicate a database schema in several databases simply by changing the connection string:

```
if (db.DatabaseExists()) {
    db.DeleteDatabase();    // Send a DROP DATABASE
}
db.CreateDatabase();
```

Remember that the database is created based on the *Table* and *Column* attributes decorating entity classes and their properties. Two of the parameters of the *Column* attribute exist only to keep definitions useful for database generation:

- **DbType**   This is the definition of the type for the column in the database. This setting overrides the type that would be automatically generated by the LINQ to SQL engine.

- **Expression**   This is the T-SQL expression that is used as an expression for a computed value in a table.

> **Important**   Remember that the *DbType* and *Expression* parameters of the *Column* attribute contain a string that is not parsed or checked by either the compiler or the LINQ to SQL engine. An error in these definitions produces an error at execution time.

Creating Entities from a Database

If you already have an existing physical data layer, you might want to create a set of entity classes for an existing database. You can use two available tools: SQLMetal and the Object Relational Designer integrated into Visual Studio 2008. We have dedicated the entire next chapter to these two tools. See Chapter 6 for further information.

Differences Between .NET and SQL Type Systems

The product documentation illustrates all types of system differences between the .NET Framework and LINQ to SQL. Many operators require a specific conversion, such as cast operations and the *ToString* method, which are converted in *CAST* or *CONVERT* operators in SQL translation. There can be significant differences if your code is sensitive to rounding differences. (*Math.Round* and *ROUND* have different logic. See the *MidpointRounding* enumeration used to control the behavior.) There are also minor differences in date and time manipulation. Above all, you need to remember that SQL Server supports *DATETIME* but not *DATE*.

> **More Info**   We covered the most important differences in the "Limitations of LINQ to SQL" section of Chapter 4.

Summary

In this chapter, we covered the CUD (Create, Update, and Delete) operations on a relational database using LINQ to SQL entities. Handling entity updates involves concurrency and transactions, and the *DataContext* class in LINQ to SQL offers the connection points to control the LINQ to SQL engine's behavior. Finally, LINQ to SQL entity serialization requires a good understanding of the change-tracking service offered by an instance of *DataContext*. An entity cannot be serialized and then deserialized in the same *DataContext*; for this reason, this chapter includes a section dedicated to attaching entities from a *DataContext*.

Chapter 6
Tools for LINQ to SQL

The best way to write queries using LINQ to SQL is by having a *DataContext*-derived class in your code that exposes all the tables, stored procedures, and user-defined functions you need as properties of a class instance. You also need entity classes that are mapped to the database objects. As you have seen in previous chapters, this mapping can be made by using attributes to decorate classes or through an external XML mapping file. However, writing this information by hand is tedious and error-prone work. You need some tools to help you accomplish this work.

In this chapter, you will learn about what file types are involved and what tools are available to automatically generate this information. The .NET 3.5 Software Development Kit (SDK) includes a command-line tool named SQLMetal. Microsoft Visual Studio 2008 offers an integrated graphical tool named the Object Relational Designer. We will examine both tools from a practical point of view.

Important   In this chapter we use the version of the Northwind database that is included in the C# samples provided with Visual Studio 2008. All the samples are contained in the Microsoft Visual Studio 9.0\Samples\1033\CSharpSamples.zip file in your program files directory if you installed Visual Studio 2008. You can also download an updated version of these samples from *http://code.msdn.microsoft.com/csharpsamples*.

File Types

There are three types of files involved in LINQ to SQL entities and a mapping definition:

- Database markup language (.DBML)
- Source code (C# or Visual Basic)
- External mapping file (XML)

A common mistake is the confusion between DBML and XML mapping files. At first sight, these two files are similar, but they are very different in their use and generation process.

DBML—Database Markup Language

The DBML file contains a description of the LINQ to SQL entities in a database markup language. Visual Studio 2008 installs a DbmlSchema.xsd file, which contains the schema definition of that language and can be used to validate a DBML file. The namespace used for this file is *http://schemas.microsoft.com/linqtosql/dbml/2007*, which is different from the namespace used by the XSD for the XML external mapping file.

> **Note**   You can find the DbmlSchema.xsd schema file in the %ProgramFiles(x86)%\Microsoft Visual Studio 9.0\Xml\Schemas folder.

The DBML file can be automatically generated by extracting metadata from an existing Microsoft SQL Server database. However, the DBML file includes more information than can be inferred from database tables. For example, settings for synchronization and delayed loading are specific to the intended use of the entity. Moreover, DBML files include information that is used only by the code generator that generates C# or Visual Basic source code, such as the base class and namespace for generated entity classes. Listing 6-1 shows an excerpt from a sample DBML file.

Listing 6-1   Excerpt from a sample DBML file

```xml
<?xml version="1.0" encoding="utf-8"?>
<Database Name="Northwind" Class="nwDataContext"
          xmlns="http://schemas.microsoft.com/linqtosql/dbml/2007">
   <Connection Mode="AppSettings"
               ConnectionString="Data Source=..."
               SettingsObjectName="DevLeap.Linq.LinqToSql.Properties.Settings"
               SettingsPropertyName="NorthwindConnectionString"
               Provider="System.Data.SqlClient" />
   <Table Name="dbo.Orders" Member="Orders">
     <Type Name="Order">
       <Column Name="OrderID" Type="System.Int32"
               DbType="Int NOT NULL IDENTITY" IsPrimaryKey="true"
               IsDbGenerated="true" CanBeNull="false" />
       <Column Name="CustomerID" Type="System.String"
               DbType="NChar(5)" CanBeNull="true" />
       <Column Name="OrderDate" Type="System.DateTime"
               DbType="DateTime" CanBeNull="true" />

       ...

       <Association Name="Customer_Order" Member="Customer"
                    ThisKey="CustomerID" Type="Customer"
                    IsForeignKey="true" />
     </Type>
   </Table>
   ...
</Database>
```

The DBML file is the richest container of metadata information for LINQ to SQL. Usually, it can be generated from a SQL Server database and then manually modified, adding information that cannot be inferred from the database. This is the typical approach when using the SQLMetal command-line tool. The Object Relational Designer included in Visual Studio 2008 offers a more dynamic way of editing this file, because programmers can import entities from a database and modify them directly in the DBML file through a graphical editor. The DBML generated by SQLMetal can also be edited with the Object Relational Designer.

The DBML file can be used to generate C# or Visual Basic source code for entities and *DataContext*-derived classes. Optionally, it can also be used to generate an external XML mapping file.

More Info   It is beyond the scope of this book to provide a detailed description of the DBML syntax. You can find more information and the whole DbmlSchema.xsd content in the product documentation at *http://msdn2.microsoft.com/library/bb399400.aspx*.

C# and Visual Basic Source Code

The source code written in C#, Visual Basic, or any other .NET language contains the definition of LINQ to SQL entity classes. This code can be decorated with attributes that define the mapping of entities and their properties with database tables and their columns. Otherwise, the mapping can be defined by an external XML mapping file. However, a mix of both is not allowed—you have to choose only one place where the mappings of an entity are defined.

This source code can be automatically generated by tools such as SQLMetal directly from a SQL Server database. The code-generation function of SQLMetal can translate a DBML file to C# or Visual Basic source code. When you ask SQLMetal to directly generate the source code for entities, internally it generates the DBML file that is converted to the entity source code. In Listing 6-2, you can see an excerpt of the C# source code generated for LINQ to SQL entities that were generated from the DBML sample shown in Listing 6-1.

Listing 6-2   Excerpt from the class entity source code in C#

```csharp
[System.Data.Linq.Mapping.DatabaseAttribute(Name="Northwind")]
public partial class nwDataContext : System.Data.Linq.DataContext {

    // ...

    public System.Data.Linq.Table<Order> Orders {
        get { return this.GetTable<Order>(); }
    }
}
 [Table(Name="dbo.Orders")]
public partial class Order : INotifyPropertyChanging, INotifyPropertyChanged {
    private int _OrderID;
    private string _CustomerID;
    private System.Nullable<System.DateTime> _OrderDate;

    [Column(Storage="_OrderID", AutoSync=AutoSync.OnInsert,
            DbType="Int NOT NULL IDENTITY", IsPrimaryKey=true,
            IsDbGenerated=true)]
```

```
public int OrderID {
    get { return this._OrderID; }
    set {
        if ((this._OrderID != value)) {
            this.OnOrderIDChanging(value);
            this.SendPropertyChanging();
            this._OrderID = value;
            this.SendPropertyChanged("OrderID");
            this.OnOrderIDChanged();
        }
    }
}

[Column(Storage="_CustomerID", DbType="NChar(5)")]
public string CustomerID {
    get { return this._CustomerID; }
    set {
        if ((this._CustomerID != value)) {
            if (this._Customer.HasLoadedOrAssignedValue) {
                throw new ForeignKeyReferenceAlreadyHasValueException();
            }
            this.OnCustomerIDChanging(value);
            this.SendPropertyChanging();
            this._CustomerID = value;
            this.SendPropertyChanged("CustomerID");
            this.OnCustomerIDChanged();
        }
    }
}

[Column(Storage="_OrderDate", DbType="DateTime")]
public System.Nullable<System.DateTime> OrderDate {
    get { return this._OrderDate; }
    set {
        if ((this._OrderDate != value)) {
            this.OnOrderDateChanging(value);
            this.SendPropertyChanging();
            this._OrderDate = value;
            this.SendPropertyChanged("OrderDate");
            this.OnOrderDateChanged();
        }
    }
}

[Association(Name="Customer_Order", Storage="_Customer",
        ThisKey="CustomerID", IsForeignKey=true)]
public Customer Customer {
    get { return this._Customer.Entity; }
    set {
        Customer previousValue = this._Customer.Entity;
        if ((previousValue != value)
            || (this._Customer.HasLoadedOrAssignedValue == false)) {
            this.SendPropertyChanging();
```

```
                        if ((previousValue != null)) {
                            this._Customer.Entity = null;
                            previousValue.Orders.Remove(this);
                        }
                        this._Customer.Entity = value;
                        if ((value != null)) {
                            value.Orders.Add(this);
                            this._CustomerID = value.CustomerID;
                        }
                        else {
                            this._CustomerID = default(string);
                        }
                        this.SendPropertyChanged("Customer");
                    }
                }
            }

        // ...
    }
```

The attributes that are highlighted in bold in Listing 6-2 are not generated in the source code file when you have SQLMetal generate both the source code file and an external XML mapping file. The XML mapping file will contain this mapping information.

More Info Attributes that define the mapping between entities and database tables are discussed in Chapter 4, "LINQ to SQL: Querying Data," and in Chapter 5, "LINQ to SQL: Managing Data."

XML—External Mapping File

An external mapping file can contain binding metadata for LINQ to SQL entities as an alternative way to store them in code attributes. This file is an XML file with a schema that is a subset of the DBML file. The DBML file also contains information useful for code generators. Attributes defined on class entities are ignored whenever they are included in the definitions of an external mapping file.

The namespace used for this file is *http://schemas.microsoft.com/linqtosql/mapping/2007*, which is different from the one used by the DBML XSD file.

Note The LinqToSqlMapping.xsd schema file should be located in the %ProgramFiles(x86)%\ Microsoft Visual Studio 9.0\Xml\Schemas folder. If you do not have that file, you can create it by copying the code from the documentation page at *http://msdn2.microsoft.com/library/ bb386907.aspx*.

In Listing 6-3, you can see an example of an external mapping file generated from the DBML file presented in Listing 6-1. We highlighted the *Storage* attribute that defines the mapping between the table column and the data member in the entity class that stores the value exposed through the member property (defined by the *Member* attribute). The value assigned to *Storage* depends on the implementation generated by the code generator; for this reason, it is not included in the DBML file.

Listing 6-3   Excerpt from a sample XML mapping file

```
<?xml version="1.0" encoding="utf-8"?>
<Database Name="northwind"
          xmlns="http://schemas.microsoft.com/linqtosql/mapping/2007">
  <Table Name="dbo.Orders" Member="Orders">
    <Type Name="Orders">
      <Column Name="OrderID" Member="OrderID" Storage="_OrderID"
              DbType="Int NOT NULL IDENTITY" IsPrimaryKey="true"
              IsDbGenerated="true" AutoSync="OnInsert" />
      <Column Name="CustomerID" Member="CustomerID" Storage="_CustomerID"
              DbType="NChar(5)" />
      <Column Name="OrderDate" Member="OrderDate" Storage="_OrderDate"
              DbType="DateTime" />

      ...

      <Association Name="FK_Orders_Customers" Member="Customers"
                   Storage="_Customers" ThisKey="CustomerID"
                   OtherKey="CustomerID" IsForeignKey="true" />
    </Type>
  </Table>
  ...
</Database>
```

> **More Info**   If a provider has custom definitions that extend existing ones, the extensions are available only through an external mapping file but not with attribute-based mapping. For example, with an XML mapping file you can specify different *DbType* values for SQL Server 2000, SQL Server 2005, and SQL Server Compact 3.5. External XML mapping files are discussed in Chapter 5.

LINQ to SQL File Generation

Usually, most of the files used in LINQ to SQL are automatically generated by some tool. The diagram in Figure 6-1 illustrates the relationships between the different file types and the relational database. In the remaining part of this section, we will describe the most important patterns of code generation that you can use.

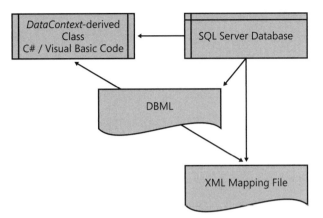

Figure 6-1   Relationships between file types and the relational database

Generating a DBML File from an Existing Database

If you have a relational database, you can generate a DBML file that describes tables, views, stored procedures, and user-defined functions, mapping them to class entities that can be created by a code generator. After it is created, the DBML file can be edited using a text editor or the Object Relational Designer included in Visual Studio 2008.

Generating an Entity's Source Code with Attribute-Based Mapping

You can choose to generate source code for class entities in C# or Visual Basic with attribute-based mapping. This code can be generated from a DBML file or directly from a SQL Server database.

If you start from a DBML file, you can still modify that DBML file and then regenerate the source code. In this case, the generated source code should not be modified because it could be overwritten in the future by code regeneration. You can customize generated classes by using a separate source code file, leveraging the *partial class* declaration of generated class entities. This is the pattern used when working with the Object Relational Designer.

If you generate code directly from a SQL Server database, the resulting source code file can still be customized using partial classes; however, if you need to modify the mapping settings, you have to modify the generated source code. In this case, you probably will not regenerate this file in the future and can therefore make modifications directly on the generated source code in C# or Visual Basic.

Generating an Entity's Source Code with an External XML Mapping File

You can choose to generate source code for class entities in C# or Visual Basic together with an external XML mapping file. The source code and the XML mapping file can be generated from a DBML file or directly from a SQL Server database.

If you start from a DBML file, you can still modify that DBML file and then regenerate the source code and the mapping file. In this case, the generated files should not be modified because they could be overwritten in the future by code regeneration. You can customize generated classes by using a separate source code file, leveraging the *partial class* declaration of the generated class entities. This is the pattern used when you work with the Object Relational Designer.

If you generate code directly from a SQL Server database, the resulting source code file can still be customized using partial classes. Because the mapping information is stored in a separate XML file, you need to modify that file to customize mapping settings. Most likely, you will not regenerate these files in the future and can therefore make modifications directly on the generated files.

Creating a DBML File from Scratch

You can start writing a DBML file from scratch. In this case, you probably would not have an existing database file and would generate the database by calling the *DataContext.CreateDatabase* method on an instance of the generated class inherited from *DataContext*. This approach is theoretically possible when you write the XML file with a text editor, but in practice we expect that it will be done only by using the Object Relational Designer.

Choosing this approach means that entity classes are more important than the database design, and the database design itself is only a consequence of the object model you designed for your application. In other words, you see the relational database as a simple persistence layer (without stored procedures, triggers, and other database-specific features), which should not be accessed directly by consumers that are not using the LINQ to SQL engine. In the real world, we have found this can be the case for applications that use the database as the storage mechanism for complex configurations or to persist very simple information, typically in a stand-alone application with a local database. Whenever a client-server or multitier architecture is involved, chances are that additional consumer applications will access the same database—for example, a tool to generate reports, such as Reporting Services. These scenarios are more database-centric and require better control of the database design, removing the DBML-first approach as a viable option. In these situations, the best way of working is to define the database schema and the domain model separately and then map the entities of the domain model on the database tables.

SQLMetal

SQLMetal is a code-generation command-line tool that can be used to do the following:

- Generate a DBML file from a database
- Generate an entity's source code (and optionally a mapping file) from a database
- Generate an entity's source code (and optionally a mapping file) from a DBML file

The syntax for SQLMetal is the following:

```
sqlmetal [options] [<input file>]
```

In the following sections, we will provide several examples that demonstrate how to use SQL-Metal.

> **More Info**   A complete description of the SQLMetal command-line options is available at *http://msdn2.microsoft.com/library/bb386987.aspx*.

Generating a DBML File from a Database

To generate a DBML file, you need to specify the */dbml* option, followed by the filename to create. The syntax to specify the database to use depends on the type of the database. For example, a standard SQL Server database can be specified with the */server* and */database* options:

```
sqlmetal /server:localhost /database:Northwind /dbml:northwind.dbml
```

Windows authentication is used by default. If you want to use SQL Server authentication, you can use the */user* and */password* options. Alternatively, you can use the */conn* option, which cannot be used with */server*, */database*, */user*, or */password*. The following command line that uses */conn* is equivalent to the previous one, which used */server* and */database*:

```
sqlmetal /conn:"Server=localhost;Database=Northwind;Integrated Security=yes"
    /dbml:northwind.dbml
```

If you have the Northwind MDF file in the current directory and are using SQL Server Express, the same result can be obtained by using the following line, which makes use of the input file parameter:

```
sqlmetal /dbml:northwind.dbml Northwnd.mdf
```

Similarly, an SDF file handled by SQL Server Compact 3.5 can be specified as in the following line:

```
sqlmetal /dbml:northwind.dbml Northwind.sdf
```

By default, only tables are extracted from a database. You can also extract views, user-defined functions, and stored procedures by using */views*, */functions*, and */sprocs*, respectively, as shown here:

```
sqlmetal /server:localhost /database:Northwind /views /functions /sprocs
    /dbml:northwind.dbml
```

> **Note**   Remember that database views are treated like tables by LINQ to SQL.

Generating Source Code and a Mapping File from a Database

To generate an entity's source code, you need to specify the */code* option, followed by the filename to create. The language is inferred by the filename extension, using *CS* for C# and *VB* for Visual Basic. However, you can explicitly specify a language by using */language:csharp* or */language:vb* to get C# or Visual Basic code, respectively. The syntax to specify the database to use depends on the type of the database. A description of this syntax can be found in the preceding section, "Generating a DBML File from a Database."

For example, the following line generates C# source code for entities extracted from the Northwind database:

```
sqlmetal /server:localhost /database:Northwind /code:Northwind.cs
```

If you want all the tables and the views in Visual Basic, you can use the following command line:

```
sqlmetal /server:localhost /database:Northwind /views /code:Northwind.vb
```

Optionally, you can add the generation of an XML mapping file by using the */map* option, as in the following command line:

```
sqlmetal /server:localhost /database:Northwind /code:Northwind.cs /map:Northwind.xml
```

> **Important** When the XML mapping file is requested, the generated source code does not contain any attribute-based mapping.

There are a few options to control how the entity classes are generated. The */namespace* option controls the namespace of the generated code. (By default, there is no namespace.) The */context* option specifies the name of the class inherited from *DataContext* that will be generated. (By default, it is derived from the database name.) The */entitybase* option allows you to define the base class of the generated entity classes. (By default, there is no base class.) For example, the following command line generates all the entities in a *LinqBook* namespace, deriving them from the *DevLeap.LinqBase* base class:

```
sqlmetal /server:localhost /database:Northwind /namespace:LinqBook
    /entitybase:DevLeap.LinqBase /code:Northwind.cs
```

> **Note** If you specify a base class, you have to be sure that the class exists when the generated source code is compiled. It is a good practice to specify the full name of the base class.

If you want to generate serializable classes, you can specify */serialization:unidirectional* in the command line, as in the following example:

```
sqlmetal /server:localhost /database:Northwind /serialization:unidirectional
    /code:Northwind.cs
```

More Info   See the section "Entity Serialization" in Chapter 5 for further information about serialization of LINQ to SQL entities, as well as Chapter 18, "LINQ and the Windows Communication Foundation."

Finally, there is a */pluralize* option that controls how the names of entities and properties are generated. When this option is specified, the entity names generated are singular, but table names in the *DataContext*-derived class properties are plural, regardless of the table name's form. In other words, the Customer (or Customers) table generates a *Customer* entity class and a *Customers* property in the *DataContext*-derived class.

Generating Source Code and a Mapping File from a DBML File

The generation of source code and a mapping file from a DBML file is identical to the syntax required to generate the same results from a database. The only change is that instead of specifying a database connection, you have to specify the DBML filename as an input file parameter of the command-line syntax. For example, the following command line generates the C# class code for the Northwind.DBML model description:

```
sqlmetal /code:Northwind.cs Northwind.dbml
```

Important   Remember to use the */dbml* option only to generate a DBML file. You do not have to specify */dbml* when you want to use a DBML file as input.

You can use all the options for generating source code and a mapping file that we described in the "Generating Source Code and a Mapping File from a Database" section.

Using the Object Relational Designer

The Object Relational Designer (O/R Designer) is a graphical editor integrated with Visual Studio 2008. It is the standard editor for a DBML file. It allows you to create new entities, edit existing ones, and generate an entity starting from an object in a SQL Server database. (There is support for tables, views, stored procedures, and user-defined functions.) A DBML file can be created by choosing the LINQ To SQL Classes template in the Add New Item dialog box, which you can see in Figure 6-2, or by adding an existing DBML file to a project (using the Add Existing Item command and picking the Data category).

The design surface allows you to drag items from a connection opened in Server Explorer. Dragging an item results in the creation of a new entity deriving its content from the imported object. Alternatively, you can create new entities by dragging items such as Class, Association, and Inheritance from the toolbox. In Figure 6-3, you can see an empty DMBL file opened in Microsoft Visual Studio. On the left are the Toolbox and Server Explorer elements ready to be dragged onto the design surface.

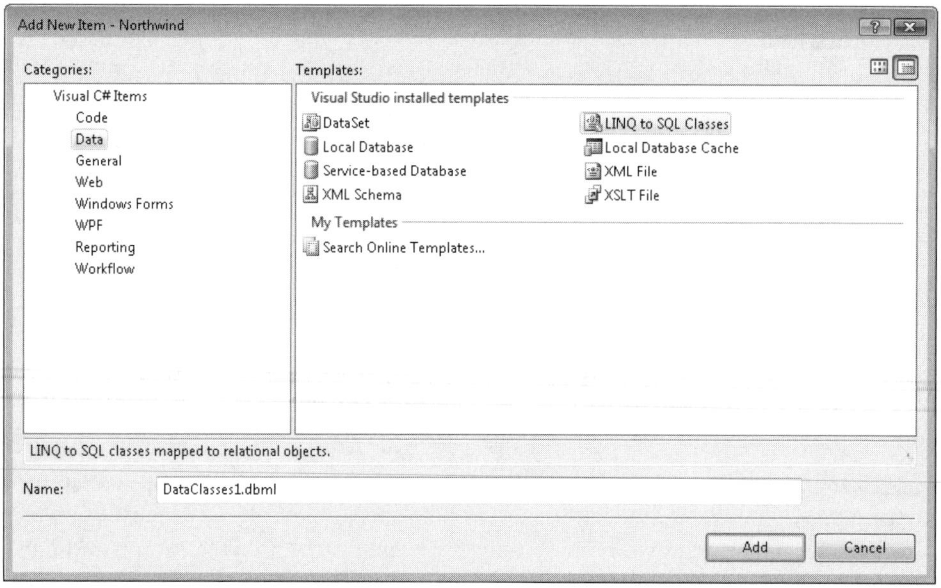

Figure 6-2   Add New Item dialog box

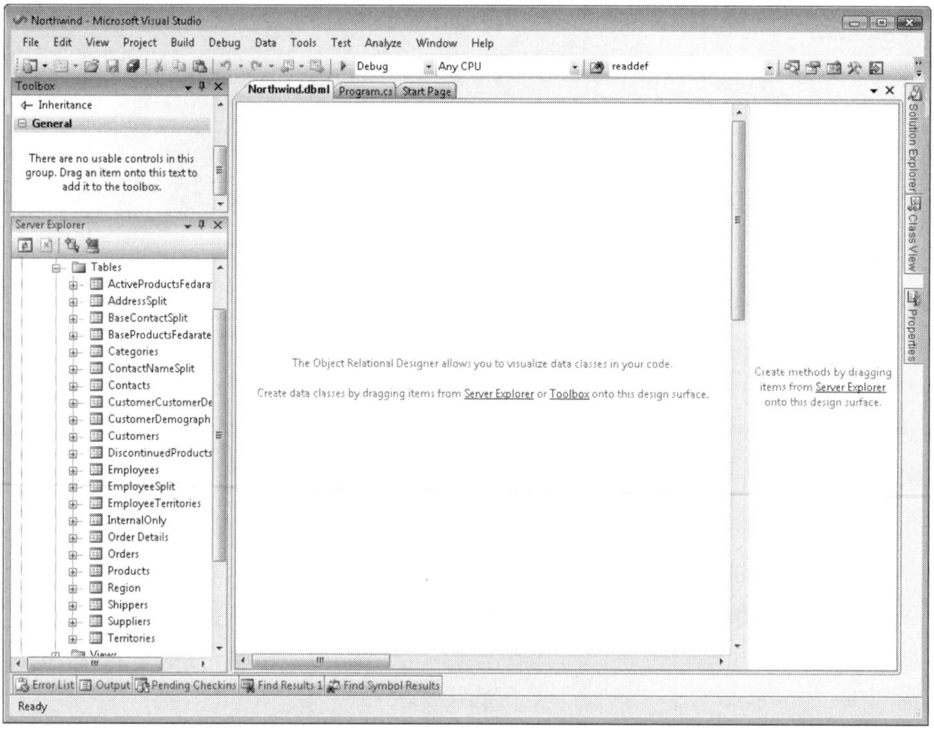

Figure 6-3   Empty DBML file opened with the Object Relational Designer

Dragging two tables, Orders and Order Details, from Server Explorer to the left pane of the DBML design surface results in a DBML file that contains two entity classes, *Order* and

Order_Detail, as you can see in Figure 6-4. Because a foreign key constraint exists in the database between the Order Details and Orders tables, an *Association* between the *Order* and *Order_Detail* entities is generated too.

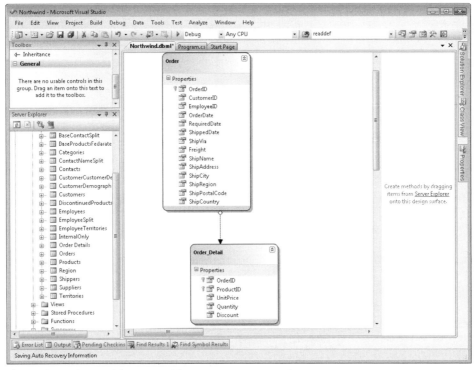

Figure 6-4   Two entities created from a server connection

You can see that plural names have been translated into singular-name entity classes. However, the names of the *Table<T>* properties in the *NorthwindDataContext* class are plural (*Orders* and *Order_Details*), as you can see in the bottom part of the Class View shown in Figure 6-5.

The Class View is updated by Visual Studio 2008 each time you save the DBML file. Every time that this file is saved, two other files are saved too: a *.layout* file, which is an XML file containing information about the design surface, and a *.cs/.vb* file, which is the source code generated for the entity classes. In other words, each time a DBML file is saved from Visual Studio 2008, the code generator is run on the DBML file and the source code for those entities is updated. In Figure 6-6, you can see the files related to our *Northwind.dbml* in Solution Explorer. We have a *Northwind.dbml.layout* file and a *Northwind.designer.cs* file.

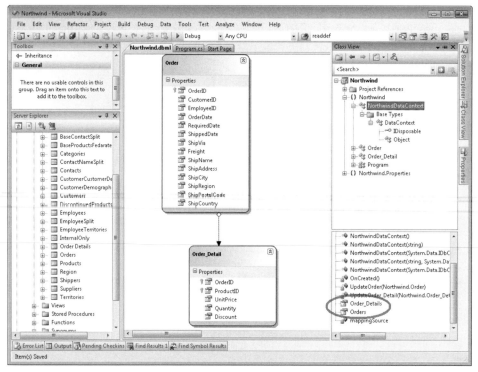

Figure 6-5   Plural names for *Table<T>* properties in a *DataContext*-derived class

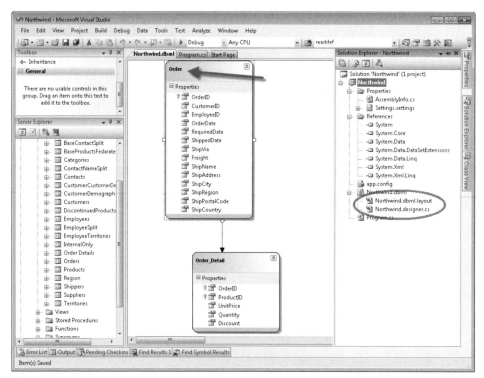

Figure 6-6   Files automatically generated for a DBML file are shown in Solution Explorer

You should not modify the source code produced by the code generator. Instead, you should edit another file containing corresponding partial classes. This file is the *Northwind.cs* file shown in Figure 6-7, which is created the first time you select the View/Code command for the currently selected item in the Object Relational Designer. In our example, we chose View, Code from the context menu on the Order entity, which is indicated by the arrow in Figure 6-6.

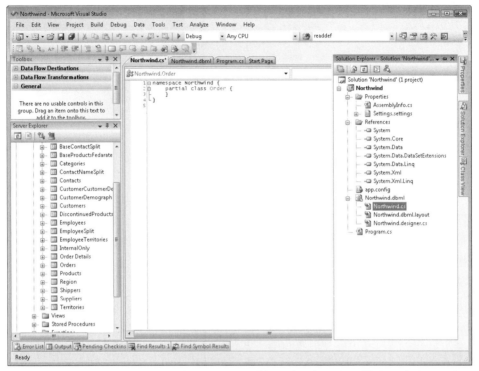

Figure 6-7   Custom code is stored in a separate file under the DBML file in Solution Explorer

At this point, most of the work will be done in the Properties window for each DBML item and in the source code. In the remaining part of this chapter, you will see the most important activities that can be performed with the DBML editor. We do not cover how an entity can be extended at the source-code level because this topic has been covered in previous chapters.

DataContext Properties

Each DBML file defines a class that inherits *DataContext*. This class will have a *Table<T>* member for each entity defined in the DBML file. The class itself will be generated following requirements specified in the Properties window. In Figure 6-8, you can see the Properties window for our *NorthwindDataContext* class.

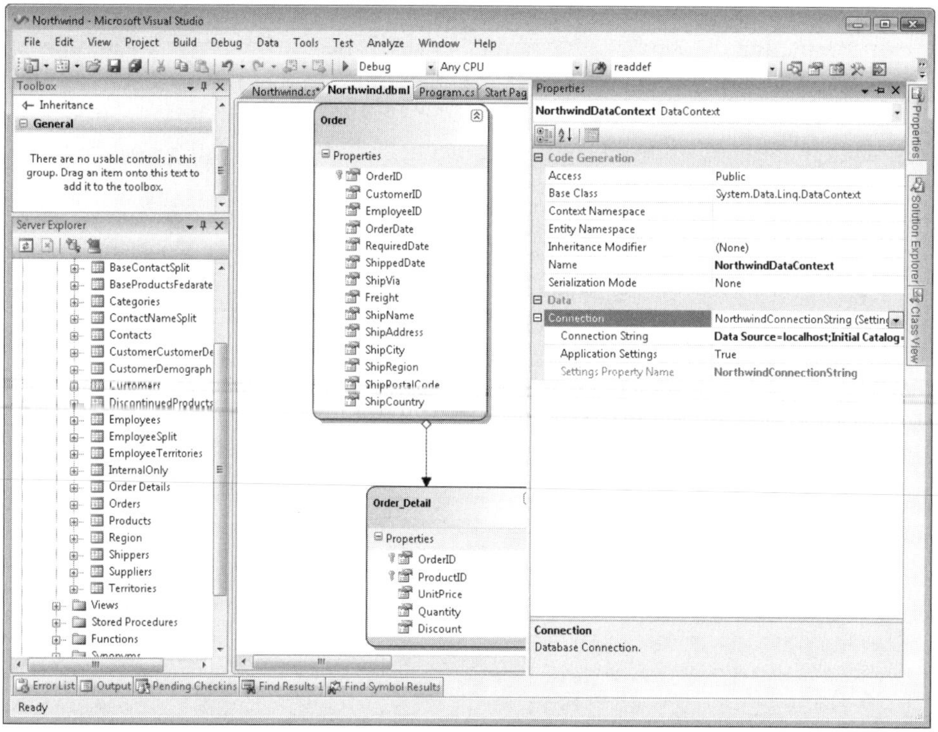

Figure 6-8 *DataContext* properties

The properties for *DataContext* are separated into two groups. The simpler one is Data, which contains the default *Connection* for *DataContext*: if you do not specify a connection when you create a *NorthwindDataContext* instance in your code, this will be the connection used. With Application Settings, you can specify whether the Application Settings file should be used to set connection information. In that case, *Settings Property Name* will be the property to use in the Application Settings file.

The group of properties named Code Generation requires a more detailed explanation, which is provided in Table 6-1.

Table 6-1   Code-Generation Properties for *DataContext*

Property	Description
Access	Access modifier for the *DataContext*-derived class. It can be only *Public* or *Internal*. By default, it is *Public*.
Base Class	Base class for the data context specialized class. By default, it is *System.Data.Linq.DataContext*. You can define your own base class, which would probably be inherited by *DataContext*.
Context Namespace	Namespace of the generated *DataContext*-derived class only. It does not apply to the entity classes. Use the same value in *Context Namespace* and *Entity Namespace* if you want to generate *DataContext* and entity classes in the same namespace.

Table 6-1   Code-Generation Properties for *DataContext*

Property	Description
Entity Namespace	Namespace of the generated entities only. It does not apply to the *DataContext*-derived class. Use the same value in *Context Namespace* and *Entity Namespace* if you want to generate *DataContext* and entity classes in the same namespace.
Inheritance Modifier	Inheritance modifier to be used in the class declaration. It can be *(None)*, *abstract*, or *sealed*. By default, it is *(None)*.
Name	Name of the *DataContext*-derived class. By default, it is the name of the database with the suffix "DataContext". For example, *Northwind-DataContext* is the default name for a *DataContext*-derived class generated for the Northwind database.
Serialization Mode	If this property is set to *Unidirectional*, the entity's source code is decorated with *DataContract* and *DataMember* for serialization purposes. By default, it is set to *None*.

Entity Class

When you select an entity class on the designer, you can change its properties in the Properties window. In Figure 6-9, you can see the Properties window for the selected *Order* entity class.

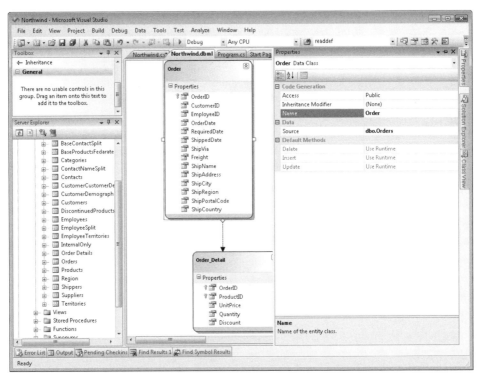

Figure 6-9   Entity class properties

The properties for an entity class are separated into three groups. The Data group contains only *Source*, which is the name of the table in the SQL Server database, including the owner or schema name. This property is automatically filled when the entity is generated by dragging a table onto the designer surface.

The Default Methods group contains three read-only properties—named *Delete*, *Insert*, and *Update*—which indicate the presence of custom Create, Update, Delete (CUD) methods. These properties are disabled if no stored procedures have been defined in the same DBML file. If you have stored procedures to be called for insert, update, and delete operations on an entity, you first have to import them into the DBML file (as described in the "Stored Procedures and User-Defined Functions" section later in this chapter). Then you can edit these properties by associating the corresponding procedure for each of the CUD operations.

Finally, the properties in the group Code Generation are explained in Table 6-2.

Table 6-2   Code-Generation Properties for an Entity Class

Property	Description
Access	Access modifier for the entity class. It can be only *Public* or *Internal*. By default, it is *Public*.
Inheritance Modifier	Inheritance modifier to be used in the class declaration. It can be *(None)*, *abstract*, or *sealed*. By default, it is *(None)*.
Name	Name of the entity class. By default, it is the singular name of the table dragged from a database in the Server Explorer window. For example, *Order* is the default name for the table named Orders in the Northwind database.
	Remember that the entity class will be defined in the namespace defined by the Entity Namespace of the related *DataContext* class.

Entity Members

When an entity is generated by dragging a table from Server Explorer, it has a set of predefined members that are created by reading table metadata from the relational database. Each of these members has its own settings in the Properties window. You can add new members by clicking on Add/Property on the contextual menu, or simply by pressing the INS key. You can delete a member by pressing the DEL key or by clicking Delete on the contextual menu. Unfortunately, the order of the members in an entity cannot be modified through the Object Relational Designer and can be changed only by manually modifying the DBML file and moving the physical order of the Column tags within a *Type*.

Warning   You can open and modify the DBML file with a text editor such as Notepad. If you try to open the DBML file with Visual Studio 2008, remember to use the Open With option from the drop-down list for the Open button in the Open File dialog box, picking the XML Editor choice to use the XML editor integrated in Visual Studio 2008; otherwise, the Object Relational Designer will be used by default. You can also use the Open With command on a DBML file shown in the Solution Explorer in Visual Studio 2008.

When you select an entity member on the designer, you can change its properties in the Properties window. In Figure 6-10, you can see the Properties window for the selected *OrderID* member of the *Order* entity class.

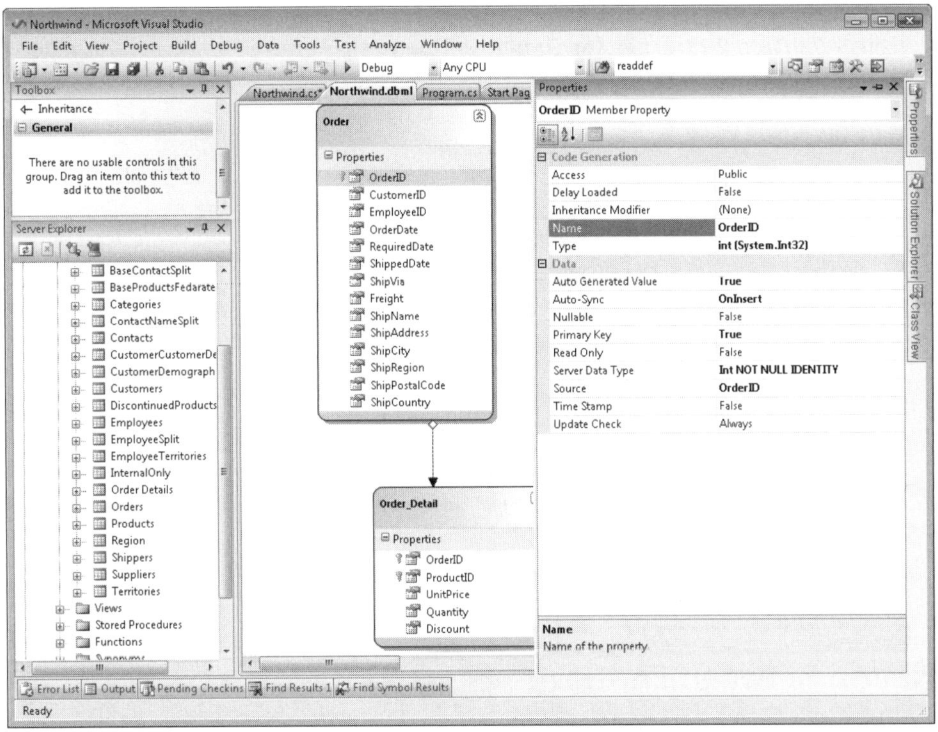

Figure 6-10   Entity member properties

The properties for an entity member are separated into two groups. The Code Generation group controls the way member attributes are generated, and its properties are described in Table 6-3.

Table 6-3   Code-Generation Properties for Data Members of an Entity

Property	Description
Access	Access modifier for the entity class. It can be *Public, Protected, Protected Internal, Internal,* or *Private.* By default, it is *Public.*
Delay Loaded	If this property is set to *true,* the data member will not be loaded until its first access. This is implemented by declaring the member with the *Link<T>* class, which is explained in the "Deferred Loading of Properties" section in Chapter 4. By default, it is set to *false.*
Inheritance Modifier	Inheritance modifier to be used in the member declaration. It can be *(None), new, virtual, override,* or *virtual.* By default, it is *(None).*
Name	Name of the member. By default, it is the same column name used in the *Source* property.
Type	Type of the data member. This type can be modified into a *Nullable<T>* according to the *Nullable* setting in the Data group or properties.

The Data group contains important mapping information between the entity data member and the table column in the database. The properties in this group are described in Table 6-4. Many of these properties correspond to settings of the *Column* attribute, which are described in Chapter 4 and Chapter 5.

Table 6-4   Data Properties for Data Members of an Entity

Property	Description
Auto Generated Value	Corresponds to the *IsDbGenerated* setting of the *Column* attribute.
Auto-Sync	Corresponds to the *AutoSync* setting of the *Column* attribute.
Nullable	If this property is set to *true*, the type of the data member is declared as *Nullable<T>*, where *T* is the type defined in the *Type* property. (See Table 6-3.)
Primary Key	Corresponds to the *IsPrimaryKey* setting of the *Column* attribute.
Read Only	If this property is set to *true*, only the *get* accessor is defined for the property that publicly exposes this member of the entity class. By default, it is set to *false*. Considering its behavior, this property could be part of the Code Generation group.
Server Data Type	Corresponds to the *DbType* setting of the *Column* attribute.
Source	It is the name of the column in the database table. Corresponds to the *Name* setting of the *Column* attribute.
Time Stamp	Corresponds to the *IsVersion* setting of the *Column* attribute.
Update Check	Corresponds to the *UpdateCheck* setting of the *Column* attribute.

Association Between Entities

An association represents a relationship between entities, which can be expressed through *EntitySet<T>*, *EntityRef<T>*, and the *Association* attribute we describe in Chapter 4. In Figure 6-4, you can see the association between the *Order* and *Order_Detail* entities expressed as an arrow that links these entities. In the Object Relational Designer, you can define associations between entities in two ways:

- When one or more entities are imported from a database, the existing foreign key constraints between tables, which are also entities of the designed model, are transformed into corresponding associations between entities.

- Selecting the Association item in the Toolbox window, you can link two entities defining an association that might or might not have a corresponding foreign key in the relational database. To build the association, you must have two data members of the same type in the related entities that define the relationship. On the parent side of the relationship, the member must also have the *Primary Key* property set to *True*.

> **Note**   An existing database might not have the foreign key relationship that corresponds to an association defined between LINQ to SQL entities. However, if you generate the relational database using the *DataContext.CreateDatabase* method of your model, the foreign keys are automatically generated for existing associations.

When you create an association or double-click an existing one, the dialog box shown in Figure 6-11 is displayed. The two combo boxes, Parent Class and Child Class, are disabled when editing an existing association; they are enabled only when you create a new association by using the context menu and right-clicking on an empty area of the design surface. Under Association Properties, you must select the members composing the primary key under the Parent Class, and then you have to choose the appropriate corresponding members in the Child Class.

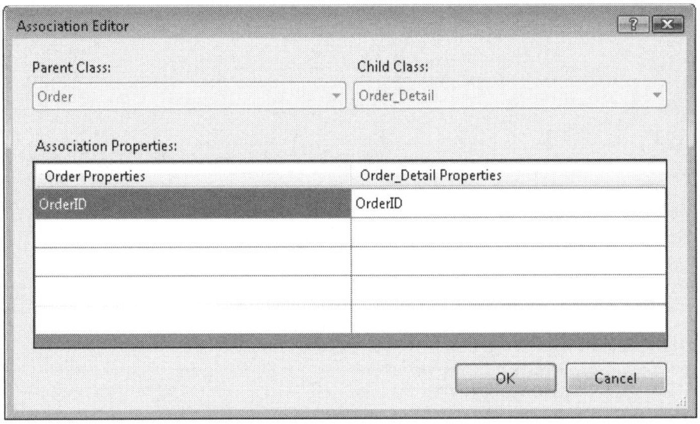

Figure 6-11   Association properties

After you have created an association, you can edit it in more detail by selecting the arrow in the graphical model and then editing it in the Properties window, as shown in Figure 6-12.

By default, the *Association* is defined in a bidirectional way. The child class gets a property with the same name as the parent class (*Order_Detail.Order* in our example), just to get a typed reference to the parent itself. In the parent class, a particular property represents the set of child elements (*Order.Order_Details* in our example). Table 6-5 provides an explanation of all the properties available in an association. As you will see, most of these settings can significantly change the output produced.

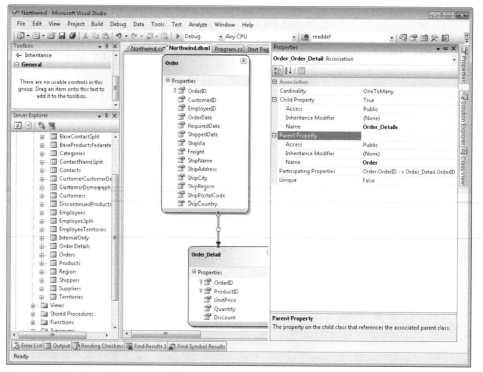

Figure 6-12 Association properties

Table 6-5   Association Properties

Property	Description
Cardinality	Defines the cardinality of the association between parent and child nodes. This property has an impact only on the member defined in the parent class. Usually and by default, it is set to *OneToMany*, which will generate a member in the parent class that will enumerate a sequence of child items. The only other possible value is *OneToOne*, which will generate a single property of the same type as the referenced child entity. See the sidebar "Understanding the Cardinality Property" for more information.
	By default, this property is set to *OneToMany*. Using the *One-ToOne* setting is recommended, for example, when you split a logical entity that has many data members into more than one database table.
Child Property	If this property is set to *False*, the parent class will not contain a property with a collection or a reference of the child nodes. By default, it is set to *True*.
Child Property/Access	Access modifier for the member children in the parent class. It can be *Public* or *Internal*. By default, it is *Public*.

Table 6-5   Association Properties

Property	Description
Child Property/Inheritance Modifier	Inheritance modifier to be used in the member children in the parent class. It can be *(None)*, *new*, *virtual*, *override*, or *virtual*. By default, it is *(None)*.
Child Property/Name	Name of the member children in the parent class. By default, it has the plural name of the child entity class. If you set *Cardinality* to *OneToOne*, you would probably change this name to the singular form.
Parent Property/Access	Access modifier for the parent member in the child class. It can be *Public* or *Internal*. By default, it is *Public*.
Parent Property/Inheritance Modifier	Inheritance modifier to be used in the parent member in the child class. It can be *(None)*, *new*, *virtual*, *override*, or *virtual*. By default, it is *(None)*.
Parent Property/Name	Name of the parent member in the child class. By default, it has the same singular name as the parent entity class.
Participating Properties	Displays the list of related properties that make the association work. Editing this property opens the Association Editor, which is shown in Figure 6-11.
Unique	Corresponds to the *IsUnique* setting of the *Association* attribute. It should be *True* when *Cardinality* is set to *OneToOne*. However, you are in charge of keeping these properties synchronized. *Cardinality* controls only the code generated for the *Child Property*, while *Unique* controls only the *Association* attribute, which is the only one used by the LINQ to SQL engine to compose SQL queries. By default, it is set to *False*.

If you have a parent-child relationship in the same table, the Object Relational Designer automatically detects it from the foreign key constraint in the relational table whenever you drag it into the model. It is recommended that you change the automatically generated name for *Child Property* and *Parent Property*. For example, importing the Employees table from Northwind results in *Employees* for the Child Property Name and *Employee1* for the Parent Property Name. You can rename these more appropriately as *DirectReports* and *Manager*, respectively.

Warning   The Child Property and Parent Property of a parent-child *Association* referencing the same table cannot be used in a *DataLoadOptions.LoadWith<T>* call because it does not support cycles.

One-to-One Relationships

Most of the time, you create a one-to-many association between two entities, and the default values of the Association properties should be sufficient. However, it is easy to get lost with a one-to-one relationship. The first point to make is about when to use a one-to-one relationship.

A one-to-one relationship should be intended as a one-to-zero-or-one relationship, where the related child entity might or might not exist. For example, we can define the simple model shown in Figure 6-13. For each *Contact*, we can have a related *Customer*, containing its amount of *Credit*. In the Properties window, you can see highlighted in bold the properties of the association between *Contact* and *Customer* that have been changed from their default values.

Figure 6-13 Association properties of a one-to-one relationship

Cardinality should already be set to *OneToOne* when you create the *Association*. However, it is always better to check it. You also have to set the *Unique* property to *True* and change the *Child Name* property to the singular *Customer* value.

The *ContactID* member in the *Contact* entity is a primary key defined as *INT IDENTITY* in the database. Thus, it has the *Auto Generated Value* set to *True* and *Auto-Sync* set to *OnInsert*. In the *Customer* entity, you have another member called *ContactID*, which is also a primary key but is not generated from the database. In fact, you will use the key generated for a *Contact* to assign the *Customer.ContactID* value. Thanks to the *Contact.Customer* and *Customer.Contact* properties, you can simply assign the relationship by setting one of these properties, without worrying about the underlying *ContactID* field. In the following code, you can see an example of two *Contact* instances saved to the *DataContext*; one of them is associated with a *Customer* instance:

```
RelationshipDataContext db = new RelationshipDataContext();

Contact contactPaolo = new Contact();
contactPaolo.LastName = "Pialorsi";
contactPaolo.FirstName = "Paolo";

Contact contactMarco = new Contact();
Customer customer = new Customer();
contactMarco.LastName = "Russo";
contactMarco.FirstName = "Marco";
contactMarco.Customer = customer;
customer.Credit = 1000;

db.Contacts.InsertOnSubmit(contactPaolo);
db.Contacts.InsertOnSubmit(contactMarco);
db.SubmitChanges();
```

We created the relationship by setting the *Contact.Customer* property, but the same result could have been obtained by setting the *Customer.Contact* property. In other words, thanks to the synchronization code automatically produced by the code generator, in our one-to-one relationship the line

```
contactMarco.Customer = customer;
```

produces the same result as writing

```
customer.Contact = contactMarco;
```

However, you have to remember that the *Customer.Contact* member is mandatory if you create a *Contact* instance, while *Contact.Customer* can be left set to the default null value if no *Customer* is related to that *Contact*. At this point, it should be clear why the direction of the association is relevant even in a one-to-one relationship. As we said, it is not really a one-to-one relationship but a one-to-zero-or-one relationship, where the association stems from the parent that always exists to the child that could not exist.

> **Warning**   A common error made when defining a one-to-one association is using the wrong direction for the association. In our example, if the association went from *Customer* to *Contact*, it would not generate a compilation error; instead, our previous code would throw an exception when trying to submit changes to the database.

Understanding the *Cardinality* Property

To better understand the behavior of the *Cardinality* property, let's take a look at the generated code. This is an excerpt of the code generated with *Cardinality* set to *OneToMany*. The member is exposed with the plural name of *Customers*.

```
public partial class Contact {
    public Contact() {
        this._Customers = new EntitySet<Customer>(
                            new Action<Customer>(this.attach_Customers),
                            new Action<Customer>(this.detach_Customers));
    }

    private EntitySet<Customer> _Customers;

    [Association(Name="Contact_Customer", Storage="_Customers",
                 ThisKey="ContactID", OtherKey="ContactID")]
    public EntitySet<Customer> Customers {
        get { return this._Customers; }
        set { this._Customers.Assign(value); }
    }
}
```

And this is the code with *Cardinality* set to *OneToOne*. The member is exposed with the singular name of *Customer*. (You need to manually change the *Child Property Name* if you change the *Cardinality* property.)

```
public partial class Contact {
    public Contact() {
        this._Customer = default(EntityRef<Customer>);
    }

    private EntityRef<Customer> _Customer;

    [Association(Name="Contact_Customer", Storage="_Customer",
                 ThisKey="ContactID", IsUnique=true, IsForeignKey=false)]
    public Customer Customer {
        get { return this._Customer.Entity; }
        set {
            Customer previousValue = this._Customer.Entity;
            if ((previousValue != value)
                || (this._Customer.HasLoadedOrAssignedValue == false)) {
                this.SendPropertyChanging();
                if ((previousValue != null)) {
                    this._Customer.Entity = null;
                    previousValue.Contact = null;
                }
                this._Customer.Entity = value;
```

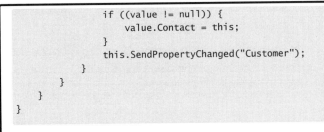

```
            if ((value != null)) {
                value.Contact = this;
            }
            this.SendPropertyChanged("Customer");
        }
      }
    }
}
```

As you can see, in the parent class we get a *Contact.Customer* member of type *Entity-Ref<Customer>* if *Cardinality* is set to *OneToOne*. Otherwise, we get a *Contact.Customers* member of type *EntitySet<Customer>* if *Cardinality* is set to *OneToMany*. Finally, the code generated for the *Customer* class does not depend on the *Cardinality* setting.

Entity Inheritance

LINQ to SQL supports the definition of a hierarchy of classes all bound to the same source table. The LINQ to SQL engine generates the right class in the hierarchy, based on the value of a specific row of that table. Each class is identified by a specific value in a column, following the *InheritanceMapping* attribute applied to the base class, as we saw in the section "Entity Inheritance" in Chapter 4.

Creating a hierarchy of classes in the Object Relational Designer starting from an existing database requires you to complete the following actions:

1. Create a Data class for each class of the hierarchy. You can drag the table for the base class from Server Explorer, and then create other empty classes by dragging a Class item from the toolbox. Rename the classes you add according to their intended use.

2. Set the *Source* property for each added class equal to the *Source* property of the base class you dragged from the data source.

3. After you have at least a base class and a derived class, create the Inheritance relationship. Select the Inheritance item in the toolbox, and draw a connection starting from the deriving class and ending with the base class. You can also define a multiple-level hierarchy.

4. If you have members in the base class that will be used only by some derived classes, you can cut and paste them in the designer. (Note that dragging and dropping members is not allowed.)

For example, in Figure 6-14 you can see the result of the following operations:

1. Drag the Contact table from Northwind.

2. Add the other empty Data classes (*Employee*, *CompanyContact*, *Customer*, *Shipper*, and *Supplier*).

3. Put the *dbo.Contacts* value into the *Source* property for all added Data classes. (Note that *dbo.Contacts* is already the *Source* value of the base class *Contact*.)

4. Define the *Inheritance* between *Employee* and *Contact* and between *CustomerContact* and *Contact*.

5. Define the *Inheritance* between *Customer* and *CompanyContact*, *Shipper* and *Company-Contact*, and *Supplier* and *CompanyContact*.

6. Cut the *CompanyName* member from *Contact*, and paste it into *CompanyContact*.

7. Set the Discriminator Property of any *Inheritance* item to *ContactType*. (See Table 6-6 for further information about this property.)

8. Set the Inheritance Default Property of any *Inheritance* item to *Contact*.

9. Set the Base Class Discriminator Value of any *Inheritance* item to *Contact*.

10. Set the Derived Class Discriminator Value to *Employee*, *Customer*, *Shipper*, or *Supplier* for each corresponding *Inheritance* item.

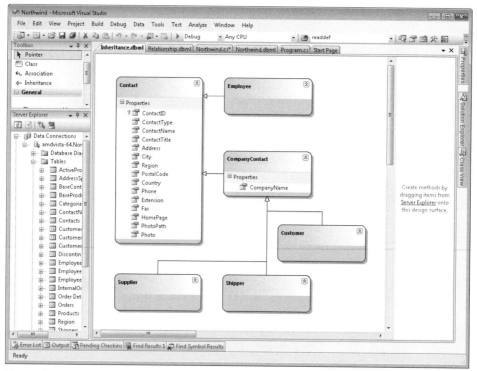

Figure 6-14   Design of a class hierarchy based on the Northwind.Contact table

Our example uses an intermediate class (*CompanyContact*) to simplify the other derived classes (*Supplier*, *Shipper*, and *Customer*). We skipped the *CompanyContact* class that sets the Derived Class Discriminator Value because that intermediate class does not have concrete data in the database table.

In Table 6-6, you can see an explanation of all the properties available for an Inheritance item. We used these properties to produce the design shown in Figure 6-14.

Table 6-6   Inheritance Properties

Property	Description
Inheritance Default	This is the type that will be used to create entities for rows that do not match any defined inheritance codes (which are the values defined for *Base Class Discriminator Value* and *Derived Class Discriminator Value*). This setting defines which of the generated *InheritanceMapping* attributes will have the *IsDefault=true* setting.
Base Class Discriminator Value	This is a value of the *Discriminator Property* that specifies the base class type. When you set this property for an *Inheritance* item, all *Inheritance* items originating from the same data class will assume the same value.
Derived Class Discriminator Value	This is a value of the *Discriminator Property* that specifies the derived class type. It corresponds to the *Code* setting of the *InheritanceMapping* attribute.
Discriminator Property	The column in the database that is used to discriminate between entities. When you set this property for an *Inheritance* item, all *Inheritance* items originating from the same data class will assume the same value. The selected data member in the base class will be decorated with the *IsDiscriminator=true* setting in the *Column* attribute.

Stored Procedures and User-Defined Functions

Dragging a stored procedure or a user-defined function from the Server Explorer window to the Object Relational Designer surface creates a method in the *DataContext* class corresponding to that stored procedure or that user-defined function. In Figure 6-15, you can see an example of the [Customer By City] stored procedure dragged onto the Methods pane of the Object Relational Designer.

 Note   You can show and hide the Methods pane by using the context menu that opens when you right-click on the design surface.

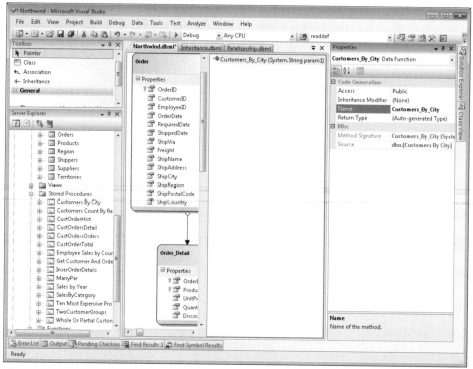

Figure 6-15   Stored procedure imported into a DBML file

When you import either a stored procedure or a user-defined function, a *Data Function* item is created in the *DataContext*-derived class. The properties of a *Data Function* are separated into two groups. The Misc group contains two read-only properties, *Method Signature* and *Source*. The *Source* property contains the name of the stored procedure or user-defined function in the database. The value of the *Method Signature* property is constructed with the *Name* property (shown in Table 6-7) and the parameters of the stored procedure or user-defined function. The group of properties named Code Generation requires a more detailed explanation, which is included in Table 6-7.

Table 6-7   Code-Generation Properties for *Data Function*

Property	Description
Access	Access modifier for the generated method in the *DataContext*-derived class. It can be *Public, Protected, Protected Internal, Internal,* or *Private.* By default, it is *Public.*
Inheritance Modifier	Inheritance modifier to be used in the member declaration. It can be *(None), new, virtual, override,* or *virtual.* By default, it is *(None).*

Table 6-7   Code-Generation Properties for *Data Function*

Property	Description
Name	Name of the method representing a stored procedure or a user-defined function in the database. By default, it is derived from the name of the stored procedure or the user-defined function, replacing invalid characters in C# or Visual Basic with an underscore (_). It corresponds to the *Name* setting of the *Function* attribute.
Return Type	Type returned by the method. It can be a common language runtime (CLR) type for scalar-valued user-defined functions, or *Class Data* for stored procedures and table-valued user-defined functions. In the latter case, by default it is *(Auto-generated Type)*. After it has been changed to an existing *Data Class* name, this property cannot be reverted to *(Auto-generated Type)*. See the "Return Type of Data Function" section for more information.

Return Type of Data Function

Usually a stored procedure or a table-valued user-defined function returns a number of rows, which in LINQ to SQL becomes a sequence of instances of an entity class. (We discussed this in the "Stored Procedures and User-Defined Functions" section in Chapter 4.) By default, the *Return Type* property is set to *(Auto-generated Type)*, which means that the code generator creates a class with as many members as the columns returned by SQL Server. For example, the following excerpt of code is part of the *Customers_By_CityResult* type automatically generated to handle the *Customer_By_City* result. (The *get* and *set* accessors have been removed from the properties declaration for the sake of conciseness.)

```
public partial class Customers_By_CityResult {
    private string _CustomerID;
    private string _ContactName;
    private string _CompanyName;
    private string _City;

    public Customers_By_CityResult() { }

    [Column(Storage="_CustomerID", DbType="NChar(5) NOT NULL",
            CanBeNull=false)]
    public string CustomerID { ... }

    [Column(Storage="_ContactName", DbType="NVarChar(30)")]
    public string ContactName { ... }

    [Column(Storage="_CompanyName", DbType="NVarChar(40) NOT NULL",
            CanBeNull=false)]
    public string CompanyName { ... }

    [Column(Storage="_City", DbType="NVarChar(15)")]
    public string City { ... }
}
```

However, you can instruct the code generator to use an existing *Data Class* to store the data resulting from a stored procedure call, setting the *Return Type* property to the desired type. The combo box in the Properties window presents all types defined in the *DataContext*. You should select a type compatible with the data returned by SQL Server.

> **Important**   *Return Type* must have at least a public member with the same name of a returned column. If you specify a type with public members that do not correspond to returned columns, these "missing" members will have a default value.

You can create an entity class specifically to handle the result coming from a stored procedure or user-defined function call. In that case, you might want to define a class without specifying a *Source* property. In this way, you can control all the details of the returned type. You can also use a class corresponding to a database table. In this case, remember that you can modify the returned entity. However, to make the *SubmitChanges* work, you need to get the initial value for all required data members of the entity (at least those with the *UpdateCheck* constraint) in order to match the row at the moment of update. In other words, if the stored procedure or user-defined function does not return all the members for an entity, it is better to create an entity dedicated to this purpose, using only the returned columns and specifying the destination table as the *Source* property.

> **Note**   To map *Return Type* to an entity during the method construction, you can drag the stored procedure or user-defined function, dropping it on the entity class that you want to use as a return type. In this way, the method is created only if the entity class has a corresponding column in the result for each of the entity members. If this condition is not satisfied, an error message is displayed and the operation is cancelled.

Mapping to Delete, Insert, and Update Operations

All imported stored procedures can be used to customize the Delete, Insert, and Update operations of the entity class. To do that, after you import the stored procedures into *DataContext*, you need to bind them to the corresponding operation in the entity class. Figure 6-16 shows the Configure Behavior dialog box that allows mapping of all the method arguments with the corresponding class properties.

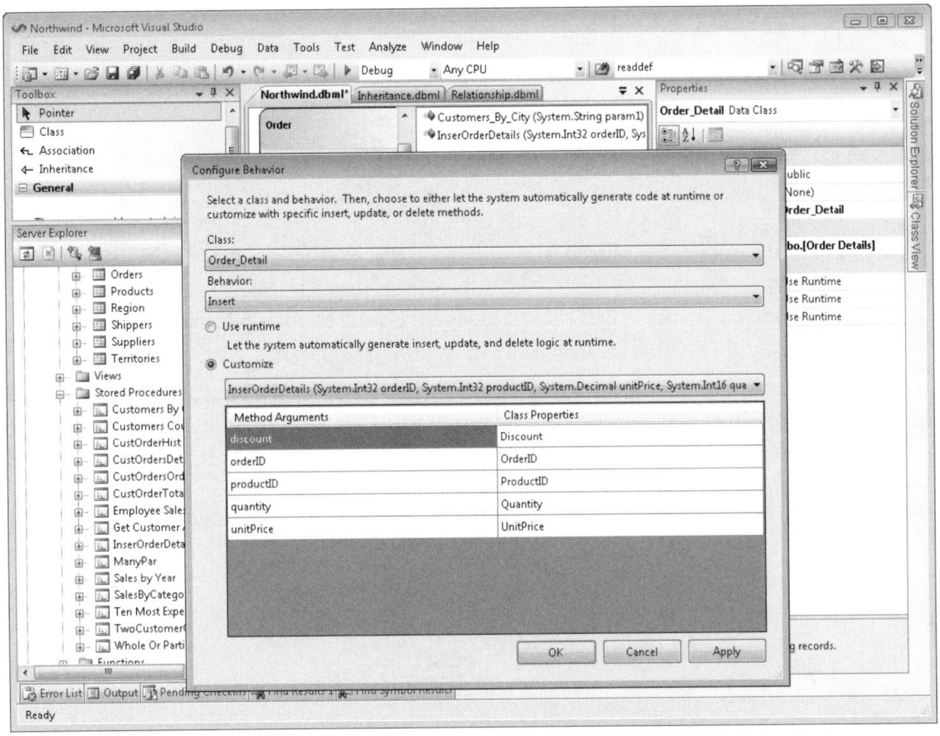

Figure 6-16   Use of a stored procedure to insert an *Order_Detail*

> **More Info**   For more information, see the "Customizing Insert, Update, and Delete" section in Chapter 5.

Views and Schema Support

All views in a database can be used to generate an entity class in the DBML file. However, LINQ to SQL does not know whether the view is updatable or not. It is your responsibility to make the right use of an entity derived from a view, trying to update instances of that entity only if they come from an updatable view.

If the database has tables in different schemas, the Object Relational Designer does not consider them when creating the name of data classes or data functions. The schema is maintained as part of the *Source* value, but it does not participate in the name construction of generated objects. You can rename the objects, but they cannot be defined in different namespaces, because all the entity classes are defined in the same namespace, which is controlled by the *Entity Namespace* property of the generated *DataContext*-derived class.

> **More Info**   Other third-party code generators might support the use of namespaces, using
> SQL Server 2005 schemas to create entities in corresponding namespaces.

Summary

In this chapter, we took a look at the tools that are available to generate LINQ to SQL entities
and *DataContext* classes. The .NET Framework SDK includes the command-line tool named
SQLMetal. Visual Studio 2008 has a graphical editor known as the Object Relational
Designer. Both allow the creation of a DBML file, the generation of source code in C# and
Visual Basic, and the creation of an external XML mapping file. The Object Relational
Designer also allows you to edit an existing DBML file, dynamically importing existing tables,
views, stored procedures, and user-defined functions from an existing SQL Server database.

Chapter 7
LINQ to DataSet

The .NET native type *System.Data.DataSet* is an in-memory representation of a set of data. It is useful for getting a disconnected copy of data that comes from an external data source. Regardless of the data source, the internal representation of a *DataSet* follows the relational model, including tables, constraints, and relationships among the tables. In other words, you can consider the *DataSet* as a sort of in-memory relational database, which makes it a good target for a LINQ implementation. In this chapter, we will see how LINQ can be used with a *DataSet*, to both query and populate it.

Introducing LINQ to DataSet

A *DataSet* is an in-memory set of objects, making it a target for LINQ to Objects. All the operations you learned about in Chapter 3, "LINQ to Objects," are applicable when you query a *DataSet*. However, a small operation is needed to query a *DataTable* contained in a *DataSet*. The *DataTable* class does not implement *IEnumerable<T>*, so you need to create a wrapper object that implements *IEnumerable<T>* and allows LINQ queries. The *Enumerable-RowCollection* is a class that does this work, and you can create it by simply calling the extension method *AsEnumerable* on a *DataTable*. This and other extension methods that we describe in this chapter, such as *AsDataView* and *CopyToDataTable*, are defined in the *Data-TableExtensions* class, which is included in the *System.Data* namespace and is part of the *System.Data.DataSetExtensions* assembly.

To use LINQ to DataSet, you need to add a reference to the *System.Data.DataSetExtensions* assembly. You also might want to include the following statement in your code:

```
using System.Data;
```

By including the preceding statement, extension methods declared in the *DataTableExtensions* class are fully visible through Microsoft IntelliSense as if they were native instance methods of the *DataSet* class.

Using LINQ to Load a *DataSet*

A *DataSet* can be loaded by querying a relational database. One possible way to do this is through a *DataAdapter*, as shown in Listing 7-1.

Listing 7-1   Loading a *DataSet* by using a *DataAdapter*

```
const string QueryOrders = @"
SELECT  OrderID, OrderDate, Freight, ShipName,
        ShipAddress, ShipCity, ShipCountry
FROM    Orders
WHERE   CustomerID = @CustomerID

SELECT      od.OrderID, od.UnitPrice, od.Quantity, od.Discount,
            p.[ProductName]
FROM        [Order Details] od
INNER JOIN  Orders o
       ON   o.[OrderID] = od.[OrderID]
LEFT JOIN   Products p
       ON   p.[ProductID] = od.[ProductID]
WHERE       o.CustomerID = @CustomerID";

DataSet ds = new DataSet("CustomerOrders");
SqlDataAdapter da = new SqlDataAdapter(QueryOrders, ConnectionString);
da.SelectCommand.Parameters.AddWithValue("@CustomerID", "QUICK");
da.TableMappings.Add("Table", "Orders");
da.TableMappings.Add("Table1", "OrderDetails");
da.Fill(ds);
```

The code in Listing 7-1 combines two *DataTable* instances into one *DataSet*, which corresponds to the orders placed by a specific customer.

Loading a *DataSet* with LINQ to SQL

If you want to load a *DataSet* using LINQ to SQL instead of a *DataAdapter*, you need to re-create the behavior of the *DataAdapter* because there is no generic method that populates a *DataTable* with an *IEnumerable<T>*. For this reason, we created the simple helper extension method named *CreateDataTable<T>*, which you can see in Listing 7-2. This method creates a *DataTable* instance and adds a new *DataRow* to the *DataTable* for each row returned by the *query* iteration.

Listing 7-2   Helper *IEnumerable<T>* extension method *CreateDataTable<T>*

```
public static DataTable CreateDataTable<T>(
                        this IEnumerable<T> query,
                        string tableName) {
    DataTable table = new DataTable(tableName);
    var fields = typeof(T).GetProperties();

    // Create columns
    foreach (var field in fields) {
        DataColumn column = new DataColumn(field.Name);
        column.AllowDBNull =
            (typeof( T ).IsSubclassOf( typeof( ValueType ) ) ) ?
                IsNullableType( typeof( T ) ) :
                true;
```

```
        table.Columns.Add(column);
    }

    // Copy rows
    foreach (var row in query) {
        object[] values = new object[fields.Length];
        for( int i = 0; i < values.Length; i++ ) {
            values[i] = fields[i].GetValue(row, null);
        }
        table.Rows.Add(values);
    }
    return table;
}
```

More Info   The MSDN documentation contains a more complete implementation of a helper function similar to our *CreateDataTable<T>* that can also add rows to an existing table. Look for the source code for *ObjectShredder<T>* and the custom method *CopyToDataTable<T>* at *http://msdn2.microsoft.com/library/bb669096.aspx*.

Using our *CreateDataTable<T>*, we can populate a *DataTable* in the same way we did using a *DataAdapter*. In Listing 7-3, you can see two LINQ to SQL queries used to populate two *DataTable* objects.

Listing 7-3   Loading *DataSet* using LINQ to SQL queries

```
NorthwindDataContext db = new NorthwindDataContext(ConnectionString);
string filterCustomerID = "QUICK";

var customerOrders =
    from o in db.Orders
    where o.CustomerID == filterCustomerID
    select new {
        o.OrderID,
        o.OrderDate,
        o.Freight,
        o.ShipName,
        o.ShipAddress,
        o.ShipCity,
        o.ShipCountry
    };

var customerOrderDetails =
    from od in db.Order_Details
    join o in db.Orders
        on od.OrderID equals o.OrderID
    join p in db.Products
        on od.ProductID equals p.ProductID
    where o.CustomerID == filterCustomerID
    select new {
        od.UnitPrice,
        od.Quantity,
```

```
        od.Discount,
        p.ProductName
    };


DataSet ds = new DataSet("CustomerOrders");
ds.Tables.Add(customerOrders.CreateDataTable("Orders"));
ds.Tables.Add(customerOrderDetails.CreateDataTable("OrderDetails"));
```

From a performance point of view, using LINQ to SQL instead of the *DataAdapter* adds a layer
to your code. Thus, response time is better using a *DataAdapter*, especially on the first call
(when the LINQ to SQL engine initializes itself for the first time). However, LINQ to SQL
avoids having unchecked SQL code in your source code, as we had in Listing 7-1.

Loading Data with LINQ to DataSet

If you need to populate a *DataTable* with the results of a query on another *DataTable*, you can
use the *CopyToDataTable<T>* extension method, which is declared as follows:

```
public static DataTable CopyToDataTable<T>(this IEnumerable<T> source)
                        where T: DataRow
```

As you can see, it is declared like our *CreateDataTable<T>* presented in Listing 7-2. However, it
requires that the generic *T* type is a *DataRow* type. This constraint permits the *CopyToData-
Table* implementation to handle original and modified values stored in the *DataRow* instances.

A simple use of *CopyToDataTable* is the one shown in Listing 7-4: the result of a LINQ query
on another table is copied into a new table.

Listing 7-4   Loading *DataSet* using LINQ on another *DataTable*

```
DataSet ds = LoadDataSetUsingDataAdapter();


var highDiscountOrders =
    from   o in ds.Tables["OrderDetails"].AsEnumerable()
    where  o.Field<float?>("Discount") > 0.2
    select o;

DataTable highDiscountOrdersTable = highDiscountOrders.CopyToDataTable();
highDiscountOrdersTable.TableName = "HighDiscountOrders";
ds.Tables.Add(highDiscountOrdersTable);
```

> **Note**   To query a *DataTable*, you need to use the *AsEnumerable* and *Field<T>* extension
> methods. We will explain them in the next section, "Using LINQ to Query a *DataSet*."

Another option when using *CopyToDataTable* is adding data to or replacing data in an existing
table. In this case, you pass the existing table as the first argument, specifying the kind of

overwrite of existing entities in the second argument. The following are two overrides of the *CopyToDataTable<T>* extension method.

```
public static DataTable CopyToDataTable<T>(this IEnumerable<T> source
                                           DataTable table,
                                           LoadOption options)
                   where T: DataRow

public static DataTable CopyToDataTable<T>(this IEnumerable<T> source
                                           DataTable table,
                                           LoadOption options,
                                           FillErrorEventHandler errorHandler)
                   where T: DataRow
```

The *LoadOption* enumeration used in the second argument has three possible values: *OverwriteChanges* overwrites both the current and original value version of the data for each column; *PreserveChanges* preserves the current value and changes only the original value version for each column; *Upsert* changes the current version of each column, leaving the original version unmodified. The default is *PreserveChanges*. In Listing 7-5, you can see an example of the *CopyToDataTable* call, which is not affected by the setting for *LoadOption* because the data is added to different rows.

Listing 7-5   Loading data into an existing *DataTable* with *CopyToDataTable*

```
DataSet ds = LoadDataSetUsingDataAdapter();

var highDiscountOrders =
    from   o in ds.Tables["OrderDetails"].AsEnumerable()
    where  o.Field<float?>("Discount") > 0.2
    select o;

DataTable selectionTable = highDiscountOrders.CopyToDataTable();

var lowDiscountOrders =
    from   o in ds.Tables["OrderDetails"].AsEnumerable()
    where  o.Field<float?>("Discount") < 0.05
    select o;

lowDiscountOrders.CopyToDataTable( selectionTable,
                                   LoadOption.PreserveChanges);
```

The level of control provided by *LoadOptions* is useful when you receive a *DataTable* containing data that might have been modified since the data's original extraction and which you still have in the destination table. However, every time you project query results into an anonymous type, you need to use a technique like those described earlier, in the section "Loading a *DataSet* with LINQ to SQL."

Using LINQ to Query a *DataSet*

A *DataTable* can be queried with LINQ, just as any other *IEnumerable<T>* list.

> **Note**   As we mentioned previously, the *DataTable* class does not implement *IEnumerable<T>*. You have to call *AsEnumerable*, which is an extension method for *DataTable*, to obtain a wrapper that implements that interface.

The list is made of *DataRow* objects, which means that you must access *DataRow* member properties to get a field value. This arrangement allows you to call any *DataRow* member instead of using a query expression over a *DataTable*. You can use the *Field<T>* accessor method instead of using a direct cast on the result of the standard *DataRow* accessor (such as *o["OrderDate"]*). The query shown in Listing 7-6 gets the orders that show a date of 1998 or later.

Listing 7-6   Querying a *DataTable* with LINQ

```
DataSet ds = LoadDataSetUsingDataAdapter();
DataTable orders = ds.Tables["Orders"];

var query =
    from   o in orders.AsEnumerable()
    where  o.Field<DateTime>( "OrderDate" ).Year >= 1998
    orderby o.Field<DateTime>( "OrderDate" ) descending
    select  o;
```

> **Note**   *AsEnumerable* and *Field<T>* are two custom extension methods for *DataTable* and *DataRow* types. They are defined in *System.Data.DataTableExtensions* and *System.Data.DataRowExtensions*, respectively.

When you have several *DataTable* objects in a *DataSet*, you might want to use some type of join. The query shown in Listing 7-7 calculates the total order amount for each order from 1998 to the present.

Listing 7-7   Joining two *DataTable* objects with LINQ

```
DataSet ds = LoadDataSetUsingDataAdapter();
DataTable orders = ds.Tables["Orders"];
DataTable orderDetails = ds.Tables["OrderDetails"];

var query =
    from   o in orders.AsEnumerable()
    join   od in orderDetails.AsEnumerable()
           on o.Field<int>( "OrderID" ) equals od.Field<int>( "OrderID" )
           into orderLines
    where  o.Field<DateTime>( "OrderDate" ).Year >= 1998
    orderby o.Field<DateTime>( "OrderDate" ) descending
```

```
select  new { OrderID = o.Field<int>( "OrderID" ),
              OrderDate = o.Field<DateTime>( "OrderDate" ),
              Amount = orderLines.Sum(
                        od => od.Field<decimal>( "UnitPrice" )
                              * od.Field<short>( "Quantity" ) ) };
```

In Listing 7-7, we specified the relationship between *orders* and *orderDetails* through the *join* syntax. If the *DataSet* contains information about existing relationships between entities, a LINQ query can take advantage of this. In Listing 7-8, we use *GetChildRows* to get the lines for the order details instead of explicitly joining the two tables.

Listing 7-8   Leveraging *DataSet* relationships in LINQ queries

```
DataSet ds = LoadDataSetUsingDataAdapter();
DataTable orders = ds.Tables["Orders"];
DataTable orderDetails = ds.Tables["OrderDetails"];
ds.Relations.Add( "OrderDetails",
                  orders.Columns["OrderID"],
                  orderDetails.Columns["OrderID"]);

var query =
    from   o in orders.AsEnumerable()
    where  o.Field<DateTime>( "OrderDate" ).Year >= 1998
    orderby o.Field<DateTime>( "OrderDate" ) descending
    select  new { OrderID = o.Field<int>( "OrderID" ),
                  OrderDate = o.Field<DateTime>( "OrderDate" ),
                  Amount = o.GetChildRows( "OrderDetails" ).Sum(
                            od => od.Field<decimal>( "UnitPrice" )
                                  * od.Field<short>( "Quantity" ) ) };
```

Inside *DataTable.AsEnumerable*

You have seen that using the *AsEnumerable* extension method for *DataTable* allows you to use a *DataTable* as a source in a LINQ query. It might be interesting to know what is returned from *AsEnumerable* to better understand what happens when you make a LINQ query over a *DataTable*.

The declaration of the *AsEnumerable* extension method is the following:

```
public static EnumerableRowCollection<DataRow> AsEnumerable(
                            this DataTable source);
```

The return type is a class named *EnumerableRowCollection,* which implements *IEnumerable<T>*. When you make a LINQ query on that class, specific extension methods for *EnumerableRow-Collection<T>* are used. They are defined in the *EnumerableRowCollectionExtensions* static class, and there are several overloaded versions of the following LINQ operators:

- *Cast*
- *OrderBy*

- *OrderByDescending*
- *Select*
- *ThenBy*
- *ThenByDescending*
- *Where*

These methods are also used to support the creation of a *DataView* instance produced by LINQ queries, as we explain in the next section, "Creating *DataView* Instances with LINQ."

Creating *DataView* Instances with LINQ

A *DataView* is a class that offers a view of a *DataTable* for sorting, filtering, searching, editing, and navigation. Usually, the view is used for data binding to elements in a user interface. A *DataView* instance does not contain a copy of data; it contains only the rules to project the results, through properties such as *Sort* and *RowFilter*. In Listing 7-9, you can see a *DataView* that filters all the orders with a date of 1998 or later and sorts orders by descending *OrderDate*.

Listing 7-9   Creation of *DataView* in the traditional way

```
DataSet ds = LoadDataSetUsingDataAdapter();
DataTable orders = ds.Tables["Orders"];

string filter = String.Format("OrderDate >= #{0:d}#",
                              new DateTime(1998, 1, 1));
string sort = "OrderDate DESC";
DataView legacyView = new DataView( orders, filter, sort,
                                    DataViewRowState.CurrentRows);
```

A *DataView* can also be created from a LINQ query on a *DataTable* by using the *AsDataView* extension method. In Listing 7-10, you can see the same *DataView* shown in Listing 7-9, although this time obtained with a LINQ query.

Listing 7-10   Creation of *DataView* using a LINQ query over a *DataTable*

```
DataSet ds = LoadDataSetUsingDataAdapter();
DataTable orders = ds.Tables["Orders"];

var query =
    from   o in orders.AsEnumerable()
    where  o.Field<DateTime>("OrderDate").Year >= 1998
    orderby o.Field<DateTime>("OrderDate") descending
    select o;

DataView view = query.AsDataView();
```

> **Note**   The *DataView* class does not support projection on anonymous types. You always need a LINQ query over a *DataTable* to be able to call the *AsDataView* extension method.

Only the LINQ operators we listed in the section "Inside *DataTable.AsEnumerable*" are supported in a LINQ query to create a *DataView*. Creating a *DataView* with LINQ offers a strongly typed way to define a *DataView*. You can see the differences from how you create a *DataView* in the traditional way by comparing Listing 7-9 and Listing 7-10. Even if we write fewer lines in the traditional approach, all the *filter* and *sort* expression strings cannot be checked during compilation. If you look at the expression necessary to filter orders having an *OrderDate* greater than or equal to 1998, you can understand that it is more difficult to write and more error-prone than the LINQ version in Listing 7-10.

When you create a *DataView* using a LINQ query, you get an instance of *LinqDataView*, which is a class that inherits *DataView*. Properties such as *RowFilter* and *Sort* are still available in *LinqDataView*, but you will not find the conversion of the filter or sort condition you defined in the LINQ query. However, if you set either of these conditions, you will change the behavior of that part of the *DataView*. For example, if you execute the following line after the code in Listing 7-10

```
view.RowFilter = String.Format( "OrderDate < #{0:d}#",
                                new DateTime(1998, 1, 1));
```

you will replace the *where* condition of the LINQ query, but you will still have the behavior of the *orderby* condition. You can also remove a filter condition by setting the *RowFilter* property to *null*:

```
view.RowFilter = null;
```

After this assignment, there are no more filters on rows, but the results would be still ordered by descending *OrderDate*, unless you also cancel the sorting clause with this statement:

```
view.Sort = null;
```

> **Note**   Remember that reading *RowFilter* and *Sort* properties on a *DataView* will not show you whether a *where* predicate or an *orderby* condition is active from the originating LINQ query. However, by assigning them you remove the corresponding behavior defined by the originating LINQ query.

Using LINQ to Query a Typed *DataSet*

A typed *DataSet* can be queried with a simpler syntax because it is not necessary to use the *Field<T>* accessor and the *AsEnumerable* method.

> **Note**   If you create the typed *DataSet* with Microsoft Visual Studio, your typed *DataTable*
> classes will be derived from the *TypedTableBase<T>* class, which implements the *IEnumerable<T>*
> interface. For this reason, it is not required to call *AsEnumerable* to get a wrapper. Extension
> methods for *TypedTableBase<T>* are defined in the *TypedTableBaseExtensions* static class.

The query shown in Listing 7-10, which we also used to leverage the existing *DataSet* relationships, can be written as shown in Listing 7-11, which uses a typed *DataSet*.

Listing 7-11   Querying a typed *DataSet* with LINQ

```
var query =
    from    o in ds.Orders
    where   o.OrderDate.Year >= 1998
    orderby o.OrderDate descending
    select  new { o.OrderID, o.OrderDate,
                  Amount = o.GetOrder_DetailsRows().Sum(
                      od => od.UnitPrice * od.Quantity ) };
```

As you can see, the query syntax is much simpler and similar to the one we used earlier to query other types of entities. However, you must use a predefined schema (the typed *DataSet*) to query a *DataSet* instance in such a way, and this prevents the use of this syntax with a *DataSet* containing a flexible schema defined at execution time. This does not mean that you should use an untyped *DataSet*; it only emphasizes that untyped *DataSets* can be queried only with the *Field<T>* accessor.

Accessing Untyped *DataSet* Data

Accessing data in an untyped *DataSet* requires the use of the *Field<T>* and *SetField<T>* accessors to get and set field values, respectively. These accessors are important because a null value in a *DataSet* is represented by the *IsNull* method returning *true*. You should check this condition each time you access a column just to avoid potential cast errors. Using *Field<T>*, a nullable type for *T* is fully supported. The use of these accessors is allowed in any *DataTable* or *DataRow* access, even outside a query expression, as you can see in Listing 7-12. This listing also uses a nullable type and tests its null value by querying the *HasValue* property of the nullable type.

Listing 7-12   Querying an untyped *DataSet* with LINQ

```
foreach (DataRow r in orderDetails.Rows) {
    double? discount = r.Field<double?>("Discount");
    if (discount.HasValue && discount.Value > 0.10) {
        r.SetField<double?>("Discount", 0.10);
    }
}
```

DataRow Comparison

Some LINQ operators need to compare *DataRow* instances. Although LINQ to SQL provides an object tracker that usually keeps the same reference for two requests of the same row from a table, *DataSet* does not offer such a mechanism. Thus, when comparing two *DataRow* instances you need to compare their content, not only the instance references. The LINQ operators that you need to do such a comparison are the following:

- *Distinct*
- *Except*
- *Intersect*
- *Union*

The *DataRowComparer* class defined in the *System.Data* namespace provides a comparer that uses the *Equals* method to compare two *DataRow* instances. The comparison is made column by column and returns true only if all corresponding columns are equal. You can use the singleton *DataRowComparer.Default* as the equality comparer for the LINQ operators that receive it as a parameter. In Listing 7-13, you can see an example of the *Intersect* operator, which internally compares *DataRow* instances.

Listing 7-13   Use of *DefaultRowComparer.Default* as an equality comparer calling the *Intersect* operator

```
var queryOldOrders =
    from   o in ds.Orders
    where  o.OrderDate.Year <= 1996
    select o;

var queryLowFreightOrders =
    from   o in ds.Orders
    where  o.Freight < 50
    select o;

DataTable oldOrders = queryOldOrders.CopyToDataTable();
DataTable lowFreightOrders = queryLowFreightOrders.CopyToDataTable();

// Find the intersection of the two queries
var queryOrders= oldOrders.AsEnumerable().Intersect(
                    lowFreightOrders.AsEnumerable(),
                    DataRowComparer.Default);

DataTable orders = queryOrders.CopyToDataTable();
```

Important   If you do not use *DataRowComparer.Default* as an equality comparer when *DataRow* comparison is involved, the comparison could be false even if the rows have the same content but a different instance reference. LINQ operators that should use this comparer are *Distinct, Except, Intersect,* and *Union*.

Summary

The *DataSet* class is a widely adopted model with which to get an in-memory set of data that is used as a cache or to bind data to the user interface. LINQ supports typed and untyped *DataSet* instances and can be used to populate a *DataSet* by querying a database with LINQ to SQL or by using other LINQ implementations such as LINQ to XML. LINQ can also be used to query a *DataSet* by querying and joining *DataTable* instances, and eventually generating *DataView* instances from LINQ queries.

Chapter 8
LINQ to Entities

LINQ to Entities is the last LINQ implementation that we describe in the "LINQ to Relational Data" section of this book. LINQ to Entities allows you to query an Entity Data Model of the ADO.NET Entity Framework using LINQ query syntax. In this chapter, we will not cover the ADO.NET Entity Framework in depth. We provide an introduction to it in Appendix A, "ADO.NET Entity Framework." If you do not already know about the ADO.NET Entity Framework, we suggest that you first read Appendix A and then come back to this chapter.

 This chapter is based on beta code!   ADO.NET Entity Framework and LINQ to Entities have not been released at the time of this writing. Because this chapter is based on beta code, some features might be changed, removed, or added in the final release. This could invalidate some of the examples shown. We kept the content updated and aligned with the most recent information we had. In any case, we will publish news and corrections about the book, together with updated code samples, at *http://www.programminglinq.com*.

Querying Entity Data Model

In this section, we will focus on LINQ query syntax and query commands that are available while querying ADO.NET Entity Framework entities with LINQ.

Overview

To better understand how LINQ to Entities works, it is helpful to take a look at its architecture. Figure 8-1 shows a schema that describes the structure of the LINQ to Entities engine.

Starting from the top of the schema, you can see that LINQ to Entities is based on the ADO.NET Entity Framework infrastructure, which is made up of a set of layered components. The Object Services and Entity SQL components are directly connected to LINQ to Entities. The Object Services layer handles the identity and state of objects, while Entity SQL provides querying capabilities over the Entity Data Model. These layers work thanks to the underlying components that are in essence those that allow the mapping between the physical persistence storage and its Entity Data Model representation. Under the covers, the Entity Framework uses the classic ADO.NET environment to connect and query the database management system (DBMS), thus leveraging implementations of *IDbConnection*, *IDbCommand*, and *IDataReader*.

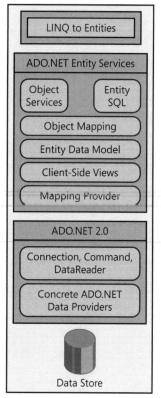

Figure 8-1   The architecture of LINQ to Entities

Imagine that you have the well-known set of Northwind customers and orders available as an Entity Data Model of the ADO.NET Entity Framework. (See Appendix A for more details about how to create an Entity Data Model.) In Listing 8-1, you can see an example of a LINQ to Entities query that extracts all customers who live in Italy.

Listing 8-1   An initial LINQ to Entities query to extract names of Northwind Italian customers

```
var northwind = new NorthwindModel.NorthwindEntities();

var italianCustomers =
    from   c in northwind.Customers
    where  c.Country == "Italy"
    select c;
```

As you can see, the LINQ query syntax is the same as you would use with LINQ to Objects or LINQ to SQL. However, here the query is converted into a command tree query of the ADO.NET Entity Framework and is then executed against the *ObjectContext*. The T-SQL query executed looks like the following one:

```
SELECT
[Extent1].[CustomerID] AS [CustomerID],
[Extent1].[CompanyName] AS [CompanyName],
```

```
[Extent1].[ContactName] AS [ContactName],
[Extent1].[ContactTitle] AS [ContactTitle],
[Extent1].[Address] AS [Address],
[Extent1].[City] AS [City],
[Extent1].[Region] AS [Region],
[Extent1].[PostalCode] AS [PostalCode],
[Extent1].[Country] AS [Country],
[Extent1].[Phone] AS [Phone],
[Extent1].[Fax] AS [Fax]
FROM [dbo].[Customers] AS [Extent1]
WHERE N'Italy' = [Extent1].[Country]
```

You can think of Listing 8-1 as code for creating an *ObjectQuery<T>* instance and executing an equivalent Entity SQL statement, just like the one shown in Listing 8-2.

Listing 8-2   The same query as Listing 8-1, but written in Entity SQL syntax using an *ObjectQuery<T>*

```
var northwind = new NorthwindModel.NorthwindEntities();

var italianCustomersObjectQuery =
  new ObjectQuery<Customers>(
    @"SELECT VALUE Customers FROM " +
    @"NorthwindEntities.Customers " +
    @"WHERE Customers.Country = 'Italy'",
    northwind);
```

The LINQ to Entities syntax is generally easier to write, compared to a free text command such as the one you use with *ObjectQuery<T>*, because of the typed approach and the availability of Microsoft IntelliSense support. In general, in all situations in which you can leverage a predefined and compiled LINQ to Entities query, it is better to use it. Whenever you need to write a dynamic query, you can use an *ObjectQuery<T>* instance and provide an Entity SQL statement. Do not assume that a LINQ to Entities query is converted into an Entity SQL query to feed an *ObjectQuery<T>* and then executed. The LINQ to Entities engine converts the LINQ query into a command tree query, just as it does with the one produced by the *ObjectQuery<T>* instance while parsing the Entity SQL syntax. Therefore, you do not have performance issues to consider when you use LINQ to Entities instead of Entity SQL.

This double approach adds a lot of flexibility to your way of writing code. One more thing to consider, as we describe in Appendix A and that you can see by reviewing the architecture schema in Figure 8-1, is that the ADO.NET Entity Framework architecture is made to support many different data storage providers. This flexibility allows your code to be independent of any particular persistence application and reusable with different DBMSs.

Query Expressions

Now that you have had a quick introduction to LINQ to Entities, let's dive into the details of LINQ to Entities query syntax. First of all, consider that LINQ to Entities is compliant with the base set of query operators and methods provided by LINQ. Thus, you have the opportunity to choose between LINQ query syntax and extension method syntax.

(See Chapter 2, "LINQ Syntax Fundamentals," and Chapter 3, "LINQ to Objects," for more details on this matter.)

If you choose to use LINQ query syntax, you can make use of almost all the commands available in the LINQ to Objects query syntax. For instance, you can do projection, filtering, grouping, joins, and so on.

On the other hand, if you prefer to use the method syntax, be aware that not all the LINQ to Object extension methods are supported by LINQ to Entities. In fact, not every common language runtime (CLR) operation can be converted into a corresponding SQL statement. For instance, all projection and restriction methods defined in LINQ to Objects that accept a positional argument are not available in LINQ to Entities because there is no guarantee that the same capability will be available on every DBMS engine. All the methods that in LINQ to Objects accept custom comparisons are unavailable because the custom comparer cannot be invoked on the DBMS. Extension methods such as *Join*, *GroupJoin*, *Contains*, *Distinct*, *Except*, *Union*, *OrderBy*, *ThenBy*, *GroupBy*, and so on support only overloads that do not require custom implementations of *IComparer* or *IEqualityComparer*.

Custom *Aggregate* methods are not available because a DBMS might not be able to execute the custom aggregation. However, predefined aggregations such as *Average*, *Count*, *Sum*, *Max*, *Min*, and so on are available.

Paging methods such as *Take* and *Skip* are supported, while *TakeWhile* and *SkipWhile* are not supported because a DBMS would not be able to accept a delegate to a custom function to evaluate.

DateTime, *String*, and nullability functions are generally supported. However, you will see later in this chapter that the evaluation of conditions and restrictions leveraging such primitive types can vary in its behavior depending on whether the query is evaluated on the client side or server side.

In this section and throughout the chapter, we will focus on some of the more interesting aspects of querying with LINQ to Entities and on how it is different from the rest of the LINQ implementations. We will not cover fully all the available methods and commands because these are covered in detail in Chapter 2.

Let's start with querying the set of Northwind customers to extract the Italian customers who placed at least 10 orders. In Listing 8-3, you can see an example of such a query.

Listing 8-3   A query to extract the Italian customers who placed at least 10 orders

```
var northwind = new NorthwindModel.NorthwindEntities();

var italianCustomerWithAtLeastTenOrders =
    from  c in northwind.Customers
    where c.Country == "Italy"
        && c.Orders.Count >= 10
    select c;
```

The query filters the result based not only on the *Country* value, but also on the *Count* property of the *Orders* collection that represents the orders submitted by each customer. The resulting T-SQL query executing against the SQL Server database is the following one:

```
SELECT
[Project2].[CustomerID] AS [CustomerID],
[Project2].[CompanyName] AS [CompanyName],
[Project2].[ContactName] AS [ContactName],
[Project2].[ContactTitle] AS [ContactTitle],
[Project2].[Address] AS [Address],
[Project2].[City] AS [City],
[Project2].[Region] AS [Region],
[Project2].[PostalCode] AS [PostalCode],
[Project2].[Country] AS [Country],
[Project2].[Phone] AS [Phone],
[Project2].[Fax] AS [Fax]
FROM ( SELECT
        [Extent1].[CustomerID] AS [CustomerID],
        [Extent1].[CompanyName] AS [CompanyName],
        [Extent1].[ContactName] AS [ContactName],
        [Extent1].[ContactTitle] AS [ContactTitle],
        [Extent1].[Address] AS [Address],
        [Extent1].[City] AS [City],
        [Extent1].[Region] AS [Region],
        [Extent1].[PostalCode] AS [PostalCode],
        [Extent1].[Country] AS [Country],
        [Extent1].[Phone] AS [Phone],
        [Extent1].[Fax] AS [Fax],
        (SELECT COUNT([Project1].[C1]) AS [A1]
         FROM ( SELECT
                    cast(1 as bit) AS [C1]
         FROM [dbo].[Orders] AS [Extent2]
         WHERE [Extent1].[CustomerID] = [Extent2].[CustomerID]
         ) AS [Project1]) AS [C1]
        FROM [dbo].[Customers] AS [Extent1]
) AS [Project2]
WHERE (N'Italy' = [Project2].[Country]) AND ([Project2].[C1] >= 10)
```

> **Note**   To view the T-SQL query sent to the DBMS, you can use a monitoring tool such as Microsoft SQL Server Profiler, or you can read the query text from the Entity Framework environment. To use the latter approach, refer to the "Query Engine" section later in this chapter.

This sample shows that, just as you do with LINQ to SQL, with LINQ to Entities you have the opportunity to make queries across the entity model, leveraging relationships. The query produced by the querying engine of LINQ to Entities does not load into memory the entire entity set, rather it loads only the required entities into memory. In LINQ to Entities, the *Orders* property of each customer entity is a collection of type *EntityCollection<Orders>*, with a deferred loading policy, as with LINQ to SQL. If you need to access the *Orders* collection of one of the customers, you can invoke the *Load* method on the collection to make the ADO.NET Entity Framework bring them up from the DBMS exactly when you need them. You can see an example of this approach in Listing 8-4.

Listing 8-4 A query to extract the Italian customers and their orders with deferred loading

```
using (var northwind = new NorthwindModel.NorthwindEntities()) {
    var italianCustomers =
        from   c in northwind.Customers
        where  c.Country == "Italy"
        select c;

    foreach (var c in italianCustomers) {
        Console.WriteLine(c.Display());

    foreach (var c in italianCustomers) {
        Console.WriteLine(c.Display());

        // Only for customers with PostalCode 42100
        if (c.PostalCode == "42100") {
            // Load their Orders if they have not yet been loaded
            if (!c.Orders.IsLoaded) {
                c.Orders.Load();
            }

            // Browse orders loaded
            foreach (Orders o in c.Orders) {
                Console.WriteLine("\tOrderID: {0} - OrderDate: {1}",
                    o.OrderID, o.OrderDate);
            }
        }
    }
}
```

If you need to load the whole set of *Orders* together with the set of selected customers, instead of explicitly loading *Orders* for each customer, you can write a different kind of LINQ to Entities query. You can leverage the *Include* method provided by *ObjectQuery<T>*, which includes other entities together with the main entity set you are querying. In Listing 8-5, you can see an example.

Listing 8-5 A query to extract the Italian customers together with their orders

```
using (var northwind = new NorthwindModel.NorthwindEntities()) {
    var italianCustomers =
        from   c in northwind.Customers.Include("Orders")
        where  c.Country == "Italy"
        select c;

    // ...

}
```

The SQL query resulting from the LINQ to Entities query in Listing 8-5 is a LEFT OUTER JOIN somewhat like the following excerpt:

```
SELECT
[Project1].[CustomerID] AS [CustomerID],
[Project1].[CompanyName] AS [CompanyName],
...
[Project1].[C1] AS [C1],
[Project1].[C2] AS [C2],
[Project1].[OrderID] AS [OrderID],
[Project1].[EmployeeID] AS [EmployeeID],
...
[Project1].[CustomerID1] AS [CustomerID1]
FROM ( SELECT
    [Extent1].[CustomerID] AS [CustomerID],
    [Extent1].[CompanyName] AS [CompanyName],
    ...
    1 AS [C1],
    [Extent2].[OrderID] AS [OrderID],
    [Extent2].[CustomerID] AS [CustomerID1],
    [Extent2].[EmployeeID] AS [EmployeeID],
    ...
    [Extent2].[ShipCountry] AS [ShipCountry],
    CASE WHEN ([Extent2].[OrderID] IS NULL)
        THEN CAST(NULL AS int) ELSE 1
    END AS [C2]
    FROM  [dbo].[Customers] AS [Extent1]
    LEFT OUTER JOIN [dbo].[Orders] AS [Extent2]
      ON [Extent1].[CustomerID] = [Extent2].[CustomerID]
    WHERE N'Italy' = [Extent1].[Country]) AS [Project1]
ORDER BY [Project1].[CustomerID] ASC, [Project1].[C2] ASC
```

Another interesting feature available only with the ADO.NET Entity Framework is the *UnionAll* method of the *ObjectQuery<T>*. This method provides the same operation as its SQL syntax counterpart, and it can be applied to an *ObjectQuery<T>* instance. It takes another *ObjectQuery<T>* argument, with the same generic *T*, creating the union of the two entity sets that results from both the queries. The smart part of this method is that the *UnionAll* operation is performed on the SQL query instead of in memory, resulting in only one roundtrip to the DBMS. In Listing 8-6, you can see an example of this method.

Listing 8-6   An example of the *UnionAll* method of *ObjectQuery<T>*

```
using (var northwind = new NorthwindModel.NorthwindEntities()) {
    var italianCustomers =
      new ObjectQuery<Customers>(
        @"SELECT VALUE Customers " +
        @"FROM NorthwindEntities.Customers " +
        @"WHERE Customers.Country = 'Italy'",
        northwind);

    var germanCustomers =
      new ObjectQuery<Customers>(
        @"SELECT VALUE Customers " +
        @"FROM NorthwindEntities.Customers " +
```

```
            @"WHERE Customers.Country = 'Germany'",
            northwind);

    foreach (var c in italianCustomers.UnionAll(germanCustomers)) {
        Console.WriteLine(c.Display());
    }
}
```

The resulting SQL command is shown in the following excerpt:

```
SELECT
[UnionAll1].[CustomerID] AS [C1],
...
[UnionAll1].[Fax] AS [C11]
FROM  (SELECT
    [Extent1].[CustomerID] AS [CustomerID],
    ...
    [Extent1].[Fax] AS [Fax]
    FROM [dbo].[Customers] AS [Extent1]
    WHERE [Extent1].[Country] = 'Italy'
UNION ALL
    SELECT
    [Extent2].[CustomerID] AS [CustomerID],
    ...
    [Extent2].[Fax] AS [Fax]
    FROM [dbo].[Customers] AS [Extent2]
    WHERE [Extent2].[Country] = 'Germany') AS [UnionAll1]
```

Unfortunately, the *UnionAll* method does not work if it is applied to a LINQ to Entities query; it works only with instances of *ObjectQuery<T>* that are explicitly created.

One last point that we want to cover about the LINQ to Entities query syntax is its capability to select anonymous types, and to do so as well as any LINQ implementation. In Listing 8-7, you can see an example of selecting the main information (CustomerID, ContactName, CompanyName) about Italian customers, together with their total order count.

Listing 8-7   Customers' main information, with total order amount and count

```
var italianCustomersWithOrdersStats =
    from c in northwind.Customers
    where c.Country == "Italy"
    select new {
        c.CustomerID,
        c.ContactName,
        c.CompanyName,
        OrdersTotalCount = c.Orders.Count
    };
```

Of course, the count of orders is made on the server side, defining a SQL query that extracts only the three customers' columns requested and the count of related orders.

You can define many other LINQ to Entities queries using grouping, joins, sorting, and so on. However, instead of writing a syntax reference for LINQ to Entities, we will focus our attention on specific and particular aspects of LINQ to Entities. To start, we will move to managing data and to the inner workings of the LINQ to Entities querying engine.

Managing Data

Typically, when you select entities through LINQ queries you not only need to present them to users, but sometime you also need to change and update the entites. In those situations, with LINQ to Entities you leverage the Object Services component of the ADO.NET Entity Framework. In Appendix A, you can find an introductory explanation about managing data with Object Services and about handling concurrency issues. Here we simply re-create such a scenario with a simple example to help you better understand some of the remaining parts of this chapter.

The example in Listing 8-8 queries the list of orders to extract only orders that need to be shipped and then marks those orders as shipped.

Listing 8-8   An example of managing data with Object Services

```
using (var northwind = new NorthwindModel.NorthwindEntities()) {
    DateTime today = DateTime.Now;

    var ordersToShip =
        from   o in northwind.Orders
        where  o.RequiredDate <= today
               && o.ShippedDate == null
        select o;

    foreach (var o in ordersToShip) {
        o.ShippedDate = today;
    }

    using (TransactionScope scope = new TransactionScope()){
        northwind.SaveChanges();
        scope.Complete();
    }
}
```

You need to invoke the *SaveChanges* method of the *ObjectContext* to persist your data changes. You can also wrap the code that submits changes to the DBMS with a *TransactionScope*, as we did in the example in Listing 8-8.

Query Engine

In this section, we will cover some aspects related to the inner workings of the LINQ to Entities querying engine. In particular, we will describe how the query engine executes queries and how to leverage compiled queries.

Query Execution

Whenever you write a LINQ to Entities query, it results in a query tree being created during execution. Under the covers, there is a LINQ query provider implemented for the *ObjectQuery<T>* class that visits the LINQ query tree and converts it to a command tree inherited from *DbCommandTree*.

> **More Info**   For further information about query providers and expression visitors, see Chapter 11, "Inside Expression Trees," and Chapter 12, "Extending LINQ."

A command tree is executed against the *ObjectContext* to return a set of data following the rules of LINQ deferred query execution. Each command tree can be evaluated on the client side as well as on the server side. Client-side evaluation of a command tree allows the replacement of expressions that need to be calculated on the client with their corresponding values. Server-side evaluation corresponds to the execution of the query on the physical DBMS using standard ADO.NET components.

In Listing 8-9, you can see an example of a query that requires evaluation on the client side first and then on the server side.

Listing 8-9   A query that is evaluated first on the client side and then on the server side

```
String country = "Italy";

var italianCustomers =
    from  c in northwind.Customers
    where c.Country == country
    select c;
```

In this example, the evaluation of the local variable *country* occurs on the client side. The remaining query is evaluated on the server side. You can also see this behavior by evaluating the T-SQL query sent to the DBMS:

```
SELECT
[Extent1].[CustomerID] AS [CustomerID],
[Extent1].[CompanyName] AS [CompanyName],
[Extent1].[ContactName] AS [ContactName],
[Extent1].[ContactTitle] AS [ContactTitle],
[Extent1].[Address] AS [Address],
[Extent1].[City] AS [City],
[Extent1].[Region] AS [Region],
[Extent1].[PostalCode] AS [PostalCode],
[Extent1].[Country] AS [Country],
[Extent1].[Phone] AS [Phone],
[Extent1].[Fax] AS [Fax]
FROM [dbo].[Customers] AS [Extent1]
WHERE [Extent1].[Country] = @prm_12b5257435894bf6a4b7acca36258f11
```

Notice that in this example the country parameter is defined as a SQL parameter, while in Listing 8-1 it was an explicit value within the query. This example suggests that whenever you want to define a parametric query to better leverage the query engine of the DBMS, you should define any value filter as a variable argument instead of using a constant value. This behavior is different from what you get with LINQ to SQL, where every constant in a LINQ query is automatically converted into a parameter of the SQL query sent to SQL Server.

After the query is executed, the results obtained through standard ADO.NET components need to be converted to CLR types. This phase is called *materialization*, and it occurs at the end of every single process of query execution. When the result of a query is a set of entities of the Entity Data Model defined in the ADO.NET Entity Framework, the entities materialized and returned to the consumer code are tracked by the *ObjectContext* and will be fully supported by the Entity Framework. This means that these entities will have change tracking, identity tracking, and so on. When the result of a query is a set of anonymous type instances or a set of primitive CLR type instances, these are not tracked by the *ObjectContext*.

Let's try to see this behavior in action with a specific example. In Listing 8-10, you can see a LINQ to Entities query that extracts the first four customers from Germany. The *ContactName* property of the first customer obtained is then changed. Remember that, as you saw in the "Managing Data" section, when you change the properties of an entity in memory you do not directly change them on the DBMS. You need to confirm the changes by invoking *SaveChanges* on the *ObjectContext*. In this example, you just change the in-memory instance, but you do not call *SaveChanges*. At the end of the example, there is one more query to extract the same set of customers.

Listing 8-10   Sample of object identity and merge options of queries sharing the *ObjectContext* instance

```
using (var northwind = new NorthwindModel.NorthwindEntities()) {
    String country = "Germany";

    var germanCustomers =
        (from   c in northwind.Customers
         where   c.Country == country
         select c).Take(4);

    foreach (var c in germanCustomers) {
        Console.WriteLine(c.Display());
    }

    // Here we are changing the in-memory customer instance
    Customers firstGermanCustomer = germanCustomers.First();
    firstGermanCustomer.ContactName += " - Modified!";

    var secondQueryForGermanCustomers =
        (from   c in northwind.Customers
         where   c.Country == country
         select  c).Take(4);
```

```
        foreach (var c in secondQueryForGermanCustomers) {
            Console.WriteLine(c.Display());
        }
    }
}
```

Here is the output of this code sample:

```
=> First query output
ALFKI - Maria Anders
BLAUS - Hanna Moos
DRACD - Sven Ottlieb
FRANK - Peter Franken
=> Second query output
ALFKI - Maria Anders - Modified!
BLAUS - Hanna Moos
DRACD - Sven Ottlieb
FRANK - Peter Franken
```

The second query output shows the first customer you modified in the code. This happens because during materialization of query results, the LINQ to Entities engine merges entities that are already loaded with those coming from the DBMS. The default behavior of this phase is to merge entities already in memory with data coming from the DBMS, following the rules of the *MergeOption* property of the *ObjectQuery<T>* type.

> **More Info**   For further details on the *MergeOption* property of the *ObjectQuery<T>*, refer to Appendix A.

You can change this behavior by configuring the *MergeOption* property of the *ObjectQuery<T>* that corresponds to the LINQ to Entities query that you are going to execute. In Listing 8-11, you can see the same sample as before, but with the assignment of the *MergeOption* property to a value of *OverwriteChanges*, which overwrites any instance already in-memory with data coming from the DBMS.

Listing 8-11   Sample of how to change the *MergeOption* configuration

```
using (var northwind = new NorthwindModel.NorthwindEntities()) {
    String country = "Germany";

    var germanCustomers =
        (from   c in northwind.Customers
         where  c.Country == country
         select c).Take(4);

    foreach (var c in germanCustomers) {
        Console.WriteLine(c.Display());
    }

    // Here we are changing the in-memory customer instance
    Customers firstGermanCustomer = germanCustomers.First();
    firstGermanCustomer.ContactName += " - Modified!";
```

```
    var secondQueryForGermanCustomers =
        (from  c in northwind.Customers
        where  c.Country == country
        select  c).Take(4);

    ((ObjectQuery<Customers>)secondQueryForGermanCustomers).MergeOption =
        MergeOption.OverwriteChanges;

    foreach (var c in secondQueryForGermanCustomers) {
        Console.WriteLine(c.Display());
    }
}
```

Here is the result of this last sample:

```
=> First query output
ALFKI - Maria Anders
BLAUS - Hanna Moos
DRACD - Sven Ottlieb
FRANK - Peter Franken
=> Second query output
ALFKI - Maria Anders
BLAUS - Hanna Moos
DRACD - Sven Ottlieb
FRANK - Peter Franken
```

This time, the customer with *CustomerID* ALFKI returned by the second query has its
original values. By using this approach, you have lost the changes you made on the variable
firstGermanCustomer because its instance is unique for the whole *ObjectContext* and it has
been overwritten by executing the *secondQueryForGermanCustomers* query.

The interesting part of Listing 8-11 is the code that changes the *MergeOption* property of the
query, shown in boldface type. You cast the query variable to *ObjectQuery<T>*, where *T* is of
type *Customers* in this example, and then you set the *MergeOption* property of the variable
resulting from the cast. This step is possible because internally every LINQ to Entities query
is represented as an instance of type *ObjectQuery<T>*. Whenever you query for entities defined
in the Entity Data Model, you also have access to the *ObjectQuery<T>* instance behind the
query. Access to this instance lets you manage its configuration.

More on *ObjectQuery<T>*

As you just saw, every LINQ to Entities query can be thought of as an *ObjectQuery<T>*
instance. However, it is not always possible to use it directly in code. Whenever the LINQ to
Entities query projects anonymous types, as in Listing 8-12, you cannot reference the anonymous type in your code to cast the query to *ObjectQuery<YourAnonymousType>*.

Listing 8-12   Type of *ObjectQuery<T>* for a query projecting anonymous types

```
using (var northwind = new NorthwindModel.NorthwindEntities()) {
    String country = "Germany";

    var germanCustomersProjection =
        from   c in northwind.Customers
        where  c.Country == country
        select new {
            c.CustomerID,
            c.ContactName,
            c.Country,
        };

    Console.WriteLine(germanCustomersProjection.GetType());

    foreach (var c in germanCustomersProjection) {
        Console.WriteLine(c);
    }
}
```

The line in boldface type in Listing 8-12 outputs to the console window the type of your query variable, as shown here:

```
System.Data.Objects.ObjectQuery`1[<>f__AnonymousType0`3[System.String,
System.String,System.String]]
```

As you can see, this type is not suitable for explicit casting in your code because you lack the capability to reference the anonymous type. The only way to cast this variable to that type would be to use reflection, but that is not exactly a user-friendly solution. However, in all cases in which the query returns nonanonymous types, it is absolutely useful to know that you can access the underlying *ObjectQuery<T>*. For instance, through this type you can gain access to the SQL query sent to the DBMS, invoking the *ToTraceString* method, as shown in Listing 8-13.

Listing 8-13   Sample to extract, via *ObjectQuery<T>*, the SQL query executed against the DBMS

```
using (var northwind = new NorthwindModel.NorthwindEntities()) {
    String country = "Germany";

    var germanCustomers =
        (from   c in northwind.Customers
         where  c.Country == country
         select c).Take(4);

    northwind.Connection.Open();
    Console.WriteLine(
        ((ObjectQuery<Customers>)secondQueryForGermanCustomers)
        .ToTraceString());

    foreach (var c in germanCustomers) {
        Console.WriteLine(c.Display());
    }
}
```

To be able to determine the SQL string that will be executed against the DBMS, you need to explicitly open the underlying connection to it, because the ADO.NET Entity Framework needs to evaluate the command tree on both the client and server. The *DbConnection* instance underlying the current *ObjectContext* is exposed through the *Connection* property of the *ObjectContext* variable, so you can easily access and open it.

One more feature provided by the ADO.NET Entity Framework is the capability to cache query plans to speed up their execution if they are frequently used in your code. This caching can be performed by configuring the *EnablePlanCaching* property of the *ObjectQuery<T>* instance used to define the query.

In LINQ to Entities, all query plans are cached by default. You can disable this behavior—when it is not useful, in cases in which queries are not executed multiple times—by using a syntax such as the following one:

```
((ObjectQuery<Customers>)query).EnablePlanCaching = false;
```

Compiled Queries

One final way to optimize LINQ to Entities query execution is to leverage compiled queries in a way that is similar to the one used by LINQ to SQL. A compiled query is a delegate to a pre-compiled *ObjectQuery<T>* instance that returns an *IQueryable<T>* result. Imagine that the query to extract customers by country has to be executed many times, and that only the country value is changed each time. In Listing 8-14, you can see an example of using compiled queries to improve performance while calling this parametric query.

Listing 8-14   Sample showing how to precompile a query

```
using (var northwind = new NorthwindModel.NorthwindEntities()) {

    var compiledQueryForCustomersByCountry =
    CompiledQuery.Compile<NorthwindEntities, String, IQueryable<Customers>>(
       (context, country) => from   c in context.Customers
                             where  c.Country == country
                             select c);

    Console.WriteLine("=> German customers");
    var germanCustomers =
            compiledQueryForCustomersByCountry(northwind, "Germany");
    foreach (var c in germanCustomers) {
      Console.WriteLine(c.Display());
    }

    Console.WriteLine("=> Italian customers");
    var italianCustomers =
            compiledQueryForCustomersByCountry(northwind, "Italy");
    foreach (var c in italianCustomers) {
      Console.WriteLine(c.Display());
    }
}
```

The main part of this sample is in boldface type. It describes the use of the *Compile* method that is available through the *CompiledQuery* type. The *Compile* method is a generic method and provides four different overloads that allow you to define precompiled queries with zero, one, two, or three typed parameters. The first argument of this method is the *ObjectContext* itself, and it is required as the first type of the generic *Compile* method. Then you can provide the type of the optional arguments of the compiled query, and you have to finish by giving the type of the result (*IQueryable<Customers>* in our example). If you need to define a query with more than three parameters, you can pass an argument of type array or a structured type such as a structure or a class.

The result of the *Compile* method gives you back a delegate that accepts the query parameters as its arguments. The result type of that delegate corresponds to the type of the last generic argument provided to the *Compile* method.

LINQ to SQL and LINQ to Entities

At first glance, LINQ to SQL and LINQ to Entities can be thought of as competitive LINQ implementations. In fact, from a LINQ query point of view, both have similar capabilities and both allow querying a DBMS with LINQ queries. However, their implementations have differences that reflect the different scenarios they target.

LINQ to SQL is a really simple and quick-to-use object relational mapper, which is usually considered to be best used in rapid application development (RAD) scenarios, where the database is only Microsoft SQL Server and the database schema does not need to be completely abstracted through an abstract entity domain model. LINQ to SQL works with entities that map 1:1 to the tables of the source database persistence layer. In this scenario, LINQ to SQL is really fast and gives you the best performance when querying Microsoft SQL Server, because it has been optimized to work with that product.

LINQ to Entities is the LINQ query provider for the ADO.NET Entity Framework, which is a more complex and powerful object relational mapper designed to be used with many different database servers. It can be used to define complex entity models without the constraint of a 1:1 mapping between entities and a database schema. With the ADO.NET Entity Framework, you can shape your entities without regard to the physical underlying data structure. You can also map the Entity Data Model with any underlying persistence layer, whether it is Microsoft SQL Server or not and regardless of whether behind a single entity there is a single table or a set of tables, multiple persistent storages, or both. Of course, these features lead the Entity Framework to define more portable queries, which at the same time can be less efficient than the ones generated by LINQ to SQL. However, you should evaluate whether the possible performance degradation affects you in a significant way by making specific tests with your own model. Do not assume that the object relational mapper implementation will be the bottleneck of your application before having tested it.

In Chapter 15, "LINQ in a Multitier Solution," you will see how to leverage both these LINQ implementations in .NET distributed architectures.

Summary

In this chapter, we provided an overview of the LINQ to Entities architecture and queries, focusing on specific aspects and behaviors rather than referencing all possible syntaxes and commands. You saw how the query engine works; how to define parametric queries, precompiled queries, or both; how to leverage specific query syntaxes; and how to access the Entity SQL query underlying each LINQ to Entities query. Finally, you saw the main differences between LINQ to SQL and LINQ to Entities.

Part III
LINQ and XML

Chapter 9

LINQ to XML: Managing the XML Infoset

Since it became available on February 10, 1998, Extensible Markup Language (XML) has been broadly supported and used. Today every development framework supports XML and its related specifications, such as the following:

- **XML Schema Definition (XSD)**   Used to define the structure of XML documents
- **Extensible Stylesheet Language for Transformations (XSLT)**   Used to transform XML documents from one schema to another
- **XPath and XQuery**   Used to search and traverse XML contents
- **Document Object Model (DOM)**   Used to manage in-memory representations of XML documents
- **Simple Object Access Protocol (SOAP) services**   Used to achieve platform interoperability using well defined and interoperable XML messages
- **XML Infoset**   Used to represent XML content as a set of information items, such as Document, Element, Attribute, Processing Instruction, Comment, etc. Each information item represents an abstract description of part of the XML content and includes a set of named properties.

Despite its widespread use, XML is still often a hostile technology for many developers because of its rigorous syntax. LINQ to XML provides a new unified application programming interface (API) to define and manage XML contents using Microsoft .NET code. The LINQ to XML programming framework is fully integrated with the .NET type system and syntax. LINQ to XML uses LINQ extension methods to read, create, search, query, and generally manage XML contents within applications using .NET code and a language-agnostic API, the same as with entities, database records, and collections of items in general.

Introducing LINQ to XML

LINQ to XML provides the power of the DOM and the expressiveness of XPath and XQuery through LINQ extension methods that you can use to manage and query in-memory XML nodes. It uses the latest enhancements to .NET languages, such as anonymous methods, generics, nullable types, and so forth. Consider the following introductory sample XML document:

```
<?xml version="1.0" encoding="UTF-16" standalone="yes"?>
<customer id="C01">
  <firstName>Paolo</firstName>
  <lastName>Pialorsi</lastName>
  <addresses>
    <address type="email">paolo@devleap.it</address>
    <address type="url">http://www.devleap.it/</address>
    <address type="home">Brescia - Italy</address>
  </addresses>
</customer>
```

Listing 9-1 shows how you can build such a document with "old-style" Document Object Model (DOM) syntax, using C#.

Listing 9-1   A sample of XML construction using DOM in C#

```
// Create the XmlDocument
XmlDocument customerDocument = new XmlDocument();

// Define processing instruction and document element (root element)
customerDocument.AppendChild(customerDocument.CreateProcessingInstruction
  ("xml", "version='1.0' encoding='UTF-16' standalone='yes'"));
customerDocument.AppendChild(customerDocument.CreateElement("customer"));
customerDocument.DocumentElement.SetAttribute("id", "C01");

// Create and add "firstName" child element to the document element
XmlElement firstNameElement = customerDocument.CreateElement("firstName");
firstNameElement.InnerText = "Paolo";
customerDocument.DocumentElement.AppendChild(firstNameElement);

// Create and add "lastName" child element to the document element
XmlElement lastNameElement = customerDocument.CreateElement("lastName");
lastNameElement.InnerText = "Pialorsi";
customerDocument.DocumentElement.AppendChild(lastNameElement);

// Create "addresses" element
XmlElement addressesElement = customerDocument.CreateElement("addresses");

// Create and add "email address" child element to the "addresses" element
XmlElement emailAddressElement = customerDocument.CreateElement("address");
emailAddressElement.SetAttribute("type", "email");
emailAddressElement.InnerText = "paolo@devleap.it";
addressesElement.AppendChild(emailAddressElement);

// Create and add "url address" child element to the "addresses" element
XmlElement urlAddressElement = customerDocument.CreateElement("address");
urlAddressElement.SetAttribute("type", "url");
urlAddressElement.InnerText = "http://www.devleap.it/";
addressesElement.AppendChild(urlAddressElement);
```

```
// Create and add "home address" child element to the "addresses" element
XmlElement homeAddressElement = customerDocument.CreateElement("address");
homeAddressElement.SetAttribute("type", "home");
homeAddressElement.InnerText = "Brescia - Italy";
addressesElement.AppendChild(homeAddressElement);

// Add "addresses" child element to the document element
customerDocument.DocumentElement.AppendChild(addressesElement);
```

As you can see, the DOM syntax requires a lot of procedural code to define each single node (information item) and to append it to its parent node. It is also a verbose syntax that it is not so agile to write and to read.

Now consider the code excerpt of Listing 9-2, where we define the same XML document but by using LINQ to XML in C# 3.0.

Listing 9-2   A sample of XML functional construction

```
XDocument customer =
    new XDocument(
        new XDeclaration("1.0", "UTF-16", "yes"),
        new XElement("customer",
            new XAttribute("id", "C01"),
            new XElement("firstName", "Paolo"),
            new XElement("lastName", "Pialorsi"),
            new XElement("addresses",
                new XElement("address",
                    new XAttribute("type", "email"),
                        "paolo@devleap.it"),
                new XElement("address",
                    new XAttribute("type", "url"),
                        "http://www.devleap.it/"),
                new XElement("address",
                    new XAttribute("type", "home"),
                        "Brescia - Italy"))));
```

The preceding example is called "functional construction," and it reveals how simple and intuitive it is to define an XML nodes hierarchy with LINQ to XML. As you can see, the code layout describes the final hierarchical structure by using nested constructors. The standard DOM approach shown previously requires you to declare and collect many objects, while this new syntax uses a single hierarchical statement to achieve this goal, allowing the developer to focus on the structure of the final output XML rather than on DOM rules. From the perspective of XML Infoset, the "functional construction" approach defines each single information item, corresponding to the various XML nodes. For instance, you can see the definition of an *XDocument* type instance, which represents a Document information item of an XML Infoset. We then define many instances of the *XElement* type, each describing an Element information item of the XML Infoset, and we create *XAttribute* instances, which map to the XML Infoset's Attribute information item.

As you can learn reading Appendix C, "Visual Basic 2008: New Language Features," Visual Basic 2008 language enhancements introduce a feature called *XML literals* that makes writing and reading XML contents even easier. In fact, the previous example, when written in Visual Basic 2008, looks like the excerpt in Listing 9-3.

Listing 9-3   A sample of Visual Basic 2008 XML literals

```
Dim customerXml As XDocument = _
  <?xml version="1.0" encoding="UTF-16" standalone="yes"?>
    <customer id="C01">
      <firstName>Paolo</firstName>
      <lastName>Pialorsi</lastName>
      <addresses>
        <address type="email">paolo@devleap.it</address>
        <address type="url">http://www.devleap.it/</address>
        <address type="home">Brescia - Italy</address>
      </addresses>
    </customer>
```

The power and expressiveness of this syntax is truly evident. We write pure XML code, even if it is inside Visual Basic 2008 code. Also, querying XML with LINQ to XML is very simple. In the following sample code, we enumerate all the *address* tags of a given customer by using C#:

```
foreach(XElement a in customer.Descendants("addresses").Elements()) {
    Console.WriteLine(a);
}
```

Using Visual Basic 2008, this query can be written using a more intuitive syntax, such as the following:

```
Dim address As XElement
For Each address In customerXml.<customer>.<addresses>.<address>
    Console.WriteLine(address.Value)
Next
```

We will come back to XML querying in Chapter 10, "LINQ to XML: Querying Nodes," but for now just notice that once again we are using an XML-like syntax within Visual Basic code. Beginning with the next section to the end of this chapter, we will cover all the features of LINQ to XML related to nodes and Infoset management.

LINQ to XML Programming

The LINQ to XML programming framework allows developers to build and manage XML contents. You can use LINQ to query over XML content, but it is completely independent, and LINQ to XML can be used as a stand-alone API. This new API is built with World Wide Web Consortium (W3C) XML Infoset instances in mind, rather than an approach that relies just on manipulating XML 1.0 string documents full of brackets. Manipulating the in-memory tree of information items of an XML Infoset is the objective of this programming framework, not the basic handling of a bare XML text file.

> **Note**   W3C defines XML Infoset as a set of information items that describes the structure of any well-formed XML document. You can think of an XML Infoset as the set of information items represented by an XML document instance, approaching the information items as the in-memory node graph description corresponding to an XML document, aside from the physical nature of the document itself. For further details on XML Infoset, read the W3C Recommendation at *http://www.w3.org/TR/xml-infoset*.

The goal of the LINQ to XML API is to provide an object-oriented approach for XML construction and management, avoiding or solving many common issues related to XML manipulation through the W3C DOM. With LINQ to XML, the approach to XML is no longer document centric, as it is in the W3C DOM. (See Listing 9-1.) Using LINQ to XML, elements can be created and can exist detached from any document, namespace usage has been simplified, and traversing the in-memory tree is like scanning any other object graph. To make all of this possible, the LINQ to XML framework is based on a set of classes, all with names prefixed by an *X* (which we will often refer to as *X* classes* in this chapter.) These classes correspond to the main common nodes of an XML document. In Figure 9-1, you can see the object model hierarchy.

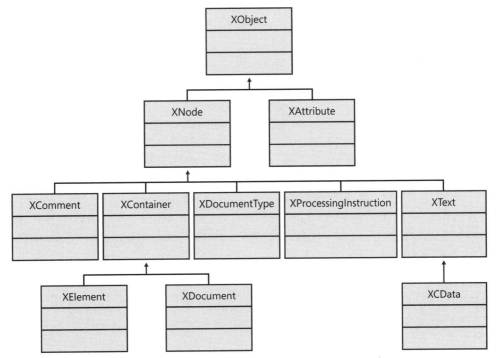

Figure 9-1   The object model hierarchy of main X* classes

To start using this new API, you must reference the *System.Xml.Linq* assembly. The following sections describe the main types defined in the corresponding *System.Xml.Linq* namespace.

XDocument

The *XDocument* class represents an XML Infoset document instance, which is the root container of a set of information items. There is exactly one Document information item in each XML Infoset, as well as in LINQ to XML. You can create document instances using the type constructors or some factory methods. Here are the supported constructors:

```
public XDocument();
public XDocument(params object[] content);
public XDocument(XDeclaration declaration, params Object[] content);
public XDocument(XDocument other);
```

As you can see, the default constructor can be used to build an empty *XDocument* instance, but the most commonly used constructors are the second and the third ones. They both accept a *params Object[]* list of objects that theoretically can be any kind of object. You should, however, use only *XElement, XProcessingInstruction, XDocumentType,* and *XComment* instances to keep the result well-formed. (We will cover those X* classes later in this chapter.)

Consider again the code excerpt in Listing 9-2. There we defined an *XDocument* instance, providing to its constructor a couple of parameters: one *XDeclaration* instance and one *XElement* instance (the *customer* element). Those X* type instances represent the whole content of the *XDocument* we are going to define.

The last constructor of the *XDocument* type supports the creation of a document based on another *XDocument* instance.

XDocument does not have a constructor with a parameter of type *XmlReader, Stream,* or whatever describes a source file or Uniform Resource Identifier (URI). In fact, *XDocument,* like *XElement,* as you will see shortly, provides a set of static *Load* methods that act as factory methods. These methods can be invoked with a document URI as a *String* parameter, rather than through an *XmlReader* or a *TextReader* argument, to directly access existing XML content. One more useful method provided by the *XDocument* type is the *Parse* static method, which allows you to parse a well-formed XML string and convert it into an *XDocument* instance.

To persist XML Infoset *XDocument* instances, you need to use one of its *Save* methods. Generally, an *XDocument* instance is useful whenever you need to create processing instructions or document type declarations on top of the XML document; otherwise, *XElement* is a better choice and is easier to use.

Important As you have already seen, Visual Basic 2008 XML literals are parsed by the Visual Basic compiler to generate standard LINQ to XML syntax. During this parsing phase, the compiler supports a subset of constructors provided by the various LINQ to XML types. For instance, whenever you need to create an *XDocument* using Visual Basic 2008 XML literals, the only constructor supported is the one that requires an initial argument of type *XDeclaration* (for example, a processing instruction) on top of the document. Any other XML literal missing the trailing *XDeclaration* is assumed to be an *XElement* instance.

One last thing to notice is that the *XDocument* type inherits from the *XContainer* class, as you can see from Figure 9-1. The *XContainer* class defines all the real implementations of the code to handle nodes and the contents of the document itself.

XElement

XElement is one of the main classes of LINQ to XML. As you can see in Figure 9-1, it has the same hierarchical level as the *XDocument* class and, like the *XDocument* type, is derived from the base *XNode* class through *XContainer*. As its name suggests, this class describes an XML element (a markup tag) and can be used as the container for any XML fragment (a well-formed excerpt of XML content) parented to a tag. It provides many constructors, which you can see in the following list:

```
public XElement(XElement other);
public XElement(XName name);
public XElement(XStreamingElement other);
public XElement(XName name, object content);
public XElement(XName name, params object[] content);
```

The first one simply creates an *XElement* instance based on an already existing *XElement*. The second constructor overload allows you to define an empty *XElement* with a specific element name. We will cover the third constructor later in this chapter when we discuss *XStreaming-Element* and focus our interest here on the last two constructors.

These constructors are the most useful because they support the functional construction of XML. The *Object content* or *params Object[] content* parameters of these constructors can be instances of simple content types (such as *String, Double, Single, Decimal, Boolean, DateTime, TimeSpan,* or *DateTimeOffset*), any type that implements *ToString*, or any type that implements *IEnumerable<T>*. The *params Object[]* list of objects also can include complex content, such as objects of type *XObject, XNode,* and *XAttribute*, which we will cover later in this chapter. Any type of content provided to these constructors will be handled as a string value unless it is an *X** type suitable to be the content of an *XElement*. In fact if you provide to these constructors an *XElement* instance to describe a tag, this tag will be added to the current element as a child. In cases in which you provide a simple content type, its string value will be used as the text content of the document element. Moreover, when you give to one of these two constructors an array of simple types—for instance an array of *Boolean* or *Integer* variables—each value contained in the array will be converted to a string and appended to the text content of the *XElement* instance.

In Listing 9-4 you can see the code to define an *XElement* named *customer*, with a child element named *firstName*.

Listing 9-4 A sample *XElement* constructed using LINQ to XML

```
XElement customerTag = new XElement("customer",
    new XElement("firstName", "Paolo"));
```

Using a standard DOM approach, we would have to define an *XmlDocument* instance, explicitly create the elements, and then append each child node to its parent by using many sentences and code lines, losing expressiveness and readability in the process. Take a look at the code block in Listing 9-5 to again compare the DOM approach and the new functional construction we have just used.

Listing 9-5   Definition of an XML element using DOM

```
XmlDocument customerDocument = new XmlDocument();
XmlElement customerElement = customerDocument.CreateElement("customer");
XmlElement firstNameElement = customerDocument.CreateElement("firstName");
firstNameElement.InnerText = "Paolo";
customerElement.AppendChild(firstNameElement);
customerDocument.AppendChild(customerElement);
```

Probably the easiest way to define this customer element is to use Visual Basic 2008 XML literals, as demonstrated in Listing 9-6.

Listing 9-6   Definition of an XML element using Visual Basic 2008 XML literals

```
Dim customerName As String = "Paolo"
Dim customerTag As XElement = _
    <customer>
      <firstName><%= customerName %></firstName>
    </customer>
```

As we describe in Appendix C, this syntax will be translated by the Visual Basic compiler into the equivalent functional construction.

There are also some static methods provided by *XElement* that act as factory methods. For instance, you can use the *Load* method of *XElement* to load the element content from an existing *XmlReader* instance to reuse existing code based on *System.Xml* classes. You can also invoke the *Load* method and give it a *TextReader* or a file URI as a *String* parameter. If you read an XML document through the static *Load* method of the *XElement* type, the internal implementation will read the XML source using an *XmlReader*, which preserves efficiency. However, the whole XML document will be loaded in memory. Later in this chapter you will see how to avoid loading the whole document into memory, delaying load operations by using a streamed approach.

There are overloads of the *Load* method that accept a *LoadOptions* parameter. This parameter defines a flag enumeration of values that allows you to define how to handle white space (*PreserveWhitespace*), line information (*SetLineInfo*), and base URI address (*SetBaseUri*) while reading the content of the *XElement* instance.

One last useful loading method of the *XElement* type is the *Parse* static method. This method, similar to the corresponding *XDocument* method, allows you to parse a well-formed XML string and convert it into an *XElement* instance ready to be plugged into an XML tree.

Whenever you need to provide a textual representation of an *XElement* instance, you can use the different overloads of the *Save* method. The possible destinations are a file, providing its path as a *String;* an *XmlWriter;* or a *TextWriter.* The default saving behavior is to ignore insignificant spaces. Alternatively, you can use overloads of the *Save* method that allow you to define specific behaviors for handling white space. Using the *SaveOptions* enumeration, you can instruct the *XElement* to serialize its content preserving insignificant white spaces; it does this by calling *Save* with a value of *DisableFormatting* for the *SaveOptions* parameter.

You can also convert an *XElement* instance to a *String* simply by invoking the *ToString* method. Moreover *XElement* also provides direct casting of its content by using a custom implementation of the *Explicit* operator. This custom operator is defined to obtain a typed version of the *Value* property of the *XElement.* Compared to classic *System.Xml.XmlElement,* direct casting is a great improvement because you can manage XML nodes typed from a .NET point of view with a value-centric approach. To better understand this concept, consider the sample code in Listing 9-7.

Listing 9-7   Sample of explicit type casting using *XElement* content

```
XElement order =
    new XElement("order",
        new XElement("quantity", 10),
        new XElement("price", 50),
            new XAttribute("idProduct", "P01"));

Decimal orderTotalAmount =
    (Decimal)order.Element("quantity") *
    (Decimal)order.Element("price");
Console.WriteLine("Order total amount: {0}", orderTotalAmount);
```

Here we use an *XElement* that describes an order. Imagine that we received this instance of the order from an order management system rather than by constructing it explicitly in code. As you can see, we extract the elements named *quantity* and *price,* and we explicitly cast them to a *Decimal* type. The conversion returns the inner *Value* of each element node, trying to cast it to *Decimal.* To handle the case of invalid content, we need to catch a *FormatException* because the various *Explicit* operator overloads internally use *XmlConvert* from *System.Xml* or *Parse* methods of .NET types. Be aware that *XElement* provides explicit conversions to the most common .NET types and also to the corresponding nullable types.

Finally, note that the *XElement* constructor automatically handles XML encoding of text. Consider Listing 9-8.

Listing 9-8   Sample of explicit escaping of XML text

```
XElement notes = new XElement("notes",
    "Some special characters like & > < <div/> etc.");
```

When you call *notes.ToString()* to get its textual representation, the result is encoded automatically through *XmlConvert* and looks like the following:

```
<notes>Some special characters like &amp; &gt; &lt; &lt;div/&gt; etc.</notes>
```

Also, node names are checked against XML naming rules and invalid names are rejected, throwing a *System.Xml.XmlException*. (For further details, see the information about the XSD types *Name* and *NMToken* on the W3C Web site at *http://www.w3.org/*.) This behavior is different from that of the old *XmlWriter*, where names were automatically encoded. We think that developers should be made aware of syntactic rules rather than always hide them under the covers. However, if you want to define "irregular" node names with LINQ to XML, you can just use the *XmlConvert* class by yourself, invoking its methods, *EncodeName* or *Encode-NmToken*, respectively. You can see an example of this approach in Listing 9-9.

Listing 9-9   Sample of manual escaping of XML names

```
XElement notes = new XElement(XmlConvert.EncodeNmToken("strange name!",
    "My parent element has a strange name!");
```

This time, calling *notes.ToString()* will give you the following output:

```
<strange_x0020_name_x0021_>My parent element has a strange
name!</strange_x0020_name_x0021_>
```

As you can see, the name of the *XElement* has been encoded correctly.

XAttribute

This class represents an XML attribute instance and can be added to any *XContainer* (i.e. *XDocument* or *XElement*) by using its constructor and LINQ to XML functional construction. Like the *XElement* class, *XAttribute* offers a rich set of conversion operators so that it can provide its content already typed from a .NET point of view. From a practical point of view, working with attributes is quite similar to working with elements. However, from an internal point of view, attributes are handled as a name/value pair mapped to the container element. Each *XAttribute* provides a couple of properties, called *NextAttribute* and *PreviousAttribute*, that are useful for browsing the sequence of attributes of an element.

In Listing 9-10 you can see an example of using the *XAttribute* type within a functional construction sentence.

Listing 9-10   Sample of using *XAttribute*

```
XElement customerTag = new XElement(
    "customer",
    new XAttribute("id", "C01"), // The attribute added to customerTag
    "Paolo Pialorsi");
```

The result of this code is an element with the name *customer* that contains the text "Paolo Pialorsi," with an attribute named *id* and the value "C01," as in the following XML fragment:

```
<customer id="C01">Paolo Pialorsi</customer>
```

XNode

XNode is the base class for many of the X* classes. It implements the entire tree-node management infrastructure, providing methods with which to add, move, remove, and replace nodes within the XML Infoset. For instance, the *AddAfterSelf* and *AddBeforeSelf* methods are useful for inserting one or more nodes after or before the current one. Listing 9-11 provides an example of these methods—specifically, it shows how to use the *AddAfterSelf* method to insert a couple of addresses for the customer in Listing 9-2, just after the first address.

Listing 9-11   Sample usage of the *AddAfterSelf* method of *XNode*

```
XElement customer = XElement.Load(@"..\..\customer.xml");

// This sentence selects the first address element, child of addresses
XElement firstAddress =
    (customer.Descendants("addresses").Elements("address")).First();

firstAddress.AddAfterSelf(
    new XElement("address",
        new XAttribute("type", "IT-blog"),
            "http://blogs.devleap.com/"),
    new XElement("address",
        new XAttribute("type", "US-blog"),
            "http://weblogs.asp.net/PaoloPia/"));
```

As you can see, we can add a set of nodes because these methods provide several overloads, which are shown here:

```
public void AddAfterSelf(Object content);
public void AddBeforeSelf(Object content);
public void AddAfterSelf(params Object[] content);
public void AddBeforeSelf(params Object[] content);
```

The first two overloads in the preceding list require a single parameter of type *Object*, while the second two overloads accept a *params Object[]* variable list of parameters. You might be wondering why these methods, like many of the constructors we have described earlier, accept the type *Object* instead of *XNode* or any other X* class instance. The answer is quite simple but very interesting: Whenever you provide an object to methods and constructors of X* classes, LINQ to XML checks to determine whether the object is an X* type instance. In cases in which the object is, LINQ to XML hangs it in the node graph if this operation is allowed by the context node. Then it checks whether the object is an array or implements *IEnumerable* to recursively handle its contents. If the object is not but can be converted to a

String by calling its *ToString* method implementation, LINQ to XML appends the string representation to the current node's text content. NULL parameters are just ignored.

Using the functional construction syntax, we can load a set of nodes, as in the following code block, using C# merged with LINQ queries. In Listing 9-12, we use the customers sequence we used in Chapter 2, "LINQ Syntax Fundamentals," to build an XML document based on those customers.

Listing 9-12   A LINQ to XML sentence merged with LINQ queries

```
XElement xmlCustomers = new XElement("customers",
    from   c in customers
    where  c.Country == Countries.Italy
    select new XElement("customer",
               new XAttribute("name", c.Name),
               new XAttribute("city", c.City),
               new XAttribute("country", c.Country)));
```

The result looks like the following XML document and can be obtained simply by calling *xmlCustomers.Save(Console.Out)*:

```
<?xml version="1.0" encoding="utf-8"?>
<customers>
  <customer name="Paolo" city="Brescia" country="Italy" />
  <customer name="Marco" city="Torino" country="Italy" />
</customers>
```

The same result can be achieved by using Visual Basic 2008 XML literals with the code shown in Listing 9-13.

Listing 9-13   A LINQ to XML sentence merged with LINQ queries, using Visual Basic 2008 XML literals

```
Dim xmlCustomers As XElement = _
    <customers>
      <%= From c In customers _
          Where (c.Country = Countries.Italy) _
          Select _
          <customer>
            <firstName><%= c.FirstName %></firstName>
          </customer> %>
    </customers>
```

Another interesting method provided by *XNode* is *DeepEqual*. It is a static method that is useful for fully comparing a couple of XML nodes for equality, as the name suggests. It works by comparing nodes through an internal abstract instance method also called *DeepEqual*. In this way, every type inherited from *XNode* implements its own *DeepEqual* behavior. For example, *XElement* compares element names, element content, and element attributes. The *XNodeEqualityComparer* class that you will see later in this chapter, within LINQ to XML queries, is based on *DeepEqual*.

XName and *XNamespace*

When defining XML contents and node graphs, usually you must also map nodes to their XML namespace. In Listing 9-14, you can see how to define nodes with an XML namespace by using a classic DOM approach.

Listing 9-14   XML namespace handling using classic DOM syntax

```
XmlDocument document = new XmlDocument();

XmlElement customer = document.CreateElement("c", "customer",
    "http://schemas.devleap.com/Customer");
document.AppendChild(customer);

XmlElement firstName = document.CreateElement("c", "name",
    "http://schemas.devleap.com/Customer");
firstName.InnerText = "Paolo Pialorsi";
customer.AppendChild(name);
```

The result of this code excerpt should be the following one:

```
<?xml version="1.0" encoding="IBM437"?>
<c:customer xmlns:c="http://schemas.devleap.com/Customer">
  <c:firstName>Paolo Pialorsi</c:name>
</c:customer>
```

As you can see, we use an overload of the *CreateElement* method, which requires three parameters: a namespace prefix, a tag local name, and the full namespace URI. The same operation can be performed for XML attributes by using the *CreateAttribute* method of *XmlDocument* or the *SetAttribute* method of *XmlElement*. To tell the truth, this way of working is not all that difficult to understand and implement. Nevertheless, developers often get confused when using this approach and complain that XML namespaces are difficult to manage. The real issue probably derives from namespace prefixes, which are just aliases to the real XML namespaces. Theoretically, prefixes are used to simplify namespace references; in reality, they can cause confusion. To address feedback from developers, LINQ to XML was designed to provide an easier way of working with XML namespaces, avoiding any explicit use of prefixes. Every node name is an instance of the *XName* class, which can be defined by a *String* or by a pairing of an *XNamespace* and a *String*. In Listing 9-15, you can see how to define XML content by using a single default XML namespace.

Listing 9-15   LINQ to XML namespace declaration

```
XNamespace ns = "http://schemas.devleap.com/Customer";
XElement customer = new XElement(ns + "customer",
    new XAttribute("id", "C01"),
    new XElement(ns + "firstName", "Paolo"),
    new XElement(ns + "lastName", "Pialorsi"));
```

The *XNamespace* definition looks like a *String*, but it is not. Internally, every *XNamespace* has a more complex behavior. Here is the output of the preceding code:

```
<?xml version="1.0" encoding="utf-8"?>
<customer id="C01" xmlns="http://schemas.devleap.com/Customer">
  <firstName>Paolo</firstName>
  <lastName>Pialorsi</lastName>
</customer>
```

Using Visual Basic 2008 syntax, we can define the namespace directly inside the XML content, as Listing 9-16 shows.

Listing 9-16   Visual Basic 2008 XML literals used to declare XML content with a default XML namespace

```
Dim customer As XDocument = _
    <?xml version="1.0" encoding="utf-8"?>
    <customer id="C01" xmlns="http://schemas.devleap.com/Customer">
      <firstName>Paolo</firstName>
      <lastName>Pialorsi</lastName>
    </customer>
```

Now consider Listing 9-17, where we use a couple of XML namespaces.

Listing 9-17   Multiple XML namespaces within a single *XElement* declaration

```
XNamespace nsCustomer = "http://schemas.devleap.com/Customer";
XNamespace nsAddress = "http://schemas.devleap.com/Address";

XElement customer = new XElement(nsCustomer + "customer",
    new XAttribute("id", "C01"),
    new XElement(nsCustomer + "firstName", "Paolo"),
    new XElement(nsCustomer + "lastName", "Pialorsi"),
    new XElement(nsAddress + "addresses",
        new XElement(nsAddress + "address",
            new XAttribute("type", "email"),
                "paolo@devleap.it"),
        new XElement(nsAddress + "address",
            new XAttribute("type", "home"),
                "Brescia - Italy")));
```

Again, the output is a document with all qualified XML nodes:

```
<?xml version="1.0" encoding="utf-8"?>
<customer id="C01" xmlns="http://schemas.devleap.com/Customer">
  <firstName>Paolo</firstName>
  <lastName>Pialorsi</lastName>
  <addresses xmlns="http://schemas.devleap.com/Address">
    <address type="email">paolo@devleap.it</address>
    <address type="home">Brescia - Italy</address>
  </addresses>
</customer>
```

At this point, you have seen that *XNamespace* is quite simple to use and that LINQ to XML automatically handles namespace declaration, avoiding the explicit use of prefixes. You are probably curious, however, about what happens when you define an *XName* as a concatenation of an *XNamespace* instance and a *String* to represent the local name of the node. Each *XName* instance can be represented as a *String* by using its *ToString* method:

```
Console.WriteLine(customer.Name.ToString());
```

Here is the result of the preceding line of code:

```
{http://schemas.devleap.com/Customer}customer
```

Let's try to use this resolved text instead of the concatenation (an *XNamespace* instance plus local name) used previously:

```
XElement testCustomer = new XElement("{http://schemas.devleap.com/Customer}customer");
Console.WriteLine(testCustomer.Name);
```

In the *System.Xml.Linq* framework, the resolved text "{namespace}local-name" is called the *expanded name* and is semantically equivalent to defining the *XNamespace* separately. The concatenation of an *XNamespace* and a *String* produces a new *XName* that is equivalent to the expanded name. By the way, writing node names by using the expanded name notation is more expensive than using an explicitly declared *XNamespace* instance.

Now we are missing only XML namespace prefixes. You have seen that LINQ to XML handles namespace declaration by itself. However, sometimes you might need to influence how to serialize nodes and represent namespaces by overriding the default behavior of LINQ to XML. To achieve this goal, you can explicitly define the prefixes to use for namespaces by using *xmlns* attributes within your elements, as we do in the example in Listing 9-18.

Listing 9-18   LINQ to XML declaration of an XML namespace with a custom prefix

```
XNamespace ns = "http://schemas.devleap.com/Customer";
XElement customer = new XElement(ns + "customer",
    new XAttribute(XNamespace.Xmlns + "c", ns),
    new XAttribute("id", "C01"),
    new XElement(ns + "firstName", "Paolo"),
    new XElement(ns + "lastName", "Pialorsi"));
```

The output looks like the following:

```
<?xml version="1.0" encoding="utf-8"?>
<c:customer xmlns:c="http://schemas.devleap.com/Customer" id="C01">
  <c:firstName>Paolo</c:firstName>
  <c:lastName>Pialorsi</c:lastName>
</c:customer>
```

As you can see, we defined "c" as the prefix for nodes associated with the *XNamespace* instance named *ns* (i.e. "http://schemas.devleap.com/Customer"). The namespace declaration leverages the *XAttribute* type, and you will always be able to query the attributes of an *XElement* instance to search for namespace declarations. You perform such a query by checking the *IsNamespaceDeclaration* property of the attributes to see whether they are effectively namespace attributes or just attributes. You can see an example in Listing 9-19, where we query the customer *XElement* defined in Listing 9-18.

Listing 9-19 LINQ to XML query for namespace against an *XElement* instance

```
var namespaces =
    from   n in customer.Attributes()
    where  n.IsNamespaceDeclaration == true
    select n;
foreach (var nsItem in namespaces) {
    Console.WriteLine("Value: {0}\nToString: {1}\nName: {2}",
        nsItem.Value,
        nsItem.ToString(),
        nsItem.Name);
}
```

The output of this code excerpt is the following:

```
Value: http://schemas.devleap.com/Customer
ToString: xmlns:c="http://schemas.devleap.com/Customer"
Name: {http://www.w3.org/2000/xmlns/}c
```

Again, we'll show you the corresponding and easiest Visual Basic 2008 syntax, which appears in Listing 9-20.

Listing 9-20 Visual Basic 2008 XML literals used to declare an XML namespace with a custom prefix

```
Dim customer As XDocument = _
<?xml version="1.0" encoding="utf-8"?>
<c:customer xmlns:c="http://schemas.devleap.com/Customer" id="C01">
  <c:firstName>Paolo</c:firstName>
  <c:lastName>Pialorsi</c:lastName>
</c:customer>
```

You might think that starting from LINQ to XML, namespaces are simpler to handle and prefixes are transparently taken out of your control. On the other hand, you might now have the impression that if you need to influence prefixes, you need to do a little more work, at least when using C# 3.0. In fact, Visual Basic 2008 XML literals also simplify namespace declaration, making use of a feature called *global XML namespaces*. This new feature allows you to globally declare an XML namespace URI with its corresponding prefix within a Visual Basic 2008 code file so that you can reuse it many times in code. In Listing 9-21 you can see an example.

Listing 9-21   Visual Basic 2008 XML literals and global XML namespaces

```
Imports System.Xml.Linq
Imports System.Linq
Imports <xmlns:c="http://schemas.devleap.com/Customer">
Public Class Program
  Private Shared Sub GlobalXmlNamespaceSample()

    Dim xmlCustomers As XDocument = _
      <?xml version="1.0" encoding="utf-8"?>
      <c:customers>
          <c:customer name="Paolo" city="Brescia" country="Italy"/>
          <c:customer name="Marco" city="Torino" country="Italy"/>
          <c:customer name="James" city="Dallas" country="USA"/>
          <c:customer name="Frank" city="Seattle" country="USA"/>
      </c:customers>

    End Sub
End Class
```

The key point of this sample is the *Imports* statement, which declares the global namespace prefix *c* for namespace *http://schemas.devleap.com/Customer*. This particular kind of *Imports* syntax can be used to declare only an XML namespace with its prefix. It is not allowed to declare a default XML namespace without a prefix.

Let's look at a final example, shown in Listing 9-22, using C# 3.0 to define a default namespace and a custom prefixed one.

Listing 9-22   C# 3.0 syntax used to define a default namespace and a custom prefix for one

```
XNamespace nsCustomer = "http://schemas.devleap.com/Customer";
XNamespace nsAddress = "http://schemas.devleap.com/Address";
XElement customer = new XElement(nsCustomer + "customer",
    new XAttribute("id", "C01"),
    new XElement(nsCustomer + "firstName", "Paolo"),
    new XElement(nsCustomer + "lastName", "Pialorsi"),
    new XElement(nsAddress + "address", "Brescia - Italy",
        new XAttribute(XNamespace.Xmlns + "a", nsAddress)));
```

The code in Listing 9-22 produces an XML fragment like the following one:

```
<?xml version="1.0" encoding="utf-8"?>
<customer id="C01">
  <firstName>Paolo</firstName>
  <lastName>Pialorsi</lastName>
  <a:address xmlns:a="http://schemas.devleap.com/Address">Brescia - Italy</a:address>
</customer>
```

To query the previous XML content for the purpose of extracting the *lastName* node, we can just write a line of code like the following:

```
XElement lastNameElement = customer.Elements(nsCustomer + "lastName");
```

Using Visual Basic 2008 and global XML namespaces, we can use code like this:

```
Dim lastNameElement As XElement = customer.<c:lastName>
```

In Chapter 10, we will examine in detail how to query XML contents using LINQ to XML queries with both C# 3.0 and Visual Basic 2008 syntax.

Other X* Classes

This new framework has other available classes that define XML declarations (*XDeclaration*), processing instructions (*XProcessingInstruction*), document types (*XDocumentType*), comments (*XComment*), and text nodes (*XText*). These classes are all derived from *XNode* except for *XDeclaration*, which is not considered a node. They are all typically used to build *XDocument* instances, as you have already seen in our description of *XDocument* constructors. *XText*, however, is not allowed to be a child of an *XDocument* unless you define it as empty or with nonsignificant characters. Notice that LINQ to XML nodes in the graph are not normalized, as in many other XML APIs. For instance, if you add a couple of *XText* nodes to an *XElement* node, they will not be merged into a single *XText* node. However, if you add two or more *String* variables to the content of an *XElement* node, their values will be merged into a unique *XText* node instance. Moreover, in LINQ to XML, empty ("") text nodes are valid and keep their existence in the XML tree. If you want to serialize an empty tag explicitly opened and closed (*<customer></customer>*), even if it has empty text content, you can simply add an empty *XText* child to it.

XStreamingElement

Sometimes you need to create XML node graphs starting from contents read from a sequence of entities or objects, and you can do this by using LINQ queries. You have already seen in Chapter 2 that LINQ queries support deferred evaluation. Now consider the following code excerpt.

```
XElement xmlOrders = new XElement("orders",
  from c in customers
  from o in c.Orders
  select new XElement("order",
    new XElement("id", o.IdProduct),
    new XElement("quantity", o.Quantity)));
```

The code defines a set of *<order/>* elements that are children of an *<orders/>* root element. Each child order element contains a couple of children, named *id* and *quantity*. These elements contain, respectively, the *IdProduct* and *Quantity* values of each *Order* instance. Using the previous syntax, the query expression, which was defined to create the list of order tags, is evaluated during the functional construction of the XML node graph. At the end of the statement, the XML output is ready and represents a point-in-time snapshot of the source values. Whenever you need to defer the LINQ query expression evaluation to its effective usage, you can use the *XStreamingElement* class, which represents a tree of *IEnumerable<T>* that will be resolved only when effectively accessed, thus deferring the XML construction as well as the evaluation of any LINQ query that is contained. Consider the sample in Listing 9-23.

Listing 9-23   Sample code showing usage of *XStreamingElement*

```
XStreamingElement xmlOrders = new XStreamingElement("orders",
    from c in customers
    from o in c.Orders
    select new XStreamingElement("order",
        new XStreamingElement("id", o.IdProduct),
        new XStreamingElement("quantity", o.Quantity)));
```

The query expression is evaluated only when saving or accessing the content of the *xmlOrders* variable. This behavior also becomes useful whenever you need to read a large source stream by using an *XmlReader*. You can use this behavior to write the source stream down, eventually applying a transformation to it by using an *XmlWriter*. In fact, even if the result is equivalent to what you can get from an *XElement*, using an *XStreamingElement* keeps a small memory footprint, leveraging *XmlReader*/*XmlWriter* instances while reading the source and writing to the destination.

In Listing 9-24 you can see an example of using *XStreamingElement* together with a chunking *XmlReader*, which loads the source XML file and chunks it, yielding each single *customer* element.

Listing 9-24   Sample code showing usage of *XStreamingElement* together with a chunking *XmlReader*

```
static void chunkingXmlReaderWithXStreamingElement() {

    var customers = ChunkCustomers("CustomersWithOrders.xml");

    XStreamingElement xmlCustomers = new XStreamingElement("customers", customers);

    xmlCustomers.Save("CustomersWithOrdersOutput.xml");
}

static IEnumerable<XElement> ChunkCustomers(String uri) {

    XmlReaderSettings settings = new XmlReaderSettings();
    // Notice the max document size (4MB) setting
    settings.MaxCharactersInDocument = (1024 * 1024) * 4; // MAX 4MB
    XmlReader xr = XmlReader.Create(uri, settings);

    while (xr.Read()){
        if ((xr.NodeType == XmlNodeType.Element)
            && (xr.Name == "customer")) {
                yield return XElement.ReadFrom(xr) as XElement;
        }
    }
}
```

The final behavior of an *XStreamingElement* is related as well to the query you are going to execute. If you define a source query for the *XStreamingElement* content by using a clause that requires you to iterate the entire data source before providing any kind of result (for instance, a LINQ to Objects *ToList()* method over an *IEnumerable<T>* data source), the entire source will be loaded into memory anyway, and you will lose the benefits of using an *XStreamingElement*. For example, in Listing 9-25, *XStreamingElement* is completely useless because of the presence of the *ToList* method against the customers collection.

Listing 9-25   Sample code showing a bad usage of *XStreamingElement*

```
static void chunkingXmlReaderWithXStreamingElement() {

    var customers = ChunkCustomers("CustomersWithOrders.xml");

    XStreamingElement xmlCustomers = new XStreamingElement("customers",
        customers.ToList()); // This is a wrong usage of XStreamingElement

    xmlCustomers.Save("CustomersWithOrdersOutput.xml");
}
```

XObject and Annotations

XObject represents the base class of the whole LINQ to XML class framework. It mainly provides methods and properties to work with annotations on nodes. Annotations are a mechanism that maps metadata to XML nodes. For instance, you can add custom user information to your nodes as shown in Listing 9-26.

Listing 9-26   Annotations applied to an *XElement* instance

```
XElement customer = XElement.Load(@"..\..\customer.xml");

CustomerAnnotation annotation = new CustomerAnnotation();
annotation.Notes = "This is a good customer!";
customer.AddAnnotation(annotation);
```

CustomerAnnotation is a custom type and can be any .NET type. You can then retrieve annotations from XML nodes by using one of the two generic methods, *Annotation<T>* or *Annotations<T>*. These generic methods search for an annotation of type *T* (or one that is derived from *T*) in the current node. If an annotation exists, *Annotation<T>* returns the first one, or *Annotations<T>* returns the full set of annotations.

```
annotation = customer.Annotation<CustomerAnnotation>();
```

Because *XObject* is the base class of every kind of X* class that is used to describe an XML node, annotations can be added to any node. Usually, annotations are used to keep state information, such as a mapping to source entities or documents used to build XML, whereas the code handles real XML content. Annotations are not part of the XML Infoset; they are not serialized or deserialized with XML content.

Another feature common to all types inherited from *XObject* are LINQ to XML events. These are an easy and common way of handling events related to changes applied to the node tree. The available events are *Changing* and *Changed*, which notify you about modifications that are going to happen and modifications that have already happened, respectively. The .NET event handler receives an instance of an *XObjectChangeEventArgs* type, which provides an *ObjectChange* property of type *XObjectChange*. *XObjectChange* is an enumeration that assumes values of *Add* for node additions, *Name* for node name modifications, *Remove* for node removals, and *Value* for node value modifications. These events can be used to monitor modifications to one node and all of its descendants. Only a modification of a tree raises an event, whereas construction of an XML tree by using functional construction does not notify events. Because the event handling infrastructure is available for any X* class inheriting from *XObject*, you can subscribe to the event of one node to catch events of all its descendants, rather than subscribing to the same event for all the nodes of the subtree. In Listing 9-27, you can see an example of how to use these events.

Listing 9-27   Example of XML tree modification events handling

```
XElement customer = XElement.Load(@"..\..\customer.xml");

// Subscribe to the changing event using a Lambda Expression
customer.Changing += (sender, e) => {
    Console.WriteLine("=> Changing event raised");
    Console.WriteLine("\tChanging of type: {0}", e.ObjectChange);

    XObject x = sender as XObject;
    Console.WriteLine("\tChanging node of type: {0}", x.NodeType);

    XElement element = sender as XElement;
    if (element != null) {
        Console.WriteLine("\tCurrent value: {0}", element.Value);
    }

    XAttribute attribute = sender as XAttribute;
    if (attribute != null) {
        Console.WriteLine("\tCurrent value: {0}", attribute.Value);
    }
};

// Subscribe to the changed event using a Lambda Expression
customer.Changed += (sender, e) => {
    Console.WriteLine("=> Changed event raised");
    Console.WriteLine("\tChanged of type: {0}", e.ObjectChange);

    XObject x = sender as XObject;
    Console.WriteLine("\tChanged node of type: {0}", x.NodeType);

    XElement element = sender as XElement;
    if (element != null) {
        Console.WriteLine("\tCurrent value: {0}", element.Value);
    }
```

```
        XAttribute attribute = sender as XAttribute;
        if (attribute != null) {
            Console.WriteLine("\tCurrent value: {0}", attribute.Value);
        }
    };


    // Look for the first address in customer
    XElement emailAddress = customer
        .Descendants("address")
        .First(a => a.Attribute("type").Value == "email");
    // Change the text content of the XML node
    emailAddress.Value = "paolo@devleap.com";
    // Change the value of the type attribute
    emailAddress.Attribute("type").Value = "externalEmail";
```

It is interesting to observe the results of the sample shown in Listing 9-25, because changing
the text content of an element raises four events: a couple of *Changing/Changed* events to
notify you of the removal of the original text content, and a couple of *Changing/Changed*
events to notify you of the addition of the new text content. Moreover, changing the value
of an attribute node raises only a set of value *Changing/Changed* events. Here is the output of
Listing 9-27:

```
=> Changing event raised
    Changing of type: Remove
    Changing node of type: Text
=> Changed event raised
    Changed of type: Remove
    Changed node of type: Text
=> Changing event raised
    Changing of type: Add
    Changing node of type: Text
=> Changed event raised
    Changed of type: Add
    Changed node of type: Text
=> Changing event raised
    Changing of type: Value
    Changing node of type: Attribute
    Current value: email
=> Changed event raised
    Changed of type: Value
    Changed node of type: Attribute
    Current value: externalEmail
```

You should not change the XML source tree while handling tree modification events because
the result could be unpredictable and unstable. Consider also that *XObject* internally adds a
specific annotation of type *XObjectChangeAnnotation* on top of nodes with an active modification-
event subscription. This can be useful for finding nodes with active event handling.

Reading, Traversing, and Modifying XML

You have seen how to create and annotate XML content using LINQ to XML. Whenever you have XML available in memory, you can also navigate and eventually modify it. To navigate XML content, you can use methods and properties of X* classes, or you can also rely on LINQ queries over an X* object. In this section, we look at the former way of working, and in the next chapter we look at the latter.

Every *XNode* provides some methods and properties by which to navigate its hierarchy. For instance, you can use the *IsAfter* or *IsBefore* method to compare ordinal positioning of nodes in a document. These methods internally use the *CompareDocumentOrder* static method of the *XNode* class and return a numeric index, of type *Integer*, that represents the "distance" between two *XNode* instances in the containing *XDocument*. It is also used by *XNodeDocument-OrderComparer*, and it is useful when ordering nodes in LINQ to XML queries.

Every *XNode* also provides a couple of properties, called *NextNode* and *PreviousNode*, that map to the next and previous nodes in the graph, as their names indicate. Pay attention to the relative cost of these properties. *NextNode* returns a reference to an internal field and is relatively cheap; *PreviousNode* requires a partial scan of the tree branch containing the current node and is a little bit more expensive. *XContainer* also provides *LastNode* and *FirstNode* properties.

Finally, every *XObject* offers a *Parent* property of type *XElement* that returns a reference to the parent element of the current node in the graph, although not all nodes have a value for their *Parent* property. For instance, the children of an *XDocument* node have a *Parent* with a null value because *XDocument* is not an *XElement*.

Whenever you find a node while traversing the document by using one of these techniques and you want to modify it, you can use methods such as *Remove* or *ReplaceWith*, which are available for any *XNode*, to remove the node itself from the graph or to replace it with a new fragment. There are also *RemoveAttributes*, *ReplaceAttributes*, and *ReplaceAll* methods for objects of type *XElement*. These methods work with their respective attributes or with the full set of child nodes. Finally, *XElement* also offers *SetAttributeValue*, *SetElementValue*, and *SetValue* to change the value of an attribute, a child element, or the entire current element, respectively.

In Listing 9-28, you can see how to replace one element with another.

Listing 9-28 Example of tag replacement using the *XElement ReplaceWith* method

```
XElement customer = new XElement("customer",
    new XAttribute("id", "C01"),
    new XElement("firstName", "Paolo"),
    new XElement("lastName", "Pialorsi"));

// Do something in the meantime ...

customer.LastNode.ReplaceWith(
    new XElement("nickName", "PaoloPia"));
```

The preceding code block changes this XML:

```xml
<?xml version="1.0" encoding="utf-8"?>
<customer id="C01">
  <firstName>Paolo</firstName>
  <lastName>Pialorsi</lastName>
</customer>
```

into this XML:

```xml
<?xml version="1.0" encoding="utf-8"?>
<customer id="C01">
  <firstName>Paolo</firstName>
  <nickName>PaoloPia</nickName>
</customer>
```

Listing 9-29 shows you how to change attribute and element values.

Listing 9-29   Example of attribute and child element management using *XElement* methods

```
customer.SetAttributeValue("id", "C02");
customer.SetElementValue("notes", "Notes about this customer");
```

By calling these methods, the LINQ to XML programming framework creates attributes or elements that do not yet exist or changes the values of ones that already exist. When the value provided to these methods is null and the nodes already exist, they are removed.

While traversing an XML tree, keep in mind that the navigation technique you use influences the result. The methods and properties shown up to this point in the chapter work directly in memory and determine their results at the time that you invoke them. If you specify to remove or replace a node, the action is taken instantly within the in-memory structure. In the case of queries over XML, based on the LINQ to XML query engine, modification methods are applied to query expression results that will be evaluated only when they are effectively used, like the ones you saw in Chapter 2.

Summary

In this chapter, you have seen how to define an XML Infoset using the LINQ to XML programming framework—by means of both functional construction and Visual Basic 2008 XML literals. You have learned how to use the main classes of the LINQ to XML programming framework to work with documents, elements, attributes, and all the information items of XML Infoset. You have seen also how to manage LINQ to XML events and annotations.

Chapter 10
LINQ to XML: Querying Nodes

Starting from what you've seen about the XML Infoset in Chapter 9, "LINQ to XML: Managing Infoset," now consider that every node set can be thought of as a sequence of nodes and queried by using LINQ queries, just as with any other sequence of type *IEnumerable<T>*. Starting from this point, we can make the case that every concept we have already applied to other sequences of items in the fields of LINQ queries (such as LINQ to Objects, LINQ to SQL, and so forth) can also be used with XML nodes. In fact LINQ to XML exposes every collection of nodes as an *IEnumerable<T>* instance.

Querying XML

You can use the standard query extension methods described in Chapter 3, "LINQ to Objects," to query XML nodes, but there are also a group of custom extension methods, declared in the *System.Xml.Linq.Extensions* class, specifically defined to be applied to sequences of *IEnumerable<X*>*. In this section, we cover these methods.

Attribute, Attributes

Each instance of *XElement* supports a set of methods to access its attributes, as shown here:

```
public XAttribute Attribute(XName name);
public IEnumerable<XAttribute> Attributes();
public IEnumerable<XAttribute> Attributes(XName name);
```

As you can see, the first method returns a single *XAttribute* instance that is retrieved by name if it exists. If it does not exist, the method returns null. The second method returns all the attributes of an *XElement* as an *IEnumerable<XAttribute>*, which is a useful type for LINQ queries. The last method returns a sequence of type *IEnumerable<XAttribute>* that contains zero or one items, whose name equals the item provided as the value of the parameter *name*. In fact, attributes of one element are a collection of uniquely named nodes; therefore, an element with multiple occurrences of the same attribute name cannot exist. Consider the following XML document, which we used also in Chapter 9:

```xml
<?xml version="1.0" encoding="UTF-16" standalone="yes"?>
<customer id="C01">
  <firstName>Paolo</firstName>
  <lastName>Pialorsi</lastName>
  <addresses>
    <address type="email">paolo@devleap.it</address>
    <address type="url">http://www.devleap.it/</address>
    <address type="home">Brescia - Italy</address>
  </addresses>
</customer>
```

In Listing 10-1 you can see an example of the *Attribute* and *Attributes* extension methods within a LINQ query expression in C# 3.0.

Listing 10-1   A sample LINQ to XML query based on the *Attribute* and *Attributes* extension methods

```
XElement xmlCustomer = XElement.Load(@"..\..\customer.xml");

Console.WriteLine("Attributes with name \"id\" count: {0}",
    xmlCustomer.Attributes().Where(a => a.Name == "id").Count());
Console.WriteLine("\"id\" attribute value: {0}",
    xmlCustomer.Attribute("id").Value);
```

The console output of this code excerpt is the following:

```
Attributes with name "id" count: 1
"id" attribute value: C01
```

As you can see, there is only one "id" attribute with a value of "C01" for the *customer* element.

Element, Elements

Every *XContainer* instance (i.e., *XDocument* and *XElement*) provides methods to return a single element by name or to select sequences of elements that are eventually filtered by their name (of type *XName*). Here are their signatures:

```
public XElement Element(XName name);
public IEnumerable<XElement> Elements();
public IEnumerable<XElement> Elements(XName name);
```

The *Element* method iterates over the child nodes of the current *XContainer* and returns the first *XElement*, whose name corresponds to the argument provided for the type *XName*. Because of the argument type (*XName*), you have to provide a valid node name, and you need to include its XML namespace URI in a case in which you are looking for a qualified element, as shown in Listing 10-2.

Listing 10-2   A sample LINQ to XML query based on the *Element* extension method

```
XNamespace ns = "http://schemas.devleap.com/Customers";
XElement xmlCustomers = new XElement(ns + "customers",
    from  c in customers
    where c.Country == Countries.Italy
    select new XElement(ns + "customer",
              new XAttribute("name", c.Name),
              new XAttribute("city", c.City),
              new XAttribute("country", c.Country)));
XElement element = xmlCustomers.Element(ns + "customer");
```

To get all the customers, you can use the *Elements* method, as shown in Listing 10-3.

Listing 10-3   Another sample LINQ to XML query based on the *Elements* extension method

```
var elements = xmlCustomers.Elements();
foreach (XElement e in elements) {
    Console.WriteLine(e);
}
```

Here is the result:

```
<customer name="Paolo" city="Brescia" country="Italy" />
<customer name="Marco" city="Torino" country="Italy" />
```

The last overload of the *Elements* method just allows filtering child elements by name. There is no way, using the *Element* or *Elements* method, to get a single *XElement* child of the current *XContainer* without providing a filtering name, given that there is more than one child element. However, you can leverage the *First* extension method of LINQ to Objects to achieve this goal. Here is an example:

```
XElement firstElement = xmlCustomers.Elements().First();
```

Because the argument of the *Element* method is an *XName* type instance, you can also use the *XNamespace* class to select elements using their fully qualified name. In Listing 10-4 you can see an example of this.

Listing 10-4   A sample LINQ to XML query based on *Elements* using a namespace

```
XNamespace ns = "http://schemas.devleap.com/Customers";
XElement xmlCustomers = new XElement(ns + "customers",
    from  c in customers
    where  c.Country == Countries.Italy
    select new XElement(ns + "customer",
        new XAttribute("name", c.Name),
        new XAttribute("city", c.City),
        new XAttribute("country", c.Country)));

XElement element = xmlCustomers.Element(ns + "customer");
```

XPath Axes "like" Extension Methods

Some of the extension methods that are defined in the *Extensions* class of the namespace *System.Xml.Linq* recall XPath Axes functions. The first two methods that we will consider are *Ancestors* and *Descendants*, which return an *IEnumerable<XElement>* sequence of elements. The *Ancestors* method extends any *IEnumerable<XNode>* instance, while *Descendants* extends any *IEnumerable<XContainer>* instance. *Descendants* returns all the elements after the current node in the document graph, regardless of their depth in the graph. *Ancestors* is somewhat complementary to *Descendants* and returns all the elements before the current node in the document graph. The signatures of both methods are shown here:

```
public static IEnumerable<XElement> Ancestors<T>
  (this IEnumerable<T> source)
    where T: XNode;
public static IEnumerable<XElement> Ancestors<T>
  (this IEnumerable<T> source, XName name)
    where T: XNode;
public static IEnumerable<XElement> Descendants<T>
  (this IEnumerable<T> source)
    where T: XContainer;
public static IEnumerable<XElement> Descendants<T>
  (this IEnumerable<T> source, XName name)
    where T: XContainer;
```

These methods are useful for querying an XML source to find a particular element after or before the current one, regardless of its position in the graph. The *Descendants* method has a counterpart instance method, available for each *XContainer* instance (document or element). Here are the available signatures for this instance method:

```
public IEnumerable<XElement> Descendants();
public IEnumerable<XElement> Descendants(XName name);
```

Consider the XML document in Listing 10-5.

Listing 10-5   An XML instance to search with LINQ to XML

```
<?xml version="1.0" encoding="UTF-8"?>
<customers>
  <customer>
    <name>Paolo</name>
    <city>Brescia</city>
    <country>Italy</country>
  </customer>
  <customer>
    <name>Marco</name>
    <city>Torino</city>
    <country>Italy</country>
  </customer>
</customers>
```

The following line of code returns 8 as the number of descendant elements of an XML document like the one in Listing 10-5:

```
Console.WriteLine(xmlCustomers.Descendants().Count());
```

The descendant elements, grouped by name, are the following: two *<customer />* elements, two *<name />* elements, two *<city />* elements, and two *<country />* elements.

The code in Listing 10-6 uses the *Descendants* method to show the nodes together with their XML content.

Listing 10-6   A sample code excerpt to browse the results of a *Descendants* method invocation.

```
XElement xmlCustomers = XElement.Load(@"..\..\Customers.xml");

foreach (var descendant in xmlCustomers.Descendants()) {
    Console.WriteLine("=> Element: {0}\n{1}",
        descendant.Name, descendant);
}
```

Executing this code you will get the following result:

```
=> Element: customer
<customer>
  <name>Paolo</name>
  <city>Brescia</city>
  <country>Italy</country>
</customer>
=> Element: name
<name>Paolo</name>
=> Element: city
<city>Brescia</city>
=> Element: country
<country>Italy</country>
=> Element: customer
<customer>
  <name>Marco</name>
  <city>Torino</city>
  <country>Italy</country>
</customer>
=> Element: name
<name>Marco</name>
=> Element: city
<city>Torino</city>
=> Element: country
<country>Italy</country>
```

As you can see, the list of descendant elements references them in the same order as they appear in the source XML document.

Two other extension methods that work like the previous ones are *AncestorsAndSelf* and *DescendantsAndSelf*. Here are their signatures:

```
public static IEnumerable<XElement> AncestorsAndSelf(
    this IEnumerable<XElement> source);
public static IEnumerable<XElement> AncestorsAndSelf(
    this IEnumerable<XElement> source, XName name);
public static IEnumerable<XElement> DescendantsAndSelf(
    this IEnumerable<XElement> source);
public static IEnumerable<XElement> DescendantsAndSelf(
    this IEnumerable<XElement> source, XName name);
```

These methods act like the previous methods, but they also return the current element. As with XPath Axes, you can retrieve all the elements of an XML source just by specifying the union of the results of *Ancestors* and *DescendantsAndSelf* or *AncestorsAndSelf* and *Descendants*.

The *XElement* type provides a couple of instance methods, *AncestorsAndSelf* and *Descendants-AndSelf*, that are the counterpart of the previously seen extension methods.

If you need to select all the descendant nodes rather than only the descendant elements, you can use methods such as *DescendantNodes*, which is suitable for *IEnumerable<XContainer>*, or *DescendantNodesAndSelf*, which extends *IEnumerable<XElement>*. Both of these methods return all descendant nodes, regardless of their node types, eventually with the *XElement* node itself for the *DescendantNodesAndSelf* method. Again, the *DescendantNodes* extension method exists also as an instance method for the *XContainer* type, and the *DescendantNodes-AndSelf* method has its counterpart instance method for the *XElement* type.

Consider the XML document shown previously in Chapter 9:

```
<?xml version="1.0" encoding="UTF-16" standalone="yes"?>
<customer id="C01">
  <firstName>Paolo</firstName>
  <lastName>Pialorsi</lastName>
  <addresses>
    <address type="email">paolo@devleap.it</address>
    <address type="url">http://www.devleap.it/</address>
    <address type="home">Brescia - Italy</address>
  </addresses>
</customer>
```

In Listing 10-7 you can see an example of how to use the *DescendantNodes* instance method.

Listing 10-7   A sample code excerpt to show the *DescendantNodes* method invocation.

```
XElement customer = XElement.Load(@"..\..\Customer.xml");

var descendantNodes = customer.DescendantNodes();
Console.WriteLine("There are {0} descendant nodes",
    descendantNodes.Count());

foreach (var descendant in descendantNodes) {
    Console.WriteLine("=> Node Type: {0}\n{1}",
        descendant.NodeType, descendant);
}
```

The console output of this code excerpt will be the list of all the nodes descending from the root *XElement* of our sample document. Take a look at the result:

```
There are 11 descendant nodes
=> Node Type: Element
<firstName>Paolo</firstName>
=> Node Type: Text
Paolo
```

```
=> Node Type: Element
<lastName>Pialorsi</lastName>
=> Node Type: Text
Pialorsi
=> Node Type: Element
<addresses>
  <address type="email">paolo@devleap.it</address>
  <address type="url">http://www.devleap.it/</address>
  <address type="home">Brescia - Italy</address>
</addresses>
=> Node Type: Element
<address type="email">paolo@devleap.it</address>
=> Node Type: Text
paolo@devleap.it
=> Node Type: Element
<address type="url">http://www.devleap.it/</address>
=> Node Type: Text
http://www.devleap.it/
=> Node Type: Element
<address type="home">Brescia - Italy</address>
=> Node Type: Text
Brescia - Italy
```

As you can see, the result contains Element and Text nodes, but it does not contain attributes because they are not considered to be nodes in LINQ to XML. In fact, the *XAttribute* type does not inherit from *XNode* but directly from the *XObject* base class.

There is also a *Nodes* extension method that extends IEnumerable<XContainer> and returns all the child nodes of that collection of *XContainer* instances, once again regardless of their node types but excluding attributes that are not nodes. The *XContainer* type offers the corresponding *Nodes* instance method.

XNode Selection Methods

The *XNode* class provides several methods that are useful for retrieving elements and nodes related to the current node itself. For instance, both the *ElementsBeforeSelf* and *ElementsAfter-Self* methods return a sequence of type IEnumerable<XElement> that contains the elements before or after the current node, respectively. They both provide an overload with a parameter of type *XName* to filter elements by name.

```
public IEnumerable<XElement> ElementsAfterSelf();
public IEnumerable<XElement> ElementsAfterSelf(XName name);
public IEnumerable<XElement> ElementsBeforeSelf();
public IEnumerable<XElement> ElementsBeforeSelf(XName name);
```

In addition, the *NodesBeforeSelf* and *NodesAfterSelf* methods return a sequence of type IEnumerable<XNode> that contains all the nodes, regardless of their node type, before or after the current one.

```
public IEnumerable<XNode> NodesAfterSelf();
public IEnumerable<XNode> NodesBeforeSelf();
```

Both these methods will return any node (*XNode*), excluding attributes as usual. In Listing 10-8 you can see an example of *NodesBeforeSelf* and *NodesAfterSelf* applied to the *address* elements of the single-customer XML we've used earlier.

Listing 10-8   A sample code excerpt to show the use of *NodesBeforeSelf* and *NodesAfterSelf*.

```
XElement customer = XElement.Load(@"..\..\customer.xml");

var firstAddress = customer.Element("addresses").FirstNode;
var nodesAfterSelf = firstAddress.NodesAfterSelf();

Console.WriteLine("Here is the first address:\n\t{0}",
    firstAddress);
Console.WriteLine("There are {0} addresses after the first address",
    nodesAfterSelf.Count());
foreach (var addressNode in nodesAfterSelf) {
    Console.WriteLine("\t{0}", addressNode);
}

Console.WriteLine();

var lastAddress = customer.Element("addresses").LastNode;
var nodesBeforeSelf = lastAddress.NodesBeforeSelf();

Console.WriteLine("Here is the last address:\n\t{0}",
    lastAddress);
Console.WriteLine("There are {0} addresses before the last address",
    nodesBeforeSelf.Count());
foreach (var addressNode in nodesBeforeSelf) {
    Console.WriteLine("\t{0}", addressNode);
}
```

The result of this code is the following:

```
Here is the first address:
        <address type="email">paolo@devleap.it</address>
There are 2 addresses after the first address
        <address type="url">http://www.devleap.it/</address>
        <address type="home">Brescia - Italy</address>

Here is the last address:
        <address type="home">Brescia - Italy</address>
There are 2 addresses before the last address
        <address type="email">paolo@devleap.it</address>
        <address type="url">http://www.devleap.it/</address>
```

Notice that the results are in document order, regardless of the direction (before or after) of the node retrieval method.

InDocumentOrder

One last extension method that needs to be explained is the *InDocumentOrder* method. It orders an *IEnumerable<XNode>* sequence of nodes related to the same *XDocument* by using an *XNodeDocumentOrderComparer* class, which bases its behavior on the *CompareDocumentOrder* method. (For more information about the inner workings of node comparison, see Chapter 9.) This extension method is very useful whenever you want to select nodes ordered on the basis of their order of occurrence in a document.

In the following example, you can see how to use it:

```
foreach (XNode a in xmlCustomers.DescendantsAndSelf().InDocumentOrder()) {
    Console.WriteLine("+ " + a);
}
```

The result of this sample code is the full list of nodes declared within the *xmlCustomers* document defined in Listing 10-5, in document order.

Deferred Query Evaluation

Under the cover, many of the extension methods described in the previous section work with deferred query evaluation, like every other LINQ query. The consequence of this mechanism is that every time you use these methods, the result can change if the source XML on which they are applied changes. Consider the example in Listing 10-9, where we output to the console window all the *city* nodes of the customers located in Italy.

Listing 10-9   A LINQ to XML query to extract all *city* nodes from a customers list

```
XElement xmlCustomers = new XElement("customers",
    from   c in customers
    where  c.Country == Countries.Italy
    select new XElement("customer",
                new XElement("name", c.Name),
                new XElement("city", c.City),
                new XElement("country", c.Country)));

var cities = xmlCustomers.DescendantsAndSelf("city");

Console.WriteLine("\nBefore XML source modification");
foreach (var city in cities) {
    Console.WriteLine(city);
}
```

The result of the query is the following:

```
Before XML source modification
<city>Brescia</city>
<city>Torino</city>
```

Now let's try to change the source of the *xmlCustomers* object. We add customers that are not located in Italy and then repeat the iteration over the *cities* query variable, representing the LINQ query over *XElements* with the XML name of *city*. The code is shown in Listing 10-10.

Listing 10-10   A LINQ to XML query to extract all *city* nodes from a customers list after adding some customers

```
xmlCustomers.Add(
    from   c in customers
    where  c.Country != Countries.Italy
    select new XElement("customer",
             new XElement("name", c.Name),
             new XElement("city", c.City),
             new XElement("country", c.Country))),

Console.WriteLine("\nAfter XML source modification");

// the query defined in cities is executed another time on the updated
// source because the foreach construct retrieves the enumerator as you
// have already seen for the usual LINQ queries
foreach (var city in cities) {
    Console.WriteLine(city);
}
```

This time the result also includes the new cities, which are outside Italy:

```
After XML source modification
<city>Brescia</city>
<city>Torino</city>
<city>Dallas</city>
<city>Seattle</city>
```

To get a static result, we can invoke one of the conversion operators we described in Chapter 3—*ToList*, *ToArray*, *ToDictionary*, or *ToLookup*—on the *cities* variable before the source is updated.

LINQ Queries over XML

You have already seen that many of the LINQ to XML methods navigate XML content and return instances of type *IEnumerable<XNode>* or *IEnumerable<XElement>*. Because LINQ queries can be applied to sequences of *IEnumerable<T>*, we can also use them to query XML content. In some of the previous examples, we used LINQ query expressions to create new XML content.

Now consider a situation in which you want to create sequences of items (objects, entities, or whatever) whose value is taken from XML content. We can use LINQ query expressions over XML nodes through LINQ to XML syntax.

Listing 10-11 is an example of a query expression applied to the well-known XML list of customers. It filters the list of *customer* elements to extract the *name* element and the *city* attribute of each customer located in Italy, ordering the result by the *name* element value.

Listing 10-11   Using LINQ to XML and query expressions to query XML content

```
var customersFromXml =
    from   c in xmlCustomers.Elements("customer")
    where  (String)c.Attribute("country") == "Italy"
    orderby (String)c.Element("name")
    select new {
            Name = (String)c.Element("name"),
            City = (String)c.Attribute("city")
    };

foreach (var customer in customersFromXml) {
    Console.WriteLine(customer);
}
```

The result is shown in the following output block:

```
{ Name = Marco, City = Torino }
{ Name = Paolo, City = Brescia }
```

This result is interesting, even if it is not all that exciting. To make these opportunities more challenging, suppose you have the same XML list of customers and also a sequence of orders defined using the following LINQ query:

```
var orders =
    from   c in customers
    from   o in c.Orders
    select new {c.Name, o.IdProduct, o.Quantity};
```

Imagine that the orders were loaded via LINQ to SQL from a Microsoft SQL Server database. You can write a complex query that joins XML nodes with entities to extract a sequence of new objects, as shown in Listing 10-12.

Listing 10-12   A LINQ query that merges LINQ to XML and LINQ to Objects

```
var ordersWithCustomersFromXml =
    from   c in xmlCustomers.Elements("customer")
    join   o in orders
    on     (String)c.Element("name") equals o.Name
    orderby (String)c.Element("name")
    select new {
            Name = (String)c.Element("name"),
            City = (String)c.Attribute("city"),
            IdProduct = o.IdProduct,
            Quantity = o.Quantity };
```

This is a new and really powerful feature of LINQ and LINQ to XML, through which we can define queries over mixed contents by using a unique language and programming environment.

If you do not like the repetition of explicit casting of XML nodes inside the LINQ query, remember that you can use the *let* clause to define a more maintainable alias, as shown in Listing 10-13.

Listing 10-13   A LINQ query that merges LINQ to XML and LINQ to Objects, simplified by using the *let* clause

```
var ordersWithCustomersFromXml =
    from    c in xmlCustomers.Elements("customer")
    let     xName = (String)c.Element("name")
    let     xCity = (String)c.Attribute("city")
    join    o in orders
    on      xName equals o.Name
    orderby xName
    select  new {
                Name = xName,
                City = xCity,
                IdProduct = o.IdProduct,
                Quantity = o.Quantity };
```

Both of the previous examples return a sequence that looks like the following when printed to the console window:

```
{ Name = Frank, City = Seattle, IdProduct = 5, Quantity = 20 }
{ Name = James, City = Dallas, IdProduct = 3, Quantity = 20 }
{ Name = Marco, City = Torino, IdProduct = 1, Quantity = 10 }
{ Name = Marco, City = Torino, IdProduct = 3, Quantity = 20 }
{ Name = Paolo, City = Brescia, IdProduct = 1, Quantity = 3 }
{ Name = Paolo, City = Brescia, IdProduct = 2, Quantity = 5 }
```

Using a LINQ query expression, you can also create a new XML graph, merging XML nodes and entities. Be careful while mixing LINQ to XML query expressions and LINQ to XML declarations over the same XML tree. In general, it is a good habit to avoid mixing declarative syntax and imperative syntax over the same node graph, whereas it is absolutely allowed and sometimes useful to generate new XML trees that query existing ones with LINQ to XML.

Querying XML Efficiently to Build Entities

Now imagine that you need to read a list of customers with their orders from an existing XML persistence layer, leveraging a set of custom entities taken from your domain model. See Listing 10-14 for the definition of the *Customer* and *Order* types.

Listing 10-14 A sample *Customer* and *Order* type definition

```
public class Customer {
    public string Name;
    public string City;
    public Countries Country;
    public Order[] Orders;

    public override string ToString(){
        return String.Format("Name: {0} - City: {1} - Country: {2}",
            this.Name, this.City, this.Country);
    }
}

public class Order {
    public int IdOrder;
    public int Quantity;
    public bool Shipped;
    public string Month;
    public int IdProduct;

    public override string ToString() {
        return String.Format("IdOrder: {0} - IdProduct: {1} - Quantity:
            {2} - Shipped: {3} - Month: {4}",
            this.IdOrder, this.IdProduct, this.Quantity, this.Shipped,
            this.Month);
    }
}
```

The XML source document, representing our hypothetical data source, could be like the
following one:

```
<?xml version="1.0" encoding="utf-8"?>
<customers>
  <customer name="Paolo" city="Brescia" country="Italy">
    <orders>
      <order id="1" idProduct="1" quantity="3" shipped="false" month="January" />
      <order id="2" idProduct="2" quantity="5" shipped="true" month="May" />
    </orders>
  </customer>
  <customer name="Marco" city="Torino" country="Italy">
    <orders>
      <order id="3" idProduct="1" quantity="10" shipped="false" month="July" />
      <order id="4" idProduct="3" quantity="20" shipped="true" month="December" />
    </orders>
  </customer>
</customers>
```

We know that with LINQ to XML we can load the XML content using an *XElement* object
and then query its nodes to build the in-memory list of *Customer* and *Order* instances.
Listing 10-15 shows an example.

Listing 10-15   A sample of loading *Customer* and *Order* instances from an XML data source via LINQ to XML

```
XElement xmlCustomers = XElement.Load("customersWithOrdersDataSource.xml");

var customersWithOrders =
    from c in xmlCustomers.Elements("customer")
    select new Customer {
        Name = (String)c.Attribute("name"),
        City = (String)c.Attribute("city"),
        Country = (Countries)Enum.Parse(typeof(Countries),
            (String)c.Attribute("country"), true),
        Orders = (
            from o in c.Descendants("order")
            select new Order {
                IdOrder = (Int32)o.Attribute("id"),
                IdProduct = (Int32)o.Attribute("idProduct"),
                Quantity = (Int32)o.Attribute("quantity"),
                Month = (String)o.Attribute("month"),
                Shipped = (Boolean)o.Attribute("shipped"),
            }
        ).ToArray()
    };

foreach (Customer c in customersWithOrders) {
    Console.WriteLine(c);
    foreach (Order o in c.Orders) {
        Console.WriteLine("  {0}", o);
    }
}
```

In this code excerpt you can see in bold the LINQ to XML methods (instance or extension) invoked. For instance, we retrieve the list of all the *customer* elements using the *Elements* instance method of the *XElement* object, which represents the document root. Then we enumerate each of these *customer* elements in order to retrieve their attributes, using the *Attributes* instance method. Finally we build the list of orders for each *Customer* type instance by using the *Descendants* instance method of the *XElement* type applied to each customer element previously selected. Notice that here again the code leverages the explicit type-casting feature offered by the *XAttribute* type to extract the typed values of the attributes.

Even if the code in Listing 10-15 is already completely functional and syntactically correct, it could be written more efficiently. In fact, with the code you've seen, we load the whole set of XML nodes in memory and then we produce the output object model. With a small data source this is not a problem, but in the case of a large or remote data source, this behavior could affect the overall performance of a solution. In this situation, it would be preferable to use a chunking reader based on an *XmlReader* instance, like the one we showed in Listing 9-24 in Chapter 9.

In Listing 10-16 you can see an example equivalent to the one presented in Listing 10-15 but using a chunking reader.

Listing 10-16   A sample of loading *Customer* and *Order* instances from XML data source using chunks

```
static IEnumerable<XElement>
ChunkedDataSourceReader(String uri, String chunkElement) {
    XmlReaderSettings settings = new XmlReaderSettings();
    XmlReader xr = XmlReader.Create(uri, settings);

    while (xr.Read()) {
        if ((xr.NodeType == XmlNodeType.Element)
            && (xr.Name == chunkElement)) {
            // For debugging and demo purposes only
            Console.WriteLine("Reading a chunk element from data source");
            yield return XElement.ReadFrom(xr) as XElement;
        }
    }
}

static void createEntitiesFromXmlUsingChunkingReader() {
    var xmlCustomers =
        ChunkedDataSourceReader("customersWithOrdersDataSource.xml",
            "customer");

    Console.WriteLine("Variable xmlCustomers defined");

    var customersWithOrders =
        from c in xmlCustomers
        select new Customer {
            Name = (String)c.Attribute("name"),
            City = (String)c.Attribute("city"),
            Country = (Countries)Enum.Parse(typeof(Countries),
                (String)c.Attribute("country"), true),
            Orders = (
                from o in c.Descendants("order")
                select new Order {
                    IdOrder = (Int32)o.Attribute("id"),
                    IdProduct = (Int32)o.Attribute("idProduct"),
                    Quantity = (Int32)o.Attribute("quantity"),
                    Month = (String)o.Attribute("month"),
                    Shipped = (Boolean)o.Attribute("shipped"),
                }
            ).ToArray()
        };

    Console.WriteLine("LINQ query expression defined");

    foreach (Customer c in customersWithOrders) {
        Console.WriteLine(c);
        foreach (Order o in c.Orders) {
            Console.WriteLine("  {0}", o);
        }
    }
}
```

The key point of this sample is the definition of the XML data source variable named *xml-Customer* through the *ChunkedDataSourceReader* method. In fact the query is exactly the same as before, except the first *from* clause, which selects directly the chunks returned by our custom function *ChunkedDataSourceReader*. Our function accepts a couple of arguments: the first one defines the XML data source URI, and the second argument gives the XPath rule to use to read each element chunk from the data source. In our sample we read the data source on a per-customer basis; thus we give an XPath rule with a "customer" value. The chunking reader will simply read the data source by using an *XmlReader* and yield every single occurrence of the requested element (*customer*), parsing it as an *XElement* by using the *ReadFrom* method of the *XNode* type. For debugging purposes, you can write a log message to the console every single time a chunking reader retrieves a new chunk.

Here is the console output of our code:

```
Variable xmlCustomers defined
LINQ query expression defined
Reading a chunk element from data source
Name: Paolo - City: Brescia - Country: Italy
  IdOrder: 1 - IdProduct: 1 - Quantity: 3 - Shipped: False - Month: January
  IdOrder: 2 - IdProduct: 2 - Quantity: 5 - Shipped: True - Month: May
Reading a chunk element from data source
Name: Marco - City: Torino - Country: Italy
  IdOrder: 3 - IdProduct: 1 - Quantity: 10 - Shipped: False - Month: July
  IdOrder: 4 - IdProduct: 3 - Quantity: 20 - Shipped: True - Month: December
```

Notice that the log of each chunk occurs just before the effective enumeration of the corresponding *Customer* instance. The solution used in Listing 10-16 is definitely more efficient than the one used in Listing 10-15, in particular when working with large or remote XML data sources.

Transforming XML with LINQ to XML

Let's apply what you have just learned about LINQ queries. Imagine that you need to transform a source document into a new schema. Listing 10-17 shows the source document.

Listing 10-17   Source XML with a list of customers

```
<?xml version="1.0" encoding="utf-8"?>
<customers>
  <customer name="Paolo" city="Brescia" country="Italy" />
  <customer name="Marco" city="Torino" country="Italy" />
  <customer name="James" city="Dallas" country="USA" />
  <customer name="Frank" city="Seattle" country="USA" />
</customers>
```

Listing 10-18 shows the output you want, where we change the namespace of the elements and filter *customer* elements on the value of *country* .

Listing 10-18   Destination XML with a list of customers transformed

```
<?xml version="1.0" encoding="utf-8"?>
<c:customers xmlns:c="http://schemas.devleap.com/Customers">
  <c:customer>
    <c:name>Paolo</c:name>
    <c:city>Brescia</c:city>
  </c:customer>
  <c:customer>
    <c:name>Marco</c:name>
    <c:city>Torino</c:city>
  </c:customer>
</c:customers>
```

You could use XSLT code to transform the source into the output. Listing 10-19 provides a really simple XSLT that would do that.

Listing 10-19   XSLT to transform XML from Listing 10-17 to Listing 10-18

```
<?xml version="1.0" encoding="UTF-8" ?>
<xsl:stylesheet version="1.0"
  xmlns:xsl="http://www.w3.org/1999/XSL/Transform"
  xmlns:c="http://schemas.devleap.com/Customers">
  <xsl:template match="customers">
    <c:customers>
      <xsl:for-each select="customer[@country = 'Italy']">
        <c:customer>
          <c:name><xsl:value-of select="@name"/></c:name>
          <c:city><xsl:value-of select="@city"/></c:city>
        </c:customer>
      </xsl:for-each>
    </c:customers>
  </xsl:template>
</xsl:stylesheet>
```

However, if you were already working with .NET code, you can avoid leaving the context of your code and instead use a simple LINQ query such as the one shown in Listing 10-20.

Listing 10-20   A functional construction used to transform XML from Listing 10-17 to Listing 10-18

```
XNamespace ns = "http://schemas.devleap.com/Customers";
XElement destinationXmlCustomers =
    new XElement(ns + "customers",
        new XAttribute(XNamespace.Xmlns + "c", ns),
        from   c in sourceXmlCustomers.Elements("customer")
        where  c.Attribute("country").Value == "Italy"
        select new XElement(ns + "customer",
                   new XElement(ns + "name", c.Attribute("name")),
                   new XElement(ns + "city", c.Attribute("city"))));
```

We personally like and appreciate XSLT features and their strong syntax, but using them requires learning another query language. We know and clearly understand that many developers are not familiar with XSLT syntax and probably will prefer the LINQ solution, which is easier for a .NET developer to write and which is also typed and checked from a compiler point of view. Finally, you can consider the Visual Basic 2008 version of this code, shown in Listing 10-21.

Listing 10-21   A Visual Basic 2008 XML literal used to transform XML from Listing 10-17 to Listing 10-18

```
Dim destinationXmlCustomers = _
    <c:customers xmlns:c="http://schemas.devleap.com/Customers">
        <%= From c In sourceXmlCustomers.<customers>.<customer> _
            Where (c.@country - "Italy") _
            Select _
            <c:customer xmlns:c="http://schemas.devleap.com/Customers">
                <c:name><%= c.@name %></c:name>
                <c:city><%= c.@city %></c:city>
            </c:customer> %>
    </c:customers>
```

This approach is probably the one that is the quickest to write and easiest to understand because you can directly think about the output XML. You can make it even easier by using global XML namespaces. Note the syntax used to select elements and attributes from the source XML document. We use a special Visual Basic 2008 syntax that you can read about in depth in Appendix C, "Visual Basic 2008: New Language Features." The syntax recalls XPath node selection. As you can see, we select all the element nodes named *customer*, which are children of the *customers* element within the *sourceXmlCustomer*, by using the following syntax:

```
sourceXmlCustomers.<customers>.<customer>
```

The Visual Basic 2008 compiler, as with XML literals, converts the syntax into a standard LINQ to XML invocation of *Elements* methods. In the same way, the syntax used to select attributes named *name* and *city* (c.@name and c.@city) recalls XPath attribute selection rules and is converted into calls of the *Attribute* method of the *XElement* type.

We want to provide one last thought about dynamic construction and transformation of XML contents. Sometimes XML schemas support optional elements or optional attributes. When we define transformations using LINQ to XML, we work at a higher level and use object instances rather than nodes. In cases in which we define an *XElement* using functional construction and assign it a null value, the result is an empty closed element, like the one shown in the following example:

```
// Where c.City == null
XElement city = new XElement("customer",
    new XAttribute("id", c.IdCustomer),
    new XElement("city", c.City));
```

The result is an empty tag - *<city />* - as shown here:

```
<customer id="10"><city /></customer>
```

In cases in which you need to omit the element declaration when it is empty (null), you can use the conditional operator, as you can see in the following sample:

```
// Where c.City == null
XElement city = new XElement("customer",
    new XAttribute("id", c.IdCustomer),
    c.City != null ? new XElement("city", c.City), null);
```

Whenever we add null content to an *XContainer*, it is skipped without throwing any kind of exception.

Support for XSD and Validation of Typed Nodes

In many of the previous examples, we used explicit casting and accessed nodes through their names as quoted strings. All those casts and quotes are not type safe and cannot be checked at compile time. However, XML document structure is often defined using an XML Schema Definition (XSD). There is a "strongly typed LINQ to XML" project, also known as "LINQ to XSD," that allows access to XML nodes using a typed and self-describing approach and is supported by Microsoft IntelliSense. For instance, the query you saw in Listing 10-13 would be written like the one in Listing 10-22.

Listing 10-22   A LINQ query over XML, based on an XSD typed approach

```
var ordersWithCustomersFromXml =
    from    c in xmlCustomers.customerCollection
    join    o in orders
    on      c.Name equals o.Name
    orderby c.Name
    select  new {
                Name = c.Name,
                City = c.City,
                IdProduct = o.IdProduct,
                Quantity = o.Quantity };
```

As you can see, when you use this approach the XML nodes graphs look like any other object graphs—regardless of whether they are made of elements, attributes, or nodes instead of objects. Keep in mind that at the time of writing this book, the "strongly typed LINQ to XML" project is still under construction.

XML schema support is also offered through some extension methods defined in the *System.Xml.Schema.Extensions* class of the *System.Xml.Linq* assembly. There are just a couple of methods with a few overloads. Those methods are *GetSchemaInfo*, which extends any *XElement* or *XAttribute* instance, and *Validate*, which extends *XDocument*, *XElement*, and

XAttribute. The *GetSchemaInfo* method returns an annotation of type *System.Xml.Schema. IXmlSchemaInfo*, taken from the current node, if present. It retrieves a schema definition mapped to the current node by using LINQ to XML annotations. The *Validate* method, as you can figure out from its name, validates the source XML node by using an *XmlSchemaSet* containing the schemas to use. Consider the XML schema shown in Listing 10-23.

Listing 10-23   An XML schema definition for our sample list of customers

```
<?xml version="1.0" encoding="utf-8" ?>
<xsd:schema id="Customer"
    targetNamespace="http://schemas.devleap.com/Customer"
    elementFormDefault="qualified"
    xmlns="http://schemas.devleap.com/Customer"
    xmlns:xsd="http://www.w3.org/2001/XMLSchema">
  <xsd:element name="customers">
    <xsd:complexType>
      <xsd:sequence>
        <xsd:element name="customer" minOccurs="0" maxOccurs="unbounded">
          <xsd:complexType>
            <xsd:attribute name="name" type="xsd:string" use="required" />
            <xsd:attribute name="city" type="xsd:string" use="required" />
            <xsd:attribute name="country">
              <xsd:simpleType>
                <xsd:restriction base="xsd:string">
                  <xsd:enumeration value="Italy" />
                  <xsd:enumeration value="USA" />
                </xsd:restriction>
              </xsd:simpleType>
            </xsd:attribute>
          </xsd:complexType>
        </xsd:element>
      </xsd:sequence>
    </xsd:complexType>
  </xsd:element>
</xsd:schema>
```

You can define an XML graph with this structure, using LINQ to XML as usual, and map the nodes to the previous schema by using an *XNamespace* instance. An example is shown in Listing 10-24.

Listing 10-24   An XML document with the schema in Listing 10-23, built using the LINQ to XML API

```
XNamespace ns = "http://schemas.devleap.com/Customer";
XDocument xmlCustomers = new XDocument(
    new XElement(ns + "customers",
        from  c in customers
        select new XElement(ns + "customer",
                    new XAttribute("city", c.City),
                    new XAttribute("name", c.Name),
                    new XAttribute("country", c.Country))));
```

At this point, you have the *xmlCustomers* variable that represents an XML Infoset instance related to the schema in Listing 10-23 and uses its corresponding XML namespace.

In Listing 10-25, you can see how to validate this *XDocument* by using the *Validate* extension method.

Listing 10-25   XML validation using the *Validate* extension method

```
static void validateXDocument() {

    // . . .

    XmlSchemaSet schemas = new XmlSchemaSet();
    schemas.Add(XmlSchema.Read(new StreamReader(@"..\..\customer.xsd"), null));
    xmlCustomers.Validate(schemas, xmlCustomers_validation);
}

static void xmlCustomers_validation(Object source, ValidationEventArgs args) {
    // In case of validation messages
    Console.WriteLine(args.Message);
}
```

The *Validate* method internally uses all the standard and common classes and tools of the *System.Xml.Schema* namespace.

You can merge the validation engine with LINQ to XML events to achieve an automatic validation behavior while changing XML tree content. In Listing 10-26, you can see an example of this idea.

Listing 10-26   XML validation using the *Validate* extension method within the *Changed* event

```
XNamespace ns = "http://schemas.devleap.com/Customer";
XDocument xmlCustomers = new XDocument(
    new XElement(ns + "customers",
        from  c in customers
        select new XElement(ns + "customer",
            new XAttribute("city", c.City),
            new XAttribute("name", c.Name),
            new XAttribute("country", c.Country))));
xmlCustomers.Save(Console.Out);
Console.WriteLine();

XmlSchemaSet schemas = new XmlSchemaSet();
schemas.Add(XmlSchema.Read(new StreamReader(@"..\..\customer.xsd"), null));

// Subscribe to Changed event on the root element
xmlCustomers.Changed += (sender, e) => {
    xmlCustomers.Validate(schemas, (source, args) => {
        if (args.Exception != null)
            throw new InvalidOperationException("Operation on XML
            inconsistent with associated schema.", args.Exception);
    });
};
```

```
    // Removes the city attribute from the first customer
    // (modification not allowed by the schema)
    xmlCustomers.Element(ns + "customers")
        .Elements(ns + "customer").First()
        .SetAttributeValue("city", null);
}
```

Whenever you change the content of the XML tree, the *Changed* event occurs and invokes the code defined in the lambda expression provided in its definition. In the case of validation issues, the validation callback defined by the inner lamba expression throws an *Invalid-OperationException*, keeping track of the inner validation exception and, indeed, blocking modifications, which make the tree invalid with respect to the assigned XML schema.

Support for XPath and *System.Xml.XPath*

One last group of extension methods offered by LINQ to XML is related to *System.Xml.XPath* integration. The *System.Xml.XPath.Extensions* class provides a few extension methods that are useful for managing *XNode* contents via XPath. The first method is *CreateNavigator*, which returns an *XPathNavigator*:

```
public static XPathNavigator CreateNavigator(this XNode node);
public static XPathNavigator CreateNavigator(this XNode node, XmlNameTable nameTable);
```

Internally, *CreateNavigator* creates an instance of an *XNodeNavigator* class, which is derived from *XPathNavigator* and is specifically defined to navigate X* class graphs. The main goal of this method is to make possible the transformation of an *XNode* using standard *System.Xml.Xsl* classes. *XslCompiledTransform* can work with *XPathNavigator*-derived classes as input. Listing 10-27 provides sample code that transforms our customers list using the XSLT we defined in Listing 10-19.

Listing 10-27   XSLT transformation using *XslCompiledTransform* and the *CreateNavigator* extension method

```
XslCompiledTransform xslt = new XslCompiledTransform();
xslt.Load(@"..\..\customerFromSourceToDestination.xslt");
xslt.Transform(sourceXmlCustomers.CreateNavigator(), null, Console.Out);
```

Another interesting method is *XPathEvaluate*, which evaluates an XPath rule against the current *XNode*, returning its value by using the internal class *XPathEvaluator*. The code in Listing 10-28 selects all attributes "*name*" from all the customers located in Italy.

Listing 10-28   Sample usage of the *XPathEvaluate* extension method

```
XElement xmlCustomers = new XElement("customers",
    from  c in customers
    select new XElement("customer",
            new XAttribute("name", c.Name),
```

```
                    new XAttribute("city", c.City),
                    new XAttribute("country", c.Country))));

var result = (IEnumerable<Object>)xmlCustomers.XPathEvaluate(
    "/customer[@country = 'Italy']/@name");

foreach (var item in result) {
    Console.WriteLine(item);
}
```

Consider that the *XPathEvaluate* method cannot determine the result of the XPath query.
Therefore, it always returns a value of type *Object*. It is your responsibility to know and
correctly cast the result type. The last two methods to take care of are *XPathSelectElement* and
XPathSelectElements. The former returns the first element corresponding to the XPath
expression provided as an argument, and the latter returns the full list of elements matching
the expression. Internally, they both use the *XPathEvaluator* class. The following example
selects all the *customer* elements located in Italy:

```
var result = xmlCustomers.XPathSelectElements(
  "/customer[@country = 'Italy']");
```

This method is sometimes useful for defining LINQ queries that work on a subset of nodes of
the source XML graph—for example, in cases in which you need to filter *customer* elements
by the *country* attribute value. An example is shown in Listing 10-29.

Listing 10-29 Sample LINQ query over the result of the *XPathSelectElements* extension method

```
var ordersOfItalianCustomersFromXml =
    from    c in xmlCustomers.XPathSelectElements(
                    "/customer[@country = 'Italy']")
    let     xName = (String)c.Element("name")
    let     xCity = (String)c.Attribute("city")
    join    o in orders
    on      xName equals o.Name
    orderby xName
    select  new {
                Name = xName,
                City = xCity,
                IdProduct = o.IdProduct,
                Quantity = o.Quantity };
```

Remember that XPath rules are checked at run time, not at compile time. Therefore, be careful
when defining them within LINQ queries. Consider also that like many other LINQ extension
methods, the XPath methods we have just evaluated also support deferred query evaluation.
Once again, keep in mind that every time you use queries that are defined using these
methods, the result is refreshed by rescanning the source XML graph, unless you copy it by
yourself using any of the conversion operators provided by LINQ for doing that (such as
ToList, ToArray, ToDictionary, or *ToLookup*).

LINQ to XML Security

LINQ to XML has been designed to handle trusted XML documents; therefore, you should avoid using LINQ to XML to manage contents received from unknown senders across the Internet. In case you need to read, traverse, or modify XML trees received from outside your environment or from untrusted people, it is better to load the nodes through an *XmlReader* class that is properly configured for security and sandboxing, thus creating a LINQ to XML tree from the *XmlReader* instance. If you need to, you can also create a LINQ to XML nodes tree from an *XmlReader* instance using a predefined memory footprint. You do this by using some custom code to read single groups of elements from the source XML and handling them with *XElement* objects as we did previously with chunking readers. You can see a brief example of this in Listing 10-30.

Listing 10-30   Sample of chunked reading of an XML tree using a secured *XmlReader*

```
static void secureChunkReaderSample () {
    var customers = ChunkCustomers(@"..\..\CustomersWithOrders.xml");
    foreach (var c in customers) {
        Console.WriteLine(c);
    }
}

static IEnumerable<XElement> ChunkCustomers(String uri) {
    XmlReaderSettings settings = new XmlReaderSettings();
    settings.XmlResolver = new XmlSecureResolver(new XmlUrlResolver(), "c:\\sources");
    settings.MaxCharactersInDocument = 1024 * 1024 * 4; // Max 4MB
    XmlReader xr = XmlReader.Create(uri, settings);
    while (xr.Read())
    {
        if ((xr.NodeType == XmlNodeType.Element)
            && (xr.Name == "customer")) {
                yield return XElement.ReadFrom(xr) as XElement;
        }
    }
}
```

As you can see, the core part of Listing 10-30 is the enumerator method named *Chunk-Customers*. This method looks like the other chunking methods we have already seen. In fact, it reads an XML file of customers that is assumed to be large by using an *XmlReader* instance, chunking the nodes on a per customer basis. The difference in this sample is the configuration of the *XmlReaderSettings* instance. Here we use an *XmlSecureResolver* instance as the *Xml-Resolver* property and a predefined maximum size of 4MB for the whole document to read. The *XmlSecureResolver* class allows you to restrict the URIs accessible from the *XmlReader* instance that uses the resolver, avoiding, for example, cross-site scripting attacks. When working with LINQ to XML, you should always consider that regardless of what you do (reading contents, transforming nodes with XSLT, validating with XSD, navigating trees with

XPath, etc.), there aren't security checks, so be very careful about denial of services realized through XSLT scripting, XSD and/or XPath processing overhead, etc. Finally, consider that for security reasons, LINQ to XML turns off DTD validation to avoid possible denial-of-service attacks made possible because of too-heavy DTDs or DTD external references.

One last thing to note about LINQ to XML security is that *XObject* annotations are visible to any assembly loaded in an XML processing pipeline. Therefore, any annotation you make on an X* type instance can be read and modified from any piece of code in your application domain, which exposes the annotation to security issues.

LINQ to XML Serialization

The *XElement* type is serializable using the *XmlSerializer* engine or *DataContractSerializer*, so it is suitable for ASP.NET Web Services and Windows Communication Foundation (WCF) service contracts and implementations. For further details about WCF contracts and services, read Chapter 18, "LINQ and the Windows Communication Foundation." For now, we will focus only on the serialization part of the discussion. In Listing 10-31, you can see an example of the code used to serialize an *XElement* that uses a *DataContractSerializer* instance.

Listing 10-31   Sample of *XElement* serialization using *DataContractSerializer*

```
XElement xmlCustomers = new XElement("customers",
    from   c in listCustomers
    select new XElement("customer",
        new XElement("name", c.Name),
        new XAttribute("city", c.City),
        new XAttribute("country", c.Country)));

MemoryStream mem = new MemoryStream();
DataContractSerializer dc = new DataContractSerializer(typeof(XElement));
dc.WriteObject(mem, xmlCustomers);
```

The result of Listing 10-31 will look like the following XML excerpt:

```
<customers><customer city="Brescia"
country="Italy"><name>Paolo</name></customer><customer city="Torino"
country="Italy"><name>Marco</name></customer><customer city="Dallas"
country="USA"><name>James</name></customer><customer city="Seattle"
country="USA"><name>Frank</name></customer></customers>
```

As you can see, it is simply the streamed representation of XML nodes. The interesting part of this section becomes apparent when you think about using *XElement* instances as the content of SOAP service messages. For example, you can use a type like the one shown in Listing 10-32 as the argument of a WCF service contract.

Listing 10-32   Sample type using *XElement*, serializable with *DataContractSerializer*

```
[DataContract(Namespace = "http://schemas.devleap.com/CustomerWithXml")]
public class CustomerWithXmlData {
    [DataMember]
    public XElement XmlData { get; set; }

    [DataMember]
    public String Name { get; set; }
}
```

The *XElement* type is the only serializable type in LINQ to XML because it implements the interface *IXmlSerializable*, as do a few other .NET types, to define a customized serialization behavior. In particular, even if the type is serializable, it does not provide any information about the schema of its nodes tree; in fact, it is configured to be exported as an "xsd:any" element section. All other LINQ to XML types are not serializable with ASP.NET Web Services or WCF.

Summary

In this chapter you have seen how to query, traverse, and transform XML nodes graphs using LINQ to XML query extensions. You discovered how to read XML contents efficiently in order to build in-memory entity models. You evaluated the support offered by *System.Xml.Linq* to XPath, XSD, and XSLT. Finally, you saw how to secure your code working with LINQ to XML and how to serialize XML nodes defined as *XElement* instances to leverage them within SOAP services.

Part IV
Advanced LINQ

Chapter 11
Inside Expression Trees

Handling and manipulating expression trees is an important skill to have because it enables you to use LINQ in an advanced way. If you want to build a dynamic filter condition, you need to be able to construct an expression tree in memory without leveraging the easy-to-use but lightweight lambda expression syntax assigned to *Expression<T>* variables. If you want to write your own LINQ provider (a topic covered in Chapter 12, "Extending LINQ"), you need to know how to navigate the nodes of an expression tree to correctly interpret its content, translating it into the operation required by your provider. Whether you want to build a dynamic filter condition, write your own LINQ provider, or simply understand what happens under the hood when the *IQueryable* interface is involved (as it is for any LINQ to SQL query), this chapter will definitely be interesting for you.

We will start this chapter with an introduction to the characteristics of expression trees and the lambda expression syntax. Then we will dissect an expression tree, analyzing the more common and important node types. Finally, we will show you some techniques for navigating (or *visiting*) and modifying an expression tree, closing the chapter with some discussion about the dynamic generation of expression trees.

 Note   In this chapter we use the term "visit" to mean the navigation of an expression tree structure. This term is derived from the kind of algorithms used, generally called "expression tree visitors."

Lambda Expressions

Lambda expressions are part of the C# 3.0 syntax, and an expression tree can be generated by the compiler starting from lambda expression syntax. You can find a more complete description of the lambda expression syntax in Appendix B, "C# 3.0: New Language Features." We will simply recap some concepts here before moving on to a more advanced analysis of lambda expressions that will enable you to better analyze expression trees.

The lambda expression syntax in C# 3.0 allows for a more concise syntax to be used to define an anonymous method. For example, the code in Listing 11-1 is based on a delegate.

Listing 11-1   Declaration of *Inc* as an anonymous method

```
delegate int IncDelegate(int x);
static void TestDelegate() {
    IncDelegate Inc = delegate(int x) { return x + 1; };
    Console.WriteLine(Inc(2));
}
```

The code in Listing 11-2 is equivalent to Listing 11-1, but it uses the lambda expression syntax.

Listing 11-2   Declaration of *Inc* as a lambda expression

```
delegate int IncDelegate(int x);
static void TestLambda() {
    IncDelegate Inc = x => x + 1;
    Console.WriteLine(Inc(2));
}
```

We defined the delegate type *IncDelegate* in both previous samples. However, lambda expressions typically are declared using one of the following *Func* delegate declarations, which are contained in the *System* namespace as part of the *System.Core* assembly (as you saw in Chapter 2, "LINQ Syntax Fundamentals"):

```
public delegate T Func<TResult>();
public delegate T Func<A0, TResult >( A0 arg0 );
public delegate T Func<A0, A1, TResult > ( A0 arg0, A1 arg1 );
public delegate T Func<A0, A1, A2, TResult >( A0 arg0, A1 arg1, A2 arg2 );
public delegate T Func<A0, A1, A2, A3, TResult >
                    ( A0 arg0, A1 arg1, A2 arg2, A3 arg3 );
public delegate T Func<A0, A1, A2, A3, A4, TResult >
                    ( A0 arg0, A1 arg1, A2 arg2, A3 arg3, A4 arg4 );
```

These *Func* declarations are simple delegates and can be used for both delegate and lambda expression syntax, because in the end you always get a delegate. Listing 11-3 shows *IncDelegate* and *IncLambda* declarations that are perfectly equivalent, except for being declared with different syntaxes.

Listing 11-3   Comparison between delegate and lambda expression syntaxes

```
static void TestFunc() {
    // Typical lambda expression using Func delegate
    Func<int, int> IncDelegate = delegate(int x) { return x + 1; };
    Func<int, int> IncLambda = x => x + 1;

    Console.WriteLine(IncDelegate(2));
    Console.WriteLine(IncLambda(2));
}
```

Lambda expressions might include several statements, but we are interested only in those that consist of an expression body, which is a single *return* statement followed by an expression. (These lambda expressions can omit the *return* statement, as we did in Listings 11-2 and 11-3.) As you will see shortly, lambda expressions defined as an expression body can be used to generate an expression tree.

> **Important**   Increment (++) and decrement (--) operators are not supported as part of an expression tree. The reason is that their presence implies an assignment to modify the incremented/decremented variable, and assignment operators are not supported in an expression tree.

Recursive Lambda Expressions

Apparently, you cannot define a recursive lambda expression. For example, to define a lambda expression for factorial evaluation you might want to write the following:

```
fac => x => x == 0 ? 1 : x * fac(x-1)
```

However, you cannot directly call the lambda expression you are defining from inside its definition. To make this syntax work, you need to define a fixed-point operator, as shown in the following *Fix* fixed-point generator:

```
static Func<T, T> Fix<T>(Func<Func<T, T>, Func<T, T>> F) {
    return t => F(Fix(F))(t);
}
```

Using *Fix*, you can obtain the recursion for the initial lambda expression:

```
Func<int, int> factorial =
    Fix<int>( fac => x => (x == 0) ? 1 : x * fac(x - 1) );
```

If you are interested in a more detailed explanation of recursive lambda expressions, you can find an excellent post by Mads Torgersen at *http://blogs.msdn.com/madst/archive/ 2007/05/11/recursive-lambda-expressions.aspx.*

For the discussion in this chapter, the important point is that you cannot directly write a recursive lambda and, hence, you cannot encode it as a lambda expression. You need a helper function such as *Fix*, and you need everyone who consumes the expression tree to understand its special significance.

What Is an Expression Tree

An expression tree is a data structure that represents an expression using nodes as operands and operators. An operand can be an expression by itself, forming a recursive structure. For example, consider the following expression:

```
9 + (5 + 6) * 3
```

This expression can be represented by an expression tree like the one represented in Figure 11-1.

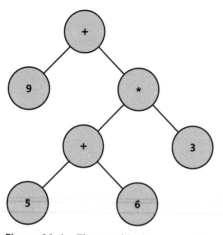

Figure 11-1   The graphical representation of an expression tree

There is a large body of literature about expression tree libraries and algorithms. The .NET Framework 3.5 has its own library to handle expression trees, which is formed by classes defined in the *System.Linq.Expressions* namespace in the *System.Core* assembly. These classes can be used directly by a programmer to create expression trees, and compilers such as C# 3.0 and Microsoft Visual Basic 2008 are able to translate an expression written in C# or Visual Basic into an expression tree created at runtime using these same classes.

Creating Expression Trees

The easiest way to create an expression tree is by leveraging language features. However, because an expression tree made up only by constants (such as the one in Figure 11-1) would be automatically converted into the result (a single constant value) at compile time, you need to build parametric expressions, such as the formula to calculate the area of a triangle:

```
b * h / 2
```

The corresponding lambda expression in C# is

```
(b, h) => b * h / 2
```

In a real C# program, you need to assign that lambda expression to some variable. At this point, you also need to define the type on which the lambda expression is defined:

```
Func<double, double, double> TriangleArea = (b, h) => b * h / 2;
```

Now you have a delegate instance, *TriangleArea*, that is no different from a regular function. However, you can get an expression tree instead of the delegate simply by declaring *Triangle-Area* as an *Expression<TDelegate>* instead of a delegate (such as the *Func<A0, A1, TResult>* you used before):

```
Expression<Func<double, double, double>> TriangleAreaExp =
    (b, h) => b * h / 2;
```

With this declaration, *TriangleAreaExp* is not a delegate but a reference to the root node of an expression tree. You can see the difference by looking at the sample code in Listing 11-4.

Listing 11-4   Difference between a lambda expression and expression tree declarations

```
static void DemoTriangleArea() {
    Func<double, double, double> TriangleArea = (b, h) => b * h / 2;
    Console.WriteLine("*** Delegate ***");
    Console.WriteLine("ToString: {0}", TriangleArea.ToString());
    Console.WriteLine("Value: {0}", TriangleArea(7, 12));

    Expression<Func<double, double, double>> TriangleAreaExp =
        (b, h) => b * h / 2;
    Console.WriteLine("*** Expression tree ***");
    Console.WriteLine("ToString: {0}", TriangleAreaExp.ToString());
    Console.WriteLine("Value: {0}", TriangleAreaExp.Compile()(7, 12));
}
```

Take a look at the following output produced by the execution of the code in Listing 11-4:

```
*** Delegate ***
ToString: System.Func`3[System.Double,System.Double,System.Double]
Value: 42
*** Expression tree ***
ToString: (b, h) => ((b * h) / 2)
Value: 42
```

TriangleArea.ToString displays the type name of the delegate class that encloses the *Triangle-Area* lambda expression. *TriangleAreaExp.ToString*, on the other hand, displays the lambda expression defined for *TriangleAreaExp* in a textual form! This is possible because the *ToString* method is overridden by the *Expression<TDelegate>* class, which *TriangleAreaExp* is an instance of. That method visits the expression tree, displaying it in a human readable form.

> **Note**   Parentheses that explicitly state operator priorities have been added with respect to the original definition of the *TriangleAreaExp* expression. These parentheses are generated by the overridden *ToString* implementation.

As you can see in Listing 11-4, an expression tree can be executed by calling the *Compile* method, which returns a delegate that is callable, just as it was in the original lambda expression assigned to *TriangleAreaExp*. This method performs work that is similar to *ToString*, visiting the whole expression tree (represented in Figure 11-2). However, instead of printing out the operands and operators found, it generates the necessary Intermediate Language (IL) code to implement the behavior described by the visited nodes, returning a reference to a delegate instance that contains that code.

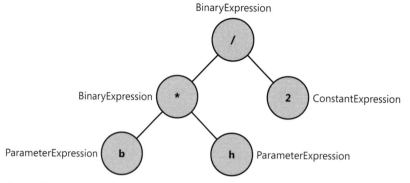

Figure 11-2 Expression tree with class names for node implementation

You can see in Figure 11-2 a graphical representation of the expression tree contained in *TriangleAreaExp*, where each node has the name of the class that implements it in the *System.Linq.Expressions* namespace. We will explore details and internals of expression trees later in this chapter.

> **Important**   In this first part of the chapter, we graphically represent only the *Body* part of a lambda expression. We will cover the entire expression tree that originates with a node of type *LambdaExpression* in the section of the chapter "Dissecting Expression Trees."

Encapsulation

Probably, many of the expressions you will use will contain calls to external methods. For example, consider the code in Listing 11-5.

Listing 11-5 Call to external methods from an expression tree

```
static int Double(int n) {
    return n * 2;
}
static void CallInExpression() {
    Expression<Func<int, int>> CallExp = (x) => Double(x) + 1;
    Console.WriteLine("ToString: {0}", CallExp.ToString());
}
```

The *Double* static method contains a simple expression that could be encapsulated into an expression tree, but because it is a method, it is opaque to the expression tree. You can see in Figure 11-3 the expression tree assigned to *CallExp*, which contains the addition of 1 to the result of a method call to *Double* using *x* as an argument.

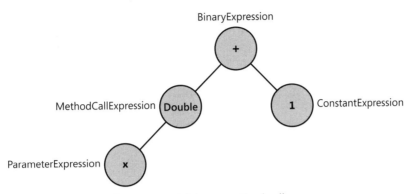

Figure 11-3   Expression tree containing a method call.

You might be tempted to "merge" an expression into an existing expression tree. Although this is possible, it is not an operation you can do by leveraging the code generated by the compiler for lambda expressions assigned to *Expression<T>*. To accomplish such a merge you could use a delegate obtained from a lambda expression instead of a function and write code like that shown in Listing 11-6.

Listing 11-6   Call to a lambda expression from an expression tree

```
static void CallInExpression() {
    Func<int,int> Double = (n) => n * 2;
    Expression<Func<int, int>> CallExp = (x) => Double(x) + 1;
    Console.WriteLine("ToString: {0}", CallExp.ToString());
}
```

This produces an expression tree similar to the one represented in Figure 11-3. The only difference is that an *InvocationExpression* node is used instead of *MethodCallExpression*.

Do you want to try declaring *Double* as an *Expression<T>*? Unfortunately, the following code does not compile:

```
Expression<Func<int, int>> Double = (n) => n * 2;
Expression<Func<int, int>> CallExp = (x) => Double(x) + 1;
```

Our intention is to create an expression tree like the one represented in Figure 11-4, where the dark gray nodes are those of the *Double* expression tree, substituting the call to *Double* in the original expression tree assigned to *CallExp*. To do this requires an expression tree manipulation, as you will see shortly.

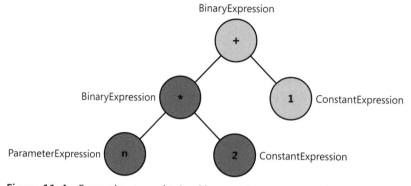

Figure 11-4   Expression tree obtained by merging two expression trees

Using the C# syntax of a lambda expression to build an expression tree, you cannot combine an existing expression tree with a new one. In a lambda expression, an expression tree has to be compiled before it can be used. Thus, you can try to "merge" two expression trees using the lambda expression syntax only by writing something like in the code contained in Listing 11-7.

Listing 11-7   Call to a lambda expression from an expression tree

```
static void CallInExpression() {
    Expression<Func<int, int>> Double = (n) => n * 2;
    Expression<Func<int, int>> CallExp = (x) => Double.Compile()(x) + 1;
    Console.WriteLine("ToString: {0}", CallExp.ToString());
}
```

However, this produces an expression tree assigned to *CallExp* that is still like the one shown in Figure 11-3, with the only difference being that an *InvocationExpression* node is used instead of *MethodCallExpression*. The *Compile* call in Listing 11-7 generates the delegate for *Double*, and after that we have the same syntax and behavior as demonstrated by Listing 11-6.

> **Important**   An expression tree is generated by the compiler only when a lambda expression with an expression body is assigned to an *Expression<T>* type instance. The compiler is not able to combine one expression tree with another. You can write the code to do that, but you will probably make some additional assumptions that the compiler might not make—in particular, you might make an assumption to solve the replacement of expression arguments.

Immutability and Modification

The nodes of an expression tree are immutable. You can change an expression tree only by creating another one, which can be made of nodes (more precisely, subtrees) of an existing tree that are tied together using newly created nodes with properties different from those in the original tree.

To help you better understand this concept, we will use an analogy comparing an expression tree and a string. Both classes produce instances that are read-only. To make a modification, you need to create a new instance. In the case of an expression tree, the implications are wider because if you want to change a part of the tree, you need to change all the nodes from the top-level node to the one that actually needs to be modified.

As an example, let's anticipate some of the concepts that will be presented later, in the section "Dissecting Expression Trees." Consider the following expression:

```
Expression<Func<int, int>> Double = (n) => (n * 2 + 1) * 4;
```

The equivalent expression tree is represented in Figure 11-5. The *BinaryExpression* type is a node type in the expression tree that has two child nodes, identified by its *Left* and *Right* properties, used to navigate the tree.

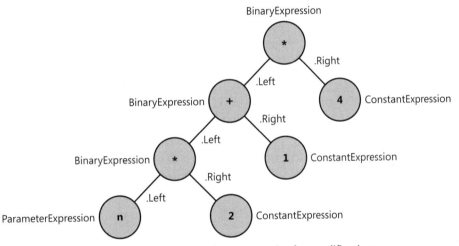

Figure 11-5   Sample expression tree used as an exercise for modifications

If you wanted to replace the 4 constant with 5, you would be tempted to write the code in Listing 11-8. First, you save in the *top* variable the top-level node of the tree; its right node is the constant 4. Then, you try to assign its *Value* property to 5, but that line of code does not compile. The *Value* property is read-only and cannot be changed.

Listing 11-8   Code that tries to modify an expression tree node but that does not compile

```
class Program {
    static void Immutability() {
        Expression<Func<int, int>> Formula = (n) => (n * 2 + 1) * 4;

        Console.WriteLine(Formula.ToString());

        Expression top = Formula.Body;
        ConstantExpression constant = top.Right() as ConstantExpression;
        Console.WriteLine(constant.Value);
```

```
                constant.Value = 5; // Compiler error - Value is a read-only property
    }

    // Other code (like Main) omitted ...
}

// Helper extension methods to simplify the code
// These helper methods are not safe - they throw exceptions
// whenever applied on nodes that are not of type BinaryExpression
public static class TreeHelper {
    public static Expression Left(this Expression exp) {
        return (exp as BinaryExpression).Left;
    }

    public static Expression Right(this Expression exp) {
        return (exp as BinaryExpression).Right;
    }
}
```

> **Note**   In Listing 11-8, we included two helper extension methods of the *Expression* class
> (*Left* and *Right*) that we will also use in the following example of expression tree modification.
> The purpose of these *Left* and *Right* helper methods is only to make the navigation code
> simpler to read. They are not intended to be used in real-world code because they throw
> exceptions if applied to nodes of types other than *BinaryExpression*.

At this point, you have two options. You can create a completely new expression tree with the
desired nodes, or you can create new nodes only for the changed part of the tree, recycling
existing nodes that are not touched by your modification. The code in Listing 11-9
implements this second option, replacing the constant node 4 with a new constant node
having a value of 5.

Listing 11-9   Substitution in an expression tree: replace 4 with 5

```
static void ReplaceLevel2() {
    Expression<Func<int, int>> Formula = (n) => (n * 2 + 1) * 4;

    // Replace 4 with 5
    // Results in
    //      (n * 2 + 1) * 5
    Expression top = Formula.Body;
    ConstantExpression newRight = Expression.Constant(5);
    Expression newTree = Expression.MakeBinary(
                            top.NodeType,
                            top.Left(),
                            newRight );
    Console.WriteLine("Original tree: {0}", top.ToString());
    Console.WriteLine("Modified tree: {0}", newTree.ToString());
}
```

The *Expression* class has static methods that are used as class factories to get new instances of expression tree nodes. In Listing 11-9, we create a new constant node with the value of 5, attach that node on the *Right* branch of a new top-level node, which is of type *Binary-Expression*, and copy the existing *Left* branch from the original expression tree. The following is the output produced by executing the code in Listing 11-9:

```
Original tree: (((n * 2) + 1) * 4)
Modified tree: (((n * 2) + 1) * 5)
```

Figure 11-6 highlights with a dark gray background the nodes that have been replaced. As you can see from the results just shown, in reality we did not change the existing tree; instead, we have created a new one, which links to the existing subtree that is kept equal in the new tree. (See the light gray nodes in Figure 11-6.)

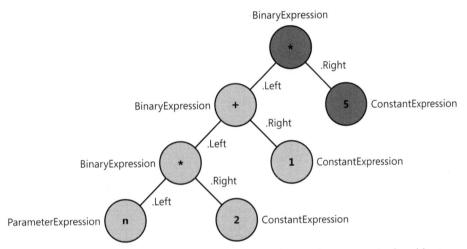

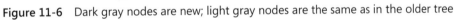

Figure 11-6   Dark gray nodes are new; light gray nodes are the same as in the older tree

The deeper you go down the tree to make changes, the more nodes there are that you need to change. You always have to replace the node from the one replaced at the top-level node. To replace the constant 4 with 5, you also need to replace the top-level node (the *BinaryExpression* that performs multiplication). If you replace the constant 1 with a value of 3, you need to replace three nodes, which you can see highlighted with a dark gray background in Figure 11-7.

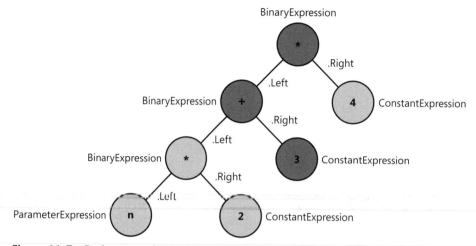

Figure 11-7 Dark gray nodes are new; light gray nodes are the same as in the older tree

The code used to replace the constant 1 with a constant of 3 is shown in Listing 11-10.

Listing 11-10 Substitution in an expression tree: replace 1 with 3

```
static void ReplaceLevel3() {
    Expression<Func<int, int>> Formula = (n) => (n * 2 + 1) * 4;

    // Replace 1 with 3
    // Results in
    //      (n * 2 + 3) * 4
    Expression top = Formula.Body;
    ConstantExpression newConstantSum = Expression.Constant(3);
    Expression newSum = Expression.MakeBinary(
                        top.Left().NodeType,
                        top.Left().Left(),
                        newConstantSum );
    Expression newTree = Expression.MakeBinary(
                        top.NodeType,
                        newSum,
                        top.Right() );
    Console.WriteLine("Original tree: {0}", top.ToString());
    Console.WriteLine("Modified tree: {0}", newTree.ToString());
}
```

The ouput produced by the execution of code in Listing 11-10 is the following:

```
Original tree: (((n * 2) + 1) * 4)
Modified tree: (((n * 2) + 3) * 4)
```

Note Having immutable nodes that can be created only by referencing child nodes makes it impossible to create circular references in an expression tree.

It should be clear now that the modification of an expression tree requires more than a few lines of code. We were able to show short samples only because we made many assumptions about the expression tree and knew exactly the tree's structure and the position of the nodes we wanted to change. In the real world, often you will need to interpret an expression without knowing its structure in advance. You might need to replace some parameters, remove some conditions, or simply combine two or more expressions together. In any case, there is a need for a more sophisticated expression tree analysis that requires a deeper knowledge of the expression tree structure.

In the remaining part of this chapter, we will introduce the most important concepts for understanding the elements that expression trees are composed of and some of the techniques to navigate and manipulate them.

Dissecting Expression Trees

An expression tree is a tree that always starts from a single top-level node, which is also the last part of the expression to be executed. Properties of this node link other nodes, and every other node might have one or more child nodes that constitute arguments of the operation that the node represents. For example, one node might be an operator that sums two operands, where each operand can be another node in the expression tree that encloses other operations. The leaves of the tree are nodes that do not have other children, such as (but not limited to) constants and parameters.

When you build an expression tree from a lambda expression, the first node is always an *Expression<T>* instance, which has a *Body* property containing another node and a *Parameters* property with an array of the parameters used in the expression tree. These parameters correspond to the parameters of the lambda expression. In the previous part of this chapter, we did not represent this first node in the graphical illustration of expression trees. Consider the following expression, which was shown earlier in Listing 11-4:

```
Expression<Func<double, double, double>> TriangleAreaExp =
    (b, h) => b * h / 2;
```

A more accurate graphical representation of this tree is shown in Figure 11-8.

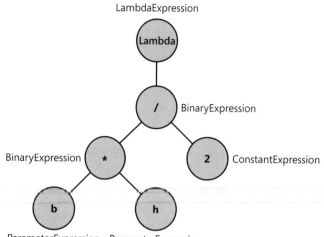

Figure 11-8   Expression tree with class names for node implementation

The top-level node is the one that corresponds to a *TriangleAreaExp* instance. This node is of the generic type *Expression<T>*, where the constructed type is *Expression<Func<double, double,double>>*. *Expression<T>* is a class that inherits from *LambdaExpression*, which inherits from the abstract class *Expression*. Any node of the expression tree is of a class that specializes *Expression*. A class such as this can have its own properties that, when the properties are of type *Expression*, define other nodes tied to the tree. Take a look at Figure 11-9 to see an example of a more complex expression tree that corresponds to the following expression:

```
Expression<Func<int, int>> Formula =
    (n) => 1 + Double(n * (n % 2 == 0 ? -1 : 1));
```

An expression tree can have nodes with 0, 1, 2, or even more child nodes. Most of the time, you will find some *BinaryExpression* instance, but the resulting tree is not always a binary tree. For example, in Figure 11-9 there is a conditional operator (IIF) with three child nodes: the condition (*Test* property) and the possible return values (*IfTrue* and *IfFalse* properties).

> **Note**   Different node types might have a different structure for navigation, and the common base class (*Expression*) does not expose public properties to navigate the child nodes, regardless of the effective instantiated class. This implies that a complete navigation of an expression tree needs a correct interpretation of all the types that might be part of the visited expression tree.

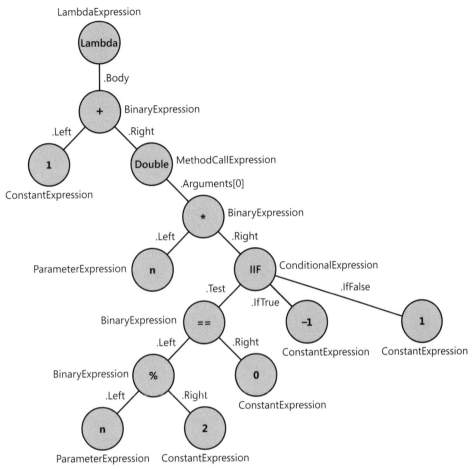

Figure 11-9   Complex expression tree

Thus, we start our dissection from the *Expression* class, defined in *System.Linq.Expressions* as part of the *System.Core* assembly.

The *Expression* Class

The *Expression* class has two roles. First, it is an abstract class inherited by all the node types. Second, it is a container for many public static methods that create tree nodes or offer helper functions. As an abstract class, its definition is very simple:

```
public abstract class Expression {
    protected Expression( ExpressionType nodeType, Type type );
    internal virtual void BuildString(StringBuilder builder);
    public override string ToString();

    // Properties
    public ExpressionType NodeType { get; }
```

```
    public Type Type { get; }

    // Static members omitted
}
```

There are neither public instance methods nor public constructors. The only way to get an instance of a node is by calling one of the public static methods of *Expression*, which creates one instance of an *Expression* derived type. The *ToString* override internally calls the virtual *BuildString* method that is typically overridden in derived classes to return a correct representation of the expression tree segment represented by the node itself. The important parts are the two public properties:

- **NodeType**   This is an instance of the *ExpressionType* enumeration, and it defines what operator is represented by the node in the expression tree. Some *Expression* derived classes always have the same value for *NodeType*, although others set this property to specify the operation that the node represents. For example, a *ConstantExpression* will always set this property to *ExpressionType.Constant*, whereas *BinaryExpression* needs to specify what operator the node defines, such as *Add*, *And*, or many others.

- **Type**   This is the type of the object resulting from the node's subtree evaluation.

Classes derived from *Expression* do not have many constraints imposed by the base class. However, these classes are already defined in the *System.Linq.Expressions* namespace and are sealed. What is more interesting for us is to understand the role and the behavior of the most important node types of an expression tree.

The static methods that are part of the *Expression* class are used as factory methods to create the various node types. We have at least one factory method for each possible *ExpressionType* value. At this level, we do not need to know the type that implements the desired operator (for example, *BinaryExpression*). It is important to know what the *ExpressionType* value is that corresponds to the desired operator (for example, *Add*). Typically, the name of the static method corresponds to the name of the member in the *ExpressionType* enumeration. For example, to create a *BinaryExpression* representing a multiplication of two expressions, you can call one of the *Expression.Multiply* factory methods (there are some overloads) that return a *BinaryExpression* instance with a *NodeType* value of *ExpressionType.Multiply*.

You are forced to use factory methods of the *Expression* class because the constructors of classes derived from *Expression* are declared as *internal*. Factory methods in the *Expression* class also conduct a sanity check of arguments before creating the node instance, throwing an exception in case of an error. You will see some examples of using factory methods later in this chapter.

Note   Another important action of the factory methods is the search for the implementation of custom operators. We do not cover detailed examples here, but operator overloading is supported by expression trees.

Expression Tree Node Types

There are 15 public classes derived from *Expression* in the *System.Linq.Expressions* namespace. Each class can represent one or more operands through the *NodeType* property, and we have a total of 46 different operands available. (This is the number of members of the *ExpressionType* enumeration.)

ExpressionType Enumeration

The *ExpressionType* enumeration defines all the possible node types of an expression tree. Each value corresponds to one or more factory methods in the *Expression* class, typically with the same name as the enumeration member. The only exception is *MemberAccess*, which has more specific factory methods, such as *Expression.Field* and *Expression.Property*. Table 11-1 shows a complete list of *ExpressionType* members, each with a short description.

Table 11-1   *ExpressionType* Enumeration Members

ExpressionType	Description
Add	Performs an arithmetic addition without overflow checking.
AddChecked	Performs an arithmetic addition with overflow checking.
And	Performs a bitwise AND operation.
AndAlso	Performs a short-circuit conditional AND operation.
ArrayIndex	Indexes an item into a one-dimensional array.
ArrayLength	Gets the length of a one-dimensional array.
Call	Performs a method call.
Coalesce	Performs a null coalescing operation.
Conditional	Performs a conditional operation. *C# 3.0: condition ? expression : expression* *Visual Basic 2008: IF(condition, expression, expression)*
Constant	Expression that has a constant value.
Convert	Performs a cast or conversion operation. If the operation is a numeric conversion, it overflows silently if the converted value does not fit the target type.
ConvertChecked	Performs a cast or conversion operation. If the operation is a numeric conversion, an exception is thrown if the converted value does not fit the target type.
Divide	Performs an arithmetic division.
Equal	Performs an equality comparison.
ExclusiveOr	Performs a bitwise XOR operation.
GreaterThan	Performs a "greater than" numeric comparison.
GreaterThanOrEqual	Performs a "greater than or equal to" numeric comparison.
Invoke	Applies a delegate or lambda expression to a list of argument expressions.
Lambda	Lambda expression.
LeftShift	Performs a bitwise left-shift operation.

Table 11-1 *ExpressionType* Enumeration Members

ExpressionType	Description
LessThan	Performs a "less than" numeric comparison.
LessThanOrEqual	Performs a "less than or equal to" numeric comparison.
ListInit	Creates a new *IEnumerable* object, initializing it from a list of elements.
MemberAccess	Reads from a field or property.
MemberInit	Creates a new object, initializing one or more of its members.
Modulo	Performs an arithmetic remainder operation.
Multiply	Performs an arithmetic multiplication without overflow checking.
MultiplyChecked	Performs an arithmetic multiplication with overflow checking.
Negate	Performs an arithmetic negation operation without overflow checking.
NegateChecked	Performs an arithmetic negation operation with overflow checking.
New	Calls a constructor to create a new object.
NewArrayBounds	Creates a new array where the bounds for each dimension are specified.
NewArrayInit	Creates a new one-dimensional array, initializing it from a list of elements.
Not	Performs a bitwise complement operation.
NotEqual	Performs an inequality comparison.
Or	Performs a bitwise OR operation.
OrElse	Performs a short-circuit conditional OR operation.
Parameter	References a parameter defined in the context of the expression.
Power	Raises a number to a power.
Quote	Expression that has a constant value of type *Expression*. A *Quote* node can contain references to parameters defined in the context of the expression it represents.
RightShift	Performs a bitwise right-shift operation.
Subtract	Performs an arithmetic subtraction without overflow checking.
SubtractChecked	Performs an arithmetic subtraction with overflow checking.
TypeAs	Provides an explicit reference or boxing conversion where null is supplied if the conversion fails.
TypeIs	Performs a type test.
UnaryPlus	Performs a unary plus operation. The result of a predefined unary plus operation is simply the value of the operand, but user-defined implementations might have nontrivial results.

Classes Derived from *Expression*

Table 11-2 illustrates all the node types that can be part of an expression tree. The table has three columns, as described in the following list:

- **Type**   This column shows the name of the class that implements the node of the element types listed in the second column. That class is defined in the *System.Linq.Expressions* namespace of the *System.Core* assembly and inherits the *Expression* abstract class.

- **NodeType**   This column lists the values of the *ExpressionType* enumeration that are supported by the *NodeType* property of the class specified in the first column, Type. Some types implement only one *ExpressionType* (such as *ConstantExpression*), although others implement many different elements (such as *BinaryExpression*).

- **Expression Properties**   This column is a list of the properties of type *Expressions* that the type exposes. These properties have to be iterated to continue the visit of a tree to the nodes related to the instance of the visited *Type*.

Table 11-2   Classes Derived from *Expression*

Type	NodeType	Expression Properties
BinaryExpression	Add; AddChecked; And; AndAlso; ArrayIndex; Coalesce; Divide; Equal; ExclusiveOr; Greater-Than; GreaterThanOrEqual; LeftShift; LessThan; LessThanOrEqual; Modulo; Multiply; MultiplyChecked; NotEqual; Or; OrElse; Power; RightShift; Subtract; SubtractChecked	Left Right
ConditionalExpression	Conditional	Test IfTrue IfFalse
ConstantExpression	Constant	-
Expression<T> **note – derives from LambdaExpression**	Lambda	Body Parameters
InvocationExpression	Invoke	Expression Arguments
LambdaExpression	Lambda	Body Parameters
ListInitExpression	ListInit	NewExpression
MemberExpression	MemberAccess	Expression
MemberInitExpression	MemberInit	NewExpression
MethodCallExpression	Call	Object Arguments
NewArrayExpression	NewArrayBounds; NewArrayInit	Expressions
NewExpression	New	Arguments
ParameterExpression	Parameter	-
TypeBinaryExpression	TypeIs	Expression
UnaryExpression	ArrayLength; Convert; ConvertChecked; Negate; NegateChecked; Not; Quote; TypeAs; UnaryPlus	Operand

Practical Nodes Guide

We included the previous two tables to give you a quick reference to node types and *Expression* implementation classes that you can have in an expression tree. We skipped a detailed explanation of each class because the product documentation provides sufficient information. We prefer to give you a guided tour of the most common and important nodes of an expression tree, introducing you to the skills necessary to handle and manipulate an expression tree. On this tour, we will refer to the following expression, which you already saw in Figure 11-9:

```
Expression<Func<int, int>> Formula =
    (n) => 1 + Double(n * (n % 2 == 0 ? -1 : 1));
```

> **Note**   If you want a tool that enables you to see a hierarchical representation of an expression tree from inside a Microsoft Visual Studio debugger or in your own application, take a look at the *LinqSamples\ExpressionTreeVisualizer* project that is part of the sample code included with Visual Studio 2008. Look for a CSharpSamples.zip package in the Samples\1033 subdirectory under the Visual Studio 2008 installation folder.

LambdaExpression and *ParameterExpression*

The first node of any expression tree generated from the C# lambda expression syntax is an instance of *LambdaExpression*. In reality, it is an instance of a constructed *Expression<T>* type, which is derived from *LambdaExpression* and does not add other members of type *Expression* to those inherited from the base *LambdaExpression* class. A *LambdaExpression* node has two properties:

```
public class LambdaExpression : Expression {
    // Other code omitted...
    public Expression Body { get; }
    public ReadOnlyCollection<ParameterExpression> Parameters { get; }
}
```

Body is the first node of the expression defined in the lambda expression. *Parameters* is a collection of *ParameterExpression*, which is derived from *Expression* and has the special purpose of referencing a parameter defined in the context of the lambda expression. These same nodes will be referenced again inside the expression tree whenever the parameter is used as an argument for an operation:

```
public sealed class ParameterExpression : Expression {
    // Other code omitted...
    public string Name { get; }
}
```

The *ParameterExpression* class does not contain references to other nodes. It is always a leaf in an expression tree. Knowing the parameters of a lambda expression is necessary for building the corresponding delegate when the expression tree is compiled because they specify the number and types of required arguments.

BinaryExpression

In our example, the *Body* property of the *LambdaExpression* references a *BinaryExpression* instance having a *NodeType* property equal to *Add*. This node defines the sum between the constant 1 and the result of a call to *Double*. The *BinaryExpression* class has the following public properties:

```
public sealed class BinaryExpression : Expression {
    // Other code omitted...

    public LambdaExpression Conversion { get; }
    public bool IsLifted { get; }
    public bool IsLiftedToNull { get; }

    public Expression Left { get; }
    public MethodInfo Method { get; }
    public Expression Right { get; }
}
```

Any binary operator has two child nodes, pointed to by the *Left* and *Right* properties of the *BinaryExpression* instance. Another important property is *Method*, which points to a custom implementation of the operator. (Whenever *Method* is null, the predefined operator is used.) In our sample extension tree (shown in Figure 11-9 earlier in the chapter), the *Left* property points to the constant of 1 and the *Right* property references the *Double* method call through an instance of the *MethodCallExpression* class.

Note   Refer to the product documentation for a deeper explanation of *Conversion*, *IsLifted*, and *IsLiftedToNull*. These properties are useful only for some node types and in some scenarios.

ConstantExpression

ConstantExpression instances are always leaves in the expression tree. In fact, this type provides only a *Value* property and no other property that would point to child nodes.

```
public sealed class ConstantExpression : Expression {
    // Other code omitted...
    public object Value { get; }
}
```

The C# compiler creates a single *ConstantExpression* whenever an expression made by constants can be resolved at compile time. For example, the expression *8 / 2 + 1* produces a single *ConstantExpression* with a value of *5*.

MethodCallExpression

The call to the *Double* static method of our expression tree is represented by an instance of *MethodCallExpression*.

```
public sealed class MethodCallExpression : Expression {
    // Other code omitted...
    public ReadOnlyCollection<Expression> Arguments { get; }
    public MethodInfo Method { get; }
    public Expression Object { get; }
}
```

This class has a *Method* property pointing to the code to execute. The *Object* property represents the instance to be used as the *this* parameter and a collection of *Arguments* to be passed for the rest of the parameters to the called method.

In our example, we have the remaining part of the expression tree stored in *Argument[0]*. In fact, the argument for *Double* is an expression tree that has a *Multiplication* as its first node:

```
Double(n * (n % 2 == 0 ? -1 : 1))
```

Keep in mind that the *Object* property of the *MethodCallExpression* class returns an *Expression*, because the instance to be used as the *this* parameter might also be the result of an expression, as in the following code:

```
string[] s = { "Linq", "Programming", "Book" };
Expression<Func<int,string>> Get = (i) => s[i].ToUpper();
```

In the preceding *Get* expression, the corresponding instance of *MethodCallExpression* references a *MethodInfo* object wrapping the *String.ToUpper* method in its *Method* property. The instance on which that method will operate is defined by the expression *s[i]* stored in the *Object* property (or an equivalent expression if s is a local variable). As always, each time we have an *Expression*, we might have a whole subtree to evaluate before obtaining the desired value.

> **Note** A local variable used in a lambda expression that is converted into an expression tree needs to reference a member of the object that is automatically generated by the compiler when an anonymous delegate is compiled. Because the lambda expression is an anonymous delegate, the string representation of a local variable (like s in our example) appears with a name that might seem different from the local variable specified in the original expression. For this reason, we talked about "an equivalent expression if s is a local variable."

ConditionalExpression

The last type we will consider in the expression tree we are analyzing is *ConditionalExpression*. C# 3.0 has a conditional expression through the *? :* syntax, although Visual Basic 2008 uses the new *IF()* statement (which is different from the legacy *IIF()* function). The *Test* expression has to be evaluated. If it is true, only the *IfTrue* expression is evaluated and returned as the result; otherwise, only the *IfFalse* expression is evaluated and returned as the result.

```
public sealed class ConditionalExpression : Expression {
    // Other code omitted...
    public Expression IfFalse { get; }
    public Expression IfTrue { get; }
    public Expression Test { get; }
}
```

Navigating an expression tree containing a *Conditional* node requires considering all three subtrees that can be tied to that operator.

InvocationExpression

One important node type that you should know about is *InvocationExpression*, which is created when a node *ExpressionType.Invoke* is requested. This node allows you to reference an external expression tree. The public properties are pretty simple:

```
public sealed class InvocationExpression : Expression {
    // Other code omitted...
    public ReadOnlyCollection<Expression> Arguments { get; }
    public Expression Expression { get; }
}
```

There is an *Expression* property with a collection of *Arguments*. When an expression tree contains such a node, we have a tree nested in another. However, these trees are still separated because moving from one to another requires a remapping of the expression tree parameters. To combine two expression trees, you need to call the *Expression.Invoke* method. You will see an example of using this method later in this chapter, in the "Combining Existing Expression Trees" section.

Visiting an Expression Tree

In the first part of this chapter, we examined the content of an expression tree assuming that we knew the type of the nodes that the tree contains. In the real world, you will probably need to analyze and manipulate an expression tree without knowing its content in advance. You need to be able to adapt to any expression tree, looking for particular nodes, inserting new conditions, and altering the expression tree. To do any of these operations, you need to know how to *visit* an expression tree, enumerating all its nodes just as you would do if you had a linear collection of nodes.

Visiting a tree is a well-covered topic, and there are several algorithms that enable you to do it. As we mentioned earlier, a peculiarity of expression trees is that they have several types of nodes, each one with different properties that affect the navigation of the tree. This peculiarity requires that you use an algorithm that knows the structure of all the types of nodes, just to be able to visit all the nodes of the tree. Let's start by considering the pattern used by the *Visitor* class published in the product documentation (specifically, in the "How to: Implement an Expression Tree Visitor" topic in the Online Help) and further developed by Matt Warren on his blog (*http://blogs.msdn.com/mattwar/archive/2007/07/31/linq-building-an-iqueryable-provider-part-ii.aspx*).

The pattern we mention consists of an abstract class, *ExpressionVisitor*, that exposes a method that visits a node and recursively calls itself for all child nodes, visiting the entire tree in this way. The specialization of this class will implement particular actions as a result of the nodes analysis. Our customized *ExpressionVisitor* class has a virtual method called *Visit*, which receives an *Expression* and returns an *Expression*. Later we will use the return value to create a new expression tree that visits an existing one. The *Visit* method simply analyzes the top-level node of the tree and dispatches it to a more specialized method, according to the node type it finds. Despite its length, the *Visit* method shown in Listing 11-11 is pretty simple.

Listing 11-11   *Visit* method in the *ExpressionVisitor* class

```
public abstract class ExpressionVisitor {
    protected ExpressionVisitor() {}

    protected virtual Expression Visit(Expression exp) {
        if (exp == null)
            return exp;
        switch (exp.NodeType) {
            case ExpressionType.Negate:
            case ExpressionType.NegateChecked:
            case ExpressionType.Not:
            case ExpressionType.Convert:
            case ExpressionType.ConvertChecked:
            case ExpressionType.ArrayLength:
            case ExpressionType.Quote:
            case ExpressionType.TypeAs:
            case ExpressionType.UnaryPlus:
                return this.VisitUnary((UnaryExpression) exp);
            case ExpressionType.Add:
            case ExpressionType.AddChecked:
            case ExpressionType.Subtract:
            case ExpressionType.SubtractChecked:
            case ExpressionType.Multiply:
            case ExpressionType.MultiplyChecked:
            case ExpressionType.Divide:
            case ExpressionType.Modulo:
            case ExpressionType.And:
            case ExpressionType.AndAlso:
            case ExpressionType.Or:
            case ExpressionType.OrElse:
            case ExpressionType.LessThan:
            case ExpressionType.LessThanOrEqual:
            case ExpressionType.GreaterThan:
            case ExpressionType.GreaterThanOrEqual:
            case ExpressionType.Equal:
            case ExpressionType.NotEqual:
            case ExpressionType.Coalesce:
            case ExpressionType.ArrayIndex:
            case ExpressionType.RightShift:
```

```
                    case ExpressionType.LeftShift:
                    case ExpressionType.ExclusiveOr:
                    case ExpressionType.Power:
                        return this.VisitBinary((BinaryExpression) exp);
                    case ExpressionType.TypeIs:
                        return this.VisitTypeIs((TypeBinaryExpression) exp);
                    case ExpressionType.Conditional:
                        return this.VisitConditional((ConditionalExpression) exp);
                    case ExpressionType.Constant:
                        return this.VisitConstant((ConstantExpression) exp);
                    case ExpressionType.Parameter:
                        return this.VisitParameter((ParameterExpression) exp);
                    case ExpressionType.MemberAccess:
                        return this.VisitMemberAccess((MemberExpression) exp);
                    case ExpressionType.Call:
                        return this.VisitMethodCall((MethodCallExpression) exp);
                    case ExpressionType.Lambda:
                        return this.VisitLambda((LambdaExpression) exp);
                    case ExpressionType.New:
                        return this.VisitNew((NewExpression) exp);
                    case ExpressionType.NewArrayInit:
                    case ExpressionType.NewArrayBounds:
                        return this.VisitNewArray((NewArrayExpression) exp);
                    case ExpressionType.Invoke:
                        return this.VisitInvocation((InvocationExpression) exp);
                    case ExpressionType.MemberInit:
                        return this.VisitMemberInit((MemberInitExpression) exp);
                    case ExpressionType.ListInit:
                        return this.VisitListInit((ListInitExpression) exp);
                    default:
                        throw new Exception(
                                    string.Format(
                                        "Unhandled expression type: '{0}'",
                                        exp.NodeType));
                }
            }
        // Other code omitted...
    }
```

A specific method is written to visit each type of node, based on the available properties
provided by the corresponding *Expression*-derived class. For each node type, the code might
have to visit properties that reference other expressions, calling their *Visit* method recursively.
In Listing 11-12, you can see the code for the *VisitBinary* method: it calls *Visit* on the *Left*, *Right*,
and *Conversion* properties. If any of these internal nodes has been changed during the visit, a
new *BinaryExpression* instance is created with the new properties; otherwise, the original node
is returned.

 Note   As we said before, node instances are immutable after their creation. The call to *Visit*
returns a node different from the one passed as the argument only as a result of a change at
any level of the visited subtree. For this reason, we have to create a new node storing the
new subtree.

Listing 11-12   *VisitBinary* method in the *ExpressionVisitor* class

```
public abstract class ExpressionVisitor {
    protected virtual Expression VisitBinary(BinaryExpression b) {
        Expression left = this.Visit(b.Left);
        Expression right = this.Visit(b.Right);
        Expression conversion = this.Visit(b.Conversion);
        if (left != b.Left || right != b.Right
            || conversion != b.Conversion) {
            if (b.NodeType == ExpressionType.Coalesce
                && b.Conversion != null)
                return Expression.Coalesce(
                        left, right,
                        conversion as LambdaExpression);
            else
                return Expression.MakeBinary(
                        b.NodeType,
                        left, right,
                        b.IsLiftedToNull, b.Method);
        }
        return b;
    }
    // Other code omitted...
}
```

Leaf nodes are those that cannot have other child nodes. They do not require another instance of *Visit* or code to check whether an internal node has been changed. This is the case for *VisitConstant* and *VisitParameter*, as you can see in Listing 11-13.

Listing 11-13   *VisitConstant* and *VisitParameter* methods in the *ExpressionVisitor* class

```
public abstract class ExpressionVisitor {
    protected virtual Expression VisitConstant(ConstantExpression c) {
        return c;
    }

    protected virtual Expression VisitParameter(ParameterExpression p) {
        return p;
    }
    // Other code omitted...
}
```

To complete the tree navigation, the presence of some node types makes it necessary to visit a list of expressions, such as the list of arguments in the case of the *MethodCallExpression* and *InvocationExpression* nodes, as you can see in Listing 11-14. The *VisitExpressionList* implementation iterates the collection of expressions and calls *Visit* for each node. (The source code for *VisitExpressionList* is not included here but is part of the book sample code.)

Listing 11-14 *VisitMethodCall* and *VisitInvocation* methods in the *ExpressionVisitor* class

```
public abstract class ExpressionVisitor {
    protected virtual Expression VisitMethodCall(MethodCallExpression m) {
        Expression obj = this.Visit(m.Object);
        IEnumerable<Expression> args =
                this.VisitExpressionList(m.Arguments);
        if (obj != m.Object || args != m.Arguments) {
            return Expression.Call(obj, m.Method, args);
        }
        return m;
    }
    protected virtual Expression VisitInvocation(InvocationExpression iv) {
        IEnumerable<Expression> args =
                this.VisitExpressionList(iv.Arguments);
        Expression expr = this.Visit(iv.Expression);
        if (args != iv.Arguments || expr != iv.Expression) {
            return Expression.Invoke(expr, args);
        }
        return iv;
    }
    // Other code omitted...
}
```

Typically, you should always start from a lambda expression node, which is visited by the *VisitLambda* method that simply pays a visit to its *Body* property. The source code for *Visit-Lambda* is shown in Listing 11-15.

Listing 11-15 *VisitLambda* method in the *ExpressionVisitor* class

```
public abstract class ExpressionVisitor {
    protected virtual Expression VisitLambda(LambdaExpression lambda) {
        Expression body = this.Visit(lambda.Body);
        if (body != lambda.Body) {
            return Expression.Lambda(lambda.Type, body, lambda.Parameters);
        }
        return lambda;
    }
    // Other code omitted...
}
```

We will not continue with all the other node types because the logic should be clear enough at this point. Even if all the nodes derive from a common base class (*Expression*), they must be interpreted type by type to be able to make a complete visit of an expression tree. The *ExpressionVisitor* class is an abstract class that implements an algorithm of *Visit* that can be specialized in a derived class for many purposes, including the following:

- To traverse the entire tree to translate the expression tree into another form. This is what the LINQ to SQL provider does to convert an in-memory expression tree into a corresponding SQL query.

- To make modifications on the properties of some node in an expression tree. Because all the nodes are immutable, this requires replacing the modified node and all the parent nodes. The replacement of parent nodes is automatically done by the *ExpressionVisitor* implementation we have just introduced.

- To add and remove nodes from a tree or combine different expression trees. These are variations of the modification of the tree we talked about in the preceding bullet point.

> **Note** The methods specialized for each type of node return a new node if any of the child nodes have been changed. Classes derived from *ExpressionVisitor* can simply specialize the behavior for a single type of node, returning a new node instance cloned from the existing one but with some differences in one or more of its properties. All the upper-level nodes referencing the new subtree are automatically built by the standard implementation of *ExpressionVisitor*.

To show an example, we created a simple derived class that displays only the expression tree content without modifying it. To do that, it intercepts the *Visit* call and displays the content of each node, indenting the node according to its depth level in the tree. Listing 11-16 shows the code for such an implementation.

Listing 11-16 *DisplayVisitor* specialization of the *ExpressionVisitor* class

```
class DisplayVisitor : ExpressionVisitor {
    private int level = 0;
    protected override Expression Visit(Expression exp) {
        if (exp != null) {
            for (int i = 0; i < level; i++) {
                Console.Write("   ");
            }
            Console.WriteLine( "{0}  -  {1}",
                exp.NodeType, exp.GetType().Name );
        }
        level++;
        Expression result = base.Visit(exp);
        level--;
        return result;
    }

    public void Display(Expression exp) {
        Console.WriteLine("===== DisplayVisitor.Display =====");
        this.Visit(exp);
    }
}
```

We tested our *DisplayVisitor* class using the code in Listing 11-17, defining the same expression represented in Figure 11-9.

Listing 11-17   Code to test the *DisplayVisitor* class

```
static int Double(int n) {
    return n * 2;
}

static void DemoExpressionVisitor() {
    Expression<Func<int, int>> Formula =
        (n) => 1 + Double(n * (n % 2 == 0 ? -1 : 1));
    Console.WriteLine( Formula.ToString() );
    DisplayVisitor visitor = new DisplayVisitor();
    visitor.Display(Formula);
}
```

The following is the output produced by the execution of the *DemoExpressionVisitor* method in Listing 11-17:

```
n => (1 + Double((n * IIF(((n % 2) = 0), -1, 1))))
===== DisplayVisitor.Display =====
Lambda  -  Expression`1
  Add  -  BinaryExpression
     Constant  -  ConstantExpression
     Call  -  MethodCallExpression
        Multiply  -  BinaryExpression
           Parameter  -  ParameterExpression
           Conditional  -  ConditionalExpression
              Equal  -  BinaryExpression
                 Modulo  -  BinaryExpression
                    Parameter  -  ParameterExpression
                    Constant  -  ConstantExpression
                 Constant  -  ConstantExpression
              Constant  -  ConstantExpression
              Constant  -  ConstantExpression
```

A further specialization of the several methods of the base class could allow for the output of more detailed information for each node, but we will see a more complex specialization of the *ExpressionVisitor* to manipulate the expression tree later in this chapter.

We have described one of the possible implementations for visiting an expression tree. This implementation will probably be used most often because it is described in the LINQ documentation and is based on a classic object-oriented approach. However, other possible implementations might be more appropriate. For example, if you want to frequently change a small piece of logic in expression tree analysis but do not want to (or cannot) create a derived class for each case, you might consider an approach based more on "functional-style" programming that we illustrate in the sidebar "An Alternative Visitor Pattern." The key point here is that you are not forced to use a specific pattern in visiting an expression tree

An Alternative Visitor Pattern

As we have already said, there are many ways to implement an algorithm to visit an expression tree. We cannot show all the possible alternatives, but we would like to introduce another implementation that differs from the previous approach and that might be preferable in some circumstances.

In Listing 11-18, you can see an excerpt of the source code for the *Visit* lambda expression that has been published by Jomo Fisher on his blog (*http://blogs.msdn.com/jomo_fisher/ archive/2007/05/23/dealing-with-linq-s-immutable-expression-trees.aspx*).

Listing 11-18 Implementation of an Expression visitor algorithm through a lambda expression

```
public static class ExprOp {
    static public Func<Expression, Expression> Visit =
        FuncOp.Create<Expression, Expression>(
            (self, expr) => {
            if (expr == null) {
                return expr;
            }
            switch (expr.NodeType) {
                case ExpressionType.Coalesce:
                    var c = (BinaryExpression) expr;
                    var left = self(c.Left);
                    var right = self(c.Right);
                    var conv = self(c.Conversion);
                    return (left == c.Left
                            && right == c.Right
                            && conv == c.Conversion)
                        ? expr
                        : Expression.Coalesce(
                                left,
                                right,
                                (LambdaExpression) conv);
                case ExpressionType.Conditional:
                    var ce = (ConditionalExpression) expr;
                    var t = self(ce.Test);
                    var it = self(ce.IfTrue);
                    var @if = self(ce.IfFalse);
                    return (t == ce.Test
                            && it == ce.IfTrue
                            && @if == ce.IfFalse)
                        ? expr
                        : Expression.Condition(t, it, @if);
                // Code for other cases has been omitted
                // handled cases are:
                //    ExpressionType.TypeIs
                //    ExpressionType.MemberAccess
                //    ExpressionType.Call
                //    ExpressionType.Lambda
```

```
//    ExpressionType.New
//    ExpressionType.NewArrayInit
//    ExpressionType.NewArrayBounds
//    ExpressionType.Invoke
//    ExpressionType.MemberInit
//    ExpressionType.ListInit
// There is no default handling, thus all the other
// node types are not handled by this switch statement
// but are intercepted by the if statements after
// the switch statement
            }
        if (expr.IsBinary()) {
            var b = (BinaryExpression) expr;
            var left = self(b.Left);
            var right = self(b.Right);
            return (left == b.Left && right == b.Right)
                    ? expr
                    : Expression.MakeBinary(
                            expr.NodeType,
                            left,
                            right);
        }
        else if (expr.IsUnary()) {
            var u = (UnaryExpression) expr;
            var op = self(u.Operand);
            return (u.Operand == op)
                    ? expr
                    : Expression.MakeUnary(
                            u.NodeType,
                            op,
                            expr.Type);
        }
        return expr;
    }
)
public static bool IsBinary(this Expression expr) {
    return expr is BinaryExpression;
}
public static bool IsUnary(this Expression expr) {
    return expr is UnaryExpression;
}
// Other code omitted...
}
```

There are some similarities between this approach and the approach used with the *ExpressionVisitor* class you saw in Listing 11-11. The *Visit* lambda expression iterates the tree nodes using a recursive approach. One major difference is that instead of having a *switch* statement with a *case* for each node type, this visitor implementation handles the two classes *BinaryExpression* and *UnaryExpression* separately. These classes enclose the majority of node types; the others should be implemented in the previous *switch* statement. We commented out some *case* statements in the *switch* statement because we were not interested in further navigating those corresponding nodes.

Note Comparing the type of the expression node with an *is* condition, as the *IsBinary* and *IsUnary* methods do, results in worse performance than a *switch* condition. Implementing them as we do in the *ExpressionVisitor* class shown in Listing 11-11 might increase the execution time of the entire visit by up to 10 percent. (The exact number strictly depends on the nodes contained in the visited expression tree.)

However, this approach is immune from the addition of new node types in a future release of these classes, because they will not break existing code. This algorithm will not visit subtrees originating from unsupported nodes, and it will handle the new nodes itself as leaf nodes, but the tree navigation will be completed without errors. For example, near the end of the .NET 3.5 development cycle, two node types were added: *Power* (for *BinaryExpression*) and *UnaryPlus* (for *UnaryExpression*). We handled them in Listing 11-11, but they were not handled in the original source code included with the online help with the release-to-market (RTM) version of the product. Listing 11-18 does not have to be fixed if a new node type is added to a future release of the .NET Framework.

Whenever you write your own visitor algorithm, you might have to decide whether you want to favor performance or compatibility with possible extensions. Finally, consider that the *Visit* lambda expression is about 3 or 4 times slower than the *ExpressionVisitor* class. This difference depends only minimally on the *switch* vs. *if/is* approach, and it is more closely related to the major resource consumption of anonymous delegates. However, remember to conduct your own performance measures to find the best tradeoff for you between execution speed and code complexity.

A more interesting characteristic of the *Visit* lambda expression in Listing 11-18 is that we do not have to define a derived class to visit (and possible modify) an expression tree. We can leverage lambda expressions to "inject" code inside the visitor algorithm, as shown in Listing 11-19, to visit the expression tree represented in Figure 11-9 using the lambda expression approach.

Listing 11-19 Expression tree visit based on a lambda expression approach

```
static void DemoVisitLambda() {
    Expression<Func<int, int>> Formula =
        (n) => 1 + Double(n * (n % 2 == 0 ? -1 : 1));
    Console.WriteLine(Formula.ToString());

    int level = 0;
    var visitFormula = ExprOp.Visit.Chain(
        (self, last, expr) => {
            if (expr != null) {
                for (int i = 0; i < level; i++) {
                    Console.Write("    ");
                }
                Console.WriteLine(
                    "{0} - {1}",
                    expr.NodeType,
                    expr.GetType().Name);
            }
            level++;
```

```
                var result = last(expr);
                level--;
                return result;
            }
    );

    visitFormula(Formula);
}
```

Each node of the tree is processed by the lambda expression passed as a parameter to the *Chain* extension method applied to the *ExprOp.Visit* lambda expression. Each node is simply displayed with the right indentation and further processed to continue the visit by calling *last(expr)*, which calls the original *Visit* lambda expression on the *expr* node.

The output produced by the execution of the *DemoVisitLambda* method in Listing 11-19 is identical to the output we obtained when executing the *DemoExpressionVisitor* method in Listing 11-17 (except for the title, of course):

```
n => (1 + Double((n * IIF(((n % 2) = 0), -1, 1))))
===== DemoVisitLambda =====
Lambda  -  Expression`1
   Add  -  BinaryExpression
      Constant  -  ConstantExpression
      Call  -  MethodCallExpression
         Multiply  -  BinaryExpression
            Parameter  -  ParameterExpression
            Conditional  -  ConditionalExpression
               Equal  -  BinaryExpression
                  Modulo  -  BinaryExpression
                     Parameter  -  ParameterExpression
                     Constant  -  ConstantExpression
                  Constant  -  ConstantExpression
               Constant  -  ConstantExpression
               Constant  -  ConstantExpression
```

The code we have seen makes use of some helper extension methods contained in a static class named *FuncOp*. For example, the illusion of having a *self* keyword that calls the same lambda expression that you are defining is the result of some helper classes and methods that are part of the *FuncOp* static class. For the sake of conciseness, we have not included the source code of *FuncOp* here. However, these methods are included in the book sample code, and you can find a detailed explanation of them in Jomo Fisher blog post at *http://blogs.msdn.com/jomo_fisher/archive/2007/05/07/visitor-revisitted-linq-function-composablity-and-chain-of-responsibility.aspx.*

The alternative *Visitor* approach that we just described is particularly useful when you have very little code to "inject" into a visitor, because it does not require you to define a new class but rather to apply a simple transformation or examination on an existing expression tree. However, when the operation you want to perform becomes more complex, we prefer the previous approach of inheriting from the *ExpressionVisitor* class because we probably would have to write a dedicated class anyway.

Dynamically Building an Expression Tree

The final part of this chapter is dedicated to exploring how you can dynamically build an expression tree. We start by analyzing how this job is performed by the compiler when it encounters an assignment of an *Expression<T>* variable. Then we describe some typical operations you might want to do when building an expression tree.

How the Compiler Generates an Expression Tree

In our opinion, one of the best ways to learn how to build an expression tree is by first understanding the way this job is performed by the compiler. Consider Listing 11-20: we have the same lambda expression

```
(n) => n + 1;
```

and we assign it, respectively, to a *Func<int,int>* variable and an *Expression<Func<int,int>>* variable.

Listing 11-20   Lambda expression and expression tree assignments

```
static void TreeConstruction() {
    Func<int, int> lambdaInc = (n) => n + 1;
    Expression<Func<int, int>> exprInc;
    exprInc = (n) => n + 1;

    Console.WriteLine("lambdaInc : {0}", lambdaInc.ToString());
    Console.WriteLine("exprInc   : {0}", exprInc.ToString());
}
```

The following is the output produced by executing *TreeConstruction* in Listing 11-20:

```
lambdaInc : System.Func`2[System.Int32,System.Int32]
exprInc   : n => (n + 1)
```

If you have carefully read this chapter up to this point, you should be ready to explain the difference between *lambdaInc* and *exprInc*. However, even a novice can understand that, for some reason, *lambdaInc* is a reference to an instance of a type probably constructed by the compiler (because we did not declare such a type), while *exprInc* is a structure that contains the definition of the expression in some readable form. But what happens under the hood when the compiler processes our *TreeConstruction* method? We will examine *lambdaInc* and *exprInc* separately.

The lambda expression is a syntax that is understood by the compiler to generate an anonymous delegate. We can declare *lambdaInc* as

```
Func<int, int> lambdaInc = delegate(int n) { return n + 1; };
```

which is the shorter form for defining a delegate. Therefore, *lambdaInc* can be written as shown in Listing 11-21, producing a result equivalent to Listing 11-20 for *lambdaInc*, with the only difference being that this time the compiler does not have to create a delegate for us.

Listing 11-21   Lambda expression assignment

```
static int IncOperation(int n) {
    return n + 1;
}

static void LambdaDelegate() {
    Func<int, int> lambdaInc = new Func<int,int>(IncOperation);
    Console.WriteLine("lambdaInc : {0}", lambdaInc.ToString());
}
```

In the end, a lambda expression is a delegate that points to some piece of code in your program. Now, if we analyze what happens when the compiler interprets the *exprInc* assignment in Listing 11-20, we will discover that the code generated is not a delegate. Our goal is to get the expression tree represented in Figure 11-10.

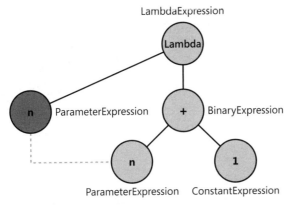

Figure 11-10   The expression tree for (n) => n + 1

In Listing 11-22, you can see an *exprInc* assignment that is equivalent to the one generated by the compiler for the code in Listing 11-20, which generates the execution tree shown in Figure 11-10.

Listing 11-22   Expression tree assignment

```
static void ExpressionAssignment() {
    Expression<Func<int, int>> exprInc;
    ConstantExpression constant = Expression.Constant(1, typeof(int));
    ParameterExpression parameter = Expression.Parameter(typeof(int), "n");
    BinaryExpression add = Expression.Add( parameter, constant );
    exprInc = Expression.Lambda<Func<int, int>>(
                add,
                new ParameterExpression[] { parameter } );
    Console.WriteLine("exprInc   : {0}", exprInc.ToString());
}
```

As you can see, the expression tree is built starting from leaves (constant *1* and parameter *n*) and then goes up to the *Add* operation, which is the *Body* of the lambda expression we assigned to *exprInc*. That lambda needs an array of parameters made by the same nodes (in this case, there is only one) used as parameters in the expression tree. The dotted line between the two *ParameterExpression* nodes in Figure 11-10 indicates that these nodes are physically represented with the same instance of *ParameterExpression*. Notice that the boldfaced code in Listing 11-22 is the expansion of this single line of Listing 11-20:

```
exprInc = (n) => n + 1;
```

The lambda expression syntax is commonly called "syntactic sugar," because it is a language addition used only to make it "sweeter" for humans to use. However, when lambda expressions are transformed into expression trees by the compiler, this sugar becomes important to us much like it is for a hypoglycemic person! Unfortunately, when you have to create an expression tree in a dynamic way, you probably need to build each node of the tree just like we did with the code in Listing 11-22.

Finally, remember that when you assign an *Expression<T>* variable with a lambda expression, the code that creates the expression tree is executed when the assignment is performed. Generated nodes are immutable, and the tree can be modified only by creating new nodes, as we already saw earlier in this chapter.

Combining Existing Expression Trees

We have just seen how you can create an expression tree starting from scratch. You can design the expression tree on a chart and then manually define all the nodes you need. However, often you might want to alter an existing tree, encapsulating it in a larger expression. As an example, consider the following lambda expression:

```
(b, h) => b * h
```

This expression can represent the formula to calculate the area of a rectangle. If you assign this lambda to an *Expression<T>* like this

```
Expression<Func<double, double, double>> rectArea = (b, h) => b * h;
```

you end up with an expression tree like the one represented in Figure 11-11.

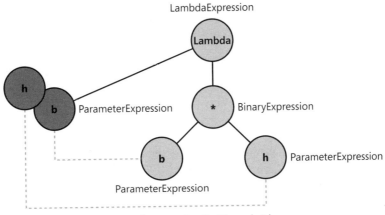

Figure 11-11   The expression tree for (b, h) => b * h

If you want to calculate a volume, you might write the following lambda expression:

```
(x, y, z) => x * y * z
```

If you let the compiler generate an expression tree for this lambda, you obtain the one represented in Figure 11-12.

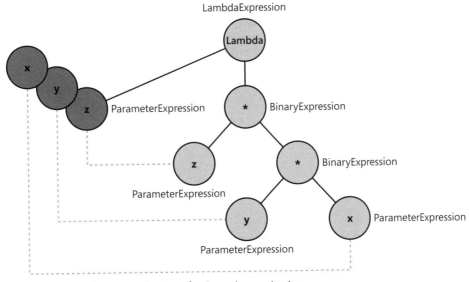

Figure 11-12   The expression tree for (x, y, z) => x * y * z

However, you might want to recycle the *rectArea* formula in this way to get the same result:

```
(x, y, z) => rectArea(x, y) * z
```

Unfortunately, that code does not compile. But if it did compile, you would obtain the expression tree represented in Figure 11-13. Even if they produce the same result, it is clear that Figure 11-12 and Figure 11-13 represent different expression trees.

We point out this difference because you might want to generate the expression trees represented in both Figure 11-12 and Figure 11-13, starting from the *rectArea* expression tree represented in Figure 11-11. However, obtaining the result that "hides" the inner expression, as in Figure 11-12, is much harder than building the tree represented in Figure 11-13 because you need to completely rebuild the encapsulated tree to substitute its parameters with those of the resulting expression tree.

Let's start with the simplest way, which incorporates the parameters of the encapsulated expression tree into those of the resulting expression tree, adding to them possible new parameters required by the added nodes. You can see this implementation in Listing 11-23. The node type that links to another expression tree is *Invoke*. To begin, add a *Multiply* node, and make a parameter mapping only from *x* to *b* and from *y* to *h*. As we said, the resulting expression tree is the one represented in Figure 11-13.

Listing 11-23 Expression tree combination

```
static void TreeCombination() {
    Expression<Func<double, double, double>> rectArea = (b, h) => b * h;

    ParameterExpression x = Expression.Parameter(typeof(double), "x" );
    ParameterExpression y = Expression.Parameter(typeof(double), "y");
    ParameterExpression z = Expression.Parameter(typeof(double), "z");
    Expression area = Expression.Invoke(rectArea, new Expression[] { x, y });
    Expression multiply = Expression.Multiply(z, area);
    Expression<Func<double,double,double,double>> volume =
        Expression.Lambda<Func<double,double,double,double>>(
            multiply,
            new ParameterExpression[] { x, y, z });

    Console.WriteLine("Area    = {0}", rectArea.ToString());
    Console.WriteLine("Volume = {0}", volume.ToString());
    Console.WriteLine("Area value    = {0}", rectArea.Compile()(20, 10));
    Console.WriteLine("Volume value = {0}", volume.Compile()(20, 10, 8));
}
```

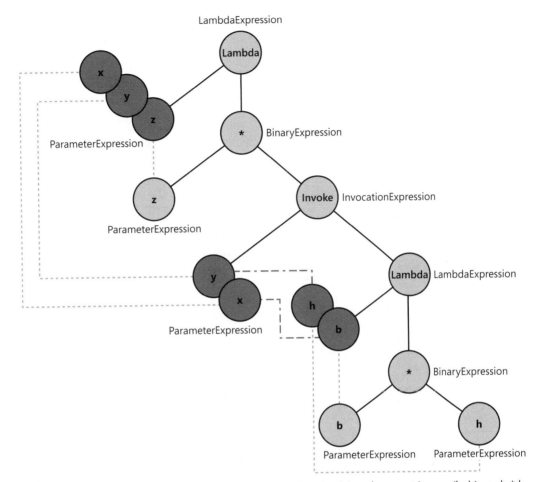

Figure 11-13 The expression tree for (x, y, z) => rectArea(x, y) * z where rectArea = (b, h) => b * h

The output produced by executing the *TreeCombination* method in Listing 11-23 is the following one:

```
Area   = (b, h) => (b * h)
Volume = (x, y, z) => (z * Invoke((b, h) => (b * h),x,y))
Area value   = 200
Volume value = 1600
```

> **Important**   Be sure you understand the role of the *Invoke* node type. To help you do this, we provided this example, which might seem useless by itself but is the simplest way to explain how to handle the *Invoke* node. In a complex expression tree, the node's behavior might appear obscure and be difficult to understand.

The second step is to obtain the expression tree shown in Figure 11-12, starting from the one we obtained in Listing 11-23 and that corresponds to the graphical representation shown in Figure 11-13. To perform the removal of *Invoke* and the parameter substitution, you need to visit the expression tree using the classes derived by *ExpressionVisitor* that are shown in Listing 11-24. The *RemoveInvokeVisitor<T>.VisitInvocation* method calls *ReplaceParameters-Visitors.Visit* to replace lambda expression parameters in the visited expression tree. The *RemoveInvokeVisitor<T>* class is the main *ExpressionVisitor*-derived class that we will use to visit the tree and to produce the required result.

Listing 11-24   Classes to remove *Invoke* and make the parameter substitution

```
class RemoveInvokeVisitor<T> : ExpressionVisitor {
    private ReadOnlyCollection<ParameterExpression> lambdaParameters;

    public RemoveInvokeVisitor(ReadOnlyCollection<ParameterExpression> parameters) {
        this.lambdaParameters = parameters;
    }

    protected override Expression VisitInvocation(InvocationExpression iv) {
        var newPars = iv.Arguments;
        LambdaExpression lambda = (iv.Expression) as LambdaExpression;
        if (lambda != null) {
            var oldPars = lambda.Parameters;
            ReplaceParametersVisitors replace =
                new ReplaceParametersVisitors(oldPars, newPars);
            return this.Visit( replace.ReplaceVisit(lambda.Body) );
        }
        else {
            return base.VisitInvocation(iv);
        }
    }

    public Expression<T> RemoveInvokeVisit(Expression<T> exp) {
        return (Expression<T>) Visit(exp);
    }
}

class ReplaceParametersVisitors : ExpressionVisitor {
    private ReadOnlyCollection<Expression> newParameters;
    private ReadOnlyCollection<ParameterExpression> oldParameters;
    public ReplaceParametersVisitors(
        ReadOnlyCollection<ParameterExpression> oldParameters,
        ReadOnlyCollection<Expression> newParameters) {
```

```
            this.newParameters = newParameters;
            this.oldParameters = oldParameters;
        }

        protected override Expression  VisitParameter(ParameterExpression p) {
            if (oldParameters != null
                && newParameters != null) {
                if (oldParameters.Contains(p)) {
                    return newParameters[oldParameters.IndexOf(p)];
                }
            }
            return base.VisitParameter(p);
        }

        public Expression ReplaceVisit(Expression exp) {
            return Visit(exp);
        }
    }
}
```

We added some lines to the code of the *TreeCombination* method you saw previously in
Listing 11-23. The excerpt in Listing 11-25 shows only the added lines, which eliminates the
Invoke node from the expression tree and makes the necessary parameter substitution.

Listing 11-25   Expression tree combination

```
static void TreeCombination() {
    // Omitted code...
    var cleaner =
        new RemoveInvokeVisitor<
                Func<double, double, double, double>>(volume.Parameters);
    var cleanVolume= cleaner.RemoveInvokeVisit(volume);
    Console.WriteLine("CleanVolume = {0}", cleanVolume.ToString());
    Console.WriteLine("CleanVolume value = {0}", cleanVolume.Compile()(20, 10, 8));
}
```

The following is the complete output produced by the execution of the new *TreeCombination*
method in Listing 11-25:

```
Area    = (b, h) => (b * h)
Volume = (x, y, z) => (z * Invoke((b, h) => (b * h),x,y))
Area value    = 200
Volume value = 1600
CleanVolume = (x, y, z) => (z * (x * y))
CleanVolume value = 1600
```

As you can see, the *CleanVolume* expression tree is in the form that is graphically represented
in Figure 11-12.

Dynamic Composition of an Expression Tree

Often, you need to create an expression tree based on conditions that occur during program execution. For example, a user makes some choices through the user interface to filter data to be queried. You might want to translate this set of conditions to an expression tree that will be passed as the predicate of a *Where* condition to a LINQ query. In this case, you know that a predicate is a lambda expression that returns a *bool*. Having some constraints for the query expression to create can simplify your code, because you can make some assumptions and base your code on that.

We prepared an example with a query of the current process, using the *System.Diagnostic.Process* class. In Listing 11 26, you can see the structure of the query executed by the *Display* method, which receives a *filterExpression* expression tree to be used as a parameter for the *Where* condition. If that argument is passed as *null*, a dummy filter that always returns *true* is used.

Listing 11-26   Query of current processes filtered by *filterExpression*

```
static void Display(Expression<Func<Process, bool>> filterExpression) {
    // If not defined, use a dummy filter
    if (filterExpression == null) {
        filterExpression = (p) => true;
    }

    Console.WriteLine("Filter : {0}", filterExpression.ToString());

    var query =
        Process.GetProcesses().AsQueryable()
        .Where(filterExpression)
        .Select(p => p.ProcessName);

    // Dump filtered processes
    foreach (var row in query) Console.WriteLine(row);
}
```

We wanted to call the *Display* method, defining its *filterExpression* parameter in a dynamic way. You can see in Listing 11-27 the *FilterSelection* method, which uses the *ProcessFilters* class (that you will see shortly) to combine different filters. *ProcessFilters* includes an *Add* method that adds a condition that operates on a *System.Diagnostic.Process* property. It executes a specific comparison with a defined constant value. In our example, we are interested only in listing processes that are responding and that have a base priority greater than 8. However, instead of hard coding filters such as these, you can build a user interface to provide more choices among properties, operators, and constant values before passing them to a more flexible *FilterSelection* method.

Listing 11-27   Use of the *ProcessFilters* class

```
static Expression<Func<Process, bool>> FilterSelection() {
    ProcessFilters pf = new ProcessFilters();

    // Set dynamic filters
    pf.Add("Responding", ExpressionType.Equal, true );
    pf.Add("BasePriority", ExpressionType.GreaterThan, 8);

    return pf.GetExpression();
}

static void Main(string[] args) {
    Expression<Func<Process, bool>> filterExpression = FilterSelection();
    Display(filterExpression);
}
```

The very last operation involved in building the expression tree is the creation of the top-level node of the tree itself. In this case, the node corresponds to a lambda expression that contains the dynamically created expression tree (*bodyFilter*) and a single parameter of type *Process*. This lambda expression is created when the *GetExpression* method is called by the *FilterSelection* method, which we illustrated earlier.

The Listing 11-28 shows the code for the *ProcessFilters* class used in the *FilterSelection* method.

Listing 11-28   Implementation of the *ProcessFilters* class

```
public class ProcessFilters {
    ParameterExpression paramExp;
    Expression bodyFilter;
    public ProcessFilters() {
        paramExp = Expression.Parameter(typeof(Process), "p");
        bodyFilter = null;
    }

    // Create a lambda expression - we always have one single parameter
    // of type Process that is declared as paramExp by the constructor
    public Expression<Func<Process, bool>> GetExpression() {
        if (bodyFilter == null) {
            return null;
        }
        Expression<Func<Process, bool>> filter;
        filter = Expression.Lambda<Func<Process, bool>>(
            bodyFilter,
            new ParameterExpression[] { paramExp });
        return filter;
    }

    // Add an AND with a filter on fieldName compared
    // with comparisonValue with the required operator
    public void Add( string fieldName,
                     ExpressionType comparisonOperator,
                     object comparisonValue) {
```

```
    switch (comparisonOperator) {
        case ExpressionType.Equal:
        case ExpressionType.NotEqual:
        case ExpressionType.LessThan:
        case ExpressionType.LessThanOrEqual:
        case ExpressionType.GreaterThan:
        case ExpressionType.GreaterThanOrEqual:
            // Supported operations                    break;
        default:
            throw new NotSupportedException(
                String.Format(
                    "Operator {0} is not supported in ProcessFilters.Add",
                    comparisonOperator.ToString()));
    } // end switch (check comparisonOperator)


    ConstantExpression comparisonConstant =
        Expression.Constant( comparisonValue,
                            comparisonValue.GetType());
    MemberExpression fieldAccess =
        Expression.Property( paramExp,
                            fieldName);
    BinaryExpression comparison =
        Expression.MakeBinary( comparisonOperator,
                                fieldAccess,
                                comparisonConstant );
    if (bodyFilter == null) {
        bodyFilter = comparison;
    }
    else {
        bodyFilter = Expression.AndAlso(bodyFilter, comparison);
    }
}
}
```

The *ProcessFilter* class holds an expression tree that saves the "current" body of the expression in the private member *bodyFilter*. The resulting expression tree will be a lambda expression with a single parameter of type *System.Diagnostic.Process*. This parameter is created by the *ProcessFilters* constructor, and it will be used to read the requested properties. (See the *field-Access* assignment in the *Add* method.)

The *Add* method of the *ProcessFilters* class simply creates a *BinaryExpression* between the property specified in *fieldName* and the constant specified in *comparisonValue*, using the operator specified by *comparisonOperator*. If the *bodyFilter* member already contains at least another node, the new top-level node is an *AndAlso* between the new comparison and the existing expression tree. We always put in an AND operator for all the conditions added to a *ProcessFilters* instance: most of the time, it is the only action required, but you could implement a more sophisticated system that allows specifying OR conditions too.

The final execution tree that is dynamically created by our sample is represented in Figure 11-14. Nodes created at the same time have the same color background. The more recent (Lambda) has the darker background; a paler background is used for older nodes. The *&& Binary-Expression* is created to perform the AND operation between the >= and == nodes.

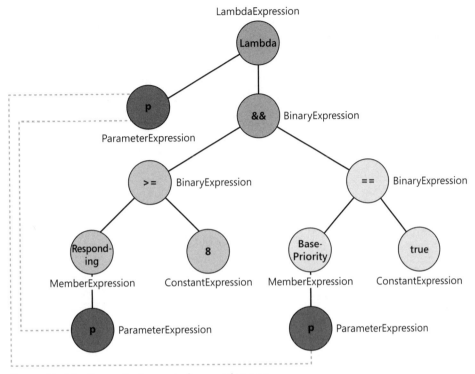

Figure 11-14 Dynamically created expression tree

The execution of the *Main* method in Listing 11-27 produces a result similar to the following one (noting that the effective result depends on the processes currently executed on the testing machine):

```
Filter : p => ((p.Responding = True) && (p.BasePriority > 8))
csrss
services
msvsmon
lsass
winlogon
csrss
smss
msvsmon
wininit
dwm
taskmgr
```

Now you can try to create your custom query on running processes by changing the *Add* calls in the *FilterSelection* method shown in Listing 11-27. More importantly, you should be able to apply the techniques you have seen in this chapter to handle and manipulate expression trees in your programs!

Summary

In this chapter, we showed you the internal behavior of lambda expressions and expression trees and how they relate to each other. We explored how to encapsulate and modify expression trees, and how to handle their immutability. We analyzed the classes contained in the *System.Linq.Expressions* namespace that support the expression trees, exploring in detail the implementation of the most common and important node types. After that, we analyzed some algorithms that are used to visit expression trees. Finally, we examined how the compiler generates expression trees from lambda expression syntax and how an expression tree can be dynamically created and manipulated.

Chapter 12
Extending LINQ

One interesting aspect of LINQ is its extensibility: you can extend LINQ by adding new operators, by writing your own implementation of standard query operators (for example, *Where*, *OrderBy*, *Distinct*, and so on), and by implementing the *IQueryable* interface to access any kind of external data.

The first two options (adding new query operators or replacing existing ones) is fundamentally a way to customize LINQ to Objects. Working with objects in memory provides for a simple replacement or extension without the need to know very much about the existing implementation of LINQ to Objects. A different scenario is involved when you use LINQ to access data that is not in-memory objects—for example, when you use LINQ to SQL. In that case, you need to implement all the operators from scratch because most of the time you need to convert the expression tree into another query language.

In this chapter, we will explore these three extensibility options for LINQ. We will describe how to create new custom operators, and then we will show an example of customizing an existing operator. Finally, we will describe how to create a custom LINQ provider by implementing the *IQueryable* interface.

Custom Operators

LINQ offers a full set of operators that cover most of the possible operations on a set of entities. However, sometimes you might require some other operator to add a particular semantic meaning to your query, especially if you can use the same operator several times in your code. As an example, we will implement a custom operator that returns, for a given collection, the element with the lowest value for a particular property.

Consider the entities *Stock* and *Quote* defined in Listing 12-1. A *Stock* instance contains a list of *Quote* instances, each with a price and time of collection.

Listing 12-1   Entities used in the custom operator example

```
public class Quote {
    public Stock Stock { get; set; }
    public decimal Price { get; set; }
    public DateTime Time { get; set; }
}

public class Stock {
    public string Ticker { get; set; }
    public string Name { get; set; }
    public decimal Shares { get; set; }
```

```
    public List<Quote> Quotes { get; set; }

    public override string ToString() {
        return String.Format(
            "{0}: {1}   MIN {2} - MAX {3}",
            Ticker,
            Shares,
            Quotes.Min(q => q.Price),
            Quotes.Max(q => q.Price));
    }
}
```

The *ToString* override in *Stock* displays the minimum and maximum price contained in the *Quotes* list. To do that, it uses the *Min* and *Max* aggregation operators. Listing 12-2 shows how to use these classes.

Listing 12-2   Quotes collection initialization

```
Stock stock = new Stock { Name = "Stock Demo", Ticker = "AGHQ", Shares = 100000M };
stock.Quotes = new List<Quote> {
    new Quote { Stock = stock, Time = new DateTime(2007, 12, 5, 11, 8, 45 ),
                Price = 57.63M },
    new Quote { Stock = stock, Time = new DateTime(2007, 12, 5, 11, 8, 56 ),
                Price = 56.92M },
    new Quote { Stock = stock, Time = new DateTime(2007, 12, 5, 11, 9, 08 ),
                Price = 57.05M },
    new Quote { Stock = stock, Time = new DateTime(2007, 12, 5, 11, 9, 23 ),
                Price = 56.87M }
};

Console.WriteLine( "Stock: {0}", stock);
```

The execution of the code in Listing 12-2 produces the following output. As you can see, it does not display the time when the minimum and maximum prices have been collected.

```
Stock: AGHQ: 100000  MIN 56,87 - MAX 57,63
```

Now consider the calculation of the minimum value. The *Min* aggregate operator we have used is defined in this way:

```
public static TResult Min<TSource, TResult> (
    this IEnumerable<TSource> source,
    Func<TSource, TResult> selector);
```

The *Min* operator returns the same type used in the comparison. However, we want to compare the *Price* property of the *Quote* class but also want to get back an instance of *Quote* with the minimum *Price* and not only the minimum *Price*. If the *Quote* class implemented the *IComparable* interface, we could have called the *Min* operator directly on the *Quotes* collection:

```
Quotes.Min()
```

This would have returned a single *Quote* instance following the comparison rules defined in the *IComparable* implementation. However, we do not want to follow this approach because the *IComparable* interface implementation could also be used for sorting quotes, and a *Quote* could be sorted by stock name, price, and time. Thus, in our scenario, we prefer not to define a semantic of automatic comparison between two *Quote* instances. Instead, we explicitly define the value to be compared (*Price*) in the *Min* call:

```
Quotes.Min(q => q.Price)
```

Because the *Min* operator returns the same type used to make the comparison, now the result of the *Min* operator is a value of the same type of *Price*. However, to still get the whole *Quote* instance, we need to use another approach. One solution is using the *Aggregate* operator, as you can see in Listing 12-3.

> **Note**   In the case of several quotes with the same price, we will get only the first one. We have not considered the need for getting all the quotes with the minimum price in this example.

Listing 12-3   Get item with the minimum price using *Aggregate*

```
Quote minQuote;

// Get the item with the minimum price using Aggregate operator
minQuote = stock.Quotes.Aggregate( (t, s) => t.Price < s.Price ? t : s );
Console.WriteLine(
    "Min item using Aggregate - {0} : {1}",
    minQuote.Time,
    minQuote.Price);
```

The use of *Aggregate* produces code that is compact and gets the job done, producing the required result:

```
Min item using Aggregate - 12/5/2007 11:09:23 AM : 56.87
```

However, the code is not easy to read. If you do not include an explicit comment, you need to read the code very carefully to understand what it is going to do. Moreover, that code is more error prone and not intuitive to write. To simplify the code we use, we need a custom operator that behaves similar to *Min* but returns the object in the sequence and not the expression value used to make the comparison. You can see the definition of this new operator, which we will call *MinPrice,* in Listing 12-4.

Listing 12-4   Definition of the *MinPrice* operator for the *Quote* class

```
static class Extensions {
    public static Quote MinPrice( this IEnumerable<Quote> source) {
        return source.Aggregate( (t, s) => t.Price < s.Price ? t : s );
    }
}
```

The *MinPrice* operator returns the *Quote* instance, which was obtained through wrapping the call to the *Aggregate* operator that compares two quotes by explicitly comparing their *Price* property. Listing 12-5 shows how to use this new operation that is extending LINQ.

Listing 12-5   Use of the *MinPrice* operator

```
// Get the item with the minimum price using a specific custom operator
Quote minQuote = stock.Quotes.MinPrice();
Console.WriteLine(
    "Min item using MinPrice  - {0} : {1}",
    minQuote.Time,
    minQuote.Price);
```

The code in Listing 12-5 produces the required result:

```
Min item using MinPrice  - 12/5/2007 11:09:23 AM : 56.87
```

Note   *MinPrice* is an extension method that is applied only to sequences of *Quote* instances because it extends the *IEnumerable<Quote>* interface, which is an instantiation of the generic *IEnumerable<T>* interface.

This approach requires a new operator definition each time we want to apply it to a type other than *Quote*, or if we want to change the property to be compared. A more generic approach requires the use of more verbose code that includes a more complex overload of the *Aggregate* operator. We call this operator *MinItem* and its implementation is shown in Listing 12-6.

Listing 12-6   Definition of the generic version of the *MinItem* operator

```
static class Extensions {
  public static TSource MinItem<TSource, TCompareValue>(
          this IEnumerable<TSource> source,
          Func<TSource, TCompareValue> comparerExpression) {

      // We get a constructed Comparer<T> instance
      // for the type to be compared
      Comparer<TCompareValue> comparer = Comparer<TCompareValue>.Default;
      // indexElement is used to execute two different pieces of code
      // in the lambda expression for Aggregate: one for the very
      // first iteration, the other for the following iterations
      int indexElement = 0;
      // The Aggregate will execute the lambda expression
      // for each element in the source sequence
      return source.Aggregate(
          default(TSource),
          (minValue, item) =>
              (indexElement++ == 0 ?
                  // First iteration - no comparison,
                  // returns item as initial minValue
                  item :
                  // Second or later  iteration: does the comparison
                  // and returns item if it is lower than the
```

```
                              // previous minValue; otherwise, returns minValue
                              (comparer.Compare( comparerExpression(item),
                                                 comparerExpression(minValue)) < 0 ?
                                                 item :
                                                 minValue)));
      }
  }
```

Using a generic *TSource* type, we have to specify its comparer by calling the *Aggregate* operator. We also need to handle the special case for the first element in the sequence, and we used *indexElement* to do that.

> **Note**   You might wonder why we simply cannot use a Boolean variable instead of an *int* to handle the special case for the first element. The reason is that in a lambda expression you have to write a single expression. The use of the post-increment operator on *indexElement* allows us to change its value without the need to define (and call) another function simply to change the state of the variable. Of course, we assume that we have less than 2^31 elements in our sequence.

The advantage of the code in Listing 12-6 is that the resulting *MinItem* operator can be applied to any type, using any expression to apply the comparison. The call to *MinItem* can specify any expression, as you can see in Listing 12-7, where we get the *Quote* instance with the lowest price and then the *Quote* instance with the oldest time.

Listing 12-7   Use of the *MinItem* operator

```
// Get the item with the minimum price using a generic custom operator
Quote minQuote = stock.Quotes.MinItem(x => x.Price);
Console.WriteLine(
    "Min item using MinItem(price) - {0} : {1}",
    minQuote.Time,
    minQuote.Price);

// Get the item with the minimum time using a generic custom operator
minQuote = stock.Quotes.MinItem(x => x.Time);
Console.WriteLine(
    "Min item using MinItem(time)  - {0} : {1}",
    minQuote.Time,
    minQuote.Price);
```

The following is the result produced by the execution of code in Listing 12-7:

```
Min item using MinItem(price) - 12/5/2007 11:09:23 AM : 56.87
Min item using MinItem(time)  - 12/5/2007 11:08:45 AM : 57.63
```

Adding new operators to LINQ is a way to extend its capabilities. Beyond adding brand new features, you can also improve code readability by wrapping existing operators into more specialized and meaningful ones.

Specialization of Existing Operators

Existing LINQ operators can be specialized for use with particular types. For example, you might want to apply a particular operator to a specific constructed type. As you will see later in this chapter, this practice is not very common because most of the time you need to implement *IQueryable* to perform complex customizations.

To start, we will describe an example of a meaningful specialization of the *Where* operator. Imagine that you have an *IVisible* interface with a *Visible* property that defines the visibility of an item in a collection. You could implement that interface in the *Customer* class, as you can see in Listing 12-8.

Listing 12-8 Definition of the *IVisible* interface and *Customer* class

```
public interface IVisible {
    bool Visible { get; set; }
}

public class Customer : IVisible {
    public Customer() {
        this.Visible = true;
    }

    public string Name { get; set; }
    public int Age { get; set; }
    public bool Visible { get; set; }

    public override string  ToString() {
        return String.Format("{0} is {1} years old", Name, Age);
    }
}
```

We want to skip any customer with *Visible* set to *false* when a query expression makes use of the *Where* operator, but without having to check the *Visible* property in the predicate expression. Listing 12-9 shows a *Where* specialization that works in this way when it is applied to types that implement the *IVisible* interface.

Listing 12-9 Specialization of the *Where* standard query operator

```
static class Extensions {
    public static IEnumerable<TSource> Where<TSource>(
            this IEnumerable<TSource> source,
            Func<TSource, Boolean> predicate)
        where TSource : IVisible {

        foreach (TSource item in source) {
            if (item.Visible && predicate(item)) {
                yield return item;
            }
        }
    }
}
```

Listing 12-10 shows the use of the customized *Where* operator in the initialization of a simple array of customers that is iterated through a query expression that explicitly filters only for customers with an age lower than 40. Moreover, customers with the *Visible* property set to *false* will be implicitly skipped by our custom *Where* operator.

Listing 12-10 Use of a specialized *Where* for types implementing the *IVisible* interface

```
Customer[] customers =
    { new Customer { Name = "John", Age = 24, Visible = false },
      new Customer { Name = "Allison", Age = 45 },
      new Customer { Name = "Brad", Age = 33 } };

var query =
    from c in customers
    where c.Age < 40
    select c;

foreach (var row in query) {
    Console.WriteLine(row);
}
```

The output produced by the code in Listing 12-10 is the following:

```
Brad is 33 years old
```

The other two customers have been skipped because they do not satisfy the condition in the *Where* predicate (Allison is more than 40 years old) or they are not visible (John).

The example we have just reviewed implements an implicit filter based on the *Visible* state of an object implementing *IVisible*. However, this filter is active only with the presence of a *Where* condition. For the specific need of skipping objects that do not have *Visible* set to *true*, an alternative (and probably simpler) way to get the same result is to write another operator to be applied to the source sequence just before the query expression itself. Instead of querying a sequence of *Customer* instances, we can query the sequence filtered by the *OnlyVisible* method defined in Listing 12-11, which filters for visible customers (*Visible* set to true) before applying any other LINQ standard operator.

Listing 12-11 Alternative way to filter for only *Visible* customers from a sequence

```
static class Extensions {
    public static IEnumerable<TSource> OnlyVisible<TSource>(
            this IEnumerable<TSource> source)
        where TSource : IVisible {

        foreach (TSource item in source) {
            if (item.Visible) {
                yield return item;
            }
        }
    }
}
```

This approach requires the query to be made on the result of a call to the *OnlyVisible* method. You can see in Listing 12-12 the query expression that uses this syntax.

Listing 12-12   Use of an *OnlyVisible* operator to get only *Visible* customers

```
var query =
    from c in customers.OnlyVisible()
    where c.Age < 40
    select c;
```

The result produced by Listing 12-12 is the same as for Listing 12-10.

As you can see, an important difference is in terms of semantics. If we specialize the *Where* operator, we also hide the internal behavior from the query. In the case of the *OnlyVisible* operator, we make this filter more explicit, but that call must be explicit in the query expression. You might have many options for implementing a similar behavior, but there are subtle differences that make one option more desirable than others depending on your requirements. In our example, if the programmer can choose to query for invisible customers, the *OnlyVisible* implementation is probably better. Otherwise, it would be preferable to use the *Where* operator or a complete control of the *Customers* collection wrapped in a method calling *OnlyVisible*.

Dangerous Practices

In this section, we want to show an example of a dangerous use of operator specialization. We can use the *MinItem* custom operator we defined early in this chapter to hijack calls to the standard *Min* operator made on a sequence of *Quote* instances. Listing 12-13 shows the implementation of such a *Min* operator specialization.

Listing 12-13   Specialization of the *Min* operator for *Quote* instances

```
static class Extensions {
    public static TSource Min<TSource, TCompareValue>(
            this IEnumerable<TSource> source,
            Func<TSource, TCompareValue> comparerExpression)
        where TSource : Quote {
        return source.MinItem(comparerExpression);
    }
}
```

This *Min* specialization applies only to *Quote* compatible types. In this way, we do not change the semantics for every type on which *Min* is applied because this could break existing code. (If it is recompiled; we cannot break compiled code because extension method resolution is made by the C# compiler during compilation.) This method allows us to write the code in Listing 12-14.

Listing 12-14   Use of the specialized *Min* operator on sequences of *Quote* instances

```
// Get item with the minimum price using a generic custom operator
Quote minQuote = stock.Quotes.Min(x => x.Price);
Console.WriteLine(
    "Min item using Min(price) - {0} : {1}",
    minQuote.Time,
    minQuote.Price);

// Get item with the minimum time using a generic custom operator
minQuote = stock.Quotes.Min(x => x.Time);
Console.WriteLine(
    "Min item using Min(time)  - {0} : {1}",
    minQuote.Time,
    minQuote.Price);
```

As we said, specializing a standard operator by changing its semantics is a dangerous practice. In this case, we are changing the semantics of the *Min* operator from this:

```
public static TCompareValue Min<TSource, TCompareValue> (
    this IEnumerable<TSource> source,
    Func<TSource, TCompareValue> selector);
```

to this:

```
public static TSource Min<TSource, TCompareValue> (
    this IEnumerable<TSource> source,
    Func<TSource, TCompareValue> selector);
```

In other words, the *Min* operator returns the source object that has the minimum value for a specified expression instead of returning the minimum value of the expression itself. This is an important semantic difference that could confuse whoever writes LINQ queries.

More generally, if you create your own version of a standard operator and do not limit the types on which it is applied, you can hide the "original" standard method in your code. This might be your intent, but if you are including code written by someone else, you have to be sure that there are no side effects caused by your changes. Be careful when overriding the behavior of existing standard operators!

Important   When you specialize a standard operator, use the same semantics and a pattern of use for parameters as well as a return type that is compatible with the existing operator you are overriding. If you need to change the semantics, consider defining a new custom operator, assigning it a specific name.

Limits of Specialization

Extending LINQ through the specialization of operators has some limitations. For example, the syntax and semantics of standard operators cannot be changed to be used in query expressions. As an example, imagine the access to a sorted dictionary by filtering only one or more keys in the *Where* condition of a query expression, as in the following pseudo-code:

```
SortedDictionary<string, string> list;

var query =
    from   l in list
    where  l.Key == "M"
    select l.Value;
```

Using a specialization of the standard *Where* operator might not be enough to improve the performance of the whole query resolution because the *Boolean* condition (*l.Key* == *"M"*) is evaluated in a "black box," which makes it impossible to understand how to optimize the access through the sorted keys collection. As we said before, adding a new operator is a better solution for this. However, we will try to analyze the predicate expression from a specialized *Where* operator. In the next part of this chapter, we will implement the *IQueryable* interface to achieve a similar purpose with a greater flexibility. A possible implementation of a faster *Where* operator on a *SortedDictionary* is illustrated in Listing 12-15 through Listing 12-20.

Listing 12-15   LINQ queries on a *SortedDictionary*

```
static void DemoSortedList() {
    SortedDictionary<string, string> list = new SortedDictionary<string, string>();
    for (char ch = 'Z'; ch >= 'A'; ch--) {
        list.Add(ch.ToString(), "Letter " + ch.ToString());
    }

    Console.WriteLine("-- queryStandard --");
    var queryStandard =
        from   l in list
        where  l.Key == "M"
        select l.Value;
    Dump(queryStandard);

    Console.WriteLine("-- queryFast --");
    var queryFast = list.WhereKey("M");
    Dump(queryFast);
}

static void Dump<T>(IEnumerable<T> sequence) {
    foreach (T item in sequence) {
        Console.WriteLine(item);
    }
}
```

Listing 12-15 includes two queries: *queryStandard* makes an iteration of all the items in our list and returns only the one with M as the key, filtering each item of the sequence through the standard *Where* operator. Conversely, *queryFast* does not perform a complete list iteration but gets only the single desired value by using the *WhereKey* operator. The implementation of this operator is shown in Listing 12-16.

Listing 12-16   Implementation of the *WhereKey* operator

```
static class Extensions {
    public static IEnumerable<TSource> WhereKey<TSource,TKey>(
            this  SortedDictionary<TKey, TSource> source,
            TKey key) {

        yield return source[key];
    }
}
```

The *WhereKey* operator differs from the standard *Where* operator because it does not get a generic *Boolean* condition to be evaluated on each item. Its semantics assume that a key value is passed to the operator and that the caller wants to receive a sequence of items that have this same key. Observing the implementation, you can see that only a single item is returned, but the *IEnumerable<T>* return type allows the projection of the results by writing code like the following:

```
var query =
    from   l in list.WhereKey("M")
    select new { Value = l, Length = l.Length };
```

The *WhereKey* implementation is faster than a regular *Where* operator because it reduces the number of comparisons needed to find the required element. To demonstrate this, we defined a class (*KeyWrapper*) to be used as a key type in the *SortedDictionary* collection. The *Key-Wrapper* class simply writes a marker each time its *Value* property is read and displays items compared when the *CompareTo* method is called. You can see its code in Listing 12-17.

Listing 12-17   Implementation of the *KeyWrapper* class

```
class KeyWrapper : IComparable {
    private string _s;
    public string Value {
        get {
            Console.Write("(" + _s + ") ");
            return _s;
        }
        set { _s = value; }
    }
    public override string ToString() {
        //Console.Write("+");
        return _s;
    }
    public KeyWrapper(string value) {
```

```
            _s = value;
        }

        public int CompareTo(object obj) {
            string operand = obj.ToString();
            Console.Write("[{0}<->{1}] ", this._s, operand);
            return _s.CompareTo(operand);
        }
    }
}
```

We have to adjust the code slightly, as shown in Listing 12-18, to use the *KeyWrapper*.

Listing 12-18 LINQ queries on a *SortedDictionary*

```
static class Extensions {
    public static IEnumerable<TSource> WhereKey<TSource >(
            this  SortedDictionary<KeyWrapper, TSource> source,
            string key) {

        yield return source[new KeyWrapper(key)];
    }
}

static void DemoSortedListTrace() {
    SortedDictionary<KeyWrapper, string> list = new
        SortedDictionary<KeyWrapper, string>();

    for (char ch = 'Z'; ch >= 'A'; ch--) {
        list.Add(new KeyWrapper(ch.ToString()), "Letter " + ch.ToString());
    }

    Console.WriteLine("-- queryStandard --");
    var queryStandard =
        from   l in list
        where  l.Key.Value == "M"
        select l.Value;
    Dump(queryStandard);

    Console.WriteLine("-- queryFast --");
    var queryFast = list.WhereKey("M");
    Dump(queryFast);
}
```

In Listing 12-18, you can see the code adapted from Listings 12-15 and 12-16 to use the new *KeyWrapper* as the key type. The following is the output produced:

```
... (other output is produced by previous operations)
-- queryStandard --
(A) (B) (C) (D) (E) (F) (G) (H) (I) (J) (K) (L) (M) Letter M
(N) (O) (P) (Q) (R) (S) (T) (U) (V) (W) (X) (Y) (Z)
-- queryFast --
[M<->S] [M<->K] [M<->O] [M<->M] Letter M
```

The output shows that the *queryStandard* case iterates the whole sequence, even after having found the desired value. The less frequent instances of access in the *queryFast* case (which calls *CompareTo*) produce a faster execution.

Now that you have seen why a new custom operator can provide faster execution, we can try to specialize the standard *Where* operator to improve its performance in accessing a *SortedDictionary* class, filtering with a single key value, as we did in the *queryStandard* case. Take a look at the definition of the standard *Where* operator:

```
public static IEnumerable<TSource> Where<TSource>(
    this IEnumerable<TSource> source,
    Func<TSource, Boolean> predicate);
```

The *predicate* is applied to each item of the *source* sequence. A standard *Where* implementation could be like the following one:

```
public static IEnumerable<TSource> Where<TSource>(
      this IEnumerable<TSource> source,
      Func<TSource, Boolean> predicate) {
    foreach (TSource item in source) {
        if (predicate(item)) {
            yield return item;
        }
    }
}
```

If we could use a constant instead of the *Boolean* predicate, we could define something like the following pseudo-code, where *MoveFirstKey* refers to a method that returns an iterator that starts from the first instance of the key passed as an argument:

```
public static IEnumerable<TSource> Where<TKey, TSource>(
      this SortedDictionary<TKey, TSource> source,
      TKey key ) {
    IEnumerator<KeyValuePair<TKey,TSource>> fastScan = source.MoveFirstKey( key );
    if (fastScan.Current.Key != null) {
        while (fastScan.Current.Key.Equals(key)) {
            yield return fastScan.Current.Value;
            fastScan.MoveNext();
        }
    }
}
```

Please note that the *SortedDictionary* collection does not have the required *MoveFirstKey* method used in the previous code snippet. Moreover, a *SortedDictionary* instance cannot have two items with the same key. The conditions used to look for possible duplicates of the same key are purely illustrative of the code required to implement that behavior in another class containing sorted objects.

However, replacing the predicate with a constant does not produce an operator that can be used through query expression syntax. In other words, you cannot write the following code:

```
var query =
    from   l in list
    where  "M"          // this produces an error
    select l.Value;
```

You still have to use it with a regular syntax:

```
var query =
    from   l in list.Where("M") // this does work
    select l.Value;
```

Nevertheless, you have already seen that specializing standard operators by changing their semantics is a dangerous practice. Therefore, we would like to analyze the expression contained in the predicate of the standard *Where* operator, catching the pattern of a comparison with the *Key* value to find an element in the dictionary. If we find such a pattern, we can substitute it with a *WhereKey* call or simply add a *WhereKey* call before the *Where* call, just to maintain full compatibility with the complete predicate. To do that, we can write a *Where* operator with the following signature:

```
public static IEnumerable<TSource> Where<TSource>(
        this IEnumerable<TSource> source,
        Expression<Func<TSource, Boolean>> predicate);
```

Here we get the *predicate* as an expression tree. (You can read more about expression tree analysis in Chapter 11, "Inside Expression Trees.") Because we want to make a specific optimization for *SortedDictionary*, we use a more specialized signature, such as the following one:

```
public static IEnumerable<KeyValuePair<TKey, TValue>> Where<TKey, TValue>(
        this SortedDictionary<TKey, TValue> source,
        Expression<Func<KeyValuePair<TKey, TValue>, Boolean>> predicate)
            where TKey : class;
```

Listing 12-19 shows the complete code for the *Where* operator optimized for *SortedDictionary*. This code visits the filter expression tree to infer whether a constant comparison of the key can be optimized by taking advantage of the *SortedDictionary* implementation as shown with the *WhereKey* operator.

Listing 12-19 Specialization of a standard *Where* operator optimized for *SortedDictionary*

```
public static IEnumerable<KeyValuePair<TKey, TValue>> Where<TKey, TValue>(
        this SortedDictionary<TKey, TValue> source,
        Expression<Func<KeyValuePair<TKey, TValue>, Boolean>> predicate)
            where TKey : class {
    // This is for trace only: we display the predicate we've found
    Trace.WriteLine("** Where predicate **");
    Trace.WriteLine(predicate.ToString());
    Trace.WriteLine("** -------------- **");
```

```
// After visiting the expression tree for the predicate, we need to
//know if a standard or an optimized Where has to be performed
bool replaceWithWhereKey = false;
TKey keyToSearch = null;


// The following expression results in a delegate that returns a copy
// of the expression tree, eliminating an expression like
//    <item>.Key == <constant>
// where <item> is an instance of KeyValuePair<TKey,TValue> (an element
// of our SortedDictionary) and <constant> is a constant value (we
// tested only strings)
var ReplaceEqual = ExprOp.Visit.Chain(
    (self, last, expr) => {
        if (expr == null) return null;
        // Visiting the expression tree, stop at a BinaryExpression
        // with an Equal comparison
        switch (expr.NodeType) {
            case ExpressionType.Equal:
                var b = (BinaryExpression) expr;
                TKey _key = null;
                MemberExpression memberAccess = null;
                // Get MemberAccess and Constant regardless of their position
                switch (b.Left.NodeType) {
                    case ExpressionType.MemberAccess:
                        memberAccess = b.Left as MemberExpression;
                        break;
                    case ExpressionType.Constant:
                        _key = (b.Left as ConstantExpression).Value as TKey;
                        break;
                }
                switch (b.Right.NodeType) {
                    case ExpressionType.MemberAccess:
                        memberAccess = b.Right as MemberExpression;
                        break;
                    case ExpressionType.Constant:
                        _key = (b.Right as ConstantExpression).Value as TKey;
                        break;
                }
                // Stops here without modifications if either
                // memberAccess or _key have not been found
                if ((memberAccess == null) || (_key == null)) {
                    return b;
                }
                // If we access the Key property of a
                // KeyValuePair<TKey,TValue> type, we can do
                // the substitution - our BinaryExpression is
                // replaced with a constant value equal to true
                if ((memberAccess.Member.ReflectedType ==
                    typeof(KeyValuePair<TKey, TValue>))
                    && (memberAccess.Member.Name == "Key")) {
                    // Set flag to replace the where condition in
                    // the caller (the Where operator)
                    replaceWithWhereKey = true;
                    keyToSearch = _key;
                    return Expression.Constant(true);
                }
```

```
                        Console.WriteLine(b.Left.ToString());
                        return b;
                    default:
                        return last(expr);
                } // end switch (expr.NodeType)
            } // end anonymous delegate
    );

    // The following call eliminates an
    //    <item>.Key == <constant>
    // comparison and makes a direct access to the Dictionary
    // using the <constant> found (saved in keyToSearch) if that
    // comparison has been found and removed
    var querySubstitution = ReplaceEqual(predicate);
    if (replaceWithWhereKey) {
        Trace.WriteLine("--- REPLACED WHERE ---");
        // Directly get the value associated with the given key
        // thanks to the SortedDictionary implementation
        var value = source[keyToSearch];
        var item = new KeyValuePair<TKey, TValue>(keyToSearch, value);
        if (predicate.Compile()(item)) {
            yield return item;
        }
    }
    else {
        // The traditional Where iteration takes place
        // if an optimized access has not been requested
        Trace.WriteLine("--- STANDARD WHERE ---");
        foreach (var item in source) {
            if (predicate.Compile()(item)) {
                yield return item;
            }
        }
    }
}
```

Despite its length, this implementation has several limitations because it supports reference types only for *TKey*, it supports one and only one *Key* comparison with a constant, and it does not support OR conditions around the *Key* comparison. There are probably other limitations, but the purpose of this sample is to illustrate the technique used to analyze and eventually change a predicate inside a *Where* operator.

Note   The code we wrote makes use of an *ExprOp* class that is not included here. The code we included in the sample code was originally written by Jomo Fisher and published on his blog at *http://blogs.msdn.com/jomo_fisher/archive/2007/05/07/visitor-revisitted-linq-function-composablity-and-chain-of-responsibility.aspx* and *http://blogs.msdn.com/jomo_fisher/archive/2007/05/23/dealing-with-linq-s-immutable-expression-trees.aspx*. Please refer to Chapter 11 for further information about expression tree analysis and manipulation.

To use our custom *Where* optimized for *SortedDictionary*, we can use the code in Listing 12-20.

Listing 12-20   Demo of queries on *SortedDictionary* using the optimized *Where* operator

```
static void DemoOptimization() {
    Trace.Listeners.Add(new TextWriterTraceListener(Console.Out));
    SortedDictionary<string, string> list = new SortedDictionary<string, string>();
    for (char ch = 'Z'; ch >= 'A'; ch--) {
        list.Add(ch.ToString(), "Letter " + ch.ToString());
    }

    Console.WriteLine("-- queryOptimized --");
    var queryOptimized =
        from   l in list
        where  l.Key == "M" && l.Value.Length > 1
        select l.Value;
    Dump(queryOptimized);
    Console.WriteLine("");

    Console.WriteLine("-- queryNotOptimized --");
    var queryNotOptimized =
        from   l in list
        where  l.Value == "Letter M" && l.Value.Length > 1
        select l.Value;
    Dump(queryNotOptimized);
    Console.WriteLine("");
}
```

We placed a trace in the *Where* operator code. The results produced by executing Listing 12-20 show that *queryOptimized* has been intercepted and optimized by our specialized *Where* operator, while *queryNotOptimized* does not satisfy the requested condition (a comparison between *Key* and a constant; in this case, we have compared the *Value* property) and executes in a standard way (you can see the "STANDARD WHERE" trace message in that case).

```
-- queryOptimized --
** Where predicate **
l => ((l.Key = "M") && (l.Value.Length > 1))
** --------------- **
--- REPLACED WHERE ---
Letter M

-- queryNotOptimized --
** Where predicate **
l => ((l.Value = "Letter M") && (l.Value.Length > 1))
** --------------- **
l.Value
--- STANDARD WHERE ---
Letter M
```

We have described only the surface of possible optimizations using custom operators. We made use of the existing *SortedDictionary* to show a potentially deeper integration of LINQ with existing indexed structures. If you want to improve LINQ queries on existing objects without having to worry too much about implementation details and which collections are used, you can take a look at the I4O (index for objects) project. That library allows the creation of indexes to get faster answers from LINQ queries over in-memory objects. The implementation is based on *IQueryable* manipulation, extensively using techniques similar to the one we have seen in our *Where* optimization.

Note The I4O project is available with source code on CodePlex at *http://www.codeplex.com/i4o*.

Creating a Custom LINQ Provider

Writing a specialized version of a standard LINQ operator is useful only when you want to operate with in-memory objects and when the intended customization does not require a comprehensive view of the query. Often the query has to be transmitted to a remote service, where "remote" is anything outside the application domain, and probably requires a specific syntax, such as SQL, XML, or simply a parameter list. In these cases, you need to analyze the query expression without executing it locally, just to convert it to an appropriate form for the service requirements. In the previous section, we showed that specializing *Where* allows the analysis of the predicate expression tree. However, this specialization is not enough if you want to comply with another operator like *Take*, which is not part of the *Where* predicate (in that case it could be part of an expression tree such as the one we manipulated earlier). You need a complete query tree for the whole query, and this requires the implementation of a LINQ provider, which typically means an implementation of the *IQueryable* interface.

Note We say "typically" because you could also implement your own LINQ provider by writing a class with a definition for all the standard operators, just as the *Queryable* and *Enumerable* classes do. Nevertheless, this approach is not very common because *Queryable* already generates an expression tree that encloses the other expression trees used in the query, such as the one in the predicate of a *Where* operator. This makes it impractical to build another LINQ implementation generating different structures to represent the query that, in the end, should always mix with expression trees. Having the query tree in the form of an expression tree is the better and faster way to get the complete representation of the query. For this reason, most LINQ providers are simply implementations of the *IQueryable* interface that make use of the existing set of extension methods defined in the *Queryable* class.

In this section, after we describe the differences between *IEnumerable* and *IQueryable* in LINQ, you will see a custom LINQ provider for a service that provides real-time flight status information.

The *IQueryable* Interface

The namespace *System.Linq* contains two important static classes. One is *Enumerable*, which contains all the LINQ standard operators that we also call LINQ to Objects. The other is *Queryable*, which contains an alternative implementation of the LINQ standard operators in which each method simply adds a node in an expression tree representing the desired operation. The final result is still an expression tree that represents the whole query tree. Given that both the *Enumerable* and *Queryable* classes are defined in the same namespace and that both contain the same set of extension methods, how does the compiler choose the implementation to use between these classes? The distinction is made through the first parameter of these methods, which defines the type that the method extends. For example, consider the following definitions:

```
public static class Enumerable {
    public static IEnumerable<T> Where<T>(
        this IEnumerable<T> source,
        Func<T, bool> predicate);
    // ...
}

public static class Queryable {
    public static IQueryable<T> Where<T>(
        this IQueryable<T> source,
        Expression<Func<T, bool>> predicate);
    // ...
}
```

In these definitions, we have two differences between *Enumerable.Where<T>* and *Queryable.Where<T>*. The first is the type of the *source* parameter, which is respectively *IEnumerable<T>* and *IQueryable<T>*. The *Enumerable.Where<T>* statement extends all the classes implementing the *IEnumerable<T>* interface, while *Queryable.Where<T>* extends all the classes implementing the *IQueryable<T>* interface. To make this clear, it is helpful to quickly recall *IEnumerable<T>* and review the *IQueryable/IQueryable<T>* interfaces:

```
public interface IEnumerable {
    IEnumerator GetEnumerator();
}
public interface IEnumerable<T> : IEnumerable {
    IEnumerator<T> GetEnumerator();
}

public interface IQueryable : IEnumerable {
    Type ElementType { get; }
    Expression Expression { get; }
    IQueryProvider Provider { get; }
}
public interface IQueryable<T> : IEnumerable<T>, IQueryable, IEnumerable {
}
```

Because *IQueryable<T>* implements *IEnumerable<T>*, the resolution of the methods in *Queryable* has precedence over those in *Enumerable* whenever the extended class implements *IQueryable<T>*. The precedence results from the compiler resolving the overload between these extension methods by favoring the more specialized interface. (The rule applied is that an implicit conversion exists from *IQueryable<T>* to *IEnumerable<T>*—see §7.4.3.4 in the C# 3.0 Language Specification for more details.)

> **Note**   In this chapter, we do not cover the *IOrderedQueryable* or *IOrderedQueryable<T>* interfaces. They are simply a specialization of *IQueryable/IQueryable<T>* that do not add new methods but simply describe that the sort order of the extracted items is significant (generally resulting from an ordering operator such as *OrderBy, OrderByDescending, ThenBy,* or *ThenByDescending*).

The second difference between the previous *Where* declarations is that the predicate parameter is passed to *Enumerable.Where<T>* as a lambda expression, but an expression tree of type *Expression<Func<T, bool>>* is passed to *Queryable.Where<T>* instead. The *Expression<T>* (in this case *Expression<Func<T, bool>>*) type instructs the compiler to build an expression tree for the enclosed lambda expression, just as we did earlier in the *Where* operator optimized for *SortedDictionary*. (See Listing 12-19.) At runtime, the call to *Queryable.Where<T>* produces a node in the expression tree that includes the predicate expression tree. In the following code, you can see the implementation of *Queryable.Where<T>*:

```
public static IQueryable<T> Where<T>(
    this IQueryable<T> source,
    Expression<Func<T, bool>> predicate) {
        MethodInfo currentMethod = (MethodInfo) MethodBase.GetCurrentMethod();
        return source.Provider.CreateQuery<T>(
            Expression.Call(
                null,
                currentMethod.MakeGenericMethod(
                    new Type[] { typeof(T) }),
                new Expression[] {
                    source.Expression,
                    Expression.Quote(predicate)
                }
            )
        );
}
```

The *CreateQuery<T>* call creates a node for an expression tree corresponding to the call to the *Where<T>* method. That call is made by a particular class that we call *Provider*. We will talk more about this class later in the chapter, but for now assume that the *Provider* class is directly related to the concrete type of *source* that implements *IQueryable<T>*. It is the role of the *IQueryable<T>.Provider* property to return an instance of the provider type that knows how to handle queries that return *IQueryable<T>*.

At this point, we know that *IQueryable* and *IEnumerable* influence the set of extension methods the compiler chooses when it compiles a query expression. As a simplification, we also know that the compiler generates an execution tree only for lambda expressions declared with an *Expression<T>* type while it generates method calls for LINQ operators. But how do they differ here?

The standard operators defined in the *Enumerable* class return an iterator that is executed when an enumerator is retrieved from the query—for example, in a *foreach* loop. (For this reason, the query expression is executed only when the loop is iterated and not when the query is defined.) The operators defined in the *Queryable* class build nodes in an expression tree corresponding to the calls of the same operators. If the expression tree is executed, it returns the original expression tree, but usually it is not executed. The expression tree generated from *Queryable* operators is visited by the linked *IQueryable* provider that generates the actions corresponding to the desired operators. For a LINQ to SQL provider, it generates a corresponding SQL query. Therefore, the role of a LINQ *IQueryable* provider (often called simply a LINQ provider) is to visit a query tree (that is, a particular execution tree) and to generate the necessary corresponding actions.

> **Important**   A method that returns an instance of *IQueryable* cannot contain a *yield* instruction. Such a method must explicitly return only an *IEnumerable* or *IEnumerator* interface. Although we do not show specific sample code for this situation, remember it when you define your own extension methods for LINQ.

From *IEnumerable* to *IQueryable* and Back

What are the differences between *IEnumerable* and *IQueryable*? Is it possible to convert an *IEnumerable* into an *IQueryable*? And is it possible to convert an *IQueryable* into an *IEnumerable*? Knowing the answers to these questions is important for using LINQ effectively and is fundamental for writing a LINQ provider. Before giving you these answers, we need to make some preliminary definitions.

Any query expression implements *IEnumerable*. Any instance of a type implementing *IEnumerable* can be converted into an *IQueryable* instance by calling *AsQueryable*. This call produces an expression tree made up of a single node that calls the original *IEnumerable* instance. This relationship is important for understanding why a complete *IQueryable* query has to be defined starting from an *IQueryable* sequence and cannot be obtained simply by applying *AsQueryable* on an existing *IEnumerable* query. Listing 12-21 shows the effects of using *AsQueryable*.

Listing 12-21   Effects of using *AsQueryable*

```
int[] numbers = { 1, 2, 3, 5, 8, 13, 21 };
IQueryable<int> query1 =
    from  n in numbers.AsQueryable()  // Typically correct use
    where  n % 2 == 0
    select n;
IQueryable<int> query2 =
    (from  n in numbers
     where  n % 2 == 0
     select n).AsQueryable();            // Typically wrong use
Console.WriteLine(query1.ToString());
Console.WriteLine(query2.ToString());
```

> **Important**   The call to *AsQueryable* produces a complete query tree only when the query is built by applying the *AsQueryable* to the source of the data (see *query1* in Listing 12-21), and not when *AsQueryable* is applied to a query already defined as *IEnumerable* (see *query2* in Listing 12-21). Usually we want to get a complete query tree, as in the first case (query1).

The execution of the code in Listing 12-21 produces the following results:

```
System.Int32[].Where(n => ((n % 2) = 0))
System.Linq.Enumerable+<WhereIterator>d__0`1[System.Int32]
```

We have a complete query tree for *query1*, where the call to *AsQueryable* is made on the numbers sequence. In this case, the call to the *Where* method is part of the expression tree that is displayed in the first row of the output. When applied to a whole query, as for *query2*, the resulting query tree only wraps the call to the iterator of *Where*, as you can see in the second row of the output. With the execution of *query1* and *query2*, we receive identical results, but only *query1* can be correctly interpreted by a LINQ provider that visits that query tree. The content of *query2* is opaque to this examination and is not interpreted correctly by a LINQ provider that, for example, has to produce an equivalent SQL query. Once again, the reason for this behavior is related to the resolution of extension method calls: the *IQueryable* interface (and hence *Queryable* extension methods) are used for all LINQ operators when the *AsQueryable* call is in the *from* clause, which defines the source for the query.

> **Note**   The *IQueryable* interface by itself does not imply that the *ToString* overload returns the query tree in a readable way. This work is charged to the LINQ provider, which should (but is not required to) implement a way to do that. For example, LINQ to SQL shows the corresponding query in SQL form. LINQ to Objects, which is the provider used in Listing 12-22, makes use of existing *ToString* capabilities of the expression tree.

The *AsQueryable* method returns an instance of *EnumerableQuery<T>*, which is a class defined in the *System.Linq* namespace that implements *IQueryable* and *IEnumerable*. This class also overrides *ToString*, calling the corresponding *ToString* method of the expression tree when created from an expression or the name of the type implementing *IEnumerable* whose instance is wrapped.

We can also convert any instance of *IQueryable* into an *IEnumerable*, although this conversion is not really necessary because *IQueryable* implements *IEnumerable* and there is an implicit conversion between those two. However, the presence of *AsEnumerable* in a query expression clearly states that using the *IEnumerable* interface is the programmer's choice and not a mistake.

Whether you call *AsEnumerable* or not, iterating an *IQueryable* requires the interpretation of the query tree and the preparation of some locally executable code. This work is done by the *GetEnumerator* method of the *IEnumerable* class: to be able to interpret the query tree, we need to know the concrete implementation of that *IEnumerable*. In the case of a LINQ to Objects query like *query1* in Listing 12-21, the call is made to *EnumerableQuery<T>.GetEnumerator*, which basically visits the expression tree, transforming *IQueryable* to *IEnumerable*, compiles the resulting expression tree in Intermediate Language (IL) code, and then executes it.

We wanted to describe these inner details to give you a more precise understanding of what really happens under the covers. Even if we did not cover all the details, keep these internals in mind when you write a new LINQ provider. If you do not need to write one, it is enough if you remember that all *IEnumerable* instances are delegates, all *IQueryable* instances are query trees, and that with some magic you can convert each one into the other. Not the full story, but enough that you can explain the differences to your buddy when you are in a hurry!

Inside *IQueryable* and *IQueryProvider*

Now that we have looked at the whole process, we can start to dig into the internals of *IQueryable*. We can start by examining member by member the *IQueryable* interface declaration, which is shown here:

```
public interface IQueryable : IEnumerable {
    Type ElementType { get; }
    Expression Expression { get; }
    IQueryProvider Provider { get; }
}
```

The *IQueryable* interface is a wrapper around an *Expression*. As we never tire of saying, a query tree is just an expression tree. The difference is made by the *IQueryable* wrapper, which contains two other members. One is *Provider*, which points to the LINQ provider that can interpret and execute the query tree. (Actually, this is the *Provider* class we previously referred to.) The other is *ElementType*, which defines the type of the result produced by the iteration over the expression tree. With the code in Listing 12-22, you can compare the different *IQueryable* implementations obtained by using *AsQueryable* in two different queries on the same array.

Listing 12-22   *IQueryable* content obtained from using *AsQueryable*

```
int[] numbers = { 1, 2, 3, 5, 8, 13, 21 };
IQueryable<int> queryEven =
    from  n in numbers.AsQueryable()
    where  n % 2 == 0
    select n;
Console.WriteLine("** queryEven **");
Console.WriteLine("Provider Type = {0}", queryEven.Provider.GetType());
Console.WriteLine("ElementType   = {0}", queryEven.ElementType);
Console.WriteLine("Expression    = {0}", queryEven.Expression);

IQueryable<int> queryNumbers = numbers.AsQueryable();
Console.WriteLine("** queryNumbers **");
Console.WriteLine("Provider Type = {0}", queryNumbers.Provider.GetType());
Console.WriteLine("ElementType   = {0}", queryNumbers.ElementType);
Console.WriteLine("Expression    = {0}", queryNumbers.Expression);
```

When you run this code, you can see the following result:

```
** queryEven **
Provider Type = System.Linq.EnumerableQuery`1[System.Int32]
ElementType   = System.Int32
Expression    = System.Int32[].Where(n => ((n % 2) = 0))
** queryNumbers **
Provider Type = System.Linq.EnumerableQuery`1[System.Int32]
ElementType   = System.Int32
Expression    = System.Int32[]
```

Notice that both queries have the same provider (*EnumerableQuery<Int32>*) and the same element type (*ElementType (Int32)*). This should be of no surprise, given that both queries originate from a call to *numbers.AsQueryable*. They differ only in the expression tree. Also keep in mind that a type that implements *IQueryable* also implements *IEnumerable*, which means that a *GetEnumerator* has to be defined in any *IQueryable* implementation.

Until now we have talked about *IQueryable* without making any distinction with *IQueryable<T>*. Take a look at its declaration:

```
public interface IQueryable<T> : IEnumerable<T>, IQueryable, IEnumerable {
}
```

The *IQueryable<T>* version adds support only to the *IEnumerable<T>* class. Most of the time, we really use *IEnumerable<T>* and *IQueryable<T>*, while the nongeneric counterparts *IEnumerable* and *IQueryable* are used only when the code is not strongly typed (which can be useful when you handle legacy classes or when the type of the data cannot be specified for whatever reason). Usually, an implementation is made on *IQueryable<T>*, implicitly supporting *IQueryable* as well.

If you want to implement *IQueryable*, you need to write a class that implements *IQueryProvider* too. Its declaration is as follows:

```
public interface IQueryProvider {
    IQueryable CreateQuery(Expression expression);
    IQueryable<T> CreateQuery<T>(Expression expression);
    object Execute(Expression expression);
    TResult Execute<TResult>(Expression expression);
}
```

In this case, the generic and nongeneric versions of the methods are part of the same interface. A "typical" *IQueryProvider* implementation redirects the generic methods to the corresponding nongeneric version, making a cast on the result. By "typical," we mean common cases in which one provider does not have a behavior depending on the *Execute* result type expected by the caller. In Listing 12-23, you can see a possible abstract class that implements this behavior. We will implement our provider deriving from this *BaseQueryProvider* class.

Listing 12-23   *IQueryProvider* implemented in a *BaseQueryProvider* abstract class

```
public abstract class BaseQueryProvider : IQueryProvider {
    public IQueryable<T> CreateQuery<T>(Expression expression) {
        if (expression == null) {
            throw new ArgumentNullException("expression");
        }
        if (!typeof(IQueryable<T>).IsAssignableFrom(expression.Type)) {
            throw new ArgumentException("Argument expression is not valid");
        }
        return (IQueryable<T>) this.CreateQuery(expression);
    }

    public TResult Execute<TResult>(Expression expression) {
        if (expression == null) {
            throw new ArgumentNullException("expression");
        }
        if (!typeof(IQueryable<TResult>).IsAssignableFrom(expression.Type)) {
            throw new ArgumentException("Argument expression is not valid");
        }
        return (TResult) this.Execute(expression);
    }

    public abstract IQueryable CreateQuery(Expression expression);
    public abstract object Execute(Expression expression);
}
```

Note   The *EnumerableQuery<T>* class implements the LINQ "standard" *IQueryable* provider we described previously. Its implementation of *CreateQuery* and *Execute* is different between generic and nongeneric versions, but its semantic meaning is the same. For that reason, we will continue by describing the *CreateQuery* and *Execute* requirements without making a distinction between generic and nongeneric versions.

The *CreateQuery* method has to create an *IQueryable* object that can evaluate the query represented by the expression tree passed as a parameter. In other words, it creates an instance of a class that implements *IQueryable*, setting its properties. The *Expression* property is set with the parameter received by *CreateQuery*. The *Provider* property is set with *this* because we are in the provider class implementation. (However, in another implementation we could have a separate class for the provider implementation.) Finally, the *ElementType* property is the type returned from the query that should correspond to the *T* for *Create-Query<T>*. The following fictitious code explains this behavior better than words (we will work on code for a real provider later):

```
public IQueryable<T> CreateQuery<T>(Expression expression) {
    IQueryable<T> result = new QueryObject();
    result.Expression = expression;
    result.ElementType = typeof(T);
    result.Provider = this;
}
```

The *Execute* method's role is to interpret the stored query expression into actions related to the nature of the provider. For example, the LINQ to SQL provider translates the expression into SQL statements. This is typically the more complex part of an *IQueryProvider* implementation, and its behavior is strictly related to the nature of the provider. The *EnumerableQuery<T>* provider that is used by the *AsQueryable* method simply compiles the expression tree in a delegate, using the same engine that compiles lambda expressions in IL code. Its *Execute* operation is called as part of the *EnumerableQuery<T>.GetEnumerator* method, and it also implements the replacement of *IQueryable* with *IEnumerable* in the expression tree before its compilation.

At this point, we are ready to write a real LINQ provider. We will focus most of the discussion on implementing the code needed to visit and interpret the query tree according to the provider requirements. We will assume that you have read Chapter 11 and understand how to visit and manipulate an expression tree. We will concentrate on the high-level operations, without covering too many details of the expression tree navigation.

Writing the *FlightQueryProvider*

First of all, we have to set the stage for our LINQ provider. Conceptually, a good candidate for a LINQ provider is any data manipulation or request that can be expressed in a declarative, standardized way, such as that offered by LINQ syntax. The most obvious providers are the ones that convert LINQ queries into existing query languages (such as SQL, CAML, and so on). However, these providers are very complex and are not good candidates for a basic example. Moreover, someone else has probably already written a provider that supports an existing, widespread query language, and you should not have the need to write another provider like that. More interesting (and more common) are situations in which an existing service to query data exists, and you want to standardize its access with LINQ. This might be a Web Service, a custom TCP/IP format, a queue-based communications system, and so on. One advantage offered by LINQ is syntax normalization. How well this normalization is done depends on your provider's implementation and its level of abstraction.

As you see, this discussion can be very long and, after a certain point, it might be very subjective. Our goal is to introduce you to a working LINQ provider that addresses a common scenario for your code.

Important   We are going to describe the existing service, and then we will examine the most important implementation details. Please note that to keep the sample easy to understand and eventually customizable by you, we used the service as a library internal to our code. In the real world, this service would probably be on a remote server, available through a communication protocol. However, the communication layer does not have a direct influence on the LINQ provider other than possible constraints on data serialization. If the service already exists, we assume that you have already solved these kinds of issues by writing some .NET types that abstract from the communication details.

If you are writing your own communication layer and want to take full advantage of LINQ and other .NET 3.5 features, look at Chapter 18, "LINQ and the Windows Communication Foundation." You might also take a look at the LINQ to TerraServer Provider Sample included in the LINQ documentation (*http://msdn2.microsoft.com/library/bb892929.aspx*), which allows access to the TerraServer Web Service through LINQ.

The *FlightStatusService* class

Our existing service describes real-time information about flight status. We have an API that allows querying for flights with specific conditions. These kinds of services are typically not persisted in a relational database. Or, when they are, there is latency on data updates—and even in that case, the database might not be accessible remotely. Hence, our constraint is to keep the existing service interface to retrieve the flight status interface. In Listing 12-24, you can see the entry point of this service, the *FlightSearch* methods in the *FlightStatusService* class.

Listing 12-24   *FlightSearch* methods are the entry points in *FlightStatusService*

```
public partial class FlightStatusService {

    public List<Flight> FlightSearch(QueryFilter pars) {
        return FlightSearch(pars, -1);
    }

    /// <summary>
    /// API to query flights status - parameters are constraints to filter
    /// only desired flights
    /// </summary>
    /// <param name="pars">Parameters for flights status search</param>
    /// <param name="maxFlights">Maximum numbers of flights in the result
    /// (-1 for all, 0 for empty result)</param>
    /// <returns>List of flights matching search parameters</returns>
    public List<Flight> FlightSearch(QueryFilter pars, int maxFlights) {
        Console.WriteLine("---- FlightQuery execution ----");
        if (maxFlights >= 0) {
            Console.WriteLine("Maximum returned flights: {0}", maxFlights);
        }
        Console.WriteLine(pars);

        // ... Implementation details ...
    }
}
```

The main *FlightSearch* implementation has two parameters: the first (*pars*) is a *QueryFilter* instance that contains the conditions for the query; the second (*maxFlights*) is the maximum number of flights desired in the result (if set to –1, it means "unlimited" and returns all the flights matching the *pars* conditions). We also have a simplified version of *FlightSearch* that has only one parameter, which defaults *maxFlights* to unlimited. The return type of these methods is a generic list of *Flight* instances. You can see the code for the *Flight* class in Listing 12-25.

Listing 12-25   *Flight* class definition, including the related *AirportInformation* class

```
public class Flight {
    public string Airline { get; set; }
    public string FlightNumber { get; set; }
    public string Aircraft { get; set; }
    public AirportInformation Departure { get; set; }
    public AirportInformation Arrival { get; set; }
```

```
        public TimeSpan TimeToArrival { get; set; }
        public int GroundSpeed { get; set; }
        public int Altitude { get; set; }

        public override string ToString() {
                return String.Format(
                    "Flight {0}{1} ({2})\n"
                    +"FROM: {3} Scheduled: {4}  Actual:    {5}\n"
                    +"TO:   {6} Scheduled: {7}  Estimated: {8}\n"
                    +"Time to arrival: {9}\n"
                    +"Ground speed/Altitude: {10} KTS / {11} feet",
                    Airline, FlightNumber, Aircraft,
                    Departure.Airport, Departure.ScheduledTime, Departure.ActualTime,
                    Arrival.Airport, Arrival.ScheduledTime, Arrival.ActualTime,
                    TimeToArrival,
                    GroundSpeed,
                    Altitude);
        }
    }

    public class AirportInformation {
        public string Airport { get; set; }
        public DateTime ScheduledTime { get; set; }
        public DateTime ActualTime { get; set; }
    }
```

Each flight has an *Airline* code, a *FlightNumber*, and an *Aircraft* type. A flight departs from some airport and arrives at another one: *Departure* and *Arrival* properties describe respective airport information such as *Airport* code, *ScheduledTime*, and actual/expected time. (We used a property named *ActualTime* that has to be interpreted as estimated time when the departure/arrival has yet to occur.) *ScheduledTime* and *ActualTime* are both in local time for the corresponding airports. *TimeToArrival* provides information about estimated time to arrival, while *GroundSpeed* and *Altitude* provide other information about the actual status of the flight. The code for the *QueryFilter* class is somewhat similar to the *Flight* content, but it uses different types and names, as you can see in Listing 12-26.

Listing 12-26   *QueryFilter* class definition

```
public partial class FlightStatusService {
    public class QueryFilter {
        public string Airline = null;
        public string FlightNumber = null;
        public string Aircraft = null;
        public string DepartureAirport = null;
        public string ArrivalAirport = null;
        public int MinMinutesToArrival = -1;
        public int MaxMinutesToArrival = -1;
        public int MinGroundSpeed = -1;
        public int MaxGroundSpeed = -1;
        public int MinAltitude = -1;
        public int MaxAltitude = -1;
```

```csharp
public override string ToString() {
    StringBuilder sb = new StringBuilder();
    sb.AppendLine("FlightStatus.QueryParameters Dump");
    DumpEqualCondition(sb, "Airline", this.Airline);
    DumpEqualCondition(sb, "FlightNumber", this.FlightNumber);
    DumpEqualCondition(sb, "DepartureAirport", this.DepartureAirport);
    DumpEqualCondition(sb, "ArrivalAirport", this.ArrivalAirport);
    DumpBetweenCondition(sb, "MinutesToArrival",
                         this.MinMinutesToArrival,
                         this.MaxMinutesToArrival);
    DumpBetweenCondition(sb, "GroundSpeed",
                         this.MinGroundSpeed,
                         this.MaxGroundSpeed);
    DumpBetweenCondition(sb, "Altitude",
                         this.MinAltitude,
                         this.MaxAltitude);
    sb.AppendLine("-----------------------");
    return sb.ToString();
}
internal void DumpEqualCondition( StringBuilder sb,
                                  string fieldName, string value) {
    if (value != null) {
        sb.Append(fieldName);
        sb.Append(" = ");
        sb.AppendLine(value.ToString());
    }
}
internal void DumpBetweenCondition( StringBuilder sb,
                                    string fieldName,
                                    int limitMin, int limitMax) {
    if ((limitMin >= 0) && (limitMax >= 0)) {
        sb.Append(fieldName);
        sb.Append(" BETWEEN ");
        sb.Append(limitMin.ToString());
        sb.Append(" AND ");
        sb.AppendLine(limitMax.ToString());
    }
    else if (limitMin >= 0) {
        sb.Append(fieldName);
        sb.Append(" >= ");
        sb.AppendLine(limitMin.ToString());
    }
    else if (limitMax >= 0) {
        sb.Append(fieldName);
        sb.Append(" <= ");
        sb.AppendLine(limitMax.ToString());
    }
}
```

Both the *Flight* and *QueryFilter* classes have a *ToString* override that displays their content in a readable form, and we have the same names in the *QueryFilter* class only for string properties contained in the *Flight* class. Actually, our service does not support filters on scheduled or actual times of departure and arrival, and we have two string properties to filter the airport code for departure and arrival. For each numeric property of *Flight*, we have two properties in *QueryFilter*—one for the minimum value and one for the maximum value—because we can define a range of values. Finally, in *QueryFilter* we have a range of minutes to filter the *TimeToArrival* of a flight (*MinMinutesToArrival*/*MaxMinutesToArrival*), and these properties are of type *int*, while *Flight.TimeToArrival* is a *TimeSpan* instance. We will come back to these differences later.

At this point, we can look at some calls to the *FlightSearch* method of the *FlightStatusService* class. We start with an "old-style" technique in Listing 12-27 that uses only C# 2.0 syntax.

Listing 12-27   Sample calls to *FlightSearch* using C# 2.0

```
static void SearchFlightsOldWay() {
    FlightStatusService flightStatus = new FlightStatusService();

    FlightStatusService.QueryFilter filterTimeSpeed =
        new FlightStatusService.QueryFilter();
    filterTimeSpeed.MaxGroundSpeed = 400;
    filterTimeSpeed.MaxMinutesToArrival = 30;

    List<Flight> flightsNearLanding =
        flightStatus.FlightSearch(filterTimeSpeed);
    Dump(flightsNearLanding);

    FlightStatusService.QueryFilter filterAltitudeAirline =
        new FlightStatusService.QueryFilter();
    filterAltitudeAirline.MinAltitude = 20000;
    filterAltitudeAirline.MaxAltitude = 30000;
    filterAltitudeAirline.Airline = "WN";

    List<Flight> flightsMediumAltitude =
        lightStatus.FlightSearch(filterAltitudeAirline);
    Dump(flightsMediumAltitude);

    string airportCode = "NRT"; // Tokyo
    FlightStatusService.QueryFilter filterTokyo =
        new lightStatusService.QueryFilter();
    filterTokyo.ArrivalAirport = airportCode;

    // Filter only 1 output rows
    List<Flight> flightsTokyo =
        flightStatus.FlightSearch(filterAltitudeAirline, 1);
    Dump(flightsMediumAltitude);
}
```

In the output produced by the execution of the code in Listing 12-27, each query has a "FlightQuery execution" header followed by a dump of the *QueryFilter* instance passed to the *FlightSearch* method. Each query exposes different challenges for our LINQ provider implementation, which we will explore later.

```
---- FlightQuery execution ----
FlightStatusService.QueryFilter Dump
MinutesToArrival <= 30
GroundSpeed <= 400
----------------------

Flight NK117 (Airbus A319)
FROM: DTW Scheduled: 25/12/2007 13.09.00  Actual:     25/12/2007 13.48.00
TO:   MCO Scheduled: 25/12/2007 15.43.00  Estimated: 25/12/2007 16.01.00
Time to arrival: 00:12:00
Ground speed/Altitude: 359 KTS / 22400 feet
-------------------
---- FlightQuery execution ----
FlightStatusService.QueryFilter Dump
Airline = WN
Altitude BETWEEN 20000 AND 30000
----------------------

Flight WN1002 (Boeing 737-700)
FROM: RNO Scheduled: 25/12/2007 12.15.00  Actual:     25/12/2007 12.24.00
TO:   SJC Scheduled: 25/12/2007 13.15.00  Estimated: 25/12/2007 13.02.00
Time to arrival: 00:18:00
Ground speed/Altitude: 447 KTS / 22000 feet
-------------------
---- FlightQuery execution ----
Maximum returned flights: 1
FlightStatusService.QueryFilter Dump
Airline = WN
Altitude BETWEEN 20000 AND 30000
----------------------

Flight WN1002 (Boeing 737-700)
FROM: RNO Scheduled: 25/12/2007 12.15.00  Actual:     25/12/2007 12.24.00
TO:   SJC Scheduled: 25/12/2007 13.15.00  Estimated: 25/12/2007 13.02.00
Time to arrival: 00:18:00
Ground speed/Altitude: 447 KTS / 22000 feet
-------------------
```

What is wrong with the code in Listing 12-27? Simply said, it is not sufficiently self-documenting, it is boring to write, and it is verbose to read. For each condition of the query, we need a C# statement. Sometimes we need to know the corresponding property of *QueryFilter* to apply a filter on a property of *Flight* because they do not always have the same name for the reasons we have mentioned before. A small syntax improvement is available using the C# 3.0 syntax, as in Listing 12-28.

Listing 12-28   Sample calls to *FlightSearch* using C# 3.0

```
static void SearchFlightsCS30() {
    FlightStatusService flightStatus = new FlightStatusService();

    var flightsNearLanding =
        flightStatus.FlightSearch(
            new FlightStatusService.QueryFilter {
```

```
                            MaxGroundSpeed = 400,
                            MaxMinutesToArrival = 30
                    });
            Dump(flightsNearLanding);

            var flightsMediumAltitude =
                flightStatus.FlightSearch(
                    new FlightStatusService.QueryFilter {
                        MinAltitude = 20000,
                        MaxAltitude = 30000,
                        Airline = "WN"
                    });
            Dump(flightsMediumAltitude);

            string airportCode = "NRT"; // Tokyo
            var flightsTokyo =
                flightStatus.FlightSearch(
                    new FlightStatusService.QueryFilter {
                        ArrivalAirport = airportCode
                    },
                    1); // Filter only 1 output rows
            Dump(flightsTokyo);
    }
```

We do not have fewer lines in Listing 12-28 than in Listing 12-27, but now the code looks nicer and is easier to read. However, we still need to document how to use the *QueryFilter* class to specify the filter conditions. We would like to query a *Flight* collection, just as we might do on any collection, even if that collection is not local to our process but is hosted remotely by our service. In the end, we want to be able to write the code in Listing 12-29, making use of the LINQ query syntax.

Listing 12-29 Sample calls to *FlightSearch* using LINQ

```
static void SearchFlightsLinq() {
    FlightStatusService flightStatus = new FlightStatusService();

    var flightsNearLanding =
        from   f in flightStatus.AsQueryable()
        where  f.GroundSpeed <= 400
               && f.TimeToArrival.TotalMinutes <= 30
        select f;
    Dump(flightsNearLanding);

    var flightsMediumAltitude =
        from   f in flightStatus.AsQueryable()
        where  f.GroundSpeed <= 400
               && f.TimeToArrival.TotalMinutes <= 30
        select f;
    Dump(flightsMediumAltitude);

    string airportCode = "NRT"; // Tokyo
    var filterTokyo =
        (from   f in flightStatus.AsQueryable()
```

```
            where  f.Arrival.Airport == airportCode
            select f)
        .Take(1); // Filter only 1 output rows
    Dump(filterTokyo);
}
```

With the query syntax, we wrote fewer lines of code, but most important is the declarative way in which we query a remote service without any knowledge of the *QueryFilter* class. We can use the well-known semantics of C# expressions in *Where* conditions acting on properties of the *Flight* class. Our provider will make the conversion to a corresponding *QueryFilter* instance to get the same results as in the previous listings. We "only" need to write an ad hoc LINQ provider implementing *IQueryable* and *IQueryProvider*. That provider will analyze the query tree and, for example, interpret the *f.Arrival.Airport == airportCode* condition as an assignment of the *airportCode* value to the *ArrivalAirport* property of a *QueryFilter* instance. We also have to write an *AsQueryable* implementation that extends the *FlightStatusService* class.

One important aspect of this scenario is the presence of the *Take* operator. (See the *filterTokyo* query in Listing 12-29.) We need to convert the *Take* operator in the *maxFlights* parameter of the *FlightSearch* call, because we want the flights to be filtered by the service and not by the client. This single requirement makes it impossible to limit our implementation to a specialization of the *Where* operator such as we did in Listing 12-19 for the *SortedDictionary* class, when we visited the *Where* predicate by receiving it as an expression tree. Now we need a real *IQueryable* implementation.

Implementing *IQueryable* in *FlightQuery*

The first step of our implementation of a LINQ provider is the definition of a class representing the query that implements the *IQueryable<T>* interface. Our provider needs to return data only for a single type, the *Flight* class. We can define the *FlightQuery* class as a constructed type implementing *IQueryable<Flight>* instead of the generic *IQueryable<T>*, as you can see in Listing 12-30.

Listing 12-30   *FlightQuery class implementing IQueryable<Flight>*

```
public class FlightQuery : IQueryable<Flight> {
    FlightQueryProvider provider;
    Expression expression;

    public FlightQuery(FlightQueryProvider provider) {
        if (provider == null) {
            throw new ArgumentNullException("provider");
        }
        this.provider = provider;
        this.expression = Expression.Constant(this);
    }
```

```
public FlightQuery(FlightQueryProvider provider, Expression expression) {
    if (provider == null) {
        throw new ArgumentNullException("provider");
    }
    if (expression == null) {
        throw new ArgumentNullException("expression");
    }
    if (!typeof(IQueryable<Flight>).IsAssignableFrom(expression.Type)) {
        throw new ArgumentOutOfRangeException("expression");
    }
    this.provider = provider;
    this.expression = expression;
}

#region IQueryable implementation
Expression IQueryable.Expression { get { return this.expression; } }
Type IQueryable.ElementType { get { return typeof(Flight); } }
IQueryProvider IQueryable.Provider { get { return this.provider; } }
#endregion IQueryable implementation

#region IEnumerable<T> implementation
public IEnumerator<Flight> GetEnumerator() {
    return ((IEnumerable<Flight>)
        this.provider.Execute(this.expression)).GetEnumerator();
}
#endregion IEnumerable<T> implementation

#region IEnumerable implementation
IEnumerator IEnumerable.GetEnumerator() {
    return ((IEnumerable)
        this.provider.Execute(this.expression)).GetEnumerator();
}
#endregion IEnumerable implementation

public override string ToString() {
    return this.provider.GetQueryText(this.expression);
}
}
```

The *FlightQuery* class is relatively easy: in fact, most of the work is delegated to the *Flight-QueryProvider* class that we still have to write! The two constructors check the parameters and save the values for the *Expression* and *Provider* properties that are implemented as part of the *IQueryable* interface. The third property defined by the *IQueryable* interface, *ElementType*, always returns *typeof(Flight)* because our provider supports only that class as a result.

You might ask what the difference is between the first and the second *FlightQuery* constructor. When you write something like this

```
var query = flightStatus.AsQueryable();
```

the *AsQueryable* implementation has to return an instance of *FlightQuery* without having an expression tree (because *flightStatus* by itself is not an expression tree). Our first constructor is used to handle this. Because we always need a valid *Expression* in an *IQueryable* object, an expression tree made of a single *ConstantExpression* node is created, pointing to the *Flight-Query* instance itself (the one represented by *flightStatus* in our *AsQueryable* call). In case we have a query tree using our *IQueryable* implementation like this:

```
var query2 = query.Where( (f) => f.GroundSpeed <= 400 );
```

we need the second constructor, which has two parameters, *provider* and *expression*. The invocation of that constructor is typically made by the *CreateQuery* methods that are part of the *IQueryProvider* implementation. That invocation will be made by the implementation of the *Where<T>* operator defined in *Queryable.Where<T>* that builds the query tree for *query2*.

Remember that you are not forced to build exactly the same constructors in another *IQueryable* implementation, but most *IQueryable* implementations will probably have a similar structure because the needs for these two constructors are very common.

At this point, we can examine the *IEnumerable/IEnumerable<T>* implementations, which are mandatory because a class that implements *IQueryable<T>* also implements *IEnumerable* and *IEnumerable<T>*. The corresponding *GetEnumerator()* methods are functionally identical; the only difference is the return value type: *IEnumerator* or *IEnumerator<T>*. Both *GetEnumerator()* methods call the *Execute* method on the *provider* member (of type *FlightQueryProvider*), passing the stored *Expression* as a parameter, and they both call *GetEnumerator()* on the result (which should always be an *IEnumerable<Flight>*). Internally, the *FlightQueryProvider* has to call the *FlightSearch* method, passing the right parameters. This will be the core part of our provider implementation.

A final note is on the *ToString* override: that method returns a textual representation of the query tree. Our goal is to leverage the existing *ToString* implementation of the *FlightStatus-Service.QueryFilter* class, wrapped in the *GetQueryText* method of our provider. The hard part is to convert the query tree into a corresponding *FlightStatusService.QueryFilter* instance, but this is the same work required to implement the *Execute* method. We will implement our provider in such a way that it is sharing the code for these two operations.

Implementing *IQueryProvider* in *FlightQueryProvider*

The core of our provider is the *IQueryProvider* implementation. This implementation will require a moderate amount of code, and for this reason we split the work into several classes. We will start by looking at our *FlightQueryProvider* implementation in Listing 12-31, which extends the *BaseQueryProvider* we defined in Listing 12-23.

Listing 12-31   *FlightQueryProvider* class implementing *IQueryProvider*

```
public class FlightQueryProvider : BaseQueryProvider {
    // Force developers to pass a FlightStatusService in the constructor
    protected FlightQueryProvider() {}

    private FlightStatusService flightStatus;
```

```
        public FlightQueryProvider(FlightStatusService flightStatus) {
            if (flightStatus == null) {
                throw new ArgumentNullException("flightStatus");
            }
            this.flightStatus = flightStatus;
        }

        #region BaseQueryProvider abstract methods implementation
        public override object Execute(Expression expression) {
            FlightQueryParameters parameters = this.Translate(expression);
            return flightStatus.FlightSearch(
                parameters.Filter,
                parameters.MaxFlights);
        }

        public override IQueryable CreateQuery(Expression expression) {
            return new FlightQuery(this, expression);
        }
        #endregion BaseQueryProvider abstract methods implementation

        public string GetQueryText(Expression expression) {
            FlightQueryParameters parameters = this.Translate(expression);
            return parameters.ToString();
        }

        private FlightQueryParameters Translate(Expression expression) {
            expression = Evaluator.PartialEval(expression);
            return new FlightQueryTranslator().Translate(expression);
        }
    }
```

The methods required by the abstract class *BaseQueryProvider* are *CreateQuery* and *Execute*. The *CreateQuery* method simply creates an instance of *FlightQuery*. The *Execute* method uses the private *Translate* method, which converts the query tree into an instance of *FlightQuery-Parameters* and executes the *FlightSearch* invocation passing the parameters obtained by the query translation. We defined the *Translate* method to share its behavior with the *GetQuery-Text* public method, which returns a textual representation of the query by making the same translation of the query tree into a *FlightQueryParameters* instance and then calling its *ToString* method. You can see the *FlightQueryParameters* definition in Listing 12-32. This class is simply a wrapper of all the possible parameters of the *FlightSearch* class.

Listing 12-32 *FlightQueryParameters* class definition

```
internal class FlightQueryParameters {
    public FlightStatusService.QueryFilter Filter { get; set; }
    public int MaxFlights { get; set; }

    public FlightQueryParameters() {
        this.Filter = new FlightStatusService.QueryFilter();
        this.MaxFlights = -1;
    }
}
```

```
    public override string ToString() {
        if (MaxFlights >= 0) {
            return String.Format(
                "{0}Maximum returned flights: {1}",
                Filter.ToString(),
                MaxFlights);
        }
        else {
            return Filter.ToString();
        }
    }
}
```

Implementing an *ExpressionVisitor* in *FlightQueryTranslator*

The most important part of our provider is the *Translate* implementation. This method
is defined within the *FlightQueryTranslator* class, which is derived from the base class
ExpressionVisitor.

> **Note**   The *ExpressionVisitor* class that we use in our Flight Status LINQ provider is the
> implementation of an expression tree visitor published by Matt Warren on his blog at
> *http://blogs.msdn.com/mattwar/archive/2007/07/31/linq-building-an-iqueryable-provider-part-
> ii.aspx*. Refer to Chapter 11 for further information about expression tree analysis and manipulation.

Because the *FlightQueryTranslator* is a long class, we will cover only the relevant code that
we want to analyze step by step. We start with an overview of the member declarations in
Listing 12-33: this listing shows the implementation of only two methods, the constructor
and *Translate*, leaving only the declaration of the others.

Listing 12-33   *FlightQueryTranslator* member declarations

```
public class FlightQueryTranslator : ExpressionVisitor {
    FlightQueryParameters queryParameters;

    internal FlightQueryTranslator() {}
    internal FlightQueryParameters Translate(Expression expression) {
        this.queryParameters = new FlightQueryParameters();
        this.Visit(expression);
        return this.queryParameters;
    }

    // ExpressionVisitor specialization
    protected override Expression VisitMethodCall(MethodCallExpression m);
    protected override Expression VisitUnary(UnaryExpression u);
    protected override Expression VisitBinary(BinaryExpression b);
    protected override Expression VisitConstant(ConstantExpression c);
    protected override Expression VisitMemberAccess(MemberExpression m);
```

```
    // Helper methods
    private void TranslateStandardComparisons(
        ExpressionType nodeType,
        ConstantExpression constant,
        MemberExpression memberAccess);

    private void TranslateAirportInformationComparison(
        ConstantExpression constant,
        MemberExpression memberAccess);

    private void TranslateTimeSpanComparison(
        ExpressionType nodeType,
        ConstantExpression constant,
        MemberExpression memberAccess);

    private static Expression StripQuotes(Expression e);
    internal static void SetIntParameter(
        int limit,
        ref int MinValue, ref int MaxValue,
        ExpressionType comparison);

    internal static int GetIntConstant(ConstantExpression constant);
    internal static double GetDoubleConstant(ConstantExpression constant);
}
```

The *Translate* method initializes the member *queryParameters*, which will be compiled by the inspection of the query tree made by the *Visit* call. The method *Visit* is defined in the *ExpressionVisitor* base class. Because we need only to intercept some nodes, the override of some methods from the base class allows us to intercept the information of interest to our provider.

First of all, in the current *FlightStatusService* implementation we can support only two LINQ operators: *Where*, which will define the content of a *FlightStatus.QueryFilter* instance, and *Take*, which will influence the *maxFlights* parameter of a *FlightSearch* call. Listing 12-34 shows the *VisitMethodCall* implementation that handles these operators and throws a *NotSupportedException* if any other operator is used in the query.

Note   We also included in Listing 12-34 the *StripQuotes* implementation. An *ExpressionType.Quote* node refers to a *UnaryExpression* instance that has a constant value of type *Expression*. Visiting the expression tree, a *MethodCallExpression* node can refer to any method. If one of the method's arguments is a lambda expression, it becomes a "quoted" expression (it is enclosed in an *ExpressionType.Quote* node type). The *Where* condition in an expression tree is represented as a *MethodCallExpression* node that stores the predicate as a quoted lambda expression. We will not need to handle this further indirection processing the *Where* predicate. The call to *StripQuotes* will provide a pure lambda expression as a predicate for the *Where* condition.

Listing 12-34   *FlightQueryTranslator.VisitMethodCall* implementation

```
/// <summary>
/// These are the only supported extension methods (Where and Take)
/// We simply visit the Where condition and the Take parameter
/// and translate them into a FlightStatus.QueryParameters instance
/// </summary>
protected override Expression VisitMethodCall(MethodCallExpression m) {
    if (m.Method.DeclaringType == typeof(Queryable)) {
        switch (m.Method.Name) {
            case "Where":
                this.Visit(m.Arguments[0]);
                LambdaExpression lambda =
                    (LambdaExpression) StripQuotes(m.Arguments[1]);
                this.Visit(lambda.Body);
                return m;
            case "Take":
                this.Visit(m.Arguments[0]);
                ConstantExpression constant =
                    m.Arguments[1] as ConstantExpression;
                if (constant == null) {
                    throw new NotImplementedException(
                        "Take supported only for constant values");
                }
                queryParameters.MaxFlights = GetIntConstant(constant);
                return m;
        }
    }
    throw new NotSupportedException(
        string.Format("The method '{0}' is not supported", m.Method.Name));
}

private static Expression StripQuotes(Expression e) {
    while (e.NodeType == ExpressionType.Quote) {
        e = ((UnaryExpression) e).Operand;
    }
    return e;
}
```

Both *Take* and *Where* operators are applied to an *IQueryable* expression: for this reason, the first common step is to continue the visit on the first parameter of these methods, which is the instance of the class that these methods are extending. In our case, it should always be an expression tree returning *IQueryable<FlightQuery>*. Then the implementation of these two operators differs.

Handling the *Take* operator is very simple: we support only a constant value, and we simply try to interpret the argument of the method call expression in *m.Arguments[1]*, saving its value in the *MaxFlights* property of the *queryParameters* instance.

To handle the *Where* condition, we need to visit its predicate, which is another expression tree, available in the second parameter of the *Where* call in *m.arguments[1]*.

> **Important**   Because we support only *Where* and *Take*, we do not need to remember that we are inside a *Where* condition when we make the call to *Visit (lambda.Body)*. In a more complex provider, we probably would need to keep track of the context in which an expression tree is visited.

A predicate in a *Where* condition is an expression that returns a *Boolean*. A query to our provider can have a meaningful predicate only by using comparison operators. If more than one comparison operator is present, we support only the AND between different conditions: our service does not have semantics that can support the OR between filter conditions. All these comparisons and logical operators are instances of *BinaryExpression* in our expression tree. The override for *VisitBinary* in Listing 12-35 filters the operations that we do not support, continuing the visit of the query tree for the left and right parts of an AND condition. In other words, the AND does not have an effect other than continuing the expression tree visit.

Listing 12-35   *FlightQueryTranslator.VisitBinary* implementation

```
/// <summary>
/// The AND condition simply continues the visit to the left and right parts
/// If there is a binary operation other than a supported comparison,
/// a NotSupportedException is thrown
/// </summary>
protected override Expression VisitBinary(BinaryExpression b) {
    switch (b.NodeType) {
        case ExpressionType.And:
        case ExpressionType.AndAlso:
            // Compare only other binary operators - we default to AND,
            // so this is not an error and does not produce other effects
            this.Visit(b.Left);
            this.Visit(b.Right);
            // We EXIT here, we do not process the condition further
            return b;
        case ExpressionType.Equal:
        case ExpressionType.LessThanOrEqual:
        case ExpressionType.GreaterThanOrEqual:
        case ExpressionType.LessThan:
        case ExpressionType.GreaterThan:
            return VisitBinaryComparison(b);
        default:
            // We DO NOT support:
            // - NotEqual
            // - Or
            throw new NotSupportedException(string.Format(
                "The binary operator '{0}' is not supported", b.NodeType));
    }
}
```

The *VisitBinaryComparison* implementation shown in Listing 12-36 has three steps. First, it evaluates the constant and the member to be compared. We do not support comparisons between *Flight* members and/or between constants or other expressions, simply because we do not have the semantics to transfer similar constraints to our *FlightStatusService*. For this reason, we assume that a binary comparison must have a constant and a member access expression (in whatever position), and it must throw an exception in all other cases.

Listing 12-36   *FlightQueryTranslator.VisitBinaryComparison* implementation

```
/// <summary>
/// Performs a sanity check of constant and memberAccess
/// Then it performs a different translation according to
/// the type of the member to be compared with
/// </summary>
private Expression VisitBinaryComparison(BinaryExpression b) {
    // FIRST STEP
    // We support only a comparison between constant
    // and a possible flight query parameter
    ConstantExpression constant =
        (b.Left as ConstantExpression ?? b.Right as ConstantExpression);
    MemberExpression memberAccess =
        (b.Left as MemberExpression ?? b.Right as MemberExpression);

    // SECOND STEP
    // Sanity check of parameters
    if ((memberAccess == null) || (constant == null)) {
        throw new NotSupportedException(
            string.Format(
                "The binary operator '{0}' must compare a valid "
                +"flight attribute with a constant",
                b.NodeType));
    }

    // We need to get the constant value
    if (constant.Value == null) {
        throw new NotSupportedException(
            string.Format(
                "NULL constant is not supported in binary operator {0}",
                b.ToString()));
    }
    switch (Type.GetTypeCode(constant.Value.GetType())) {
        case TypeCode.String:
        case TypeCode.Int16:
        case TypeCode.Int32:
        case TypeCode.Double:
            break;
        default:
            throw new NotSupportedException(
                string.Format(
                    "Constant {0} is of an unsupported type ({1})",
                    constant.ToString(),
                    constant.Value.GetType().Name));
    }

    // THIRD STEP
    // Look for member name through Reflection
    // We assume that string properties in Flight have the same name
```

```
        // in QueryParameters
        // We have a special check for Flight members of complex types
        if (memberAccess.Member.ReflectedType == typeof(TimeSpan)) {
            TranslateTimeSpanComparison(b.NodeType, constant, memberAccess);
            return b;
        }
        else if (memberAccess.Member.ReflectedType == typeof(AirportInformation)) {
            TranslateAirportInformationComparison(constant, memberAccess);
            return b;
        }
        else if (memberAccess.Member.ReflectedType != typeof(Flight)) {
            throw new NotSupportedException(
                    string.Format(
                        "Member {0} is not of type Flight",
                        memberAccess.ToString()));
        }
        TranslateStandardComparisons(b.NodeType, constant, memberAccess);
        return b;
    }
```

The second step is simply a sanity check of the *memberAccess* and *constant* expressions. Something more complex happens during the third step. The simplest case is the comparison of a *Flight* member with a primitive type, such as *string* or *int*. Here is an example of such a query:

```
var query =
    from   f in flightStatus.AsQueryable()
    where  f.Airline == "UA" && f.Altitude >= 10000
    select f;
```

This standard case is handled by the *TranslateStandardComparisons* shown in Listing 12-37. We have special cases when we compare the *Departure*, *Arrival*, or *TimeToArrival* members of the *Flight* class with some constant values, as in the following query:

```
var query =
    from   f in flightStatus.AsQueryable()
    where  f.Arrival.Airport == "NRT"
           && f.TimeToArrival.TotalHours >= 2
    select f;
```

The code in Listing 12-36 intercepts these cases by analyzing the type of the member access expression. We have two different methods for handling these cases, *TranslateAirportInformation-Comparison* and *TranslateTimeSpanComparison*, whose implementation is included in Listing 12-38.

Listing 12-37 *FlightQueryTranslator.TranslateStandardComparisons* implementation

```
/// <summary>
/// The standard case supports an equal condition for strings
/// and other comparisons for GroundSpeed and Altitude integers
/// </summary>
private void TranslateStandardComparisons(
    ExpressionType nodeType,
```

```csharp
        ConstantExpression constant,
        MemberExpression memberAccess) {

        string stringFieldName =
            (from field in typeof(Flight).GetProperties()
             where Type.GetTypeCode(field.PropertyType) == TypeCode.String
                 && field.Name == memberAccess.Member.Name
             select field.Name).FirstOrDefault();

        // Loop for all strings (Airline, FlightNumber and Aircraft)
        if (stringFieldName != null) {
            if (nodeType != ExpressionType.Equal) {
                throw new NotSupportedException(
                    string.Format(
                        "The binary operator '{0}' is not supported on {1} member",
                        nodeType,
                        memberAccess.Member.Name));
            }
            queryParameters.Filter.GetType()
                .GetField(stringFieldName)
                .SetValue(queryParameters.Filter, constant.Value);
        }
        else {
            // String not found
            switch (memberAccess.Member.Name) {
                case "GroundSpeed":
                    SetIntParameter(
                        GetIntConstant(constant),
                        ref queryParameters.Filter.MinGroundSpeed,
                        ref queryParameters.Filter.MaxGroundSpeed,
                        nodeType);
                    break;
                case "Altitude":
                    SetIntParameter(
                        GetIntConstant(constant),
                        ref queryParameters.Filter.MinAltitude,
                        ref queryParameters.Filter.MaxAltitude,
                        nodeType);
                    break;
                default:
                    throw new NotSupportedException(
                        string.Format("Condition on member {0} is not supported",
                        memberAccess.ToString()));
            }
        }
    }

internal static void SetIntParameter(
    int limit,
    ref int minValue,
    ref int maxValue,
    ExpressionType comparison) {
```

```
switch (comparison) {
    case ExpressionType.Equal:
        MinValue = limit;
        MaxValue = limit;
        break;
    case ExpressionType.LessThan:
        MaxValue = limit - 1;
        break;
    case ExpressionType.LessThanOrEqual:
        MaxValue = limit;
        break;
    case ExpressionType.GreaterThan:
        MinValue = limit + 1;
        break;
    case ExpressionType.GreaterThanOrEqual:
        MinValue = limit;
        break;
    default:
        throw new NotSupportedException(
            string.Format(
                "The binary operator '{0}' is not supported",
                comparison));
    }
}
```

At this point, the code speaks for itself. Sometime we use reflection to find members in the *FlightStatus.QueryFilter* structure or to explore the types of the member access expression we are visiting.

Listing 12-38   *TranslateAirportInformationComparison* and *TranslateTimeSpanComparison* implementation

```
/// <summary>
/// We currently support only the filter on the Airport code
/// </summary>
private void TranslateAirportInformationComparison(
    ConstantExpression constant,
    MemberExpression memberAccess) {

    MemberExpression parent = memberAccess.Expression as MemberExpression;
    if (parent.Member.ReflectedType != typeof(Flight)) {
        throw new NotSupportedException(
            string.Format(
                "Member {0} is not of type Flight",
                memberAccess.ToString()));
    }
    // We support only Airport ...
    if (memberAccess.Member.Name == "Airport") {
        switch (parent.Member.Name) {
            case "Departure":
                queryParameters.Filter.DepartureAirport =
                    constant.Value.ToString();
                break;
```

```
                    case "Arrival":
                        queryParameters.Filter.ArrivalAirport =
                            constant.Value.ToString();
                        break;
                }
            }
    }


    /// <summary>
    /// We support only a TotalMinutes and TotalHours comparison
    /// </summary>
    private void TranslateTimeSpanComparison(
        ExpressionType nodeType,
        ConstantExpression constant,
        MemberExpression memberAccess) {

        MemberExpression parent = memberAccess.Expression as MemberExpression;
        if (parent.Member.ReflectedType != typeof(Flight)) {
            throw new NotSupportedException(
                string.Format(
                    "Member {0} is not of type Flight",
                    memberAccess.ToString()));
        }
        // We support only TotalMinutes for this simple provider
        if ((memberAccess.Member.Name == "TotalMinutes")
            && (parent.Member.Name == "TimeToArrival")) {
            SetIntParameter(
                (int) GetDoubleConstant(constant),
                ref queryParameters.Filter.MinMinutesToArrival,
                ref queryParameters.Filter.MaxMinutesToArrival,
                nodeType);
        }
        else if ((memberAccess.Member.Name == "TotalHours")
            && (parent.Member.Name == "TimeToArrival")) {
            SetIntParameter(
                (int) GetDoubleConstant(constant) * 60,
                ref queryParameters.Filter.MinMinutesToArrival,
                ref queryParameters.Filter.MaxMinutesToArrival,
                nodeType);
        }
        else {
            throw new NotSupportedException(
                string.Format(
                    "Query on {0} expression is not supported",
                    memberAccess.ToString()));
        }
    }
```

Finally, we do not support expression trees that do not match the pattern of predicates that we support. For that reason, the implementations of *VisitUnary*, *VisitConstant*, and *VisitMemberAccess* (all included in Listing 12-39) throw an exception—these expressions are already handled by the helper methods called inside the *VisitBinary* method.

Listing 12-39 *VisitUnary, VisitConstant,* and *VisitMemberAccess* implementations in *FlightQueryTranslator*

```
protected override Expression VisitUnary(UnaryExpression u) {
    throw new NotSupportedException(
        string.Format(
            "The unary operator '{0}' is not supported",
            u.NodeType));
}

protected override Expression VisitConstant(ConstantExpression c) {
    if (c.Value is IQueryable) {
        // Assumes constant nodes implementing IQueryable
        // are flight sequences
        return c;
    }
    throw new NotSupportedException(
        string.Format(
            "The constant for '{0}' is not supported",
            c.ToString()));
}

protected override Expression VisitMemberAccess(MemberExpression m) {
    throw new NotSupportedException(
        string.Format(
            "The member '{0}' is not supported",
            m.Member.Name));
}
```

Working with the *FlightQueryProvider*

Our LINQ provider is almost ready. We only need to extend our *FlightStatusService* with the *AsQueryable* operator. Because we assume that we do not own the code for the *FlightStatus-Service* class, we use the extension method syntax shown in Listing 12-40.

Listing 12-40 *AsQueryable* definition as an extension method of *FlightStatusService*

```
public static class FlightStatusExtension {
    public static IQueryable<Flight> AsQueryable(
        this FlightStatusService flightStatus ) {

        FlightQueryProvider context =
            new FlightQueryProvider(flightStatus);
        return new FlightQuery(context);
    }
}
```

The *AsQueryable* operator creates an instance of *FlightQueryProvider* bound to the *flightStatus* instance, and it returns a new instance of the *FlightQuery* class. Each call to *AsQueryable* creates a new instance for both the *FlightQueryProvider* and *FlightQuery* classes. This is specific to our implementation: another provider could implement some caching techniques on the *IQueryProvider* implementation, but usually the cost of objects implementing *IQueryProvider* is very light, such as the *DataContext* in LINQ to SQL. The *AsQueryable* operator itself is not mandatory: you can always get a *FlightQuery* instance by calling the *IQueryProvider.Create-Query* method.

At this point, we can finally execute our LINQ queries on our *FlightStatusService*. Now the code we originally wrote in Listing 12-29 can be executed successfully. We can also get the query translated from a LINQ implementation to a textual representation. The code in Listing 12-41 is an example of that.

Listing 12-41   Samples of LINQ queries applied to *FlightStatusService*

```
FlightStatusService flightStatus = new FlightStatusService();

var query1 =
    from    f in flightStatus.AsQueryable()
    where   f.Airline == "UA" && f.Altitude >= 10000
    select f;
Console.WriteLine("** query1 **");
Console.WriteLine(query1);

var query2 =
    (from    f in flightStatus.AsQueryable()
     where   f.Arrival.Airport == "NRT"
             && f.TimeToArrival.TotalHours >= 2
     select f).Take(2);
Console.WriteLine("** query2 **");
Console.WriteLine(query2);
```

The execution of Listing 12-41 produces the following results:

```
** query1 **
FlightStatusService.QueryFilter Dump
Airline = UA
Altitude >= 10000
-----------------------

** query2 **
FlightStatusService.QueryFilter Dump
ArrivalAirport = NRT
MinutesToArrival >= 120
-----------------------
Maximum returned flights: 2
```

Having a textual representation of a query expression is very important for debugging and also to build unit tests. In our *FlightQueryProvider* implementation, this feature comes almost for free because most of the work is done by the *Translate* method that is shared between the *GetQueryText* and *Execute* methods.

Cost-Benefit Balance of a Custom LINQ Provider

Some final thoughts are dedicated to the cost-benefit balance evaluation. Implementing a LINQ provider is not an easy task. You need to deeply understand how to interpret the expression tree representing the query. Moreover, subtle bugs can remain hidden for years and when they explode, you have to understand what is happening on many different levels of abstraction just to isolate the bug. Also consider the possible errors in a query passed to a custom LINQ provider. These kinds of errors (just think of all our examples of *NotImplemented-Exception*) can be checked only at execution time and not at compile time. Therefore, using the *IQueryable* interface somewhat exposes your code to errors that can be intercepted only during query execution.

Important   *IQueryable* query expressions cannot be completely checked at compile time, especially when they use unsupported operators and/or expressions.

Thus, a new LINQ provider definitely has a high cost. But what are the benefits?

Generally speaking, having LINQ queries is a good thing because programmers express their will in a declarative form instead of an iterative one. LINQ abstracts the code from the data source's internal implementation, providing a more affordable abstraction from any specific data layer. Finally, LINQ is part of the .NET Framework, and we can imagine that in a few years, reading and writing LINQ queries will be part of the standard skills of the large majority of .NET programmers.

But is the cost for implementing a LINQ provider justified by its benefits?

Obviously, it depends. A LINQ provider used only by the programmer who is using a service could be very expensive. On the other hand, if a library will be used by hundreds of other people or over several different data layers, the presence of a LINQ provider can lower the learning curve and produces a better return on investment. These improvements become more important as the complexity of the underlying data model increases because the simplification, readability, and maintainability of LINQ queries better amortize the cost of writing a custom LINQ provider.

Note   We did not mention the performance implications of using LINQ. Adding a layer to the software usually does not improve performance, unless it provides a sort of cache service (for example, like that provided by the LINQ to SQL provider through *DataContext* entities). It is a developer's responsibility to evaluate whether the performance cost involved in using LINQ is affordable. Typically, calling a remote service has other bottlenecks, like latency in communication, and using LINQ should not be an issue. However, each scenario deserves a dedicated analysis.

Summary

In this chapter, you saw how to build custom operators, how to specialize existing operators, and finally how to build a custom LINQ provider. Creating new LINQ operators and specializing one or more of the existing ones does not require complete control over query expressions. Defining a custom LINQ provider implementing *IQueryable* and *IQueryProvider* requires many more resources (time and competencies first and foremost). A custom LINQ provider is necessary whenever you want to implement an external service whose API cannot be changed. To establish whether a LINQ provider is worth the time required to build it, you have to evaluate the cost-benefit balance for your own scenario.

Chapter 13
Parallel LINQ

Parallel Language Integrated Query (PLINQ, also known as Parallel LINQ) is an implementation of LINQ to Objects that executes queries in parallel. It is based on the Parallel Extensions to the .NET Framework. Both these framework components had been released as part of a Community Technology Preview at the time of this writing (February 2008). In this chapter, we will introduce the basic concepts of the Parallel Extension to the .NET Framework and describe the syntax and common uses of PLINQ. When PLINQ is released, it will be a very interesting way to write parallel code in a declarative way. For this reason, it is important to give you a preview of what the implications will be of adopting this technology.

> **This chapter is based on beta code!**   Parallel LINQ and the Parallel Extension to the .NET Framework had not been released at the time of this writing. Because this chapter is based on beta code, performance measures might change and some features might be changed, removed, or added in the final release. These differences could invalidate some of the examples shown in this chapter. We kept the information updated and aligned with the most recent information we had. In any case, we will publish news and corrections regarding book content together with updated code samples at *http://www.programminglinq.com*.

Parallel Extensions to the .NET Framework

The Parallel Extensions to the .NET Framework are the foundation of PLINQ. These extensions are implemented in an assembly named *System.Threading*. To start using them, you need to reference System.Threading.dll in your project. This same assembly also contains the PLINQ implementation.

> **Note**   You can download the "Microsoft Parallel Extensions to .NET Framework 3.5, December 2007 Community Technology Preview" from *http://www.microsoft.com/downloads/ details.aspx?FamilyID=e848dc1d-5be3-4941-8705-024bc7f180ba&displaylang=en*. Please check whether a newer version is available before installing it. The installation of this framework is necessary to compile and execute the code in this chapter.

Parallel.For and *Parallel.ForEach* Methods

The Parallel Extensions provides classes and methods that simplify the parallelization of code, without requiring you to deal with details about threads, thread pools, and synchronization. The first example that you can see in Listing 13-1 is the *For* method of the *System.Threading.Parallel* class.

Listing 13-1 *Parallel.For statement*

```
static void SequentialFor() {
    Stopwatch sw = Stopwatch.StartNew();
    for (int index = 0; index < 10 0; index++) {
        ProcessData(index);
    }
    long elapsed = sw.ElapsedMilliseconds;
    Console.WriteLine("Sequential for: {0} milliseconds", elapsed);
}

static void ParallelFor() {
    Stopwatch sw = Stopwatch.StartNew();
    Parallel.For(0, 100, (index) => {
        ProcessData(index);
    });
    long elapsed = sw.ElapsedMilliseconds;
    Console.WriteLine("Parallel for: {0} milliseconds", elapsed);
}
```

The *Parallel.For* call in the *ParallelFor* method replaces the *for* statement of the *SequentialFor* method. We ran this code on a dual-processor machine, with the following results:

```
Sequential for: 3893 milliseconds
Parallel for: 2461 milliseconds
```

As you can see, the *Parallel.For* implementation makes use of different threads to run the code inside the original *for* loop, which in this case calls the *ProcessData* method. In a multicore machine, this results in faster execution. In a single-core machine, the overhead for parallelism makes the *Parallel.For* call slower than the original *for* statement. However, we are simulating a heavy processing operation in the *ProcessData* method. If the process operation executes operations involving the suspension of threads, such as any I/O operation, the resulting response time could be better even on a single-core machine.

 Note   If the processor has to wait for an external resource or for synchronizing with another thread, the current thread is suspended. In this case, another thread can be served by the same processor that was serving the suspended thread.

The *Parallel.ForEach* method implements a parallel execution for what would be a simple *foreach* statement, as you can see in Listing 13-2.

Listing 13-2 *Parallel.ForEach statement*

```
static void SequentialForEach(int[] data) {
    Stopwatch sw = Stopwatch.StartNew();
    foreach (int value in data) {
        ProcessData(value);
    }
```

```
        long elapsed = sw.ElapsedMilliseconds;
        Console.WriteLine("Sequential foreach: {0} milliseconds", elapsed);
    }

    static void ParallelForEach(int[] data) {
        Stopwatch sw = Stopwatch.StartNew();
        Parallel.ForEach(data, (value) => {
            ProcessData(value);
        });
        long elapsed = sw.ElapsedMilliseconds;
        Console.WriteLine("Parallel foreach: {0} milliseconds", elapsed);
    }
```

The *Parallel.ForEach* method is similar to the *Parallel.For* method. They both execute the delegate passed as the last argument on possibly different threads. This results in a faster response time for the entire loop if the code is executed on a multicore machine or if there are operations inside the loop that can suspend the thread. The following is the result obtained running the code on a dual-core workstation:

```
Sequential for: 3944 milliseconds
Parallel for: 2213 milliseconds
```

The use of the *Parallel.For* and *Parallel.ForEach* methods requires that the operation for each cycle be independent from the others. In other words, you cannot assume that *ProcessData* will be called receiving 2 as an argument after it has been called receiving the argument 1. More importantly, if the code executed in several cycles has to store results in a shared object, such as an *int* or a *List<T>* or any other one, you have to make sure that access to shared objects is protected against concurrency. The Parallel Extensions to the .NET Framework provide some simplifications in this kind of scenario, as we will show you later in this chapter.

Do Method

The *Parallel.Do* method receives an array of delegates that can be executed in any order and in different threads. Decisions about order and threads are automatically made and are based on the available resources and duration of each delegate. Thanks to the C# 3.0 syntax, you can use *Parallel.Do* by writing code such as that shown in Listing 13-3.

Listing 13-3   *Parallel.Do* statement

```
static int Operation(int index) {
    DataCalculation(index);
    Console.WriteLine("Operation {0}", index);
    return i * 10;
}

static void DemoDo_Sequential() {
    Console.WriteLine("=== Sequential calls ===");
    Operation(1);
```

```
        Operation(2);
        Operation(3);
        Operation(4);
    }

    static void DemoDo_Parallel() {
        Console.WriteLine("=== Parallel.Do calls ===");
        Parallel.Do(
            () => Operation(1),
            () => Operation(2),
            () => Operation(3),
            () => Operation(4));
    }
```

> **Note**   In this example, we do not use the values returned by calls to *Operation*, but we will use them in an example later in the chapter.

The calls to *Operation* made inside *DemoDo_Parallel* can be called in different threads and in a nondeterministic order. In fact, you can see that the output produced by calling *DemoDo_Sequential* and then *DemoDo_Parallel* demonstrates that in the latter case the calls have been made using different threads:

```
=== Sequential calls ===
Operation 1
Operation 2
Operation 3
Operation 4
=== Parallel.Do calls ===
Operation 2
Operation 1
Operation 3
Operation 4
```

The implementation of *Parallel.Do* creates several instances of the *Task* class, without exposing them to the control of the programmer.

Task Class

The *System.Threading.Tasks.Task* class represents an asynchronous operation. It is a wrapper for a delegate that includes information such as the end of execution (*IsCompleted*, *IsCanceled*) and methods to stop the execution of a *Task* (*Cancel*). The previous code for *DemoDo_Parallel*, shown in Listing 13-3, can be written by instantiating *Task* objects, as shown in Listing 13-4.

Listing 13-4   Use of the *Task* class

```
static void DemoTask() {
    Console.WriteLine("=== Task calls ===");
    Task t1 = Task.Create(delegate { Operation(1); });
    Task t2 = Task.Create(delegate { Operation(2); });
```

```
        Task t3 = Task.Create(delegate { Operation(3); });
        Task t4 = Task.Create(delegate { Operation(4); });
        TaskCoordinator.WaitAll( new Task[] { t1, t2, t3, t4 } );
    }
```

The *TaskCoordinator.WaitAll* method waits until the end of the execution of all the tasks that were created before and passed as an array of the *Task* argument. Each *Task* can be executed in a different thread. A possible result of executing the *DemoTask* method in Listing 13-4 is the following (although this output might be different for each execution):

```
=== Task calls ===
Operation 2
Operation 1
Operation 4
Operation 3
```

The *Task* class is useful when you want to control asynchronous operations with the ability to cancel one or more of them, without having to implement a custom handling of that scenario.

Future<T> Class

The *Future<T>* class inherits from the *Task* class, and it adds semantics to read a value resulting from an asynchronous operation without having to write synchronization code.

In both Listings 13-3 and 13-4, we did not care about handling the result of the *Operation* method call. To handle the result, we need to store the result of the *Operation* call in the *Task* instance (and to do that, we need to create a custom class that inherits *Task*). Then we need to read that value from the *Task* object consumer. All these operations are already implemented using the *Future<T>* class. With this class, we can write code like that shown in Listing 13-5.

Listing 13-5   Use of the *Future<T>* class

```
static void DemoFuture() {
    Console.WriteLine("=== Future<T> calls ===");
    var f1 = Future.Create(() => Operation(1));
    var f2 = Future.Create(() => Operation(2));
    var f3 = Future.Create(() => Operation(3));
    var f4 = Future.Create(() => Operation(4));

    int result = f1.Value + f2.Value + f3.Value + f4.Value;
    Console.WriteLine("Future result is {0}", result);
}
```

The static *Future.Create* method returns a new instance of the *Future<T>* class. The *T* type is inferred from the delegate passed as an argument. In our example, *Operation* is a method that returns an *int*; for this reason, instances of *Future<int>* are generated. Access to the *Future<T>.Value* property executes a *Task.Wait* call if the task is still not complete. This means that accessing several *Value* properties, as we did in Listing 13-5, executes a series of *Wait* calls instead of a single *WaitAll* call. Because *Future<T>* inherits *Task*, we can always call *WaitAll* before accessing the *Value* property. For example, the following two lines guarantee a single wait operation:

```
TaskCoordinator.WaitAll(new Task[] { f1, f2, f3, f4 });
int result = f1.Value + f2.Value + f3.Value + f4.Value;
```

Regardless of the read order of the *Value* properties, the call to *Operation* can execute and complete in any order. The following output is a possible result of the execution of Listing 13-5:

```
=== Future<T> calls ===
Operation 2
Operation 1
Operation 3
Operation 4
```

Using *Future<T>* hides most of the details of thread synchronization that are necessary when an asynchronous operation needs to return data to another thread.

Concurrency Considerations

Writing multithreaded code exposes a programmer to a wider range of possible errors. A program that correctly runs in a single thread might be affected by any sort of concurrency issues if moved into a multithreaded environment. The most common issue is concurrent write access to a shared object. A piece of code is thread-safe if it functions correctly during simultaneous execution by multiple threads, but almost all the classes in .NET are not thread-safe by design (and performance is one of the reasons for that). Using Parallel Extensions to the .NET Framework, you still need to synchronize these kinds of access. However, thread synchronization is an expensive operation that also limits scalability. A better approach is to write code that does not share data, but it is not always possible to do that.

Consider the code in Listing 13-6, which implements a simple sum of the results returned from the *Operation* method called inside a *Parallel.For* call.

Listing 13-6 Example of a race condition in a parallel operation

```
static void DemoConcurrency_RaceCondition() {
    Console.WriteLine("=== DemoConcurrency_RaceCondition ===");
    int sum = 0;
    Parallel.For(0, 10, (index) => {
        int local = sum;
        local += Operation(index);
        sum = local;
    });
    Console.WriteLine("Final sum: {0}", sum);
}
```

As you can see, *sum* is a variable that is local to the *DemoConcurrency* method. However, it is used by concurrent methods (the delegate that implements the cycle of the *For* method), and it can be accessed by several threads at the same time. The code in Listing 13-6 should produce a final sum of 450. (*Operation* returns the valued received as the argument multiplied by 10.) However, running the code in Listing 13-6 on a multicore machine should produce a final result lower than the expected value, as in the following output, where the final sum is 280:

```
=== DemoConcurrency_RaceCondition ===
Operation 8
Operation 9
Operation 0
Operation 1
Operation 2
Operation 3
Operation 4
Operation 5
Operation 6
Operation 7
Final sum: 280
```

There are several approaches to solve this issue. The most common approach is to use some synchronization statements that protect data from concurrent access (for example, using the *lock* statement in C#):

```
object sync = new object();
// ...
Parallel.For(0, 10, (index) => {
    lock (sync) {
        int local = sum;
        local += Operation(index);
        sum = local;
    }
});
```

However, using synchronization between concurrent threads can limit scalability. An alternative and more scalable approach is to avoid the concurrent access entirely. This approach does not require the use of a particular application programming interface (API), but it affects the way the code is designed. It is important to think about these kinds of issues before writing code because refactoring a design issue after it has occurred is much more expensive than adding synchronization code. In Listing 13-7, you can see a possible implementation of the code in Listing 13-6 that uses parallel execution without concurrency issues.

Listing 13-7   Safe code without race condition

```
static void DemoConcurrency_Safe() {
    Console.WriteLine("=== DemoConcurrency_Safe ===");
    int sum = 0;
    int[] results = new int[10];
    Parallel.For(0, 10, (index) => {
        results[index] = Operation(index);
    });
    sum = results.Sum();
    Console.WriteLine("Final sum: {0}", sum);
}
```

Each cycle of the *Parallel.For* stores the result of the call to *Operation* in a different memory zone. When the loop is finished, the results array contains all the values returned from each *Operation* call, and only at this point are these values summed together, executing the *Sum* method in a single thread.

The truly difficult part about using parallelization techniques is finding the right balance between scalability and resource consumption. The solution shown in Listing 13-7 is more scalable, but it works by allocating an array of *int* that is not necessary with the synchronization approach. A dedicated analysis is required to find the best solution on a case-by-case basis.

More Info   A valuable source of information for multithreaded programming in .NET is Jeffrey Richter's book *CLR via C#*, Second Edition (Microsoft Press, 2006)

Using PLINQ

PLINQ is an implementation of LINQ to Objects that executes queries in parallel using the classes of the Parallel Extensions to the .NET Framework that we described in the preceding section.

Starting to use PLINQ is very simple. Consider this code:

```
int[] numbers = ...
var oddNumbers =
    from   i in numbers
    where  i % 2 == 1
    select i;
```

The *oddNumbers* query returns all the odd integers contained in the *numbers* array. To do that, it performs a sequential scan of *numbers*, and the result maintains the same order as the original source. This operation is executed in a single thread.

To use PLINQ, you simply call the *AsParallel* extension method on the data source, which in this case is the *numbers* array:

```
var oddNumbers =
    from   i in numbers.AsParallel()
    where  i % 2 == 1
    select i;
```

At this point, the scan of *numbers* is no longer implemented as a single sequential scan. Instead, the array scan can be split into several threads, using more CPU cores than the single one used with the sequential approach. Although most of the syntax-related explanation of PLINQ ends here (we will present some additional details about *AsParallel* arguments later), the implications of using such techniques of implicit parallelization require much more information, which we will describe in the following sections.

Threads Used by PLINQ

We think that a better way to understand PLINQ is by analyzing how many threads are involved when a PLINQ query is executed. First of all, let's look at the behavior of a query consumer when it does not make use of PLINQ and instead uses a standard LINQ to Objects query, as in Listing 13-8.

Listing 13-8   Simple LINQ to Object query

```
static void StandardLinq() {
    Console.WriteLine("=== StandardLinq ===");
    int[] data = LoadData(100000000);
    var query =
        from   i in data
        where  i % 12345678 == 0
        select new { Value = i, ThreadID = Thread.CurrentThread.ManagedThreadId };

    Stopwatch sw = Stopwatch.StartNew();
    foreach (var number in query) {
        Console.WriteLine("{0} - from ThreadId={1}",
                          number,
                          Thread.CurrentThread.ManagedThreadId);
    }
    long elapsed = sw.ElapsedMilliseconds;
    Console.WriteLine("Elapsed time   : {0} milliseconds", elapsed);
    Console.WriteLine("CurrentThreadId: {0}",
        Thread.CurrentThread.ManagedThreadId);
}
```

We initialize a huge array of type *int* and look for the few members that can be divided by 12345678. On the dual-core workstation we used for our tests, this was the result:

```
=== StandardLinq ===
{ Value = 0, ThreadID = 1 } - from ThreadId=1
{ Value = 12345678, ThreadID = 1 } - from ThreadId=1
{ Value = 24691356, ThreadID = 1 } - from ThreadId=1
{ Value = 37037034, ThreadID = 1 } - from ThreadId=1
{ Value = 49382712, ThreadID = 1 } - from ThreadId=1
{ Value = 61728390, ThreadID = 1 } - from ThreadId=1
{ Value = 74074068, ThreadID = 1 } - from ThreadId=1
{ Value = 86419746, ThreadID = 1 } - from ThreadId=1
{ Value = 98765424, ThreadID = 1 } - from ThreadId=1
Elapsed time   : 4310 milliseconds
CurrentThreadId: 1
```

The elapsed time is interesting to compare with the parallelized version. Take a look at the two points at which we captured the managed thread ID. The projection of the query creates an anonymous type, which will save the number found and the thread used to execute the code to generate the anonymous type itself. The *CurrentThreadId* value informs us of the thread ID used by the *foreach* loop that enumerates the query. This same ID is shown after the output of a number that is found (see *"from ThreadId=..."*). In this sample, all the code is executed in the same thread.

At this point, we can make a simple change to the query, adding *AsParallel* to the *data* source in the LINQ query, as you can see in Listing 13-9.

Listing 13-9   Simple PLINQ query

```
static void SamplePLinq() {
    Console.WriteLine("=== SamplePLinq ===");
    int[] data = LoadData(100000000);
    var query =
        from   i in data.AsParallel()
        where  i % 12345678 == 0
        select new { Value = i, ThreadID = Thread.CurrentThread.ManagedThreadId };

    Stopwatch sw = Stopwatch.StartNew();
    foreach (var number in query) {
        Console.WriteLine("{0} - from ThreadId={1}",
                          number,
                          Thread.CurrentThread.ManagedThreadId);
    }
    long elapsed = sw.ElapsedMilliseconds;
    Console.WriteLine("Elapsed time    : {0} milliseconds", elapsed);
    Console.WriteLine("CurrentThreadId: {0}",
        Thread.CurrentThread.ManagedThreadId);
}
```

The execution of this code produces a different result. If you have a single-core machine, you should obtain something like this:

```
=== SamplePLinq ===");
{ Value = 0, ThreadID = 3 } - from ThreadId=1
{ Value = 12345678, ThreadID = 3 } - from ThreadId=1
{ Value = 24691356, ThreadID = 3 } - from ThreadId=1
{ Value = 37037034, ThreadID = 3 } - from ThreadId=1
{ Value = 49382712, ThreadID = 3 } - from ThreadId=1
{ Value = 61728390, ThreadID = 3 } - from ThreadId=1
{ Value = 74074068, ThreadID = 3 } - from ThreadId=1
{ Value = 86419746, ThreadID = 3 } - from ThreadId=1
{ Value = 98765424, ThreadID = 3 } - from ThreadId=1
Elapsed time    : 3828 milliseconds
CurrentThreadId: 1
```

With a dual-core machine, you should get a result similar to the following one, which has been produced using the same hardware that was used to execute the sequential query in Listing 13-8:

```
=== SamplePLinq ===");
{ Value = 61728390, ThreadID = 4 } - from ThreadId=1
{ Value = 74074068, ThreadID = 4 } - from ThreadId=1
{ Value = 86419746, ThreadID = 4 } - from ThreadId=1
```

```
{ Value = 98765424, ThreadID = 4 } - from ThreadId=1
{ Value = 0, ThreadID = 3 } - from ThreadId=1
{ Value = 12345678, ThreadID = 3 } - from ThreadId=1
{ Value = 24691356, ThreadID = 3 } - from ThreadId=1
{ Value = 37037034, ThreadID = 3 } - from ThreadId=1
{ Value = 49382712, ThreadID = 3 } - from ThreadId=1
Elapsed time   : 2113 milliseconds
CurrentThreadId: 1
```

In both cases, the thread used to execute the *foreach* loop and, consequently, the *WriteLine* is different from the thread or threads used to execute the PLINQ query. This difference could have been the result of a performance penalization, at least for the first case with a single thread, because communication between threads introduces a new cost that is not present in the traditional LINQ version. In this case, we had a performance gain anyway, lowering to 3828 milliseconds the initial 4310 milliseconds. The reason is that only a few members have been returned from the query, and the execution of the *WriteLine* command (executed in *ThreadId* = 1) in this case did not suspend the query itself, which was executed in another thread (*ThreadId* = 3). Remember that the *WriteLine* is a suspensive operation because it makes an I/O call to the console device (in *ThreadId* 1), and during this call the other thread can continue its work (in *ThreadId* 3). Using a dual-core machine, we got a real and visible performance improvement, going down to 2113 milliseconds, half of our initial time! However, we will not always be so lucky. Do not assume that *AsParallel* always improves response time. Usually, the block of computation necessary to return at least a row is not nearly as long as in this case (where we return only 9 members out of an array of 100 million elements).

Now that the differences between LINQ and PLINQ in terms of thread usage are clear, we can start to dig into more details of PLINQ.

PLINQ Implementation

When we added the *AsParallel* call to the data source in the query, we simply called the *AsParallel* extension method defined in *ParallelQuery*, which is included in the *System.Linq* namespace:

```
namespace System.Linq {
public static class ParallelQuery {
    public static IParallelEnumerable<T> AsParallel<T>(this IEnumerable<T> source);
    public static IParallelEnumerable<object> AsParallel(this IEnumerable source);
    public static IParallelEnumerable<T> AsParallel<T>(this IEnumerable<T> source,
                           int degreeOfParallelism);
    public static IParallelEnumerable<T> AsParallel<T>(this IEnumerable<T> source,
                           ParallelQueryOptions options);
    public static IParallelEnumerable<T> AsParallel<T>(this IEnumerable<T> source,
                           ParallelQueryOptions options,
                           int degreeOfParallelism);
    public static IEnumerable<T> AsSequential<T>(
                           this IParallelEnumerable<T> source);
}
}
```

As you can see, there are several overloaded versions of *AsParallel* that allow you to specify these parameters:

- *int degreeOfParallelism*: This is the maximum number of threads to be used in the query. (This number is also limited by the *PLINQ_DOP* environment variable.)

- *ParallelQueryOptions options*: This enumeration actually specifies only whether the order of results has to be preserved (*PreserveOrdering*) or not (*None*). The default is *None*.

The only other extension method defined in *ParallelQuery* is *AsSequential<T>*, which transforms a PLINQ query (*IParallelEnumerable<T>*) into a standard LINQ to Objects query (*IEnumerable<T>*).

The type returned from *AsParallel* implements the *IParallelEnumerable<T>* interface, which is defined as follows:

```
public interface IParallelEnumerable<T> : IEnumerable<T>, IEnumerable {
    IEnumerator<T> GetEnumerator(bool usePipelining);
}
```

IParallelEnumerable<T> implements *IEnumerable<T>* and *IEnumerable*, adding a *GetEnumerator* method that is specific to a PLINQ implementation (which we will say more about in the next section). From the consumer point of view, the presence of the *IParallelEnumerable<T>* interface simply enables extension methods to call the implementation defined in the *ParallelEnumerable* class. This class, which is defined in the System.Threading.dll assembly, is similar to the *Enumerable* class defined in System.Core.dll. Both classes implement LINQ operators as extension methods and are defined in the *System.Linq* namespace. However, *Enumerable* extends *IEnumerable<T>* and *ParallelEnumerable* extends *IParallelEnumerable<T>*.

At this point, it is clear that a single data source in a query directly defines what the extension method is to be called (LINQ or PLINQ, for example). But what happens when a query joins two sources? In this case, the left-most data source is the one that defines the implementation to use. In other words, if a data source that implements *IParallelEnumerable<T>* is used on the left side of a join, even if the other side only implements *IEnumerable<T>*, the *ParallelQuery* implementation is used and the query is handled by PLINQ instead of LINQ to Objects.

PLINQ Use

The execution of a PLINQ query begins only when the program starts to process the output of the query, just as LINQ to Objects does. In the section "Threads Used by PLINQ," we discussed the difference between the thread that processes the output of the query (the one executing the *foreach* statement in our example) and the threads that produce this output, implementing all the requested operations on the original data source. However, we have observed only one of the three modes of query processing offered by PLINQ.

Pipelined Processing

Pipelined processing is the default processing model that we observed earlier. There is a set of worker threads executing the query and a separate thread that consumes the query result. The consumer thread processes data as soon as the worker threads start to produce results. This is the behavior obtained using the well-known *foreach* statement.

Stop-and-Go Processing

With stop-and-go processing, the consumer waits for all the worker threads to finish their work before consuming data. In this way, the consumer thread does not contend for CPU resources with worker threads, and this often results in better execution time for getting all the results—even if the time to get the first element from the query is the same as the time to execute the entire query. Because the consumer does not need to use the CPU, the thread used by the consumer is used as a worker thread during query execution. This is clearly visible in Listing 13-10.

Listing 13-10   PLINQ query using the stop-and-go processing model

```
static void SamplePLinq_StopAndGo() {
    Console.WriteLine("=== SamplePLinq_StopAndGo ===");
    int[] data = LoadData(100000000);
    var query =
        from   i in data.AsParallel()
        where  i % 12345678 == 0
        select new { Value = i, ThreadID = Thread.CurrentThread.ManagedThreadId };

    Stopwatch sw = Stopwatch.StartNew();
    using (var e = query.GetEnumerator(false)) {
        // The first call to MoveNext waits for the execution
        // of the entire query. After that call, data is enumerated
        // from an in-memory list
        while (e.MoveNext()) {
            Console.WriteLine("{0} - from ThreadId={1}",
                        e.Current,
                        Thread.CurrentThread.ManagedThreadId);
        }
    }
    long elapsed = sw.ElapsedMilliseconds;
    Console.WriteLine("Elapsed time   : {0} milliseconds", elapsed);
    Console.WriteLine("CurrentThreadId: {0}",
        Thread.CurrentThread.ManagedThreadId);
}
```

As you can see from the source code, *GetEnumerator* is called by passing *false* to the *usePipelining* argument. This is possible only by explicitly writing the enumeration loop, without using the *foreach* statement (which by default ends by using *true* for this argument). It is interesting to see the output produced by the execution of the code in Listing 13-10:

```
=== SamplePLinq_StopAndGo ===
{ Value = 0, ThreadID = 3 } - from ThreadId=1
{ Value = 12345678, ThreadID = 3 } - from ThreadId=1
{ Value = 24691356, ThreadID = 3 } - from ThreadId=1
{ Value = 37037034, ThreadID = 3 } - from ThreadId=1
{ Value = 49382712, ThreadID = 3 } - from ThreadId=1
{ Value = 61728390, ThreadID = 1 } - from ThreadId=1
{ Value = 74074068, ThreadID = 1 } - from ThreadId=1
{ Value = 86419746, ThreadID = 1 } - from ThreadId=1
{ Value = 98765424, ThreadID = 1 } - from ThreadId=1
Elapsed time    : 1752 milliseconds
CurrentThreadId: 1
```

The thread with ID 1 has been used for both the consumer loop and to produce part of the query result. In this way, we waited to see the first row appear on the console, but when it arrived, the query completed almost immediately and the overall required time went down to 1752 milliseconds, almost 20 percent better than using the pipelined processing model. This is not an optimization measure that you can always expect, but it is interesting to know that a performance benefit exists.

The stop-and-go processing model is automatically used by PLINQ when *ToArray* or *ToList* is called. Also, a sort in the query forces the use of a stop-and-go operation.

Note   The automatic use of the stop-and-go processing model when calling *ToArray* or *ToList* explains why you can observe a performance gain by calling one of these methods and then iterating the resulting collection, instead of iterating the result of a PLINQ query. However, remember that the stop-and-go processing model does not return any item until all the items have been processed.

Inverted Enumeration

Until now, we always executed the code that consumes the query results in a specific thread. In some circumstances (but not in our simple example), this thread might become a real bottleneck in your architecture. You can gain a higher degree of parallelism by invoking the consumer code in the same thread that produced an item during the query execution. You cannot do this using the standard syntax of C# 3.0, but you can with an extension method named *ForAll*, which is declared in the *ParallelEnumerable* class. This extension method gets a single argument of type *Action<T>*. This argument usually represents a delegate that will be executed for each row of the result. You can see in Listing 13-11 an example of the *ForAll* syntax.

Listing 13-11   PLINQ query using an inverted processing model

```
static void SamplePLinq_Inverted() {
    Console.WriteLine("=== SamplePLinq_Inverted ===");
    int[] data = LoadData(100000000);
    var query =
        from   i in data.AsParallel()
        where  i % 12345678 == 0
        select new { Value = i, ThreadID = Thread.CurrentThread.ManagedThreadId };

    Stopwatch sw = Stopwatch.StartNew();
    query.ForAll((number) => {
        Console.WriteLine("{0} - from ThreadId={1}",
                          number,
                          Thread.CurrentThread.ManagedThreadId);
    } );
    long elapsed = sw.ElapsedMilliseconds;
    Console.WriteLine("Elapsed time    : {0} milliseconds", elapsed);
    Console.WriteLine("CurrentThreadId: {0}",
        Thread.CurrentThread.ManagedThreadId);
}
```

Looking at the output produced by the execution of the code in Listing 13-11, you can see that now some *Console.WriteLine* calls are not executed in the same "consumer" thread. In fact, they are executed in the same thread used to produce the output row. Obviously, the code inside a *ForAll* should be thread-safe.

```
=== SamplePLinq_Inverted ===");
{ Value = 0, ThreadID = 4 } - from ThreadId=4
{ Value = 12345678, ThreadID = 4 } - from ThreadId=4
{ Value = 61728390, ThreadID = 1 } - from ThreadId=1
{ Value = 24691356, ThreadID = 4 } - from ThreadId=4
{ Value = 74074068, ThreadID = 1 } - from ThreadId=1
{ Value = 37037034, ThreadID = 4 } - from ThreadId=4
{ Value = 86419746, ThreadID = 1 } - from ThreadId=1
{ Value = 49382712, ThreadID = 4 } - from ThreadId=4
{ Value = 98765424, ThreadID = 1 } - from ThreadId=1
Elapsed time    : 1714 milliseconds
CurrentThreadId: 1
```

This result tells us that performance has been further optimized. In this case, we gained a few milliseconds compared to stop-and-go processing. The inverted enumeration does not pay the overhead of the context switch between threads to execute consumer code. However, this difference might vary for each execution. In fact, the *Console.WriteLine* we are calling uses some synchronization techniques to protect against concurrent execution. Having code in the consumer part that does not require synchronization should result in a more predictable gain in performance.

> **Note**   The use of inverted enumeration should be considered when the cost for context switching between worker threads and consumer threads is high, or when using a single consumer thread becomes the performance bottleneck. Both of these conditions will likely be more frequent with a query that returns a large number of elements. Another reason to use inverted enumeration might be the lower latency between the generation of an element and its processing (that is, no context switching, even when the query returns a small number of elements).

Side Effects of Parallel Execution

The most common and visible side effect of a PLINQ query execution is the order of results. Unless you use a constraint (such as an *orderby* condition), the order of results produced by a PLINQ query is not predictable and is not the same as the original data source. In this section, we will explore how you can order results, and you will also see why operators used by a PLINQ query should not modify the state of a shared resource.

Order of Results

In LINQ to Objects, the enumeration over the data source usually results in the order of the original data being maintained in the result produced by the LINQ query. This is not true in PLINQ, and if you want to control the output order you have two choices. The first is the use of an *orderby* clause in the PLINQ query, like in Listing 13-12.

Listing 13-12   PLINQ query using the *orderby* operator

```
static void SamplePLinq_OrderBy() {
    Console.WriteLine("=== SamplePLinq_OrderBy ===");
    int[] data = LoadData(100000000);
    var query =
        from    i in data.AsParallel()
        where   i % 12345678 == 0
        orderby i
        select  new { Value = i, ThreadID = Thread.CurrentThread.ManagedThreadId };

    Stopwatch sw = Stopwatch.StartNew();
    foreach (var number in query) {
        Console.WriteLine("{0} - from ThreadId={1}",
                    number,
                    Thread.CurrentThread.ManagedThreadId);
    }
    long elapsed = sw.ElapsedMilliseconds;
    Console.WriteLine("Elapsed time   : {0} milliseconds", elapsed);
    Console.WriteLine("CurrentThreadId: {0}",
        Thread.CurrentThread.ManagedThreadId);
}
```

The execution of Listing 13-12 implicitly uses a stop-and-go processing model and produces the following output:

```
=== SamplePLinq_OrderBy ===
{ Value = 0, ThreadID = 4 } - from ThreadId=1
{ Value = 12345678, ThreadID = 4 } - from ThreadId=1
{ Value = 24691356, ThreadID = 4 } - from ThreadId=1
{ Value = 37037034, ThreadID = 4 } - from ThreadId=1
{ Value = 49382712, ThreadID = 4 } - from ThreadId=1
{ Value = 61728390, ThreadID = 1 } - from ThreadId=1
{ Value = 74074068, ThreadID = 1 } - from ThreadId=1
{ Value = 86419746, ThreadID = 1 } - from ThreadId=1
{ Value = 98765424, ThreadID = 1 } - from ThreadId=1
Elapsed time    : 1760 milliseconds
CurrentThreadId: 1
```

Another option you have is to use the *ParallelQueryOptions.PreserveOrdering* argument by calling the *AsParallel* extension method on the data source. In our example, the data source is already sorted—thus, we can try to use this argument instead of specifying the *orderby* condition. Listing 13-13 shows the code for this test.

Listing 13-13   PLINQ query using the *ParallelQueryOptions.PreserveOrdering* argument

```
static void SamplePLinq_PreserveOrdering() {
    Console.WriteLine("=== SamplePLinq_PreserveOrdering ===");
    int[] data = LoadData(100000000);
    var query =
        from   i in data.AsParallel(ParallelQueryOptions.PreserveOrdering)
        where  i % 12345678 == 0
        select new { Value = i, ThreadID = Thread.CurrentThread.ManagedThreadId };

    Stopwatch sw = Stopwatch.StartNew();
    foreach (var number in query) {
        Console.WriteLine("{0} - from ThreadId={1}",
                          number,
                          Thread.CurrentThread.ManagedThreadId);
    }
    long elapsed = sw.ElapsedMilliseconds;
    Console.WriteLine("Elapsed time    : {0} milliseconds", elapsed);
    Console.WriteLine("CurrentThreadId: {0}",
        Thread.CurrentThread.ManagedThreadId);
}
```

The output produced keeps the original order, but in this case there is a higher cost in terms of performance:

```
=== SamplePLinq_PreserveOrdering ===
{ Value = 0, ThreadID = 4 } - from ThreadId=1
{ Value = 12345678, ThreadID = 4 } - from ThreadId=1
{ Value = 24691356, ThreadID = 4 } - from ThreadId=1
{ Value = 37037034, ThreadID = 4 } - from ThreadId=1
```

```
{ Value = 49382712, ThreadID = 4 } - from ThreadId=1
{ Value = 61728390, ThreadID = 1 } - from ThreadId=1
{ Value = 74074068, ThreadID = 1 } - from ThreadId=1
{ Value = 86419746, ThreadID = 1 } - from ThreadId=1
{ Value = 98765424, ThreadID = 1 } - from ThreadId=1
Elapsed time    : 12918 milliseconds
CurrentThreadId: 1
```

Our query is now slower than the original single-threaded version. The reason is that we have a large number of elements in the data source and a query that filters only a few elements from there. The *ParallelQueryOptions.PreserveOrdering* argument has an impact on the way the data is read and processed from the data source, whereas if we used *orderby* the impact is only on the produced results (which is very few elements in our case). This does not mean that *ParallelQueryOptions.PreserveOrdering* is not an option; in fact, it could be the only way to keep the right order if data comes, for example, from streaming. This option does not have a big performance penalty if the cost of processing elements in the query is much higher than the cost of extracting the elements from the data source.

> **Important**   Using either *orderby* or *ParallelQueryOptions.PreserveOrdering* is not relevant if you use an inverted enumeration processing model by calling the *ForAll* extension method to process query results. The execution of the delegate passed as an argument to *ForAll* does not respect the requested order.

Changes in Data During Execution

Working in a multithreading context requires that you pay more attention to any possible race condition you might create in your program. Usually, you write a query assuming that the data source does not change its content during query execution. If a query uses only *pure functions*, your only concerns are about possible external modifications during query execution. A pure function is a function that has no side effects and does not depend on any state beyond its local scope. For example, a projection or predicate expression that contains code that modifies a shared resource might be a source of race conditions. Consider the following code:

```
int accumulator = 0;
var query =
    from   i in data.AsParallel(ParallelQueryOptions.PreserveOrdering)
    select new { Aggregated = accumulator += i, Value = i };
```

As you can see, this query should produce a column named *Aggregated*, which contains the aggregate of *Value* up until the displayed row. However, with PLINQ we have two issues here. First, when splitting the order of execution into several threads, the *accumulator* is not incremented with the right order. Second, the write access to *accumulator* has the same kind of race condition we described when we were talking about Listing 13-6.

> **Important**   Code in a PLINQ query must not change data that can be shared across differ-
> ent threads. This includes expressions written inside the query, methods called by these
> expressions, and code for custom operators.

Processing Query Results

Instance members of most .NET Framework classes are not thread safe. For example, filling
data in a collection class such as *List<T>* requires you to call the *List<T>* instance members in
a safe way. When you use PLINQ, you have to be careful about these kinds of issues.

For example, this is a safe way to load a list:

```
List<int> result = new List<int>();
var query =
    from   i in data.AsParallel()
    where  i % 2 == 0
    select i;
foreach (var number in query) {
    result.Add(number);
}
```

The preceding code uses pipelined processing. The calls to *List<T>.Add* in the *foreach* loop
will always be made from the same thread that has created the *List<T>* instance itself. You
might be tempted to use code such as the following, which is faster but which is unsafe with
regard to its use of the *result* instance of *List<T>*:

```
List<int> result = new List<int>();
var query =
    from   i in data.AsParallel()
    where  i % 2 == 0
    select i;
query.ForAll((number) => {
    result.Add(number);
});
```

Because *ForAll* will execute the code in several threads, there might be a race condition resulting from calling the *List<T>.Add* method from different threads at the same moment. To avoid
this risk and to get the minimum overhead in performance for synchronization, you can
call the *ToList<T>* extension method on any PLINQ query, as in the following code:

```
var query =
    from   i in data.AsParallel()
    where  i % 2 == 0
    select i;
List<int> result = query.ToList();
```

This is the fastest and a much safer way to populate a *List<T>* from a PLINQ result. Other
similar extension methods available are *ToArray<T>*, *ToDictionary<T>*, and *ToLookup<T>*.

Exception Handling with PLINQ

Throwing an exception during a PLINQ query execution cannot immediately stop all PLINQ query activities. The processing of a PLINQ query usually involves several threads. When an exception is thrown in one of those threads, the system tries to stop all other threads in execution serving the PLINQ query. However, in the meantime, other threads can throw other exceptions. In the end, more than one exception might be thrown from a PLINQ query before you can catch the first one. For this reason, all exceptions thrown inside a PLINQ query are gathered into a single instance of *AggregateException*, which is thrown after the PLINQ query has been stopped. An *AggregateException* contains a list of all the exceptions thrown in the PLINQ query in its *InnerExceptions* property. Listing 13-14 shows an example of a PLINQ query that throws several divide-by-zero exceptions during its execution.

Listing 13-14   Exception handling for a PLINQ query

```
static void SamplePLinq_ExceptionHandling() {
    int[] data = LoadData(100);
    var query =
        from   i in data.AsParallel()
        where  i % 5 == 0
        select new { Value = i * 2 / (i % 10),
                     ThreadID = Thread.CurrentThread.ManagedThreadId };

    try {
        foreach (var number in query) {
            Console.WriteLine("{0} - from ThreadId={1}",
                              number,
                              Thread.CurrentThread.ManagedThreadId);
        }
    }
    catch (AggregateException ex) {
        Console.WriteLine(ex.Message);
        Console.WriteLine(
            String.Format( "AggregateException with {0} inner exceptions",
                           ex.InnerExceptions.Count ) );
        int counter = 0;
        foreach (var innerException in ex.InnerExceptions) {
            Console.WriteLine("({0})--> {1} : {2}",
                              ++counter,
                              innerException.GetType().Name,
                              innerException.Message);
        }
    }
}
```

The following output is produced on a dual-core machine:

```
one or more parallel tasks failed
AggregateException with 2 inner exceptions
(1)--> DivideByZeroException : Attempted to divide by zero.
(2)--> DivideByZeroException : Attempted to divide by zero.
```

With a traditional execution in LINQ to Objects, we would have had only one *DivideByZero-Exception*. In PLINQ, you always have an *AggregateException*, even when only one exception has been thrown inside the PLINQ query.

PLINQ and Other LINQ Implementations

When you use PLINQ with other LINQ providers, you have to make sure that they operate in a compatible way. In general, all the data sources implementing *IEnumerable<T>* can operate as data sources for a PLINQ query. For example, a LINQ to XML query can be parallelized, as you can see in Listing 13-15.

Listing 13-15   PLINQ used with a LINQ to XML query

```
static void XmlPLinq() {
    XElement doc = XElement.Load(@"..\..\NorthwindCustomersWithOrders.xml");
    var query =
        from   c in doc.Elements("customer").AsParallel()
        where  c.Element("country").Value == "Italy"
        select new {
            CompanyName = c.Element("companyName").Value,
            ThreadID = Thread.CurrentThread.ManagedThreadId
        };

    foreach (var item in query) {
        Console.WriteLine("{0} - from ThreadId={1}",
                          item,
                          Thread.CurrentThread.ManagedThreadId);
    }
}
```

The result produced by executing the code in Listing 13-15 can be similar to the following one, which was obtained using a dual-core machine:

```
{ CompanyName = Franchi S.p.A., ThreadID = 4 } - from ThreadId=1
{ CompanyName = Magazzini Alimentari Riuniti, ThreadID = 3 } - from ThreadId=1
{ CompanyName = Reggiani Caseifici, ThreadID = 3 } - from ThreadId=1
```

Warning   If you use a parallel query as an argument to *XStreamingElement*, it will use a parallel query when you serialize the XML tree by using methods of this class. This can result in an unexpected order for the nodes in the XML tree that is produced.

Some different issues need to be considered when you use a provider operating with *IQueryable*, such as LINQ to SQL. In these cases, you need to materialize the query result by calling *AsEnumerable*, and only then can you call *AsParallel*. If you do not take this step and apply *AsParallel* to the data source, you will end up loading all the table rows in memory and the query will be executed using PLINQ. For example, consider the following LINQ to SQL query:

```
var query =
    from   c in db.GetTable<Customer>()
    where  c.Country == "Italy"
    select new { c.CompanyName };
```

This query produces the following SQL code, which is sent to the Microsoft SQL Server database:

```
SELECT [t0].[CompanyName]
FROM    [Customers] AS [t0]
WHERE   [t0].[Country] = "Italy"
```

If you apply *AsEnumerable* to the data source, the whole query becomes a PLINQ query and the *Customers* table is queried in its entire form (all columns and all rows) from the SQL Server database. In other words, if you write this LINQ query

```
var query =
    from   c in db.GetTable<Customer>().AsParallel()
    where  c.Country == "Italy"
    select new { c.CompanyName };
```

the SQL query sent to the database will be the following one:

```
SELECT [t0].[CustomerID], [t0].[CompanyName], [t0].[City],
       [t0].[Region] AS [State], [t0].[Country]
FROM    [Customers] AS [t0]
```

If you want to send an optimized query to SQL Server and process its result in a parallel way, you can call *AsParallel* on the entire LINQ to SQL query:

```
var query =
    from row in
        (from c in db.GetTable<Customer>()
         where c.Country == "Italy"
         select new { c.CompanyName }
        ).AsParallel()
    select new {
        row.CompanyName,
        ThreadID = Thread.CurrentThread.ManagedThreadId
    };
```

Applying parallelism to the result of a LINQ to SQL query (or to any other *IQueryable* provider) should not be a very frequent occurrence. Only if the processing of data coming from these queries is particularly heavy does it make sense to parallelize it. Usually, the *IQueryable* provider is in charge of the optimization of the query execution. One scenario in which this could be useful is when you have a query that combines data coming from SQL Server with data coming from other sources, such as LINQ to XML or LINQ to Objects.

Summary

Parallel LINQ (PLINQ) is a LINQ implementation that allows for the parallelization of a LINQ query. Only queries operating in memory can take advantage of PLINQ, and queries to *IQueryable* providers can use PLINQ only on their results. PLINQ is based on the Parallel Extensions to the .NET Framework. Using PLINQ requires an understanding of the implications of using multithread programming and of the side effects of query execution, such as write access to shared objects.

Chapter 14

Other LINQ Implementations

LINQ represents an important change in the way we write code. As we have said several times in this book, if LINQ were only a new version of Embedded SQL for the new millennium, its impact would be limited to a relatively small layer of application architecture. It is very likely, however, that the impact of LINQ will become increasingly pervasive in the everyday life of a programmer. At least this is our prediction, and we are so convinced of it that we have dedicated more than two years of our lives to studying LINQ and writing books about it.

In this chapter, we will give you an idea of how relevant the impact of LINQ is going to be for programmers and developers. We will make our point by showing you some early alternative LINQ implementations. We have divided this chapter into sections that group LINQ implementations by category of service and the type of data handled. Most of these implementations are community-driven projects; some are just proof-of-concept exercises. The goal of describing these examples is to give you a broad view of the enormous potential of LINQ.

Important   LINQ implementations referenced in this chapter were not written or released by Microsoft. At the date of this writing (March 2008), they are publicly available and most are open to contributions of other programmers. We cannot guarantee the quality and reliability of the LINQ implementations we reference in this chapter.

Database Access

As you know, LINQ to SQL supports only Microsoft SQL Server databases (including the Compact 3.5 version) and LINQ to Entities supports all the databases supported by the ADO.NET Entity Framework. If you have a database other than Microsoft SQL Server, the simplest way to access it through LINQ is by looking for an ADO.NET Entity Framework provider for the database you are using. If you have a provider, you can access your data using LINQ to Entities. However, if for any reason LINQ to Entities is not a good choice for you, an alternative LINQ implementation might offer the support you need. As we described in Chapter 12, "Extending LINQ," you sometimes need a custom LINQ provider. The only one currently available that supports other types of databases is DbLinq (*http://code2code.net/DB_Linq/*), which supports LINQ queries over MySQL, Oracle, PostgreSQL, and SqlLite databases.

The reason there are not more alternative LINQ implementations that directly implement database access is twofold. First, writing a LINQ provider that generates SQL statements supporting all LINQ (and SQL) operators is a very tough job. Second, the existence of the

ADO.NET Entity Framework pushes third-party database vendors to write their providers to support that framework—which offers a broader range of support for tools and applications—rather than LINQ, which is included through LINQ to Entities.

Data Access Without a Database

The title of this section might sound strange. However, it is not that strange if you consider that sometimes you might need to access data without directly accessing a database—even if your data in the end is likely to be stored in some relational engine. The first example we will look at deals with this scenario by using ADO.NET Data Services, formerly code named Astoria (*http://astoria.mslivelabs.com*). ADO.NET Data Services is described as "a combination of patterns and libraries that enables any data store to be exposed as a flexible data service that can be consumed by consumers within a corporate network or across the Internet. ADO.NET Data Services uses URIs to point to pieces of data and simple, well-known formats to represent that data, such as JSON [JavaScript Object Notation] and ATOM/APP [Atom Publishing Protocol]." Through the support of the Entity Data Model that you can define in the ADO.NET Entity Framework, ADO.NET Data Services can be accessed using LINQ to Entities. In this way, your program does not have to handle details such as HTTP verbs (for example, GET, POST, or DELETE) that are used to interact with the service.

Another example of remote data storage is the one provided by services such as Amazon SimpleDB and Microsoft SQL Server Data Services (SSDS). These services offer a pay-per-use model to store data on a remote platform that is completely managed by the hosting provider. Each of these services has its own application programming interface (API), but it is natural that their LINQ support makes them easier to use. Although SSDS natively offers a managed library to support LINQ queries, there is also a LINQ provider for SimpleDB (*http://www.codeplex.com/LinqToSimpleDB*). Considering that each of these services has a proprietary API and does not use standard SQL as the query language, their LINQ compatibility might ease the difficulty of adopting these kinds of platforms, lowering the learning curve for developers who opt to use them.

Another common source of data is Microsoft Office Excel. An interesting study about a LINQ provider to access Excel data is the LINQ to Excel provider (*http://www.codeplex.com/xlslinq*). This provider is still a simple prototype that does not have complete functionality, but it is interesting because it directly accesses Excel files without using the existing OLE DB provider. This approach makes it possible to define custom LINQ operators and custom entities that are specific to Excel, something that would be difficult to do if you were trying to perform data access through a standard SQL query. This is not to say that using SQL for data access is the wrong approach. However, sometimes you do not have access to all the information available in an Excel document when using the Excel OLE DB provider, which is the standard way to query Excel data using SQL. For instance, you cannot use OLE DB to get a list of worksheets in a workbook, but this list is obtainable when using the following *sheets* query in LINQ to Excel:

```
XlsWorkbook book = new XlsWorkbook("sample.xls");
var sheets = from   s in book.Worksheets
             select s;
```

It is worth mentioning that accessing the Excel object model is also possible with LINQ to Objects, but a custom provider for LINQ can simplify access because it uses a more simplified and data-oriented object model.

Microsoft Office SharePoint Server (and Windows SharePoint Services) deserve separate mention. Queries to SharePoint can be defined using the Collaborative Application Markup Language (CAML), which is an XML-based language that is used in Windows SharePoint Services to define the fields and views used in sites and lists, as well as to define queries over them. It is natural to expect that there would be a LINQ provider that generates CAML queries, just as LINQ to SQL generates SQL queries. And, in fact, one does exist: the LINQ to SharePoint project (*http://www.codeplex.com/LINQtoSharePoint*) supports a query provider that translates LINQ queries to CAML. In the future, it might provide support for updating entities obtained from LINQ to SharePoint queries. Considering the wide adoption of SharePoint, which is becoming one of the primary repositories of business information in many companies, the ease of accessing SharePoint data through LINQ is very important to integrating SharePoint into existing applications.

Similar to SharePoint, Microsoft Dynamics CRM is another important repository of data. It is accessible through FetchXML, which is an XML-based query language used in Microsoft CRM (customer relationship management). The LINQ to CRM project (*http://www.codeplex.com/LinqtoCRM*) implements a LINQ provider that translates queries into FetchXML.

LINQ to Entity Domain Models

The ADO.NET Entity Framework provides a set of tools and libraries for designing and using an entity-relationship data model. LINQ to Entities exposes this model with LINQ syntax. The ADO.NET Entity Framework can be considered an Object Relational Mapping (ORM) solution. Other ORMs are available on the market. The most well-known one is probably NHibernate (*http://www.nhibernate.org*). LINQ integration for this tool is expected in the upcoming NHibernate 2.0 release. (At the time of this writing, the current release is 1.2.) Another ORM for .NET is LLBLGen Pro (*http://www.llblgen.com*), which is also nearing release and directly supports LINQ. You can find many interesting technical posts about the LINQ to LLBLGen implementation at *http://weblogs.asp.net/fbouma/archive/2008/03/07/developing-linq-to-llblgen-pro-part-14.aspx*. Finally, support for LINQ is already present in the Genome ORM (*http://www.genom-e.com*).

The key point here is that most of the existing ORM tools are going to provide full LINQ support. This is a clear indication that the wide adoption of LINQ for accessing data is taken for granted, at least by ORM vendors and communities.

LINQ to Services

In Chapter 12, we showed the implementation of a LINQ provider that simplifies access to a fictitious FlightStatus service. This exercise was useful for providing you with the knowledge to build LINQ wrappers for your favorite services. In the real world, there are already implementations for widely used services. Most of these implementations are community based and are not officially supported by single-service providers. But we want to emphasize again how LINQ can become the preferred access layer for any kind of data source, even if it is a remote service.

One of the first LINQ wrappers to an external service was LINQ to Amazon (*http:// linqinaction.net/blogs/main/archive/2007/12/12/linq-in-action-samples-source-code.aspx*). With this service, you can look for books in the Amazon catalog, filtering them by attributes such as publisher, price, title, and so on. Similarly, LINQ to Flickr (*http://www.codeplex.com/ LINQFlickr*) allows you to search for photos stored in the Flickr photo-sharing service. LINQ to Flickr also offers support for adding or deleting photos, which is a feature that is not directly tied to the LINQ query syntax but is conceptually similar to the entities you can manage in LINQ to SQL.

Another source for accessing data through remote services is Google. The LINQ to Google implementation (*http://www.codeplex.com/glinq*) actually supports only queries to Google Base, which is a search engine that allows indexing of structured entities decorated with customizable attributes. The presence of attributes that decorate entities makes the use of LINQ meaningful because these attributes can be part of a LINQ query, as shown in the following example:

```
GoogleItems.GoogleContext gc = new GoogleItems.GoogleContext(key);
var r = from    car in gc.products
        where   car.Brand == "Ferrari"
                && car.Price < 200000
        select new { car.Title, car.Price };
```

Another LINQ implementation that could be useful for accessing remote services is LINQ to JSON, which is part of the Json.NET 2.0 library (*http://www.codeplex.com/Json*). This implementation provides a model integrated with LINQ to access data serialized with JSON from a .NET application.

Simplifying access to remote services that provide integration with LINQ queries is an area that will likely see great expansion in the future. The service provider does not need to define its own LINQ wrapper; any user of a service can write his own wrapper for LINQ. However, we expect that the most widely used services will be supported directly by service providers or by projects that are supported by communities.

LINQ for System Engineers

Applications that control an existing infrastructure or that automate administrative tasks might be able to take advantage of LINQ while accessing specific services and APIs useful for their needs.

LINQ to Active Directory (*http://www.codeplex.com/LINQtoAD*) is an implementation that simplifies access to Active Directory APIs, such as *System.DirectoryServices* (.NET) and *ActiveDs* (COM). The same author originally wrote (and analytically described) a more general implementation of LINQ to LDAP (*http://community.bartdesmet.net/blogs/bart/archive/ 2007/04/05/the-iqueryable-tales-linq-to-ldap-part-0.aspx*).

Another interesting LINQ implementation is one that provides access to Windows Management Instrumentation (WMI). An early implementation of a LINQ to WMI provider has been provided at *http://bloggingabout.net/blogs/emile/archive/2005/12/12/10514.aspx*. It was based on a beta version of LINQ and was not feature complete. Recently that code has been upgraded to the released version of .NET Framework 3.5 (*http://www.ridgway.co.za/archive/ 2008/01/02/an-updated-linq-to-wmi-implementation.aspx*). We hope to see a more complete LINQ to WMI implementation very soon.

Dynamic LINQ

The standard result of a LINQ query is considered to be static. It does not change after query execution. However, there are situations in which the definition of a LINQ query should be more dynamic, acting more as a filter in a stream of data or making the query result "live."

The LINQ to Streams implementation (*http://www.codeplex.com/Slinq*) is focused on streaming data, which changes in real time. Currently, it is a simple prototype, but the approach seems interesting for particular scenarios such as network monitors, financial services, and real-time data acquisition.

Another approach to the same issue is the one used in SyncLINQ. This implementation is focused more on data binding over LINQ queries. To support dynamic updates of the query result, a SyncLINQ query returns collections implementing *INotifyCollectionChanged*, which is the interface provided by the .NET Framework to notify listeners of dynamic changes. The SyncLINQ implementation should establish compatibility with existing user interface components that support *INotifyCollectionChanged*.

These implementations do not provide a solution for every tier of an application architecture, but they are an interesting approach to solving some of the issues regarding the use of a common programming pattern (LINQ queries). These implementations attempt to simplify and encapsulate the work necessary to handle dynamic updates to data returned from a query.

Other LINQ Enhancements and Tools

The last section of this chapter is dedicated to other LINQ-related implementations and tools that do not fit into the classifications in the previous sections.

DryadLINQ (*http://research.microsoft.com/research/sv/DryadLINQ*) is a research project that uses LINQ to access Dryad, a distributed execution engine. DryadLINQ compiles lambda expressions into DLLs and routes the DLLs to remote machines for execution. This is a more complex form of parallelism than the one offered by PLINQ and is an interesting implementation for very CPU-intensive applications.

Indexed LINQ, also known as I4O (*http://www.codeplex.com/i4o*), is a class library that allows you to create indexes on objects that are queried using LINQ to Objects. This implementation is particularly interesting for applications that load and maintain a great number of objects in memory. In Chapter 12, we provided an example of one service that belongs in this category: the FlightStatusService, which monitors all the flights around the world in real time. (There are thousands of flights around the world in any moment.) Using optimizations like the one provided by I4O, any object graph in memory can seem like an in-memory database, even if the issues of concurrent access in a multithreaded environment are not automatically solved by LINQ and I4O.

A tool for building LINQ providers is LINQ Extender (*http://www.codeplex.com/LinqExtender*). The LINQ to Flickr provider we mentioned earlier was created using this tool. It is interesting because it provides an extensible model that supports an object-tracking service similar to the one that exists in LINQ to SQL. Another interesting part of LINQ Extender is that it does not require you to extend a parser for an expression tree. The existing parser converts an expression tree into a simpler object that describes the query itself. It is a simplification that might not be good for every application, but you will probably encounter many cases in which a simple provider cannot support complex queries just because the service that it wraps has very simple and limited query semantics.

A library that allows manipulation of a LINQ query is MetaLinq, also called LINQ to Expressions (*http://www.codeplex.com/metalinq*). Unfortunately, the code is based on a beta version of .NET 3.5 and at the time of this writing has not been updated to the released version. However, it is provided with source code and could be adapted by hand. This library offers an object model that allows the manipulation of an expression tree (which could be a query tree) without the limitations imposed by a real expression tree, which is made of immutable objects. The final stage of this manipulation is the creation of an equivalent immutable expression tree that can be used with LINQ.

A very useful tool for writing and testing LINQ queries is LINQPad (*http://www.linqpad.net*). It is an interactive editor and an execution environment for LINQ and SQL queries. It supports queries written using LINQ to SQL, LINQ to Objects, and LINQ to XML. Another interesting tool is LINQ over C# (*http://www.codeplex.com/LinqOverCSharp*), which provides a parser for C# that can be used together with LINQ as a solid base for refactoring code and creating software QA tools.

Finally, LINQ to Geo (*http://www.codeplex.com/LinqToGeo*) is a LINQ implementation for geospatial data, and LINQ to Lucene (*http://www.codeplex.com/linqtolucene*) supports the Lucene Information Retrieval System, which is a free open source search engine.

Summary

In this chapter, we provided an overview of the LINQ implementations, extensions, and tools available at the time of this writing (March 2008). The goal of this chapter was to provide you with a guide to start exploring other LINQ implementations.

You saw alternative LINQ implementations for accessing data in databases and also for accessing data stored in systems other than relational databases. We presented LINQ implementations that support ORMs other than the ADO.NET Entity Framework, and we also described existing wrappers that allow LINQ queries over remote services such as Amazon and Flickr, as well as other standard services, such as Active Directory and WMI. Finally, we described other LINQ implementations and tools that can improve the performance of LINQ providers or simplify the creation of new LINQ providers.

Part V
Applied LINQ

Chapter 15
LINQ in a Multitier Solution

With this chapter, we begin the section "Applied LINQ," which is focused on practical LINQ applications. We will pay particular attention to the effective use of LINQ in common software scenarios. The goals of this part of the book are to show you how to leverage LINQ in everyday solutions and to evaluate the impact of LINQ on modern software architectures and implementations.

We will start by describing some architectural patterns and rules, concentrating on matters related to the data access layer and the business layer. In the upcoming chapters, we will consider the presentation and communication layers, covering the most commonly available and most often used technologies (ASP.NET, Windows Presentation Foundation/Silverlight, and Windows Communcation Foundation) in these fields.

Characteristics of a Multitier Solution

A multitier solution is a software project that usually targets multiple concurrent users and is divided into *n* layers, at least two or three layers in general. In a two-tier scenario, a software application is also referred to as *client-server* software. One layer is represented by the back-end *server* infrastructure, which is generally made up of a database persistence layer. The other layer, the so-called *client*, includes all the code that is required to connect to the back-end database. Generally, in two-tier scenarios, the business logic and domain knowledge required for the solution is implemented within the client software. Sometimes the solution also includes database logic such as intelligent stored procedures, triggers, and so on. A client-server architecture is suitable for a solution being implemented for a small number of users.

We will not cover the client-server scenario in detail because it has many limitations compared to other architectural solutions. In particular, it is limited in terms of scalability. We define software as *scalable* if its performance remains constant and independent regardless of the number of users. Scalable software is not necessarily fast—it simply has a fixed performance score regardless of the number of customers served. The nature of a client-server solution prevents it from being a scalable solution—specifically, an increase in the number of users can have a huge impact on the back-end database layer.

Over the past several years, it has become more and more common to define architectures with at least three tiers to address the need to have scalable solutions. In the Internet era, many software solutions are widely offered on a network and are targeted to a large and unpredictable number of concurrent users. The layers of a three-tier solution are the data access layer, the business layer, and the presentation layer. The data access layer (DAL) represents the set of code and data structures used to implement information persistence.

The business layer (BIZ) defines business logic, business workflows, and rules that drive the behavior of the application. The presentation layer, or user interface (UI) layer, is the part of the software targeted to the end user, and it can be implemented in many different ways, one for each kind of consumer (Web, Windows, smart device, and so on). In general, DAL and BIZ are deployed on specific and dedicated application servers, while the UI can be deployed on any consumer device (Windows, smart device, and so on) or to specific publishing application servers (Web applications on front-end Web servers).

Technologies such as Simple Object Access Protocol (SOAP) services, smart clients, smart phones, workflow services, and so on have influenced many software architects to add other layers. In this way, we have reached a commonly accepted definition of *n*-tier solution architecture as one in which *n* designates a value greater than or at least equal to three. In general, as you can see from Figure 15-1, these *n* layers are targeted to meet specific application requirements such as security, workflow definition, communication, and so on.

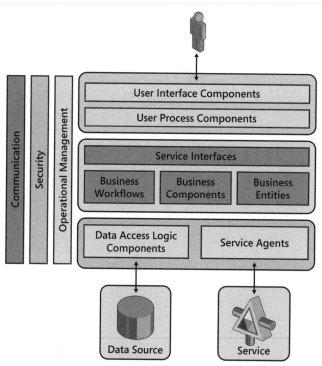

Figure 15-1   Schema of an *n*-tier architecture

The main reason for dividing a software solution's architecture into layers is to improve maintainability, availability, security, and deployment.

Maintainability results from the ability to change and maintain small portions (for example, single layers) of an application without needing to touch the other layers. This way of working allows you to lessen maintenance time and also assess the cost of a fix or a feature change by focusing your attention only on the layers involved in the change. Client-server software is less easy to maintain because every fix or modification of the code needs to be deployed to each client, which results in a high cost of ownership. A well-defined multitier solution is also available to users more often because critical or highly stressed layers can be deployed in a redundant infrastructure.

From a security perspective, a layered solution can make use of different security modules, each one tightly aligned with a particular software layer to make the solution stronger. Last but not least, multitier software is usually deployed more easily because each layer can be configured and sized somewhat independently from each other.

> **Note**   In this chapter, we will use the well-known Northwind database as the persistence storage location for a sample multitier solution.

LINQ to SQL in a Two-Tier Solution

From a LINQ perspective, the architecture of a two-tier solution is one of the ideal hosts for a LINQ to SQL implementation. You can use LINQ to SQL entities to model each database table, as well as to query and manage these entities (server tables) from the consumer (client). In a two-tier solution you can also leverage the extensibility of the LINQ to SQL *DataContext* object, which is available through partial methods.

For instance, consider the Customers and Orders tables of the Northwind database and the corresponding domain model entities (shown in Figure 15-2).

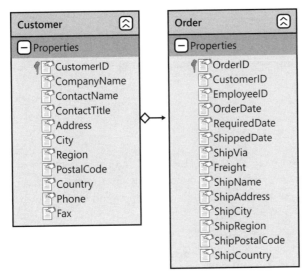

Figure 15-2   The domain model used in LINQ to SQL examples

If you want to save a single *Customer* instance with its related *Order* instances, you can use the approach we described in Chapter 5, "LINQ to SQL: Managing Data." The Object Relational Designer integrated into Microsoft Visual Studio 2008 automatically generates some partial methods that are useful for defining a customized behavior for customer and order insertion, deletion, and updating. Listing 15-1 contains a code excerpt taken from an autogenerated *DataContext* type.

Listing 15-1   The partial methods of an autogenerated *DataContext*

```
[System.Data.Linq.Mapping.DatabaseAttribute(Name="Northwind")]
public partial class NorthwindDataContext : System.Data.Linq.DataContext {

    private static System.Data.Linq.Mapping.MappingSource mappingSource =
        new AttributeMappingSource();

    #region Extensibility Method Definitions
    partial void OnCreated();
    partial void InsertCustomer(Customer instance);
    partial void UpdateCustomer(Customer instance);
    partial void DeleteCustomer(Customer instance);
    partial void InsertOrder(Order instance);
    partial void UpdateOrder(Order instance);
    #endregion
    // ...
    }
```

As you can see, the partial methods *Insert*TYPE, *Delete*TYPE, and *Update*TYPE are generated and made available to make it easier for you to customize the behavior of the *DataContext* object during the most common data modification operations.

LINQ in an *n*-Tier Solution

In this section we will evaluate the role of the various LINQ implementations in an *n*-tier solution, where in general *n*-tier refers to three or more layers. We will start from the data access layer and then move to the business layer.

LINQ to SQL as a DAL Replacement

The first step in defining any *n*-tier solution architecture is to identify and describe the domain model, which is the set of entities used by the system. If you want to drive a database design from a domain model, you can create the physical database from the LINQ to SQL entity model by using the *CreateDatabase* method of the *DataContext* object. On the other hand, if your database structure has already been defined or you prefer to use specific database features in your domain model (such as triggers, functions, views, stored procedures, and so on), you can model LINQ to SQL entities starting from existing tables.

More Info   More details about the different ways of working with LINQ to SQL and the tools you can use can be found in Chapter 6, "Tools for LINQ to SQL."

Regardless of the way in which you define the physical database and the corresponding LINQ to SQL entity model, using LINQ to SQL as your data layer results in LINQ to SQL entities being used by the entire application architecture. This last point means that the types defined for LINQ to SQL, such as the *Customer* and *Order* entities discussed earlier, will be used throughout the application. For instance, a presentation layer implemented using WPF will share these types with LINQ to SQL and be able to perform data binding against a sequence of type *IEnumerable<Customer>* that is obtained by executing a LINQ query over an instance of *Table<Customer>* provided by a *DataContext* instance.

This situation has both advantages and disadvantages. The advantages come from the agility and ease of use offered by LINQ to SQL. By taking a closer look at the code generated and defined by LINQ to SQL tools (such as SQLMetal or the Object Relational Designer in Microsoft Visual Studio 2008), you can see that these types implement a set of interfaces targeted to UI data binding: *INotifyPropertyChanging* and *INotifyPropertyChanged*.

On the other hand, the nature of LINQ to SQL means that the data layer will be tightly integrated with the Microsoft SQL Server database. This level of integration might be your goal for a single-database-platform solution, but it can also pose limitations for your architecture.

In general, a data layer is defined as an abstraction of the physical persistence layer, thus allowing changes to the back-end implementation that are transparent to the layers above it. The abstraction from the physical persistence layer is usually achieved by defining a domain model that is independent from the database, enabling the DAL and BIZ layers to communicate by using the entities that belong to the independent domain model. However, when using LINQ to SQL as a pure data layer replacement, you are forced to work with Microsoft SQL Server and your entities will be widely marked in code with attributes mapping to Microsoft SQL Server specific information. In addition, at times you might already have a domain model defined simply because you are extending an existing application or because you do not want to mark your domain model with data-layer-specific (LINQ to SQL) attributes.

To avoid these issues, you can take a few steps forward in the direction of real abstraction by using one of the techniques illustrated in the next sections.

Abstracting LINQ to SQL with XML External Mapping

To accomplish abstraction from the database layer, the first step you can take is to define an external XML mapping for your LINQ to SQL entities. We describe an example of this approach at the end of Chapter 5, in the "Binding Metadata" section. By using an external XML mapping, you can keep your entities free from any LINQ to SQL code attributes, and you can leverage already existing entities, mapping them to LINQ to SQL. Listing 15-2 recalls sample excerpts from Chapter 5 for your convenience.

Listing 15-2   The code to define a *DataContext* based on an external XML mapping file

```
public partial class Northwind : System.Data.Linq.DataContext {

    // Extensibility Method Definitions

    public Northwind(string connection,
        System.Data.Linq.Mapping.MappingSource mappingSource) :
            base(connection, mappingSource) {
        OnCreated();
    }

    public Northwind(System.Data.IDbConnection connection,
        System.Data.Linq.Mapping.MappingSource mappingSource) :
            base(connection, mappingSource) {
        OnCreated();
    }

    public System.Data.Linq.Table<Customer> Customers {
        get {
            return this.GetTable<Customer>();
        }
    }

    public System.Data.Linq.Table<Order> Orders {
        get {
            return this.GetTable<Order>();
        }
    }
}
```

As you can see, the *DataContext* type provides a couple of constructors, both of which require an argument of type *MappingSource*. This argument represents a link to an external XML mapping file such as the one illustrated in Listing 15-3.

Listing 15-3   The XML mapping file for the Northwind *DataContext*

```
<?xml version="1.0" encoding="utf-8"?>
<Database Name="northwind"
 xmlns="http://schemas.microsoft.com/linqtosql/mapping/2007">
  <Table Name="dbo.Customers" Member="Customers">
    <Type Name="Customer">
      <Column Name="CustomerID" Member="CustomerID" Storage="_CustomerID"
              DbType="NChar(5) NOT NULL" CanBeNull="false"
              IsPrimaryKey="true" />
      <Column Name="CompanyName" Member="CompanyName"
              Storage="_CompanyName" DbType="NVarChar(40) NOT NULL"
              CanBeNull="false" />
      <Column Name="ContactName" Member="ContactName"
              Storage="_ContactName" DbType="NVarChar(30)" />

      ...

      <Association Name="FK_Orders_Customers" Member="Orders"
                Storage="_Orders" ThisKey="CustomerID"
```

```
                        OtherKey="CustomerID" DeleteRule="NO ACTION" />
    </Type>
  </Table>
  <Table Name="dbo.Orders" Member="Orders">
    <Type Name="Orders">
      <Column Name="OrderID" Member="OrderID" Storage="_OrderID"
              DbType="Int NOT NULL IDENTITY" IsPrimaryKey="true"
              IsDbGenerated="true" AutoSync="OnInsert" />
      <Column Name="CustomerID" Member="CustomerID" Storage="_CustomerID"
              DbType="NChar(5)" />
      <Column Name="OrderDate" Member="OrderDate" Storage="_OrderDate"
              DbType="DateTime" />

      ...

      <Association Name="FK_Orders_Customers" Member="Customers"
                   Storage="_Customers" ThisKey="CustomerID"
                   OtherKey="CustomerID" IsForeignKey="true" />
    </Type>
  </Table>
    ...
</Database>
```

To load a *DataContext* instance with an external XML mapping file, you can call its constructor and provide an *XmlMappingSource* instance, as we do in Listing 15-4.

Listing 15-4   The code to load the Northwind *DataContext* with a custom XML mapping file

```
NorthwindDataContext nwind = new NorthwindDataContext(
    ConfigurationManager.ConnectionStrings["Northwind"].ConnectionString,
    XmlMappingSource.FromUrl(
        ConfigurationManager.AppSettings["NorthwindModelUrl"]));
```

The *XmlMappingSource* class is just one class inherited from the abstract *MappingSource* type. The *DataContext* constructor accepts any type derived from *MappingSource*, which means you can define your own mapping using any kind of custom entity schema definition.

Using an external mapping schema might seem to be a practice that satisfies the needs of abstraction and entity independence, but it is not a real solution. The source code that defines the entities still needs to be specific to LINQ to SQL. For instance, consider the relationship between each *Customer* and his *Order* instances. In Listing 15-5, you can see that the *Customer* type requires a field of type *EntitySet<Order>*. Also, the *Order* type, omitted from the following example, has a field of type *EntityRef<Customer>*. Those types and fields are completely tied to LINQ to SQL.

Listing 15-5   Code excerpt of the *Customer* type based on external XML mapping

```
public partial class Customer : INotifyPropertyChanging, INotifyPropertyChanged {

    private string _CustomerID;
    private string _CompanyName;
```

```
    // ... code omitted ...

    private EntitySet<Order> _Orders;
    // Extensibility Method Definitions
    // ... code omitted ...

    public EntitySet<Order> Orders {
        get {
            return this._Orders;
        }
        set {
            this._Orders.Assign(value);
        }
    }

    // ... code omitted ...
    private void attach_Orders(Order entity) {
        this.SendPropertyChanging();
        entity.Customer = this;
    }

    private void detach_Orders(Order entity)
    {
        this.SendPropertyChanging();
        entity.Customer = null;
    }
}
```

The resulting class is still not truly independent and abstracted from LINQ to SQL. Even so, using an external mapping source is useful whenever you want to separate the entity source code from the mapping information. For example, you might want to translate type names from the database structure to the software architecture, to join a custom mapping source with a LINQ to SQL entity model, or to specify provider-specific attributes that differentiate SQL Server 2000 from SQL Server 2005 databases that use the source code from the same entities.

Using LINQ to SQL Through Real Abstraction

When you need to truly and effectively hide the LINQ to SQL implementation from the upper layers, you should create a real object-oriented abstraction. For instance, you can define your domain model to be independent from any particular data layer implementation, including LINQ to SQL or anything else, by defining a dedicated assembly with your own custom entities. Using this approach, you implement what is known as *persistence ignorance*. In Listing 15-6, you can see an example of *Customer* and *Order* types of this kind.

Listing 15-6   The *Customer* and *Order* types defined in an independent domain model

```
namespace DevLeap.Linq.Architecture.NTier.DomainModel {
    public abstract class BaseEntity {
        // Here there could be some common behaviors and properties
    }
    public class Customer : BaseEntity {
        public String CustomerID { get; set; }
        public String CompanyName { get; set; }
```

```
        public String ContactName { get; set; }
        public String ContactTitle { get; set; }
        public String Address { get; set; }
        public String City { get; set; }
        public String Region { get; set; }
        public String PostalCode { get; set; }
        public String Country { get; set; }
        public String Phone { get; set; }
        public String Fax { get; set; }
        public List<Order> Orders { get; set; }
    }
    public class Order : BaseEntity {
        public Int32 OrderID { get; set; }
        public String CustomerID { get; set; }

        // ... code omitted ...
    }
}
```

These types are simple and look like data transfer objects (DTO) rather than domain model entities. However, remember that this example is just for the sake of illustration. In a real solution, these entities will probably include some domain model logic such as validation rules, constraints, and so on. In Figure 15-3, you can see the class diagram corresponding to the actual domain model.

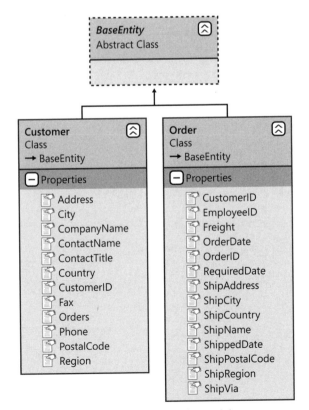

Figure 15-3   The abstract domain model

In the sample code that follows, we will work only with *Customer* instances, and any *Order* instance will be available only through its corresponding *Customer* object. To begin, consider the implementation of the data layer as a set of Data Mappers, each one providing a kind of CRUD (Create, Read, Update and Delete) operation for each domain model entity.

> **Note**   A Data Mapper is a software layer that transfers data between the database and in-memory objects. You can find the definition of a Data Mapper at *http://www.martinfowler.com/eaaCatalog/dataMapper.html.*

To keep the business layer independent from the data layer implementation and from the persistence storage, you can define an interface and a *Factory* that creates Data Mapper instances implementing a specific interface. An example is shown in Listing 15-7.

Listing 15-7   An abstract interface for a Data Mapper acting as a CRUD on the *Customer* entity

```
namespace DevLeap.Linq.Architecture.NTier.DataLayer {
    public interface ICustomerDal {
        /// <summary>
        /// Adds a new customer to the persistence storage
        /// </summary>
        /// <param name="item">The customer instance to add</param>
        /// <returns>The customer that has just been added</returns>
        Customer Add(Customer item);

        /// <summary>
        /// Reads a customer instance from the persistence storage
        /// </summary>
        /// <param name="key">The key to extract the customer instance</param>
        /// <returns>The customer instance if it exists</returns>
        Customer Read(String key);

        /// <summary>
        /// Reads all the available customer instances from the
        /// persistence storage
        /// </summary>
        /// <returns>The list of existing customers</returns>
        /// <remarks>In a real scenario, there could be a filtering condition,
        /// eventually expressed using a LINQ query expression</remarks>
        List<Customer> ReadAll();

        /// <summary>
        /// Updates a customer into the persistence storage
        /// </summary>
        /// <param name="item">The customer instance to update</param>
        /// <returns>The customer that has just been updated</returns>
        Customer Update(Customer item);

        /// <summary>
        /// Deletes a customer from the persistence storage
        /// </summary>
```

```
        /// <param name="item">The customer to delete</param>
        /// <returns>The result of the deleting operation</returns>
        Boolean Delete(Customer item);
    }
}
```

In Listing 15-7, we defined a simplified interface dedicated to the *Customer* entity. We could do this for every single entity of the domain model that requires a dedicated Data Mapper. However, starting with .NET 2.0, we can use generic types to define a kind of code "prototype." Thus, we can replace the code in Listing 15-7 with a generic interface suitable for many of the entities in the domain model. You can see how to do this in Listing 15-8.

Listing 15-8   An abstract and generic interface defining a Data Mapper for every entity in the domain model

```
namespace DevLeap.Linq.Architecture.NTier.DataLayer {
    public interface IDal<TEntity, TEntityList, TKey>
        where TEntity : BaseEntity, new()
        where TEntityList : IEnumerable<TEntity> {

        /// <summary>
        /// Adds a new entity to the persistence storage
        /// </summary>
        /// <param name="item">The entity  instance to add</param>
        /// <returns>The entity that has just been added</returns>
        TEntity Add(TEntity item);

        /// <summary>
        /// Reads an entity instance from the persistence storage
        /// </summary>
        /// <param name="key">The key to extract the entity instance</param>
        /// <returns>The entity instance if it exists</returns>
        TEntity Read(TKey key);

        /// <summary>
        /// Reads all the available entity instances from the persistence storage
        /// </summary>
        /// <returns>The list of existing entities</returns>
        /// <remarks>In a real scenario, there could be a filtering condition,
        /// eventually expressed using a LINQ query expression</remarks>
        TEntityList ReadAll();

        /// <summary>
        /// Updates an entity in the persistence storage
        /// </summary>
        /// <param name="item">The entity instance to update</param>
        /// <returns>The entity that has just been updated</returns>
        TEntity Update(TEntity item);

        /// <summary>
        /// Deletes an entity from the persistence storage
        /// </summary>
```

```
        /// <param name="item">The entity to delete</param>
        /// <returns>The result of the deleting operation</returns>
        Boolean Delete(TEntity item);
    }
}
```

This generic interface can be implemented for each entity to define the entity's generic arguments. *TEntity* is the type of the entity, which should be inherited from *BaseEntity* and requires a default constructor. *TEntityList* is the type used to represent a sequence of entities and should implement *IEnumerable<TEntity>* to be queryable from the business layer using LINQ to Objects. *TKey* is the type of the unique key, which is useful for uniquely identifying an entity of type *TEntity*.

From the business layer point of view, the data layer will be just a set of classes implementing this generic interface. In this way, the BIZ will completely ignore how the real data layer constructed by the factory is implemented.

We won't cover the implementation of the data layer factory here, but you can find a fully functional example in the sample source code of this book. Of course, the solution we are presenting is fictitious and is useful just to illustrate LINQ concepts. This architecture should be revised and completed to be used in a real solution.

Now let's move our attention to the role of LINQ to SQL within this infrastructure. To completely abstract our solution from any specific data layer, including a LINQ to SQL implementation, we need to define the real data layer implementation in a dedicated assembly that will be loaded through the data layer factory instead of being directly referenced. Inside this referenced assembly, there will be the code using LINQ to SQL. Only domain model entities will travel across the boundaries between any DAL implementation and the BIZ layer consumer: not data tables, not LINQ to SQL entities, and not anything else.

To meet this last requirement, the LINQ to SQL–based data layer will translate back and forth all its own entities to the domain model entities. To better organize the code, we defined a *BaseDal* abstract and generic class from which every entity-specific data layer type will be derived. In Listing 15-9, you can see a possible implementation of the *BaseDal* type.

Listing 15-9   A hypothetical implementation of the *BaseDal* type

```
using System;
using System.Collections.Generic;
using System.Linq;
using System.Text;
using DomainModel = DevLeap.Linq.Architecture.NTier.DomainModel;

namespace DevLeap.Linq.Architecture.NTier.DataLayer.LinqToSql {
    public class BaseDal<TEntity, TEntityList, TKey>:
        IDal<TEntity, TEntityList, TKey>
        where TEntity : BaseEntity, new()
        where TEntityList : IEnumerable<TEntity> {
```

```
        private NorthwindDataContext _northwind;
        protected NorthwindDataContext Northwind {
            get { return this._northwind; }
        }

        protected BaseDal(){
            _northwind = new NorthwindDataContext(nwConnectionString);
        }

        #region IDal<TEntity,TEntityList,TKey> Members
        // ... Code omitted ...
        #endregion
    }
}
```

The definition of the read-only protected property named *Northwind* corresponds to an instance of the LINQ to SQL *DataContext*. Seeing that every LINQ to SQL data-layer class will need to access the *DataContext*, and given that the *DataContext* should be instantiated and destroyed for each unit of work, in this sample we decided to use a *DataContext* instance dedicated to each data layer domain model entity, assuming that we are in a loosely coupled environment because of the *n*-tier architecture.

Every data layer type will inherit the *BaseDal* abstract class, implementing the real behavior related to the entity to manage. For instance, in Listing 15-10 you can see an excerpt of the *Read* method in the *CustomerDal* type.

Listing 15-10   The first hypothetical implementation of a part of the *CustomerDal* type

```
using System;
using System.Collections.Generic;
using System.Linq;
using System.Text;
using DomainModel = DevLeap.Linq.Architecture.NTier.DomainModel;
namespace DevLeap.Linq.Architecture.NTier.DataLayer.LinqToSql {
    public class CustomerDal :
        BaseDal<DomainModel.Customer, List< DomainModel.Customer>, String>

        // ... Code omitted ...

        public override DomainModel.Customer Read(string key) {

            // Get the first LINQ to SQL customer entity
            // instance with the provided key
            var linqCustomer = this.Northwind.Customers
                .First(c => c.CustomerID == key);

            // Convert it into a Domain Model customer
            var result = new DomainModel.Customer {
                    CustomerID = linqCustomer.CustomerID,
                    Address = linqCustomer.Address,
                    City = linqCustomer.City,
                    CompanyName = linqCustomer.CompanyName,
                    ContactName = linqCustomer.ContactName,
                    ContactTitle = linqCustomer.ContactTitle,
```

```
                        Country = linqCustomer.Country,
                        Fax = linqCustomer.Fax,
                        Phone = linqCustomer.Phone,
                        PostalCode = linqCustomer.PostalCode,
                        Region = linqCustomer.Region
                    };

            result.Orders = new List<DomainModel.Order>();

            // Convert every order obtained from LINQ to SQL
            // into an Order of the Domain Model
            foreach (var o in linqCustomer.Orders) {
                result.Orders.Add(new DomainModel.Order {
                    OrderID - o.OrderID,
                    CustomerID = o.CustomerID,
                    EmployeeID = o.EmployeeID,
                    Freight = o.Freight,
                    OrderDate = o.OrderDate,
                    RequiredDate = o.RequiredDate,
                    ShipAddress = o.ShipAddress,
                    ShipCity = o.ShipCity,
                    ShipCountry = o.ShipCountry,
                    ShipName = o.ShipName,
                    ShippedDate = o.ShippedDate,
                    ShipPostalCode = o.ShipPostalCode,
                    ShipRegion = o.ShipRegion,
                    ShipVia = o.ShipVia
                });
            }
            return (result);
        }

        // ... Code omitted ...

    }
}
```

The code in Listing 15-10 is completely functional and syntactically correct. However, it is a little bit verbose and redundant. Never underestimate the power and expressiveness of LINQ syntax! In Listing 15-11, you can see the same method implemented using a single LINQ query expression.

Listing 15-11 The final implementation of a part of the *CustomerDal* type

```
using System;
using System.Collections.Generic;
using System.Linq;
using System.Text;
using DomainModel = DevLeap.Linq.Architecture.NTier.DomainModel;

namespace DevLeap.Linq.Architecture.NTier.DataLayer.LinqToSql {
    public class CustomerDal :
        BaseDal<DomainModel.Customer, List< DomainModel.Customer>, String>
```

```
        // ... Code omitted ...

    public override DomainModel.Customer Read(string key) {
        // Convert the first LINQ to SQL customer
        // into a Domain Model customer using a
        // LINQ query expression
        var result =
            (from c in this.Northwind.Customers
             where c.CustomerID == key
             select new DomainModel.Customer {
                 CustomerID = c.CustomerID,
                 Address = c.Address,
                 City = c.City,
                 CompanyName = c.CompanyName,
                 ContactName = c.ContactName,
                 ContactTitle = c.ContactTitle,
                 Country = c.Country,
                 Fax = c.Fax,
                 Phone = c.Phone,
                 PostalCode = c.PostalCode,
                 Region = c.Region,
                 // Converts the list of orders of the
                 // LINQ to SQL customer into the list of
                 // orders defined in the Domain Model
                 // using a LINQ subquery
                 Orders = new List<DomainModel.Order>(
                     from o in c.Orders
                     select new DomainModel.Order {
                         OrderID = o.OrderID,
                         CustomerID = o.CustomerID,
                         EmployeeID = o.EmployeeID,
                         Freight = o.Freight,
                         OrderDate = o.OrderDate,
                         RequiredDate = o.RequiredDate,
                         ShipAddress = o.ShipAddress,
                         ShipCity = o.ShipCity,
                         ShipCountry = o.ShipCountry,
                         ShipName = o.ShipName,
                         ShippedDate = o.ShippedDate,
                         ShipPostalCode = o.ShipPostalCode,
                         ShipRegion = o.ShipRegion,
                         ShipVia = o.ShipVia
                     })
             }).First();

        return (result);
    }

    // ... Code omitted ...

    }
}
```

The difference between Listing 15-10 and Listing 15-11 is just syntactical; the performance of both method implementations is the same because they both query Microsoft SQL Server with the same queries. However, this is only a simple example. There could be more complex situations in which using a single query expression would give you better performance, allowing the LINQ to SQL engine to execute optimized SQL queries. Working with legacy-style procedural code does not allow for any kind of implicit platform optimization.

The key point of this example is that you can replace the LINQ to SQL data layer implementation with any kind of data layer that supports the same contracts (interfaces, base classes, and domain model entities). The technology used within the data access layer is completely transparent to the upper layers, so you are realizing a real abstraction over the DAL and LINQ to SQL without losing the power and simplicity of LINQ to SQL programming. In the book's sample code, you can find the full implementation of the LINQ to SQL–based data layer.

LINQ to XML as the Data Layer

To demonstrate the real abstraction achieved in the previous section, we built a LINQ to XML–based data layer suitable for a full and transparent substitution of the actual data layer based on LINQ to SQL.

Imagine having an XML file that stores customers and orders (NorthwindCustomersWithOrders.XML). In Listing 15-12, you can see an excerpt of this file.

Listing 15-12   An excerpt of the NorthwindCustomersWithOrders.XML persistence file

```xml
<?xml version="1.0" encoding="utf-8"?>
<Northwind>
  <customer>
    <customerID>ALFKI</customerID>
    <address>Obere Str. 57</address>
    <city>Berlin</city>
    <companyName>Alfreds Futterkiste</companyName>
    <contactName>Maria Anders</contactName>
    <contactTitle>Sales Representative</contactTitle>
    <country>Germany</country>
    <fax>030-0076545</fax>
    <phone>030-0074321</phone>
    <postalCode>12209</postalCode>
    <region />
    <orders>
      <order>
        <orderId>10643</orderId>
        <employeeID>6</employeeID>
        <freight>29.4600</freight>
        <orderDate>1997-08-25T00:00:00</orderDate>
        <requiredDate>1997-09-22T00:00:00</requiredDate>
        <shipAddress>Obere Str. 57</shipAddress>
        <shipCity>Berlin</shipCity>
        <shipCountry>Germany</shipCountry>
        <shipName>Alfreds Futterkiste</shipName>
```

```
        <shippedDate>1997-09-02T00:00:00</shippedDate>
        <shipPostalCode>12209</shipPostalCode>
        <shipRegion />
        <shipVia>1</shipVia>
      </order>
      <order>
        <!-- XML code omitted -->
      </order>
    </orders>
  </customer>
  <!-- XML code omitted -->
  <customer>
    <customerID>WOLZA</customerID>
    <address>ul. Filtrowa 68</address>
    <city>Warszawa</city>
    <companyName>Wolski  Zajazd</companyName>
    <contactName>Zbyszek Piestrzeniewicz</contactName>
    <!-- XML code omitted -->
  </customer>
</Northwind>
```

We can build a data layer that works with LINQ to XML and provides data mapping functionalities to the BIZ by abstracting it from the physical persistence storage. In Listing 15-13, you
can see a sample implementation of the *CustomerDal* type for the LINQ to XML data layer
implementation.

Listing 15-13   An excerpt of the *Read* method of the *CustomerDal* based on LINQ to XML

```
namespace DevLeap.Linq.Architecture.NTier.DataLayer.LinqToXml {
  public class CustomerDal :
    BaseDal<DomainModel.Customer,
    IEnumerable<DomainModel.Customer>, String> {

    // ... Code omitted ...

    public override DomainModel.Customer Read(string key) {
      var result =
        (from x in this.NorthwindXml.Descendants("customer")
        where x.Element("customerID").Value == key
        select new DomainModel.Customer {
          CustomerID = (String)x.Element("customerID"),
          Address = (String)x.Element("address"),
          City = (String)x.Element("city"),
          CompanyName = (String)x.Element("companyName"),
          ContactName = (String)x.Element("contactName"),
          ContactTitle = (String)x.Element("contactTitle"),
          Country = (String)x.Element("country"),
          Fax = (String)x.Element("fax"),
          Phone = (String)x.Element("phone"),
          PostalCode = (String)x.Element("postalCode"),
          Region = (String)x.Element("region"),
          // Converts the list of orders of the LINQ to SQL customer
          // into the list of orders defined in the Domain Model
```

```
        Orders = new
          List<DevLeap.Linq.Architecture.NTier.DomainModel.Order>(
            from ox in x.Element("orders").Elements("order")
            select new DomainModel.Order {
              OrderID = (Int32)ox.Element("orderID"),
              CustomerID = (String)x.Element("customerID"),
              EmployeeID = (String.IsNullOrEmpty(
                  ox.Element("employeeID").Value) ? null :
                  (Int32?)ox.Element("employeeID")),
              Freight = (String.IsNullOrEmpty(
                  ox.Element("freight").Value) ? null :
                  (Decimal?)ox.Element("freight")),
              OrderDate = (String.IsNullOrEmpty(
                  ox.Element("orderDate").Value) ? null :
                  (DateTime?)ox.Element("orderDate")),
              RequiredDate = (String.IsNullOrEmpty(
                  ox.Element("requiredDate").Value) ? null :
                  (DateTime?)ox.Element("requiredDate")),
              ShipAddress = (String)ox.Element("shipAddress"),
              ShipCity = (String)ox.Element("shipCity"),
              ShipCountry = (String)ox.Element("shipCountry"),
              ShipName = (String)ox.Element("shipName"),
              ShippedDate = (String.IsNullOrEmpty(
                  ox.Element("shippedDate").Value) ? null :
                  (DateTime?)ox.Element("shippedDate")),
              ShipPostalCode = (String)ox.Element("shipPostalCode"),
              ShipRegion = (String)ox.Element("shipRegion"),
              ShipVia = (String.IsNullOrEmpty(
                  ox.Element("shipVia").Value) ? null :
                  (Int32?)ox.Element("shipVia")),
            })
          }).First();
        return (result);
      }
      // ... Code omitted ...
    }
  }
}
```

As you can see, the *Read* method implementation works with a LINQ to XML query to extract the required customer element, and it converts the customer element into the domain model *Customer* entity by using a LINQ query expression. The *CustomerDal* type has a base class that simply implements the light logic to load and save the *XElement* that corresponds to the entire XML storage file. In Listing 15-14, you can see its implementation.

Listing 15-14   An excerpt of the *BaseDal* abstract base class for a LINQ to XML–based data layer

```
namespace DevLeap.Linq.Architecture.NTier.DataLayer.LinqToXml {
    public abstract class BaseDal<TEntity, TEntityList, TKey>:
        IDal<TEntity, TEntityList, TKey>
            where TEntity : BaseEntity, new()
            where TEntityList : IEnumerable<TEntity> {
        private XElement _northwindXml;
        protected XElement NorthwindXml {
```

```
            get { return (this._northwindXml); }
        }

        protected BaseDal() {
            _northwindXml = XElement.Load(XmlDataSourcePath);
        }

        protected void Save() {
            this.NorthwindXml.Save(XmlDataSourcePath);
        }

        #region IDal<TEntity,TEntityList,TKey> Members
        // ... Code omitted ...
        #endregion
    }
}
```

LINQ to Entities as the Data Layer

One more option is to use LINQ to Entities and the ADO.NET Entity Framework to query and manage data in the persistence storage component, leveraging one of the main features of the ADO.NET Entity Framework: database platform independence. LINQ to Entities supports many different data providers out of the box, and there are many third-party software companies planning to support it. (For more information, go to *http://blogs.msdn.com/adonet/ archive/2007/12/17/the-ado-net-entity-framework-not-just-for-sql-server.aspx.*)

 More Info   For more details on LINQ to Entities and the ADO.NET Entity Framework, see Chapter 8, "LINQ to Entities," and Appendix A, "ADO.NET Entity Framework."

Because of the native abstraction provided by LINQ to Entities, you probably would choose to use its infrastructure whenever you really need to abstract from the data layer, and this would be OK. On the other hand (and one more time), this decision could have an impact on your domain model, thus causing you to miss out on one of the main requirements for real data layer abstraction: the persistence ignorance of the domain model. In fact, by now the ADO.NET Entity Framework (which is at the beta stage at the time of writing this book) supports many providers through an open and public query provider model. However, it is still missing support for complete persistence ignorance. Technically speaking, the ADO.NET Entity Framework supports two different scenarios:

- **Prescriptive classes**, which are types inheriting a specific base class, which works directly with the persistence storage. Usually, these classes are automatically generated using a supporting tool.

- **IPOCO (Interface-Based Plain Old CLR Objects)**, which are entity types that need to implement certain specific interfaces to support features such as persistence, change tracking, relationships, identifying keys, and so on.

You cannot use your own domain model entities as they are; instead, you need to partially change their implementation to make them usable with the ADO.NET Entity Framework and queryable through LINQ to Entities. These considerations lead us to conclude that it is wise to consider LINQ to Entities in its first released version as a data layer replacement, in addition to LINQ to SQL. LINQ to Entities makes it easier to support different persistence storage platforms simply by changing the mapping configuration, while LINQ to SQL supports only Microsoft SQL Server. However, if you need real and complete persistence ignorance, you still need to define an abstraction layer of your own.

LINQ in the Business Layer

Regardless of how you implement your data and persistence layers, modern *n*-tier solutions have a business layer that is useful for many reasons. The benefits of having a well-defined business layer include:

- **Security enforcement.** Every single activity or operation made by any user should come through the business layer, which should be the central place where you enforce security policies. In this way, regardless of the presentation layer (WPF, Silverlight, Windows Forms, ASP.NET, etc.) and the communication infrastructure (WCF, ASMX, .NET Remoting, etc.) you use, there will be one place where security policies will be checked and enforced. This behavior helps avoid ambiguity and improves maintainability too.

- **Business logic validation and rules enforcement.** In addition to security policies, business logic validation policies and business rules should be enforced in a single place. The business layer is the right place to check these policies and rules. Declarative rules in the domain model, such as attributes, constraints, and referential integrity checks, are only part of the possible logic that a complex application requires. They should be considered complimentary (sometimes redundant) to the rules defined in the business logic layer.

- **Business processes coordination.** Quite often during the last few years, and probably more and more in the next few years, business logic consists of complex business processes that coordinate other business components and external services (think about SOA, SaS, and S+S).

- **Transaction coordination.** As we just mentioned, a business process can coordinate many different services and business components and can involve many different data providers. Consequently, the business layer is the only place where a business process can determine the outcome of a transactional activity, regardless of whether it is a local or a distributed transaction.

- **Simplified maintenance.** If all the logic, processes, and rules are defined in a unique place (the business layer), you also gain benefits in maintenance. Any logic or process modification will affect only the business layer, making both testing and deployment of changes faster.

LINQ to Objects to Write Better Code

The business layer works with your domain model entities, transferring them back and forth from the data layer and using them in business logic, processes, and rules. On top of the business layer, an application could have a communication layer to separate physical software layers, or there could be the UI. In both cases you can use LINQ query expressions in the BIZ code to more easily write algorithms and procedures.

For instance, imagine having a business process to print refund forms for all orders shipped later than the *RequiredDate*. The process filters for customers by country. Working with classic procedural code, you would probably extract from the data layer all customers grouped by country, query all the orders that have been delivered late, and then create a refund form, saving the result back to the persistence layer. Because this business process occurs periodically, it is defined as a *Refund* method of the *CustomersBiz* class. In Listing 15-15, you can see a "legacy style" implementation for such a business method.

Listing 15-15   A "legacy style" business method to refund customers for late delivered orders

```
public void RefundLegacy() {
    // Temporary repository for delayed orders, grouped by country
    SortedDictionary<String, List<Order>> ordersToRefundByCountry =
        new SortedDictionary<String, List<Order>>();

    // Get the full list of customers
    // In real life be careful on this kind of "full scan" methods!
    var customers = this._dal.ReadAll();
    foreach (var c in customers) {
        foreach (var o in c.Orders) {
            // If the order is late
            if (o.RequiredDate < o.ShippedDate) {
                // Check if the current customer country already exists
                if (!ordersToRefundByCountry.ContainsKey(c.Country)) {
                    // Otherwise create it
                    ordersToRefundByCountry[c.Country] = new List<Order>();
                }
                // Add the order to the list
                ordersToRefundByCountry[c.Country].Add(o);
            }
        }
    }

    Int32 itemsCount = 0;
    foreach (var itemsGroup in ordersToRefundByCountry) {
        foreach (var item in itemsGroup.Value) {
            // Imagine that here you create and send the refund form
            Console.WriteLine("Country: {0} - CustomerID: {1} - OrderID:
                {2} - DelayedDays: {3}",
                itemsGroup.Key, item.CustomerID, item.OrderID,
```

```
        ((TimeSpan)item.ShippedDate.Value.Subtract(item.RequiredDate.Value)).Days);
                itemsCount++;
            }
        }

        Console.WriteLine("Total count of orders to refund: {0}", itemsCount);
    }
```

The same business method could be re-written using LINQ to Objects and LINQ queries. In Listing 15-16, you can see a hypothetical LINQ style implementation.

Listing 15-16   A "LINQ style" business method to refund customers for orders delivered late

```
public void Refund() {
    var customersWithOrdersToRefund =
        (from c in this._dal.ReadAll()
        group c by c.Country into customersByCountry
            from i in customersByCountry
            from o in i.Orders
            where o.RequiredDate < o.ShippedDate
            orderby i.Country
                select new {
                        i.Country,
                        i.CustomerID,
                        o.OrderID,
                        DelayedDays =
((TimeSpan)o.ShippedDate.Value.Subtract(o.RequiredDate.Value)).Days }).ToList();

    foreach (var item in customersWithOrdersToRefund) {
        // Imagine that here you create and send the refund form
        Console.WriteLine(item);
    }

    Console.WriteLine("Total count of orders to refund: {0}",
        customersWithOrdersToRefund.Count());
}
```

As you can see, the code is more readable. It can also be more efficient, even if only under specific circumstances and conditions, as you will see in the next section.

IQueryable<T> versus *IEnumerable<T>*

Until now, we have worked with LINQ to SQL in the data layer and LINQ to Objects in the business layer. The methods that read the entities from the persistence storage return objects of type *IEnumerable<T>*, where *T* is the type of the entities to manage. As you know, every *IEnumerable<T>* implementation can leverage the benefits of LINQ to Objects. However, the *IQueryable<T>* interface implements *IEnumerable<T>* and can be used to represent LINQ queries as expression trees instead of resolving their definition into LINQ to Objects extension method invocations. Every LINQ query over a LINQ to SQL *DataContext* returns a type implementing *IQueryable<T>*. Thus, we can try to return this type from our data layer types instead of *IEnumerable<T>* or *List<T>*.

> **More Info**   *IEnumerable<T>* is described in Chapter 3, "LINQ to Objects." *IQueryable<T>* is covered in detail in Chapter 11, "Inside Expression Tress", and Chapter 12, "Extending LINQ."

Consider Listing 15-17, where you can see an excerpt of a possible implementation of the *ReadAll* method in the *CustomerDal* class. It is based on LINQ to SQL and returns an *IEnumerable<Customer>* to the caller, which should be the BIZ.

Listing 15-17   The LINQ based implementation of the *ReadAll* method of *CustomerDal*

```
public override IEnumerable<DomainModel.Customer> ReadAll() {
    // Convert the LINQ to SQL customers
    // into Domain Model customers using a
    // LINQ query expression
    var result =
        from c in this.Northwind.Customers
        select new DomainModel.Customer {
            CustomerID = c.CustomerID,
            Address = c.Address,
            City = c.City,
            CompanyName = c.CompanyName,
            ContactName = c.ContactName,
            ContactTitle = c.ContactTitle,
            Country = c.Country,
            Fax = c.Fax,
            Phone = c.Phone,
            PostalCode = c.PostalCode,
            Region = c.Region,
            // Converts the list of orders of the LINQ to SQL customer
            // into the list of orders defined in the Domain Model
            Orders = new List<DevLeap.Linq.Architecture.NTier.DomainModel.Order>(
                from o in c.Orders
                select new DomainModel.Order {
                    OrderID = o.OrderID,
                    CustomerID = o.CustomerID,
                    EmployeeID = o.EmployeeID,
                    Freight = o.Freight,
                    OrderDate = o.OrderDate,
                    RequiredDate = o.RequiredDate,
                    ShipAddress = o.ShipAddress,
                    ShipCity = o.ShipCity,
                    ShipCountry = o.ShipCountry,
                    ShipName = o.ShipName,
                    ShippedDate = o.ShippedDate,
                    ShipPostalCode = o.ShipPostalCode,
                    ShipRegion = o.ShipRegion,
                    ShipVia = o.ShipVia
                })
        };
    return (result);
}
```

If you try to analyze the SQL statements sent to the database when calling this method, you will notice that whenever you enumerate the result of the *ReadAll* method, a query for the whole set of customers and orders is sent to the database. For example, imagine having a business method called *GetCustomersByCountry* that returns a set of customers filtered by the value of *Country*. In Listing 15-18, you can see the implementation of this method.

Listing 15-18   Implementation of the *GetCustomersByCountry* method in the BIZ

```
public IEnumerable<DomainModel.Customer> GetCustomersByCountry(String country) {
    // Check authorization policies

    // Select the data using a LINQ query expression
    var result =
        from c in this._dal.ReadAll()
        where c.Country == country
        select c;

    // Eventually check and personalize the entity for the caller

    // Return the resulting customer instance to the caller
    return (result);
}
```

In Listing 15-19, you can see how to use the *GetCustomersByCountry* method to extract some fields (*CustomerID*, *ContactName*, *Country*) from the list of Italian customers.

Listing 15-19   A code excerpt calling the *GetCustomersByCountry* business method

```
private static void ReadItalianCustomers() {
    CustomersBiz cb = new CustomersBiz();

    // Query the list of customers to extract italian ones
    var query =
        from c in cb.GetCustomersByCountry("Italy")
        select new { c.CustomerID, c.ContactName, c.Country };
    foreach (var c in query) {
        Console.WriteLine(c);
    }
}
```

With the current code, all the customers and their orders will be selected from the database persistence layer. The filter by country will be applied to in-memory entities using LINQ to Objects. Here is the SQL query sent to the database:

```
SELECT [t0].[CustomerID], [t0].[CompanyName], [t0].[ContactName], [t0].[ContactTitle], [t0].
[Address], [t0].[City], [t0].[Region], [t0].[PostalCode], [t0].[Country], [t0].[Phone], [t0].
[Fax], [t1].[OrderID], [t1].[CustomerID] AS [CustomerID2], [t1].[EmployeeID], [t1].[OrderDate],
[t1].[RequiredDate], [t1].[ShippedDate], [t1].[ShipVia], [t1].[Freight], [t1].[ShipName],
[t1].[ShipAddress], [t1].[ShipCity], [t1].[ShipRegion], [t1].[ShipPostalCode], [t1].
[ShipCountry], (
```

```
    SELECT COUNT(*)
    FROM [dbo].[Orders] AS [t2]
    WHERE [t2].[CustomerID] = [t0].[CustomerID]
    ) AS [value]
FROM [dbo].[Customers] AS [t0]
LEFT OUTER JOIN [dbo].[Orders] AS [t1] ON [t1].[CustomerID] = [t0].[CustomerID] ORDER BY
[t0].[CustomerID], [t1].[OrderID]
```

It would definitely be better to extract only the Italian customers and eventually only the fields really used by the consumer. In fact, in real scenarios you could extract millions of lines of customers and orders if you filter by *Country* only on the BIZ side. One possible solution to this behavior is to move the query to the data layer, defining an ad hoc selection method to extract and project exactly the data that is really needed. However, this approach moves the filtering logic from the business layer to the data layer, making the BIZ dependant on the DAL. Another possible solution is returning an *IQueryable<T>* from the data layer instead of an *IEnumerable<T>*. The only difference in this approach is the signature of the *ReadAll* method defined in Listing 15-16. The following is the new method signature:

```
public override IQueryable<DomainModel.Customer> ReadAll() {
    // ... exactly the same code as the one in Listing 15-16
}
```

If you execute the code in Listing 15-19 again with only the signature changed, you will see that now the SQL code sent to SQL Server is exactly what we are looking for.

```
SELECT [t0].[CustomerID], [t0].[ContactName], [t0].[Country]
FROM [dbo].[Customers] AS [t0]
WHERE [t0].[Country] = @p0
```

What happens under the covers is that the data layer returns an *IQueryable<T>* that represents an expression tree, not the real set of entities. The *GetCustomersByCountry* method adds a filtering condition to the expression tree, while the code in Listing 15-19 adds a custom projection to the same expression tree. Finally, the enumeration (*foreach*) of the query expression determines the conversion of the expression tree into the corresponding ad hoc SQL statement.

What we have just described can be really powerful and can dramatically improve an application's performance and scalability. However, as you have already seen in Chapter 11, moving *IQueryable<T>* instances outside the LINQ to relational world can also lead to unpredictable results and issues. For instance, the *Refund* method will stop working in this case because the filtering condition based on customer orders, which are of type *List<Order>*, cannot be converted into a SQL statement by the LINQ to SQL query provider.

 Note   The *Orders* property declared in our *Customer* attribute is of type *List<Order>*. The LINQ to SQL entity classes uses *EntitySet<T>* to define properties that map a one-to-many relationship. However, *EntitySet<T>* is specific to the LINQ to SQL implementation and cannot be used to define DAL-independent entity classes.

One more thing to consider: if you decide to use *IQueryable<T>* within your data layer interfaces, you should support it from any persistence layer. For example, the data access layer based on LINQ to XML that we presented previously needs to convert its results into something compliant with *IQueryable<T>*. To satisfy this requirement, you can leverage the *Queryable.AsQueryable* method, which converts any instance of *IEnumerable<T>* into a constant expression queryable via *IQueryable<T>*. However, remember again that not every type can be used within an expression tree and queried by a provider for *IQueryable<T>*.

We recommend that you consider the opportunities offered by using *IQueryable<T>*, but be very careful and use it only through ad hoc methods and in situations where it is really useful.

Identifying the Right Unit of Work

Another possible matter that arises from working with LINQ to SQL in an *n*-tier distributed architecture is to correctly identify the boundaries of a unit of work. A unit of work "keeps track of everything you do during a business transaction that can affect the database" (from "Patterns of EEA," which you can read at *http://www.martinfowler.com/eaaCatalog/unitOfWork.html*). As you learned in the chapters dedicated to LINQ to SQL, the *DataContext* represents a unit of work. Thus, it should be created and used only for single units of work. In general, creating a unique *DataContext* instance and sharing it across multiple user requests is not a good practice.

In our examples, we created a *DataContext* instance for each Data Mapper instance that is used by a single business component instance. In this way, different business transactions require different business component instances.

Another option to keep units of work isolated is to apply the *ThreadStatic* attribute to an instance of *DataContext* in order to share it across many different domain model entities, identifying the unit of work with the single thread calling the application server infrastructure. This solution could help in defining services or Web applications, where each user request is mapped to a specific processing thread. However, caching a *DataContext* instance for several service requests might require some additional checks when attaching entities, as we will see shortly.

Whatever technique you define to keep track of the current unit of work, remember that to really abstract and separate the business layer from the data layer, you should make transparent to the BIZ the solution you adopted because the unit of work relates only to the specific DAL implementation.

It is up to you to correctly define the boundaries of your application units of work and their activation policies, thinking about your business rules and processes. In this chapter, we have provided just some hypothetical examples. It is important to underline that the choice you make could affect the code you have to write, in particular in the data layer. For instance, if you keep the *DataContext* in memory across multiple requests, then when attaching changed entities you should check for their existence in the *DataContext*.

Handling Transactions

In Chapter 5, you saw how to handle transactions while working with LINQ to SQL. Generally in distributed *n*-tier architectures the outcome of transactional activities is determined by the business layer because only the business logic can determine whether a complex business process has been completed correctly or has to be cancelled, rolling back any related data modifications. For the same reasons, any activity or operation that involves data modifications through the configured data layer should be wrapped with a *TransactionScope* from *System.Transaction* from .NET 2.0 and you should avoid using explicit transactions in the LINQ to SQL data layer.

Concurrency and Thread Safety

One last consideration goes to thread-safety. Keep in mind that good software solutions work asynchronously on the application server and on the client side. From a LINQ-based architecture point of view, you need to consider that LINQ to SQL and LINQ to Entities are not thread-safe, so it is up to you to determine a correct threading policy. In general it is better to avoid sharing instances (like a *DataContext* and entities) between different threads, otherwise you will need to use *Lock*, *Mutex*, *ReaderWriteLock* and *ReaderWriteLockSlim*, etc. to synchronize the access to resources. We will not cover here how to leverage these classes, but it is important that you remember this.

> **More Info**   To learn more about threading, synchronization, concurrency, etc. in the Microsoft .NET Framework, we suggest that you read Jeffrey Richter's book *Applied Microsoft .NET Framework Programming*, published by Microsoft Press.

Summary

In this chapter, we discussed the various techniques available to define two-tier, three-tier, and *n*-tier architectures using LINQ. You learned how to develop an abstract data layer and how to leverage custom entities. You also experienced the power of expression trees when defining custom *IQueryable<T>* variables. Finally, we discussed how to manage a unit of work with LINQ, how to handle transactions, and what to do in order to achieve thread-safety.

Chapter 16
LINQ and ASP.NET

ASP.NET 3.5 is one of the areas of the .NET Framework in which LINQ has been deeply embedded. In this chapter, we will focus on the new features available in ASP.NET 3.5 targeting LINQ—in particular, for LINQ to SQL and LINQ to Objects.

ASP.NET 3.5

In this section, we will cover some of the new features and capabilities available in ASP.NET 3.5 and Microsoft Visual Studio 2008. These features are not all related to LINQ itself, but we will use them during the remaining parts of this chapter. If you are already familiar with ASP.NET 3.5, you can skip or read quickly through this section.

ASP.NET 3.5 extends the ASP.NET 2.0 control and class framework by providing new controls such as *ListView* and *DataPager* and a set of new AJAX-enabling controls. Other improvements involve the IDE of Visual Studio 2008, with new HTML and cascading style sheets (CSS) designers, improved Microsoft IntelliSense, and the capability to design nested master pages.

ListView

ListView is a new control that takes the place of the *DataGrid*, *GridView*, *DataList*, and *Repeater* controls. It allows full control over the data template used to render data binding contents, including the container. This new control allows you to define data binding editing, insertion, deletion, selection, paging, and sorting with full control over the HTML generated. It should be used in place of many of the other controls available prior to ASP.NET 3.5. In fact, using *ListView* you can bind items as you do with *DataGrid*, *GridView*, *DataList*, or *Repeater*, or you can define a freer layout by declaring a set of user-defined HTML/ASPX templates.

The *ListView* control allows you to define a rich set of templates. *LayoutTemplate* and *ItemTemplate* are mandatory, while all the others are optional. Let's start with an ASPX page used to render a set of Northwind customers, shown in Listing 16-1.

Listing 16-1   A sample ASPX page using a *ListView* control instance.

```
<%@ Page Language="C#" AutoEventWireup="true" CodeFile="Listing16-1.aspx.cs"
    Inherits="Listing16_1" %>
<!DOCTYPE html PUBLIC "-//W3C//DTD XHTML 1.0 Transitional//EN"
  "http://www.w3.org/TR/xhtml1/DTD/xhtml11-transitional.dtd">
<html xmlns="http://www.w3.org/1999/xhtml">
<head runat="server">
    <title>Listing 16-1</title>
</head>
```

```
<body>
    <form id="form1" runat="server">
    <div>
    <asp:ListView ID="customersList" runat="server"
        DataSourceID="customersDataSource">
        <LayoutTemplate>
            <ul>
                <asp:PlaceHolder ID="itemPlaceholder" runat="server" />
            </ul>
        </LayoutTemplate>
        <ItemTemplate>
            <li>
                <b><asp:Label runat="server" Text='<%# Eval("CustomerId") %>' /></b> -
                <asp:Label runat="server" Text='<%# Eval("ContactName") %>' /><hr />
                <asp:Label runat="server" Text='<%# Eval("CompanyName") %>' />
                [<asp:Label runat="server" Text='<%# Eval("Country") %>' />]
            </li>
        </ItemTemplate>
    </asp:ListView>
    <asp:SqlDataSource ID="customersDataSource" runat="server"
    ConnectionString="<%$ ConnectionStrings:NorthwindConnectionString %>"
    SelectCommand="SELECT [CustomerID], [CompanyName], [ContactName], [Country]
                FROM [Customers]" />
    </div>
    </form>
</body>
</html>
```

As you can see, we have defined an *<asp:ListView />* element, bound to a *SqlDataSource* control, with a couple of templates in it. The first one, named *LayoutTemplate*, declares how to render the full layout of the container of data items. It could be a TABLE, DIV, SPAN, UL, OL, or any other element you want to use to wrap your set of data. Any data-bound content you are going to render through the *ListView* is rendered as defined in the *ItemTemplate* element. As you can see, the *LayoutTemplate* contains an *<asp:PlaceHolder />* control with an ID *"itemPlaceholder"*. This control will be used as the placeholder for each data-bound item to render. The value of *"itemPlaceholder"* for the ID of the placeholder can be configured, but the key point here is that *ItemTemplate* defines how to render each data-bound item, placing the result of its rendering inside the *LayoutTemplate* result, where a placeholder control has been defined.

The following is the full list of the templates available while defining a *ListView* control:

- *ItemSeparatorTemplate*: As its name implies, this template defines the content to render between data-bound items.

- *AlternatingItemTemplate*: Defines alternate content to distinguish between consecutive items.

- *SelectedItemTemplate*: Defines how to render a selected item to differentiate it from the others.

- *EditItemTemplate*: Defines the content to render in place of the *ItemTemplate*, for an item that has editing status.

- *InsertItemTemplate*: Defines the content to render to insert a new item. By configuring the *InsertItemPosition* property of the *ListView* control, you can decide to render the *InsertItemTemplate* at the top or at the bottom of the rendered list.

- *GroupTemplate*: Defines the content to render to wrap a set of *ItemTemplate* or *EmptyItemTemplate* items. This template is useful for defining output such as multicolumn lists, where output is grouped in rows made of columns. The *GroupTemplate* defines how to wrap a set of data-bound items, where the number of items for each group is defined by the property *GroupItemCount*.

- *GroupSeparatorTemplate*: Defines the content to render between each group of data-bound items.

- *EmptyItemTemplate*: Rendered whenever there is an empty item to render in a group. Imagine a situation in which you have to render a set of items grouped in rows of three columns each, but your data source is not arranged in multiples of three. You will end your data-bound list with one or two empty columns. This template declares how to render those empty columns.

- *EmptyDataTemplate*: Rendered when the data source is empty.

All the template elements in the preceding list use the common and well-known ASP.NET data-binding expressions to define which fields or properties to display.

In Listing 16-2, you can see an example of a *ListView* control rendering a list of items in a grid with multiple rows and columns.

Listing 16-2   A sample ASPX page using a *ListView* control instance to render a list with multiple rows and columns.

```
<%@ Page Language="C#" AutoEventWireup="true" CodeFile="Listing16-2.aspx.cs"
    Inherits="Listing16_2" %>
<!DOCTYPE html PUBLIC "-//W3C//DTD XHTML 1.0 Transitional//EN"
  "http://www.w3.org/TR/xhtml1/DTD/xhtml1-transitional.dtd">
<html xmlns="http://www.w3.org/1999/xhtml">
<head runat="server">
    <title>Untitled Page</title>
</head>
<body>
    <form id="form1" runat="server">
    <div>
    <asp:ListView ID="customersList" runat="server"
        ItemPlaceholderID="dataItemPlaceholder"
        GroupPlaceholderID="groupPlaceholder"
        DataSourceID="customersDataSource" GroupItemCount="5">
        <LayoutTemplate>
            <table cellpadding="2" cellspacing="3">
                <asp:PlaceHolder ID="groupPlaceholder" runat="server" />
            </table>
```

```
            </LayoutTemplate>
            <GroupTemplate>
                <tr>
                    <asp:PlaceHolder ID="dataItemPlaceholder" runat="server" />
                </tr>
            </GroupTemplate>
            <ItemTemplate>
                <td align="center" style="background-color: LightGreen;">
                    <b><asp:Label ID="Label1" runat="server"
                                Text='<%# Eval("CustomerId") %>' /></b> -
                    <asp:Label ID="Label2" runat="server"
                                Text='<%# Eval("ContactName") %>' /><br />
                    <asp:Label ID="Label3" runat="server"
                                Text='<%# Eval("CompanyName") %>' />
                    [<asp:Label ID="Label4" runat="server"
                                Text='<%# Eval("Country") %>' />]
                </td>
            </ItemTemplate>
            <EmptyItemTemplate>
                <td align="center" style="background-color: LightGreen;"> </td>
            </EmptyItemTemplate>
        </asp:ListView>
        <asp:SqlDataSource ID="customersDataSource" runat="server"
        ConnectionString="<%$ ConnectionStrings:NorthwindConnectionString %>"
        SelectCommand="SELECT [CustomerID], [CompanyName], [ContactName], [Country]
                    FROM [Customers]" />
    </div>
    </form>
</body>
</html>
```

In Listing 16-2, you can see how to declare a custom value for the ID of the element to use as the data-bound item placeholder, using the *ItemPlaceholderID* attribute. One more thing to notice in Listing 16-2 is the attribute *GroupingPlaceholderID*, which is used to declare the ID of the placeholder describing each group of data items.

ListView Data Binding

The *ListView* control can be bound to any data source control available in ASP.NET, including the *LinqDataSource* control, which we will cover in detail later in this chapter, or any data source that implements the *IEnumerable* interface.

To bind *ListView* to a data source control, you simply need to assign the ID of the data source control to the *DataSourceID* property of the *ListView* instance. You can see this in Listing 16-1 and Listing 16-2, where we bind a *ListView* control to a *SqlDataSource* control instance.

To bind *ListView* to a data source that implements the *IEnumerable* interface, you need to programmatically set the *DataSource* property, referencing the enumeration of items and invoking the *DataBind* method of the control instance.

In Listing 16-3, you can see a sample ASPX page using this technique, while in Listing 16-4 you can see the corresponding C# code, which sets the *DataSource* property and invokes the *DataBind* method.

Listing 16-3 A sample ASPX page excerpt using a *ListView* control bound to a data source by user code.

```
<asp:ListView ID="customersList" runat="server">
    <LayoutTemplate>
        <ul>
            <asp:PlaceHolder ID="itemPlaceholder" runat="server" />
        </ul>
    </LayoutTemplate>
    <ItemTemplate>
        <li>
            <b><asp:Label ID="Label1" runat="server"
                    Text='<%# Eval("CustomerId") %>' /></b> -
            <asp:Label ID="Label2" runat="server"
                    Text='<%# Eval("ContactName") %>' /><br />
            <asp:Label ID="Label3" runat="server"
                    Text='<%# Eval("CompanyName") %>' />
            [<asp:Label ID="Label4" runat="server"
                    Text='<%# Eval("Country") %>' />]
        </li>
    </ItemTemplate>
</asp:ListView>
```

Listing 16-4 The code-behind class of the ASPX page shown in Listing 16-3.

```
public partial class Listing16_3 : System.Web.UI.Page {
    protected void Page_Load(object sender, EventArgs e) {
        if (!this.IsPostBack) {
            NorthwindDataContext dc = new NorthwindDataContext();
            customersList.DataSource = dc.Customers;
            customersList.DataBind();
        }
    }
}
```

One interesting feature of the *ListView* control is its capability, while it is bound to a data source, to manage a set of data keys to identify each data-bound item. This is useful for data sources where each item has multiple values for its primary key or identifier. To leverage this feature, you can set the *DataKeyNames* property of the *ListView* instance with an array of *String* variables, representing the fields that are part of the item identifier (the record primary key fields in the case of a data base record set). Later in your code, you can get the identifier of each data-bound item from the *ListView* control instance, retrieving the value from the read-only indexer property *DataKeys* of the *ListView* or retrieving the value of the *Selected-DataKey* property. In Listing 16-5, you can see the code-behind class of a sample page that uses this feature to extract the identifier of the item currently selected by the user by leveraging the *ListView* control's selection events. The data source of this sample is the Northwind's Order Details table, where each order detail is identified by the *OrderID* and *ProductID* fields.

Listing 16-5   The code-behind class of the ASPX page using the *DataKeyNames* and *DataKeys* properties.

```
public partial class Listing16_6 : System.Web.UI.Page {
    protected void orderDetailsList_SelectedIndexChanged(Object sender, EventArgs e) {
        Int32? selectedItemOrderID =
                    ((Int32?)orderDetailsList.SelectedDataKey.Values[0]) ?? null;
        Int32? selectedItemProductID =
                    ((Int32?)orderDetailsList.SelectedDataKey.Values[1]) ?? null;

        selectedItemId.Text = String.Format("Selected item ID: {0} - {1}",
            selectedItemOrderID,
            selectedItemProductID);
    }
}
```

In Listing 16-6, you can see the ASPX page corresponding to the code shown in Listing 16-5.

Listing 16-6   The ASPX code of the page using the *DataKeyNames* property.

```
<%@ Page Language="C#" AutoEventWireup="true" CodeFile="Listing16-6.aspx.cs"
    Inherits="Listing16_6" %>
<!DOCTYPE html PUBLIC "-//W3C//DTD XHTML 1.0 Transitional//EN"
  "http://www.w3.org/TR/xhtml1/DTD/xhtml1-transitional.dtd">
<html xmlns="http://www.w3.org/1999/xhtml">
<head runat="server">
    <title>Untitled Page</title>
</head>
<body>
    <form id="form1" runat="server">
    <div>
    <asp:ListView ID="orderDetailsList" runat="server"
        DataKeyNames="OrderID, ProductID"
        DataSourceID="orderDetailsDataSource"
        OnSelectedIndexChanged="orderDetailsList_SelectedIndexChanged">
        <LayoutTemplate>
            <table border="1" cellpadding="2" cellspacing="3">
                <tr>
                    <th style="text-align: center;">Action Command</th>
                    <th style="text-align: center;">OrderID + ProductID</th>
                    <th style="text-align: center;">UnitPrice</th>
                    <th style="text-align: center;">Quantity</th>
                    <th style="text-align: center;">Total</th>
                </tr>
                <asp:PlaceHolder ID="itemPlaceholder" runat="server" />
            </table>
        </LayoutTemplate>
        <ItemTemplate>
            <tr>
```

```
                    <td style="text-align: center;">
                        <asp:Button CommandName="Select"
                        Text="Select" runat="server" />
                    </td>
                    <td style="text-align: center;">
                        <b><asp:Label runat="server"
                        Text='<%# Eval("OrderID") %>' /> -
                        <asp:Label runat="server"
                        Text='<%# Eval("ProductID") %>' /></b><br />
                    </td>
                    <td style="text-align: center;">
                        <asp:Label runat="server"
                        Text='<%# Eval("UnitPrice", "{0:c}") %>' />
                    </td>
                    <td style="text-align: center;">
                        <asp:Label runat="server"
                        Text='<%# Eval("Quantity") %>' />
                    </td>
                    <td style="text-align: right;">
                        <asp:Label runat="server"
                        Text='<%# Eval("Total", "{0:c}") %>' />
                    </td>
                </tr>
        </ItemTemplate>
        <SelectedItemTemplate>
            <tr style="background-color: LightGreen;">
                <td style="text-align: center;">
                    <asp:Button ID="Button1" CommandName="Select"
                        Text="Select" runat="server" />
                </td>
                <td style="text-align: center;">
                    <b><asp:Label ID="Label1" runat="server"
                    Text='<%# Eval("OrderID") %>' /> -
                    <asp:Label ID="Label2" runat="server"
                    Text='<%# Eval("ProductID") %>' /></b><br />
                </td>
                <td style="text-align: center;">
                    <asp:Label ID="Label3" runat="server"
                    Text='<%# Eval("UnitPrice", "{0:c}") %>' />
                </td>
                <td style="text-align: center;">
                    <asp:Label ID="Label4" runat="server"
                    Text='<%# Eval("Quantity") %>' />
                </td>
                <td style="text-align: right;">
                    <asp:Label ID="Label5" runat="server"
                    Text='<%# Eval("Total", "{0:c}") %>' />
                </td>
            </tr>
        </SelectedItemTemplate>
    </asp:ListView>

<asp:SqlDataSource ID="orderDetailsDataSource" runat="server"
    ConnectionString="<%$ ConnectionStrings:NorthwindConnectionString %>"
    SelectCommand="SELECT TOP 20 [OrderID], [ProductID], [UnitPrice],
```

```
            [Quantity], [UnitPrice] * [Quantity] AS [Total]
            FROM [Order Details]" />
    </div>
    <div>
        <asp:Label ID="selectedItemId" runat="server" />
    </div>
    </form>
</body>
</html>
```

DataPager

One more new control available in ASP.NET 3.5 is *DataPager*, which is useful for automating paging tasks in data-bound controls. This new control can be applied only to controls implementing the *IPageableItemContainer* interface, like the new *ListView* control we just described. This interface provides a couple of properties—one to set the current page size (*MaximumRows*) and one to set the starting record index (*StartRowIndex*)—one method (*SetPageProperties*) to set those properties, and an event (*TotalRowCountAvailable*) to notify you of the availability of that information as well as the total number of rows. In Listing 16-7, you can see the definition of the *IPageableItemContainer* interface.

Listing 16-7   The *IPageableItemContainer* interface definition.

```
public interface IPageableItemContainer {
    // Events
    event EventHandler<PageEventArgs> TotalRowCountAvailable;

    // Methods
    void SetPageProperties(int startRowIndex, int maximumRows, bool databind);

    // Properties
    int MaximumRows { get; }
    int StartRowIndex { get; }
}
```

The *DataPager* control uses this interface to talk with its paged control.

> **Note**   The *DataPager* control by itself does not paginate the data source; instead, it informs the bound control to paginate it. In the case of smart data sources, such as the *LinqDataSource*, which we will cover later in this chapter, the result is efficient and the query extracts exactly the required fields. However, with controls not designed or configured for paging, the paging task occurs in memory—thus, eventually creating performance issues on large sets of data.

To map a *DataPager* instance to a data-binding control, you can set the *PagedControlID* property of the pager control or, in the case of a *ListView* control, you can define the *DataPager* element inside the *LayoutTemplate* of the paged control. In Listing 16-8, you can see an ASPX page using a *DataPager* instance to paginate a list of records bound to a *ListView* control.

Listing 16-8   A sample ASPX page using a *ListView* control paged by a *DataPager* control.

```
<%@ Page Language="C#" AutoEventWireup="true" CodeFile="Listing16-8.aspx.cs"
    Inherits="Listing16_8" %>
<!DOCTYPE html PUBLIC "-//W3C//DTD XHTML 1.0 Transitional//EN"
  "http://www.w3.org/TR/xhtml1/DTD/xhtml1-transitional.dtd">
<html xmlns="http://www.w3.org/1999/xhtml">
<head runat="server">
    <title>Untitled Page</title>
</head>
<body>
    <form id="form1" runat="server">
    <div>
    <asp:ListView ID="customersList" runat="server"
        DataSourceID="customersDataSource">
        <LayoutTemplate>
            <table cellpadding="2" cellspacing="3">
                <tr>
                    <th style="text-align: center">CustomerId</th>
                    <th style="text-align: center">CompanyName</th>
                    <th style="text-align: center">ContactName</th>
                    <th style="text-align: center">Country</th>
                </tr>
                <asp:PlaceHolder ID="itemPlaceholder" runat="server" />
            </table>
        </LayoutTemplate>
        <ItemTemplate>
            <tr>
                <td style="text-align: center">
                    <asp:Label runat="server" Text='<%# Eval("CustomerId") %>' />
                </td>
                <td style="text-align: center">
                    <asp:Label runat="server" Text='<%# Eval("CompanyName") %>' />
                </td>
                <td style="text-align: center">
                    <asp:Label runat="server" Text='<%# Eval("ContactName") %>' />
                </td>
                <td style="text-align: center">
                    <asp:Label runat="server" Text='<%# Eval("Country") %>' />
                </td>
            </tr>
        </ItemTemplate>
    </asp:ListView>

    <asp:DataPager ID="customersListPager" runat="server"
        PagedControlID="customersList" PageSize="5">
        <Fields>
            <asp:NumericPagerField ButtonCount="20" />
        </Fields>
    </asp:DataPager>
```

```
        <asp:SqlDataSource ID="customersDataSource" runat="server"
            ConnectionString="<%$ ConnectionStrings:NorthwindConnectionString %>"
            SelectCommand="SELECT [CustomerID], [CompanyName], [ContactName],
            [Country] FROM [Customers]" />

        </div>
        </form>
    </body>
    </html>
```

As you can see from Listing 16-8, the *DataPager* control provides a *PageSize* property to define the number of records to show for each page. Under the covers, this property sets the *MaximumRows* property of the *DataPager* itself and also for the paged control, using the corresponding property of the *IPageableItemContainer* interface.

The pager control renders the paging UI using a set of fields that can be defined within the *DataPager* element. These fields describe what kind of paging buttons to provide to the user. For instance, there is a *NextPreviousPagerField* that describes the appearance of the buttons to be used to move to the next page, previous page, first page, and last page. This field also enables you to define the CSS style, the images used, and the visibility of the paging buttons. There is also a *NumericPagerField* that describes the appearance, CSS style, and visibility of the numeric paging buttons. In Listing 16-9, you can see an example of using *DataPager* with a custom set of fields defined.

Listing 16-9 A sample ASPX page showing an excerpt of a *DataPager* control with configured pager fields.

```
<asp:DataPager ID="customersListPager" runat="server"
    PagedControlID="customersList" PageSize="5">
    <Fields>
        <asp:NextPreviousPagerField ButtonType="Link"
            FirstPageText="&lt;&lt;" PreviousPageText="&lt;"
            ShowFirstPageButton="true" ShowLastPageButton="false"
            ShowPreviousPageButton="true" ShowNextPageButton="false" />
        <asp:NumericPagerField ButtonCount="20" ButtonType="Link" />
        <asp:NextPreviousPagerField ButtonType="Link"
            LastPageText="&gt;&gt;" NextPageText="&gt;"
            ShowFirstPageButton="false" ShowLastPageButton="true"
            ShowPreviousPageButton="false" ShowNextPageButton="true" />
    </Fields>
</asp:DataPager>
```

If you need to customize the paging fields to a great extent, you can define a *TemplatePagerField*, which enables you to freely define the layout of the paging UI. In such a situation, the template will be able to manage the properties of the *DataPager* to be aware of its properties—such as *StartRowIndex*, *PageSize*, and *TotalRowCount*—so that it can generate the appropriate HTML output. In Listing 16-10, you can see an example of using a custom field template to render pages in a drop-down list.

Listing 16-10   A sample ASPX page excerpt using a *DataPager* control with a custom template for pager fields.

```
<asp:DataPager ID="customersListPager" runat="server"
    PagedControlID="customersList" PageSize="5">
    <Fields>
      <asp:TemplatePagerField>
        <PagerTemplate>
            Go to page:
            <uc:PagerDropDownList runat="server" AutoPostBack="true"
                TotalPageCount="<%# Math.Ceiling
                    ((double)Container.TotalRowCount / Container.PageSize) %>" />
        </PagerTemplate>
      </asp:TemplatePagerField>
    </Fields>
</asp:DataPager>
```

In the code in Listing 16-10, the *<uc:PagerDropDownList />* element refers to a custom user control that we defined to handle page numbers that are rendered inside a common drop-down list. In Listing 16-11, you can see the source code of this custom user control.

Listing 16-11   The code of a custom user control to render page numbers in a drop-down list.

```
public class PagerDropDownList : DropDownList {

    public Int32 TotalPageCount { get; set; }

    protected override void OnPreRender(EventArgs e) {
        base.OnPreRender(e);

        for (Int32 c = 1; c <= TotalPageCount; c++) {
            this.Items.Add(new ListItem(c.ToString("00")));
        }

        DataPager pager = ((DataPagerFieldItem)this.Parent).Pager;
        Int32 currentPageIndex = (Int32)Math.Ceiling(
            (double)pager.StartRowIndex / pager.PageSize);

        this.Items[currentPageIndex].Selected = true;
    }

    protected override void OnSelectedIndexChanged(EventArgs e) {
        base.OnSelectedIndexChanged(e);

        Int32 currentPageIndex = Int32.Parse(this.SelectedValue);
        DataPager pager = ((DataPagerFieldItem)this.Parent).Pager;
        pager.SetPageProperties((currentPageIndex - 1) * pager.MaximumRows,
            pager.MaximumRows, true);
    }
}
```

Note that all the pager fields inherit from the abstract base class *DataPagerField*; thus, you can define your own fields if you need to.

One last thing to note about the *DataPager* control is that it provides you with the capability to use a querystring field to receive the current page number to show. By default, the *DataPager* uses HTTP POST commands to navigate through the pages. By the way, sometimes it can be useful to make paging available through querystring parameters. Think about a Web site publishing products grouped by pages. With HTTP POST–based paging, which is the default for *DataPager*, search engines crawl just the first page of each set of products. Using an HTTP GET–based rendering pattern allows for the indexing of contents, based on different URLs for each single page, thereby improving the efficiency of content crawling. To leverage this feature, you need to set the value of the *QueryStringField* property of the *DataPager* control. In the case of a null or empty string value for this property, the *DataPager* control uses HTTP POST; otherwise, it looks for a querystring field declaring the page to show. The name of this querystring field will be the value assigned to the *QueryStringField* property of the *DataPager* instance. In the case of an ASPX page with multiple data sources, data bound controls, and *DataPager* controls, you should set different values of this property for each *DataPager* instance; otherwise, unexpected paging behavior could occur. Consider also that using a querystring-based paging technique forces the *DataPager* fields to render paging buttons as *HyperLink* controls, ignoring any explicit setting of the *ButtonType* property of the fields. In Listing 16-12, you can see an example of using the *QueryStringField* property.

Listing 16-12   A sample ASPX page excerpt with a *DataPager* control using querystring paging.

```
<asp:DataPager ID="customersListPager" runat="server"
    PagedControlID="customersList" PageSize="5"
    QueryStringField="page">
    <Fields>
        <asp:NextPreviousPagerField ButtonType="Link"
            FirstPageText="&lt;&lt;" PreviousPageText="&lt;"
            ShowFirstPageButton="true" ShowLastPageButton="false"
            ShowPreviousPageButton="true" ShowNextPageButton="false"  />
        <asp:NumericPagerField ButtonCount="20" ButtonType="Link" />
        <asp:NextPreviousPagerField ButtonType="Link"
            LastPageText="&gt;&gt;" NextPageText="&gt;"
            ShowFirstPageButton="false" ShowLastPageButton="true"
            ShowPreviousPageButton="false" ShowNextPageButton="true" />
    </Fields>
</asp:DataPager>
```

> **Note**   If you want to delve deeper into ASP.NET development techniques, we suggest you read the great book *Essential ASP.NET 2.0* by Fritz Onion with Keith Brown (Addison-Wesley Professional, 2006). To improve your knowledge about ASP.NET 3.5 in particular, we suggest you read the book *Microsoft ASP.NET 3.5 Developer Reference* by Dino Esposito (Microsoft Press, 2008).

LinqDataSource

The biggest news concerning ASP.NET 3.5 from a LINQ point of view is the *LinqDataSource* control. This new control implements the *DataSource* control pattern and allows you to use LINQ to SQL or LINQ to Objects to data bind any bindable rendering control using an ASPX declarative approach. For instance, you can use the *LinqDataSource* control to bind a *Data-Grid*, *GridView*, *Repeater*, *DataList*, or *ListView* control. This control resembles the *SqlDataSource* and *ObjectDataSource* from previous versions of ASP.NET, but it targets a LINQ to SQL data model or a custom set of entities using LINQ to Objects.

If you have ever used the *SqlDataSource* and *ObjectDataSource* controls, you probably know that you have to define custom queries or methods, respectively, to provide data querying, inserting, editing, and deleting features. With the *LinqDataSource* control, you can leverage the out-of-the-box LINQ environment to get all of these functionalities, without having to write specific code. Of course, you can always decide to customize this behavior, but it is important to know that it is your choice and it is not mandatory.

For instance, imagine that you have the list of customers from the Northwind database. In Figure 16-1, you can see the complete LINQ to SQL data model schema.

The DBML file can be directly added to the *App_Code* folder of the ASP.NET Web project, or it can be defined in a separate and dedicated class library project. In the case of a sample prototypal solution or a simple Web application, you can declare the data model within the Web project itself. If you are developing an enterprise solution, it is better to divide the layers of your architecture into dedicated projects, thus defining a specific class library for the data model definition.

> **Note**   For an enterprise-level solution, read Chapter 15, "LINQ in a Multitier Solution," which discusses how to deal with architectural and design matters related to LINQ adoption.

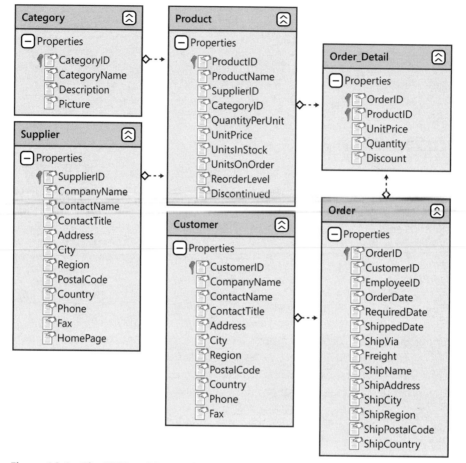

Figure 16-1   The LINQ to SQL Database Model (DBML) schema used in the samples of this chapter

Consider the ASPX page shown in Listing 16-13, where we retrieve a set of customers and bind it to a *GridView* control. As you can see, the *LinqDataSource* control declares a *ContextType-Name* property that maps to the previously defined *NorthwindDataContext* type, and a *Table-Name* property that corresponds to the *Customers* property of the *DataContext* instance, representing a class of type *Table<Customer>* of LINQ to SQL.

Listing 16-13   A sample ASPX page using a *LinqDataSource* control to render the list of Northwind customers into a *GridView* control.

```
<%@ Page Language="C#" AutoEventWireup="true" CodeFile="Listing16-13.aspx.cs"
    Inherits="Listing16_13" %>
<!DOCTYPE html PUBLIC "-//W3C//DTD XHTML 1.0 Transitional//EN"
  "http://www.w3.org/TR/xhtml1/DTD/xhtml1-transitional.dtd">
<html xmlns="http://www.w3.org/1999/xhtml">
<head runat="server">
    <title>Listing 16-13</title>
</head>
```

```
<body>
    <form id="form1" runat="server">
    <div>
        <asp:GridView runat="server" DataSourceID="customersDataSource" />
        <asp:LinqDataSource ID="customersDataSource" runat="server"
            ContextTypeName="NorthwindDataContext"
            TableName="Customers" />
    </div>
    </form>
</body>
</html>
```

Using Microsoft Visual Studio 2008, you can define these and many other properties using the graphical page designer. In Figure 16-2 and Figure 16-3, you can see the steps for graphically configuring a *LinqDataSource* control by using a designer wizard. To start the wizard you simply need to insert a *LinqDataSource* control into an ASPX page, click on the control task menu, and choose the Configure Data Source task activity. In the first step, presented in the Choose A Context Object screen, you can define the main source for the control.

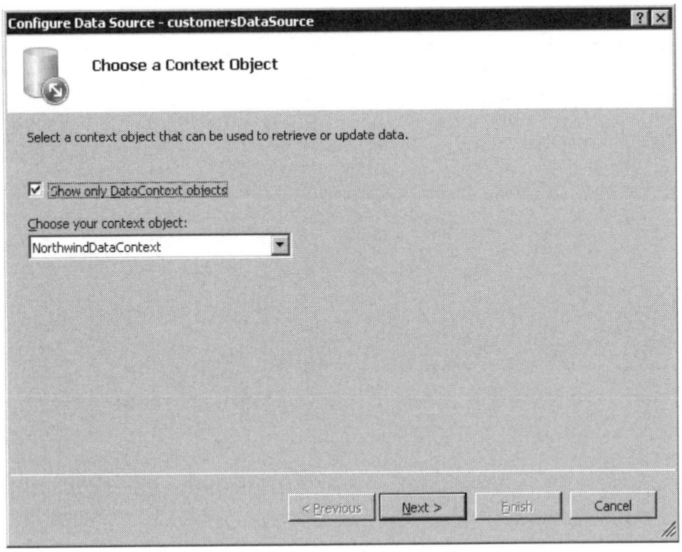

Figure 16-2   The Choose A Context Object screen of the *LinqDataSource* control configuration designer

If you keep the Show Only DataContext Objects option selected, the drop-down list will show only objects inheriting from the LINQ to SQL *DataContext* type, like the *NorthwindData-Context* shown in Figure 16-1. If you clear that option, the designer shows you any .NET type available in the project or in the user-defined projects referenced, including custom entities that can eventually be queried by using LINQ to Objects or any instance of *IEnumerable<T>*.

> **Note**   When referencing user-defined class libraries, remember that the *LinqDataSource*
> designer works with compiled assemblies. Therefore, you need to compile your solution to
> access newly created or modified types.

In this last case, the drop-down list will also show all the entity types defined in the LINQ to SQL data model, not only the *DataContext* type. This is useful to query a property of type *EntitySet<T>* offered by a specific LINQ to SQL entity—for example, the set of orders of a specific customer instance in a master-detail rendering page.

After clicking the Next button in the designer wizard, you are presented with the Configure Data Selection configuration panel, shown in Figure 16-3.

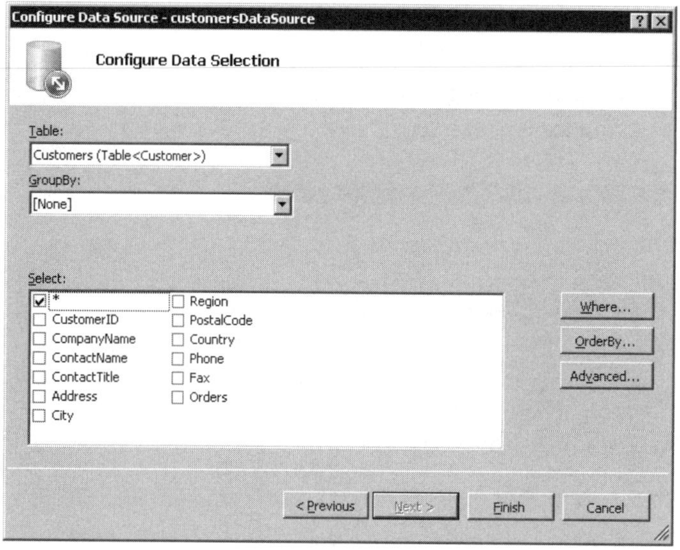

Figure 16-3   The Configure Data Selection screen of the *LinqDataSource* control configuration designer

Here you can define the whole set of configuration parameters of the *LinqDataSource* control. The Table drop-down list allows you to select the *Table<T>* to query, in the case of a *Data-Context*, or the *IEnumerable* property of a custom type to query with LINQ to Objects. The GroupBy drop-down list is used to define a grouping rule, eventually with an inner ordering for each group. The Select section provides a list that allows you to choose the fields or properties to select while querying the data source. By default, the *LinqDataSource* control projects all the fields (*), but you can define a custom projection predicate. There are also a set of buttons to define selection rules (the Where button) and ordering conditions (the OrderBy button). Through those buttons, you can define static filtering and ordering rules, but you can also define dynamic parameters, mapping their values to other controls, cookie values, form input elements, ASP.NET *Profile* variables, querystring parameters, or ASP.NET *Session* variables. This behavior is exactly the same as all the other *DataSource* controls, such as *SqlDataSource* and *ObjectDataSource*.

There is one last command, named Advanced, that determines whether you allow automatic inserts, deletes, or updates. By default, the *LinqDataSource* control simply selects data in a read-only manner. Keep in mind that automatic data modification is allowed only when the following conditions are satisfied: the projection returns all the data source items (having *Select* of "*" enabled), there are no grouping rules, the Context Object is set to a class inheriting from *DataContext,* and consequently the queried collection is of type *Table<T>*. If any of these conditions is not true, a custom LINQ query will occur, and the projected results will be an *IEnumerable<T>*, where *T* is an anonymous type, which is a read-only type by design.

> **Note**   Think carefully about the previous conditions. Whenever you need to query an updatable set of items using the automatic engine of the *LinqDataSource* control, you need to query its full set of fields/properties (SELECT * FROM …) even if you need to change a few of them. It is a behavior that is acceptable in very simple solutions with only one full table mapped directly to the UI, but in more complex and common solutions it is better to use custom selection and data updating rules.

After configuring the *LinqDataSource* control, you are ready to bind it to any bindable control, as we did in Listing 16-13.

All the parameters available through the UI designer can be defined in markup inside the ASPX source code of the page. In fact, the result of using the designer affects the markup definition of the *LinqDataSource* control instance. In Listing 16-14, you can see an example of a *LinqDataSource* control bound to the list of *CompanyName, ContactName*, and *Country* for Northwind's customers. The list is filtered by *Country*, mapped to a drop-down list with automatic post-back enabled, and ordered by *ContactName* value.

Listing 16-14   A sample ASPX page using a *LinqDataSource* control to render the list of Northwind's customers into a *GridView* control with some filtering and ordering rules.

```
<%@ Page Language="C#" AutoEventWireup="true" CodeFile="Listing16-14.aspx.cs"
    Inherits="Listing16_14" %>
<!DOCTYPE html PUBLIC "-//W3C//DTD XHTML 1.0 Transitional//EN"
  "http://www.w3.org/TR/xhtml1/DTD/xhtml1-transitional.dtd">
<html xmlns="http://www.w3.org/1999/xhtml">
<head runat="server">
    <title>Listing 16-14</title>
</head>
<body>
    <form id="form1" runat="server">
    <div>
        <br />Country: 
        <asp:DropDownList ID="ddlCountries" runat="server"
            AutoPostBack="True" DataSourceID="countriesDataSource"
            DataTextField="Country" DataValueField="Country" />
        <br />
```

```
        <asp:GridView ID="customersGrid" runat="server"
            DataSourceID="customersDataSource" AutoGenerateColumns="False">
            <Columns>
                <asp:BoundField DataField="CompanyName"
                    HeaderText="CompanyName" ReadOnly="True"
                    SortExpression="CompanyName" />
                <asp:BoundField DataField="ContactName"
                    HeaderText="ContactName" ReadOnly="True"
                    SortExpression="ContactName" />
                <asp:BoundField DataField="Country"
                    HeaderText="Country" ReadOnly="True"
                    SortExpression="Country" />
            </Columns>
        </asp:GridView>
        <asp:LinqDataSource ID="customersDataSource" runat="server"
            ContextTypeName="NorthwindDataContext"
            Select="new (CompanyName, ContactName, Country)"
            TableName="Customers" Where="Country == @Country">
            <WhereParameters>
                <asp:ControlParameter ControlID="ddlCountries"
                    Name="Country" PropertyName="SelectedValue"
                    Type="String" />
            </WhereParameters>
        </asp:LinqDataSource>
        <br />
        <asp:LinqDataSource ID="countriesDataSource" runat="server"
            ContextTypeName="NorthwindDataContext" GroupBy="Country"
            OrderGroupsBy="key" Select="new (key as Country)"
            TableName="Customers">
        </asp:LinqDataSource>
    </div>
    </form>
</body>
</html>
```

Under the covers of this page, the *LinqDataSource* control converts its configuration to a dynamic query expression executed against the source context.

Paging Data with *LinqDataSource* and *DataPager*

If you define a *DataPager* control that is applied to a rendering control such as a *ListView* and mapped to a *LinqDataSource* control instance, you will be able to paginate the data source at the level of the LINQ query. In fact, the *LinqDataSource* control will be configured to select a maximum number of records (*MaximumRows*) starting from a start record index (*StartRow-Index*), depending on the *DataPager* configuration. Internally, the *LinqDataSource* control will translate these parameters into a query ending with a *.Skip(StartRowIndex).Take(Maximum-Rows)* expression.

In Listing 16-15, you can see a sample ASPX page querying the list of Northwind's customers, filterable by country using a drop-down list, and paged with a page size of five customers per page.

Listing 16-15   A sample ASPX page using a *LinqDataSource* control to render the list of Northwind's customers into a *ListView* control with filtering and paging through a *DataPager* control.

```
<%@ Page Language="C#" AutoEventWireup="true" CodeFile="Listing16-15.aspx.cs"
    Inherits="Listing16_15" %>
<!DOCTYPE html PUBLIC "-//W3C//DTD XHTML 1.0 Transitional//EN"
  "http://www.w3.org/TR/xhtml1/DTD/xhtml1-transitional.dtd">
<html xmlns="http://www.w3.org/1999/xhtml">
<head runat="server">
    <title>Listing 16-15</title>
</head>
<body>
    <form id="form1" runat="server">
    <div>
        <br />Country: 
        <asp:DropDownList ID="ddlCountries" runat="server"
            AutoPostBack="True" DataSourceID="countriesDataSource"
            DataTextField="Country" DataValueField="Country" />
        <br />
        <asp:ListView ID="customersList" runat="server"
            DataSourceID="customersDataSource">
            <LayoutTemplate>
                <table cellpadding="5" cellspacing="0" border="1">
                    <tr>
                        <th style="text-align: center">CustomerId</th>
                        <th style="text-align: center">CompanyName</th>
                        <th style="text-align: center">ContactName</th>
                        <th style="text-align: center">Country</th>
                    </tr>
                    <asp:PlaceHolder ID="itemPlaceholder" runat="server" />
                </table>
            </LayoutTemplate>
            <ItemTemplate>
                <tr>
                    <td style="text-align: center">
                        <asp:Label ID="Label1" runat="server"
                            Text='<%# Eval("CustomerId") %>' />
                    </td>
                    <td style="text-align: center">
                        <asp:Label ID="Label2" runat="server"
                            Text='<%# Eval("CompanyName") %>' />
                    </td>
                    <td style="text-align: center">
                        <asp:Label ID="Label3" runat="server"
                            Text='<%# Eval("ContactName") %>' />
                    </td>
                    <td style="text-align: center">
                        <asp:Label ID="Label4" runat="server"
                            Text='<%# Eval("Country") %>' />
                    </td>
                </tr>
            </ItemTemplate>
        </asp:ListView>
        <asp:LinqDataSource ID="customersDataSource" runat="server"
            ContextTypeName="NorthwindDataContext"
```

```
            Select="new (CustomerID, CompanyName, ContactName, Country)"
            TableName="Customers" Where="Country == @Country">
            <WhereParameters>
                <asp:ControlParameter ControlID="ddlCountries"
                    Name="Country" PropertyName="SelectedValue"
                    Type="String" />
            </WhereParameters>
        </asp:LinqDataSource>
        <asp:DataPager ID="customersPager" PagedControlID="customersList"
            runat="server" PageSize="5">
            <Fields>
                <asp:NumericPagerField ButtonCount="5" ButtonType="Link" />
            </Fields>
        </asp:DataPager>
        <br />
        <asp:LinqDataSource ID="countriesDataSource" runat="server"
            ContextTypeName="NorthwindDataContext" GroupBy="Country"
            OrderGroupsBy="key" Select="new (key as Country)"
            TableName="Customers">
        </asp:LinqDataSource>
    </div>
    </form>
</body>
</html>
```

In Figure 16-4, you can see the HTML output of the page shown in Listing 16-15.

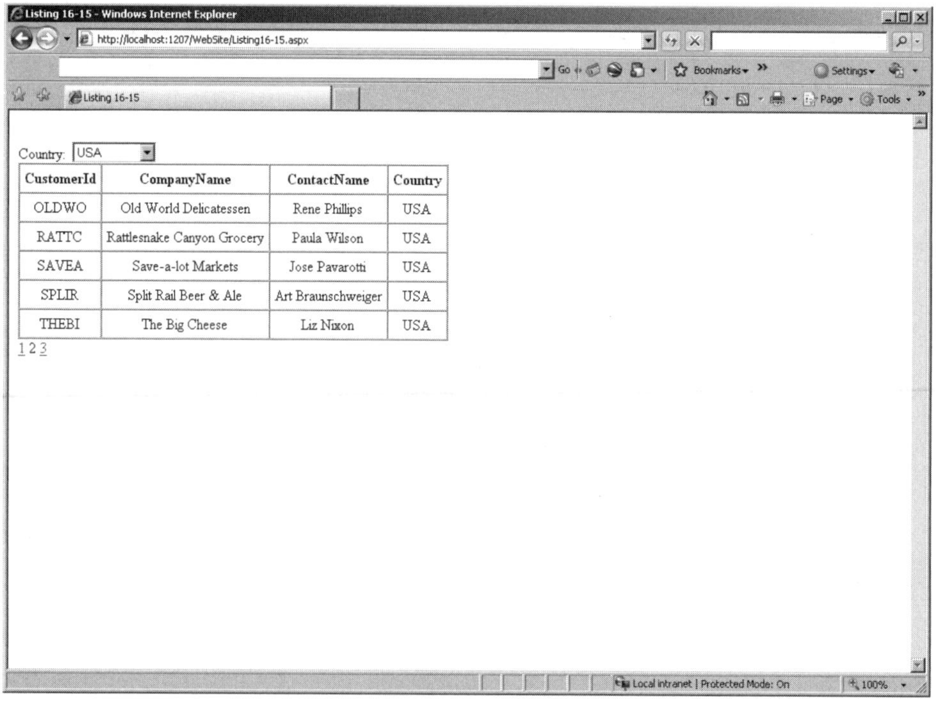

Figure 16-4   The HTML output of the page shown in Listing 16-15.

You can take a closer look at this behavior by subscribing to the *Selecting* event offered by each *LinqDataSource* control instance. This event allows you to inspect the actual selecting, filtering, ordering, grouping, and paging parameters of the executing query. Within the event code, you can also personalize the values of these parameters by customizing the query result before its execution. In Listing 16-16, you can see an example of using the *Selecting* event to define a custom filtering parameter. The *Arguments* property of the *LinqDataSourceSelect-EventArgs* instance, received by the event handler, describes the paging configuration.

> **Note**   The technique used for pagination by combining a *DataPager* and a *LinqDataSource* is a good approach from an ASP.NET point of view because it requests only the data displayed in one page from the data source. However, if the query is made on a large table without filters in a relational database such as a SQL Server database and the user selects the last page, the resulting query requires a complete scan of the table. Even with an existing index corresponding to the desired order, this operation consumes resources of the database server and time to complete.
>
> Additionally, if the query is the result of complex filters on a large table, each movement in the pages of the *DataPager* control could still require long execution times, because the query is executed every time the user requests a new page. In scenarios where the table size is large and/or the filter operation requires a particular amount of time, you might need to use a more complex architecture with temporary data caching of the results of such a queries.

Listing 16-16   An example of using the *Selecting* event of a *LinqDataSource* control.

```
public partial class Listing16_16 : System.Web.UI.Page {
    protected void customersDataSource_Selecting(Object sender,
        LinqDataSourceSelectEventArgs e) {
        // Forces sorting by ContactName
        e.Arguments.SortExpression = "ContactName";
    }
}
```

Handling Data Modifications with *LinqDataSource*

Whenever you need to modify data through a *LinqDataSource* instance, you need to configure it with a type inherited from *DataContext* as its *ContextTypeName*, a *TableName* corresponding to the name of a property of type *Table<T>* belonging to the *DataContext* type, a null or empty value for the *Select* property, and a null value for the *GroupBy* property. You also need to set to true the *EnableDelete*, *EnableInsert*, or *EnableUpdate* flags to support deletion, insertion, or modification of data items, respectively. As you have already seen, you can enable these flags using the designer interface or the ASPX markup. Regardless of the way in which you configure the *LinqDataSource* instance, after enabling data modifications you will be able to change the data source by using a data-bound control that supports editing, such as *GridView*, *ListView*, or *DetailsView*. In Listing 16-17, you can see an example of an ASPX page that uses an editable *GridView* to show the list of Northwind's customers.

Listing 16-17   A sample ASPX page excerpt using an editable *LinqDataSource* control.

```
<form id="form1" runat="server">
    <div>
        <asp:GridView ID="customersGrid" runat="server"
            DataKeyNames="CustomerID" DataSourceID="customersDataSource"
            AutoGenerateEditButton="true" AutoGenerateColumns="true" />

        <asp:LinqDataSource ID="customersDataSource" runat="server"
            ContextTypeName="NorthwindDataContext" TableName="Customers"
            OrderBy="ContactName" EnableUpdate="true" />

    </div>
</form>
```

If you need to modify or examine the values of the fields before effectively executing data modification tasks, you can subscribe to the events *Deleting*, *Inserting*, *Selecting*, and *Updating*. When you want to examine field values after data modification, you can handle the corresponding post-events, such as *Deleted*, *Inserted*, *Selected*, and *Updated*. Keep in mind that if you want to specify a default value for empty fields, during modification of the data source you can add parameters to the *InsertParameters*, *UpdateParameters*, and *DeleteParameters* of the control.

The events occurring before the data modification receive event arguments specific to each modification operation. For instance, a *Selecting* event handler receives a *LinqDataSourceSelect-EventArgs* object, allowing you to customize the query parameters as well as the result, as you will see in the next section.

A *Deleting* event handler receives an argument of type *LinqDataSourceDeleteEventArgs*. This type provides an *OriginalObject* property that contains the data item that will be deleted. It also provides a property named *Exception*, of type *LinqDataSourceValidationException*, that describes any exception related to data validation that occurred within the entity before its deletion. If you want to handle such an exception by yourself and do not want to throw it again, you can set to true the *ExceptionHandled* Boolean property of the event argument.

An *Inserting* event handler receives an argument of type *LinqDataSourceInsertEventArgs*. This type provides the data item that is going to be inserted as the value of its *NewObject* property, while the *Exception* and *ExceptionHandled* properties work just like those for the *Deleting* event argument, obviously referencing validation exceptions related to data item insertion.

An *Updating* event handler receives an event argument of type *LinqDataSourceUpdateEvent-Args*, describing the original and actual state of the data item through the *OriginalObject* and *NewObject* properties, respectively. Again, the handling of any kind of validation exception is based on the *Exception* property and *ExceptionHandled* flag.

Maybe you are wondering how the *LinqDataSource* control keeps track of the original values of entities between page postbacks. Under the covers, the *LinqDataSource* control saves each entity field's original value into the page *ViewState*, except for fields that are marked as

UpdateCheck.Never in the data model. For more details about *UpdateCheck* configuration, refer to Chapter 6, "Tools for LINQ to SQL." Using this technique, the *LinqDataSource* control is able to transparently handle data concurrency checks.

In Listing 16-18, you can see an example of code validating the updating of customer information, before any real data modification occurs.

Listing 16-18   The code-behind class of a page handling a custom validation rule while updating customer information through an editable *LinqDataSource* control.

```
protected void customersDataSource_Updating(object sender,
    LinqDataSourceUpdateEventArgs e) {
    if (((Customer)e.OriginalObject).Country != (((Customer)e.NewObject).Country)) {
        e.Cancel = true;
    }
}
```

The interesting part of this approach is that all the plumbing is handled transparently by the *LinqDataSource* control. Later in this chapter, you will see how to manually handle data selections based on custom LINQ queries.

While each pre-event handler receives a specific event argument type instance, all the post-event handlers receive an event argument of type *LinqDataSourceStatusEventArgs*, which allows you to examine the result of the data modification task. In fact, this event argument type provides the resulting data item in its *Result* property in the case of a successful modification. In the case of data modification failure, the post-event argument will have a null value for the *Result* property and will provide the exception that occurred in its *Exception* property. As with pre-events, you can set an *ExceptionHandled* Boolean property of the event argument to not throw the exception again. In Listing 16-19, you can see an excerpt of code handling a concurrency exception while updating a data item.

Listing 16-19   Sample code handling a concurrency exception while editing a data item through a *LinqDataSource* control.

```
protected void customersDataSource_Updated(object sender,
    LinqDataSourceStatusEventArgs e) {
    if ((e.Result == null) && (e.Exception != null)) {
        if (e.Exception is ChangeConflictException) {
            // Handle data concurrency issue
            // TBD ...

            // Stop exception bubbling
            e.ExceptionHandled = true;
        }
    }
}
```

There are three final events that are useful while handling the *LinqDataSource* control: *Context-Creating*, *ContextCreated*, and *ContextDisposing*. The first two occur when the *DataContext* is going to be created or has been created, respectively. When *ContextCreating* occurs, you can specify a custom *DataContext* instance, setting the *ObjectInstance* property of the event argument of type *LinqDataSourceContextEventArgs* you receive. If you ignore this event, the *LinqDataSource* control will create a *DataContext* by itself, based on the type name provided through the *ContextTypeName* property. You can use this event if you want to customize the *DataContext* creation—for instance, to provide a custom connection string, a user-defined *SqlConnection* instance, or a custom *MappingSource* definition. The *ContextCreated* event, on the other hand, allows you to customize the *DataContext* instance already created. It receives a *LinqDataSourceStatusEventArgs*, like post-event data modification events, but in this case the *Result* property of the event argument contains the *DataContext* type instance. In the case of errors while creating the *DataContext*, you will find an exception in the *Exception* property of the event argument and a value of null for the *Result* property. Listing 16-20 shows an example of handling the *ContextCreated* event to define a custom data shape for querying data.

Listing 16-20 Sample code customizing the *DataContext* of a *LinqDataSource* control, just after its creation.

```
protected void customersDataSource_ContextCreated(object sender,
    LinqDataSourceStatusEventArgs e) {
    NorthwindDataContext dc = e.Result as NorthwindDataContext;
    if (dc != null) {
        // Instructs the DataContext to load orders of current year with
        // each customer instance
        DataLoadOptions dlo = new DataLoadOptions();
        dlo.AssociateWith<Customer>(c => c.Orders
            .Where(o => o.OrderDate.Value.Year == DateTime.Now.Year));

        dc.LoadOptions = dlo;
    }
}
```

The *ContextDisposing* event is useful for handling custom or manual disposing of the *DataContext* type instance and receives an event argument of type *LinqDataSourceDisposeEventArgs*. This event occurs during the *Unload* event of the *LinqDataSource* control and provides the *DataContext* that is going to be disposed of in the *ObjectInstance* property of the event argument.

Note Because the *LinqDataSource* control is hosted by an ASP.NET environment, internally the *DataContext* used to query the data source is created and released for each single request with a pattern similar to the one shown later in this chapter and in Chapter 18, "LINQ and the Windows Communication Foundation." In the case of an uneditable *LinqDataSource* control, the *ObjectTrackingEnabled* property of the *DataContext* instance is set to false; otherwise, it is left to its default value of true.

Using Custom Selections with *LinqDataSource*

Sometimes you need to select data by using custom rules or custom user-defined stored procedures. Whenever you are using a *LinqDataSource* in these situations, you can subscribe to the *Selecting* event of the data source control. The *Selecting* event handler receives a *Linq-DataSourceSelectEventArgs* instance that can be used to change the selection parameters, as you saw in the previous section. However, it can also be used to return a completely customized selection by setting the *Result* property of the event argument to a custom value. In Listing 16-21, you can see an example of code handling the *Selecting* event to return the result of a custom stored procedure instead of a standard LINQ to SQL query.

Listing 16-21   The code-behind class of a page handling a custom selection pattern for a *LinqDataSource* control using a stored procedure.

```
protected void customersOrdersDataSource_Selecting(object sender,
    LinqDataSourceSelectEventArgs e) {
    NorthwindDataContext dc = new NorthwindDataContext();
    e.Result = dc.CustOrdersOrders("ALFKI");
}
```

In the case of an editable *LinqDataSource* control, the custom selection code should return a set of items with the same type *T* referenced by the *Table<T>* type of the *TableName* property of the data source control. The code to select the custom result could be any code returning a set of items consistent with the configured *TableName*; thus, you can use a stored procedure as well as customized explicit LINQ to SQL queries. Listing 16-22 shows a *Selecting* event implementation that uses a custom LINQ query to select a customized data source.

Listing 16-22   The code-behind class of a page handling a custom selection pattern for a *LinqDataSource* control using an explicit LINQ query.

```
protected void customersDataSource_Selecting(object sender,
    LinqDataSourceSelectEventArgs e) {
    NorthwindDataContext dc = new NorthwindDataContext();

    e.Result =
        from   c in dc.Customers
        where  c.Country == "USA" && c.Orders.Count > 0
        select c;
}
```

One more thing to notice is that in the case of data paging, the custom result will be paged too. This paging occurs because the *Result* property of the *Selecting* event argument will be managed by the *LinqDataSource* engine anyway, applying any paging rule to it. In the case of an *IQueryable<T>* result, as in Listing 16-22, the paging will occur on the LINQ query expression tree, preserving performance and efficiency.

When you programmatically set a custom result during the *Selecting* event, the *ContextCreated* event of the *LinqDataSource* control is not raised.

Using *LinqDataSource* with Custom Types

A common usage of the *LinqDataSource* control is querying data available through LINQ to SQL, but it can also be used to query custom types and entities. If you define a *ContextType-Name* that does not correspond to a type inherited from the LINQ to SQL *DataContext*, the *LinqDataSource* will switch from LINQ to SQL to LINQ to Objects queries. Consider the code in Listing 16-23, which describes user-defined *Customer* and *Order* types and is not related to a LINQ to SQL data model.

Listing 16-23   User-defined *Customer* and *Order* entities not related to a LINQ to SQL data model.

```
public class Customer {
    public Int32 CustomerID { get; set; }
    public String FullName { get; set; }
    public List<Order> Orders { get; set; }
}

public class Order {
    public Int32 OrderID { get; set; }
    public Int32 CustomerID { get; set; }
    public Decimal EuroAmount { get; set; }
}
```

Now consider a *CustomerManager* class offering a property named *Customers* and of type *List<T>*, where *T* is a *Customer* type, as shown in Listing 16-24.

Listing 16-24   A *CustomerManager* type providing a property of type *List<Customer>*.

```
public class CustomerManager {

    public CustomerManager() {
        this.Customers = new List<Customer> {
            new Customer { CustomerID = 1, FullName = "Paolo Pialorsi",
                Orders = new List<Order> {
                    new Order { OrderID = 1, CustomerID = 1, EuroAmount = 100},
                    new Order { OrderID = 2, CustomerID = 1, EuroAmount = 200}
                }
            },
            new Customer { CustomerID = 2, FullName = "Marco Russo",
                Orders = new List<Order> {
                    new Order { OrderID = 3, CustomerID = 2, EuroAmount = 150},
                    new Order { OrderID = 4, CustomerID = 2, EuroAmount = 250},
                    new Order { OrderID = 5, CustomerID = 2, EuroAmount = 130},
                    new Order { OrderID = 6, CustomerID = 2, EuroAmount = 220}
                }
            },
            new Customer { CustomerID = 3, FullName = "Andrea Pialorsi",
                Orders = new List<Order> {
                    new Order { OrderID = 7, CustomerID = 3, EuroAmount = 900},
                    new Order { OrderID = 8, CustomerID = 3, EuroAmount = 2500}
                }
            }
```

```
        };
    }

    public List<Customer> Customers { get; set; }
}
```

You can use the *CustomerManager* type as the value for the *ContextTypeName* of a *LinqData-Source* control, while the "Customers" string could be the value for the *TableName* property of the *LinqDataSource* control. Internally, the data source control queries the collection of items returned from the *CustomerManager* class, allowing your code to query a custom set of entities instead of a LINQ to SQL data model. Nevertheless, keep in mind that using LINQ to Objects instead of LINQ to SQL requires you to load into memory the whole set of data—before any filtering, sorting, or paging task. Be careful using this technique because it could be very expensive for your CPU and memory if your code is processing a large amount of data or many page requests. In Listing 16-25, you can see an ASPX page using this kind of configuration.

Listing 16-25   A sample ASPX page using a *LinqDataSource* control linked to a set of user-defined entities.

```
<%@ Page Language="C#" AutoEventWireup="true" CodeFile="Listing16-25.aspx.cs"
    Inherits="Listing16_25" %>

<!DOCTYPE html PUBLIC "-//W3C//DTD XHTML 1.0 Transitional//EN"
  "http://www.w3.org/TR/xhtml11/DTD/xhtml11-transitional.dtd">

<html xmlns="http://www.w3.org/1999/xhtml">
<head runat="server">
    <title>Listing 16-25</title>
</head>
<body>
    <form id="form1" runat="server">
    <div>

        <asp:GridView ID="customersGrid" runat="server"
            DataSourceID="customersDataSource">
        </asp:GridView>

        <asp:LinqDataSource
            ID="customersDataSource" runat="server"
            ContextTypeName="DevLeap.Linq.Web.DataModel.CustomerManager"
            TableName="Customers" />

    </div>
    </form>
</body>
</html>
```

Binding to LINQ queries

At this point, we have worked with LINQ using the new *LinqDataSource* control. However, in ASP.NET you can bind a bindable control to any kind of data source that implements the *IEnumerable* interface. Every LINQ query, when it is enumerated, provides a result of type *IEnumerable<T>*, which internally is also an *IEnumerable*. Therefore, any LINQ query can be used as an explicit data source in user code. In Listing 16-26, you can see an example of a page using a LINQ query in its *Page_Load* event to bind a custom list of Northwind products to a *GridView* control.

Listing 16-26   A sample page code based on a user-explicit LINQ query in the *Page_Load* event.

```
public partial class Listing16_26 : System.Web.UI.Page {
    protected void Page_Load(object sender, EventArgs e) {
        NorthwindDataContext dc = new NorthwindDataContext();

        var query =
            from   c in dc.Customers
            where  c.Country == "USA" && c.Orders.Count > 0
            select new {
                c.CustomerID, c.ContactName,
                c.CompanyName, c.Country,
                OrdersCount = c.Orders.Count };

        customersGrid.DataSource = query;
        customersGrid.DataBind();
    }
}
```

These considerations enable you to use the complete LINQ query syntax, particularly LINQ to SQL and LINQ to XML, to query custom data shapes and many different content types, binding the results to an ASP.NET control. For instance, Listing 16-27 shows the code-behind class of an ASPX page that renders the list of posts from one blog via LINQ to XML applied to the blog RSS feed.

Listing 16-27   The code-behind class of a page reading an RSS feed using a LINQ to XML query.

```
public partial class Listing16_27 : System.Web.UI.Page {
    protected void Page_Load(object sender, EventArgs e) {
        XElement feed = XElement.Load(
            "http://introducinglinq.com/blogs/MainFeed.aspx");

        var query =
            from   f in feed.Descendants("item")
            select new {
                Title = f.Element("title").Value,
                PubDate = f.Element("pubDate").Value,
                Description = f.Element("description").Value
            };
```

```
            blogPostsGrid.DataSource = query;
            blogPostsGrid.DataBind();
        }
    }
```

Querying data sources of any kind and shape using the many different flavors of LINQ is a challenging activity. However, the most common use of user-defined explicit LINQ queries is in the field of LINQ to SQL. Sooner or later, almost every Web application will need to query a set of records from a database. What is of most interest occurs when the data needs to be updated. Using the *LinqDataSource* control, we saw that everything is automated and that the data source control handles updates, insertions, deletions, and selections by itself, eventually raising a concurrency exception when data concurrency issues occur.

When querying data manually, you need to take care of many details by yourself. First of all, consider that ASP.NET is an HTTP-based development platform. Therefore, every request you handle can be considered independent from any other, even if it comes from the same user/browser. Given this, you need to keep track of changes applied to your data between multiple subsequent requests, possibly avoiding use of *Session* variables or shared (static) objects, because this can reduce the scalability of your solution. On the other hand, you should not keep an in-memory instance of the *DataContext* used to query a LINQ to SQL data model. You should instead create, use, and dispose of the *DataContext* for each request, as the *LinqData-Source* control does. In Listing 16-28, you can see an example of this technique for explicitly querying the list of Northwind's customers.

Listing 16-28   The code-behind class of a page explicitly querying Northwind's customers via LINQ to SQL.

```
public partial class Listing16_28 : System.Web.UI.Page {
    protected void Page_Load(object sender, EventArgs e) {
        NorthwindDataContext dc = new NorthwindDataContext();

        var query =
            from   c in dc.Customers
            select new {
               c.CustomerID, c.ContactName, c.Country, c.CompanyName};

        customersGrid.DataSource = query;
        customersGrid.DataBind();
    }
}
```

In this sample, we use the query result to bind a *GridView* control, configured to be editable. Listing 16-29 shows the corresponding ASPX page source code.

Listing 16-29 The ASPX page code excerpt based on the code-behind class shown in Listing 16-28.

```
<body>
    <form id="form1" runat="server">
    <div>

        <asp:GridView ID="customersGrid" runat="server"
            AutoGenerateEditButton="true"
            AutoGenerateColumns="true" />

    </div>
    </form>
</body>
```

Now here's the interesting part. Imagine that your user decides to change some fields for the currently selected customer, using an editable *GridView* like the one shown in Figure 16-5.

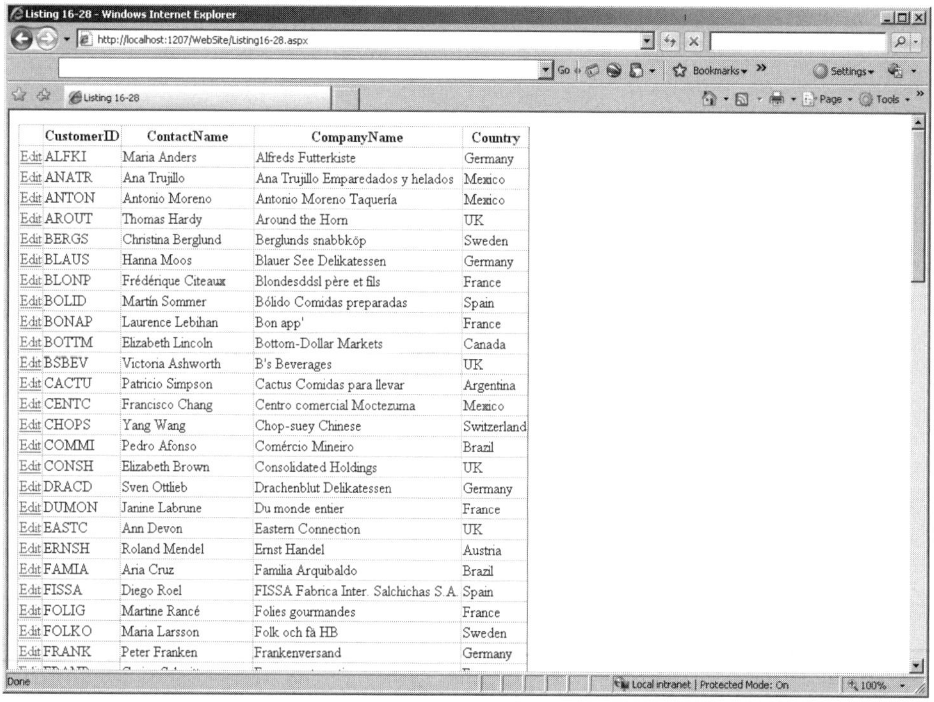

Figure 16-5 The HTML output of the page defined by Listings 16-28 and 16-29.

What you get back when the user presses the Update button on the page is the index of the selected/edited item in the *GridView*, as well as the values of the controls rendering the editable row. To update the data source, you need to create a new *DataContext* instance, which will be used during the entire unit of work that handles this single page request, and query the *DataContext* to get the entity corresponding to the data item that is going to be updated.

After you have retrieved the data item entity from the original store, you can explicitly change its properties, handling the user modifications, and then you can submit changes to the persistence layer, using the *SubmitChanges* method of the *DataContext* object. In Listing 16-30, you can see an example of the required code.

Listing 16-30   The code-behind class of a page explicitly updating a Northwind's customer instance with LINQ to SQL.

```
protected void UpdateCustomerInstance(String customerID,
        String contactName, String country, String companyName) {
    NorthwindDataContext dc = new NorthwindDataContext();

    Customer c = dc.Customers.First(c => c.CustomerID == customerID);
    if (c != null) {
        c.ContactName = contactName;
        c.Country = country;
        c.CompanyName = companyName;
    }

    dc.SubmitChanges();
}
```

The preceding example is missing an important part of the process: the concurrency check. In fact, we simply use the input coming from the user to modify the persistence layer. However, we have no guarantees about the exclusiveness of the operation we are performing. When the user decides to update a data item, you can leverage a specific *DataContext* method, called *Attach*. This method allows you to attach an entity to a *DataContext* instance, eventually providing its original state to determine whether any modification happened or simply to notify the *DataContext* that the entity has been changed. If the entity type has an *UpdateCheck* policy defined (see Chapter 6 for further details), the *DataContext* will be able to reconcile the entity with the one actually present in the database. In Listing 16-31, you can see an example of a code-behind class using this technique.

Listing 16-31   The code-behind class of a page updating a Northwind customer instance with LINQ to SQL, tracking the original state of the entity.

```
protected void AttachAndUpdateCustomerInstance(String customerID,
    String contactName, String country, String companyName) {

    NorthwindDataContext dc = new NorthwindDataContext();

    Customer c = new Customer();
    c.CustomerID = customerID;
    c.ContactName = contactName;
    c.Country = country;
    c.CompanyName = companyName;

    // The Boolean flag indicates that the item has been changed
    dc.Customers.Attach(c, true);
    dc.SubmitChanges();
}
```

Summary

This chapter showed you how to leverage the new features and controls available in ASP.NET 3.5 to develop data-enabled Web applications, using LINQ to SQL and LINQ in general. Consider that what you have seen is really useful for rapidly defining Web site prototypes and simple Web solutions. On the other hand, in enterprise-level solutions you will probably need at least one intermediate layer between the ASP.NET presentation layer and the data persistence one, represented by LINQ to SQL. In real enterprise solutions, you usually also need a business layer that abstracts all business logic, security policies, and validation rules from any kind of specific persistence layer. And you will probably have a Model-View-Controller or Model-View-Presenter pattern governing the UI. In this more complex scenario, chances are that the LinqDataSource control will be tied to entities collections more often than to LINQ to SQL results.

Chapter 17
LINQ and WPF/Silverlight

In this chapter, we will cover the support provided by Microsoft Windows Presentation Foundation (WPF) and Silverlight to Language Integrated Query (LINQ). As you will see, LINQ helps address many situations in which you need to manage data, either as XML or as a collection of entities, to solve data binding needs, rendering needs, or both.

Using LINQ with WPF

In this section, we will focus on data binding using LINQ to SQL and LINQ to Entities.

Binding Single Entities and Properties

Windows Presentation Foundation provides solid and wide support for data binding, allowing user interface designers to bind elements to entities, XML, controls, and so on. In WPF, you can achieve data binding simply by configuring a data source against a target property that supports binding. A property can be bound whenever it is implemented as a *DependencyProperty*. For instance, you can bind the *Text* property of a *TextBox*, but you can also bind the *Text* property of a *TextBlock*, or the *Background* property of an *AccessText* element. In Listing 17-1, you can see an example of XAML code that binds the *Text* property of a couple of *TextBox* elements to the properties of a variable of type *Contact*.

Listing 17-1   A XAML sample window with a simple data-binding definition

```
<Window x:Class="DevLeap.Linq.WPF.SampleBinding"
    xmlns="http://schemas.microsoft.com/winfx/2006/xaml/presentation"
    xmlns:x="http://schemas.microsoft.com/winfx/2006/xaml"
    xmlns:c="clr-namespace:DevLeap.Linq.WPF"
    Title="SampleBinding" Height="146" Width="300">

    <Window.Resources>
        <c:Contact x:Key="myContact"
            FirstName="Andrea" LastName="Pialorsi" />
    </Window.Resources>

    <Grid Height="106">
        <Canvas Name="canvas1">
            <TextBox Name="firstName"
    Text="{Binding Source={StaticResource myContact}, Path=FirstName}"
    Canvas.Left="10" Canvas.Top="12" Height="29" Width="250" />
            <TextBox Name="lastName"
```

```
         Text="{Binding Source={StaticResource myContact}, Path=LastName}"
         Canvas.Left="10" Canvas.Top="61" Height="29" Width="250" />
            </Canvas>
         </Grid>
      </Window>
```

Listing 17-2 contains the *Contact* type definition.

Listing 17-2   The *Contact* type definition

```
public class Contact {
    public String FirstName { get; set; }
    public String LastName { get; set; }
}
```

In Figure 17-1, you can see the resulting window.

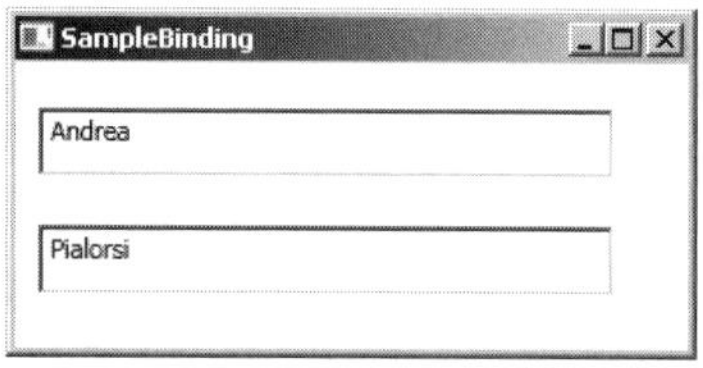

Figure 17-1   The rendering of the XAML window with simple data binding

Starting from this really simple example, it becomes interesting to evaluate how WPF binding works when the binding source is a LINQ to SQL or LINQ to Entities entity, instead of being a static resource.

Let's consider the well-known Northwind set of customers and imagine having a XAML window bound to a *Customer* instance. In Listing 17-3, you can see the XAML code for the window.

Listing 17-3   A XAML window with data binding against a Northwind customer instance

```
<Window x:Class="DevLeap.Linq.WPF.SingleCustomer"
    xmlns="http://schemas.microsoft.com/winfx/2006/xaml/presentation"
    xmlns:x="http://schemas.microsoft.com/winfx/2006/xaml"
    Title="SingleCustomer" Height="222" Width="300" Loaded="Window_Loaded">

    <Grid>
        <Canvas Name="canvas1" Margin="0,0,0,121">
            <TextBlock Height="16" Canvas.Left="10"
                Canvas.Top="14" Width="68.69">Customer ID:</TextBlock>
            <TextBox Name="CustomerID"
                Text="{Binding Path=CustomerID}" Canvas.Left="10"
                Canvas.Top="30" Height="29" Width="250" />
            <TextBlock Height="16" Canvas.Left="10"
                Canvas.Top="64" Width="79">Contact Name:</TextBlock>
            <TextBox Name="ContactName"
                Text="{Binding Path=ContactName}" Canvas.Left="10"
```

```
                    Canvas.Top="79" Height="29" Width="250" />
            <TextBlock Height="16" Canvas.Left="10"
                Canvas.Top="111" Width="88">Company Name:</TextBlock>
            <TextBox Name="CompanyName"
                Text="{Binding Path=CompanyName}" Canvas.Left="10"
                Canvas.Top="128" Height="29" Width="250" />
        </Canvas>
    </Grid>

</Window>
```

In Listing 17-4, you can see the code to bind the first Northwind customer to the window *DataContext*.

Listing 17-4   The C# source code corresponding to the window created with XAML in Listing 17-3

```
public partial class SingleCustomer : Window {
    public SingleCustomer() {
        InitializeComponent();
    }

    private void Window_Loaded(object sender, RoutedEventArgs e) {
        NorthwindDataContext dc = new NorthwindDataContext();
        this.DataContext = dc.Customers.First();
    }
}
```

As you can see, the binding of the *Text* properties of the three *TextBox* elements is almost identical to the static binding shown in Listing 17-1. The only difference is that in the sample just shown the *Source* of the *Binding* is configured by code, instead of being a *StaticResource* within the XAML window. In WPF, the binding source of a control can be explicitly set against the control itself, or it can be set higher in the control hierarchy. In fact, WPF bubbles the *DataContext* lookup across the entire control hierarchy. It is important to emphasize that you can bind a set of XAML elements against a hierarchical data structure, such as a customer with a collection of orders in it, eventually relate it to a collection of products, and so on. In fact, a WPF binding path can reference any depth level in an object graph.

For the sake of completeness, in Figure 17-2 you can see the window resulting from the code samples shown in Listing 17-3 and Listing 17-4.

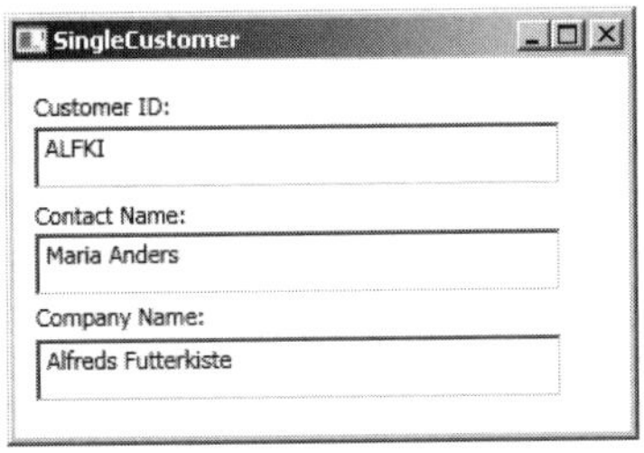

Figure 17-2   The rendering of the XAML window with simple data binding

The interesting part of this discussion emerges when you think about changing entities bound to a XAML window. LINQ to SQL entities, as well as LINQ to Entities entities, implement a couple of interfaces useful for data-binding purposes. These interfaces are *INotifyProperty-Changing* and *INotifyPropertyChanged*. The first of these interfaces notifies the data-binding environment that a property of a currently bound item is going to be changed, while the latter interface notifies the environment about a property change that has already happened. In Listing 17-5, you can see the signatures of these interfaces, together with the classes involved in their definition.

Listing 17-5 The signatures of the *INotifyPropertyChanging* and *INotifyPropertyChanged* interfaces, together with their related types

```
public interface INotifyPropertyChanging {
    event PropertyChangingEventHandler PropertyChanging;
}

public delegate void PropertyChangingEventHandler(object sender,
    PropertyChangingEventArgs e);

public class PropertyChangingEventArgs : EventArgs {
    public PropertyChangingEventArgs(string propertyName);
    public virtual string PropertyName { get; }
}

public interface INotifyPropertyChanged {
    event PropertyChangedEventHandler PropertyChanged;
}

public delegate void PropertyChangedEventHandler(object sender,
    PropertyChangedEventArgs e);

public class PropertyChangedEventArgs : EventArgs {
    public PropertyChangedEventArgs(string propertyName);
    public virtual string PropertyName { get; }
}
```

This behavior, which is available both for LINQ to SQL and LINQ to Entities, implies that the WPF environment is able to intercept and handle any data modification related to data-bound entities, and thus that it is able to dynamically and automatically refresh portions of the user interface to be consistent with data changes as soon as they occur.

To test this behavior, we can simply add a *Button* to the window created in Listing 17-3, as shown in the XAML excerpt presented in Listing 17-6.

Listing 17-6 A XAML excerpt to define a *Button* element

```
<Button Canvas.Left="10" Canvas.Top="171" Height="37"
    Name="changeCurrentCustomer" Width="250"
    Click="changeCurrentCustomer_Click">Change Current Customer</Button>
```

In Listing 17-7, you can see the code corresponding to the *Click* event of the *Button* element.

Listing 17-7   The *Click* event of the *Button* element

```
private void changeCurrentCustomer_Click(object sender,
    RoutedEventArgs e) {
        ((Customer)this.DataContext).ContactName += " modified!";
}
```

As soon as you press the Change Current Customer button, you will see that the *TextBox* displaying the *ContactName* synchronizes its value with the actual *Customer* instance.

In Figure 17-3, you can see the result, just after pressing the button.

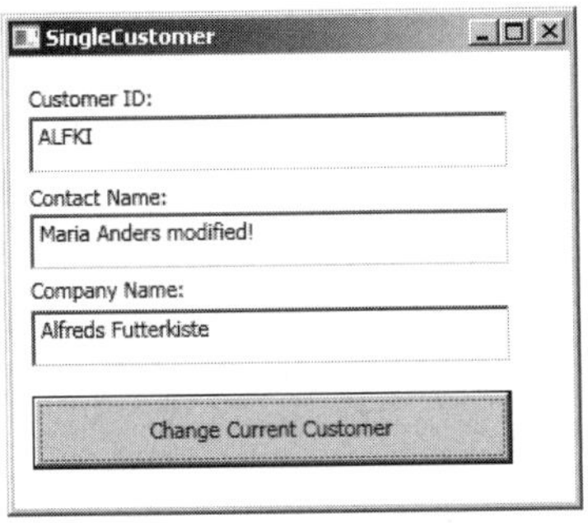

Figure 17-3   The rendering of the XAML window with simple data binding

This feature allows you to define user interfaces that are fully synchronized with their binding sources. Keep in mind that this behavior is automatically available only with autogenerated entities of both LINQ to SQL and LINQ to Entities. If you define your own entities, it is your responsibility to support this useful behavior.

On the other hand, you need a client-server application architecture to leverage this behavior, and in modern applications you will probably have LINQ to SQL or LINQ to Entities on the application server and client-side entities in the consumer environment. For this reason, communication frameworks such as Windows Communication Foundation (WCF), or even ASMX, provide the capability to automatically generate data binding–enabled client-side entities. This capability is provided by implementing *INotify** interfaces on the entities derived from communication contracts, such as those that are part of Web Services Description Languages (WSDLs) and Extensible Schema Definitions (XSDs). For further details about LINQ and WCF, refer to Chapter 18, "LINQ and the Windows Communication Foundation."

Binding Collections of Entities

So far, we have discussed how to use single entities as binding sources. Another interesting type of data binding is one used against a collection of items. From a WPF point of view, every type implementing the *IEnumerable* interface can be used as a binding source. However, only types implementing the *INotifyCollectionChanged* interface can automatically send notifications to the user interface about the insertion and deletion of items. In Listing 17-8, you can see the signature of this interface, together with the related types.

Listing 17-8   The signature of the *INotifyCollectionChanged* interface, together with its related types

```
public interface INotifyCollectionChanged {
    event NotifyCollectionChangedEventHandler CollectionChanged;
}

public delegate void NotifyCollectionChangedEventHandler(object sender,
    NotifyCollectionChangedEventArgs e);

public class NotifyCollectionChangedEventArgs : EventArgs {
    // Public constructors
    // ...

    // Public properties
    public NotifyCollectionChangedAction Action { get; }
    public IList NewItems { get; }
    public int NewStartingIndex { get; }
    public IList OldItems { get; }
    public int OldStartingIndex { get; }
}
```

WPF provides a type named *ObservableCollection<T>* that already implements the *INotify-CollectionChanged* interface, thus offering a set of events useful for monitoring the collection status. In general, this type can be used as the base class for any collection that needs to be bound in WPF, supporting the whole set of features available.

Unfortunately, the collections of entities in both LINQ to SQL and LINQ to Entities do not inherit the *ObservableCollection<T>* class or implement the *INotifyCollectionChanged* interface. This implies that you will not be able to automatically handle user-interface updates when the data sources change, which happens whenever you use the *Table<T>* and *DataQuery<T>* classes of LINQ to SQL or the *ObjectQuery<T>* class of LINQ to Entities as sources for binding elements in WPF. This also happens with any LINQ query based on either of these LINQ query providers. To visualize this behavior, consider the sample XAML code shown in Listing 17-9.

Listing 17-9   Sample XAML code of a WPF window with a *ListBox* bound to a LINQ to SQL set of entities

```
<Window x:Class="DevLeap.Linq.WPF.ComplexBinding"
  xmlns="http://schemas.microsoft.com/winfx/2006/xaml/presentation"
  xmlns:x="http://schemas.microsoft.com/winfx/2006/xaml"
  Title="WPF LINQ Sample Application" Height="418" Width="616"
  Loaded="Window_Loaded">

  <Window.Resources>
    <DataTemplate x:Key="CustomerTemplate">
```

```
      <Grid>
        <Grid.ColumnDefinitions>
          <ColumnDefinition Width="50" />
          <ColumnDefinition Width="200" />
          <ColumnDefinition Width="*"/>
        </Grid.ColumnDefinitions>
        <TextBlock Grid.Column="0" Text="{Binding Path=CustomerID}" />
        <TextBlock Grid.Column="1" Text="{Binding Path=ContactName}" />
        <TextBlock Grid.Column="2" Text="{Binding Path=CompanyName}" />
      </Grid>
    </DataTemplate>
  </Window.Resources>

  <Canvas>
    <TextBlock Canvas.Top="8" Height="18.96"
      Canvas.Left="9.183" Width="113">Customer ID:</TextBlock>
    <TextBox Canvas.Top="5" Name="CustomerID"
      Text="{Binding Path=CustomerID}" Height="21.96"
      Canvas.Left="127" Width="84" />
    <TextBlock Canvas.Top="40" Height="19"
      Canvas.Left="9.183" Width="113">Contact Name:</TextBlock>
    <TextBox Canvas.Top="37" Name="ContactName"
      Text="{Binding Path=ContactName}" Height="22"
      Canvas.Left="127" Width="171" />
    <TextBlock Canvas.Top="72" Height="19"
      Canvas.Left="8" Width="114.183">Company Name:</TextBlock>
    <TextBox Canvas.Top="69" Name="CompanyName"
      Text="{Binding Path=CompanyName}" Height="22"
      Canvas.Left="127" Width="171" />
    <Button Canvas.Left="8" Canvas.Top="105" Height="28"
      Name="reloadCustomersList" Width="151"
      Click="reloadCustomersList_Click">Reload Customers</Button>
    <Button Canvas.Left="176" Canvas.Top="105" Height="28"
      Name="addNewCustomer" Width="151"
      Click="addNewCustomer_Click">Add a new Customer</Button>
    <Button Canvas.Left="344" Canvas.Top="105" Height="28"
      Name="deleteCustomer" Width="151"
      Click="deleteCustomer_Click">Delete selected Customer</Button>
    <StackPanel Margin="8,120,11,10" Name="panelCustomers"
      Grid.ColumnSpan="2"
      Height="233" Canvas.Left="0" Canvas.Top="27" Width="582">
      <ListBox IsSynchronizedWithCurrentItem="True"
        ItemsSource="{Binding}"
        ItemTemplate="{StaticResource CustomerTemplate}"
        Height="233" Width="582" />
    </StackPanel>
  </Canvas>
</Window>
```

As you can see, this XAML code defines a *DataTemplate* element that defines how to render each *Customer* instance of Northwind customers. Later in the code, the template is applied to each item of a *ListBox* element. Moreover, there are three *TextBox* elements that are bound to the *Customer* instance currently selected within the *ListBox* element. Finally, there are three buttons that allow you to refresh the list of customers, add a new *Customer* instance, and delete the currently selected *Customer* instance, respectively. In Listing 17-10, you can see the source code behind the XAML in Listing 17-9.

Listing 17-10   The code behind the *ComplexBinding* XAML of Listing 17-9

```
public partial class ComplexBinding : Window {
    private NorthwindDataContext dc;

    public ComplexBinding() {
        InitializeComponent();
    }

    private void Window_Loaded(object sender, RoutedEventArgs e) {
        dc = new NorthwindDataContext();
        bindWindow();
    }

    private void reloadCustomersList_Click(object sender,
        RoutedEventArgs e) {
        bindWindow();
    }

    private void bindWindow() {
        this.DataContext =
            from   c in dc.Customers
            select c;
    }

    private void addNewCustomer_Click(object sender, RoutedEventArgs e) {
        Customer c = new Customer {
            CustomerID = "DLEAP",
            ContactName = "Paolo Pialorsi",
            CompanyName = "DevLeap",
            Country = "Italy",
        };

        dc.Customers.InsertOnSubmit(c);
        dc.SubmitChanges();
    }

    private void deleteCustomer_Click(object sender, RoutedEventArgs e) {
        Customer c = dc.Customers
            .First(i => i.CustomerID == CustomerID.Text);
        if (c != null) {
            dc.Customers.DeleteOnSubmit(c);
            dc.SubmitChanges();
        }
    }
}
```

In Figure 17-4, you can see this WPF window in action.

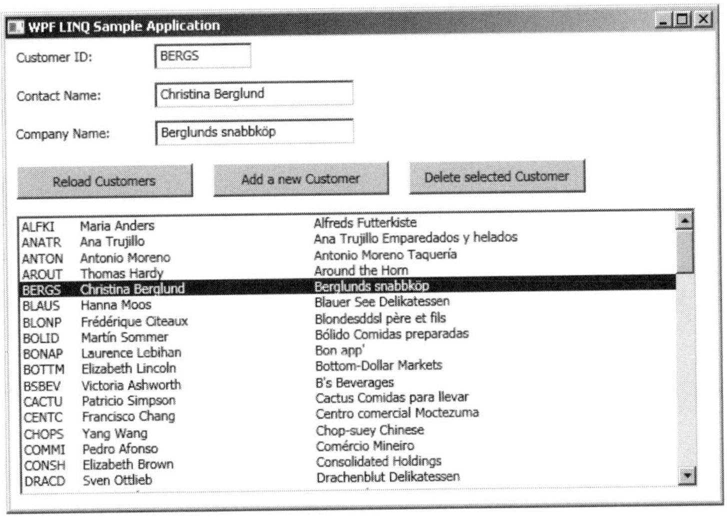

Figure 17-4   The rendering of the XAML window with complex (list and detail) data binding

It is really interesting to note that whenever you select a *Customer* instance within the *ListBox* element and change its content using one of the three *TextBox* elements, the *ListBox* content is automatically updated too. This happens because each single entity returned by the query (*DataQuery<T>* in our example) implements both *INotifyPropertyChanging* and *INotifyProperty-Changed* interfaces, which allows it to automatically notify the user interface of its changes.

However, if you click the Add A New Customer button, you will see that the newly created *Customer* instance will not appear in the bound list. Because the collection returned by LINQ to SQL does not implement the *INotifyCollectionChanged* interface, it does not notify the user interface of any change. To see the user interface updated, you need to click the Reload Customers button. The same behavior would take place with LINQ to Entities.

In our opinion, this is not really an issue unless you are writing a simple prototype or demo. As we already stated with regard to single entity binding, in modern software architectures you will never have a client-server scenario, but you will probably have a consumer application that consumes an application server leveraging an abstract communication layer. On the consumer side, there will be entities and collections of entities different from the ones on the application server side. The entities on the consumer side will be specifically designed to be bound correctly to the user interface (Windows Forms, WPF, ASP.NET, and so on).

Using LINQ with Silverlight

Silverlight is the cross-browser, cross-platform, and cross-device plug-in that Microsoft promotes as a technology for delivering rich, media-based Web solutions. At the time of this writing, the released version of Silverlight is 1.0, which is mostly suitable for interactive video and streaming solutions. However, Microsoft is hard at work on the Silverlight 2.0 release. In this upcoming release of the product, there will be support for both LINQ to Objects and LINQ to XML, as well as ASP.NET AJAX support. This will allow you to define really rich Web 2.0 client solutions, leveraging the syntax and tools that are also available on the server side.

Neither LINQ to SQL nor LINQ to Entities implementations will be available in Silverlight 2.0 because plug-ins built on top of such a framework will work on the client-side, within the browser. For security reasons (browser sandboxing) as well as for location reasons (usually, the database management system is not available to the Web client), there is no way to connect to a remote database management system from these types of implementations. However, for a Silverlight application it should be possible for you to use LINQ providers that access remote services. (We presented an example of this with the *FlightStatusService* provider in Chapter 12, "Extending LINQ.")

Summary

In this chapter, we demonstrated how to use entities and collections of entities of both LINQ to SQL and LINQ to Entities as sources for data binding in WPF. In particular, we showed you that single entities are ideal for data-binding tasks in WPF, while collections and LINQ queries of such entities are not as good.

We also demonstrated that, in general, both LINQ to SQL and LINQ to Entities work on the application server side, and only pure client-server solutions can leverage LINQ to Relational entities as data-binding sources. Client-server solutions are in general out-of-date and legacy solutions when compared to modern multitier solutions. Finally, we noted that the upcoming release of Silverlight (version 2.0) will include native support for LINQ to Objects and LINQ to XML, but there will not be support for LINQ to Relational implementations.

Chapter 18

LINQ and the Windows Communication Foundation

Language Integrated Query (LINQ) is a pervasive technology that you will find useful within any other .NET environment, including Windows Communication Foundation (WCF) services. When considering how to use LINQ with WCF, two of the main questions are whether queries can be sent across application layer boundaries and whether you can use LINQ to SQL or LINQ to Entities objects on smart clients and disconnected applications.

In this chapter we will try to answer these and other questions. We will describe how to use LINQ with WCF-based services and how to use the new query language to simplify services development. In the first section we provide a quick overview of the basics of WCF as context for the remaining sections of the chapter, where we will cover WCF and LINQ to SQL, WCF and LINQ to Entities, and the serialization of query expressions. If you already know about WCF in .NET 3.5, you can skip the next section and move directly to the section "WCF and LINQ to SQL." Otherwise you should carefully read the section "WCF Overview" to understand the remaining parts of this chapter.

WCF Overview

Windows Communication Foundation is a basic framework for developing distributed solutions based on a solid communication infrastructure. It can be used to define service-oriented solutions as well as to implement communication layers in a .NET environment. WCF represents the evolution and merging of many previous frameworks, such as COM+ Serviced Components, ASMX Web Services, WSE SOAP Services, .NET Remoting, and (to a degree) MSMQ. The key benefits of WCF (also known as ServiceModel because of the name of its namespace, *System.ServiceModel*) when compared to its ancestors are the unified programming model that it provides and its design and architecture that lead to a fully configurable and maintainable framework.

> **More Info** To learn more about Windows Communication Foundation, we suggest that you read, in the following order, the books *Microsoft Windows Communication Foundation Step by Step* by John Sharp (Microsoft Press); *Windows Communication Foundation Unleashed* by Craig McMurtry, Marc Mercuri, Nigel Watling, Matt Winkler (Sams); and *Inside Windows Communication Foundation* by Justin Smith (Microsoft Press).

From a ServiceModel point of view, services are provided by service hosts and consumed by service consumers. Each service implements one or more contracts, shared with its consumers and published through a specific endpoint.

WCF Contracts and Services

In WCF a contract is a type (which might be an interface or a class) that is decorated with specific attributes. The code in Listing 18-1 shows a simple contract.

Listing 18-1   A sample service contract definition

```
[ServiceContract(Namespace = "http://schemas.devleap.com/OrderService")]
public interface IOrderService {
    [OperationContract()]
    int InsertOrder(Order o);
}
```

Notice the *ServiceContract* and *OperationContract* attributes. These attributes instruct the Ser-viceModel infrastructure to publish the contract with a specific XML namespace for messages and with a particular operation, named *InsertOrder*. An implementation of this service could be similar to Listing 18-2.

Listing 18-2   A sample service implementation

```
public class OrderService: IOrderService {
    public int InsertOrder(Order o) {
        // Implementation details hidden ...
    }
}
```

Each operation in WCF implements a specific message exchange pattern (MEP), which can be a request/reply pattern, a receive-only pattern, or a send-only pattern, depending on the operation's signature. Our example of a service works with a request/reply MEP. Regardless of the type of MEP your service implements, communication is based on messages. The ServiceModel defines a very low-level concept of a message, which is implemented by the *System.ServiceModel.Channels.Message* type. The *Message* type describes a SOAP message as an XML Infoset and provides properties and methods with which to navigate through the SOAP nodes. Internally, all services work with instances of this type, but managing SOAP messages manually, as classic XML, is often too complicated, even if it is actually possible.

Instead, in real-world solutions WCF services publish contracts that work with "serializable" types. For instance, the service contract we defined works with a type *Order* that needs to be serializable. We have many different choices for serialization, depending on what we want to do with the service and what kind and level of interoperability we want to achieve with other platforms. If we need to communicate from .NET to .NET, as we could do with .NET Remoting in the past, we can add a *SerializableAttribute* on top of the *Order* type, as shown in Listing 18-3.

Listing 18-3   A runtime serializable *Order* type

```
[Serializable]
public class Order {
    public int Id { get; set; }
    public decimal Amount { get; set; }
    public string CustomerCode { get; set; }
}
```

On the other hand, if we want to define the order as an XML contract, we would start from its XSD definition, as in Listing 18-4.

Listing 18-4   The XML schema definition of an order

```
<?xml version="1.0" encoding="utf-8" ?>
<xsd:schema
    targetNamespace="http://schemas.devleap.com/Order"
    elementFormDefault="qualified"
    xmlns="http://schemas.devleap.com/Order"
    xmlns:xsd="http://www.w3.org/2001/XMLSchema">
    <xsd:element name="Order">
        <xsd:complexType>
            <xsd:sequence>
                <xsd:element name="Id" type="xsd:int" />
                <xsd:element name="Amount" type="xsd:decimal" />
                <xsd:element name="CustomerCode" type="xsd:string" />
            </xsd:sequence>
        </xsd:complexType>
    </xsd:element>
</xsd:schema>
```

In this case, we could then use a command line tool called SVCUTIL.EXE to convert the XSD definition to a .NET type. Here is the syntax for that operation:

```
C:\>SVCUTIL.EXE /dconly OrderSchema.xsd
```

The result, often called a *data contract*, is shown in the following excerpt:

```
using System.Runtime.Serialization;
[DataContract(Namespace = "http://schemas.devleap.com/Order")]
public partial class Order {
    [DataMember (IsRequired=true)]
    public int Id { get; set; }

    [DataMember (IsRequired=true, Order=1)]
    public decimal Amount { get; set; }

    [DataMember (IsRequired=true, EmitDefaultValue=false, Order=2)]
    public string CustomerCode { get; set; }
}
```

One more possibility is to engage the "legacy" SOAP serialization engine, used by ASP.NET ASMX Web Services and based on the class *XmlSerializer* from the *System.Xml.Serialization* namespace. In this case you can start again from the XSD schema and generate the serializable .NET type by using the XSD.EXE command line tool:

```
C:\>XSD.EXE -c OrderSchema.xsd
```

The *-c* flag instructs the tool to create the code corresponding to the XML schema provided. Here is an excerpt of the result:

```
using System.Xml.Serialization;
[XmlRoot(Namespace = "http://schemas.devleap.com/Order")]
public partial class Order {
    [XmlElement()]
    public int Id { get; set; }

    [XmlElement()]
    public decimal Amount { get; set; }

    [XmlElement()]
    public string CustomerCode { get; set; }
}
```

The autogenerated type is very similar to the one obtained by using SVCUTIL.EXE. The main difference is that it is decorated with attributes from the *System.Xml.Serialization* namespace rather than the *DataContract* and *DataMember* attributes.

> **Note**   There are also other differences about extensibility that we will not cover in this book.

If you want to use the *XmlSerializer* serialization engine, you also need to modify the contract definition by explicitly declaring your intention.

```
[ServiceContract(Namespace = "http://schemas.devleap.com/OrderService")]
[XmlSerializerFormat()]
public interface IOrderService {
    [OperationContract()]
    int InsertOrder(Order o);
}
```

One last opportunity offered by WCF is to work with types that describe the SOAP message structure (a set of optional headers and a mandatory body) from a wider perspective than pure XML. In fact, in this case you can work with types known as *message contracts,* which use a different set of attributes that are useful for defining what to put within the SOAP message body and what to put in the optional collection of headers. However, in using these types, you do not have access to the low-level XML Infoset.

Listing 18-5 shows an example of such a contract, once again describing our order.

Listing 18-5   The message contract describing the order insertion

```
using System.Xml.Serialization;
[MessageContract(IsWrapped = true, WrapperName = "Order",
    WrapperNamespace = "http://schemas.devleap.com/Order")]
public class OrderRequestMessage {
    [MessageHeader (MustUnderstand = true)]
    public Guid TransactionId { get; set; }

    [MessageBodyMember (Order = 0)]
    public int Id { get; set; }

    [MessageBodyMember (Order = 1)]
    public decimal Amount { get; set; }

    [MessageBodyMember (Order = 2)]
    public string CustomerCode { get; set; }
}
```

Here the *MessageContract* attribute declares the type of contract we are describing, and the *MessageHeader* and *MessageBody* attributes declare what to put in the SOAP header and the SOAP body, respectively.

From a service-oriented point of view, contracts should usually be based on message contracts or data contracts, eventually expressed in the legacy *XmlSerializer* compliant style. Of course, you can simply define parameters as you would with common methods, or you can use run-time serializable types, but this approach would be tightly coupled to the .NET environment and would not really be interoperable and service oriented, even if suitable for WCF solutions in the .NET Remoting style.

Service Oriented Contracts

To be completely service oriented, our sample service needs to have the contract shown in Listing 18-6:

Listing 18-6   The order service contract

```
[ServiceContract(Namespace = "http://schemas.devleap.com/OrderService")]
public interface IOrderService {
    [OperationContract()]
    OrderResult InsertOrder(Order o);
}
```

Here the *OrderResult* type is another data contract type, generated from its XSD (shown in Listing 18-7), that describes the result of the order insertion.

Listing 18-7   The *OrderResult* data contract XML schema definition

```xml
<?xml version="1.0" encoding="utf-8" ?>
<xsd:schema
    targetNamespace="http://schemas.devleap.com/OrderResult"
    elementFormDefault="qualified"
    xmlns="http://schemas.devleap.com/OrderResult"
    xmlns:xsd="http://www.w3.org/2001/XMLSchema">
    <xsd:element name="OrderResult">
        <xsd:complexType>
            <xsd:sequence>
                <xsd:element name="Id" type="xsd:int" />
                <xsd:element name="Result">
                    <xsd:simpleType>
                        <xsd:restriction base="xsd:string">
                            <xsd:enumeration value="Inserted" />
                            <xsd:enumeration value="BackOrder" />
                            <xsd:enumeration value="Rejected" />
                        </xsd:restriction>
                    </xsd:simpleType>
                </xsd:element>
            </xsd:sequence>
        </xsd:complexType>
    </xsd:element>
</xsd:schema>
```

Listing 18-8 shows the essential part of the corresponding service implementation:

Listing 18-8   The order service implementation

```csharp
public class OrderService: IOrderService {
    OrderResult InsertOrder(Order o) {
        // Implementation details omitted ...
    }
}
```

Endpoint and Service Hosting

To publish a service such as this, you need to define a service host, which can be any type of application that is able to offer the service through one or more endpoints. An endpoint consists of an address at which the service is available, a binding that you can see as the transport protocol with its configured features, and a reference to a specific contract to use while communicating with the consumers. The WCF object model provides a class to implement a service host, named *ServiceHost* as well. Listing 18-9 shows a sample of its use, publishing the service over HTTP.

Listing 18-9   A sample code-configured service host for the order service

```
public static SampleHostApplication
    static void Main() {
        using (ServiceHost host = new ServiceHost(typeof(OrderService))) {
            host.AddServiceEndpoint(typeof(IOrderService),
                new WSHttpBinding(),
                "http://localhost:8000/OrderService");
            host.Open();
            // Wait for connections ... code hidden
        }
    }
}
```

The previous example defines the service host configuration by using code. You can also use a .config file to provide all the details about the endpoint to keep the code free from deployment details. In this second case the service host code would look like the code in Listing 18-10.

Listing 18-10   A sample service host for the order service with a separated configuration file

```
public static SampleHostApplication
    static void Main() {
        using (ServiceHost host = new ServiceHost(typeof(OrderService))) {
            host.Open();
            // Wait for connections ... code hidden
        }
    }
}
```

As you can see, the endpoint configuration code is missing because its definition has been moved into the .config file, shown in Listing 18-11.

Listing 18-11   The configuration file for the order service

```
<?xml version="1.0" encoding="utf-8" ?>
<configuration>
    <system.serviceModel>
        <services>
            <service name="DevLeap.Linq.WCF.OrderService">
                <endpoint
                    address="http://localhost:8000/OrderService"
                    binding="wsHttpBinding"
                    contract="DevLeap.Linq.WCF.IOrderService" />
            </service>
        </services>
    </system.serviceModel>
</configuration>
```

In this example, the *ServiceModel* configuration section declares the existence of a service published through a particular endpoint over a WS-* compliant HTTP-based binding. A *service* element can have many endpoint child nodes as a means to publish the same service with different contracts, bindings, or addresses. For instance, you might be interested in making the service available via HTTP for remote consumers, while preferring to consume the service through TCP within your local area network. Listing 18-12 shows an example.

Listing 18-12   Another configuration file for the order service, publishing a couple of endpoints

```xml
<?xml version="1.0" encoding="utf-8" ?>
<configuration>
    <system.serviceModel>
        <services>
            <service name="DevLeap.Linq.WCF.OrderService">
                <endpoint
                    address="http://localhost:8000/OrderService"
                    binding="wsHttpBinding"
                    contract="DevLeap.Linq.WCF.IOrderService" />
                <endpoint
                    address="net.tcp://localhost:35001/OrderService"
                    binding="netTcpBinding"
                    contract="DevLeap.Linq.WCF.IOrderService" />
            </service>
        </services>
    </system.serviceModel>
</configuration>
```

In Visual Studio 2008, you do not need to manually define a service host, especially if you are using it only for testing purposes. In fact, you can simply create a WCF Service Library project and implement the WCF service in it. We suggest that you maintain a separate project for the contracts to keep your solution better organized. This kind of project template automatically provides an out-of- the-box service host application, called WCF Service Host, that works like the ASP.NET Development Server for ASP.NET Web projects in Visual Studio 2005. To test your service you just need to press F5 and start using it.

Service Consumers

To consume a service you need a .NET service consumer. Again using Visual Studio 2008 and a project of type WCF Service Library, you can make use of an out- of-the-box client, called WCF Test Client, that allows you to invoke the service operations using a dedicated client, which is also capable of tracing the SOAP requests and responses. Figure 18-1 shows an example in Visual Studio 2008.

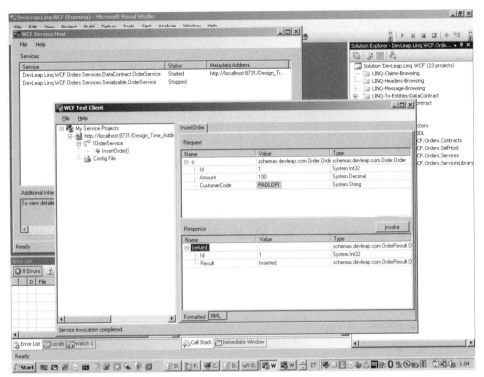

Figure 18-1   The WCF Service Host and WCF Test Client provided by Visual Studio 2008

In addition to this useful utility, you can define consumers in a couple of ways in WFC. The
first approach assumes an abstraction from the service itself and is based on the platform
independent WSDL contract definition. You start from the WSDL service description, which
can be automatically generated by the ServiceModel infrastructure (if adequately configured)
or defined by using the SVCUTIL.EXE command line tool. Here is an example of the command line parameters necessary to build a consumer-side contract from a service-side one:

```
C:\>SVCUTIL.EXE DevLeap.Linq.WCF.OrderServiceContracts.dll
```

Here the given DLL assembly contains the contract's definition for our service. The result of
this command is a set of WSDL and XSD files describing the service contract from an XML
abstract point of view. Invoking SVCUTIL.EXE one more time, with the generated files as
input, creates the consumer-side proxy classes.

```
C:\>SVCUTIL.EXE OrderServiceContracts.wsdl Order.xsd OrderResult.xsd
```

The result of this command is an *OrderServiceClient* class and all its related types (*Order, Order-
Result*, etc.), which we can use to invoke the service. The tool will also generate an app.config
file that defines the consumer-side configuration of the ServiceModel. The auto-generated
code (shown in Listing 18-13) hides from us the background, and the beauty, of the WCF
communication infrastructure.

Listing 18-13   The code on the client that consumes the service referenced through its WSDL contract

```
Order o = new Order() { Id = 1, Amount = 100, CustomerCode = "PP001"};
OrderServiceClient svcClient = new OrderServiceClient();
OrderResult result = svcClient.InserOrder(o);
```

The same result could have been reached by using the Add Service Reference menu command, available in Visual Studio 2008 through the Solution Explorer. This command requires you to specify the URI of the service to download its metadata through WS-MetadataExchange (if supported by the service) or to request its WSDL and XSDs through the old-fashioned "?WSDL" querystring HTTP request. Any of these solutions requires you to enable metadata publishing on the service side, through configuration or code. Listing 18-14 shows how to enable metadata through configuration, which in general is a more maintainable solution.

Listing 18-14   A service-side configuration file enabling metadata publishing

```
<?xml version="1.0" encoding="utf-8" ?>
<configuration>
    <system.serviceModel>
        <services>
            <service name="DevLeap.Linq.WCF.OrderService"
                behaviorConfiguration="OrderServiceBehavior">
                <endpoint
                    binding="wsHttpBinding"
                    contract="DevLeap.Linq.WCF.IOrderService" />
                <endpoint
                    address="mex"
                    binding="mexHttpBinding"
                    contract="IMetadataExchange" />
                <host>
                    <baseAddresses>
                        <baseAddress
                            value="http://localhost:8000/OrderService" />
                    </baseAddresses>
                </host>
            </service>
        </services>
        <behaviors>
            <serviceBehaviors>
                <behavior name="OrderServiceBehavior">
                    <serviceMetadata allowHttpGet="true" />
                </behavior>
            </serviceBehaviors>
        </behaviors>
    </system.serviceModel>
</configuration>
```

This new configuration declares a custom behavior configuration. From a ServiceModel point of view, behaviors are configurations for the whole service or for any particular endpoint. They determine how the service behaves in terms of security, metadata publishing, throttling, session management, etc.

In this particular configuration we enabled metadata publishing via HTTP GET and also through a specific endpoint supporting WS-MetadataExchange over HTTP. We also defined a base address URI for service publishing and a custom relative address for the service itself and for its WS-MetadataExchange publishing.

While a service host with this configuration is running, we can reference the service directly via the Add Service Reference command.

Whenever you consume WCF services from a WCF environment, without any need for interoperability, you can choose not to decouple the service and the consumer through WSDL and XSD. In fact, you can directly share the contract types, referencing the assembly that defines them on the service side. To use these shared contracts on the consumer side, you use an ad hoc ServiceModel factory type called *ChannelFactory*, shown in Listing 18-15.

Listing 18-15   A sample of *ChannelFactory<TChannel>* usage on the consumer side

```
ChannelFactory<IOrderService> svcClientFactory =
    new ChannelFactory<IOrderService>(
        new WSHttpBinding(),
        "http://localhost:8000/OrderService");
IOrderService svcClientChannel = svcClientFactory.CreateChannel();
Order o = new Order() { Id = 1, Amount = 100, CustomerCode = "PP001"};
OrderResult result = svcClient.InserOrder(o);
```

In this example, the generic *ChannelFactory* builds a communication channel for us to establish communication with the service. The *IOrderService* interface and the *Order* type, however, are the same as we have on the service side. Of course, this way of working is in contrast to one of the main service-oriented tenents (services should share contracts not types), but in this situation our goal is not to provide a truly service-oriented solution, but to consume a remote service, making the physical location of the service transparent. To completely achieve the goal of "location and binding transparency," we can use a configuration file and simply reference it while constructing the channel factory. Listing 18-16 shows a sample configuration file.

Listing 18-16   A consumer side configuration file to define a remote service

```
<?xml version="1.0" encoding="utf-8" ?>
<configuration>
    <system.serviceModel>
        <client name="OrderServiceEndpoint">
            <endpoint
                address="http://localhost:8000/OrderService"
                binding="wsHttpBinding"
                contract="DevLeap.Linq.WCF.IOrderService" />
        </client>
    </system.serviceModel>
</configuration>
```

In Listing 18-17 you can see the revised code to use the configuration shown in Listing 18-16 while instantiating the factory.

Listing 18-17   The code to consume a service via *ChannelFactory< TChannel>* using a .config file

```
IOrderService svcClientChannel = svcClientFactory.CreateChannel(
    "OrderServiceEndpoint");
Order o = new Order() { Id = 1, Amount = 100, CustomerCode = "PP001"};
OrderResult = svcClientChannel.InserOrder(o);
```

Starting from these concepts, we can now evaluate how LINQ and WCF can work together to improve services development.

WCF and LINQ to SQL

One use of WCF is to move entities obtained from LINQ to SQL from the application server to a consumer. However, there are some constraints in doing this that we will explore in the following section about serialization. After we cover serialization, we will describe how to effectively combine WCF and LINQ to SQL.

LINQ to SQL Entities and Serialization

To use LINQ to SQL entities within WCF services, you need to check how those entities behave in relation to the serialization engine in WCF. In fact, one of the main questions that arises when talking about the relationship between WCF and LINQ is what happens regarding serialization with LINQ to SQL entities and LINQ queries. To examine this matter, we will move through some different serialization scenarios, analyzing the behavior of LINQ and LINQ to SQL entities.

First of all, imagine that you have a LINQ to SQL entity model based on the well-known Northwind sample database. Now execute a query over the Customers table like the one shown here:

```
var customersFromUSA =
  from   c in dc.Customers
  where  c.Country == "USA" && c.Orders.Count > 3
  select c;
```

Now try to serialize *customersFromUSA* using a *BinaryFormatter* or a *DataContractSerializer*. Both operations fail with specific exceptions. The runtime formatter raises a *SerializationException* stating that the generic type *System.Data.Linq.DataQuery`1[]* is not marked as a serializable type. The *DataContractSerializer* throws an *InvalidDataContractException* declaring a similar issue (type not marked with the *DataContract* attribute). These exceptions occur because the query we defined is of a type that is not serializable and transferable across application domains or machines. (In fact, query expressions by design are not serializable, a topic we will cover in more depth later in the chapter.)

One possible solution is to try to convert the query result into an explicit list by using the *ToList* extension method and then serialize its result. Unfortunately, this step is not a complete solution because the entity types automatically generated by the LINQ to SQL toolset (SQL-Metal or the Visual Studio 2008 designer) are not serializable by default as well. However, you can solve that issue simply by changing a configuration parameter in the entity model designer (shown in Figure 18-2) for the DBML file, setting the value of Serialization Mode to Unidirectional. Unidirectional refers to the direction of serialization when you are serializing entities containing relationships. As you will see in more detail later, relationships are unidirectionally serialized from parent to child entities but not from child to parent.

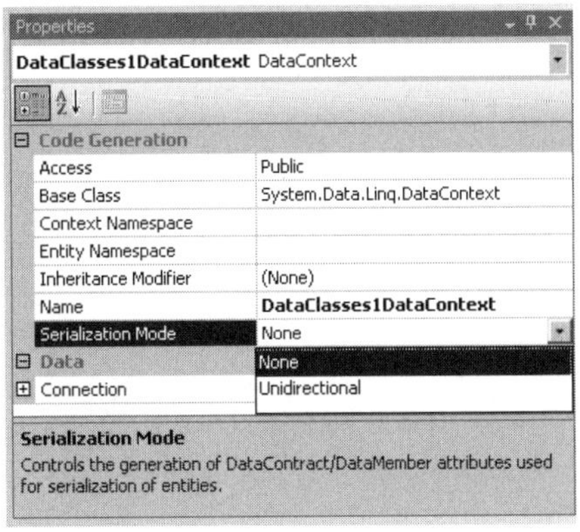

Figure 18-2   The Serialization Mode parameter of the DataContext model

If you prefer to use the SQLMetal tool, you can specify the "/serialization:unidirectional" parameter at the command line as follows:

```
C:\>SQLMETAL.EXE /server:yourserver /database:northwind /code:nwind.cs
    /namespace:nwind /serialization:unidirectional
```

Listing 18-18 is an excerpt of a LINQ to SQL entity describing the Northwind Customer table with the unidirectional serialization option configured.

Listing 18-18   An excerpt of the code generated by LINQ to SQL for the Customer entity of Northwind

```
[Table(Name="dbo.Customers")]
[DataContract()]
public partial class Customer : INotifyPropertyChanging, InotifyPropertyChanged {
    // ...
    private string _CustomerID;
    // ...

    [Column(Storage="_CustomerID", DbType="NChar(5) NOT NULL",
        CanBeNull=false, IsPrimaryKey=true)]
    [DataMember(Order = 1)]
    public string CustomerID {
```

```
            get { return this._CustomerID; }
            set {
                if ((this._CustomerID != value)) {
                    this.OnCustomerIDChanging(value);
                    this.SendPropertyChanging();
                    this._CustomerID = value;
                    this.SendPropertyChanged("CustomerID");
                    this.OnCustomerIDChanged();
                }
            }
        }
    }
    // Code omitted ...
    [Association(Name="Customer_Order", Storage="_Orders", OtherKey="CustomerID")]
    [DataMember(Order = 12)]
    public EntitySet<Order> Orders {
        get {
            return this._Orders;
        }
        set {
            this._Orders.Assign(value);
        }
    }
}
```

As you can see, the type is not marked with the *SerializableAttribute;* indeed, it is not serializable through the common runtime serialization based on .NET formatters. However, it is marked with *DataContract* and *DataMember* attributes, which makes it serializable with *DataContractSerializer* and useful for WCF applications. Also look at the collection of *Orders,* of type *EntitySet<Order>*: it is marked as a *DataMember,* a subject that we will describe in more detail later in this chapter.

At this point, we can argue that even LINQ queries are not serializable and thus not suitable for WCF applications. However, LINQ to SQL entities are serializable through *DataContractSerializer,* which means that we can make use of them in WCF.

One other type of entities you might need to serialize are anonymous types. A typical situation you might face is a query returning a set of anonymous types instead of a set of entities taken from the entity model. Here is a simple query of this kind, for testing purposes:

```
var customersFromUSA =
  from   c in dc.Customers
  where  c.Country == "USA" && c.Orders.Count > 3
  select new { c.CustomerID, c.ContactName };
```

Unfortunately, anonymous types are not serializable. However, as an alternative solution you can define your own serializable types in cases in which a custom entity shape projection is needed. For example, you can define your own *SerializableCustomer* type such as the one shown in Listing 18-19.

Listing 18-19   A custom serializable customer type

```
[DataContract]
[Serializable]
public class SerializableCustomer {
    [DataMember]
    public String CustomerID { get; set; }

    [DataMember]
    public String CompanyName { get; set; }

    [DataMember]
    public String ContactName { get; set; }
}
```

You could then declare the query to project instances of your type:

```
var customersFromUSA =
  from   c in dc.Customers
  where  c.Country == "USA" && c.Orders.Count > 3
  select new SerializableCustomer {
    CustomerID = c.CustomerID,
    ContactName = c.ContactName
    CompanyName = c.CompanyName };
```

In this last situation the result of the LINQ query, calling the *ToList* method, will be serializable because our custom type is serializable as well. The query itself, however, is still not serializable.

To summarize, the behavior of LINQ and LINQ to SQL with regard to serialization is the following:

- LINQ queries are not serializable at all.

- LINQ to SQL entities are serializable only with *DataContractSerializer* but not with .NET runtime serialization through formatters.

- Anonymous types are not serializable at all.

- Custom serializable types are serializable, by definition, and can be used to project serializable data from LINQ queries.

Keep these rules in mind because we will refer to them during the remaining parts of the chapter.

Publishing LINQ to SQL Entities with WCF

Now let's consider a WCF service that exchanges entities with its consumers using LINQ to SQL types marked as unidirectional serializable. This service could be a kind of CRUD (Create, Read, Update, Delete) service that is not a pure service-oriented solution. However, service-oriented solutions are not always a requirement—for example, in situations in which you simply need to move data across layers in a proprietary solution that does not need to be interoperable and service oriented, you could effectively use a service with a CRUD behavior. Listing 18-20 shows the service contract:

Listing 18-20 The service contract of the CRUD service based on LINQ to SQL

```
[ServiceContract(Namespace = "http://schemas.devleap.com/CustomerService")]
interface ICustomerService {
    [OperationContract()]
    Customer GetCustomer(CustomerSelector selector);

    [OperationContract()]
    Customer AddCustomer(Customer customer);

    [OperationContract()]
    Customer UpdateCustomer(Customer customer);

    [OperationContract()]
    DeletionResult DeleteCustomer(Customer customer);
}

[DataContract(Namespace = "http://schemas.devleap.com/NW/CustomerSelector")]
public class CustomerSelector {
    [DataMember(Name = "CustomerID", Order = 0, IsRequired = true)]
    public String CustomerID { get; set; }
}

[DataContract(Namespace = "http://schemas.devleap.com/NW/DeletionResult")]
public class DeletionResult {
    [DataMember(Name = "Result", Order = 0, IsRequired = true)]
    public Boolean Result { get; set; }
}
```

The *CustomerSelector* and *DeletionResult* types are simply *DataContracts* useful for the definition of our CRUD service. The *Customer* type is the LINQ to SQL generated entity.

Let's concentrate on the customer retrieval operation. A hypothetical service implementation could be based on a back-end business layer enforcing all the security and validation rules, handling custom events and handlers, and executing the real business tasks. Listing 18-21 shows a sample implementation of the service.

Listing 18-21 An excerpt of the service implementation of the CRUD service based on LINQ to SQL

```
public class CustomerService: ICustomerService {
    public Customer GetCustomer(CustomerSelector selector) {
        CustomerBiz cb = new CustomerBiz();
        return (cb.GetCustomer(selector.CustomerID));
    }
    // Code omitted ...
}
```

Listing 18-22 shows the business component implementation of the *GetCustomer* method, based on a LINQ to SQL query.

Listing 18-22   The business component implementation of the *GetCustomer* method

```
public class CustomerBiz {
    public Customer GetCustomer(String customerID) {
        using (NorthwindDataContext northwind = getDataContext()) {
            var customer =
                northwind.Customers.Single(c => c.CustomerID == customerID);

            return (customer);
        }
    }
    // Code omitted ...
}
```

Using the diagnostic tools in WCF, we can see that on the wire each customer instance is transferred as an XML message like the one shown in Listing 18-23.

Listing 18-23   The XML message transferred on the wire by WCF

```
<GetCustomerResponse xmlns="http://schemas.devleap.com/CustomerService">
    <GetCustomerResult
      xmlns:b="http://schemas.datacontract.org/2004/07/
      DevLeap.Linq.WCF.LinqToSQL.NorthwindModel"
      xmlns:i="http://www.w3.org/2001/XMLSchemainstance">
        <b:CustomerID>Al FKI</b:CustomerID>
        <b:CompanyName>Alfreds Futterkiste</b:CompanyName>
        <b:ContactName>Maria Anders</b:ContactName>
        <!-- XML Omitted ... -->
        <b:Orders>
            <b:Order>
                <b:OrderID>10643</b:OrderID>
                <b:CustomerID>ALFKI</b:CustomerID>
                <b:EmployeeID>6</b:EmployeeID>
                <!-- XML Omitted ... -->
                <b:Order_Details>
                    <b:Order_Detail>
                        <b:OrderID>10643</b:OrderID>
                        <b:ProductID>28</b:ProductID>
                        <b:UnitPrice>45.6000</b:UnitPrice>
                        <b:Quantity>15</b:Quantity>
                        <b:Discount>0.25</b:Discount>
                    </b:Order_Detail>
                    <!-- XML Omitted ... -->
                </b:Order_Details>
            </b:Order>
            <!-- XML Omitted ... -->
        </b:Orders>
    </GetCustomerResult>
</GetCustomerResponse>
```

As you can see, the customer serialization contains not only the customer itself but also the object graph, including orders and order_details. Using a tool such as the Microsoft SQL Server Profiler, we can see that under the hood the LINQ query, executed within the business layer, simply queries the database engine for the customer record, as we have described in the chapters about LINQ to SQL in Part 2. Moreover, when the *DataContractSerializer* engine serializes the entity, it also tries to serialize its properties of type *EntitySet<T>* because they are marked with the *DataMember* attribute (see Listing 18-18). In this way, the collection of orders and the collection of order_items that are contained in each order are loaded during serialization. You can turn off this behavior simply by setting to *false* the *DeferredLoadingEnabled* property of the data context. Only in this case the collection of *Orders* will be left empty. Of course, as you have seen in the chapters about LINQ to SQL, when deferred loading is disabled and you try to access the *Orders* property by yourself it will also not be loaded.

Something different happens to the properties of type *EntityRef<T>*. Consider, for instance, the *Customer* property of each *Order* instance:

```
[Table(Name="dbo.Orders")]
[DataContract()]
public partial class Order :
    INotifyPropertyChanging, INotifyPropertyChanged {

    // Code omitted ...

    private EntityRef<Customer> _Customer;

  [Association(Name="Customer_Order",
    Storage="_Customer", ThisKey="CustomerID", IsForeignKey=true)]
  public Customer Customer {
        get { // Code omitted ... }
        set { // Code omitted ... }
    }
    // Code omitted ...
}
```

As you can see, the LINQ to SQL auto-generated code does not mark these properties with the *DataMember* attribute. These properties will not be serialized and they will not be loaded during serialization, regardless of the deferred loading configuration. One reason for this behavior is to avoid circular references during serialization. From this behavior comes the unidirectional definition of the serialization configuration.

Consuming LINQ to SQL Entities with WCF

Up to this point, we have described the behavior of LINQ to SQL and WCF from the service-side point of view. Now let's move to the consumer side, which offers additional challenges. We can consume our service with a classic service reference (based on a WSDL or on WS-MetadataExchange), and we can also consume it with a *ChannelFactory<T>*-based consumer.

Regardless of the type of consumer we define, it is worth noting that we can present the entities we receive from LINQ to SQL through WCF to users not only in read-only fashion but also for modification. The service contract we defined declares a full CRUD set of methods. Because the service implementation relies on the underlying business component, we will focus on it instead of the simpler and shorter operations.

Let's start with the *AddCustomer* operation. Take a look at the fundamental part of the entity addition code, shown in Listing 18-24.

Listing 18-24   The main implementation of the *AddCustomer* method of the business component

```
public class CustomerBiz {
    private NorthwindModel.NorthwindDataContext getDataContext() {
        NorthwindDataContext northwind = new NorthwindDataContext();
        northwind.DeferredLoadingEnabled = false;
        northwind.ObjectTrackingEnabled = true;
        return (northwind);
    }
    // Code omitted ...
    public Customer AddCustomer(Customer customer) {
        using (NorthwindDataContext northwind = getDataContext()) {
            northwind.Customers.Add(customer);
            northwind.SubmitChanges();
            return (customer);
        }
    }
    // Code omitted ...
}
```

The main parts of the code are the call to the *Add* method of the *Customers* table and the invocation of the *SubmitChanges* method on the *DataContext*. (See Chapter 4, "LINQ to SQL: Querying Data," and Chapter 5, "LINQ to SQL: Managing Data," for more details).

It is important to emphasize that our business component does not cache the *DataContext* object; instead it creates a new instance whenever it needs one. This behavior might seem strange, but consider that in our scenario, the consumer side is completely disconnected from the application server. It would be useless to track and keep in memory instances of our entities between different service invocations. Keeping a permanent instance of the *DataContext* would also reduce the scalability of the solution.

> **Note**   In a two-tier application, it is better to use a single *DataContext* instance to complete a unit of work, performing queries over entities and changing those entities within the same context.

The second operation we want to describe is the *DeleteCustomer* method, which is defined in Listing 18-25.

Listing 18-25   The implementation of the *DeleteCustomer* method of the business component

```
public Boolean DeleteCustomer(Customer customer) {
    using (NorthwindDataContext northwind = getDataContext()) {
        northwind.Customers.Attach(customer);
        northwind.Customers.Remove(customer);
        northwind.SubmitChanges();
        return (true);
    }
}
```

Here the behavior is a little bit different (and strange at first sight) from entity insertion: an *Attach* invocation precedes the *Remove* call! But there is an explanation for this. The entity received by the service for removal originally comes from the service side and has been moved across the wire to be handled by the consumer, which then gives the entity back to the service. During the entity's trip, the *DataContext* of the business layer is destroyed just after returning the entity instance to the consumer. When we receive the entity instance back in the service, we need to attach to the new *DataContext* the customer entity that is going to be removed. After attaching the customer to the actual context, we can remove it to make the LINQ to SQL engine aware of the deletion to execute during the next call to the *SubmitChanges* method.

The most complex situation is in the *UpdateCustomer* method. Here we need to attach the customer to the *Customers* table of the context, just as we did for deletion, but we also have some other considerations.

Usually, working in an always-connected environment (where the *DataContext* instance is shared and common to each data operation), you can change entities and call *SubmitChanges* directly through that context. However, in WCF we operate in a disconnected environment and, as you have already seen, the context is constructed and destroyed for each request. This leads to the need to attach the customer coming from the consumer side, as we did during deletion. Moreover, when updating the entity we also need to notify the context that the customer entity has to be considered as an updated version of a previously existing one. As you saw in Chapter 5, the *Attach* method offers three different overloads, two of them designed for this purpose.

The first *Attach* overload that is interesting in our scenario requires a couple of parameters: the entity and a *Boolean* variable stating whether the entity has been modified or not. This method also has some requirements for how the entity is defined within the model. It assumes that the entity has a version member or does not have an update check policy. In other words, you can have an entity with a row version, time stamp, or anything else useful for identifying concurrency conflicts, or you should configure the whole entity to not have concurrency checks at all. You can do this in the designer of the DBML model, configuring the *Update Check* property for each property of the entity to the value Never, as shown in Figure 18-3.

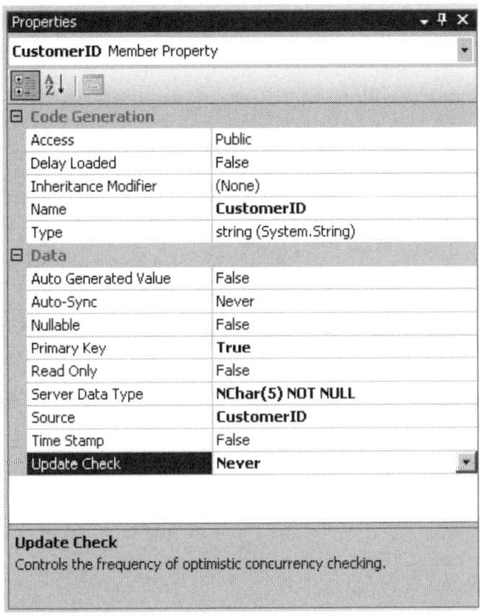

Figure 18-3   The Update Check parameter of the entity members of the data model

This configuration instructs the LINQ to SQL engine to not check concurrency issues. In the following excerpt, you can see the code generated by changing this parameter. Keep track of the *UpdateCheck* property in the *ColumnAttribute* definition (shown in bold).

Listing 18-26   The LINQ to SQL entity model for the *Customer* type with a concurrency check disabled

```
[Table(Name="dbo.Customers")]
[DataContract()]
public partial class Customer : INotifyPropertyChanging, INotifyPropertyChanged {

    // Code omitted ...

    [Column(Storage="_CustomerID", DbType="NChar(5) NOT NULL",
        CanBeNull=false, IsPrimaryKey=true, UpdateCheck=UpdateCheck.Never)]
    [DataMember(Order=1)]
    public string CustomerID {
        get {
            return this._CustomerID;
        }
        set {
            if ((this._CustomerID != value)) {
                this.OnCustomerIDChanging(value);
                this.SendPropertyChanging();
                this._CustomerID = value;
                this.SendPropertyChanged("CustomerID");
                this.OnCustomerIDChanged();
            }
        }
    }
    // Code omitted ...
}
```

The difference between having a concurrency check based on a version member and not having any kind of concurrency check is not trivial because this could affect the validity of your data. Usually we suggest implementing a concurrency check with a version member mapped to a row version/time-stamp field.

The second *Attach* method overload also requires a couple of arguments, both of the type of the attaching entity. The first parameter represents the entity to attach, and the second defines the original entity instance that will be used to compare the new one and determine the changes that occurred. Because we are in a disconnected environment, we do not have the original entity available unless we query it from the DBMS. For this reason, it is preferable to use the first overloaded method in the WCF scenario. Listing 18-27 shows the *UpdateCustomer* method using the first overload for *Attach*.

Listing 18-27   The *UpdateCustomer* method of the business component

```
public Customer UpdateCustomer(Customer customer) {
    NorthwindDataContext northwind = getDataContext();
    northwind.Customers.Attach(customer, true);
    northwind.SubmitChanges();
    return(customer);
}
```

One last situation to consider is the retrieval of a list of entities instead of a single one. In this case the service will return a *DataContract* serializable type containing a generic *List<T>*, where *T* is the entity type of the list—for instance, the *Customer* type. Returning the list instead of a single item is equivalent to the previous *GetCustomer* method implementation, but you need to convert the query result into a *List<Customer>*, applying the *ToList* extension method to the LINQ query. In cases in which you need to give the list of entities back to the service, you will find the two overloads of the *AttachAll* method of the LINQ to SQL *Table<T>* type useful. Both methods accept an *IEnumerable<T>* as their first argument and iterate the items, invoking the *Attach* method for each of them, eventually with a modification flag in the overload with the richest set of arguments.

As you can see, it is possible to transfer LINQ to SQL entities across the wire leveraging WCF and *DataContract* serialization. However, you need to address specific constraints and rules about entities configuration, such as the unidirectional behavior and the concurrency check policy you want to implement.

LINQ to Entities and WCF

In LINQ to Entities, as in LINQ to SQL, you might have a need to serialize queries and their results. As we mentioned previously, however, expression trees are not serializable, which means that in LINQ to Entities you cannot move queries across application domains or machines. A more interesting discussion concerns the serialization of ADO.NET Entity Framework entities. Those entities are marked with both *SerializableAttribute* and *DataContractAttribute*, which means that you can use the result of a LINQ to Entities query as the content of a WCF communication.

This section is based on Beta code!   The ADO.NET Entity Framework had not been
released at the time of writing. Because this section is based on beta code, some features
might be changed, removed, or added in the final release. This could invalidate some of the
examples shown in this section. We tried to keep this content updated and aligned with
the most recent information we had. In any case, we will publish news and corrections for the
book together with updated code samples at *http://www.programminglinq.com*.

Let's start by modeling the same part of the Northwind database that we used before, this
time by using the ADO.NET Entity Framework, creating entities for Customers, Orders,
Order_Details, and Products, as shown in Figure 18-4.

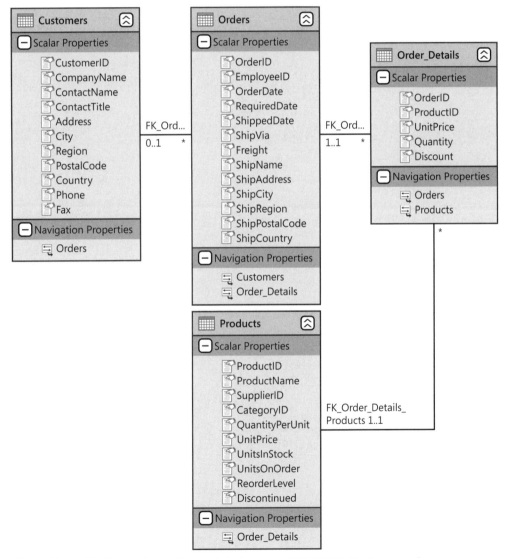

Figure 18-4   The Northwind entity model schema in ADO.NET Entity Framework

Now imagine that you need to define a WCF service to query the list of customers filtered by country, by region, or by both. Listing 18-28 contains the hypothetical service contract.

Listing 18-28   The service contract of a service to query the list of Northwind customers

```
[ServiceContract(Namespace = "http://schemas.devleap.com/NW/CustomersService")]
public interface ICustomersService {
    [OperationContract()]
    CustomersList ListCustomers(CustomersFilter request);
}
```

In this contract, the types *CustomersList* and *CustomersFilter* are serializable through *Data-ContractSerializer* and are defined as shown in Listing 18-29.

Listing 18-29   The contract types for the service to query the list of Northwind customers

```
[CollectionDataContract(
    Name = "Customers",
    Namespace = "http://schemas.devleap.com/NW/Customers",
    ItemName = "Customer")]
public class CustomersList: List<Customers> {
    public CustomersList() { }
    public CustomersList(IEnumerable<Customers> source): base(source) { }
}

[DataContract(Namespace = "http://schemas.devleap.com/NW/CustomersFilter")]
public class CustomersFilter {
    [DataMember(Name = "Country", Order = 0, IsRequired = false)]
    public String Country { get; set; }

    [DataMember(Name = "Region", Order = 1, IsRequired = false)]
    public String Region { get; set; }
}
```

We defined *CustomersList* as a custom list, extending the generic *List<T>*, to be sure that the corresponding XML has a defined namespace and that each item has a consistent name, using the proper *DataContract* attributes. (In general, it is a good habit to uniquely identity XML messages with a specific XML namespace. Even though these are introductory samples related to LINQ and not to XML, we decided to define appropriate contracts.) *CustomersFilter* is a classic data contract type with a couple of optional properties.

The *CustomersList* type describes a list of items of type *Customers*, where *Customers* is the entity automatically generated by the Entity Framework to represent a single customer instance. Listing 18-30 shows a simplified excerpt of this type.

Listing 18-30   An excerpt of the Entity Framework designer's auto-generated code for the *Customers* entity

```
[global::System.Data.Objects.DataClasses.EdmEntityTypeAttribute(
    NamespaceName="NorthwindModel", Name="Customers")]
[global::System.Runtime.Serialization.DataContractAttribute()]
[global::System.Serializable()]
public partial class Customers:
    global::System.Data.Objects.DataClasses.EntityObject {

    public static Customers CreateCustomers(
        string customerID, string companyName) {
        Customers customers = new Customers();
        customers.CustomerID = customerID;
        customers.CompanyName = companyName;
        return customers;
    }

    [global::System.Data.Objects.DataClasses.EdmScalarPropertyAttribute(
        EntityKeyProperty=true, IsNullable=false)]
    [global::System.Runtime.Serialization.DataMemberAttribute()]
    public string CustomerID {
        get {
            return this._CustomerID;
        }
        set {
            this.OnCustomerIDChanging(value);
            this.ReportPropertyChanging("CustomerID");
            this._CustomerID =
                global::System.Data.Objects.DataClasses
                .StructuralObject.SetValidValue(value, false, 5);
            this.ReportPropertyChanged("CustomerID");
            this.OnCustomerIDChanged();
        }
    }
    private string _CustomerID;
    partial void OnCustomerIDChanging(string value);
    partial void OnCustomerIDChanged();

    // Code omitted ...
    [global::System.Data.Objects.DataClasses
        .EdmRelationshipNavigationPropertyAttribute("NorthwindModel",
            "FK_Orders_Customers", "Orders")]
    [global::System.Xml.Serialization.XmlIgnoreAttribute()]
    [global::System.Xml.Serialization.SoapIgnoreAttribute()]
    [global::System.ComponentModel.BrowsableAttribute(false)]
    public global::System.Data.Objects.DataClasses
        .EntityCollection<Orders> Orders {
        get {
            return ((global::System.Data.Objects.DataClasses
                .IEntityWithRelationships)(this)).RelationshipManager
                .GetRelatedCollection<Orders>(
                    "NorthwindModel.FK_Orders_Customers", "Orders");
        }
    }
}
```

Keep your attention on the attributes that extend the *Orders* property of the *Customers* type. We will examine these in more detail later in this section.

As we did in LINQ to SQL, and with respect to how software architecture should be defined, these contracts are compiled within a dedicated assembly that references the entity framework modeling assembly. A separate assembly describes the service implementation, which internally uses a business layer component to execute the real business tasks and queries in the context of security and validation requirements. The final layout of assemblies on the service side could be the following:

- **DevLeap.Linq.WCF.EntityFrameworkModel** contains the entity model.

- **DevLeap.Linq.WCF.Biz** defines the business components and references the DevLeap.Linq.WCF.EntityFrameworkModel assembly.

- **DevLeap.Linq.WCF.Contracts** defines the WCF contracts and references the DevLeap.Linq.WCF.EntityFrameworkModel assembly, in order to use entities within data contracts.

- **DevLeap.Linq.WCF.Services** implements the service contracts through concrete services and references DevLeap.Linq.WCF.Biz, DevLeap.Linq.WCF.Contracts and DevLeap.Linq.WCF.EntityFrameworkModel.

Listing 18-31 shows the simple service implementation, with only a few lines of code calling the backend infrastructure, just as every service should.

Listing 18-31 The implementation of the service to query the list of *Customers*

```
public class CustomersService: ICustomersService {
    public CustomersList ListCustomers(CustomersFilter request) {
        CustomersBiz cb = new CustomersBiz();
        return (cb.ListCustomers(request));
    }
}
```

The core functionality is defined inside the *CustomersBiz* component to keep it unique and common to every component, service, or presentation layer. The business component will use a LINQ to Entities query to extract the correct set of customers. Listing 18-32 shows the implementation.

Listing 18-32 The implementation of the business component to query the list of *Customers*

```
public class CustomersBiz {
    public CustomersList ListCustomers(CustomersFilter request) {
        // Code omitted ...
        var customers =
            from c in northwind.Customers
            where (  (String.IsNullOrEmpty(request.Country)
                        || c.Country == request.Country)
                  && (String.IsNullOrEmpty(request.Region)
```

```
                          || c.Region == request.Region))
            select c;

        return (new CustomersList(customers));
    }
}
```

On the consumer side, regardless of whether you use a channel factory or a service reference pattern, you will receive a set of *Customers* entities. If you use a channel factory, the entities will be instances of the same type as we have in the entity model. In the case of a service reference, the customers entities on the consumer side will be a consumer-side type regenerated from the WSDL for the service.

If we take a closer look at the XML that is crossing the boundaries of our communication infrastructure, we can see that the XML that is sent is the same, regardless of the consumer type. Listing 18-33 shows an excerpt of the response SOAP message returned by the service.

More Info   To trace the SOAP messages exchanged between the service and the consumer, you can enable the WCF tracing feature by using the WCF Configuration Editor in Visual Studio 2008 or manually configuring the app.config file of your host application. If you use the new WCF Service Host tool provided by Visual Studio 2008, you can trace the messages using the WCF Test Client application offered by the Visual Studio 2008 environment.

Listing 18-33   The SOAP message moving across the wire with the list of *Customers*

```
<s:Envelope xmlns:a="http://www.w3.org/2005/08/addressing"
  xmlns:s="http://www.w3.org/2003/05/soap-envelope">
  <s:Header>
    <!-- SOAP Headers omitted for simplicity -->
  </s:Header>
  <s:Body>
    <ListCustomersResponse
      xmlns="http://schemas.devleap.com/NW/CustomersService">
      <ListCustomersResult xmlns:d4p1="http://schemas.devleap.com/NW/Customers"
          xmlns:i="http://www.w3.org/2001/XMLSchema-instance"
          xmlns:d4p3="http://schemas.datacontract.org/2004/07/NorthwindModel">
        <d4p1:Customer>
      <EntityKey
        xmlns:d6p1="http://schemas.datacontract.org/2004/07/System.Data"
        xmlns="http://schemas.datacontract.org/2004/07/System.Data.Objects.
          DataClasses">
    <d6p1:EntityContainerName>NorthwindEntities</d6p1:EntityContainerName>
      <d6p1:EntityKeyValues>
        <d6p1:EntityKeyMember>
          <d6p1:Key>CustomerID</d6p1:Key>
          <d6p1:Value xmlns:d9p1="http://www.w3.org/2001/XMLSchema"
            i:type="d9p1:string">GREAL</d6p1:Value>
        </d6p1:EntityKeyMember>
```

```
        </d6p1:EntityKeyValues>
      <d6p1:EntitySetName>Customers</d6p1:EntitySetName>
        </EntityKey>
            <d4p3:Address>2732 Baker Blvd.</d4p3:Address>
            <d4p3:City>Eugene</d4p3:City>
            <d4p3:CompanyName>Great Lakes Food Market</d4p3:CompanyName>
            <d4p3:ContactName>Howard Snyder</d4p3:ContactName>
            <d4p3:ContactTitle>Marketing Manager</d4p3:ContactTitle>
            <d4p3:Country>USA</d4p3:Country>
            <d4p3:CustomerID>GREAL</d4p3:CustomerID>
            <d4p3:Fax i:nil="true"></d4p3:Fax>
            <d4p3:Phone>(503) 555-7555</d4p3:Phone>
            <d4p3:PostalCode>97403</d4p3:PostalCode>
            <d4p3:Region>OR</d4p3:Region>
        </d4p1:Customer>

        <!-- All other customers omitted for the sake of simplicity -->

      </ListCustomersResult>
    </ListCustomersResponse>
  </s:Body>
</s:Envelope>
```

There are a couple of big differences here when compared to the XML content returned by an implementation based on LINQ to SQL. The first difference is that the *DataContract* serialization will never contain child collections. In fact, if you double check the code in Listing 18-30 defining the *Customers* entity, you will notice that the *Orders* property is marked with *XmlIgnoreAttribute* and *SoapIgnoreAttribute*. These attributes instruct the WCF serialization engine to skip these complex properties while serializing the entity. On the other hand, if you serialize Entity Framework entities using a *BinaryFormatter*, related objects will also be serialized if they exist.

The second difference is that there is an *EntityKey* element describing the identity key of each serialized entity within the serialized XML. The *EntityKey* element comes from the base class *EntityObject,* from which all the entities generated by the Entity Framework EDMX designer are derived. Of course, if you implement your own entities by using an IPOCO approach such as we illustrate in Appendix A "ADO.NET Entity Framework," this behavior could be different. Moreover, the *ObjectState* of the entity is missing from its XML serialization. Thus, when deserialized with LINQ to Entities, the entity will be reconstructed as a detached entity, and you will need to attach it to LINQ to Entities before you can handle it.

The presence of *EntityKey* within the entity serialization allows you to exchange the entity back and forth between the consumer and the service. As an illustration, let's consider the CRUD-like service contract shown in Listing 18-34.

Listing 18-34 A service contract for a CRUD-like service based on LINQ to Entities

```
[ServiceContract(Namespace = "http://schemas.devleap.com/NW/CustomerManagerService")]
public interface ICustomerManagerService {
    [OperationContract()]
```

```
    Customers GetCustomer(CustomerKey key);

    [OperationContract]
    Customers UpdateCustomer(Customers customer);

    [OperationContract]
    Customers InsertCustomer(Customers customer);

    [OperationContract]
    DeletionResult DeleteCustomer(Customers customer);
}
```

As we did with LINQ to SQL based services, the implementation of this service makes use of a back-end business layer that uses LINQ to Entities. To start with the simplest operation, Listing 18-35 shows the implementation of the *GetCustomer* business method.

Listing 18-35   The *GetCustomer* implementation within the business component

```
public Customers GetCustomer(String customerID) {
    var northwind = getContext();

    var customer =
        (from  c in northwind.Customers
         where  c.CustomerID == customerID
         select c).First();

    return (customer);
}
```

The implementation of this method is very similar to the implementation in LINQ to SQL. Here again, because of the disconnected environment we are working in and to improve the scalability of the solution, we use a per-call created *ObjectContext* in order not to charge the service-side with state management.

The *InsertCustomer* and *DeleteCustomer* methods are a little bit more interesting because they use some methods from the Entity Framework engine. These implementations are shown in Listing 18-36.

Listing 18-36   The *InsertCustomer* and *DeleteCustomer* implementations within the business component

```
public Customers InsertCustomer(Customers customer) {
    var northwind = getContext();

    northwind.AddObject("Customers", customer);
    northwind.SaveChanges(true);

    return (customer);
}
```

```
public Boolean DeleteCustomer(Customers customer) {
    var northwind = getContext();

    northwind.AttachTo("Customers", customer);
    northwind.DeleteObject(customer);
    northwind.SaveChanges(true);

    return (true);
}
```

The insertion of a new customer entity is really simple. It uses the *AddObject* method of the *ObjectContext* to add to the tracking engine the newly created item and then confirms the addition by invoking the *SaveChanges* method.

The deletion of an existing entity occurs through the invocation of the *AttachTo* method of the *ObjectContext*. This method is specifically designed for attaching entities to the graph of tracked entities of the *ObjectContext*, whenever those entities are missing an explicit key to map them with an entity set. In fact, we need to provide the name of the entity set explicitly. We use this method because, as we mentioned previously, every single time we move an entity across the wire, serializing it with the *DataContractSerializer*, its state is marked as Detached. Another method, called *Attach*, is also useful for attaching an entity to the *ObjectContext* when the entity already has an entity key. This allows for an automatic mapping to the correct entity set.

After attaching the entity, we are ready to inform the context of our intention to delete it, invoking the *DeleteObject* method and confirming the action with a *SaveChanges* method call.

Now comes the implementation of the *UpdateCustomer* business method, which is the most interesting one. Listing 18-37 shows the code.

Listing 18-37 The *UpdateCustomer* implementation within the business component

```
public Customers UpdateCustomer(Customers customer) {
    var northwind = getContext();

    northwind.AttachTo("Customers", customer);

    // These lines to force the entity as modified
    // because it is marked as "unchanged" just after AttachTo
    ObjectStateEntry entry = northwind.ObjectStateManager
        .GetObjectStateEntry(customer.EntityKey);
    if (entry != null)
        entry.SetModified();

    // Refresh the entity keeping consumer-side changes
    northwind.Refresh(RefreshMode.ClientWins, customer);

    northwind.SaveChanges(true);
    return(customer);
}
```

As we did in the *DeleteCustomer* method, we attach the received entity to the context. However, here we need to inform the *ObjectContext* that the entity has been modified. You might wonder why we need to take care of this behavior. Why doesn't the framework derive this information itself by looking at the attached entity? We do this for one specific reason: whenever we attach an entity to the context, its state is set to a value of Unchanged, thus any modification is lost. This is why, just after attaching the entity, we mark its state as Modified by invoking the corresponding *SetModified* method of the *ObjectStateManager* of the Entity Framework object model. Nevertheless, this step is not enough to persist the modification. The entity is now marked as modified, but the tracking engine is not aware of what has been effectively modified. One solution to this situation is to refresh the entity state with its original state in the DBMS by invoking the *Refresh* method of the *ObjectContext*, keeping track of client modifications, and setting the *RefreshMethod* to *ClientWins*. This behavior requires that you query the DBMS one more time before sending the final SQL UPDATE statement, which is produced by the *SaveChanges* method invocation. Another solution would be to iterate over the entity's properties and explicitly change their values to make the *ObjectStateManager* aware of the changes.

All the operations we have just described are available regardless of the consumer-side pattern you adopt, making it possible to leverage SOAP communication through WCF services with legacy ASMX or any other kind of SOAP consuming platform, in addition to .NET consumers.

Query Expression Serialization

In this chapter we have mentioned that a query expression is not serializable within .NET runtime serialization, either through DataContract or XML serialization. The main reason for this behavior is that a query expression consists of a graph of expression type instances. Those items might be instances of *BinaryExpression*, *ConditionalExpression*, *ConstantExpression*, *LambdaExpression*, *MethodCallExpression*, etc. Not all of these expression types are transparently transferable across the wire, however. It is easy to imagine an XML representation for the following lambda expression that checks whether a variable x is a multiple of 2:

```
Expression<Func<int, bool>> expr = x => x % 2 == 0;
```

The hypothetical XML representation would be similar to the following:

```
<Expression>
    <Body>
        <ExpressionEqual>
            <Right>
                <ExpressionModulo>
                    <Left>
                        <ExpressionParameter>x</ExpressionParameter>
                    </Left>
                    <Right>
                        <ExpressionConstant>2</ExpressionConstant>
                    </Right>
                </ExpressionModulo>
```

```
            </Right>
            <Left>
                <ExpressionConstant>0</ExpressionConstant>
            </Left>
        </ExpressionEqual>
    </Body>
</Expression>
```

Unfortunately, expressions are not always so trivial. Imagine what might happen in the case of an expression that is a little bit more complex than the previous example, such as the following one:

```
Expression<Func<int, int, double>> expr = (x, y) => x * Utility.Calc(y);
```

This expression calculates a *double* value, starting from a couple of *integer* arguments, and invokes a custom function offered by the *Utility* static class. To perform this operation, the expression tree contains a *MethodCallExpression* to call the static method *Calc* of the *Utility* type. But in this second example we have no guarantee that we will find the same *Utility* type on the other side of the wire after sending an XML serialized expression to someone else. This is just a simple example that illustrates that query expressions are not made to be serializable because of their architecture—and not only for a lack of serialization attributes.

However, in the case of LINQ queries that do not use external methods or components, you can think about a kind of serialization surrogate. Such a surrogate could iteratively visit the query tree with a visitor pattern, such as an *IQueryable* / *IQueryProvider* engine does (see Chapter 11, "Inside Expression Trees," and Chapter 12, "Extending LINQ"), constructing the corresponding XML serialization. By doing this, however, you need to accept a reduced set of features.

Summary

In this chapter we briefly described WCF, the different types of WCF service contracts, how to build a service host, and how to consume a service with a service reference based on a WSDL contract or through channel factories. You have also seen how to use LINQ to SQL and LINQ to Entities objects as the content of WCF messages and how to move entities back and forth by using the ServiceModel.

It is important to note that we did not use any kind of transactional context or exception handling techniques in the samples illustrated, simply for the sake of brevity. In real solutions you should implement a transactional context within the business component and you should define an exception management infrastructure consistent with WCF and the SOAP faults environment.

Remember also that any real service-oriented solution should implement an architecture that decouples the application server layer from the communication layer. In other words, even if you can send LINQ to SQL and LINQ to Entities objects back and forth through WCF, you should use services like the ones we illustrated in this chapter only in your own homogeneous environment based on the .NET Framework. In real service-oriented solutions, it is better to implement a communication layer that abstracts from the concrete back-end, defining communication entities different from the application server and service consumers.

Last but not least, you should evaluate how to use the new capabilities offered by LINQ to SQL and LINQ to Entities to publish services oriented toward real business rules that can satisfy and handle complex data structures based on the services you are going to offer. For instance, instead of implementing CRUD-like services for each of your entities, you could define a smaller set of services capable of handling entity graphs, which can be detached from and attached to a single unit of work represented by a *DataContext / ObjectContext* per-request instance. This approach leads to more business-oriented solutions, rather than mechanisms involving single entities and entity-oriented atomic activities.

Part VI
Appendixes

Appendix A
ADO.NET Entity Framework

In this appendix, we will evaluate the new data access framework—the ADO.NET Entity Framework—provided by Microsoft ADO.NET. In particular, we will focus on the capability it provides to manage and query entities, which is something you can do with a standard relational data source, but only with deep abstraction from the physical data layer.

This chapter is based on Beta code!   The ADO.NET Entity Framework has not been released at the time of this writing. Because this chapter is based on beta code, some features might be changed, removed, or added in the final release. This could invalidate some of the examples shown in this chapter. We kept this appendix updated and aligned with the most recent information we had. In any case, we will publish news and corrections for the book, together with updated code samples, at *http://www.programminglinq.com*.

You can download ADO.NET Entity Framework Beta 3 from *http://www.microsoft.com/downloads/details.aspx?FamilyId=15DB9989-1621-444D-9B18-D1A04A21B519&displaylang=en*. You also need the ADO.NET Entity Framework Tools, which you can download from *https://www.microsoft.com/downloads/details.aspx?FamilyId=D8AE4404-8E05-41FC-94C8-C73D9E238F82&displaylang=en*. When you read this book, the ADO.NET Entity Framework might already have been released. Please check whether a newer version is available before installing it. The installation of the ADO.NET Entity Framework is necessary to compile and execute the code in this appendix.

ADO.NET Standard Approach

Consider a common example of an order management application based on the Microsoft SQL Server Northwind sample database. In Figure A-1, you can see a subset of the database schema for the order management side.

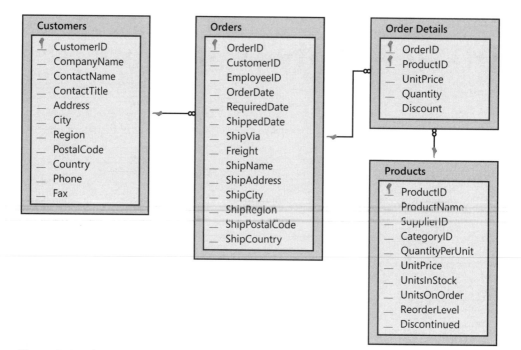

Figure A-1   The Northwind orders database schema

If you want to query the data from a standard .NET application using ADO.NET 2.0, you can choose a connected or disconnected approach, using a *SqlCommand* with a *SqlDataReader* for the connected approach or a *SqlDataAdapter* and a *DataSet* instance for the disconnected approach. Imagine that you are developing an online e-commerce Web application and you decide to use a connected approach. You will probably need to query the list of orders placed and submit new orders. Each order made is a main order row (in the Orders table) mapped to a set of order items (in the Order Details table).

In the following example, you can see a simplified query for extracting all the orders placed by each customer:

```
SELECT c.CustomerID, c.CompanyName, c.ContactName,
       o.OrderID, o.OrderDate
FROM Customers AS c
INNER JOIN Orders AS o
    ON c.CustomerID = o.CustomerID
```

Here are two simplified parametric queries to insert orders and order items:

```
-- Order insert statement
INSERT INTO [Northwind].[dbo].[Orders]
  ([CustomerID] ,[EmployeeID], [OrderDate] ,[RequiredDate)
VALUES
  (@CustomerID, @EmployeeID, @OrderDate, @RequiredDate)
-- Order Detail insert statement
```

```
INSERT INTO [Northwind].[dbo].[Order Details]
  ([OrderID], [ProductID], [UnitPrice], [Quantity], [Discount])
VALUES
  (@OrderID, @ProductID, @UnitPrice, @Quantity, @Discount)
```

In Listing A-1, you can see how to invoke the first selection query—for instance, to bind the result to an ASP.NET 2.0 *GridView*.

Listing A-1   A classic ADO.NET 2.0 query using a *SqlDataReader*

```
SqlConnection cn = new SqlConnection(NWindConnectionString);
SqlCommand cmd = new SqlCommand("SELECT c.CustomerID, c.CompanyName, " +
"c.ContactName, o.OrderID, o.OrderDate FROM Customers AS c INNER JOIN " +
"Orders AS o ON c.CustomerID = o.CustomerID", cn );

using (cn) {
    cn.Open();

    using (SqlDataReader dr = cmd.ExecuteReader(
                               CommandBehavior.CloseConnection)) {
        gridCustomersOrders.DataSource = dr;
        gridCustomersOrders.DataBind();
    }
}
```

This appendix is not the right place to discuss whether it is better to use a *DbDataReader* or a *DataSet* to achieve the best balance between performance and scalability. For this reason, we will skip these kinds of considerations. However, we do want to highlight some possible issues with this approach to querying.

First, we are querying the database persistence layer directly from our application code (the ASPX page, in this example), and we are tied to a particular kind of database engine (Microsoft SQL Server 2005). You probably know that ADO.NET 2.0 code can leverage *DbProviderFactories* to be more independent from the physical database. This flexibility is enormously helpful in our efforts to write more flexible code and to reuse our applications against different database persistence layers. On the other hand, even when using *DbProviderFactories*, we are working with code that mixes typed .NET syntax and untyped SQL code, as shown in Listing A-2.

Listing A-2   A classic ADO.NET 2.0 query using *DbProviderFactories*

```
DbProviderFactory dbFactory =
    DbProviderFactories.GetFactory(NWindProviderName);
DbConnection cn = dbFactory.CreateConnection();
cn.ConnectionString = NWindConnectionString;
DbCommand cmd = cn.CreateCommand();
cmd.CommandText = "SELECT c.CustomerID, c.CompanyName, c.ContactName, " +
    "o.OrderID, o.OrderDate FROM Customers AS c INNER JOIN Orders AS o " +
    "ON c.CustomerID = o.CustomerID";

using (cn) {
    cn.Open();
```

```
    using (DbDataReader dr = cmd.ExecuteReader(
                            CommandBehavior.CloseConnection)) {
        gridCustomersOrders.DataSource = dr;
        gridCustomersOrders.DataBind();
    }
}
```

The first issues we are facing are the lack of strongly typed code and the need to merge different kinds of code and syntaxes (C#, SQL, and so on). Consider also that each order consists of a main header row and a set of items. With regard to the physical database, these records are retrieved from different database tables (Orders and Order Details). When querying orders, we can just execute a multiple-resultset query. However, if the application requirements involve common needs such as paging, sorting, and custom ordering in querying items, we will probably need to write queries that are not trivial (even if any good database developer should be able to do that). Finally, another problem in this code is that we are too close to the database within our application code. As you already saw in Chapter 15, "LINQ in a Multitier Solution," modern applications are often logically and physically divided into layers.

In such architectures, we usually cannot transfer data between layers using *DbDataReader* instances because we do not want to keep database connections open for a long time and because the physical layers could be deployed on different machines (servers). Therefore, it is not convenient to marshal or serialize *DbDataReader* instances over the wire. You could use a *DataSet* or a typed *DataSet* to avoid these issues. However, what happens when your physical data layer consists of more than a database or an XML file? And what other issues will you encounter when you have different physical persistence layers that eventually describe the same conceptual information (such as Orders and Order Details) with different database structures?

For instance, you could have a Microsoft SQL Server 2000 database that describes, with a normalized relational data structure, custom options (color, size, and so on) of each order detail, while you might also have an XML field with SQL Server 2005/2008 to be more versatile. Modern architectures, for these and many other reasons, tend to use custom entities to describe at a conceptual level what you need to manage. The physical layer is just another detail from this point of view, and the overall application architecture should be independent from it.

We have discussed some common issues related to data retrieval for orders already placed. Now consider the other goal of our application: placing orders. We need a data structure to store orders while customers are placing them—the common and classic shopping basket. When the customer confirms his shopping basket, we need to save the header row and each child order detail within the persistence layer using an ACID (Atomic, Consistent, Isolated, Durable) transaction. Once again, we could use a *DataSet* to solve this problem, updating the database with a *DbDataAdapter*. However, keep in mind the same considerations we made regarding data retrieval. As an alternative, we could use custom entities to describe our concept of an order. These orders would be made of various pieces of information, some of which might have multiple occurrences.

Abstracting from the Physical Layer

In Figure A-2, you can see a short conceptual definition (illustrated with a Microsoft Visual Studio 2008 class diagram) of some of our entities, which can be convenient if we decide to provide a conceptual definition of our application domain.

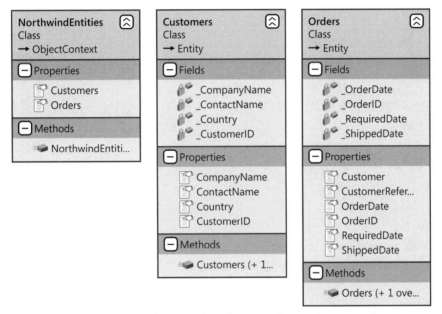

Figure A-2   The Visual Studio 2008 class diagram of our order system from a conceptual point of view

In Listing A-3, you can see a C# representation of this conceptual description.

Listing A-3   A sample object-oriented definition of our conceptual entities

```
namespace NorthwindModel {
    public partial class NorthwindEntities {
        public List<Customer> Customers {
            // ...          }

        public List<Order> Orders {
            // ...          }
    }

    public partial class Customer {

        public string CustomerID { get; set; }
```

```
        public string CompanyName { get; set; }

        public string ContactName { get; set; }

        public string Country { get; set; }

        public List<Order> Orders
        {
            get {
                // ...
            }
        }
    }

public partial class Order {

        public int OrderID { get; set; }

        public DateTime? OrderDate { get; set; }

        public DateTime? RequiredDate { get; set; }

        public DateTime? ShippedDate { get; set; }

        public Customer Customer {
            get {
                // ...
            }
            set {
                // ...
            }
        }
    }
}
```

The real problem is how to load and manage entities like the ones we have just defined (which involves reading their contents from a database) in a way that is independent from the nature and structure of the database itself. Using standard programming languages, we have to define, write, test, and maintain a lot of plumbing to achieve this goal.

We also have to deal with several issues. For instance, whenever we load a parent entity (such as a *Customer*), is it best to also load its children (*Orders* for *Customer* instances, *Order Details* for *Orders*)? Or is it better to load children only when we really need to access them? The answer is probably, "It depends," because when we access a *Customer*, we do not automatically also want her *Orders*. On the other hand, many times when accessing one *Order* we also need to enumerate its *Details*. Every time we need a *Customer*, is it better to execute a single query and load it from the database, or is it easier and faster to reuse an in-memory instance of that particular *Customer*? If we reuse object instances, do we need to worry about concurrency issues? We could go on for hours with questions like these. Unfortunately, there are no absolute solutions for every problem and application. There are just a few patterns and rules that suggest the most common and reasonable solutions. The best solution might be using a data access framework that allows us to decide on a case-by-case basis.

Entity Data Modeling

The first feature of the ADO.NET Entity Framework that we will examine is the capability it provides to model entities from a conceptual level of abstraction. This approach is based on an Entity Model definition that can be created using a Visual Studio 2008 integrated designer and wizard or a manual command-line tool. Regardless of which tool you use, sooner or later the result will be a set of three files defining the conceptual schema and its mapping against the physical schema.

Entity Data Model Files

Each entity data model is internally based on a set of XML schemas (which are useful for defining entities), and the model maps them to the physical persistence layer. These XML files will be parsed by a tool to generate the corresponding .NET implementation code. These processes are know as *Entity Data Modeling* (EDM). The first XML metadata file we will examine is the Conceptual Schema Definition Language (CSDL) file, which defines the entity side of our application framework. A file of this type describes each *EntityType* (a specific entity), *EntitySet* (group of entities), and *Association* (relationship between entities).

In Listing A-4, you can see an excerpt of our Northwind CSDL metadata file, describing the *Customer* and *Order* entities.

Listing A-4   The *Customer* and *Order* entity type definitions within Northwind.CSDL

```xml
<Schema Namespace="NorthwindModel" Alias="Self"
xmlns="http://schemas.microsoft.com/ado/2006/04/edm">
  <EntityContainer Name="NorthwindEntities">
    <EntitySet Name="Customers" EntityType="NorthwindModel.Customers" />
    <EntitySet Name="Orders" EntityType="NorthwindModel.Orders" />
    <AssociationSet Name="FK_Orders_Customers"
                    Association="NorthwindModel.FK_Orders_Customers">
      <End Role="Customers" EntitySet="Customers" />
      <End Role="Orders" EntitySet="Orders" />
    </AssociationSet>
  </EntityContainer>
  <EntityType Name="Customers">
    <Key>
      <PropertyRef Name="CustomerID" />
    </Key>
    <Property Name="CustomerID" Type="String"
              Nullable="false" MaxLength="5" FixedLength="true" />
    <Property Name="CompanyName" Type="String"
              Nullable="false" MaxLength="40" />
    <Property Name="ContactName" Type="String" MaxLength="30" />
```

```
        <Property Name="ContactTitle" Type="String" MaxLength="30" />
        <Property Name="Address" Type="String" MaxLength="60" />
        <Property Name="City" Type="String" MaxLength="15" />
        <Property Name="Region" Type="String" MaxLength="15" />
        <Property Name="PostalCode" Type="String" MaxLength="10" />
        <Property Name="Country" Type="String" MaxLength="15" />
        <Property Name="Phone" Type="String" MaxLength="24" />
        <Property Name="Fax" Type="String" MaxLength="24" />
        <NavigationProperty Name="Orders"
                            Relationship="NorthwindModel.FK_Orders_Customers"
                            FromRole="Customers" ToRole="Orders" />
    </EntityType>
    <EntityType Name="Orders">
      <Key>
        <PropertyRef Name="OrderID" />
      </Key>
      <Property Name="OrderID" Type="Int32" Nullable="false" />
      <Property Name="EmployeeID" Type="Int32" />
      <Property Name="OrderDate" Type="DateTime" />
      <Property Name="RequiredDate" Type="DateTime" />
      <Property Name="ShippedDate" Type="DateTime" />
      <Property Name="ShipVia" Type="Int32" />
      <Property Name="Freight" Type="Decimal" Precision="19" Scale="4" />
      <Property Name="ShipName" Type="String" MaxLength="40" />
      <Property Name="ShipAddress" Type="String" MaxLength="60" />
      <Property Name="ShipCity" Type="String" MaxLength="15" />
      <Property Name="ShipRegion" Type="String" MaxLength="15" />
      <Property Name="ShipPostalCode" Type="String" MaxLength="10" />
      <Property Name="ShipCountry" Type="String" MaxLength="15" />
      <NavigationProperty Name="Customers"
                          Relationship="NorthwindModel.FK_Orders_Customers"
                          FromRole="Orders" ToRole="Customers" />
    </EntityType>
    <Association Name="FK_Orders_Customers">
      <End Role="Customers" Type="NorthwindModel.Customers" Multiplicity="0..1" />
      <End Role="Orders" Type="NorthwindModel.Orders" Multiplicity="*" />
    </Association>
  </Schema>
```

This file defines an *EntityContainer*, named *NorthwindEntities*, which contains a couple of *EntitySets*, called *Customers* and *Orders*. *Customers* is a list of entities of type *Customer*, and *Orders* is a set of *Order* instances. There is also a relationship, called *Relationship_Orders_Customers*, that describes how to traverse the object graph of *Customer* and *Order* instances, using the definition of an *Association* between them.

As you can see, this code fragment describes only entities, without any kind of reference to the database, and all the *Customer* and *Order* properties are defined using only .NET types. The schema also describes validation rules and constraints that will also be made available in our code, as specific validation code.

A second XML metadata file to consider is the Storage Schema Definition Language (SSDL) file, which describes the physical data layer. Listing A-5 provides an example.

Listing A-5   The physical data layer *Customer* and *Order* definitions within Northwind.SSDL

```
<Schema Namespace="NorthwindModel.Store" Alias="Self"
ProviderManifestToken="09.00.3042"
xmlns="http://schemas.microsoft.com/ado/2006/04/edm/ssdl">
  <EntityContainer Name="dbo">
    <EntitySet Name="Customers"
               EntityType="NorthwindModel.Store.Customers" />
    <EntitySet Name="Orders" EntityType="NorthwindModel.Store.Orders" />
    <AssociationSet Name="FK_Orders_Customers"
                    Association="NorthwindModel.Store.FK_Orders_Customers">
      <End Role="Customers" EntitySet="Customers" />
      <End Role="Orders" EntitySet="Orders" />
    </AssociationSet>
  </EntityContainer>
  <EntityType Name="Customers">
    <Key>
      <PropertyRef Name="CustomerID" />
    </Key>
    <Property Name="CustomerID" Type="nchar" Nullable="false" MaxLength="5" />
    <Property Name="CompanyName" Type="nvarchar" Nullable="false" MaxLength="40" />
    <Property Name="ContactName" Type="nvarchar" MaxLength="30" />
    <Property Name="ContactTitle" Type="nvarchar" MaxLength="30" />
    <Property Name="Address" Type="nvarchar" MaxLength="60" />
    <Property Name="City" Type="nvarchar" MaxLength="15" /
    <Property Name="Region" Type="nvarchar" MaxLength="15" />
    <Property Name="PostalCode" Type="nvarchar" MaxLength="10" />
    <Property Name="Country" Type="nvarchar" MaxLength="15" />
    <Property Name="Phone" Type="nvarchar" MaxLength="24" />
    <Property Name="Fax" Type="nvarchar" MaxLength="24" />
  </EntityType>
  <EntityType Name="Orders">
    <Key>
      <PropertyRef Name="OrderID" />
    </Key>
    <Property Name="OrderID" Type="int" Nullable="false"
              StoreGeneratedPattern="Identity" />
    <Property Name="CustomerID" Type="nchar" MaxLength="5" />
    <Property Name="EmployeeID" Type="int" />
    <Property Name="OrderDate" Type="datetime" />
    <Property Name="RequiredDate" Type="datetime" />
    <Property Name="ShippedDate" Type="datetime" />
    <Property Name="ShipVia" Type="int" />
    <Property Name="Freight" Type="money" />
    <Property Name="ShipName" Type="nvarchar" MaxLength="40" />
    <Property Name="ShipAddress" Type="nvarchar" MaxLength="60" />
    <Property Name="ShipCity" Type="nvarchar" MaxLength="15" />
    <Property Name="ShipRegion" Type="nvarchar" MaxLength="15" />
    <Property Name="ShipPostalCode" Type="nvarchar" MaxLength="10" />
    <Property Name="ShipCountry" Type="nvarchar" MaxLength="15" />
  </EntityType>
  <Association Name="FK_Orders_Customers">
    <End Role="Customers" Type="NorthwindModel.Store.Customers"
```

```
                Multiplicity="0..1" />
        <End Role="Orders" Type="NorthwindModel.Store.Orders"
                Multiplicity="*" />
        <ReferentialConstraint>
          <Principal Role="Customers">
            <PropertyRef Name="CustomerID" />
          </Principal>
          <Dependent Role="Orders">
            <PropertyRef Name="CustomerID" />
          </Dependent>
        </ReferentialConstraint>
      </Association>
  </Schema>
```

Unlike the CSDL file, this XML document has explicit references to the physical data structure—such as primary keys, nullability rules, identities, foreign key constraints, and data types related to the SQL Server side. In this example, the two CSDL and SSDL files are quite similar because we are defining a very simple situation. In real-world applications, these files will probably hold more complex and less symmetric code.

The last metadata file to consider is the Mapping Schema Language (MSL) file, which simply maps the two previous metadata definition files. In Listing A-6, you can see a sample mapping file.

Listing A-6   CSDL and SSDL mapping described by Northwind.MSL

```
<Mapping Space="C-S" xmlns="urn:schemas-microsoft-com:windows:storage:mapping:CS">
  <EntityContainerMapping StorageEntityContainer="dbo"
                          CdmEntityContainer="NorthwindEntities">
    <EntitySetMapping Name="Customers">
      <EntityTypeMapping TypeName="IsTypeOf(NorthwindModel.Customers)">
        <MappingFragment StoreEntitySet="Customers">
          <ScalarProperty Name="CustomerID" ColumnName="CustomerID" />
          <ScalarProperty Name="CompanyName" ColumnName="CompanyName" />
          <ScalarProperty Name="ContactName" ColumnName="ContactName" />
          <ScalarProperty Name="ContactTitle" ColumnName="ContactTitle" />
          <ScalarProperty Name="Address" ColumnName="Address" />
          <ScalarProperty Name="City" ColumnName="City" />
          <ScalarProperty Name="Region" ColumnName="Region" />
          <ScalarProperty Name="PostalCode" ColumnName="PostalCode" />
          <ScalarProperty Name="Country" ColumnName="Country" />
          <ScalarProperty Name="Phone" ColumnName="Phone" />
          <ScalarProperty Name="Fax" ColumnName="Fax" />
        </MappingFragment>
      </EntityTypeMapping>
    </EntitySetMapping>
    <EntitySetMapping Name="Orders">
      <EntityTypeMapping TypeName="IsTypeOf(NorthwindModel.Orders)">
        <MappingFragment StoreEntitySet="Orders">
          <ScalarProperty Name="OrderID" ColumnName="OrderID" />
          <ScalarProperty Name="EmployeeID" ColumnName="EmployeeID" />
          <ScalarProperty Name="OrderDate" ColumnName="OrderDate" />
```

```
                <ScalarProperty Name="RequiredDate" ColumnName="RequiredDate" />
                <ScalarProperty Name="ShippedDate" ColumnName="ShippedDate" />
                <ScalarProperty Name="ShipVia" ColumnName="ShipVia" />
                <ScalarProperty Name="Freight" ColumnName="Freight" />
                <ScalarProperty Name="ShipName" ColumnName="ShipName" />
                <ScalarProperty Name="ShipAddress" ColumnName="ShipAddress" />
                <ScalarProperty Name="ShipCity" ColumnName="ShipCity" />
                <ScalarProperty Name="ShipRegion" ColumnName="ShipRegion" />
                <ScalarProperty Name="ShipPostalCode" ColumnName="ShipPostalCode" />
                <ScalarProperty Name="ShipCountry" ColumnName="ShipCountry" />
          </MappingFragment>
        </EntityTypeMapping>
      </EntitySetMapping>
      <AssociationSetMapping Name="FK_Orders_Customers"
                        TypeName="NorthwindModel.FK_Orders_Customers"
                        StoreEntitySet="Orders">
        <EndProperty Name="Customers">
          <ScalarProperty Name="CustomerID" ColumnName="CustomerID" />
        </EndProperty>
        <EndProperty Name="Orders">
          <ScalarProperty Name="OrderID" ColumnName="OrderID" />
        </EndProperty>
        <Condition ColumnName="CustomerID" IsNull="false" />
      </AssociationSetMapping>
    </EntityContainerMapping>
  </Mapping>
```

You can see that this last file explicitly maps metadata between the conceptual model (*CdmEntityContainer*) and the physical storage (*StorageEntityContainer*), defining the containing table (TableName) and column (ColumnName) for each scalar property (*Name*) of each entity (*TypeName*).

The result of this set of files is a code file that can be automatically generated by the Visual Studio 2008 wizard or manually generated through a command-line tool. This code file contains the definitions of all the *EntityType*, *EntitySet*, and *Association* types defined within the CSDL file. While CSDL is converted into code, SSDL and MSL remain in XML so that you can change the physical layer without changing the conceptual model.

Entity Data Model Designer and Wizard

The ADO.NET Entity Framework provides a Visual Studio 2008 integrated designer and wizard, which is useful for creating conceptual schemas from scratch or from an existing and supported database persistence layer. To start the designer wizard, you simply need to add a file of type "ADO.NET Entity Data Model" to a Visual Studio 2008 project. In Figure A-3, you can see the first step of the proposed wizard.

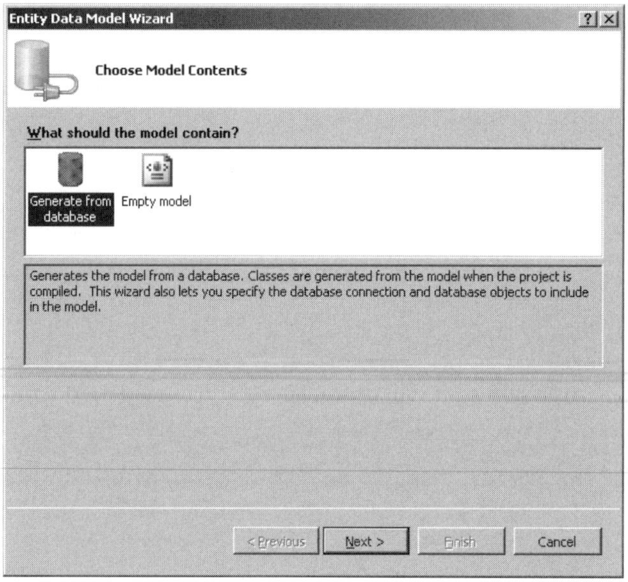

Figure A-3   First step of the ADO.NET Entity Data Model designer wizard

Here you have the opportunity to connect to an existing database schema rather than define an empty model starting from scratch. If you choose to use an existing database, you will be prompted with the step shown in Figure A-4.

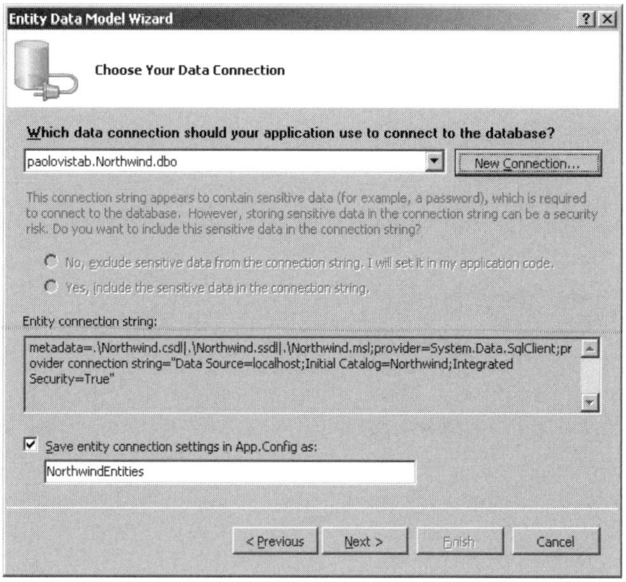

Figure A-4   Second step of the ADO.NET Entity Data Model designer wizard

This second step allows you to select the database connection to use, eventually creating a new connection. Either you use an existing connection or you create a new one. You can save the connection string in the application configuration file, and the wizard allows you to define the configuration key to use for this purpose. The last step in the wizard allows you to choose the objects (tables, views, stored procedures) to import into the model. In Figure A-5, you can see a screen shot of this last step.

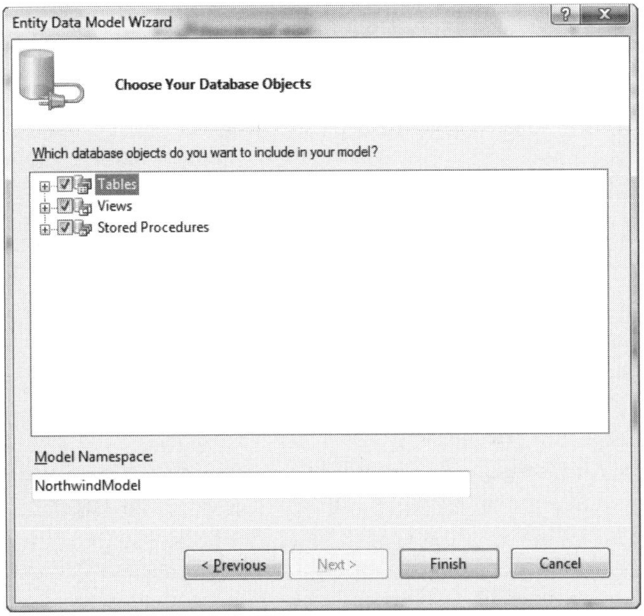

Figure A-5   Last step of the ADO.NET Entity Data Model designer wizard

The result of running the wizard is an .EDMX file that is simply an XML file that internally represents the whole set of the model files (CSDL, SSDL, MSL). In Listing A-7, you can see an excerpt of this file.

Listing A-7   Excerpt of the .EDMX file for the Northwind entity model

```xml
<?xml version="1.0" encoding="utf-8"?>
<edmx:Edmx Version="1.0"
xmlns:edmx="http://schemas.microsoft.com/ado/2007/06/edmx">
  <edmx:Designer xmlns="http://schemas.microsoft.com/ado/2007/06/edmx">
    <edmx:Connection>
      <DesignerInfoPropertySet>
        <DesignerProperty Name="MetadataArtifactProcessing"
                          Value="CopyToOutputDirectory" />
      </DesignerInfoPropertySet>
    </edmx:Connection>
    <edmx:Options>
      <DesignerInfoPropertySet>
        <DesignerProperty Name="ValidateOnBuild" Value="true" />
      </DesignerInfoPropertySet>
```

```
        </edmx:Options>
        <edmx:ReverseEngineer />
        <edmx:Diagrams>
          <!-- Designer configuration here ... -->
          <!-- ... -->
        </edmx:Diagrams>
      </edmx:Designer>
      <edmx:Runtime>
        <!-- CSDL content -->
        <edmx:ConceptualModels>
          <!-- ... -->
        </edmx:ConceptualModels>
        <!-- SSDL content -->
        <edmx:StorageModels>
          <!-- ... -->
        </edmx:StorageModels>
        <!-- C-S mapping content -->
        <edmx:Mappings>
          <!-- ... -->
        </edmx:Mappings>
      </edmx:Runtime>
    </edmx:Edmx>
```

Every time you build your solution, the Visual Studio integrated designer will generate the three corresponding source files in the bin\Debug or bin\Release directory of your current project or solution. In this situation, you should not modify these files by hand; instead, you should maintain the model (EDMX) in Visual Studio 2008 and rebuild the project or solution when necessary. However, generated files can be changed after development to adapt the model to other sources.

Whenever you define an EDMX file as an Entity Data Model Item Template in an ASP.NET Web project, the EDMX file will be placed in the App_Code folder of the Web application and a specific build action will embed the source files (CSDL,SSDL, MSL) as resources.

Through the EDMX designer, you can configure the mapping of an entity's fields by using the Entity Mapping Details window shown in Figure A-6. As you can see, this window allows you to define the mapping of each property of the entity to the corresponding table and column of the storage schema.

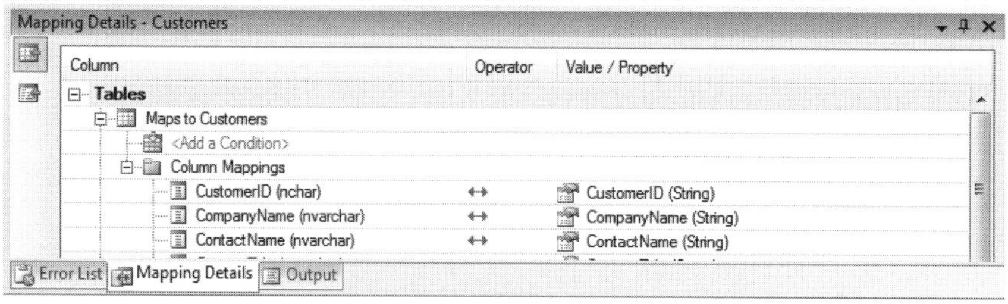

Figure A-6   Entity Mapping Details window of the ADO.NET Entity Data Model designer

The designer also provides an Entity Model Browser window that allows you to browse the model graph, grouping the nodes into two main sets that describe the conceptual model and the target database storage model. In Figure A-7, you can see the browser window.

Figure A-7   Entity Model Browser window of the ADO.NET Entity Data Model designer

Last but not least, from the designer surface you can manage an entity's associations and their corresponding cardinality. Consider that every time you import tables with relationships into the model, the designer infers those relationships and associates the tables in the model. If you have two tables related through a many-to-many relationship table, the designer omits that table and represents the underlying relation in the entity model schema.

One last thing to notice about the designer is its capability to resync against modifications of the persistence storage schema. In fact, if you remove one or more tables from the database schema, you can refresh the entity model and those tables will be removed from the model too. If you add new tables to the schema, again refreshing the entity model, you will be able to add mapping to them in the entity model. To synchronize the model against the database schema, you need to select the Update Model From Database command from the Entity Model Browser window's context menu. Nevertheless, keep in mind that a database schema and an entity model conceptual schema should not change on a day-to-day basis. They should be designed and defined after a wise and accurate analysis.

If you need to change the model with a low-level approach, you can always open the EDMX file using an XML editor, and you will be able to do everything you want with respect to its XML schema.

Note   The XML schemas used by the EDMX file are automatically installed and configured by the ADO.NET Entity Framework Tools setup. However you can find the XSD files in the Visual Studio 2008 common schemas folder (c:\Program Files (x86)\Microsoft Visual Studio 9.0\xml\Schemas).

The environment, by default, validates the file during the next build, or you can re-open the designer and validate the model by selecting the Validate command from the Entity Model Browser window's context menu.

Entity Data Model Generation Tool

There is a tool named EdmGen.EXE, available in the .NET Framework 3.5 directory, which is useful for manually producing an entity data model definition. You can execute it against any existing database instance supported by the ADO.NET Entity Framework. The result is the set of files constituting the Entity Data Model (CSDL, SSDL, MSL). The same tool can also be used to validate an existing model or to generate a source code file corresponding to a specific CSDL definition or to the entire set of definition files (CSDL, SSDL, MSL). Consider that the EdmGen tool always includes in the output files all the objects defined in the source database schema. If you want to model just a subset of the objects in the source database schema, you need to use the Visual Studio 2008 designer, running the wizard or starting from an empty model. In the following excerpt, you can see a sample of the syntax needed to invoke the tool to build the model of the Northwind database, using the local default SQL Server instance:

```
EdmGen /mode:FullGeneration /project:NorthwindEntities
/provider:System.Data.SqlClient
/connectionstring:"server=localhost;integrated security=true; database=northwind"
```

Note   There are many arguments you can provide to the EdmGen tool. They are all well documented in the product documentation, so we will not reference all of them here.

Entity Data Model Rules and Definition

The ADO.NET Entity Framework requires that all the entities have identifying keys. This requirement is generally satisfied by mapping tables that have primary keys in the storage engine. However, when there are entities derived from tables missing a primary key, the EDM tools attempt to infer a key for the entity and still leave the entity in a read-only state. You can manually change the read-only state, changing the model source files via the XML editor, but it is at your own risk and it is your responsibility to define the identifying key of the entity or accept the one proposed by the EDM tools.

Before moving forward and using the entity model that is defined, remember that in real enterprise-level solutions you will probably start the entity model definition from an empty designer surface, rather than from an existing database schema. One of the main features of the ADO.NET Entity Framework is its capability to keep your entity model independent of and decoupled from the physical database schema. However, if you define the model as a 1:1 mapping of the tables available in the database, the result is not really independent. The right way of working is to define your conceptual model from scratch, focusing your attention on the business goals of the application you are defining. After having defined the conceptual schema, you should determine the best way to persist it against database storage that is well defined and normalized. And finally, you should map these schemas (conceptual and storage) by leveraging the real power of Object Relational Mapping (ORM) techniques.

Querying Entities with ADO.NET

You have seen how to model your data layer to the right level of abstraction, using the ADO.NET metadata files and the EDM schema tools and designers.

The ADO.NET Entity Framework also provides a set of classes that allows you to work with the entities produced by parsing the metadata files. Starting from the already defined and broadly adopted architecture of ADO.NET, this latest version provides a new ADO.NET managed provider to manage entities instead of records.

> **Note**   An ADO.NET managed provider is a set of classes defined to manage a particular kind of data source. There are providers for SQL Server, Oracle, ODBC, OLE DB, and so on. All of them implement common interfaces defined by ADO.NET. Every developer can use them from an abstract point of view—accessing their members through common interfaces instead of using explicit type casting. The *DbProviderFactories* engine that we saw previously is mainly based on this concept.

This new managed provider, defined within the *System.Data.EntityClient* namespace of the *System.Data.Entity* assembly, offers an *EntityConnection* class that inherits from *System.Data.Common.DbConnection*, like any other ADO.NET connection does (for example, *SqlConnection*, *OleDbConnection*, and so on). *EntityConnection* accepts a particular connection string that requires not only a database connection, but also a path to the set of XML metadata files (CSDL, SSDL, and MSL) and the type of the provider to use for the physical data layer. Here is a sample connection, defined in an *App.Config* file, for an *EntityConnection* instance:

```
<connectionStrings>
  <add name="Northwind"
    connectionString="
      metadata=.\Northwind.csdl|.\Northwind.ssdl|.\Northwind.msl;
      provider=System.Data.SqlClient;provider connection string=&quote;Data
      Source=.;Initial Catalog=Northwind;Integrated Security=True;
      multipleactiveresultsets=true&quote;"
      providerName="System.Data.EntityClient"/>
</connectionStrings>
```

Pay attention to the *MultipleActiveResultsets* feature configured in the connection string. With that setting, the *EntityClient* provider can leverage multiple parallel queries to dynamically load the entities. Later in the appendix we will cover this matter in more detail.

EntityConnection can be used by an *EntityCommand* instance to select a set of entities instead of a set of records. In Listing A-8, you can see an example of a query that retrieves the full list of Northwind customer entities.

Listing A-8   A sample query against a set of entities, using *EntityCommand* and *EntityConnection*

```
using (EntityConnection cn = new EntityConnection(NwindConnectionString)) {
    EntityCommand cmd = new EntityCommand(
        "SELECT c FROM NorthwindEntities.Customers AS c", cn);

    cn.Open();
    using (DbDataReader dr =
               cmd.ExecuteReader(CommandBehavior.SequentialAccess)) {
        while (dr.Read()) {
            Console.WriteLine(((DbDataRecord)dr.GetValue(0))[0]);
        }
    }
}
```

The query provided as an argument to the *EntityCommand* constructor is interesting. It looks like a classic SQL query, but it is not. In reality, it is an Object Query that is a query against the *EntitySets* of the conceptual model. *NorthwindEntities* is the *EntityContainer*, and *Customers* is the *EntitySet* of all the *Customer* instances. The result of this query is a list of *DbDataRecord* instances, each of which describes a customer.

So far, this code is not very interesting. In fact, it is not much different from any other code to query a database using ADO.NET. Nevertheless, consider the code that is automatically generated from the model. It defines a .NET type (a class) for each *Entity* defined in the model (or in the source CSDL file). For instance, consider the *Customers* type shown in Listing A-9.

Listing A-9   An excerpt of the *Customers* type autogenerated from the entity model

```
[global::System.Data.Objects.DataClasses.EdmEntityTypeAttribute(
  NamespaceName="NorthwindModel", Name="Customers")]
[global::System.Runtime.Serialization.DataContractAttribute()]
[global::System.Serializable()]
public partial class Customers :
global::System.Data.Objects.DataClasses.EntityObject {

    // ... code omitted ...

    [global::System.Data.Objects.DataClasses.EdmScalarPropertyAttribute(
      EntityKeyProperty=true, IsNullable=false)]
    [global::System.Runtime.Serialization.DataMemberAttribute()]
    public string CustomerID {
        get {
            return this._CustomerID;
        }
        set {
```

```
            this.OnCustomerIDChanging(value);
            this.ReportPropertyChanging("CustomerID");
            this._CustomerID = global::System.Data.Objects.DataClasses
                .StructuralObject.SetValidValue(value, false, 5);
            this.ReportPropertyChanged("CustomerID");
            this.OnCustomerIDChanged();
        }
    }
    private string _CustomerID;
    partial void OnCustomerIDChanging(string value);
    partial void OnCustomerIDChanged();

    // ...
    [global::System.Data.Objects.DataClasses
        .EdmRelationshipNavigationPropertyAttribute("NorthwindModel",
        "FK_Orders_Customers", "Orders")]
    [global::System.Xml.Serialization.XmlIgnoreAttribute()]
    [global::System.Xml.Serialization.SoapIgnoreAttribute()]
    [global::System.ComponentModel.BrowsableAttribute(false)]
    public global::System.Data.Objects.DataClasses
        .EntityCollection<Orders> Orders {
        get {
            return ((global::System.Data.Objects.DataClasses
                .IEntityWithRelationships)(this)).RelationshipManager
                .GetRelatedCollection<Orders>
                ("NorthwindModel.FK_Orders_Customers", "Orders");
        }
    }
}
```

The *Customers* type inherits from the base class *EntityObject* defined in the common namespace *System.Data.Objects.DataClasses*. This base class provides all the features to manage object state, change events, validation rules, and so on. The code is decorated with .NET attributes taken from the same namespace as the *EntityObject* base class for the purpose of defining the behavior of each property that will be compliant with the EDM definition. For instance, you can see that the *CustomerID* property is marked with an *EdmScalarProperty-Attribute* instance. This marking indicates that from a conceptual point of view the property is the unique identifier of each *Customer* instance. Moreover, these types are serializable as a *DataContract* of *System.Runtime.Serialization* version 3.0; thus, they can be used as message content in Windows Communication Foundation (WCF) services, as you have already seen in Chapter 18, "LINQ and the Windows Communication Foundation." They are also serializable using the old-style runtime serialization based on *IFormatter* implementations.

The code also defines a root .NET type called *NorthwindEntities*—which is described in the model files—that acts as a container for all the *EntitySet* instances. In Listing A-10, you can see an excerpt of its definition.

Listing A-10   An excerpt of the *NorthwindEntities* type autogenerated from the model files

```
public partial class NorthwindEntities: System.Data.Objects.ObjectContext {

    public NorthwindEntities()
        : base("name=NorthwindEntities", "NorthwindEntities") { }

    public NorthwindEntities( string connectionString )
        : base(connectionString, "NorthwindEntities") { }

    public NorthwindEntities(global::System.Data.EntityClient.EntityConnection
        connection )
        : base(connection, "NorthwindEntities") { }

    //     code omitted ...

    [global::System.ComponentModel.BrowsableAttribute(false)]
    public System.Data.Objects.ObjectQuery<Customer> Customers {
        get {
            if ((this._Customers == null)) {
              this._Customers = base.CreateQuery<Customer>("[Customers]");
            }
            return this._Customers;
        }
    }

    private global::System.Data.Objects.ObjectQuery<Customer> _Customers;

    // ... code omitted ...

    [global::System.ComponentModel.BrowsableAttribute(false)]
    public System.Data.Objects.ObjectQuery<Order> Orders {
        get {
            if ((this._Orders == null)) {
              this._Orders = base.CreateQuery<Order>("[Orders]");
            }
            return this._Orders;
        }
    }

    private global::System.Data.Objects.ObjectQuery<Order> _Orders;

    // ... code omitted ...

}
```

The class inherits from *System.Data.Objects.ObjectContext*, and it internally defines the *Customers* and *Orders* sets as instances of the generic type *ObjectQuery*. *ObjectQuery* describes a typed result of a query over a set of entities. We can use instances of *NorthwindEntities* to access and query all the typed and object-oriented entities. In Listing A-11, you can see an example of querying the list of *Customers* objects to extract all the customers.

Listing A-11   An ADO.NET Entities query to extract all the customers

```
using (NorthwindEntities db = new NorthwindEntities()) {

    var customers = db.CreateQuery<DbDataRecord>(
        "SELECT c FROM NorthwindEntities.Customers AS c");

    foreach (var c in customers) {
        Console.WriteLine( ((Customers)c[0]).Display() );
    }
}
```

We create the query over entities by invoking the *CreateQuery* generic method of the *North-windEntities* object. The *CreateQuery* method is defined in the base *ObjectContext* class and does not return its result immediately; instead, it defines a query tree that will be evaluated when it is enumerated. This behavior suggests a potential conjunction with LINQ queries, which you will see later in this appendix. The result of the query is a set of *DbDataRecord* objects, each of which contains a single column row representing a single *Customers* instance. In fact, we cast the zero column of each row into a *Customers* instance and invoke a custom extension method to display the result.

We are working with a typed environment, and *Customers* is not a database row but a defined and known entity. Therefore, we can invoke the *CreateQuery* method, assigning to its generic type the *Customers* type itself, as shown in Listing A-12.

Listing A-12   An ADO.NET Entities query to extract all the typed customers

```
using (NorthwindEntities db = new NorthwindEntities()) {

    var customers = db.CreateQuery<Customers>(
        "SELECT VALUE c FROM NorthwindEntities.Customers AS c");

    foreach (var c in customers) {
        Console.WriteLine(c.Display());
    }
}
```

We used the VALUE keyword to ask for an already typed and fully compiled *Customers* instance—for each item in the physical data storage—as a result from the query engine.

We can also filter entities based on conditions, which are eventually mapped to parameters. Consider the sample code in Listing A-13, in which we extract all the customers located in Italy.

Listing A-13 An ADO.NET Entities query to extract all the customers located in Italy

```
using (NorthwindEntities db = new NorthwindEntities()) {

    var customers = db.CreateQuery<Customers>(
        "SELECT VALUE c FROM NorthwindEntities.Customers AS c " +
        "WHERE c.Country = 'Italy'");

    foreach (var c in customers) {
        Console.WriteLine(c.Display());
    }
}
```

We can also use parameters to feed a parametric query instead of using explicitly declared values. In Listing A-14, you can see a parametric query used to filter customers on the basis of the *Country* property.

Listing A-14 An ADO.NET Entities query to extract all the customers of a particular country

```
using (NorthwindEntities db = new NorthwindEntities()) {

    var customers = db.CreateQuery<Customers>(
        "SELECT VALUE c FROM NorthwindEntities.Customers AS c " +
        "WHERE c.Country = @Country");

    customers.Parameters.Add(new ObjectParameter("Country", country));
    foreach (Customers c in customers) {
        Console.WriteLine(c.Display());
    }
}
```

Under the covers, the *System.Data.EntityClient* framework parses the queries over entities and converts them, using a database-specific provider, to SQL queries to extract from the physical data layer the data mapped on the entities. After this, it loads the entities with the content received from the database server. In the end, this is a smart and maintainable surrogate for a custom data layer. In the following block, you can see the SQL code produced to execute the query described in Listing A-14:

```
SELECT
[Extent1].[CustomerID] AS [CustomerID],
[Extent1].[CompanyName] AS [CompanyName],
[Extent1].[ContactName] AS [ContactName],
[Extent1].[ContactTitle] AS [ContactTitle],
[Extent1].[Address] AS [Address],
[Extent1].[City] AS [City],
[Extent1].[Region] AS [Region],
[Extent1].[PostalCode] AS [PostalCode],
[Extent1].[Country] AS [Country],
[Extent1].[Phone] AS [Phone],
[Extent1].[Fax] AS [Fax]
FROM [dbo].[Customers] AS [Extent1]
WHERE [Extent1].[Country] = @Country
```

> **Important**   The SQL queries generated by the ADO.NET Entity Framework that we
> illustrate in this appendix are only illustrative. Microsoft reserves the right to change the SQL
> code that is generated, and sometimes we simplify the text. Therefore, you should not rely
> on it. To see the generated query yourself, you can invoke the *ToTraceString* method of the
> *ObjectQuery* type, after opening the *Connection* related to the current *ObjectContext* instance.

You can probably appreciate that the querying engine of *EntityClient* tries to optimize query
plans and avoids SQL injection by using parametric queries. However, if you need to execute
custom stored procedures, instead of autogenerated SQL code, for security reasons or
performance matters, consider that you can define procedures in the EDM and invoke them
as if they were methods of the *ObjectContext*. The EDM also defines relationships between
entities. Consider the example in Listing A-15, in which we retrieve all orders filtered by
customers of a specific country.

Listing A-15   An ADO.NET Entities query to extract all the orders of customers of a specific country

```
using (NorthwindEntities db = new NorthwindEntities()) {

    ObjectQuery<Orders> orders = db.CreateQuery<Orders>(
        "SELECT VALUE o FROM NorthwindEntities.Orders AS o " +
        "WHERE o.Customers.Country = @Country");
    orders.Parameters.Add(new ObjectParameter("Country", country));

    foreach (Orders o in orders) {
        Console.WriteLine(o.Display());
    }
}
```

In this last example, we traverse the object graph to filter each of the *Orders* on the basis of the
Customers property. There are many other opportunities for querying entities. For instance, in
Listing A-16 we extract all customers who placed orders in the last 10 years, leveraging the
NAVIGATE keyword to traverse an object relationship between *Customers* and *Orders*
instances.

Listing A-16   An ADO.NET Entities query to extract all the customers who placed orders in the last
10 years

```
using (NorthwindEntities db = new NorthwindEntities()) {

    var customers = db.CreateQuery<Customers>(
        "SELECT VALUE c FROM NorthwindEntities.Customers AS c " +
        "WHERE EXISTS( " +
        "SELECT VALUE o " +
        "FROM NAVIGATE(c, NorthwindModel.FK_Orders_Customers) " +
        "AS o " +
        "WHERE o.OrderDate > @Date)");
    customers.Parameters.Add(new ObjectParameter("Date",
        DateTime.Now.AddYears(-10)));
```

```
        foreach (var c in customers) {
            Console.WriteLine(c.Display());
        }
    }
```

Another feature of the *ObjectQuery* class is its capability to cache the query plan generated on the Entity Query provided for execution. Caching can be done by setting the *EnablePlan-Caching* Boolean property of the *ObjectQuery* instance. In Listing A-17, you can see an example of query plan caching.

Listing A-17   An example of query plan caching

```
using (NorthwindEntities db = new NorthwindEntities()) {

    var customers = db.CreateQuery<Customers>(
        "SELECT VALUE c FROM NorthwindEntities.Customers AS c " +
        "WHERE EXISTS( " +
        "SELECT VALUE o " +
        "FROM NAVIGATE(c, NorthwindModel.FK_Orders_Customers) " +
        "AS o " +
        "WHERE o.OrderDate > @Date)");
    customers.Parameters.Add(new ObjectParameter("Date",
        DateTime.Now.AddYears(-10)));
    customers.EnablePlanCaching = true;
    foreach (var c in customers) {
        Console.WriteLine(c.Display());
    }
}
```

Querying ADO.NET Entities with LINQ

You have seen how ADO.NET Entities can be queried using text queries based on an SQL "dialect" specifically and intentionally defined for querying entities. However, entities are a typed representation of conceptual information, and it would be great to write queries using a fully typed approach. As we describe in Chapter 8, "LINQ to Entities," you can leverage LINQ to Entities to query ADO.NET Entities using a LINQ query approach. Listing A-18 offers a quick review of these capabilities, showing a way to translate the query used in Listing A-17 into LINQ to Entities.

Listing A-18   A LINQ to Entities query to extract all the customers who placed orders in the last 10 years

```
using (NorthwindEntities db = new NorthwindEntities()) {

    DateTime referenceDate = DateTime.Now.AddYears(-10);
    var customers = (from   o in db.Orders
                     where  o.OrderDate > referenceDate
                     select o.Customers).Distinct();
```

```
        foreach (var c in customers) {
            Console.WriteLine(c.Display());
        }
    }
}
```

The LINQ approach enables you to write fully typed code, as you can see from the typed *DateTime* filter.

Managing Data with Object Services

Now think about updating entities and persisting their state back to the physical data layer. The ADO.NET Entity Framework transparently monitors object state and instancing whenever you change an object's contents, leveraging the base class *EntityObject* from which every single entity type generated from the EDM tools inherits. The *EntityObject* base class together with the *ObjectContext* base class are part of the Object Services component. This component is part of the ADO.NET Entity Framework, it is implemented by classes from the *System.Data.Objects* and *System.Data.Objects.DataClasses* namespaces, and it enables querying, adding, updating, and deleting entities using a strongly typed approach with Entity SQL and LINQ to Entities. Let's start with Listing A-19, which provides an example of how to modify an entity instance.

Listing A-19   Entity modification and data persistence

```
using (NorthwindEntities db = new NorthwindEntities()) {

    var customer = (from   c in db.Customers
                    where  c.CustomerID == "ALFKI"
                    select c).AsEnumerable().First();

    Console.WriteLine("Customer ContactName: {0}", customer.ContactName);
    Console.WriteLine("Customer state: {0}", customer.EntityState);

    customer.ContactName = "Maria Anders - Changed";

    Console.WriteLine("Customer ContactName: {0}", customer.ContactName);
    Console.WriteLine("Customer state: {0}", customer.EntityState);

    db.SaveChanges();

    Console.WriteLine("Customer state: {0}", customer.EntityState);
}
```

The output of this code is similar to the following:

```
Customer ContactName: Maria Anders
Customer state: Unchanged
Customer ContactName: Maria Anders - Changed
Customer state: Modified
Customer state: Unchanged
```

You can see that as soon as we change the customer instance, we implicitly also change its *EntityState* value, which keeps track of the entity status throughout its lifetime. This property can assume the classical values of *Added*, *Deleted*, *Detached*, *Modified*, and *Unchanged*. The entity status is tracked by the *ObjectContext* engine. In fact, we are working inside a *using* block applied to a *NorthwindEntities* object, and every query is executed against the current context. Whenever a user queries for an entity instance, the *ObjectContext* base engine checks to determine whether the object has already been loaded into memory. If the object is already available, the engine returns that instance; otherwise, it retrieves the instance from the physical database and keeps track of it. Whenever a piece of code changes the object instance, the *ObjectContext* is notified and tracks the information. In Listing A-20, you can see the instancing and object concurrency policy in action.

Listing A 20 Entity status and concurrency

```
using (NorthwindEntities db = new NorthwindEntities()) {

    var customer1 = (from   c in db.Customers
                    where  c.CustomerID == "ALFKI"
                    select c).AsEnumerable().First();

    Console.WriteLine("Customer 1 ContactName: {0}", customer1.ContactName);
    Console.WriteLine("Customer 1 state: {0}", customer1.EntityState);

    customer1.ContactName = "Maria Anders - Changed";

    Console.WriteLine("Customer 1 ContactName: {0}", customer1.ContactName);
    Console.WriteLine("Customer 1 state: {0}", customer1.EntityState);

    var customer2 = (from   c in db.Customers
                    where  c.CustomerID == "ALFKI"
                    select c).AsEnumerable().First();

    Console.WriteLine("Customer 2 ContactName: {0}", customer2.ContactName);
    Console.WriteLine("Customer 2 state: {0}", customer2.EntityState);

    db.SaveChanges();

    Console.WriteLine("Customer 1 state: {0}", customer1.EntityState);
    Console.WriteLine("Customer 2 state: {0}", customer2.EntityState);
    Console.WriteLine("Customer 1 HashCode: {0}", customer1.GetHashCode());
    Console.WriteLine("Customer 2 HashCode: {0}", customer2.GetHashCode());

    Console.WriteLine("Customer 1 Equals Customer 2? {0}",
        customer1.Equals(customer2));
}
```

The result of the preceding code excerpt is the following:

```
Customer 1 ContactName: Maria Anders
Customer 1 state: Unchanged
Customer 1 ContactName: Maria Anders - Changed
```

```
Customer 1 state: Modified
Customer 2 ContactName: Maria Anders - Changed
Customer 2 state: Modified
Customer 1 state: Unchanged
Customer 2 state: Unchanged Customer 1 HashCode: 7765704
Customer 2 HashCode: 7765704
Customer 1 Equals Customer 2? True
```

The object instances that hold *customer1* and *customer2* are the same. They have the same *HashCode*, and *Equals* returns *true*. Perhaps you are wondering how *ObjectContext* identifies object instances. It uses the key of the entity, and this is why it is so important to correctly define identifying keys within the entity model.

Every time you need to change an entity, you can simply update its properties or invoke its methods. Behind the scenes, the Object Services engine guarantees that you do not have multiple instances of the same entity, thereby helping you to avoid concurrency issues within your own application. It does this by validating input against the EDM you defined and keeping track of every kind of change you make over entity instances. Changes are made in memory, and none of them are directly persisted to the physical storage until you invoke the *SaveChanges* method of the *ObjectContext* instance. Only when you invoke this method is the data sent to the database.

Your actions could be concurrent with those of other users or applications. *ObjectContext* prevents your code from being concurrent, but someone else could change an entity on the persistence layer that you have changed in memory. In this situation, an *OptimisticConcurrencyException* is thrown.

Object Identity Management

Every time you make a query to extract some entities from the persistence storage, those entities are cached and tracked by the Object Services component. The service that maintains objects' identities is the *ObjectStateManager*, and there is one instance of this object for each *ObjectContext*. Whenever you query or attach an entity to an *ObjectContext* instance, the *ObjectStateManager* checks to see whether it is new or a duplicate. If it is a new object, the entity will be cached; otherwise, the behavior is configurable through a *MergeOption* parameter. This parameter can assume the following values:

- *AppendOnly*   Appends only new entities, skipping duplicates. This is the default behavior.

- *OverwriteChanges*   The already existing object instance will be overwritten by the new one coming from the store. Any change previously made to the entity will be lost, and the entity will be reverted to the store status.

- *PreserveChanges*   Original values will be replaced with the new ones, but any eventually changed field will be preserved.

- *NoTracking*   Will not modify the *ObjectStateManager* cache.

This behavior becomes useful whenever you want to merge entities or revert user modifications back to the original state. On the other hand, consider that the default behavior means that objects already in memory will never be synchronized with the database, unless you dispose of the *ObjectContext* and create a new instance of it.

Transactional Operations

Whenever you need to perform transactional activities, you can use either a *TransactionScope* or an old-style explicit *DbTransaction* object. We suggest that you adopt the new transactional framework of .NET Framework 2.0 (*System.Transactions*), but providing a transaction management explanation is not one of the goals of this book. Simply consider the example in Listing A-21, in which we use *TransactionScope* to cover the result of an entity modification sentence.

Listing A-21   Entity modification using *TransactionScope*

```
using (NorthwindEntities db = new NorthwindEntities()) {
    using (TransactionScope scope = new TransactionScope()) {

        var customer = (from   c in db.Customers
                        where  c.CustomerID == "ALFKI"
                        select c).AsEnumerable().First();

        customer.ContactName = "Paolo Pialorsi";
        db.SaveChanges();
        scope.Complete();
    }
}
```

Manually Implemented Entities

There are situations in which you need to use self-implemented entities instead of the ones generated by EDM tools. For instance, when you want to leverage already existing entities, domain models, or both. As we described in Chapter 15, the Object Services component allows you to do that by using an Interface-based Plain Old CLR Objects (IPOCO) approach. In fact, the *EntityObject* class, used as the base class for each EDM tools–generated entity, inherits a class named *StructuralObject* and implements three ADO.NET Entity Framework functional-specific interfaces (*IEntityWithKey*, *IEntityWithChangeTracker*, *IEntityWithRelationships*). The *StructuralObject* class provides a set of methods for supporting designer-generated types, and it implements common user-interface (UI) notification tasks through the implementation of the interfaces *INotifyPropertyChanging* and *INotifyPropertyChanged*. ADO.NET Entity Framework–specific interfaces define the following entities' behaviors:

- **IEntityWithKey**   Used to expose the entity identifying key to Object Services.

- ■ *IEntityWithChangeTracker*   Defines the minimum set of features to track object state with Object Services.

- ■ *IEntityWithRelationships*   Defines the minimum set of features needed to have relationships to other types.

Because of these infrastructural requirements, you do not have real and full persistence ignorance in your self-implemented entities. However, you have quite a wide degree of flexibility—you are able to determine which behaviors to support, and you can selectively implement the corresponding interfaces.

LINQ to SQL and ADO.NET Entity Framework

You should be concerned about a partial overlap of LINQ to SQL and ADO.NET Entity Framework/LINQ to Entities. Although they operate at different levels of an application architecture, they have similar functionalities—such as the tracking of changes made to object entities. You should consider LINQ to SQL as a "simple" ORM that targets Microsoft SQL Server database management systems (DBMSs) only, and that has a 1:1 mapping between typed entities and database schema. On the other hand, the ADO.NET Entity Framework targets more complex scenarios, where there is not always a 1:1 mapping between entities and the physical database schema. And also, with the ADO.NET Entity Framework, you target many different DBMSs, leveraging specific providers that are or will soon be available in the marketplace.

Summary

In this appendix, we described what the ADO.NET Entity Framework is and how to use it to realize a conceptual abstraction from the physical data layer. You saw how to define EDM schemas using the EDM tools and designers, as well as some of the code automatically generated by Visual Studio 2008 for these entity model metadata files. The entities generated from the metadata can be queried with an SQL-like query language called Entity Query, and they can also be queried using LINQ to Entities. Finally, you saw how to change and persist entities—including how to handle concurrency and transactions—using the Object Services infrastructure. We also introduced concepts to help you understand how LINQ to Entities works. However, the ADO.NET Entity Framework is really a big matter and deserves a complete book.

Appendix B
C# 3.0: New Language Features

A full knowledge of the C# 3.0 language enhancements is not necessary to use Language Integrated Query (LINQ). For example, none of the new language features require a modification of the common language runtime (CLR). LINQ relies on new compilers (C# 3.0 or Microsoft Visual Basic 2008), and these compilers generate intermediate code that works well on Microsoft .NET 2.0, given that you have the LINQ assemblies available.

However, in this appendix, we provide short descriptions of C# features (ranging from C# 1.*x* to C# 3.0) that you need to clearly understand in order to work with LINQ most effectively.

C# 2.0 Revisited

C# 2.0 improved the original C# language in many ways. For example, the introduction of generics enabled developers to use C# to define methods and classes having one or more type parameters. Generics are a fundamental pillar of LINQ.

In this section, we describe several C# 2.0 features that are important to LINQ: generics, anonymous methods (which are the basis of lambda expressions in C# 3.0), the *yield* keyword, and the *IEnumerable* interface. You need to understand these concepts well to best understand LINQ.

Generics

Many programming languages handle variables and objects by defining specific types and strict rules about converting between types. Code that is written in a strongly typed language lacks something in terms of generalization, however. Consider the following code:

```
int Min( int a, int b ) {
    if (a < b) return a;
    else return b;
}
```

We need a different version of *Min* for each type of parameter we want to compare. Developers who are accustomed to using objects as placeholders for a generic type (which is common with collections) might be tempted to write a single *Min* function such as this:

```
object Min( object a, object b ) {
    if (a < b) return a;
    else return b;
}
```

Unfortunately, the *less than* operator (<) is not defined for the *System.Object* type (which in C# can be identified with the *object* keyword). We need to use a common (or generic) interface to do that:

```
IComparable Min( IComparable a, IComparable b ) {
    if (a.CompareTo( b ) < 0) return a;
    else return b;
}
```

However, even if we solve this problem, we are faced with a bigger issue: the indeterminate result type of the *Min* function. A caller of *Min* that passes two integers should make a type conversion from *IComparable* to *int*, but this might raise an exception (if the returned type is not an *int*) and surely would involve a CPU cost because of boxing and unboxing:

```
int a = 5, b = 10;
int c = (int) Min( a, b );
```

C# 2.0 solved this problem with generics. The basic principle of generics is that type generation is moved from the C# compiler to the jitter. Here is the generic version of the *Min* function:

```
T Min<T>( T a, T b ) where T : IComparable<T> {
    if (a.CompareTo( b ) < 0) return a;
    else return b;
}
```

> **Note**   The *jitter* is the run-time compiler that is part of the .NET runtime. It translates Intermediate Language (IL) code to machine code. When you compile .NET source code, the compiler generates an executable image containing IL code, which is compiled in machine code instructions by the jitter at some point before the first execution.

Moving type generation to the jitter is a good compromise: the jitter can generate many versions from the same code, one for each type that is used. This approach is similar to a macro expansion, but it differs in the optimizations used to avoid code proliferation—all versions of a generic function that use reference types as generic types share the same compiled code because the binary representation of a reference is always the same as *object*, while the difference is maintained against callers to grant type checking.

With generics, instead of writing code such as this:

```
int a = 5, b = 10;
int c = (int) Min( a, b );
```

you can write code such as this:

```
int a = 5, b = 10;
int c = Min<int>( a, b );
```

The cast for the *Min* result has disappeared, and the code will run faster. Moreover, the compiler can infer the generic *T* type of the *Min* function from the parameters, and we can write this simpler form:

```
int a = 5, b = 10;
int c = Min( a, b );
```

Type Inference in Generics   Type inference in generics is a key feature. It allows you to write more abstract code, making the compiler handle details about types. Nevertheless, the C# implementation of type inference does not remove type safety and can intercept incorrect code (for example, a call that uses incompatible types, such as passing an *int* and a *string* that both implement *IComparable* but are different types) at compile time.

Generics can also be used with type declarations (as classes and interfaces) and not only to define generic methods. As we said earlier, a detailed explanation of generics is not the goal of this appendix, but we want to emphasize that you have to be comfortable with generics to work well with LINQ.

Delegates

A delegate is a class that encapsulates one or more methods. Internally, one delegate stores a list of method pointers, each of which can be paired with a reference to an instance of the class containing an instance method.

A delegate can contain a list of several methods, but our attention in this section is on delegates that contain only one method. From an abstract point of view, a delegate of this type is like a code container. The code in that container is not modifiable, but it can be moved along a call stack or stored in a variable until its use is no longer necessary. It stores a context of execution (the object instance), extending the lifetime of the object until the delegate is no longer referenced.

The syntax evolution of delegates is the foundation for anonymous methods, which we will cover in the next section. The declaration of a delegate actually defines a type that will be used to create instances of the delegate itself. The delegate declaration requires a complete method signature. In the code in Listing B-1, we declare three different types: each one can be instantiated only with references to methods with the same signatures.

Listing B-1   Delegate declaration

```
delegate void SimpleDelegate();
delegate int ReturnValueDelegate();
delegate void TwoParamsDelegate( string name, int age );
```

Delegates are a typed and safe form of old-style C function pointers. With C# 1.x, a delegate instance can be created only through an explicit object creation, such as those shown in Listing B-2.

Listing B-2   Delegate instantiation (C# 1.x)

```
public class DemoDelegate {
    void MethodA() { . . . }
    int MethodB() { . . . }
    void MethodC( string x, int y ) { . . . }

    void CreateInstance() {
        SimpleDelegate a = new SimpleDelegate( MethodA );
        ReturnValueDelegate b = new ReturnValueDelegate ( MethodB );
        TwoParamsDelegate c = new TwoParamsDelegate ( MethodC );
        // . . .
    }
}
```

The original syntax required to create a delegate instance is tedious: you always have to know the name of the delegate class, even if the context forces the requested type, because it does not allow any other. This requirement means, however, that the delegate type can be safely inferred from the context of an expression.

C# 2.0 is aware of this capability and allows you to skip part of the syntax. The previous delegate instances we have shown can be created without the *new* keyword. You only need to specify the method name. The compiler infers the delegate type from the assignment. If you are assigning a *SimpleDelegate* type variable, the *new SimpleDelegate* code is automatically generated by the C# compiler, and the same is true for any delegate type. The code for C# 2.0 shown in Listing B-3 produces the same compiled IL code as the C# 1.x sample code in Listing B-2.

Listing B-3   Delegate instantiation (C# 2.0)

```
public class DemoDelegate {
    void MethodA() { . . . }
    int MethodB() { . . . }
    void MethodC( string x, int y ) { . . . }

    void CreateInstance() {
        SimpleDelegate a = MethodA;
        ReturnValueDelegate b = MethodB;
        TwoParamsDelegate c = MethodC;
        // . . .
    }
    // . . .
}
```

You can also define a generic delegate type, which is useful when a delegate is defined in a generic class and is an important capability for many LINQ features, such as predicates and projection definitions in a LINQ query.

The common use for a delegate is to inject some code into an existing method. In Listing B-4, we assume that *Repeat10Times* is an existing method that we do not want to change.

Listing B-4   Common use for a delegate

```
public class Writer {
    public string Text;
    public int Counter;
    public void Dump() {
        Console.WriteLine( Text );
        Counter++;
    }
}

public class DemoDelegate {
    void Repeat10Times( SimpleDelegate someWork ) {
        for (int i = 0; i < 10; i++) someWork();
    }

    void Run1() {
        Writer writer = new Writer();
        writer.Text = "C# chapter";
        this.Repeat10Times( writer.Dump );
        Console.WriteLine( writer.Counter );
    }
    // . . .
}
```

The existing callback is defined as *SimpleDelegate*, but we want to pass a string to the injected method and we want to count how many times the method is called. We define the *Writer* class, which contains instance data that acts as a sort of parameter for the *Dump* method. As you can see, we need to define a separate class just to put together code and data that we want to use. A simpler way to code a similar pattern is to use the anonymous method syntax.

Anonymous Methods

In the previous section, we illustrated a common use for a delegate. C# 2.0 established a way to write the code shown in Listing B-4 more concisely by using an anonymous method. Listing B-5 shows an example.

Listing B-5   Using an anonymous method

```
public class DemoDelegate {
    void Repeat10Times( SimpleDelegate someWork ) {
        for (int i = 0; i < 10; i++) someWork();
    }
```

```
        void Run2() {
            int counter = 0;
            this.Repeat10Times( delegate {
                Console.WriteLine( "C# chapter" );
                counter++;
            } );
            Console.WriteLine( counter );
        }
        // . . .
    }
```

In this code, we no longer declare the *Writer* class. We simply define a method inside the *Repeat10Times* call, which might seem as though we are really passing a piece of code as a parameter. Nevertheless, the compiler converts this code into a pattern similar to the common delegate example with an explicit *Writer* class, as shown in Listing B-4. The only evidence for this conversion in our source code is the *delegate* keyword before the code block. This syntax is called an *anonymous method*. Behind the scenes, the compiler automatically creates a hidden type for us that implements a method with the same code as that inside the *delegate* code block. This method is passed as a parameter to construct the delegate object received by *Repeat10Times*.

> **Note**   Remember that a delegate instance cannot contain code, it is only a pointer to some code. Anonymous methods seem to be a means to put code into a variable and move it around, but this is not what really happens under the covers: at the end, anonymous methods are simply a nice and easy syntax with which to make the compiler generate delegate instances for you.

The *delegate* keyword for anonymous methods precedes the code block. When we have a method signature for a delegate that contains one or more parameters, this syntax allows us to define the names of the parameters for the delegate. The code in Listing B-6 defines an anonymous method for the *TwoParamsDelegate* delegate type.

Listing B-6   Parameters for an anonymous method

```
public class DemoDelegate {

    void Repeat10Times( TwoParamsDelegate callback ) {
        for (int i = 0; i < 10; i++) callback( "Linq book", i );
    }

    void Run3() {
        Repeat10Times( delegate( string text, int age ) {
            Console.WriteLine( "{0} {1}", text, age );
        } );
    }
    // . . .
}
```

We are now passing two implicit parameters to the delegate inside the *Repeat10Times* method. Think about it: if you were to remove the declaration for the *text* and *age* parameters, the delegate block would generate two errors related to undefined names.

Enumerators and Yield

C# 1.*x* defines two interfaces to support enumeration. The namespace *System.Collections* contains these declarations, shown in Listing B-7.

Listing B-7   *IEnumerator* and *IEnumerable* declarations

```
public interface IEnumerator {
      bool MoveNext();
      object Current { get; }
      void Reset();
}

public interface IEnumerable {
      IEnumerator GetEnumerator();
}
```

An object that implements *IEnumerable* can be enumerated through an object that implements *IEnumerator*. You can perform the enumeration by calling the *MoveNext* method of the object returned by *GetEnumerator* until *false* is returned.

The code in Listing B-8 defines a class that can be enumerated in this way. As you can see, the *CountdownEnumerator* class is more complex, and it implements the enumeration logic in a single place. In this sample, the enumerator does not really enumerate anything but simply returns descending numbers starting from the *StartCountdown* number defined in the *Countdown* class (which is also the enumerated class).

Listing B-8   Enumerable class

```
public class Countdown : IEnumerable {
    public int StartCountdown;

    public IEnumerator GetEnumerator() {
        return new CountdownEnumerator( this );
    }
}

public class CountdownEnumerator : IEnumerator {
    private int _counter;
    private Countdown _countdown;

    public CountdownEnumerator( Countdown countdown ) {
        _countdown = countdown;
        Reset();
    }
```

```
public bool MoveNext() {
    if (_counter > 0) {
        _counter--;
        return true;
    }
    else {
        return false;
    }
}

public void Reset() {
    _counter = _countdown.StartCountdown;
}

public object Current {
    get {
        return _counter;
    }
}
}
}
```

The real enumeration happens only when *CountdownEnumerator* is used by a code block. For example, one possible use is shown in Listing B-9.

Listing B-9   Sample enumeration code

```
public class DemoEnumerator {
    public static void DemoCountdown() {
        Countdown countdown = new Countdown();
        countdown.StartCountdown = 5;

        IEnumerator i = countdown.GetEnumerator();

        while (i.MoveNext()) {
            int n = (int) i.Current;
            Console.WriteLine( n );
        }
        i.Reset(); // NOT A GOOD PRACTICE - SEE BOOK TEXT
        while (i.MoveNext()) {
            int n = (int) i.Current;
            Console.WriteLine( "{0} BIS", n );
        }
    }
    // . . .
}
```

The *GetEnumerator* call returns the enumerator object. We make two loops on it just to show the use of the *Reset* method. We need to cast the *Current* return value to *int* because we are using the nongeneric version of the enumerator interfaces.

Note   C# 2.0 introduced enumeration support through generics. The namespace *System.Collections.Generic* contains generic *IEnumerable<T>* and *IEnumerator<T>* declarations. These interfaces eliminate the need to convert data into and out of an *object* type. This capability is important when enumerating value types because there are no more boxing or unboxing operations that might affect performance.

Since C# 1.*x*, enumeration code can be simplified by using the *foreach* statement. The code in Listing B-10 produces a result equivalent to the previous example.

Listing B-10   Enumeration using a *foreach* statement

```
public class DemoEnumeration {
    public static void DemoCountdownForeach() {
        Countdown countdown = new Countdown();
        countdown.StartCountdown = 5;

        foreach (int n in countdown) {
            Console.WriteLine( n );
        }
        foreach (int n in countdown) {
            Console.WriteLine( "{0} BIS", n );
        }
    }
    // . . .
}
```

When you use *foreach*, the compiler generates an initial call to *GetEnumerator* and a call to *MoveNext* before each loop. The real difference is that the code generated by *foreach* never calls the *Reset* method: two instances of *CountdownEnumerator* objects are created instead of one. It is a good practice to not use the *Reset* method of an *IEnumerator* implementation (as we did in Listing B-9), because some of those objects are compiler-generated and do not implement the *Reset* method. We explain this in more detail in the sidebar "Avoid Reuse of Enumerator Objects" at the end of this section.

Note   The *foreach* statement can also be used with classes that do not expose an *IEnumerable* interface but that have a public *GetEnumerator* method.

C# 2.0 introduced the *yield* statement through which the compiler automatically creates for you a class implementing the *IEnumerator* interface. The corresponding *GetEnumerator* implementation that is generated then returns an instance of this class. The *yield* statement can be used only immediately before the *return* or *break* keyword. The code in Listing B-11 generates a class equivalent to the previous *CountdownEnumerator*.

Listing B-11   Enumeration using a *yield* statement

```
public class CountdownYield : IEnumerable {
    public int StartCountdown;

    public IEnumerator GetEnumerator() {
        for (int i = StartCountdown - 1; i >= 0; i--) {
            yield return i;
        }
    }
}
```

From a logical point of view, the *yield return* statement is equivalent to suspending execution, which is resumed at the next *MoveNext* call. Remember that the *GetEnumerator* method is called only once for the whole enumeration, and it returns an instance of a class that implements the *IEnumerator* interface. Only that class really implements the behavior defined in the method that contains the *yield* statement.

Compiler-Generated Code for the *yield* Statement

The *yield* keyword can be used in any method that returns an *IEnumerable* or *IEnumerator* interface. (In our example, we are considering *IEnumerator*.) The compiler generates code for a class that implements *IEnumerator* and contains the logic in the *GetEnumerator* method.

The *GetEnumerator* method in Listing B-11 is transformed by the compiler in the code shown in Listing B-12.

Listing B-12   Compiler-transformed *GetEnumerator* code

```
public class CountdownYield : IEnumerable {
    public int StartCountdown;

    public IEnumerator GetEnumerator() {
        CY_Enumerator enumerator = new CY_Enumerator( 0 );
        enumerator.__this = this;
        return enumerator;
    }
}
```

The compiler generated *CY_Enumerator* class is shown in Listing B-13. For the sake of readability, we substituted compiler-generated names with simpler names, such as *CY_Enumerator*, __state, __current, and so on. Compiler-generated names are not accessible from regular C# code. (The use of Reflection to bypass members and type visibility is not considered "regular" C# code.)

Listing B-13   Compiler-generated *Enumerator* for a *yield* statement

```csharp
private sealed class CY_Enumerator : IEnumerator<object>, IEnumerator, IDisposable {
    // Fields
    private int __state;
    private object __current;
    public CountdownYield __this;
    public int __i;

    // Methods
    public CY_Enumerator(int state) {
        this.__state = state;
    }

    private bool MoveNext() {
        switch (this.__state) {
            case 0:
                this.__state = -1;
                this.__i = this.__this.StartCountdown - 1;
                while (this.__i >= 0) {
                    this.__current = this.__i;
                    this.__state = 1;
                    return true;
                Label_0057:
                    this.__state = -1;
                    this.__i--;
                }
                break;
            case 1:
                goto Label_0057;
        }
        return false;
    }

    void IEnumerator.Reset() {
        throw new NotSupportedException();
    }

    void IDisposable.Dispose() {}

    // Properties
    object IEnumerator<object>.Current {
        get { return this.__current; }
    }

    object IEnumerator.Current {
        get { return this.__current; }
    }
}
```

A method that contains *yield* statements is called an *iterator*. An iterator can include many *yield* statements. The code in Listing B-14 is perfectly valid and is functionally equivalent to the previous *CountdownYield* class with a *StartCountdown* value of 5.

Listing B-14   Multiple *yield* statements

```
public class CountdownYieldMultiple : IEnumerable {
    public IEnumerator GetEnumerator() {
        yield return 4;
        yield return 3;
        yield return 2;
        yield return 1;
        yield return 0;
    }
}
```

By using the generic version of *IEnumerator*, it is possible to define a strongly typed version of the *CountdownYield* class, shown in Listing B-15.

Listing B-15   Enumeration using *yield* (typed)

```
public class CountdownYieldTypeSafe : IEnumerable<int> {
    public int StartCountdown;

    IEnumerator IEnumerable.GetEnumerator() {
        return this.GetEnumerator();
    }
    public IEnumerator<int> GetEnumerator() {
        for (int i = StartCountdown - 1; i >= 0; i--) {
            yield return i;
        }
    }
}
```

The strongly typed version contains two *GetEnumerator* methods: one is for compatibility with nongeneric code (returning *IEnumerable*), and the other is the strongly typed one (returning *IEnumerator<int>*).

The internal implementation of LINQ to Objects makes extensive use of enumerations and *yield*. Even if they work under the covers, keep their behavior in mind while you are debugging code.

Avoid Reuse of Enumerator Objects

We noted that *foreach* creates a new instance of an object implementing *IEnumerator* each time, never making use of the *IEnumerator.Reset* method. In general, you should not call the *Reset* method on an instance of a class that implements *IEnumerator*, just as the *foreach* statement does, because that implementation might not support the *Reset* method. This is the case for the compiler itself, which generates *IEnumerator* implementations for iterators containing this code:

```
void IEnumerator.Reset() {
    throw new NotSupportedException();
}
```

> If you are not sure of the *IEnumerator* implementation of *Enumerator* objects, do not reuse them. Using *foreach* is a good practice because it does not call the *Reset* method. Moreover, each time *foreach* is used, it gets a new *Enumerator* object by calling the *GetEnumerator* method.

C# 3.0 Features

C# 3.0 moves C# in the direction of a functional language, supporting a more declarative style of coding. LINQ makes extensive use of all the new features, which also let you use a higher level of abstraction in your code in areas other than LINQ.

Note   You can read an interesting post about C# and functional languages written by Mads Torgersen, a program manager for the C# language at Microsoft, on his blog at *http://blogs.msdn.com/madst/archive/2007/01/23/is-c-becoming-a-functional-language.aspx.*

Automatically Implemented Properties

Most of the properties in a type are simple wrappers around a private data member of the same type. Code generation and integrated development environment (IDE) tools are available to accelerate the writing of code such as the following:

```
private string _name;
public string Name {
    get { return _name; }
    set { _name = value; }
}
```

With C# 3.0 you can get the same result (a property wrapping a private data member) with a single line of code:

```
public string Name { get; set; }
```

The syntax just shown asks the compiler to generate the underlying data member and accessors code. The only difference with the explicit property declaration is the name of the private data member, which is not *name* but is autogenerated and not accessible from the class code, even if it is private to the class itself.

If in a future release of your program you need to modify the accessor code, you can return to the explicit syntax. In that case, you must declare the data member. This declaration does not break any existing code because the name of the autogenerated private data member is not accessible from any code. For this reason, the new syntax cannot be used for read-only or write-only properties because your own code would have the same limitations. However, you can always differentiate *get* and *set* accessibility, as in the following code:

```
public string Name { get; private set; }
```

Local Type Inference

Type inference is a wonderful feature for any language. It preserves type safety while allowing you to write more "relaxed" code. In other words, you can define variables and use them without worrying too much about their types, leaving it to the compiler to determine the correct type of a variable by inferring it from the expression assigned to the variable itself.

The price for using type inference might be less explicit code against the types you want to use. However, in our opinion, this feature simplifies code maintenance of local variables where explicit type declaration is not particularly meaningful.

C# 3.0 offers type inference that allows you to define a variable by using the *var* keyword instead of a specific type. This might seem to be equivalent to defining a variable of type *object*, but it is not. The following code shows you that an *object* type requires the boxing of a value type (see the *b* declaration), and in any case it requires a cast operation when you want to operate with the specific type (see the *d* assignment):

```
var a = 2;       // a is declared as int
object b = 2;    // Boxing an int into an object
int c = a;       // No cast, no unboxing
int d = (int) b; // Cast is required, an unboxing is done
```

When *var* is used, the compiler infers the type from the expression used to initialize the variable. The IL code generated by the compiler contains the inferred type. For another example, consider this excerpt:

```
int a = 5;
var b = a;
```

It is perfectly equivalent to the following example:

```
int a = 5;
int b = a;
```

Why is this important? The *var* keyword calls to mind the Component Object Model (COM) type VARIANT, which was used pervasively in Microsoft Visual Basic 6.0. In reality, however, it is *absolutely* different because it is a type-safe declaration. In fact, as you write your code in Visual Studio, the type is inferred and IntelliSense reflects the real type of the variable and provides you with the list of the members of that type. As we have just explained, when the code is compiled, the generated IL code uses the inferred type, which is why this feature does not break the type safety of the language. To some, *var* might seem to be a tool for the lazy programmer. Nevertheless, *var* is the only way to define an anonymous type variable, as we describe later.

> **Note**   Variants were a way in COM to implement late binding with the type of a variable. There was no compile check using variants, and this caused a lot of nasty bugs that were revealed only when code was executed (most of the time, only when it was executed by end users if you had not implemented a good unit test plan).

The *var* keyword can be used only within a local scope. In other words, a local variable can be defined in this way, but not a member or a parameter. The following code shows some examples of valid uses of *var*: the *x*, *y*, and *r* variables are *double*; *d* and *w* are *decimal*; *s* and *p* are *string*; and *l* is an *int*. Please note that the constant 2.3 defines the type inferred by three variables, and the *default* keyword is a typed *null* that allows the compiler to infer the correct type for *p*.

```
public void ValidUse( decimal d ) {
    var x = 2.3;                // double
    var y = x;                  // double
    var r = x / y;              // double
    var s = "sample";           // string
    var l = s.Length;           // int
    var w = d;                  // decimal
    var p = default(string);    // string
}
```

The next sample shows some cases in which the *var* keyword is not allowed:

```
class VarDemo {
    // invalid token 'var' in class, struct or interface member declaration
    var k = 0;

    // type expected in parameter list
    public void InvalidUseParameter( var x ) {}

    // type expected in result type declaration
    public var InvalidUseResult() {
        return 2;
    }
    public void InvalidUseLocal() {
        var x;              // Syntax error, '=' expected
        var y = null;       // Cannot infer local variable type from 'null'
    }
    // . . .
}
```

The *k* type can be inferred by the constant initializer, but *var* is not allowed on type members. The result type of *InvalidUseResult* could be inferred by the internal *return* statement, but even this syntax is not allowed.

This simple language feature allows us to write code that virtually eliminates almost all local variable type declarations. Although this simplifies code writing, it can make reading code more difficult. For example, if you are going to call an overloaded method with versions of the method that differ in parameter types, it could be unclear by reading the code which version of the method is being called. Similar problems are generated from the poor use of method overloading: you should use different method names when the behavior (and the meaning) of the methods is different.

Best Practices Using Local Type Inference

We have not found consistent best practices for using local type inference in C#. We agree that using *var* everywhere for local variable declaration, even if syntactically correct, is not good practice. In general, you should use the *var* keyword when it is unavoidable (for example, to store instances of anonymous types, which we will describe later). Conversely, you should use an explicit type when there is no initializer, when a type cannot be inferred (for example, if the initializer is a lambda expression), or when the inferred type is not the one you want (for example, it is too specific).

In any case, you should choose between *var* and an explicit type and use the one that improves code readability and maintenance. In the following list, we offer our opinion about what practices result in more readable code. However, we understand that a programmer accustomed to untyped languages might prefer using *var* everywhere—but this is not recommended. Please note that the following list points to anonymous types and query expressions, which will be covered later in this appendix.

- Do use *var* for anonymous types.

  ```
  var c3 = new { Name = "Tom", Age = 31 };
  ```

- Do use *var* for query expressions.

  ```
  var query = from c in customers where c.Discount > 3 select c;
  ```

- Do use *var* for complex generic types (which is a more general case that includes query expressions)—in such cases, repeating a long type in declaration and initialization on the same line does not improve readability.

  ```
  var ordersByCustomer = new Dictionary<string, List<Orders>>();
  ```

- You can but should not use *var* for *new* results in the case of a known type instance.

  ```
  var customer = new Customer();
  var numbers = new int[] { 1, 3, 5, 9 };
  ```

- Do not use *var* for a constant.

  ```
  var x = 5;   // Bad Practice
  ```

- Do not use *var* for simple expression assignments.

  ```
  var amount = customer.Amount;      // Bad Practice
  var x = y / z;                     // Bad Practice
  var count = list.Count();          // Bad Practice
  ```

Lambda Expressions

C# 2.0 introduced the capability to "pass a pointer to some code" as a parameter by using anonymous methods. This concept is a powerful one, but what you really pass in this way is a reference to a method, not exactly a piece of code. That reference points to strongly typed code that is generated at compile time. Using generics, you can obtain more flexibility, but it is hard to apply standard operators to a generic type.

C# 3.0 introduces lambda expressions, which let you define anonymous methods using more concise syntax. Lambda expressions can also optionally postpone code generation by creating an *expression tree*. An expression tree allows other operations (such as scans and the creation of similar trees) before code is actually generated, which happens at execution time. An expression tree can be generated only for the particular pieces of code that are expressions.

More Info   For more information about expression trees, see Chapter 11, "Inside Expression Trees."

The following code shows a simple use of an anonymous method:

```csharp
public class AggDelegate {
    public List<int> Values;
    delegate T Func<T>( T a, T b );

    static T Aggregate<T>( List<T> l, Func<T> f ) {
        T result = default(T);
        bool firstLoop = true;
        foreach( T value in l ) {
            if (firstLoop) {
                result = value;
                firstLoop = false;
            }
            else {
                result = f( result, value );
            }
        }
        return result;
    }

    public static void Demo() {
        AggDelegate l = new AggDelegate();
        int sum;
        sum = Aggregate(
                l.Values,
                delegate( int a, int b ) { return a + b; }
            );
        Console.WriteLine( "Sum = {0}", sum );
    }

    // . . .
}
```

In the following examples, we use similar versions of the *Aggregate* method, so we will not reproduce it each time. The anonymous method passed as a parameter to *Aggregate* defines the aggregate operation that is executed for each element of the *List* object that is used.

Using lambda expression syntax, we can write the *Aggregate* call as shown in Listing B-16.

Listing B-16   Explicitly typed parameter list

```
sum = Aggregate(
        l.Values,
        ( int a, int b ) => { return a + b; }
    );
```

You can read this formula as, "Given a and b, both integers, return a + b that is the sum of a and b."

We removed the *delegate* keyword before the parameter list and added the -> token between the parameter list and the method code. At this stage, the difference is only syntactical because the compiled code is identical to the result of the anonymous method syntax. However, lambda expression syntax allows you to write the same code as shown in Listing B-17.

Listing B-17   Implicitly typed parameter list

```
sum = Aggregate(
        l.Values,
        ( a, b ) => { return a + b; }
    );
```

> **Note**   The pronunciation of the => token has no official definition. A few developers use "such that" when the lambda expression is a predicate and "becomes" when it is a projection. Other developers say generically "goes to."

You can read this formula as "given a and b, return a + b, whatever '+' means for the type of a and b." (The "+" operator must exist for the concrete type of a and b—inferred from the context—otherwise, the code will not compile.)

Although we removed parameter types from the parameter list, the compiler will infer parameter types from the *Aggregate* call. We are calling a generic method, but the generic type *T* is defined from the *l.Values* parameter, which is a *List<int>* type. In this call, *T* is an *int*; therefore, the *Func<T>* delegate is a *Func<int>*, and both *a* and *b* are of type *int*.

You can think of this syntax as more similar to a *var* declaration than to another form of generic use. The type resolution is made at compile time. If a parameter type is generic, you cannot access operators and members other than those allowed by type constraints. If it is a regular type, you have full access to operators (such as the "+" operator we are using) and members eventually defined on that type.

A lambda expression can define a body in two ways. We have seen the statement body, which requires brackets like any other block of code and a *return* statement before the expression that has to be returned. The other form is the expression body, which can be used when the code inside the block is only a *return* followed by an expression. You can simply omit the brackets and the *return* statement, as shown in Listing B-18.

Listing B-18 Expression body

```
sum = Aggregate(
        l.Values,
        ( a, b ) => a + b
    );
```

When we worked with lambda expressions for the first time, we felt some confusion until we realized that they are only a more powerful syntax with which to write an anonymous method. This is an important concept to remember because you can always access identifiers that are not defined in the parameter list. In other words, remember that the parameter list defines the parameters of the anonymous method. Any other identifier inside the body (either a statement or an expression) of a lambda expression has to be resolved within the anonymous method definition. The following code shows an example of this. (The *Aggregate-Single<T>* method uses a slightly different delegate for the second parameter, declared as delegate *T FuncSingle<T>(T a)*).

```
int sum = 0;
sum = AggregateSingle(
        l.Values,
        ( x ) => sum += x
    );
```

This lambda expression has only the *x* parameter; *sum* is a local variable of the containing method, and its lifetime is extended over the lifetime of the delegate instance that points to the anonymous method defined by the lambda expression itself. Remember that the result of the corresponding *return sum += x* statement will be the value of *sum* after the sum of *x*.

When a lambda expression has only one parameter, the parentheses can be omitted from the parameter list, as in this example:

```
int sum = 0;
sum = AggregateSingle(
        l.Values,
        x => sum += x
    );
```

If there are no parameters for a lambda expression, two parentheses are required before the => token. The code in Listing B-19 shows some of the possible syntaxes.

Listing B-19 Lambda expression examples

```
( int a, int b ) => { return a + b; } // Explicitly typed, statement body
( int a, int b ) => a + b;             // Explicitly typed, expression body
( a, b ) => { return a + b; }          // Implicitly typed, statement body
```

```
( a, b ) => a + b                  // Implicitly typed, expression body
( x ) => sum += x                  // Single parameter with parentheses
x => sum += x                      // Single parameter no parentheses
() => sum + 1                      // No parameters
```

Predicate and Projection

Some lambda expressions have a particular name based on their purpose:

■ A *predicate* is a Boolean expression that is intended to indicate membership of an element in a group. For example, it is used to define how to filter items inside a loop:

```
// Predicate
( age ) => age > 21
```

■ A *projection* is an expression that returns a type different from the type of its single parameter:

```
// Projection: takes a string and returns an int
( s ) => s.Length
```

A practical use of lambda expressions is in writing small pieces of code inside the parameter list of a method call. The following code shows an example of a predicate passed as a parameter to a generic *Display* method that iterates an array of elements and displays only those that make the predicate true. The predicate and its use appear in boldface type in the code. The *Func* delegate shown in Listing B-20 is explained in the following pages.

Listing B-20 Lambda expression as a predicate

```
public static void Demo() {
    string[] names = { "Marco", "Paolo", "Tom" };
    Display( names, s => s.Length > 4 );
}

public static void Display<T>( T[] names, Func<T, bool> filter ) {
    foreach( T s in names) {
        if (filter( s )) Console.WriteLine( s );
    }
}
```

The execution results in a list of names having more than four characters. The conciseness of this syntax is one reason for using lambda expressions in LINQ; the other reason is the potential to create an expression tree.

To this point, we have considered the difference between the statement body and the expression body only as a different syntax that can be used to retrieve the same code, but there is something more. A lambda expression can also be assigned to a variable of these delegate types:

```
public delegate T Func<T>();
public delegate T Func<A0, T>( A0 arg0 );
public delegate T Func<A0, A1, T> ( A0 arg0, A1 arg1 );
public delegate T Func<A0, A1, A2, T>( A0 arg0, A1 arg1, A2 arg2 );
public delegate T Func<A0, A1, A2, A3, T> ( A0 arg0, A1 arg1, A2 arg2, A3 arg3 );
```

There are no requirements for defining these delegates in a particular way. LINQ defines such delegates within the *System.Linq* namespace, but lambda expression functionality does not depend on these declarations. You can make your own, even with a name other than *Func*, except in one case: if you convert a lambda expression to an expression tree, the compiler emits a binary representation of the lambda expression that can be navigated and converted into executable code at execution time. An expression tree is an instance of a *System.Linq .Expressions.Expression<D>* class, where *D* is the delegate that the expression tree represents.

In many ways, the use of lambda expressions to create an expression tree makes lambda expressions similar to generic methods. The difference is that generic methods are already described as IL code at compile time (only the type parameters used are not completely specified), while an expression tree becomes IL code only at execution time. Only lambda expressions with an expression body can be converted into an expression tree, and this conversion is not possible if the lambda expression contains a statement body.

Listing B-21 shows how the same lambda expression can be converted into either a delegate or an expression tree. The lines that appear in boldface type show the assignment of the expression tree and its use.

Listing B-21   Use of an expression tree

```
class ExpressionTree {
    delegate T Func<T>( T a, T b );
    public static void Demo() {
        Func<int> x = (a, b) => a + b;
        Expression<Func<int>> y = (a, b) => a + b;

        Console.WriteLine( "Delegate" );
        Console.WriteLine( x.ToString() );
        Console.WriteLine( x( 29, 13 ) );
        Console.WriteLine( "Expression tree" );
        Console.WriteLine( y.ToString() );
        Console.WriteLine( y.Compile()( 29, 13 ) );
    }
}
```

Here is the output of the *Demo* execution. The result of the invocation is the same (42), but the output of the *ToString()* invocation is different.

```
Delegate
ExpressionTree+Func`1[System.Int32]
42
```

```
Expression tree
(a, b) => (a + b)
42
```

The expression tree maintains a representation of the expression in memory. You cannot use the compact delegate invocation on an expression tree as we did on the *x* delegate syntax. When you want to evaluate the expression, you need to compile it. The invocation of the *Compile* method returns a delegate that can be invoked through the *Invoke* method (or the compact delegate invocation syntax we used in the preceding example).

Deferred query evaluation is an important foundation for many parts of LINQ. For example, LINQ to SQL has methods that navigate an expression tree and convert it into an SQL statement. That conversion is made at execution time and not at compile time. If you need to execute an expression tree many times, it is better to save the compiled form to avoid the compilation cost for each call.

Expression Trees Are Immutable

An expression tree cannot be directly manipulated: once it is created by the compiler, it is immutable. Each object that makes up part of an expression tree has read-only properties and methods, thus its state cannot be changed once it is created.

This situation has pros and cons. The advantage is that any expression tree (or any branch of the tree) can be referenced by another expression tree. The disadvantage is that an expression tree can be manipulated only by building a new copy of it. However, only the branch of an expression tree that contains a modification is required to be rebuilt, while the other unmodified parts can use the same reference to tree nodes already used by the original tree.

Some good examples of the algorithms that allow navigation and manipulation of an expression tree can be found on blogs by Jomo Fischer and Matt Warren. (See *http:// blogs.msdn.com/jomo_fisher/archive/2007/05/23/dealing-with-linq-s-immutable-expression- trees.aspx* and *http://blogs.msdn.com/mattwar/archive/2007/07/31/linq-building-an- iqueryable-provider-part-ii.aspx*.) On CodePlex there is a library called MetaLinq – LINQ to Expressions (*http://www.codeplex.com/metalinq*), which contains classes to create a modifiable expression tree in memory, generating a "real" expression tree by calling the *AsExpression()* method. Finally, another useful resource is the source code for the Expression Tree Visualizer that is included in LINQ sample code for C#, which is part of the Visual Studio 2008 complete installation. That code navigates an expression tree and represents it in a hierarchical form in a Windows Forms control.

Extension Methods

C# is an object-oriented programming language that allows the extension of a class through inheritance. Nevertheless, designing a class that can be inherited in a safe way and maintaining that class in the future is hard work. A good way to write code that can be safely inherited is to declare all classes as *sealed* unless they are designed as inheritable. In that case, safety is set against agility.

> **More Info**   Microsoft .NET allows class B in assembly Y.DLL to be derived from class A in assembly X.DLL. This capability implies that a new version of X.DLL should be designed to be compatible even with older versions of Y.DLL. C# and .NET have many tools to help in this effort. However, if you want to allow a class's derivation, you should design the class as inheritable; otherwise, you run the risk that making a few changes in the base classes will break existing code in derived classes. If you do not design a class to be inheritable, it is better to make the class *sealed*, or at least *private* or *internal*.

C# 3.0 introduces a syntax that conceptually extends an existing type (either reference or value) by adding new methods without deriving it into a new type. Some might consider the results of this change to be only syntactic sugar, but this capability makes LINQ code more readable and easier to write. The methods that extend a type can use only the public members of the type itself, just as you can do from any piece of code outside the target type.

The following code shows a traditional approach to writing two methods (*FormattedUS* and *FormattedIT*) that convert a *decimal* value into a string formatted with a specific culture:

```
static class Traditional {
    public static void Demo() {
        decimal x = 1234.568M;
        Console.WriteLine( FormattedUS( x ) );
        Console.WriteLine( FormattedIT( x ) );
    }

    public static string FormattedUS( decimal d ) {
        return String.Format( formatIT, "{0:#,0.00}", d );
    }

    public static string FormattedIT( decimal d ) {
        return String.Format( formatUS, "{0:#,0.00}", d );
    }

    static CultureInfo formatUS = new CultureInfo( "en-US" );
    static CultureInfo formatIT = new CultureInfo( "it-IT" );
}
```

There is no link between these methods and the *decimal* type other than the methods' parameters. We can change this code to extend the *decimal* type. It is a value type and not inheritable, but we can add the *this* keyword before the first parameter type of our methods, and in this way use the method as if it was defined inside the decimal type. Changes appear in boldface type in the code shown in Listing B-22.

Listing B-22 Extension methods declaration

```
static class ExtensionMethods {
    public static void Demo() {
        decimal x = 1234.568M;
        Console.WriteLine( x.FormattedUS() );
        Console.WriteLine( x.FormattedIT() );
        Console.WriteLine( FormattedUS( x ) ); // Traditional call allowed
        Console.WriteLine( FormattedIT( x ) ); // Traditional call allowed
    }

    static CultureInfo formatUS = new CultureInfo( "en-US" );
    static CultureInfo formatIT = new CultureInfo( "it-IT" );
    public static string FormattedUS( this decimal d ) {
        return String.Format( formatIT, "{0:#,0.00}", d );
    }

    public static string FormattedIT( this decimal d ) {
        return String.Format( formatUS, "{0:#,0.00}", d );
    }
}
```

An extension method must be *static* and *public*, must be declared inside a *static* class, and must have the keyword *this* before the first parameter type, which is the type that the method extends. The *this* modifier can be used only for the first parameter of a method, which becomes the *instance* parameter. Extension methods are public because they can be (and normally are) called from outside the class where they are declared.

Although this is not a big revolution, one advantage is Microsoft IntelliSense support, which is capable of showing all extension methods accessible to a given identifier. However, the result type of the extension method might be the extended type itself. In this case, you can extend a type with many methods, all working on the same data. LINQ very frequently uses extension methods in this way.

We can write a set of extension methods to *decimal* as shown in Listing B-23.

Listing B-23 Extension methods for native value types

```
static class ExtensionMethods {
    public static decimal Double( this decimal d ) {
        return d + d;
    }
    public static decimal Triple( this decimal d ) {
        return d * 3;
    }
    public static decimal Increase( this decimal d ) {
        return d + 1;
    }
    public static decimal Decrease( this decimal d ) {
        return d - 1;
    }
}
```

```
public static decimal Half( this decimal d ) {
    return d / 2;
}
// . . .
}
```

In Listing B-24, we can compare the two calling syntaxes: the classical one (*y*) and the new one (*x*).

Listing B-24   Extension methods call order

```
decimal x = 14M, y = 14M;
x = Half( Triple( Decrease( Decrease( Double( Increase( x ) ) ) ) ) );
y = y.Increase().Double().Decrease().Decrease().Triple().Half();
```

The result for both *x* and *y* is 42. The classical syntax requires several nested calls that have to be read from the innermost to the outermost. The new syntax acts as though our new methods are members of the decimal class. The call order follows the read order (left to right) and is much easier to understand.

> **Note**   Be aware that extension methods come at a price. When you call an instance method of a type, you can expect that the instance state can be modified by your call. But an extension method can do that only by calling public members of the extended type, as we mentioned previously. When the extension method returns the same type as it extends, you can assume that the instance state of the type should not be changed—and it cannot be changed if it is a value type because the extension method operates on a copy of the value and not on the original. However, we cannot assume it for any reference type because the related cost (creating a copy of an object for each call) could be too high.

An extension method is not always selected by the compiler, which follows these rules to resolve a method for an identifier in your code:

1. **Instance method:** If an instance method exists, it has priority.

2. **Extension method:** The search for an extension method is made through all static classes in the current namespace and then in all namespaces included in active *using* directives. (*Current namespace* refers to the innermost namespace when the call is made.) If two types contain the same extension method, the compiler raises an error. The search order for extension methods starts from the ones that are lexically closer because the *using* clauses are closer to the calling code in the nesting structure. In the following code, any applicable extension method *Ext* in *N2* is preferred over one in *N1*:

```
class A {
    using N1;
    class B {
        using N2;
```

```
        void M( string s ) {
            s.Ext();
        }
    }
}
```

The most common use of extension methods is to define them in static classes in specific namespaces, importing them into the calling code by specifying one or more *using* directives in the module.

The precedence rules used to resolve a method call define a feature that is not apparent at first sight. When an extension method exists both for a type and for its base or any ancestor type, the compiler always selects the method targeting the most derived type. In all cases, extension methods are not used when the type itself implements a method with the same name.

We can see this behavior in a few examples. The first code example contains an extension method for the *object* type; in this way, you can call *Display* on an instance of any type. We call it on our own *Customer* class instance:

```
public class Customer {
    protected int Id;
    public string Name;

    public Customer( int id ) {
        this.Id = id;
    }
}

static class Visualizer {
    public static void Display( this object o ) {
        string s = o.ToString();
        Console.WriteLine( s );
    }
}

static class Program {
    static void Main() {
        Customer c = new Customer( 1 );
        c.Name = "Marco";
        c.Display();
    }
}
```

The result of executing this code is the class name *Customer*.

We can customize the behavior of the *Display* method for the *Customer* class, defining an overloaded extension method, as shown in Listing B-25. (We could define an overloaded extension method in another namespace if this namespace had a higher priority in the resolution order.)

Listing B-25   Extension methods overload

```
static class Visualizer {
    public static void Display( this object o ) {
        string s = o.ToString();
        Console.WriteLine( s );
    }
    public static void Display( this Customer c ) {
        string s = String.Format( "Name={0}", c.Name );
        Console.WriteLine( s );
    }
}
```

This time the more specialized version is executed, as we can see from the execution output, shown here:

```
Name=Marco
```

Without removing these extension methods, we can add other special behavior to *Display* by implementing it as an instance method in the *Customer* class. This implementation, shown in Listing B-26, will have precedence over any other extension method for a type equal to or derived from *Customer*.

Listing B-26   Instance method over extension methods

```
public class Customer {
    protected int Id;
    public string Name;

    public Customer( int id ) {
        this.Id = id;
    }

    public void Display() {
        string s = String.Format( "{0}-{1}", Id, Name );
        Console.WriteLine( s );
    }
}
```

The execution output, shown here, illustrates that the instance method is now called:

```
1-Marco
```

At first glance, this behavior seems to overlap functionality provided by virtual methods. It does not, however, because an extension method has to be resolved at compile time, while virtual methods are resolved at execution time. This means that if you call an extension method on an object defined as a base class, the instance type of the contained object is not relevant. If a compatible extension method exists (even if it is a derived class), it is used in place of the instance method. The code in Listing B-27 illustrates this concept.

Listing B-27   Extension methods resolution

```
public class A {
    public virtual void X() { Console.WriteLine("A.X"); }
}
public class B : A {
    public override void X() { Console.WriteLine("B.X"); }
    public void Y() { Console.WriteLine("B.Y"); }
}

static public class E {
    static void X( this A a ) { Console.WriteLine("E.X"); }
    static void Y( this A b ) { Console.WriteLine("E.Y"); }

    public static void Demo() {
        A a = new A();
        B b = new B();
        A c = new B();

        a.X(); // Call A.X
        b.X(); // Call B.X
        c.X(); // Call B.X

        a.Y(); // Call E.Y
        b.Y(); // Call B.Y
        c.Y(); // Call E.Y
    }
}
```

The *X* method is always resolved by the instance method. It is a virtual method, and for this reason *c.X()* calls the *B.X* overridden implementation. The extension method *E.X* is never called on these objects.

The *Y* method is defined only on the *B* class. It is an extension method for the *A* class, and therefore only *b.Y()* calls the *B.Y* implementation. Note that *c.Y()* calls *E.Y* because the *c* variable is defined as an *A* type (even if it contains an instance of type *B*) and *Y* is not defined in class *A*.

A final point to consider regarding a generic extension method is that when you use a generic type as the parameter that you mark with the *this* keyword, you are extending not only a class but a whole set of classes. We found that this operation is not very intuitive when you are designing a components library, but it is a comfortable approach when you are writing the code that uses them. The following code is a slightly modified version of a previous example of lambda expressions. We added the *this* keyword to the *names* parameter and changed the invocation of the *Display* method. Important changes appear in boldface type in the code shown in Listing B-28.

Listing B-28   Lambda expression as predicate

```
public static void Display<T>( this T[] names, Func<T, bool> filter ) {…}

public static void Demo() {
    string[] names = { "Marco", "Paolo", "Tom" };
    names.Display( s => s.Length > 4 );
    // It was: Display( names, s => s.Length > 4 );
}
```

The *Display* method can be used with a different class (for example, an array of type *int*), and it will always require a predicate with a parameter that is the same type as the array. The following code uses the same *Display* method, showing only the even values:

```
int[] ints = { 19, 16, 4, 33 };
ints.Display( i => i % 2 == 0 );
```

As you learn more about extension methods, you can start to see a language that is more flexible but still strongly typed.

Object Initialization Expressions

C# 1.*x* allows the initialization of a field or a local variable in a single statement. The syntax shown here can initialize a single identifier:

```
int i = 3;
string name = "Unknown";
Customer c = new Customer( "Tom", 32 );
```

When an initialization statement of this kind is applied to a reference type, it requires a call to a class constructor that has parameters that specify how to initialize the inner state of the instance created (with the only exception being *string*, which accepts a literal). Initialization of value types can occur by using literals or by calling a specific constructor (as with reference types).

When you want to initialize an object (either a reference or value type), you need a constructor with enough parameters to specify the initial state of the object you want to initialize. Consider this code:

```
public class Customer {
    public int Age;
    public string Name;
    public string Country;
    public Customer( string name, int age ) {
        this.Name = name;
        this.Age = age;
    }
    // . . .
}
```

The *customer* instance is initialized through the *Customer* constructor, but we set only the *Name* and *Age* fields. If we want to set *Country* but not *Age*, we need to write code such as that shown in Listing B-29.

Listing B-29 Standard syntax for object initialization

```
Customer customer = new Customer();
customer.Name = "Marco";
customer.Country = "Italy";
```

C# 3.0 introduces a shorter form of object initialization syntax that generates functionally equivalent code, shown in Listing B-30.

Listing B-30 Object initializer

```
// Implicitly calls default constructor before object initialization
Customer customer = new Customer { Name = "Marco", Country = "Italy" };
```

Note The syntaxes used to initialize an object (standard and object initializers) are equivalent after code is compiled. Object initializer syntax produces a call to a constructor for the specified type (either a reference or value type): this is the default constructor whenever you do not place a parenthesis between the type name and the open bracket. If that constructor makes assignments to the member fields successively initialized, the compiler still performs that work, although the assignment might not be used. An object initializer does not have an additional cost if the called constructor of the initialized type is empty.

The names assigned in an initialization list can correspond to either fields or properties that are public members of the initialized object. The syntax also allows for specifying a call to a non-default constructor, which might be necessary if the default constructor is not available for a type. Listing B-31 shows an example.

Listing B-31 Explicit constructor call in object initializer

```
// Explicitly specify constructor to call before object initialization
Customer c1 = new Customer() { Name = "Marco", Country = "Italy" };

// Explicitly specify non-default constructor
Customer c2 = new Customer( "Paolo", 21 ) { Country = "Italy" };
```

The *c2* assignment just shown is equivalent to this one:

```
Customer c2 = new Customer( "Paolo", 21 );
c2.Country = "Italy";
```

> **Note**   The real implementation of an object initializer creates and initializes the object into a temporary variable and, only at the end, it copies the reference to the destination variable. In this way, the object is not visible to another thread until it is completely initialized.

One of the advantages of the object initializer is that it allows for writing a complete initialization in a functional form: you can put it inside an expression without using different statements. Therefore, the syntax can also be nested, repeating the syntax for the initial value of a member into an initialized object. The classic *Point* and *Rectangle* classes example shown in Listing B-32 (part of the C# 3.0 specification document) illustrates this.

Listing B-32   Nested object initializers

```
public class Point {
    public int X { get; set; }
    public int Y { get; set; }
}

public class Rectangle {
    public Point TL { get; set; }
    public Point BR { get; set; }
}

// Possible code inside a method
Rectangle r = new Rectangle {
    TL = new Point { X = 0, Y = 1 },
    BR = new Point { X = 2, Y = 3 }
};
```

The compiled initialization code for *r* is equivalent to the following:

```
Rectangle rectangle2 = new Rectangle();
Point point1 = new Point();
point1.X = 0;
point1.Y = 1;
rectangle2.TL = point1;
Point point2 = new Point();
point2.X = 2;
point2.Y = 3;
rectangle2.BR = point2;
Rectangle r = rectangle2;
```

Now that you have seen this code, it should be clear when using the shortest syntax has a true advantage in terms of code readability. The two temporary variables, *point1* and *point2*, are also created in the object initializer form, but we do not need to explicitly define them.

The previous example used the nested object initializers with reference types. The same syntax also works for value types, but you have to remember that a copy of a temporary *Point* object is made when the *TL* and *BR* members are initialized.

> **Note** Copying value types can have performance implications on large value types, but this is not related to the use of object initializers.

The object initializer syntax can be used only for assignment of the initial value of a field or variable. The *new* keyword is required only for the final assignment. Inside an initializer, you can skip the *new* keyword in an object member's initialization. In this case, the code uses the object instance created by the constructor of the containing object, as shown in Listing B-33.

Listing B-33 Initializers for owned objects

```
public class Rectangle {
    Point tl = new Point();
    Point br = new Point();
    public Point TL { get { return tl; } }
    public Point BR { get { return br; } }
}

// Possible code inside a method
Rectangle r = new Rectangle {
    TL = { X = 0, Y = 1 },
    BR = { X = 2, Y = 3 }
};
```

The *TL* and *BR* member instances are implicitly created by the *Rectangle* class constructor. The object initializer for *TL* and *BR* does not have the *new* keyword. In this way, the initializer works on the existing instance of *TL* and *BR*.

In the examples so far, we have used some constant within the object initializers. You can also use other calculated values, as shown here:

```
Customer c3 = new Customer{
    Name = c1.Name, Country = c2.Country, Age = c2.Age };
```

C# 1.*x* included the concept of initializers that used a similar syntax, but it was limited to arrays:

```
int[] integers = { 1, 3, 9, 18 };
string[] customers = { "Jack", "Paolo", "Marco" };
```

The same new object initializer syntax can also be used for collections. The internal list can be made of constants, expressions, or other initializers, like any other object initializer we have already shown. If the collection class implements the *System.Collections.Generic.ICollection<T>* interface, for each element in the initializer a call to *ICollection<T>.Add(T)* is made with the same order of the elements. If the collection class implements the *IEnumerable* interface, the

Add() method is called for each element in the initializer. As an example, the following syntax explicitly initializes *list* with three instances of *Customer*:

```
var list = new List<Customer>;
list.Add( x );
list.Add( y );
list.Add( z );
```

This syntax is equivalent to the following:

```
var list = new List<Customer> { x, y, z };
```

If there are two or more arguments for the *Add()* method, they must be specified between a nested pair of braces. In fact, you can also use braces around each single element in the previous syntax, but doing so is less readable:

```
var list = new List<Customer> { { x }, { y }, { z } };
```

This syntax is required in the case of a *Dictionary*, where the *Add()* method has two parameters:

```
public class Dictionary<TKey, TValue> ... {
    public void Add(TKey key, TValue value) {...}
}
```

The equivalent initializer is something like this pseudocode:

```
TKey key1, key2;
// assign values to key1 and key2

TValue value1, value2;
// assign values to value1 and value2

var dictionary = new Dictionary<TKey, TValue> { {key1, value1}, {key2, value2} };
```

To initialize such a *Dictionary* collection you can use the following syntax:

```
var dictionary = new Dictionary<int, string> {
                { 0, "zero" },
                { 1, "one" },
                { 2, "two" } };
```

The previous examples should make it clear that braces only encapsulate *Add()* method parameters in a more compact syntax.

The code in Listing B-34 shows some complete examples of using collection initializers.

Listing B-34   *Collection initializers*

```
// Collection classes that implement ICollection<T>
List<int> integers1 = new List<int> { 1, 3, 9, 18 };
```

```
List<Customer> list1 = new List<Customer> {
    new Customer( "Jack", 28 ) { Country = "USA"},
    new Customer { Name = "Paolo" },
    new Customer { Name = "Marco", Country = "Italy" }
};

Dictionary<int, Customer> customers;
customers = new Dictionary<int, Customer> {
    { 1, new Customer( "Jack", 28 ) { Country = "USA"} },
    { 2, new Customer { Name = "Paolo" } },
    { 3, new Customer { Name = "Marco", Country = "Italy" } }
};

// Collection classes that implement IEnumerable
ArrayList integers2 = new ArrayList() { 1, 3, 9, 18 };

ArrayList list2 = new ArrayList {
    new Customer( "Jack", 28 ) { Country = "USA"},
    new Customer { Name = "Paolo" },
    new Customer { Name = "Marco", Country = "Italy" }
};
```

In summary, object and collection initializers allow the creation and initialization of a set of objects (eventually nested) within a single function. LINQ makes extensive use of this feature, especially through anonymous types.

Anonymous Types

An object initializer can also be used without specifying the class that will be created with the *new* operator. Doing that, a new class—an anonymous type—is automatically defined for you by the compiler. Consider the example shown in Listing B-35.

Listing B-35 Anonymous types definition

```
Customer c1 = new Customer { Name = "Marco" };
var c2 = new Customer { Name = "Paolo" };
var c3 = new { Name = "Tom", Age = 31 };
var c4 = new { c2.Name, c2.Age };
var c5 = new { c1.Name, c1.Country };
var c6 = new { c1.Country, c1.Name };
```

The variables *c1* and *c2* are of the *Customer* type, but the type of variables *c3*, *c4*, *c5*, and *c6* cannot be inferred simply by reading the printed code. The *var* keyword should infer the variable type from the assigned expression, but this one has a *new* keyword without a type specified. As you might expect, that kind of object initializer forces the compiler to generate a new class.

The generated class has a public property and an underlying private field for each argument contained in the initializer: its name and type are inferred from the object initializer itself.

When the name is not explicit, it is inferred from the initialization expression, as in the definitions for *c3*, *c4*, *c5*, and *c6*. This shorter syntax is called a *projection initializer* because it projects not just a value but also the name of the value.

That class is the same for all possible anonymous types whose properties have the same names and types in the same order. We can see the type names used and generated in this code:

```
Console.WriteLine( "c1 is {0}", c1.GetType() );
Console.WriteLine( "c2 is {0}", c2.GetType() );
Console.WriteLine( "c3 is {0}", c3.GetType() );
Console.WriteLine( "c4 is {0}", c4.GetType() );
Console.WriteLine( "c5 is {0}", c5.GetType() );
Console.WriteLine( "c6 is {0}", c6.GetType() );
```

The following is the output that is generated:

```
c1 is Customer
c2 is Customer
c3 is <>f__AnonymousType0`2[System.String,System.Int32]
c4 is <>f__AnonymousType0`2[System.String,System.Int32]
c5 is <>f__AnonymousType5`2[System.String,System.String]
c6 is <>f__AnonymousTypea`2[System.String,System.String]
```

The anonymous type name cannot be referenced by the code (because you do not know the generated name), but it can be queried on an object instance. The variables *c3* and *c4* are of the same anonymous type because they have the same fields and properties. Even if *c5* and *c6* have the same properties (type and name), they are in a different order, and that is enough for the compiler to create two different anonymous types.

> **Important**   Usually in C#, the order of members inside a type is not important; even standard object initializers are based on member names and not on their order. Because of the need for LINQ to get a different type for two classes that differ only in the order of their members, C# 3.0 anonymous types are also influenced by the order of the properties. LINQ requires this behavior in order to represent an ordered set of fields, as in a SELECT statement.

The syntax to initialize a typed array has been enhanced in C# 3.0. Now you can declare an array initializer and infer the type from the initializer content. This mechanism can be combined with anonymous types and object initializers, as in the code shown in Listing B-36.

Listing B-36   Implicitly typed arrays

```
var ints = new[] { 1, 2, 3, 4 };
var cal = new[] {
    new Customer { Name = "Marco", Country = "Italy" },
    new Customer { Name = "Tom", Country = "USA" },
    new Customer { Name = "Paolo", Country = "Italy" }
};
```

```
var ca2 = new[] {
    new { Name = "Marco", Sports = new[] { "Tennis", "Spinning"} },
    new { Name = "Tom", Sports = new[] { "Rugby", "Squash", "Baseball" } },
    new { Name = "Paolo", Sports = new[] { "Skateboard", "Windsurf" } }
};
```

> **Note**   The syntax of C# 1.x needs the assigned variable to be a definite type. The syntax of
> C# 3.0 allows the use of the *var* keyword to define the variable initialized in such a way.

While *ints* is an array of *int* and *ca1* is an array of *Customers*, *ca2* is an array of anonymous types, each containing a string (*Name*) and an array of strings (*Sports*). You do not see a type in the *ca2* definition because all types are inferred from the initialization expression. Once again, note that the *ca2* assignment is a single expression, which can be embedded in another one.

Anonymous Types Are Immutable

An instance of an anonymous type is immutable. The generated class uses exclusively read-only properties to access data members. Consider the following line of code:

```
var customer = new { Name = "Marco", Country = "Italy" };
```

The anonymous type assigned to *customer* corresponds to a class similar to the following one:

```
internal sealed class AnonymousTypeCustomer {
    // Fields
    private readonly string fieldCountry;
    private readonly string_fieldName;
// . . .
    // Properties
    public string Country {
        get { return this.fieldCountry; }
    }

    public string Name {
        get { return this.fieldName; }
    }
}
```

The C# compiler generates read-only fields and properties for the anonymous type. The only possible initialization is the one offered by the anonymous type constructor. This means that you cannot modify an instance of an anonymous type in C#:

```
var customer = new { Name = "Marco", Country = "Italy" };
customer.Name = "Paolo"; // This line generates a compiler error
```

Thanks to the immutability of anonymous types, concurrent access in a multithreading environment does not require synchronization and, more importantly, it is assumed that the

GetHashCode method will always return the same number for an instance of an anonymous type. This improves the efficiency of using anonymous types in collections such as *Dictionary* and *HashTable*. It also simplifies the comparison between different instances of an anonymous type.

Equality and hashcode semantics for anonymous types are automatically defined by the type structure and cannot be customized by the programmer. The *GetHashCode* function computes the hash with an algorithm that iterates all fields, making a call to *GetHashCode* for each of them. If a field could change its value, the consequence would be a different hash result for the entire anonymous type instance. Imagine the consequences if such an instance were inserted into a collection such as a *HashTable*.

As you can see in Appendix C, "Visual Basic 2008: New Language Features," Visual Basic 2008 differs from C# 3.0 because instances of anonymous types defined in Visual Basic 2008 can be modified even after construction, unless you do not use the *Key* modifier. With Visual Basic 2008, only fields marked with *Key* are read-only and take part in the equality and identity logic for an instance of an anonymous type.

Anonymous Type Internals

The implementation of anonymous types is based on generics. When you implicitly use an anonymous type with the *new {}* syntax, the compiler might define a new type on your behalf. The class generated by the compiler for the following line:

```
var c1 = new { Name = "Marco", Country = "Italy" };
```

is in reality similar to the syntax shown in the following code:

```
internal sealed class AnonymousType0<TName, TCountry> {
    // Fields
    private readonly TCountry fieldCountry;
    private readonly TName_fieldName;

    // Properties
    public TCountry Country {
        get { return this.fieldCountry; }
    }

    public TName Name {
        get { return this.fieldName; }
    }

    // Other methods
    // . . .
}
```

The compiler takes advantage of generics to parameterize a type based on the field names. This step avoids the creation of unnecessary types because a new unbound generic type is defined only for a unique sequence of field names, regardless of their type.

If you write the following line of code after the definition of *c1*:

```
var c2 = new { Name = 5, Country = "Italy" };
```

no new generic type needs to be defined because *c1* and *c2* both define an anonymous type with the same fields/properties in the same order. These two declarations are equivalent to the following:

```
var c1 = new A0<string,string> { Name = "Marco", Country = "Italy" };
var c2 = new A0<int,string> { Name = 5, Country = "Italy" };
```

with *A0* being a shortened form of the real compiler-generated type name.

However, the following declaration of *c3*:

```
var c3 = new { Age = 5, Country = "Italy" };
```

requires a new unbound generic type because the first field *Age* does not have the same name as the first field of *c1* and *c2*. Here is the equivalent code using the automatically generated anonymous type (with *A1* being the shortened form of the real compiler-generated type name):

```
var c3 = new A1<int,string> { Age = 5, Country = "Italy" };
```

Knowing the logic of the internal implementation is not required to write programs, but it can be useful when debugging or analyzing post-mortem call stack dumps in the case of unexpected exceptions.

Query Expressions

C# 3.0 also introduces *query expressions*, which have a syntax similar to the SQL language and are used to manipulate data. This syntax is converted into regular C# 3.0 syntax that makes use of specific classes, methods, and interfaces that are part of the LINQ libraries. We do not cover all the keywords in detail because it is beyond the scope of this appendix. We cover the syntax of query expressions in more detail in Chapter 2, "LINQ Syntax Fundamentals."

In this section, we introduce the transformation that the compiler applies to a query expression simply to describe how the code is interpreted.

Here is a typical LINQ query:

```
// Declaration and initialization of an array of anonymous types
var customers = new []{
    new { Name = "Marco", Discount = 4.5 },
    new { Name = "Paolo", Discount = 3.0 },
    new { Name = "Tom", Discount = 3.5 }
};
```

```
var query =
  from    c in customers
  where   c.Discount > 3
  orderby c.Discount
  select  new { c.Name, Perc = c.Discount / 100 };

foreach( var x in query ) {
    Console.WriteLine( x );
}
```

A query expression begins with a *from* clause (in C#, all query expression keywords are case sensitive) and ends with either a *select* or *group* clause. The *from* clause specifies the object on which LINQ operations are applied, which must be an instance of a class that implements the *IEnumerable<T>* interface.

That code produces the following results:

```
{ Name = Tom, Perc = 0.035 }
{ Name = Marco, Perc = 0.045 }
```

C# 3.0 interprets the *query* assignment as if it was written in this way:

```
var query = customers
            .Where( c => c.Discount > 3)
            .OrderBy( c => c.Discount )
            .Select( c=> new { c.Name, Perc = c.Discount / 100 } );
```

Each query expression clause corresponds to a sequence of calls to extension methods. Therefore, the query expression syntax is similar to a macro expansion, even if it is a more intelligent one because it infers many definitions, like the names of parameters in lambda expressions.

Query expressions introduce new keywords that have a special meaning only in that context: *from*, *where*, *join*, *on*, *equals*, *into*, *let*, *orderby*, *ascending*, *descending*, *select*, *group*, and *by*. Although it is better to avoid using these names as identifiers, the prefix "@" can be used to disambiguate an identifier from a keyword in a query expression. For example, without the "@" prefix before the *group* identifier, the following code generates an error when compiling:

```
int[] group = { 1, 2, 3 };
var query = from i in @group select i;
```

At this point, it should be clear why the features of C# 3.0 that allow you to write complex actions into a single expression are so important to LINQ. A query expression calls many methods in a chain, where each call uses the result of the previous call as a parameter. Extension methods simplify the syntax, avoiding nested calls. Lambda expressions define the logic for some operations (such as *where*, *orderby*, and so on). Anonymous types and object initializers define how to store the results of a query. Local type inference is the glue that holds these pieces together.

Partial Methods

The last feature of C# 3.0 we want to consider in this appendix is not strictly necessary to implement LINQ, but it is useful enough in many circumstances (the most common is event handling) to deserve a brief description.

C# 2.0 introduced partial class definitions. You can have different parts of the same class split in several definitions that usually are written in different source files. (You can use the same source file for partial class definitions, but it is not as useful.) Here is an example:

```
public partial class Customer {
    public void SendMail() { . . . }
    public void SendFax() { . . . }
}

public partial class Customer {
    public virtual void OnPhoneCall() { . . . }
    public virtual void OnOrder() { . . . }
}
```

The news in C# 3.0 is the syntax for partial methods. A method can be declared without a body, just as in an interface. This is called a *defining declaration* and must include the *partial* keyword:

```
partial void Log( string s );
```

In another part of your class, you can declare a real implementation for the *Log* method. This is called an *implementing declaration* and requires the *partial* keyword as well:

```
partial void Log( string s ) {
    Console.WriteLine( s );
}
```

Partial methods must follow some rules:

- They are implicitly *private* and cannot define access modifiers.
- They cannot have an *out* modifier (but *ref* is allowed).
- Their return type must be *void*.
- The *partial* keyword must appear right before the *void* type (otherwise, *partial* wouldn't be recognized as a keyword at all).

Usually, partial methods are used in conjunction with partial classes. If the class has only a declaration for a partial method, without an implementation, any call to the partial method will be removed by the compiler as well as the evaluation of the arguments. This optional status of a partial method explains the rules about its parameters and return type, because the compiler would not be able to remove the calls otherwise.

In the following code, you can see a number of calls to a partial method:

```
Log( String.Format( "{0} : Init", DateTime.Now ) );
Init();
Log( String.Format( "{0} : ReadData", DateTime.Now ) );
ReadData();
Log( String.Format( "{0} : ProcessData", DateTime.Now ) );
ProcessData();
Log( String.Format( "{0} : WriteResults", DateTime.Now ) );
WriteResults();
```

If the *Log* method is not implemented but only declared as a partial method, the resulting code is similar to the following example, without any call to either the *Log* or *String.Format* method:

```
Init();
ReadData();
ProcessData();
WriteResults();
```

This behavior is similar to the one offered by the *Conditional* attribute in C#. The difference is that it is easier to use whenever you have a lot of small events, most of them not used. Compared with virtual methods, it has the advantage of being more efficient because there are no calls to empty methods and (most importantly) the arguments in the call are not evaluated at all. For example, classes generated for LINQ to SQL make extensive use of this feature. The code in Listing B-37 shows some of these classes. Instead of declaring the *OnXXX* methods as virtual, they are declared as partial. In this way, the compiler removes all references to the methods from the code calling them if they are not defined at execution time.

Listing B-37   Defining declaration in a class autogenerated by the Visual Studio 2008 designer

```
[Table(Name="dbo.Products")]
public partial class Product : INotifyPropertyChanging, INotifyPropertyChanged {
    // . . .
    partial void OnLoaded();
    partial void OnValidated();
    partial void OnCreated();
    partial void OnProductIDChanging(int value);
    // . . .
}
```

As you can see, partial methods are very useful in combination with autogenerated code that needs to be manipulated and used by a programmer. The reasons for using them are better performance and a smaller memory footprint for the executable code. If the programmer implements only the *OnCreated()* method, as in Listing B-38, all other partial methods will not appear in the compiled class, and therefore do not consume space for names, virtual method tables, and so on.

Listing B-38   Implementing declaration in a partial class

```
[Table(Name="dbo.Products")]
public partial class Product : INotifyPropertyChanging, INotifyPropertyChanged {
    // . . .
    partial void OnCreated() {
        // Do some work
    }
}
```

Summary

In this appendix, we reviewed some C# 1.x and 2.0 concepts, such as generics, anonymous methods, and iterators and *yield*. These concepts are all very important to understanding the C# 3.0 extensions. We also covered the new features of C# 3.0 that are the basis for LINQ: local type inference, lambda expressions, extension methods, object initializers, and anonymous types.

The more visible changes in C# 3.0 are query expressions. We cover their syntax in detail in Chapter 2, together with an explanation of the LINQ architecture.

Appendix C
Visual Basic 2008: New Language Features

The release of Microsoft Visual Basic 2008 introduces enhancements to the language to better support Language Integrated Query (LINQ). As with C# 3.0, the changes to Visual Basic 2008 do not require modification of the common language runtime (CLR).

> **More Info**   For more information about C# 3.0, see Appendix B, "C# 3.0: New Language Features."

In this appendix, we examine the new syntax available in Visual Basic 2008, comparing it to the C# equivalent whenever possible. As you will see, there are some differences between these languages, and some features are not present in both. Even if you are a C# programmer, please take a look at this appendix. You will discover that sometimes you can take advantage of Visual Basic 2008 rather than C#, or at least you will be able to read Visual Basic code for LINQ.

If you prefer to use Visual Basic, remember that knowledge of the whole set of Visual Basic 2005 features is necessary to effectively use the new Visual Basic 2008 syntax. The ability to read C# code is also important for reading the chapters in this book (because LINQ examples are written in C#) and for understanding the differences between C# 3.0 and Visual Basic 2008.

> **Note**   Visual Basic 2008 is also known as Visual Basic 9.0. Visual Basic 2005 is also known as Visual Basic 8.0.

Visual Basic 2008 and Nullable Types

Visual Basic 2008 includes features that have been available in C# since version 2.0. One of these features—nullable types—is often useful with LINQ. Since the introduction of generics in Microsoft .NET 2.0, the CLR has offered the generic class *Nullable(Of T As Struct)* to programmers who need to add the semantic of NULL to a value type. Declaring a variable of this type, you can assign the NULL "value" without having to define a new type for this sole purpose. In this way, handling NULLs in data becomes similar to how they are handled in SQL.

C# 2.0 added direct support in the language to enable the use of this type: if you simply add the question mark (?) suffix to the name of the type, your compiled code will use the *Nullable* generic class instantiated for the requested type. Visual Basic 2008 offers the same capabilities with a similar syntax, as you can see in Listing C-1.

Listing C-1   Nullable type declarations

```
Dim a As Integer? = 18
Dim b As Integer? = 24
Dim c As Integer? = Nothing
Dim d As Integer?
d = a + c  ' d = 18 + Nothing = Nothing
c = a + b  ' c = 18 + 24 = 42
```

A regular *Integer* variable cannot be assigned to *Nothing* because *Integer* is a value type. In Listing C-1, we assigned *c* to *Nothing*, and we used it in a calculation to assign *d*. The result of *a + c* is *Nothing*, showing the three-valued logic that is typical of nullable types. The NULL "value" (represented by *Nothing* in Visual Basic) is propagated into an expression, with some exceptions, using logical operators.

The conversion between nullable and non-nullable types depends on the *Option Strict* setting. With *Option Strict On*, a nullable value cannot be assigned to the corresponding non-nullable type and requires a conversion through *CType* syntax. The code in Listing C-2 shows the required conversions.

Listing C-2   Nullable type conversions (with *Option Strict On*)

```
' Behavior with Option Strict On
Dim k As Integer? = 16
Dim p As Integer = k                        ' Compiler error
Dim q As Integer = DirectCast( k, Integer ) ' Compiler error
Dim r As Integer = CType( k, Integer )      ' Ok (exception if k is Nothing)
```

With *Option Strict Off*, a nullable value can be assigned to the corresponding non-nullable type, but it can throw an exception if the assigned value is true. Conversely, *DirectCast* generates a compiler error if a nullable type is assigned to the corresponding non-nullable type, assuring you that an exception will not be thrown during execution. The code in Listing C-3 shows the possible conversions with *Option Strict Off*.

Listing C-3   Nullable type conversions (with *Option Strict Off*)

```
' Behavior with Option Strict Off
Dim k As Integer? = 16
Dim p As Integer = k     ' Ok (throws an exception if k is Nothing)
Dim q As Integer = DirectCast( k, Integer ) ' Compiler error
Dim r As Integer = CType( k, Integer )      ' Ok (exception if k is Nothing)
```

Refer to the Visual Basic documentation for more information about the nullable types in Visual Basic 2008. We expect this feature to be used extensively in code that manipulates data back and forth from a relational database.

The *If* Operator

Visual Basic 2008 has a new operator called *If*, which can act like both the coalesce operator in C# (*??*) and the classical *IIf* operator in Visual Basic depending on the number of parameters it is called with.

In C# 2.0, the following code uses the coalesce operator, which assigns the 0 value if the expression preceding the *??* operator is null:

```
int?    temperature = 42;
int?    speed = null;
string  firstName = "Marco";
string  lastName = null;
int     t = temperature ?? 0; // t = 42
int     s = speed ?? 0;       // s = 0
string name = (firstName ?? "").ToLower()
            + " "
            + (lastName ?? "").ToUpper();
```

This code shows a way to safely convert a nullable value into a corresponding non-nullable type (nulls are converted into a valid value), as we did for *t* and *s*. Another use of the coalesce operator is to get a valid reference when there is a null reference, just as we did for *name* in the previous example.

The same coalesce behavior is obtained in Visual Basic 2008 by calling the *If* operator with two arguments, as shown in Listing C-4.

Listing C-4   *If* operator used as a coalesce operator

```
Dim temperature As Integer? = 42
Dim speed As Integer? = Nothing
Dim firstName As String = "Marco"
Dim lastName As String = Nothing

Dim t As Integer = If(temperature, 0) ' t = 42
Dim s As Integer = If(speed, 0)       ' s = 0
Dim name As String
name = If(firstName, "").ToLower() _
     + " " _
     + If(lastName, "").ToUpper()
```

The *If* operator can also be called with three arguments, in which case the first argument must be Boolean, and the operator behaves like the *IIf* operator, returning the second argument if the first argument is true and the third argument otherwise.

The difference between *If* and *IIf* is that *If* evaluates only the required argument, while *IIf* evaluates all arguments regardless of the value of the Boolean passed as a first argument. The behavior of *If*, also called *short-circuit evaluation*, allows you to write expressions that would raise an exception if written within an *IIf* operator. The code in Listing C-5 shows an example of the difference between *If* and *IIf*.

Listing C-5   *If* operator used as *IIf* with short-circuit evaluation

```
Dim num As Integer = 42
Dim den As Integer = 0
Dim resultOld As Integer
Dim resultNew As Integer

resultNew = If(den <> 0, num \ den, 0)   ' No error
resultOld = IIf(den o 0, num \ den, 0) ' Division by Zero Exception
```

The only caution when substituting *If* for *IIf* is to consider possible side effects of not calling the unused argument: if the unused argument is a function call, it might change the state of other objects, resulting in a different behavior when executing code. This situation should not occur very frequently, but its presence has to be checked before you use *IIf* rather than *If*.

Visual Basic 2008 Features Corresponding to C# 3.0

Most of the new Visual Basic 2008 features have a C# 3.0 equivalent. For the sake of conciseness, this section concentrates on the specific Visual Basic 2008 syntax. Considerations about the implications and possible uses of these new features are the same as we offered in Appendix B for the corresponding C# 3.0 features.

Local Type Inference

The local type inference feature is also called *implicitly typed local variables*. It allows the definition of variables by inferring types from the assigned expression. At first sight, a Visual Basic developer might think that this is the same behavior that is obtained with *Option Strict Off*. In fact, you still get a strongly typed variable if you assign a value in the declaration statement. The example in Listing C-6 shows you this syntax; the comments indicate the effective type of the variable declared.

Listing C-6   Local type inference

```
Dim x = 2.3        ' Double
Dim y = x          ' Double
Dim r = x / y      ' Double
Dim s = "sample"   ' String
Dim l = s.Length   ' Integer
Dim w = d          ' Decimal
Dim o              ' Object - allowed only with Option Strict Off
```

You can see the same behavior here as in C#. The syntax for Visual Basic simply omits the *As type* part of the declaration. The declaration of *o* is not valid if you enable *Option Strict On*. Note that even with *Option Strict Off* active, all the variables types are those inferred by the initialization expression. In fact, that setting would compile the example even with Visual Basic 2005, but all variables would be of the *Object* type, boxing the value assigned in the initialization expression.

> **Note**   We recommend that you use *Option Strict On* unless you have a good reason to avoid it. For example, when you access a Component Object Model (COM) object through interop without having a primary interop assembly, the late-binding behavior of *Option Strict Off* could be useful to call methods implemented only through the *IDispatch* interface that are not exposed in the type library of the COM object.

The use of *Option Strict On* can help you avoid some possible errors. For example, consider the code in Listing C-7.

Listing C-7   Behavior changed from Visual Basic 2005 to Visual Basic 2008

```
Option Strict Off
Module LocalTypeInference
    Sub BeCareful()
        Dim a = 10
        a = "Hello"
        Console.WriteLine(a)
    End Sub
    '  . . .
End Module
```

In Visual Basic 2005, the *a* variable is of type *Object*; therefore, we can always change the assigned value type because it is eventually boxed. Executing the *BeCareful* method in Visual Basic 2005, we display the string *Hello*. In Visual Basic 2008, using *Option Strict Off*, we get an exception when we try to assign a *String* (that does not contain a number) to an *Integer* variable:

```
Unhandled Exception: System.InvalidCastException:
Conversion from string "Hello" to type 'Integer' is not valid.
---> System.FormatException: Input string was not in a correct format
```

If you use *Option Strict On*, you get a compile error for the code in Listing C-7. Visual Basic 2005 does not accept the *a* declaration; Visual Basic 2008 does not like the *Hello* string to be assigned to an integer variable. Be careful when you migrate existing Visual Basic code to LINQ if you have always used *Option Strict Off*.

> **Important**   You can disable local type inference by specifying *Option Infer Off*. By default, a new Visual Basic 2008 project uses *Option Infer On*. To avoid possible issues in code migration, *Option Infer Off* is used by default when you are migrating code from a previous version of Visual Basic. A default value for *Option Infer* can also be specified with the compiler option */optioninfer*.

Extension Methods

Extension methods can be defined in Visual Basic 2008 with a technique that produces results similar to those obtained in C#. We concentrate only on syntax differences here. The code in Listing C-8 uses traditional method declarations and calls to convert a *decimal* value into a string formatted with a specific culture.

Listing C-8   Standard method declaration and use

```
Module Demo
    Sub DemoTraditional()
        Dim x As Decimal = 1234.568
        Console.WriteLine(FormattedIT(x))
        Console.WriteLine(FormattedUS(x))
    End Sub
End Module

Public Class TraditionalMethods
    Shared Function FormattedIT(ByVal d As Decimal) As String
        Return String.Format(formatIT, "{0:#,0.00}", d)
    End Function

    Shared Function FormattedUS(ByVal d As Decimal) As String
        Return String.Format(formatUS, "{0:#,0.00}", d)
    End Function

    Shared formatUS As CultureInfo = New CultureInfo("en-US")
    Shared formatIT As CultureInfo = New CultureInfo("it-IT")
End Class
```

As with C#, we can change this Visual Basic code to extend the *decimal* type. Instead of adding a keyword as in C#, which uses *this* before the first argument, in Visual Basic we decorate the extension method with the attribute *System.Runtime.CompilerServices.Extension*. To use a shorter attribute name, we can add the *Imports System.Runtime.CompilerServices* statement, as you can see in Listing C-9.

Listing C-9   Extension method declaration

```
Imports System.Runtime.CompilerServices

<Extension()> _
Public Module ExtensionMethods
```

```
    <Extension()> _
    Public Function FormattedIT(ByVal d As Decimal) As String
        Return String.Format(formatIT, "{0:#,0.00}", d)
    End Function

    <Extension()> _
    Public Function FormattedUS(ByVal d As Decimal) As String
        Return String.Format(formatUS, "{0:#,0.00}", d)
    End Function

    Private formatUS As CultureInfo = New CultureInfo("en-US")
    Private formatIT As CultureInfo = New CultureInfo("it-IT")
End Module
```

Note   Visual Basic requires the use of the *Extension* attribute to decorate the declaration of an extension method. In C# an extension method is indicated by using the *this* keyword before the first argument in a method declaration. Both syntaxes produce the same results in terms of code and attributes.

An extension method must be defined in a *Module*, and the method must be decorated with the *Extension* attribute. The same attribute will be automatically generated for the enclosing class and assembly. The first parameter type is the type that the method extends. Usually, extension methods and containing modules are public because they can be (and normally are) called even from outside the assembly in which they are declared.

Note   At this point, the compiled code for the *ExtensionMethods* module contains metadata because we have defined a class with both the *MustInherit* and *NotInheritable* keywords, which is a syntax that is not allowed by the compiler. When decompiling the code with Intermediate Language Disassembler (ILDASM) or Reflector, you have to interpret this condition as the equivalent of a static class in C#. ILDASM is a tool that is part of the .NET Framework SDK. Reflector is a free decompiler that supports several languages, including C# and Visual Basic, and is available at *http://www.aisto.com/roeder/dotnet*.

Using an extension method from Visual Basic code requires that the class containing extension methods be used as a parameter of an *Imports* statement. This requirement is different from C#, which requires a *using* statement for the containing namespace and not for the specific class. In Listing C-10, you can see the call of the extension methods we declared in the previous sample. We use *Imports ExtensionVB.ExtensionMethods* because the containing namespace is *ExtensionVB* (it is either the name of our assembly or the name of the root namespace), and *ExtensionMethods* is the name of the class containing our extension methods.

Listing C-10   Extension method use

```
Imports ExtensionVB.ExtensionMethods

Module Demo
    Sub DemoExtension()
        Dim x As Decimal = 1234.568
```

```
            Console.WriteLine(x.FormattedIT())
            Console.WriteLine(x.FormattedUS())
        End Sub
    End Module
```

Almost all the considerations about extension methods that we covered in Appendix B are valid here, with the only exceptions being the syntax differences that we have highlighted.

Object Initialization Expressions

Visual Basic 2008 offers a new syntax to initialize multiple members of the same type instance. The *With* syntax does the same work, but the object initializer in Visual Basic 2008 allows the initialization of multiple members in a single expression. This functionality is necessary to initialize anonymous types, as we will see later.

We will use the class shown in Listing C-11 in our examples.

Listing C-11   Sample class for object initializers

```
Public Class Customer
    Public Age As Integer
    Public Name As String
    Public Country As String
    Public Sub New(ByVal name As String, ByVal age As Integer)
        Me.Age = age
        Me.Name = name
    End Sub
    ' . . .
End Class
```

If you want to initialize *Country* but not *Age* on a new instance of *Customer*, in Visual Basic 2005 you can write the code based on the *With* statement shown in Listing C-12.

Listing C-12   Initialization using the *With* statement

```
    Dim customer As New Customer
    With customer
        .Name = "Marco"
        .Country = "Italy"
    End With
```

The new object initializer syntax in Visual Basic 2008 allows initialization in a different form, as you can see in Listing C-13.

Listing C-13   Object initializer syntax

```
    Dim customer As Customer
    customer = New Customer With {.Name = "Marco", .Country = "Italy"}
```

The object initializer syntax expects the keyword *With* after the object creation, followed by brackets containing a list of members to initialize. Each member is assigned by specifying its name prefixed by a dot, followed by an equals sign (=) and then the initialization expression. Multiple members are separated by a comma (,). You can also write the previous example in a single line, like this:

```
Dim customer As New Customer With {.Name = "Marco", .Country = "Italy"}
```

If you are a C# developer, you should be aware that splitting an expression on multiple lines in Visual Basic always requires the line continuation notation, which is a special character (an underscore) at the end of each line. You can see how to use them in Listing C-14.

Listing C-14   Object initializer syntax on multiple lines

```
Dim customer As Customer = _
    New Customer With { _
        .Name = "Marco", _
        .Country = "Italy"}
```

The use of line continuations can negate the benefits of object initializers. We generally prefer to use the new object initializer syntax rather than the traditional *With* statement in cases in which we can write everything on a single line. For example, we can leverage local type inference to write the code in Listing C-15.

Listing C-15   Object initializer syntax and local type inference

```
Dim customer = New Customer With {.Name = "Marco", .Country = "Italy"}
```

Object initializers can use constants or other expressions for the assigned values. Moreover, you can use a nondefault constructor followed by an object initializer. The example in Listing C-16 illustrates these concepts.

Listing C-16   Object initializers using expressions

```
Dim c1 = New Customer With {.Name = "Marco", .Country = "Italy"}
Dim c2 = New Customer("Paolo", 21) With {.Country = "Italy"}
Dim c3 = New Customer With {.Name = "Paolo", .Age = 21, .Country = "Italy"}
Dim c4 = New Customer With {.Name = c1.Name, .Country = c2.Country, .Age = c2.Age}
```

Because an object initializer is an expression, it can be nested. Listing C-17 shows an example.

Listing C-17   Nested object initializers

```
' In Point and Rectangle classes, we collapsed parts of implementation
Public Class Point
    Private _x, _y As Integer
    Public Property X ... ' Integer - implementation collapsed
    Public Property Y ... ' Integer - implementation collapsed
End Class
```

```
Public Class Rectangle
    Private _tl, _br As Point
    Public Property TL() ... ' Point - implementation collapsed
    Public Property BR() ... ' Point - implementation collapsed
End Class

' Possible code inside a method
    Dim r = New Rectangle With { _
            .TL = New Point With {.X = 0, .Y = 1}, _
            .BR = New Point With {.X = 2, .Y = 3} _
        }
```

Anonymous Types

An anonymous type is a type that is declared without an identifier. Anonymous types in Visual Basic 2008 offer all the corresponding C# 3.0 features with two differences. First, all members are writable by default. Second, the comparison of anonymous type instances considers only read-only properties, which must be explicitly defined using the *Key* keyword. Through the use of *Key*, Visual Basic gives you the flexibility to define mutable, immutable, and partially mutable anonymous types. In C#, anonymous type instances are always immutable because their fields are read-only.

You can use object initializers without specifying the class that will be created with the *New* operator. When you do this, a new class (an anonymous type) is created. Consider Listing C-18.

Listing C-18   Anonymous type definition

```
Dim c1 As New Customer With {.Name = "Marco"}
Dim c2 = New Customer With {.Name = "Paolo"}
Dim c3 = New With {.Name = "Tom", .Age = 31}
Dim c4 = New With {c2.Name, c2.Age}
Dim c5 = New With {c1.Name, c1.Country}
Dim c6 = New With {c1.Country, c1.Name}
```

The variables *c1* and *c2* are of the *Customer* type, but the type of variables *c3*, *c4*, *c5*, and *c6* cannot be inferred simply by reading the printed code. The local type inference should infer the variable type from the assigned expression, but we do not have an explicit type after the *New* keyword for these expressions. That kind of object initializer generates a new class.

The generated class has a public property and an underlying private field for each argument contained in the initializer; the property's name and type are inferred from the object initializer. That class is the same for all possible anonymous types that have the same names, accessibility, and types in the same order for their properties. We can see the type names used and generated with this code:

```
Console.WriteLine("c1 is {0}", c1.GetType())
Console.WriteLine("c2 is {0}", c2.GetType())
```

```
Console.WriteLine("c3 is {0}", c3.GetType())
Console.WriteLine("c4 is {0}", c4.GetType())
Console.WriteLine("c5 is {0}", c5.GetType())
Console.WriteLine("c6 is {0}", c6.GetType())
```

The output generated is the following:

```
c1 is AnonymousTypes.Customer
c2 is AnonymousTypes.Customer
c3 is VB$AnonymousType_0`2[System.String,System.Int32]
c4 is VB$AnonymousType_0`2[System.String,System.Int32]
c5 is VB$AnonymousType_1`2[System.String,System.String]
c6 is VB$AnonymousType_2`2[System.String,System.String]
```

The anonymous type name cannot be referenced by the code (because you do not know the generated name), but it can be queried on an object instance. The variables *c3* and *c4* are of the same anonymous type because they have the same fields and properties. Even if *c5* and *c6* have the same properties (type and name), they are in a different order, and that is enough for the compiler to create two different anonymous types.

If you want to create an array of anonymous types, you have to address the issue that the array initializer syntax does not support anonymous types. However, by defining a helper method, you can leverage the *ParamArray* flexible parameter list and generics, writing the code shown in Listing C-19.

Listing C-19 Anonymous type definition

```
Sub DemoArray()
    Dim ca = MakeArray( _
            New With {.Name = "Marco", .Country = "Italy"}, _
            New With {.Name = "Tom", .Country = "USA"}, _
            New With {.Name = "Paolo", .Country = "Italy"})
    Console.WriteLine("ca is {0}", ca.GetType())
End Sub

Function MakeArray(Of T)(ByVal ParamArray params As T()) As T()
    Return params
End Function
```

MakeArray generates an array of types of the same type as the arguments they are being passed to. Remember that all the parameters must be of the same type; because they are anonymous types, they have to be *identical* (same order, name, and type of properties). The output generated from the execution of the *DemoArray* method in Listing C-19 demonstrates that we defined an array of anonymous type instances:

```
ca is VB$AnonymousType_1`2[System.String,System.String][]
```

Anonymous Types Are Not Immutable in Visual Basic 2008

Until now, we created anonymous types whose instances are modifiable. This process is different from C#, where anonymous type instances are immutable. To make a property of an anonymous type read-only, the keyword *Key* must precede the member name. (See Listing C-20.) These properties are called *key properties*. An anonymous type in which all members are key properties is immutable, just like an anonymous type generated by the C# 3.0 compiler.

Listing C-20   Anonymous types with and without key properties

```
Dim c7 = New With {.Name = "Marco", .Country = "USA"}
Dim c8 = New With {Key .Name = "Marco", .Country = "USA"}
c7.Country = "France"
c7.Name = "Claude"
c8.Country = "Italy"
c8.Name = "Roberto" ' Compiler error - Name is read-only
```

As you can see in Listing C-20, the *Name* property of the *c8* instance cannot be written because it is a key property, and therefore read-only. Another important consideration is that *c7* and *c8* are instances of different types. Consider this code:

```
Console.WriteLine("c7 is {0}", c7.GetType())
Console.WriteLine("c8 is {0}", c8.GetType())
```

The result demonstrates that the types for *c7* and *c8* are different:

```
C7 is VB$AnonymousType_1`2[System.String,System.String]
c8 is VB$AnonymousType_3`2[System.String,System.String]
```

As we said before, the accessibility designation of a property (read-only or writable) participates in the anonymous type definition, as do its name, types, and order of its properties.

Key properties also affect the way comparisons are made. The *GetHashCode* and *Equals* methods are implemented by the compiler for each anonymous type and consider only the key properties. In other words, two instances of a writable anonymous type will be considered equal only if they are exactly the same instance. You can see a comparison of several kinds of anonymous types in Listing C-21.

Listing C-21   Anonymous type comparisons and key properties

```
Dim h1 = New With {.Name = "Marco", .Country = "USA"}
Dim h2 = New With {.Name = "Marco", .Country = "Italy"}
Dim h3 = New With {Key .Name = "Marco", .Country = "USA"}
Dim h4 = New With {Key .Name = "Marco", .Country = "Italy"}
Dim h5 = New With {Key .Name = "Marco", Key .Country = "USA"}
Dim h6 = New With {Key .Name = "Marco", Key .Country = "Italy"}

Console.WriteLine("h1 and h2 are {0}", If(h1.Equals(h2), "equals", "different"))
Console.WriteLine("h3 and h4 are {0}", If(h3.Equals(h4), "equals", "different"))
Console.WriteLine("h5 and h6 are {0}", If(h5.Equals(h6), "equals", "different"))
```

Listing C-21 produces the following result in output:

```
h1 and h2 are different
h3 and h4 are equals
h5 and h6 are different
```

The *h1* and *h2* instances are different because the comparison is made on references and not on instance content because there are no key properties. The *h3* and *h4* instances are equal because only the *Name* property is considered in comparison, regardless of the different values for *Country,* which is not a key property. The *h5* and *h6* instances are different because *Country* is a key property and its value is different in considered objects.

Query Expressions

Visual Basic 2008 supports the concept of query expressions (a syntax similar to the SQL language that is used to manipulate data) just as C# 3.0 does. Preliminary documentation of Visual Basic 2008 talks about query comprehension in identifying this language-integrated syntax for queries. A detailed explanation of all the keywords valid in a query expression is presented in Chapter 2, "LINQ Syntax Fundamentals." This section illustrates the main syntax differences in query expressions between C# and Visual Basic 2008. Some of the specific details will be clearer after you read Chapter 3, "LINQ to Objects."

A LINQ query can be written in Visual Basic using the *From... Where... Select...* pattern, as shown in Listing C-22.

Listing C-22   Simple LINQ query

```vb
Dim customers() = MakeArray( _
    New With {.Name = "Marco", .Discount = 4.5}, _
    New With {.Name = "Paolo", .Discount = 3.0}, _
    New With {.Name = "Tom", .Discount = 3.5} _
)

Function MakeArray(Of T)(ByVal ParamArray params As T()) As T()
    Return params
End Function

' The Following declaration is into a Sub
Dim query = _
    From c In customers _
    Where c.Discount > 3 _
    Select c.Name, Perc = c.Discount / 100
```

The *Where* and *Select* clauses are optional, but *From* is mandatory. If the *Where* clause is present, the predicate used as the *Where* condition is transformed into a lambda expression (as shown in the next section) by the compiler. Another nested function is generated for the projection (the code that follows the *Select* keyword).

Listing C-22 show the simpler syntax for the *Select* projection. The compiled code is equivalent to:

```
Dim query = _
        From c In customers _
        Where c.Discount > 3 _
        Select New With {c.Name, .Perc = c.Discount / 100}
```

If the *Select* clause is not specified, the range variable is automatically selected. For example, if you write this code:

```
Dim query = _
        From c In customers _
        Where c.Discount > 3 _
```

the compiler will automatically generate code corresponding to:

```
Dim query = _
        From c In customers _
        Where c.Discount > 3 _
        Select c
```

For the *Order By* clause, the order of keywords can be different than in C# 3.0. For example, consider the C# 3.0 code shown in Listing C-23.

Listing C-23   *Order By* in C# 3.0

```
var query =
    from    c in customers
    where   c.Discount > 3
    orderby c.Discount
    select  new {c.Name, Perc = c.Discount / 100)
```

The code in Listing C-23 can be written in a very similar way in Visual Basic 2008, as shown in Listing C-24.

Listing C-24   *Order By* in Visual Basic 2008

```
Dim query = _
    From c In customers _
    Where c.Discount > 3 _
    Order By c.Discount _
    Select c.Name, Perc = c.Discount / 100
```

Moreover, Visual Basic 2008 allows the use of *Order By* after *Select*. In that case, projected values can be used in the *Order By* clause. In Listing C-25, the order is made using *Perc*, which would not be a valid expression using *Order By* before *Select*.

Listing C-25   *Order By* used with *r.Perc* in Visual Basic 2008

```
Dim query = _
    From c In customers _
    Where c.Discount > 3 _
```

```
Select r = New With {c.Name, .Perc = c.Discount / 100} _
Order By Perc
```

Visual Basic 2008 also reserves special query expression keywords for features that are accessible only through specific method calls in C# 3.0. These keywords are reserved only in the context of queries themselves; they are not reserved words for the rest of the language. The reserved keywords are the following:

- *Aggregate*
- *Distinct*
- *Group By*
- *Group Join*
- *Skip*
- *Skip While*
- *Take*
- *Take While*

These keywords and other details about minor differences between Visual Basic 2008 and C# 3.0 in the syntax of query expressions are covered in Chapter 2 and Chapter 3.

Lambda Expressions

C# 3.0 allows you to explicitly write a lambda expression using this syntax:

```
(c) => c.Country == "USA"
( a, b ) => a + b
```

The corresponding syntax in Visual Basic 2008 is based on the keyword *Function*, as you can see in Listing C-26.

Listing C-26   Lambda expressions in Visual Basic 2008

```
Function(c) c.Country = "USA"
Function( a, b ) a + b
```

Using lambda expressions, you can write more complex query expressions, as shown in Listing C-27.

Listing C-27   Use of lambda expressions in query expressions

```
Dim customers As New List(Of Customer)
' Load customers with data...
Dim query = customers.FindAll( Function(c) c.Country = "USA" );
```

Closures

When a query expression contains a delegate as a parameter, in C# 3.0 you use a lambda expression to define the delegate in a shorter and easier way. You can use lambda expressions also in Visual Basic 2008, and the compiler produces a similar result by creating *closures*, which are delegates that capture their surrounding context and pass them to the underlying method call. For example, with the query in Listing C-28, the compiler generates two lambda expressions that represent the delegate to be passed to the *Select* and *Where* functions.

Listing C-28   Closures with query expressions

```
Dim maxPlayers = 2
Dim players = _
    From customer In customers _
    Where customer.Sports.Count > maxPlayers _
    Select customer.Name
```

The two lambda expressions generate two corresponding closures. These closures have the same scope as the method that contains the *players* variable assignment, which uses the lambda expressions. This setup is necessary to access the *maxPlayers* variable. The generated code is equivalent to the following, which uses the delegate syntax:

```
Dim players = _
    Enumerable.Select( _
        Enumerable.Where( _
            customers, _
            Function(customer) customer.Sports.Count > maxPlayers ), _
        Function(customer) customer.Name )
```

A closure is an object that encapsulates all the local variables. Using a closure, references to a local variable become references to the closure. The closure generated in the previous example is equivalent to the following code, which expands the lambda expression into regular delegate calls:

```
Friend Class _Closure
    Public Sub New()
    End Sub

    Public Sub New(ByVal other As _Closure)
        If (Not other Is Nothing) Then
            Me._maxPlayers = other._maxPlayers
        End If
    End Sub

    Public Function _Lambda_1(ByVal customer As Customer) As Boolean
        Return (customer.Sports.Count > Me._maxPlayers)
    End Function

    Public _maxPlayers As Integer
End Class
```

```
' The previous excerpt of code is expanded in the Main method
Module Demo
    Private Shared Function _Lambda_2(ByVal customer As Customer) As String
        Return customer.Name
    End Function

    Sub Main()
        Dim customers As Customer() = ... ' Initialization of customers

        ' The next two lines correspond to the "Dim maxPlayers = 2" line
        Dim _ClosureVariable As New _Closure
        _ClosureVariable._maxPlayers = 2

        Dim players = _
            Enumerable.Select( _
                Enumerable.Where(customers, _
                    AddressOf _ClosureVariable._Lambda_1), _
                AddressOf _Lambda_2)
        ' ...
    End Sub
End Module
```

Partial Methods

Visual Basic 2008 supports partial methods with a syntax slightly different from C# 3.0. Although the *Partial* keyword has to be used on both the class definition and in the defining declaration, it must not be present in the implementing declaration. (C# 3.0 requires the *partial* keyword on both declarations.)

In Listing C-29, you can see the defining declaration of two partial methods, both called by the *Name* property setter. A partial method has to be a *Sub* and cannot be a *Function*. Moreover, its method body must be empty.

Listing C-29   Partial class definition containing a defining declaration

```
Partial Class DemoPartial
    Private _Name As String
    Property Name() As String
        Get
            Return _Name
        End Get
        Set(ByVal value As String)
            Dim good As Boolean = True
            OnNameValidation(good)
            If Not good Then
                Exit Property
            End If
            _Name = value
            OnNameChanged()
        End Set
    End Property
```

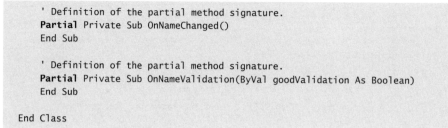

```
    ' Definition of the partial method signature.
    Partial Private Sub OnNameChanged()
    End Sub

    ' Definition of the partial method signature.
    Partial Private Sub OnNameValidation(ByVal goodValidation As Boolean)
    End Sub

End Class
```

The defining declaration is like that of a regular method, without requiring the *Partial* keyword. An example is shown in Listing C-30. The class declaration might or might not have the *Partial* keyword too. The important point is that at least one of the class declarations begins with the *Partial* keyword: this is enough to consider the class partial for all its declarations in the same project.

Listing C-30   Partial class definition containing an implementing declaration

```
Partial Class DemoPartial      ' Partial here is optional
    Private Sub OnNameChanged()
        Console.WriteLine("Name is changed to {0}", Name)
    End Sub
End Class
```

Remember that calls to partial methods are generated by the compiler only if there is an implementing declaration. In the case of the *DemoPartial* class shown in Listings C-29 and C-30, the call to *OnNameValidation* in the *Name* property setter is not generated by the compiler because there is no corresponding implementation.

Visual Basic 2008 Features Without C# 3.0 Counterparts

Visual Basic 2008 has some features that do not have an equivalent counterpart in C# 3.0. Some of these features are partially related to LINQ. One of these features is XML support, which has a large impact if you use LINQ to XML. Another, which we have already seen in the "Query Expressions" section, is that some keywords in LINQ queries are present only in Visual Basic 2008 (*Aggregate, Distinct, Group By, Group Join, Skip, Skip While, Take, and Take While*).

XML Support

Visual Basic 2008 is a language that implements particular syntax support for LINQ to XML, consisting of XML literals and late binding over XML. To describe these features, we will use some classes that are part of LINQ to XML: *XDocument, XElement,* and *XAttribute*. We cover these classes in detail in Chapter 9, "LINQ to XML: Managing Infoset" and Chapter 10, "LINQ to XML: Querying Nodes." For the purpose of describing XML support, it is sufficient to know that these classes represent an XML document, element, and attribute, respectively.

XML Literals

In Visual Basic 2008, an *XML literal* is considered an expression. If you want to assign a value to an object representing an XML tree, you can simply write that value as an assigned expression, as shown in Listing C-31.

Listing C-31   XML literal used as a constant

```
Dim ourBook As XElement
ourBook = _
    <Book Title="Programming LINQ">
        <Author>Marco Russo</Author>
        <Author>Paolo Pialorsi</Author>
    </Book>
```

We have assigned to *ourBook* an *XElement* instance named *Book* that has an attribute *Title* containing "Programming LINQ" and two inner *Author* elements containing our names. The code in Listing C-31 is translated by the compiler into code that is equivalent to this:

```
Dim book As XElement
book = New XElement("Book", _
            New XAttribute("Title", "Programming LINQ"), _
            New XElement("Author", "Marco Russo"), _
            New XElement("Author", "Paolo Pialorsi"))
```

In reality, the Visual Basic 2008 compiler generates code that is less readable but that performs better than the previous example, which uses a more common pattern. The following is the real code generated:

```
Dim book As New XElement(XName.Get("Book", ""))
book.Add(New XAttribute(XName.Get("Title", ""), "Programming LINQ"))
Dim author As New XElement(XName.Get("Author", ""))
author.Add("Marco Russo")
book.Add(author)
author = New XElement(XName.Get("Author", ""))
author.Add("Paolo Pialorsi")
book.Add(author)
```

Important   As we said earlier, XML literals are expressions in Visual Basic 2008. These expressions do not require a line continuation character when defined across multiple lines. More importantly, either an underscore character or a comment in an XML literal is considered part of the XML and not a line continuation or a comment. This is a big exception compared to standard Visual Basic syntax. The end of the expression is defined by the closing tag matching the initial tag.

As usual, we can infer the variable type by placing the initial assignment into the declaration. In the following assignment, we can also see an XML literal defined in a single line:

```
Dim book = <Book Title="Programming LINQ"></Book>
```

XML literals are converted into method calls by the compiler, and the compiler expects a valid XML syntax. An invalid XML literal produces a compiler error. As you can see in Listing C-32, the XML literal assigned to *a* has an invalid *Title* attribute (it's missing a "), and the one assigned to *b* has a missing closing tag. (It should be *</Book>* instead of *<Book>*.)

Listing C-32   Invalid XML literals

```
Dim a = <Book Title="Invalid Title></Book> ' Error
Dim b = <Book Title="Good Title"><Book>    ' Error
```

Visual Basic 2008 leverages XML literals, thereby enabling the calls for other expressions. In other words, an XML literal can be an expression that will be evaluated at execution time and not only a constant in the code. For example, imagine that you want to generate an XML literal dynamically for a book and use a string to assign the book title attribute. To do that, you need to "break" the XML literal with a regular Visual Basic 2008 expression, using the special <%= and %> tags. The code in Listing C-33 shows how to assign attributes and element content with regular Visual Basic 2008 expressions.

Listing C-33   XML literal in a dynamic expression

```
Dim bookTitle = "Programming LINQ"
Dim author1 = "Marco Russo"
Dim author2 = "Paolo Pialorsi"
Dim book = _
    <Book Title=<%= bookTitle %>>
        <Author><%= author1 %></Author>
        <Author><%= author2 %></Author>
    </Book>
```

Warning   Leave a space after <%= tags and before %> tags; otherwise, the compiler cannot interpret the expression correctly.

The <%= and %> tags define *embedded expressions* in an XML literal. The embedded expressions are evaluated and substituted at execution time. In this example, embedded expressions are placeholders equivalent to the parameters of an *XElement*, *XAttribute*, or *XDocument* constructor. You can place into these embedded expressions any expression that is valid in those contexts.

For example, you can define in a dynamic way not only the element and attribute content, but also their names, as shown in Listing C-34. We also use a string concatenation to assign the *Authors* element, combining two strings with our names, separated by a comma.

Listing C-34   Dynamic XML tags in an XML literal

```
Dim bookTitle = "Programming LINQ"
Dim author1 = "Marco Russo"
Dim author2 = "Paolo Pialorsi"
Dim tagBook = "Book"
Dim attrName = "Title"
Dim tagAuthors = "Authors"
Dim book = _
    <<%= tagBook %> <%= attrName %>=<%= bookTitle %>>
        <<%= tagAuthors %>><%= author1 & ", " & author2 %></>
    </>
```

In our opinion, the example in Listing C-34 is not the best way to use XML literals. Filling the code with angular brackets and embedded expressions is not the best way to make code readable. The same *book* assignment is more explicit and clearer if written with the code shown in Listing C-35. (For the sake of brevity, we skipped variable declarations.)

Listing C-35   Dynamic XML tags in explicit method calls

```
Dim book = _
    New XElement(tagBook, _
        New XAttribute(attrName, bookTitle), _
        New XElement(tagAuthors, author1 & ", " & author2))
```

> **Note**   We are not saying that you should not use expressions to assign a tag name in an XML literal. Our intention is to emphasize that embedded expressions in XML literals are convenient when the resulting XML structure is immediately understandable. At the extreme, you could define an XML literal without any constant inside (as we did earlier), but we do not think this is significantly more readable than regular method calls. In the examples we provided, Listing C-33 shows a good use of an XML literal and embedded expressions. If you do not have constant values for tag names, as in Listing C-34, the use of XML literals and embedded expressions can offer no greater convenience.

If you use an embedded expression to define XML element names, you have to be careful with the syntax required for the closing tag. In such a case, the closing tag must not have the tag name inside. As you can see in Listing C-36, the closing tag is only </>, without the dynamic tag name defined by the *tagElement* variable.

Listing C-36   Closing tag for dynamic XML tags

```
Dim tagElement = "Description"
Dim sample = <<%= tagElement %>>Sample element</>
```

An embedded expression in an XML literal can embed only one expression. Because an XML literal is an expression, you can write this apparently useless syntax:

```
Dim book = _
    <Book Title="Programming LINQ">
        <%= <Publisher>Microsoft Press</Publisher> %>
    </Book>
```

In this case, the *Publisher* element is an XML literal encapsulated in an embedded expression of the external *Book* element, another XML literal. This example is useful for observing an important syntax detail. The <%= tag must have the evaluated expression on the same line; otherwise, it requires a line continuation character. The %> tag must be on the same line as the end of the evaluated expression; otherwise, you need a line continuation character in the preceding line.

The following code is not valid:

```
Dim book = _
    <Book Title="Programming LINQ">
        <%=
            <Publisher>Microsoft Press</Publisher>
        %>
    </Book>
```

But we can separate code in different lines by using line continuation characters, as in the following example. Note that line continuation is always external to XML literals.

```
Dim book = _
    <Book Title="Programming LINQ">
        <%= _
            <Publisher>Microsoft Press</Publisher> _
        %>
    </Book>
```

If you want to put more expressions into a single embedded expression, you must define an array of elements. For example, to put two separate *Author* elements into a single embedded expression, you can enclose a list of XML literals between brackets, as shown in Listing C-37. Note the use of the line continuation character after the first element in the array initializer and the explicit declaration of an array of *XElement*.

Listing C-37 Nested list of XML literals

```
Dim book = _
    <Book Title="Programming LINQ">
        <%= New XElement() { _
            <Author>Marco Russo</Author>, _
            <Author>Paolo Pialorsi</Author> } %>
    </Book>
```

We just used an array to put a list of *Author* elements into a *Book* element. Therefore, we can leverage other methods that generate an *IEnumerable* object to put a list of XML elements into another XML element.

In the statements shown in Listing C-38, we use a LINQ query to get the list of authors from an array of people. As you can see, an XML literal can embed a query expression that returns a sequence of XML literals, which are built with another embedded expression that references each row returned from the query.

Listing C-38   Query embedded into an XML literal

```
Dim team = {New {Name := "Marco Russo", Role := "Author"}, _
            New {Name := "Paolo Pialorsi", Role := "Author"}, _
            New {Name := "Roberto Brunetti", Role := "Reviewer"}}
Dim book = _
    <Book Title="Programming LINQ">
        <%= From person In team _
            Where person.Role = "Author" _
            Select <Author><%= person.Name %></Author> %>
    </Book>
```

By combining LINQ syntax and XML literals, you can generate simple and complex XML data structures containing query results in an easy and efficient way.

Late Binding over XML

When you want access to XML data, you probably need to navigate into an object tree that represents the hierarchical structure of the XML document. Visual Basic 2008 offers some syntax that simplifies this kind of operation—that is, late-binding operations over XML.

We'll start by considering an XML list of movies. Each movie item must have one *Title* (as an attribute) and one *Director* (as an element), plus one list of genres. The following code shows part of the initialization in our sample code:

```
Dim movies = _
<Movies>
    <Movie Title="Fight Club">
        <Genre>Crime</Genre>
        <Genre>Drama</Genre>
        <Genre>Thriller</Genre>
        <Director>David Fincher</Director>
    </Movie>
    <!-other movies not shown here -->
</Movies>
```

The first dedicated XML syntax that we want to show is the *child axis*. If we write *movie.<Genre>*, we get all the genres of the chosen *movie*, as you can see in Listing C-39.

Listing C-39   Child axis

```
Dim fightClub = _
    (From movie In movies.<Movie> _
    Where movie.@Title = "Fight Club" _
    Select movie).First()
```

```
' Get the first genre
Dim firstGenre = fightClub.<Genre>(0).Value
' Corresponds to: firstGenre = fightClub.Elements("Genre")(0).Value
Console.WriteLine("First = {0}", firstGenre)

' Display all genres
' Corresponds to: fightClub.Elements("Genre")
For Each g In fightClub.<Genre>
    Console.WriteLine(g.Value)
Next
```

If the query provides only one row, or if we are interested only in the first row of results, we can access the first element of the collection. For example, *fightClub.<Genre>(0)* allows access to a corresponding *XElement* instance. If we need the value of an element or an attribute, we need to read the *Value* property. However, this syntax might return more than one row. In such a case, a loop that iterates over all rows in the sequence might access all of them.

The child axis syntax is translated into a call to *Elements*, specifying the name of the element as an argument. For syntax details, refer to the comments in Listing C-39.

You can access an attribute through the *attribute axis*. If you write *fightClub.@Title*, you get a string with the value of the attribute, as shown in Listing C-40.

Listing C-40   Attribute axis

```
' Display the Title attribute of Fight Club movie
Console.WriteLine(fightClub.@Title)
' Corresponds to: Console.WriteLine(fightClub.Attribute("Title").Value)
```

The attribute axis syntax is translated into a call to *Attribute*, specifying the name of the attribute as an argument.

The last operation introduced here is the *descendants axis*. It allows you to get all children of an element, regardless of their position in the hierarchy. You can see in Listing C-41 that the syntax is similar to the one for the child axis, but you use three dots instead of one.

Listing C-41   Descendants axis

```
' List of Directors
Dim directors = movies...<Director>
For Each director In directors
    Console.WriteLine(director)
Next
```

In this case, the output of Listing C-41 (the descendants axis) shows possible duplicates. We could use the *Distinct* operator to clean up the output. We provide more details about this in the discussion of LINQ operators in Chapter 3.

> **More Info**   We analyze the integration of .NET compilers with XML in more detail in Chapter 9 and Chapter 10.

Relaxed Delegates

In Visual Basic version 2005 and earlier, if you wanted to bind a method to a delegate, the two signatures (method and delegate) had to be exactly the same. This is not necessary in C#—the method simply needs a compatible signature. For example, less specialized types in parameters are allowed. Visual Basic 2008 removes the previous limitation, and you can now legally write code such as that shown in Listing C-42.

Listing C-42   Relaxed delegates

```
Public Delegate Sub EventHandler(ByVal s As Object, ByVal e As EventArgs)

Public Class DemoEvent
    Public Event Click As EventHandler
End Class

Module Application
    Public WithEvents A As DemoEvent

    Sub DemoOnClick(ByVal s As Object, ByVal e As Object) Handles A.Click
        Console.WriteLine("Hello World")
    End Sub
    ' . . .
End Module
```

In Listing C-42, we have highlighted in bold the line that produces a compilation error in Visual Basic 2005. For the line to be compiled with Visual Basic 2005, it should have been written as shown in the following code (in which we have highlighted in bold the changed type of the second parameter):

```
Sub DemoOnClick(ByVal s As Object, ByVal e As EventArgs) Handles A.Click
```

If you do not use the parameters inside the method bound to a delegate, you can skip the whole parameter list from the method declaration. The *Handles* keyword infers the real signature of the method from the corresponding delegate declaration. In Listing C-43, you can see an alternative way to write the previous *DemoOnClick* method. C# does not permit such syntax because C# does not have an equivalent to the *Handles* keyword that can be used to infer the missing signature.

Listing C-43   Relaxed delegates with signature inference

```
    Sub RelaxedOnClick2() Handles A.Click
        Console.WriteLine("Hello World from")
    End Sub
```

C# 3.0 Features Without Visual Basic 2008 Counterparts

C# 3.0 has some features that do not have an equivalent in Visual Basic 2008. These features are the *yield* keyword and anonymous methods. Neither of these features is fundamental to supporting LINQ, even if they are useful in many situations that are common when writing code that uses LINQ.

The *yield* Keyword

Visual Basic 2008 does not have a feature that corresponds to the C# 2.0 *yield* keyword. You can implement iterators in Visual Basic 2008 by using an iterator design pattern. Remember that *yield* does not require support from the CLR. It is implemented by the compiler that generates the code necessary for implementing the iterator.

Anonymous Methods

Anonymous methods are not available in Visual Basic 2008 as a stand-alone feature, but sometimes lambda expressions can be used as a substitute. Closures for lambda expressions are generated by the compiler in a way that is similar to that used by the C# compiler with anonymous methods. However, lambda expressions cannot replace anonymous delegates in every situation.

> **More Info**   For more information about closures, see the "Closures" section earlier in this appendix.

Summary

In this appendix, we covered the most important new features of Visual Basic 2008, dividing them into four main sections. The first was about nullable types, which have been part of C# since version 2.0. The second section discussed features matching C# 3.0: local type inference, extension methods, object initialization expressions, anonymous types, query expressions, lambda expressions, closures, and partial methods. The third section covered features present only in Visual Basic 2008: XML literals, late binding over XML, and relaxed delegates. The final section was dedicated to features present in C# 3.0 but not in Visual Basic 2008: the *yield* keyword and anonymous methods.

Index

Symbols

! (not operator), 148
? (question mark), 75
@ prefix, 609
++ (increment) operator, 307
– (decrement) operator, 307
== operator, 35
=> token, 588

A

AccessText class, 495
Active Directory, 429
ADO.NET 2.0
   abstracting from physical layer, 545–546
   querying entities, 557–564
   querying entities with LINQ, 564–565
   standard approach, 541–544
ADO.NET Data Services, 426
ADO.NET Entity Framework
   caching query plans, 247
   data access without databases, 426
   database access, 425
   entity data modeling, 547–556
   LINQ to Entities, 453–454
   LINQ to SQL, 569
   managing data, 565–568
   manually implemented entities, 568–569
   Object Services component, 233, 241
   ORM support, 427
   query providers, 248
   querying an Entity Data Model, 233–240
   release information, 541
   WCF example, 528–529
Aggregate clause (Visual Basic),
   40, 82–85, 627
Aggregate operator
   extending LINQ, 353–355
   functionality, 81–83
   LINQ to SQL limitations, 146
aggregate operators
   Aggregate clause (Visual Basic), 40, 82–85
   Aggregate operator, 81–83, 146, 353–355
   Average operator, 79–81, 236
   Count operator, 75
   functionality, 74
   LINQ to SQL limitations, 146–147
   LongCount operator, 75

Max operator, 78–79, 236
Min operator, 78–79, 236,
   352–353, 358–359
Sum operator, 75–77, 140, 236
AggregateException, 420
All operator, 88–89
ALTER TABLE statement (SQL), 185
AlternatingItemTemplate (ASP.NET), 464
Amazon SimpleDB, 426
animations, 272–274
anonymous delegates, 26, 326
anonymous methods
   C# feature, 575–577, 638
   lambda expressions, 305, 587
anonymous types
   best practices, 586
   C# feature, 604–608
   compiled queries, 137
   defined, 73
   Equals method, 624
   GetHashCode method, 606, 624
   immutability, 606–607
   LinqDataSource control, 479
   Name property, 625
   serialization, 518–519
   Visual Basic feature, 622–625
Any operator, 88
APIs (application programming interfaces),
   5, 253, 426
ArgumentException, 102
ArgumentNullException, 53, 79
ArgumentOutOfRangeException, 95
AsEnumerable operator,
   98–100, 421–422
ASP.NET
   binding to LINQ queries, 490–494
   DataPager control, 470–475, 480–484
   LinqDataSource control, 475–490
   ListView control, 463–466
   ListView data binding, 466–468
   Profile variables, 478
   Session variables, 478, 491
   Web Services, 301–302, 475
Association attribute
   Access modifier, 208–209
   Cardinality property, 208, 212–213
   EntityRef wrapper class, 118
   functionality, 118, 175, 206–207

About the Authors

Paolo Pialorsi is a consultant, trainer, and author who specializes in developing distributed applications architectures and service-oriented architecture solutions. He is a founder of DevLeap, a company focused on providing content and consulting to professional developers. Paolo wrote *Introducing Microsoft LINQ* with Marco Russo and is the author of three books in Italian about XML and Web Services. He is also a regular speaker at industry conferences.

Marco Russo is a founder of DevLeap. He is a regular contributor to developer user communities and is an avid blogger on Microsoft SQL Server Business Intelligence and other Microsoft technologies. Marco provides consulting and training to professional developers on the Microsoft .NET Framework and Microsoft SQL Server. He wrote *Introducing Microsoft LINQ* with Paolo Pialorsi and is the author of two books in Italian about C# and the common lanaguage runtime.

What do you think of this book?

We want to hear from you!

Do you have a few minutes to participate in a brief online survey?

Microsoft is interested in hearing your feedback so we can continually improve our books and learning resources for you.

To participate in our survey, please visit:

www.microsoft.com/learning/booksurvey/

...and enter this book's ISBN-10 or ISBN-13 number (located above barcode on back cover*). As a thank-you to survey participants in the United States and Canada, each month we'll randomly select five respondents to win one of five $100 gift certificates from a leading online merchant. At the conclusion of the survey, you can enter the drawing by providing your e-mail address, which will be used for prize notification only.

Thanks in advance for your input. Your opinion counts!

*Where to find the ISBN on back cover

ISBN-13: 000-0-0000-0000-0
ISBN-10: 0-0000-0000-0

0 0 0 0 0

0 000000 000000

Example only. Each book has unique ISBN.

Microsoft®
Press

No purchase necessary. Void where prohibited. Open only to residents of the 50 United States (includes District of Columbia) and Canada (void in Quebec). For official rules and entry dates see:

www.microsoft.com/learning/booksurvey/